McNamara at War

McNamara at War

at War

A New History

Philip Taubman *and*

William Taubman

W. W. NORTON & COMPANY

Independent Publishers Since 1923

For information about permission to reproduce selections from
this book, write to Permissions, W. W. Norton & Company, Inc.,
500 Fifth Avenue, New York, NY 10110

For information about special discounts for bulk purchases, please contact
W. W. Norton Special Sales at specialsales@wwnorton.com or 800-233-4830

Manufacturing by Lakeside Book Company
Book design by Daniel Lagin
Production manager: Ramona Wilkes

ISBN 978-1-324-00716-6

W. W. Norton & Company, Inc.
500 Fifth Avenue, New York, NY 10110
www.wwnorton.com

W. W. Norton & Company Ltd.
15 Carlisle Street, London W1D 3BS

10 9 8 7 6 5 4 3 2 1

To our parents, Nora and Howard Taubman, who would have loved the idea of our writing a book together.

And we are here as on a darkling plain
Swept with confused alarms of struggle and flight,
Where ignorant armies clash by night.

FROM "DOVER BEACH"
MATTHEW ARNOLD

The hand that signed a paper felled a city;
Five sovereign fingers taxed the breath,
Doubled the globe of dead and halved a country;
These five kings did a king to death.

FROM "THE HAND THAT SIGNED THE PAPER"
DYLAN THOMAS

TWO OF ROBERT S. MCNAMARA'S FAVORITE POEMS

CONTENTS

SECTION III
AFTERMATH
1968–2009

McNamara at War

Introduction

Astooped old man with thinning hair trudged about a mile and a half every weekday morning from the Watergate apartment complex on the Potomac River to Thirteenth and I Street, NW, in downtown Washington and then returned toward evening. His small office, given to him by Corning Glass, on whose board of directors he had once served, came with a secretary who later recalled that he "stayed in his own space" and most mornings came into the office with "his head bowed."[1] Sometimes the old man was recognized by other pedestrians or denizens of office buildings along the way (one of us, Philip Taubman, saw the figure frequently passing near *The New York Times'* Washington bureau), some doing double takes to see if it was really the man they had seen so often on television and newspaper front pages in years past, but he paid no attention to those who noticed him. Staring straight ahead, he looked, according to one observer who knew him and had once struggled to keep up with his fast, powerwalking pace, like "Ichabod Crane, hunched over, old and shaky, wearing a shabby trench coat with its belt hanging down."[2]

He was not only well into his eighties, he was depressed. More than anything else he was tormented by trauma that had occurred nearly three decades earlier, by his failure to master the biggest challenge he had ever faced. Throughout his life, he had surmounted almost every challenge he had encountered. But not this one. "It was the big heavy albatross around his neck," his second wife later recalled. "And he couldn't get rid of it. It was suffocating him. It was killing him."[3]

=====

IN HIS LAST YEARS, ROBERT S. MCNAMARA WAS NOT THE MAN THE world knew at the height of his fame when he was US secretary of defense and the dominant figure in the cabinets of Presidents John F. Kennedy and Lyndon B. Johnson. Nor the man who was president of the Ford Motor Company before being summoned to Washington in 1960 by Kennedy. Nor he who led the World Bank from 1968 to 1981 after leaving the Pentagon. During those years, especially during his time at the Defense Department, he seemed brilliant but distant, cold, and arrogant, a "computer with legs," as Senator Barry Goldwater once dubbed him,[4] a man who presided over much of the Vietnam War in which some 58,000 Americans and millions of Vietnamese died. As early as 1965, McNamara had ceased to believe that that war could be won militarily, but he continued to manage the conflict as Johnson's principal wartime adviser rather than urging the president to exit it. He chose not to resign, with or without a howl of protest, and then mostly refused to talk about the war for nearly two decades afterward.

Russell Baker, longtime columnist for *The New York Times*, saw McNamara at the zenith of his powers as an archetypical American figure, a leader in over his head who mesmerizes those around him, draws them into his orbit, then leads them to ruin. "People like this are not uncommon," Baker observed. "Their schoolhouse intellectual powers dazzle sensible people, disarming our normal healthy instinct to be skeptical when faced with any product that's being sold too vigorously. . . . We all marvel at the speed of their rise." Baker compared McNamara to the seemingly omniscient owl in a James Thurber fable who enchanted other animals only to lead them to slaughter when he fails to see a truck bearing down on them on a country road. "Thurber understood McNamara before there was a McNamara," Baker said.[5]

Baker may have overstated the case a bit, yet McNamara's mastery and commanding presence at the peak of his career were undeniable. But there was another side to McNamara, mostly unknown. He could be warm and emotional, especially with close friends. He was overwhelmingly powerful in defending his own views, but later condemned himself with equal fury for not welcoming more debate about them. His confidence and self-confidence before the war awed and intimidated his associates. But, especially when first called to Washington, he was politically naive and felt insecure. He came across as incredibly intense, without revealing that much of that tension reflected the acute stress he himself was feeling. As Arthur M. Schlesinger Jr., his Kennedy administration colleague, put it more than three decades later, "I have known for a long time that underneath that disciplined exterior, McNamara is a man filled with tense and pent-up emotion," so "wound up" that in his later years, "he is almost out of control."[6]

McNamara tried to hold himself to the highest ethical standards, but he repeatedly violated them and chastised himself for doing so. After he left the Pentagon, driven in part by a deep sense of repentance, he applied his extraordinary energy to trying to eradicate global poverty as president of the World Bank. After that, he struggled for nearly three decades to understand the folly of the Vietnam War and its lessons for the future. "We were wrong, terribly wrong" about Vietnam, he confessed in his memoir, *In Retrospect: The Tragedy and Lessons of Vietnam*, published in 1995.[7] But his admission of grave error, virtually unprecedented in the annals of retired leaders, never came with a heartfelt apology for the war. His admission of error provoked critics to charge he was even more evil because, despite concluding that the war was unwinnable, he continued to send brave soldiers to their deaths. The lessons he derived from Vietnam produced insights that, had they been taken into account by his successors, could have helped the United States avoid disasters in Iraq and Afghanistan. The danger that unwavering loyalty to presidents on national security matters can lead to calamity should prove instructive to current and future commanders in chief. But not only have such lessons been disregarded, they failed to comfort McNamara himself, who was overwhelmed with personal anguish and a sense of guilt at the end of his life. The striking success he had long aspired to achieve ended up fracturing his family. The war he presided over sundered for several years his relations with his son, stressed his ties with his daughters, and, he believed, sickened and in effect killed his beloved wife. In that sense, it was his very rise that brought about his fall.

Much was written about him during his time in the Pentagon, a great deal of it, like David Halberstam's *The Best and the Brightest* (1972), cuttingly critical. At least three biographies exist, by Henry L. Trewhitt (1971), Deborah Shapley (1993), and Paul Hendrickson (1996). He also looms large in several films, for example, Errol Morris's *The Fog of War* (2003), Ken Burns's documentary about the Vietnam War (2017), and Steven Spielberg's *The Post* (2017). Most recently, McNamara's son Craig published his own wrenching memoir, *Because Our Fathers Lied: A Memoir of Truth and Family, from Vietnam to Today* (2022). But the full story of the psychological and emotional forces that shaped McNamara's life and career remains to be told.

Why is it so important? After all, McNamara was not fully in charge of the American defense policy or of US conduct of the Vietnam War. Those responsibilities were reserved for Presidents John F. Kennedy and Lyndon B. Johnson, both of whom jealously guarded their prerogatives as commanders in chief. Moreover, both McNamara and his bosses (as well as their colleagues Secretary of State Dean Rusk, National Security Adviser McGeorge Bundy, and others in the administration and elsewhere in Washington's national security elite) were practically prisoners of a Cold War ideology that they felt required them to "defend freedom" as well as American security in Vietnam.

But McNamara was more than just a presidential adviser. He was the star of both the Kennedy and Johnson cabinets, viewed by both JFK and LBJ as a close personal friend as well as an invaluable counselor. As a result, he became the key advocate of American escalation in Vietnam in 1965. And yet, after he himself turned against the war in late 1965, he couldn't bring himself to make an all-out case for ending it. Why did he fight so hard to escalate a war that he soon realized was beyond winning? Why did he decide the war was unwinnable? Why didn't he fight to end it? Why did he refuse for so long to criticize it? These questions are more than personal. The answers are central to understanding the war and American foreign policy in general.

McNamara's personal contradictions are not, of course, the whole story of the war. But it is crucial to comprehend them. Where did they come from? How many of them can be traced back to his childhood? How did they evolve when he was in high school, college, and graduate school, as a young faculty member at Harvard Business School, and during his stint in the military during World War II? How did they shape and reflect his roles and policies at Ford and the World Bank as well as the Pentagon? How did they affect, and how were they affected by, his close relations with Kennedy and Johnson? How did he cope with their painful legacy in his last years?

These are among the reasons we have chosen to write a new political and psychological portrait of McNamara. But what makes us the ones to do so? Both of us lived through the Vietnam War, although we did not serve in it as a result of educational and medical deferments. Philip Taubman followed American politics and foreign policy as a correspondent and editor of *The New York Times* for three decades, 1979–2008. He is the author of three books about Cold War history—on the development of America's space-based surveillance satellites, efforts by five prominent Cold Warriors later in their lives to abolish nuclear weapons, and the life and career of a former secretary of state, George Shultz.[8] William Taubman's biographies of Nikita Khrushchev and of Mikhail Gorbachev trace the influence of their personalities on their efforts to reform the Soviet Union and their leading roles in the Cold War and, in Gorbachev's case, ending the Cold War.[9] Our research benefited from access to materials previously unavailable to McNamara biographers, including letters from McNamara's mother, Claranel, to him over the years; letters that McNamara exchanged with his wife, Margy, as newlyweds during World War II; admiring letters that Jackie Kennedy wrote to McNamara during the Kennedy and Johnson presidencies and beyond; and the secret diary of John McNaughton, his closest Pentagon aide on Vietnam policy matters.

We realize that our reconsideration of McNamara's life will not satisfy—nor should it—those who have rightfully never forgiven him, especially those who grew only more bitter at him upon learning that he sent so many American soldiers to die in a war in which he no longer believed. McNamara's mechanical prosecution of the Vietnam War, his baldly deceptive public reports on the conflict, his unstinting loyalty to President Lyndon Johnson, his obsessive and misplaced reliance on statistical data in making decisions—all these characteristics, described and denounced by contemporaries and chroniclers of the Kennedy and Johnson administrations, are both undeniable and indefensible. Although he was not the chief American decision maker about the war, the conflict was, as his critics said at the time, "McNamara's War."[10] History has properly judged his role in Vietnam as a terrible and costly failure of leadership.

But these failures raise further questions we will address: What was the source of the misplaced confidence that McNamara initially brought to Vietnam? How close did he come to an emotional breakdown while still serving as defense secretary? Moreover, with the help of newly available sources, we will also explore questions never raised before by McNamara biographers, such as the nature of his relationship with Jacqueline Kennedy, a relationship that clearly meant a great deal to them both and deepened through the emotional support he gave her after the assassination of her husband. How was it that the coldest Kennedy cabinet member became Jackie's warmest cabinet friend? What, exactly, did he do to earn her trust and affection? What was it about McNamara that led Jackie to tell him she wanted him to be a role model for her son, John Kennedy Jr.? And perhaps most importantly, how did her affection for him and her growing opposition to the Vietnam War, and his fondness for her, influence his own doubts about the war and his decision to remain in the Johnson administration to try to wind it down rather than publicly breaking with Johnson over the war? More broadly, how did McNamara, who knew no member of the Kennedy clan before his appointment as defense secretary, including the president, become part of the Kennedy inner circle and Georgetown social circuit, just months after settling in Washington? After the 1963 assassination of John Kennedy, a man he greatly admired and respected, why did he so faithfully serve Lyndon Johnson, whom he later described as "crude, mean, vindictive, scheming and untruthful"?[11] And was his close association after the assassination with Robert Kennedy and Johnson, raw political rivals, ultimately a betrayal of both men?

The McNamara we found in our research was a complicated figure riven by internal contradictions, suppressed emotions, periods of melancholy, zealous loyalty to the presidents he served, and a profound inability to understand and overcome his weaknesses. He was capable of great affection—for his wife, his children, and Jackie Kennedy and the women he courted after his wife died—but he struggled at times to connect emotionally with his children. Yet, after emotionally fraught periods, they reconnected. Despite the intervals of estrangement, Craig, looking back at his relationship with his father, and speaking for his sisters as well, said, "We never doubted his love for us. And in turn, I don't think that he ever doubted our love for him."[12] His effort to compartmentalize his life, rarely speaking to his family about the enormous pressure he faced at work or the stress he felt, left him isolated and without adequate emotional support. Yes, his lifetime reliance on cold data betrayed him when it came to running a war. But the rise and fall of Robert McNamara were propelled in larger measure by other factors that in the end devoured him. It seems clear to us that the combination of McNamara's disabling personality traits and Lyndon Johnson's own psychological perturbations produced a misshapen partnership that generated fatally flawed decisions about the Vietnam War.

Yet another issue insufficiently appreciated until now is McNamara's fascination with poetry and what it reveals about him. Not only did he read it throughout his life, he collected his favorites in an album. What makes that important is not his taste (it was conventional and relentlessly premodern, without Ezra Pound, e. e. cummings, or the early T. S. Eliot) but that it was replete with sentiment, that it constituted a kind of private repository of emotions of the sort that McNamara was loath to reveal in public, or even in private, partly because he viewed that as a sign of weakness.

MORE THAN A DECADE AFTER HIS DEATH IN 2009, DEAR COLORADO friends of McNamara's, Edgar and Elizabeth Boyles, wondered whether he might have been spared the torment that marred much of his life if he had acted on the injunction in the Gnostic Gospel of Thomas: "If you bring forth what is within you, what you bring forth will save you. If you do not bring forth what is within you, what you do not bring forth will destroy you."[13]

McNamara's war was not only in Vietnam. He was also at war with himself. Our aim in this book is neither to bury McNamara nor to praise him. It is to better understand him and thereby understand a man who had a decisive influence on US and world history.

SECTION I

PATHWAY TO POWER

=◆=

1916–1960

CHAPTER ONE

Driven to Excel

"How you get Bob McNamara out of that pair of people, I don't know. Maybe it was just an aberrant gene, like [McNamara's sister] Peg's red hair."[1] That was how a woman who knew McNamara well in college and married one of his best childhood friends contrasted him with his parents.

McNamara did differ from his parents, particularly in the intellectual and administrative brilliance that propelled him to the heights of business and public life. But his personality clearly reflected theirs. He shared or adopted some of their traits because his parents exemplified them or pressed them upon him; others he rejected and in the process made the opposite his own. His father was cold and aloof, his mother intense and highly emotional. It may seem contradictory, and it didn't manifest itself clearly until much later in life, but a combination of both his parents' qualities turned out to be the essence of their son.

McNamara's father, Robert James McNamara, twenty-two years older than his wife and age fifty-three when his son was born, was described by one friend of his son as "an indrawn, withdrawn, in-turning person," "sitting silently in a chair in the parlor," "very austere," and "terribly polite," paying little attention to his son's friends. A McNamara biographer, Paul

Hendrickson, portrayed Robert James as "closed-off and of another time, trying as best he could to parent children as an old man, an old man whom nobody seems ever to have witnessed tossing a ball to his children or getting down on the floor to roughhouse." "He might have," a boyhood friend of Bob McNamara, Dick Quigley, remembered, "but I never saw it. And I was over there pretty much with my own dad."[2] Bob McNamara never learned how to be a father, his son, Craig, believed, because he "did not have a role model of a loving father."[3] But Robert James's example did convey how to work hard, to be tolerant of people of various races and creeds, and to respect high culture.

McNamara's mother, Claranel Strange McNamara, hovered over him like a helicopter parent in a pre-helicopter age, smothering him with attention and instruction while pushing him relentlessly to greater heights. According to Vern Goodin, a close friend of McNamara, her son did not respect her intellectually as much as he did his father.[4] But he seemed to internalize much of her drive, her passion, and her vaulting ambition for him as well as her insistence that he live up to impossibly high standards of rectitude.

McNamara himself struck his friends as smart, even brilliant, incredibly hardworking, serious, and ambitious—but certainly not as "the human machine" a high school girlfriend, Annalee Whitmore, later read about.[5] Rather, in 1967, she remembered him as "one of the most gay, fun-loving, adventurous, intelligent young men I ever dated," as "one of the best dancers" at Piedmont High School, a guy with "natural rhythm, a ready sense of humor, high standards, a great intelligence—he was real fun, with spontaneous wit and gaiety." "People who think that Bob McNamara is stuffy or self-righteous just don't know him. He loathes phonies, stuffed shirts, status symbols, glad handers. . . . If I had the choice of one public servant to decide the future of this country, I'd choose Bob McNamara because he makes decisions on the basis of knowledge and humanity."[6] Another high school friend recalled him as "so painfully good. He was so neat, so clean; he was the kind of boy you'd trust with either your money or your sick kittens. But when I say that I make him sound like a square. Yet he wasn't, he wasn't—a square is an object of ridicule, and Bob was a great talker, a good dancer; it was always fun to have him around. He was never left out of anything."[7]

====

MCNAMARA'S GRANDFATHER, JEREMIAH MCNAMARA, FLED THE potato famine in County Cork, Ireland, and found refuge in East Boston in the middle of the nineteenth century. A year or two later he was working as a cobbler in Stoughton, Massachusetts, south of Boston. Together with his wife, Margaret, and their four children, he managed to make it to California in 1868, probably in search of Gold Rush riches; family legend has it that part of the trek was on the back of mules across Panama. Robert James McNamara, their fourth child, was then about four years old; four more children were born in California. Jeremiah McNamara settled in a predominantly Irish neighborhood of San Francisco, making a living by working in a shoe factory and by delivering milk.[8]

Robert James quit school after the eighth grade. Following his father into the shoe business, he rose steadily over the next six decades: first, cutting leather; next, as a traveling salesman; and then, secretary in a wholesaler's central office, western regional manager at another firm, Williams-Marvin, and finally, in 1927, sales manager of one of the biggest shoe manufacturers on the West Coast, Buckingham and Hecht.[9] One of his brothers worked as a postman in Oakland, another in a pottery mill, while the third died young.[10] (His two sisters married and ended up living in Hawaii, where Ray Ward, who married first one of them, and then, after the first one died, the other, became a senior vice president of the Dole Pineapple Company.)[11] In that sense, Robert James was a success, especially compared with some of his son's friends' fathers who lost their jobs during the Great Depression, and more than one of whom committed suicide.[12] Dick Quigley recalled a story his father Fred (Robert James's best friend) heard from a higher-up in Robert James's firm: "Every year, Bob McNamara goes out with one of the salesmen on his route and it's a matter of several weeks. The sales on that territory rise so much that it practically equals our cushion of profit for the year. So we all pray that he will do well for years to come because he's a miraculous salesman."[13]

For a time, at least, Robert James also set an example for selflessness, working to support his parents and siblings. On June 29, 1914, he got married to Claranel Strange, a secretary at the shoe firm where he worked, only after he had fulfilled his family obligations.[14] But his slowness to marry may also have reflected his pretentious self-image and his fussiness about finding someone worthy. Claranel (who later preferred to be called Nell) was twenty-two years his junior. For him, it may have seemed the last chance to wed. What motivated Nell, her daughter Peg thought, was fear that she would never marry if she didn't soon, plus the prospect of a union with a decorous, respectable older man who would protect her. The fact that he spent so much time traveling wasn't a drawback; he left her in charge of the household (except for its finances), in which she was clearly the dominant force. "My parents didn't have a very loving relationship," Peg remembered. It didn't help that Nell felt she married beneath her.[15]

Dick Quigley remembered Robert James as "a very smooth man," who carried himself gracefully, wore a pince-nez attached to a ribbon and tailor-made clothes, and had marvelous manners. Quigley recalled how "Uncle Bob used to come over to our house every Sunday morning for at least ten or fifteen years when we lived in Oakland. . . . I can picture him. He was very precise. He was always immaculately dressed as though he was going to a business meeting, although it was Sunday and he was just going to chew the fat with an old friend." (On Sundays, his wife took the children, Bob and Peggy, to the First Presbyterian Church.) "He had some of the mannerisms that President [Theodore] Roosevelt had. When he spoke, he spoke with his hands as well as his voice. His cigarette would go like this . . . there was this great curvy elegance to it. He'd blow smoke at the ceiling, he'd talk through the puffs." Young Quigley used to think, "How graceful, how wonderful to grow up and do that, which I never did."[16]

Peg McNamara, Bob's younger sister, described her father's other affectations to Paul Hendrickson: severely starched collars and cuffs, a ring with three diamonds in a row on a band of gold, plus another ring that Peg spotted in an old photo of him. ("Oh my, he's wearing two rings, isn't he?" she gasped just after assuring her interviewer that her father wasn't flashy.) In addition, Robert James had at least six personalized canes, one of them with "an elk's head for a handle carved from ivory, smooth as scrimshaw; sporting huge [deer's] antlers and a fierce flying eye," another ivory-and-gold one, and yet another, a black tapered cane with a gold top.[17] McNamara biographer Deborah Shapley describes other photographs of Robert James as "an impeccable figure in waistcoat, coat, tie, shined shoes, sometimes spats. The face is round yet severe and shielded by round-rimmed glasses and a hat. No one who describes him mentions humor, and . . . no one recalls him reading a book."[18] Robert McNamara himself confirms that he never saw either of his parents reading a book, except when his mother was helping him do his homework in the second or third grade.[19] His own devotion to reading was a kind of rebellion.

Hendrickson describes another photo of Robert James: "A small man, maybe five foot six or five foot seven, with a high collar and plastered hair [which his son emulated] is leaning back on a rococo table in a turn-of-the-century photo parlor."[20] Adds Hendrickson: "He was in thrall to ocean crossings and lounging robes. He owned a profusion of stickpins." At the dinner table he was just as finicky: once, on a sales trip in Oregon with one of his salesmen, he rejected prunes brought to the table by a waitress as "much too wrinkled."[21]

McNamara's finances were tight, but Robert James regularly sailed to Hawaii to visit his sisters on one of the Matson Lines steamships. He was said to know the captain of the *Lurline* personally and to pride himself on dining nightly at the captain's table. He also enjoyed yearly vacations at a sanitarium in wine country north of San Francisco. At St. Helena, according to Hendrickson, "there were white-uniformed boys to hold the quiver" for archery, and "burly figures in chalky shoes and starched trousers" helped guests into steam cabinets.[22] Bob McNamara doesn't refer to his father's expensive affectations, let alone condemn them, in his recollections, but his own insistence on frugality may have constituted another kind of rebellion.

Robert James was also fond of music. He liked to play records on the windup mahogany Victrola in the family's living room, especially those featuring the famous tenor Enrico Caruso, and was said to have performed in a light opera group in Oakland.[23] Robert James bought a piano and loved to have his daughter "play me something sweet at the piano."[24] But in general, he kept his distance from his children, his son's lifetime friend Vern Goodin remembered. All those mornings "chewing the fat" with the Quigleys, Dick Quigley thought, showed "Uncle Bob needed to get away from the house."[25] He was not only old-fashioned but prudish: coming home from work, he always stopped, Peggy remembered, doffed his hat, and kissed his wife, but never with any passion. Once when Peggy dared to walk across the living room with the back of her blouse not carefully tucked into her skirt, her father gasped in a horrified tone that Peggy reproduced in an interview decades later: "Peggy, is that your *skin*?"[26]

Bob McNamara characterized his own relationship with his father gently: Robert James "really was less closely associated [than my mother] with my early days in primary school and high school."[27] But McNamara's classmates and fraternity brothers at Berkeley didn't mince words: they "would have sworn that his dad wasn't alive—they'd never seen or even heard about him."[28] Will Goodwin noticed that Bob showed "great respect" for his father because he knew that although "the old man wasn't always right, you better not question it."[29] Bob didn't relish revealing that his father had been a shoe salesman. "If you watch his face," recalled Goodwin's wife Mary Jo, "he seems embarrassed sometimes when his family comes up, and there is this kind of jerky twitching motion . . ."[30]

Robert James's pretentious façade concealed a sense of insecurity that he revealed to the Quigleys. He "was always concerned," Dick Quigley recalled. "He used to come over and get my dad to give him a fight talk before he went out on the road. My dad knew how to pep him up a little bit." One time before Robert James embarked on a sales trip to Texas, "he was worried stiff," Dick Quigley remembered. Dick's father Fred "tried to calm him down. He said, 'Now Bob, you've been doing this for years. When you get down there, you'll get the inspiration as to how to go in.'" But Robert James didn't calm down. "'I don't know what to push when I go down there,'" he insisted. But on his return he claimed he had "knocked them dead" by selling boots made of polished leather to Texans, who were used to cowboy boots made of rough leather.[31]

This combination of insecurity and boastfulness irritated one of Robert James's salesmen, C. H. O'Brien, who told his family, "Oh, Mac is driving me crazy again. I'm trying to explain something to him, but he won't look at it my way, he can only see it his." He'd tell Robert James, "you can't deal with these country people this way. You have to be more informal and down-to-earth with them." But "he was hard as hell to get through to sometimes because of his fixed opinions."[32]

Bob McNamara must have sensed his father's insecurity. Indeed, it foreshadowed his own, which seemed to underlie his drive to please his teachers, his bosses, and eventually the presidents he served. Bob McNamara tried so hard to conceal that insecurity that he ended up projecting the opposite, namely, an intimidating sense of confidence and superiority. But the ache of his inner doubts was reflected in the sharp pity he felt for his father. Five decades later, while attending a performance of Arthur Miller's *Death of a Salesman*, Bob McNamara shocked the lady friend sitting next to him by suddenly weeping "openly and startlingly" at the story of Willy Loman's desperate but doomed efforts to portray himself to himself and to his family as a master salesman.[33]

Despite the distance between them, McNamara's father fostered his son's respect for art. Robert James went to plays and to the opera. And despite his dandyish exterior, he exemplified respect for work—"not just work for monetary reward," his son would say, "but academic work, public sector work and diligence in one's private activities was expected." McNamara's parents never discussed international events or domestic politics with their children.[34] "It was not an intellectual environment of discussing ideas or values or even events," McNamara recalled. But his father's behavior seemed to set high standards. "One was expected to work hard," Bob McNamara recalled, "for what it would bring you and your family, but also because that was the way responsible people behaved in our society. It was a responsibility to oneself and one's society. . . . I never questioned this. I never really thought there was any other way of behaving."[35]

Experiencing the Depression sharpened these lessons. "I didn't come from a 'poor' family," Bob McNamara recalled, "but I came from a family with limited means. I can remember, for example, in my teens not being able to go to Scout camp for two weeks because it cost $12 a week. And in those days, $25 for two weeks was something that at that particular moment of time we didn't have."[36] Robert James's children may not have been fully aware of the indulgences he permitted himself. But young Bob knew that the crash of 1929 had reduced the country to "a godawful mess." Indeed, the crash taught him "the need for safety nets and hence the merits of the Rooseveltian social legislation, and the need for each of us to move thriftily through life—[lessons] which have never left me and which, I think, on balance, have been very good."[37]

It also encouraged him, with more than a little prompting from his father, "to recognize the problem of labor." In the summer of 1934, after his first year in college, he wanted to work as a seaman. Although such jobs were scarce, he managed to get one "through my father's assistance." But striking longshoremen shut down the docks in every West Coast port and ships couldn't move. "It was a hell of a mess," McNamara remembered. He lost his job, but after several weeks the maritime companies hired scabs and "I went over and signed on as strikebreaker. I came home that night very proud to get a job in that kind of environment. My father just gave me unshirted hell. He said no son of his was ever going to be a strikebreaker! Now the point is he was not particularly prolabor either; it was just that was not going to happen in his family."[38]

NELL'S GRANDFATHER, GIDEON STRANGE, HAD MOVED FROM MIS-souri to Yuba City, California, about forty-five miles north of Sacramento, in 1870. His son, William, Nell's father, had five children, a son and four daughters. Shelby Strange, Bob McNamara's uncle, attended Stanford University, worked as a pharmacist, and then went to medical school and practiced in San Francisco. William Strange's eldest daughter, Bess, also went to Stanford, finishing in its second graduating class, and eventually supervised mathematics education in the San Francisco school system. Nell told Peg that she, too, would have gone to Stanford except that she had withdrawn from high school in 1902 because of what Peg believed was a case of typhoid, graduating only three years later when she was almost twenty-one. But Hendrickson speculates that a searing family feud may have delayed Nell's school career—her parents divorced after William Strange beat his daughter Ida so badly he knocked her "across the room and onto the floor," threatened to beat Bess's brains out, and raged so fiercely against his wife Martha that Nell's mother took her five children and left him, moving them from one apartment to another (four in all) over the course of seven years.[39]

The Strange family were Southern Methodists, which elevated their social status over the Irish Catholic McNamaras. Robert James's family insisted that he be married by a priest, a concession Nell accepted, but the ceremony took place below the communion rail rather than at the altar because the marriage was "mixed."[40]

Childhood friends of McNamara remembered his mother as a powerful woman. She was "a very strong person," recalled Joseph Cooper, a college classmate, "intense" but "charming." When Nell entertained, Cooper said, "it was like a hotel setting." Added Peg McNamara: "Garnishes perfect on the plate, grated carrots, every jot and tittle." "You went to her house for dinner," said Cooper, "and you could hardly move afterwards–everything from soup to nuts, onion soup for appetizer, every fork properly laid." Phil Pierpont, who once stayed with the McNamaras for a couple of weeks while looking for a summer job, recalled that he never saw either a grain of dust or a drop of alcohol in the house, but there was always some huge sweet, like a strawberry mousse, in the fridge.[41]

Dick Quigley remembered Nell as "a person of very positive ideas and opinions" that she gave "freely," not about politics but about "whether a sauce was made correctly or whether there were too many calories in this or that."

"She wasn't too tall," added Quigley's sister, Gwynn. "She was always beautifully dressed and quick moving. She fought being plump. I wouldn't say she was intellectual. Very nice person. A lady in that day and age."[42] According to her daughter, Nell "was president of everything she ever joined." "She was in the King's Daughters [an interdenominational Christian service organization that built healthcare facilities for the elderly], she was always in the PTA of every school we ever went to, she was president of the Mothers' Association, and she was very active in the Presbyterian Church."[43]

Nell doted on her first child. Bobby (as his mother called him when she wasn't cooing "Little Man" or "Little Robert") was born on June 9, 1916. His progress after that, as chronicled by his adoring mother in a book called *The Record of Our Baby Boy*, illuminates her character more than his. She records his first word, "Mamma," confessing her sorrow that "I cannot write, 'Daddy' in that space," which is "certainly no fault of your mother's"; after all, she had been saying " 'Da-da-da' to you constantly since birth, but 'what's the use?' " Bobby's first tooth was cause for celebration: his mother registered its arrival on January 11, 1917, his "two uppers" when they appeared on February 23, "a birthday gift to mother," and every tooth after that until all had arrived. She recorded his first gift, a little red chair that Bobby, "speaking" through his mother, welcomed warmly: "I think it's fine. My first chair"; "his first chum," a big toy soldier doll; his first shoes—"tan kid with white buttons and brown silk tassels—and how fond he is of them"—from his father's firm, presented by Robert James himself. She kisses his little foot on September 3, 1916, and two months later whispers in his ear, "Do you love your mother?" and imagines how adoringly he would reply if he could.[44]

Another story that Nell used to tell about her son reached and impressed his high school friends. Recalled Gwynn Quigley: "He didn't talk until he was two"—as if waiting until he could excel. "He didn't say a word, and then he finally said, 'I've been able to talk all the time, if I'd have wanted to.' That was his mother's favorite story."[45]

Nell McNamara pushed both her children to excel. She told them "they were the top of the world," said Gwynn Quigley, "maybe a little bit too much."[46] Peggy took adult sewing classes, swimming lessons at the Y, went to dancing school, and had other classes at the California School of Arts and Crafts.[47] According to Vern Goodin, Nell "took perfect care" of her son; she "spoiled him," added Gwynn. "She was an intense person," recalled Joe Cooper, and "she was very interested in Bob."[48] McNamara himself recalled both parents, but particularly his mother, exerting "strong pressure, if you will, to excel academically from my earliest years, pressure that "lasted throughout their entire lives and my entire educational experience," pressure epitomized by "If I had come home with an A—: 'Why wasn't it an A+?'"[49]

Moreover, Nell didn't just want her son to excel in school, she insisted that he behave properly. "Religious values," McNamara says, "were an important part" of what he acquired as he was growing up. Although his parents had different religious affiliations (he Catholic, she Protestant), they sent him and his sister to Presbyterian Sunday school, which he recalled attending "religiously"—so much so that "I received a medal for ten years of not perfect, but at least good attendance at Sunday school." The church, McNamara continued, had "a tremendous impact on my life."

According to his daughter Margy, her father was a "very religious man." "He never discussed that with us," she continued, but he took the family to church every Sunday. "We sat as a family, Dad took notes, but we never asked why." Among the books piled high on his nightstand, along with history, economics, poetry, and literature was religion.[50] He didn't consider himself "an intently religious person," he confessed late in life. He didn't believe in "God, the Father and Son and Holy Ghost," but he did believe that "beyond an individual's selfish interests and desire to advance the interests, in material ways, of himself or his family[,] I do believe there's something beyond that. And that came out of church, very, very important."

Another thing that came out of churchgoing was tolerance—"religious tolerance, ethnic tolerance, racial tolerance. I don't think we talked much about it," but "my friends were of various races and various religions and from my earliest years it was just accepted that one should be tolerant, that one should help one's fellow man—both individually and generally, that one should maximize one's own capacity and one's own use of one's faculties. Those values were inculcated at the earliest age."[51]

Values like these were admirable, but Nell McNamara's preaching could also be narrow and leave scars. To discourage him (and anyone else who entered their house) from drink, she banned liquor. In one of a series of interviews he did with Brian VanDeMark, a historian who helped him write his memoirs, McNamara, as if "out of the blue," suddenly described the "tremendous stress" he had experienced throughout his life. It began, he told VanDeMark, with his mother's "very strict dictates on behavior, language, and sex, among other things." He had joined the Boy Scouts in response to his mother's wishes, but when he found that dirty language and sex loomed large there, too, that made him feel "conflicted."[52] Conflicted or not, he satisfied not only the Scouts that he lived up to their exemplary standards, but his best friends, too. His oldest friend, Will Goodwin, insisted to Deborah Shapley that Bob was the epitome of "the Boy Scout Law," whose twelve requirements were that scouts be "trustworthy, loyal, helpful, friendly, courteous, kind, obedient, cheerful, thrifty, brave, clean, and reverent," with the only caveat being that "he is indeed reverent in his own way."[53]

According to Paul Hendrickson, "he learned to lie at his mother's knee." "For all of Nell's sense of what was proper, she was an incredible exaggerator and embellisher."[54] McNamara supposedly not having said a word until he was able to speak perfectly at age two was one such fib. And there would be other fantasies, such as claiming that a Harvard University president traveled all the way to California to recruit her son to its faculty, and that the wartime letters that she boasted Bob sent her every day from overseas actually existed.

Late in life he confessed to an interviewer that if he "grew up not communicating," his mother was also responsible. "She expected me to do certain things and live in certain ways and her ideas were—were not practical. I had the most wonderful group of friends, but they weren't what she visualized young men should be, but I never talked about it because—so I got into the habit of withholding things."[55]

McNamara's mother not only pressured her son; more than three decades later she was policing her grandson, Craig. He recalled "an incident when I said something inappropriate in front of her, and she hauled me up to the tiled bathroom of our two-story Tudor home [in Ann Arbor, Michigan] to wash my mouth out with soap." Which later led Craig to wonder "if she treated my father this harshly. I don't think that Dad even attended her funeral. What kind of childhood brutalities did she inflict on him?"[56] Craig's conclusion: His father's mother was "very, very over-bearing" and a "very spiteful woman." And that with little or no love from his father and moving away from his mother, he "let that part of his life go and never embraced them in our life."[57]

═══

ACCORDING TO HENRY TREWHITT, ONE OF BOB MCNAMARA'S HIGH school teachers thought that "Bob felt [his mother] had pushed him too hard and that Bob had told his mother so."[58] But he not only succumbed to much of that pressure, he convinced himself that many of the habits and strictures his mother preached, especially the duty to excel in school, were so important that he adopted them as part of his own creed.

For McNamara's first seven years, the family lived in San Francisco in a flat between Sixteenth Avenue and Clement Street in the Central Richmond district, not far from where the Golden Gate Bridge was built some years later. Peggy was told that her brother had been "sort of sickly with bronchial trouble" and had been homeschooled by his mother before attending elementary school.[59] McNamara remembered the school as a wooden building called "The Shack," which was overcrowded with prod-ucts of the post–World War One baby boom. But he recalled his first-grade teacher, whose values echoed those of his parents, as "superb." She "gave the class an examination every month in the first grade and then reseated the class based on the results of the examination. The rows were vertical rows and she put the person with the highest grades every month in the first chair in the lefthand row. I worked like heck to be in that chair."[60]

McNamara's main competitors for the coveted chair were "Chinese, Japanese and Jews," he recalled, and "five days a week I'd work like hell to beat them." But on the sixth day, Saturday, when McNamara rested and played with his neighborhood friends, his rivals attended their "ethnic schools" where they studied their language, their culture, and their val-ues, so that on Monday, he said, primed with extra learning, they were "determined to beat that goddamned Irishman." Was all this pressure at school, on top of what he was feeling at home, healthy for a first grader? McNamara insists he welcomed it, at least in retrospect, regarding it as "a tremendous influence on me," showing that "even in the first grade I was oriented to and motivated by a determination to achieve academic excellence." The intense environment "stimulated my interest" in excelling and "supported the value I placed on it. This was true throughout all my years in grade school, in high school, the university, and graduate school."[61]

When McNamara was seven, his family moved to San Rafael, in Marin County across the bay from San Francisco, where the climate was a bit sunnier and drier and better for his health.[62] Peggy remembered their new home as a "large, brown-shingled house" with "quite a bit of land and we had a lot of trees," including apricot, peach, and lemon trees.[63] It was "a pleasanter place to bring up children," McNamara recalled, "more rural" and "quite attractive," but requiring a more extended commute for his father: a train from San Rafael to Sausalito, and then a ferry to San Francisco. So a year later, the family moved again, this time to Oakland.[64]

McNamara attended Westlake Junior High School, where his social studies teacher, Marie Carriker, remembered him as "a student of perfection. When he did research on different countries, he would make beautiful books. He sat in the last seat in the back row, but you knew he was there. He was conspicuous for his scholarship, not his personality. What I mean is, he was not pushy, but when you called on him, he was ready."[65]

The Oakland house, 1036 Annerley Road, was a two-story structure with a cement exterior, a big living room in the front, a dining room and kitchen facing the rear, and three bedrooms upstairs.[66] "It wasn't a mansion," Dick Quigley remembered, "but it was a substantial home" in "an area in Oakland that just borders—perhaps half a block—from Piedmont."[67] Visited in 2022, the house was still "very comfortable," as its current occupant, an eighty-five-year-old widow, described it. "Very large, very comfy, very sunny," with lots of windows and woodwork. And the neighborhood "hasn't changed at all," she added, since she and her husband moved in more than fifty years before. All that could be heard on Annerley Road in the middle of the day in 2022 was the whirring of leaf blowers and the chirping of birds.[68] As for Piedmont, McNamara recalled it as "the Westchester County [an affluent suburb of New York

City] of the Bay Area," a location, it turned out, that was pivotal in his life because it gave him access to Piedmont High School.[69] Piedmont, nestled in the East Bay hills that rise from the flatlands of Oakland, was much wealthier than Oakland, with better schools. Piedmont High resembled a prep school with well-kept grounds surrounding its yellow stucco building, paintings hanging in corridors, and many female students wearing "middy blouses with ties, simple skirts and white buck or saddle shoes."[70] According to McNamara's high school friend Stanley Johnson, the school had an art program and a concert series in which "famous artists" came and played, a precursor of the kind of cultural offerings that McNamara cherished later in life. "It was just sort of expected that you would go on to college, and students studied with that in mind."[71]

Peggy's impression was that her parents intended to move to Piedmont, but the people who sold them the house didn't tell them it was actually in Oakland. Or did Nell realize that a house on the Oakland-Piedmont border would be cheaper while offering her children the chance to attend Piedmont High? In any event, McNamara recalled, "my mother managed to obtain entrance for my sister and me to the Piedmont school system."[72]

By the time McNamara entered Piedmont in the tenth grade, he was already a star. "He was very smart," Peggy remembered. "I think everyone always knew that he would be very successful at what he did, he was that kind of a child. He was active in everything," including the Boy Scouts. Their parents "were very interested in everything he did . . . and consequently he tried to live up to their expectations."[73] "I was a member of the Piedmont Scouts, not Oakland," added McNamara, neglecting to recall, at least on this occasion, the dirty talk and sex talk that had made him so uncomfortable in the Scouts, "and that was a very, very important character-forming experience." Not only was he an Eagle Scout, he was a counselor at Scout camp for a couple of years.[74]

Piedmont itself, as McNamara's high school classmate Annalee Whitmore remembered, was a small town with a gas station, a drugstore "where we could eat lunches, and a grocery store named Cheatham's—maybe that was it." "We could look down and see the Golden Gate," she continued. "Millionaires lived there. There were huge, huge mansions." One of the millionaires was Stanley Dollar, owner of the Dollar Steamship Lines. Annalee remembered "a great party" at Diana Dollar's house during which the kids played " 'sardines'—in which someone has to hide and the lights are out and you have to go around feeling where people are, and then when you find the 'it' who is hiding you have to just squeeze in and hide with them" until, at the end, "there was a great bulge of humanity somewhere in a corner behind a chest of drawers or something." When Diana gave a block party, "the whole street was closed off and smoothed and soaked. A big band was brought in under a tent. It was a marvelous dance."[75]

In keeping with his Puritan ethic, McNamara later played down his proximity to the "rich kids" who lived up the hill. "Those children didn't have anything I wanted my children to have."[76] But according to his teacher Anna Lee Guest, the students who lived on the hill had a head start academically: "It would take a strong student from lower Piedmont to make it up there on the hill, let alone excel, but Bob did." "I could pick them out pretty well as they came along," she told Hendrickson. "All I know is that [Bob] did everything he was supposed to do and he did it right."[77] Not only did he compile an academic record at Piedmont that his wealthier classmates envied, he threw himself with gusto into an imposing array of extracurricular activities, and made friends with his most promising peers. Twenty-six A's and only seven B's (four of them in French, two in physical education, and one in junior English) adorned his academic transcript. Anna Lee thought, although she wasn't sure, that "in order to get an A in art, Bob took afterschool lessons in weaving, which we all thought indicated remarkable devotion." Like his mother, he joined almost every available organization: the Board of Control (the student council), the Boys' Council (a more social organization), and the Alpha Clan Council (executive committee of the honor society). He was editor of the 1933 school yearbook, the *ClanO-Log*, a member of the Glee Club and the Opera, and president of *Rigma*, a secret fraternity committed to service that a teacher later described as "more of a nuisance than any-thing else," and president of the French Club, despite his having received four of his seven grades of B in French.[78] The teacher who selected him as yearbook editor, Miss Lane, regarded him as the best she ever picked.

His "organizational ability," she said, was "simply amazing." He arrived early and stayed late at work on *ClanO-Log*, and when she asked him if he needed anything, he would say he was getting along fine.[79]

McNamara's best friends at Piedmont High included other high achievers such as Vern Goodin, later a San Francisco trial lawyer, and Annalee, whose high school memberships included twelve extracurricular activities compared to McNamara's eight, and took up five lines in the yearbook compared to McNamara's three. She would become a *Time-Life* correspondent in the Pacific and cowrote *Thunder Out of China* with Theodore White.[80] McNamara dated Annalee, who remembered the time she and Bob "drove to San Francisco with another couple . . . to dance, probably at the Mark Hopkins [Hotel]. We went down to the beach after[ward] to eat something—chili, I don't remember—and ride on a roller coaster and missed the last ferry back and didn't arrive home until just about dawn." Her father was coming out the door when they got home, and "thank heavens my father just said, 'Good morning' and left." "We had marvelous times," Annalee remembered.[81]

Bob also dated Hallie Booth, whom many boys considered the most beautiful girl in the school. Annalee later described her as "lovely to look at—beautiful features: light brown, curly, wavy hair; ultrafeminine. She would look up at you through her long eyelashes and say, 'Would you help me with this?' And it would melt anyone's heart."[82] But Hallie was no extracurricular slouch either; she was vice president and secretary of the student body and editor of the student newspaper, *The Highlander*, secretary of the Alpha Clan, and a member of the Interclass Council, among other things.[83]

Goodin recalled McNamara as a supersmart student: always brief and to the point on his exams; he once submitted a half-page essay for which he received a grade of A, whereas Goodin got a C for a five-pager.[84] But McNamara wasn't aggressive in class. He respected his teachers, Guest remembered, he waited to speak until he was called on, and, unlike in first grade where his teacher rewarded him with a seat in the first row, he chose to sit in the back of the room, as if not to flaunt his brilliance.[85] Dick Quigley described McNamara as "kind of reticent, sort of a holdback person," but he had "a hunch that he was always looking to the best chance for Bob in whatever he did." Added Gwynn Quigley: "He was brought up that way. I think his mother must have just hammered that he would be the top."[86] Stan Johnson, president of the Piedmont student body and later another San Francisco lawyer, disagreed: "Bob came to the surface because of his abilities. He didn't work his way deliberately into prominent positions. He arrived because of his natural qualities, but he refused to exploit them for personal advancement." Another classmate recalled him as "not aloof, but self-contained." "Still missing," comments McNamara's early biographer, Trewhitt, "was the awesome drive that became famous later." Classmates and adults who knew McNamara during this period assumed that the special drive he did show came from his mother, who "appeared at the school to clear up any questions about grades." And when she appeared, a teacher told Trewhitt with a grin, "it was a good idea to have answers."[87] "I can tell you this," Guest insisted, "all [his mother] wanted was for Bob to succeed. She wanted everything for those kids."[88] Stanley Johnson "never saw signs of anything but a close, informal family relationship." But according to Johnson, "Bob never actually discussed his father and mother."[89] Nor did he later with his son, Craig: "I can't tell you more than two words about my grandfather," said Craig. "I'm asking you, why wouldn't my father have told me about his father? I think I've seen one photograph."[90]

By his senior year at Piedmont High, McNamara was eager to head to college and start an independent life. He wound up not far from home, still within his mother's gravitational force.

CHAPTER TWO

Golden Bear

"I applied for admission to Stanford," McNamara recalled. "Stanford at the time was one of the very few universities in the country that had entrance exams. I . . . took the entrance exams, was accepted, but couldn't go because I couldn't afford it. I would like to have, but I think it was very fortunate that I didn't. I went to Berkeley instead. Berkeley cost at the time $26 a semester—$52 a year for all tuition-related expenses. Actually, they said that tuition was $0 and these were fees for towels and whatever. $52 a year plus living [expenses], but I lived at home, so it was a very inexpensive way to get a magnificent education."[1] Stanford tuition for a full year was $300.[2]

His father, firmly in charge of family finances, vetoed Stanford. Robert James made the choice easier by buying his son a used car that Annalee Whitmore recalled as a black Model A Ford with green wire wheels. Most days he left home before eight, fortified by breakfast prepared by his mother (a glass of orange juice with a raw egg in it, unconventional fare he swallowed every morning throughout his life), picked up his friend Vern Goodin (who lived a block and a half away), and drove through the dense morning fog that frequently cloaked the area, stinting on use of the car's headlamps to conserve the battery. On the way home, Bob would sometimes detour through the Oakland Hills to glimpse farms nestled in the Moraga Valley, then head downhill, coasting as much as possible to save gas, but being sure to be on time on days when he had promised to pick up his father at the Lake Shore and Trestle Glen trolley stop on his way home from work.[3]

"Cal" Berkeley was a mammoth state university, the first and flagship campus of the University of California system that was already one of the nation's elite academic institutions. It had some 25,000 students, half of them undergraduates, some 3,000 of them in McNamara's freshman class. It boasted an activist president, Robert Gordon Sproul, who lured star professors like nuclear physicist Robert Oppenheimer (the future "father of the atomic bomb") and Ernest O. Lawrence (constructor of the first cyclotron) to the faculty; it also had a fabled football team and championship crew.

Berkeley was a huge new world compared to Piedmont High. In the beginning it intimidated even McNamara. Fran Helmer, who grew up across Annerley Road from the McNamaras, thought he felt inadequate at first; since his personality didn't bowl people over, he tried to impress his peers with his grades, by joining every possible campus organization, and by taking up all sorts of other activities, like skiing, and sticking with them until he got good at them.[4] The ambition, talent, and drive that had propelled him to the top in high school eventually made him a star in college, as well. He recalled being "gripped by the excitement of expanding my understanding of the world" as his understanding of that world "exploded," and he confessed he had a "tremendous drive to succeed in grades."[5] His intelligence, eagerness to learn, and straight-arrow sense of duty and decency led professors and administrators to admire him. But performing on the big new stage also displayed other sides of him: the warmth and sensitivity that lay beneath a sometimes aloof exterior, social awkwardness heightened by his being a year younger than most other students, and being a commuter rather than in residence. He also revealed a kind of naivete and the insecurity that went with it. There was also his effort to ingratiate himself with important men, in this case the university president and provost, that loomed large later in life as he cultivated his relations with Henry Ford II, John F. Kennedy, and Lyndon Johnson.

=====

MCNAMARA'S FIRST-YEAR GRADES WEREN'T ALL STELLAR: HE GOT A's in math and philosophy, but a C and a B in English courses and another C in French—the latter revealing, biographer Deborah Shapley says, "a lifelong tin ear for languages" that, one should add, didn't help him decode Vietnamese (or even French) culture during his many trips to the country in the 1960s.[6] By his sophomore year he was emphasizing courses in philosophy and math; his favorite course, significantly, "Moral and Civil Polity," taught by philosopher George Plimpton Adams, drew on items in the day's newspaper to pose problems of "conflict of obligation," that is, the grounds on which one should make decisions.[7] He thought a logic course taught by Adams was "terrific . . . I enjoyed it immensely."[8] Planning to major in economics, he was becoming accustomed to thinking in quantitative terms, he told Shapley, to talking and thinking in numbers.[9] This approach paid off in outstanding sophomore grades: nine A's and one B. Many years later McNamara boasted: "I was elected a member of Phi Beta Kappa at the University of California at the end of my sophomore year. There were only three out of a class of whatever—3500—that were elected Phi Beta Kappa at the end of sophomore year. And that came about because I had gone to a good high school, was going to a good university, and I was highly motivated to achieve excellence in scholarship."[10]

McNamara's teachers admired him. Malcolm Davisson, who taught him economics, recalled him as "very broadly based. He read widely outside his courses. Frankly, he didn't have to work too hard for his grades, so he had resources to spend elsewhere. I regarded him as a genuine intellectual, and I fully expected him to become a teacher."[11] "He had something different," Davisson said later, "some breadth of intellectual curiosity that was different from his friend Vernon Goodin. I could tell it." McNamara returned the compliment. It was after taking Davisson's courses, he said, that he consciously adopted the style of thinking and talking quantitatively.[12]

Others, too, noticed McNamara. During his sophomore year he was invited to serve on the high-status Student Affairs Committee. Accepting the appointment dutifully, he wrote to the president of the Associated University Students of California: "I wish to express my appreciation of the honor. . . . I shall endeavor to perform my duties conscientiously and wisely." During the mid-thirties, as student radicals pressed for change at the university as well as in society, McNamara saw himself as "part of a liberal branch of my class, the liberal element of the student government, we were the responsible student leaders trying to avoid tearing the university apart."[13]

The Order of the Golden Bear was one of several quasi-secret societies at Berkeley; Triune and Winged Helmet were two others. Triune was a sophomore organization, Winged Helmet enrolled juniors, and Golden Bear, seniors. To be invited to join any of them was an honor, but Golden Bear most of all. Its members had to be leaders of established campus groups. "If you had the choice of just one thing," recalled one former member, "you'd rather be Golden Bear than Phi Beta Kappa or Skull and Keys or anything else." "We thought we were really helping the administration to run the university." "The fraternity wanted you to achieve Golden Bear. . . . The fraternities were very anxious to have their members occupy important positions in college activities."[14] "They were known and people knew you were in them," Joe Cooper remembered, "but they were not discussed. They were not secret societies; they were more or less confidential. . . . They were related to the problems we felt the university had; they related to even details of whatever was going on in the university. On occasion, there was a situation in which you wanted to commend them, but that doesn't take as much discussion as ones where you thought there could be improvement."[15]

As the most select of these societies, the Golden Bear met with leading university administrators in a rustic log cabin, called Senior Men's Hall, located along Strawberry Creek upstream of the faculty club. "In the early days of the building, Professor of History Henry Morse Stephens likened Senior Hall to the 'heart' of the University, situated close to the 'mind' of the Faculty Club."[16] Although the Golden Bear focused on university matters, members were burnishing their personal resumes and advancing their career prospects. President Sproul preached the virtues of public service but also endorsed society membership as "a profitable investment . . . from which [Golden Bear members] must expect their dividends of personal happiness and public leadership in later life."[17] Sproul often met with the Golden Bear and the Student Affairs Committee, sometimes over breakfast at the faculty club or at a reception in his home. "He knew that we were interested in campus problems, or he may have been interested in our ideas," McNamara's friend Stan Johnson recalled. But the university provost, Monroe Deutsch, a professor of classics, was "the one we had most of our contacts with." He struck Johnson and his friends as a "very affable, pleasant, understanding type of person, who was interested in students and in seeing that students not only learned scholarship, but learned how to get along in the world after they got out of school." It was in service of this noble aim, presumably, that on one memorable occasion Deutsch recited stanzas from Rudyard Kipling's "The Palace," a poem to which McNamara often returned later in life, in which an elderly king, learning from the his own and his predecessor's hubris, admits his mistakes and warns his successors, "After me cometh a Builder. Tell him, I too have known."[18]

If this wasn't the beginning of McNamara's lifelong love of poetry, it was an early example thereof, foreshadowing lessons he learned later in life and meriting inclusion in the album of poems he collected. Deutsch read the powerful poem with such emotion as to reduce McNamara, who was the Golden Bear's warden, to tears.[19] But the provost had noticed him long before then. As a freshman, McNamara was invited to tea by Provost and Mrs. Deutsch. "I was always taught to be prompt" (presumably by his parents), he later told Shapley. So he arrived early at the Deutsches' home, only to discover that he was the first and for the time being the only guest. Observing the hosts introducing themselves to the next few guests with a smile and a handshake, McNamara positioned himself next to them and began shaking hands and informing each arrival of his own name.

McNamara laughed as he recounted this story to Shapley many years later, but he must have been mortified when he discovered his error.[20] Or was he already arrogant enough not to be embarrassed? By the time he was a senior, he was not just more adept at dealing with Cal's highest administrators but more than a little overconfident. President Sproul's longtime secretary, Agnes Robb, told Hendrickson how McNamara once dropped by Sproul's office to tell him (in Hendrickson's paraphrase) "how he should run the university." After McNamara departed, Sproul "shook his head [and] laughed out loud," incredulous, but still apparently liking his uppity young friend.[21]

Being head of the Student Judicial Committee, which investigated and adjudicated student misbehavior, was the perfect assignment for a believer, like McNamara, in the Boy Scout Law. On November 11, 1936, the *San Francisco Chronicle* reported that his committee had unearthed "pilfering of other people's property from gym lockers." What the *Chronicle* labeled "wholesale cheating" during an exam on American institutions became the subject of an April 11, 1937, investigative report by McNamara.[22] His committee convicted a star football player for academic cheating. Charles T. Post, editor of *The Daily Cal*, thought such severity reflected a kind of innocence, as if McNamara naively counted on his fellow students always to do the right thing.[23] But the football coach went out of his way to praise McNamara, whether sincerely or because once the verdict was announced he had to endorse it.[24]

McNamara's choice of a fraternity to pledge in his freshman year reflected his initial innocence, awkwardness, and eagerness to be accepted. Fraternities were central to Berkeley social life. Veritable mansions, they were located along the upper end of the campus on leafy but busy streets. The most prestigious houses sought out the classiest candidates while they were still local high schoolers, inviting the most promising ones on all-day yacht excursions. McNamara's best friends at Cal—like Will Goodwin, Stan Johnson, and Walter "Wally" Haas from the wealthy family that owned Levi Strauss & Co.—all joined fancier frats while McNamara quickly settled for Phi Gamma Delta, because, reports Hendrickson, "they got hold of him early, rushed him ahead of the more likely houses, and the socially unsure boy said yes."[25] FIJI (as it was known) "was kind of a wild bunch," one of its members, Carson Magill, recalled. "Prohibition having been repealed when Roosevelt came in, there was a lot of drinking. It was just like, oh boy, now we can [have] alcohol! A lot of people tried to see how much they could drink the first two weeks. A lot of boozing."[26]

McNamara tried on occasion to lift the intellectual level of his brothers. In the fall of 1936, according to a YMCA bulletin (called "The Y's Bear") that kept track of fraternity doings, he stimulated several fraternities including his own to invite faculty members to speak at their houses. And the next spring he and Will Goodwin led weekly discussions in their fraternities on "Plato's principles."[27] Some of his raucous frat brothers came to respect him: "He was definitely of the more serious group," Magill observed. "Nobody resented it. He wasn't singled out as a bookish person; he just did his thing and tolerated those who wanted to play more than he did."[28] Or, as Magill put it to Hendrickson on another occasion, "Everybody knew he was so damn smart, we respected Bob for that. It was as if we all had said to ourselves, 'You don't have to be like us, Bob, because we know you're so damn bright.' The one or two times I doubled with him, I got mighty thirsty."[29]

But others looked down on McNamara as a dull "day dog."[30] "I'll tell you what it was," remembered one brother. "He was missing a feeling he was anybody. As soon as he got a sense of that, that turned him on. He was like a guy who came to a cocktail party ten drinks behind. . . . You sort of passed him. . . . He never seemed to enjoy it. It wasn't that he was unpopular, he was a nonentity in a sense."[31]

Opting for Phi Gam was a bad choice, but, characteristically, McNamara determined to stick it out. Whether or not he enjoyed the FIJIs, he struggled to win their respect. He chaired their Mardi Gras dance, the first big bash of the year, when he was a freshman, and later served on the "Vigilante Committee," whose mandate (believe it or not!) was to revive hazing on the campus. He loyally attended Monday suppers and meetings, took part in Saturday morning cleanups, parked his car in the Phi Gam driveway on Bancroft Way, and posed with the rest of the brothers for group photos, usually (Hendrickson reports) in the second

row, in a cardigan and white bucks, "looking glum."[32] He even ended up
as house manager.[33]

His mother joined Phi Gam's Mother's Committee, the better to follow the next steps in her boy's irresistible rise. (Magill remembered Mrs.
McNamara as "a very pleasant little whitehaired lady; she was a very regular
attendant at the mothers' club.")[34] Despite Nell's strictures against inde-
cent language, her son got off a memorable line about his inability to book
a hall for a big event: he and his friends were like a fat man wearing tight
pants—no ball room.[35] And McNamara even proved his mettle in "class
fights." "The upper class would make us go three rounds with each other,"
Magill recalled. "I'd transferred up from Santa Clara; I'd taken some box-
ing down there, so I hit him right in the chin about the first minute of our
engagement and knocked him down. He was my friend. I didn't want to
hurt him or anything, so I thought, well, maybe I'll take it easy. Instead,
boy, he came on strong and I had my hands full the rest of the fight. We
really had a good go. You know, he was a good guy."[36]

Given his principles, on the one hand, and his need to be accepted on
the other, plus his habit of obeying his parents and yet wanting to make
his own way, McNamara must have felt conflicted about Phi Gam. Years
later, when the Phi Gam "nonentity" was a top Ford Motor Company
executive and then US secretary of defense, he got his revenge. Magill, by
then a successful advertising executive in San Francisco, sent "greetings
from an old fraternity brother back in California."

"Yeah, who's that?" McNamara asked an aide.

"Carson Magill," he was told.

"Oh, that's nice."

A later note from Magill brought no response either. Nor did a con-
gratulatory note when McNamara joined the Kennedy administration.[37]

———

SPORTS WAS ANOTHER ARENA IN WHICH MCNAMARA TESTED HIM-
self at Berkeley, seeking to excel and not giving up easily when the challenge was more than he could handle. He tried out for the Cal crew, which
had competed for the United States in both the 1928 and 1932 Olympics.

According to the coach, Carroll (Ky) Ebright, who was something of a martinet, McNamara was "a good kid, tenacious," but he "wasn't big enough. He weighed less than 160 and was only five feet eleven. He couldn't beat out the bigger fellows."[38] On top of that, McNamara recalled, "I had to take four hours out of my day to drive from the Berkeley campus down to the Alameda Estuary [in San Francisco Bay] to do the crew practice and then drive back home."[39] But he was "pushing himself to the limit," his friend Will Goodwin recalled, and managed to make it as stroke of the second freshman boat and then served as crew manager during his second and third years, until he was replaced by a classmate in his senior year.[40] Many years later, recounting his rowing history for a *Washington Post* story about the athletic New Frontiersmen of the Kennedy administration, McNamara exaggerated his prowess a bit, telling the reporter, "I liked the sport except for those last damned 200 strokes. But I had to give it up as a sophomore. I didn't have time."[41]

Meanwhile, McNamara challenged himself in other outdoor activities. Prompted by Will Goodwin, he took up mountain climbing and skiing in the Sierra Nevada Mountains and pursued them ferociously. "Bob was bound and determined to be a good skier," Stan Johnson recalled. "He kept practicing whatever was weakest."[42] McNamara "loved the mountains," Joe Cooper remembered. "When he'd go on a trip into the mountains, he would enjoy every part of it. He loved the mountains. He loved to look at them. He loved to walk hard and fast and long through them." These initial forays into the high country of the Sierra Nevada range were the beginning of a lifetime love of mountain hiking and skiing—but not fly-fishing—that eventually extended to the Colorado Rockies and became an important way for McNamara to challenge himself physically. At the time, his friend Joe Cooper thought "there was a little too much general love of the whole thing to let him specialize enough to become the type of fly-fisherman I am. I think Bob's eyes were too much open [to everything] around him to maybe concentrate enough on fishing."

Cooper invited McNamara to spend time at his family's ranch in northern California. Cooper's father set out to teach McNamara to fish and thought at first he had made a convert: "I think we got him. I think he

lost that fish and I heard him swear. I think maybe he's going to make it."
Cooper's father didn't make a convert, but McNamara himself did. When
Cooper brought his friend back to the ranch a week later, father and son
were mixing drinks in the pantry when the elder Cooper whispered: "You
know, Joey, you've brought a lot of nice young boys up here before, but last
weekend you brought a real man up here."[43]

The "real man" also tried prospecting for gold. With local newspapers
reporting how people who had lost their jobs and found themselves on
relief were panning old tailings in the mountains, McNamara and Johnson "thought that would be sort of fun to try and do it, and maybe learn
something about gold-panning." They bought a gold pan, packed camping
gear and a pick and shovel in Bob's car, and drove up to an old Piedmont
Scout camp on Spanish Creek, one of many streams in the forested landscape along the western slopes of the Sierra. There they found an old miner
who spent summers panning a few dollars' worth of gold and was grateful
for company; he showed them how to set up a sluice box and where to dig.
"We learned quite a little bit about how to actually pan for gold," Johnson remembered, "and we actually did get a little gold." After hoisting the
sluice box on the back of Bob's car, they headed across the Western Sierra
looking for more. But on the way the sluice box broke and they lost the
bottle into which they had deposited the few nuggets they had found.[44]

Shipping out to sea as an ordinary seaman—not just once but three
times—was another challenge McNamara set for himself. The summer
before his first year at Berkeley, when he was just seventeen, he worked on
a ship that sailed to New York and back through the Panama Canal. His
second attempt, in 1934, failed owing to the longshoremen's strike, but
the next summer, with the strike over, he sailed again, this time on the SS
Peter Kerr. "Nobody wanted the damned jobs," McNamara recalled, "they
were terrible jobs." The pay was around twenty dollars a month, there was
no fresh running water in the crew's quarters, the bunks were so infested
with bedbugs that one morning he counted nineteen bites (overall, he
had "forty bedbug bites on one leg between the ankle and the knee"), and
the food was "inedible." He lost about thirteen pounds that summer, but
since "I'd been rowing on the Cal crew I was in topnotch shape."[45]

After graduation, McNamara returned to the sea again, this time with his friend Will Goodwin. First, they worked on a freighter, the *Mandalay*, on a trip to Hawaii, and then on the SS *President Hoover*, the Dollar Line cruise ship that was said to be the biggest one plying the Pacific. Living conditions in the crew's quarters were somewhat better this time: there were thirteen bunks in the "ordinary seaman's foxhole," three or four on each of four sides, plus, a red cross on one of the showers, which McNamara and Goodwin took to mean it was safe for sailors who didn't have venereal disease. In fact, it was for those who contracted VD, who of course, did not include McNamara or Goodwin. The work on the ship was hard: throwing off lines, swabbing decks, pulling watch duty on the midnight-to-four "dog watch." But according to Goodwin, the chief mate liked McNamara so much he occasionally let him take the helm.[46]

The trip provided McNamara his first encounter with Asian poverty, colonialism, and war. Wandering around Shanghai in 1937 he saw "malnourished, unhealthy, ill-housed, illiterate" people living in "hovels made of sticks," whereas in the "islands of luxury" of the British and French concessions he saw signs declaring, "No cats, dogs or Chinese allowed."[47] While the *Hoover* was anchored at the mouth of the Yangtze River, a Chinese plane mistook it for a Japanese troopship and bombed the deck, killing two men and wounding others. McNamara was so intent on photographing the incident that he had to be dragged belowdecks.[48] Was this uncharacteristic recklessness on his part, or a sign of incipient fascination with war and violence?

═══

THE OVERALL IMPRESSION MCNAMARA MADE ON HIS CLOSEST COLlege friends, like the one he made on high school friends, differs substantially from his public image later in life. Joe Cooper thought he was "a very honest man, a very sound man, a very smart man, an extremely congenial man, and a man with the best of principles. All of that sounds kind of stuffy, but he wasn't stuffy; he was a very warm man with a great sense of humor." And "his ethics were excellent." He would judge everything as to "what should be done and with very good reasons. He would approach anything from a long-term perspective" and ask "what was a 'good' thing. . . . And he was a very good judge of that."[49]

According to Vern Goodin, as paraphrased by Van DeMark, McNamara was "intensely loyal to all his old friends" and "a fascinating raconteur" who told stories with "a total recall of detail." He was a person of "absolute, total integrity and morality—without being judgmental about other people's failings."[50] Hendrickson asked Goodin, who was elected president of the sophomore class, whether everyone was in awe of McNamara's intelligence. Goodin's answer: "He didn't seem so much smarter, although I did look over once and see Bob with a one-page blue book answer while the rest of us were filling up page after page. That worried me."[51]

To Stan Johnson, McNamara remained what he had been in high school, "both quiet and outgoing. . . . He wasn't standoffish, but he wasn't a gladhander or a big rah-rah boy by any means. . . . He was serious-minded and rather dedicated toward making a success of life. . . . He seemed to be his own boss as far as ideas were concerned, but he wasn't, on the other hand, somebody who intruded on anybody else."[52]

Not much is known about McNamara's "love life" while at Berkeley— perhaps because, given his total dedication to his classes and his extracurricular activities, there wasn't much of it. Annalee Whitmore attended Stanford and though he drove down the peninsula to visit her there, they were just friends. Hallie Booth's sister Jean, who told Hendrickson that Hallie dated McNamara off and on through college, sounded as if their relationship blossomed more the next year when he wrote her "all the time" from Harvard Business School.

With the Depression still on, political activists of all sorts swarmed the Berkeley campus, distributing leaflets, trying to sign up supporters. "We had Communists," Cooper recalled. "We had every side to it. I would say Bob and I tended to be on the conservative side—probably I a little more blindly than Bob. . . . I don't think Bob had to have the university to come up with [his] values because I think Bob made his own values by reasoning and with a strong ethical sense [with] which he would direct himself toward what was the right thing to do."[53]

As McNamara remembered it, his time at Berkeley during the Depression made him something of a left-winger. "I am a much better person for having gone to Berkeley than Stanford because Berkeley was a hotbed of radicalism."[54] In fact, of course, he was more of a liberal than a radical: "I grew up in an environment of economic distress and to some degree, of strife—labor/management strife." And "I think with hindsight that was a plus. I learned some lessons about values," about "the need for safety nets and hence the merits of the Rooseveltian social legislation."[55] He came out of that period, he later told British journalist Henry Brandon, "with a strong feeling that the laissez faire philosophy of the past century was no longer a proper or sound philosophical basis for the individual or society to move on into the middle of the twentieth century and that both the individual and the institutions of society needed to be shaped toward the requirements of the nation."[56]

McNamara didn't hide his views, but he didn't proclaim them from the hilltop either, as another classmate recalled. "I was more liberal," said Leonard W. Charvet, "more likely to fly off the handle. He was more thoughtful, working his way through issues. But he was not a stuffed shirt. He had time for those who were less quick than he. None of us was as quick as he was, that was obvious."[57]

These recollections fit the profile of a boy scout in the best sense of that term, of a young man determined, as his parents had taught him, to do the right thing. What would he do when that clashed with his strong need to be accepted by his fellow students and to be respected by powerful college professors and administrators? For the time being, this potential contradiction remained mostly latent. What would happen when ambition required him to violate his own high ethical standards remained to be seen.

College also gave McNamara his first exposure to the military in the form of the Reserve Officers Training Corps (ROTC). A land-grant college operating at public expense, Berkeley required two years of military training for every male student. McNamara, as usual, sought more than the minimum, applying for an optional four-year navy program, but when the navy rejected him for poor eyesight, he settled for two years in the

Army ROTC, in which about 2,000 students studied "military history, marksmanship, military tactics, and map-reading."[58] ROTC was deeply unpopular at this time in Berkeley's history. A 1940 straw poll among undergraduates showed 2,828 favored abolition of compulsory ROTC, while 997 favored its retention.[59] What McNamara himself learned, the future Pentagon chief remembered, was that "nobody took the military seriously. My friends and I saw it as a pointless ritual, irrelevant to our world. On the day of our final parade, when we had to march before the president of the university, we threw down our rifles as soon as we were done—the hell with it!"[60]

Given all his college accomplishments (academic, extracurricular, athletic), McNamara applied for a Rhodes Scholarship to continue his studies in England at Oxford University. Provost Deutsch's letter of recommendation praised him as "always honorable and straightforward in his designs, courageously ready to set forth his opinions although without bumptiousness," but also referred to "his great sense of loyalty and consciousness of obligation to his fellows."[61] Despite McNamara's sterling credentials, the Rhodes Committee chose Bruce Waybur, a Sacramento farm boy who wowed them by giving a hog call during his interview. McNamara later denied being disappointed. "I didn't want to go to Oxford," he said, perhaps easing the pain of rejection by denying his eagerness to be accepted, "although I did apply . . . under tremendous pressure from the provost of the University of California, whom I loved."[62] But later in life he seemed particularly proud that many of his friends and protégés had proven themselves as Rhodes scholars.[63] Having failed to garner a Rhodes, McNamara opted for another prestigious institution on his list—winning admission the next fall to Harvard Business School, presumably the high road to success and riches in the world of finance. For the time being, however, he would need some help, so he applied for fellowships, unsuccessfully asking his friend Vern Goodin's father for a personal loan. He then approached his own father, who, after demanding that he prepare a budget ($600 for tuition, $3,000 for cross-country travel and room and board), wrote a check for what his son needed.[64]

Vern Goodin was shocked that the old man came through. But that summer, while beavering away on the SS *President Hoover*, McNamara confessed to Will Goodwin that he aspired to something greater than business success. Goodwin had been admitted to Johns Hopkins Medical School that fall. "Willie," McNamara admitted, "I kind of envy you going into medicine, because that means you know exactly what you're going to do. You know that you're going to be taking care of people and you're going to be helping people. I'd like to do that, too, but I'd like to do it on a big scale . . . on a worldwide scale."[65]

What McNamara meant by that, Goodwin thought correctly, was that he wanted to serve humanity in general—another ethical goal that, theoretically at least, could provide him with the influence, recognition, and power to which he also aspired.

CHAPTER THREE

"The Happiest Days of Our Lives"

In 1937, Harvard Business School was one of only four universities in the United States for training businessmen (it had no female students, McNamara remembered).[1] Initially established in 1908 within the Faculty of Arts and Sciences, it was confirmed as a separate school in 1913.[2] As a latecomer to Harvard, which offered a degree after only two years, it felt condescended to by the distinguished Graduate School of Arts and Sciences, but to an incoming student like McNamara it still seemed elite. Its redbrick buildings were located directly across the Charles River from Harvard College, Harvard Yard, and Harvard Square. When McNamara arrived, he was assigned a small single room in Gallatin Dormitory with a window opening onto a courtyard. Two of his friends, Wally Haas and Bill Hewitt, who had been fraternity brothers together at Berkeley (not in McNamara's frat, but in the more prestigious Alpha Delta Phi), roomed together in a suite down the hall. The three of them, along with another first-year student, formed a study group that gathered in the Haas-Hewitt living room to grapple with the notorious case studies that were the centerpiece of the curriculum. During these evening sessions, McNamara quickly proved himself the leader. "We'd get to the foothills of the Sierras with him," Haas recalled metaphorically, "then he would take off for the mountains."[3] McNamara's professors soon were similarly impressed: "I almost got the feeling he was ingesting these systems as if he'd somehow known them all before, in another consciousness," recalled Edmund Learned.[4]

It wasn't as if the curriculum were easy. "There was an immense amount of pressure," McNamara remembered, "particularly in the first year. Huge amounts of material to assimilate. Lots of report writing. Deadlines, very tight deadlines. So, it was a heavy workload. But . . . I enjoyed it."[5]

Although Harvard Business School was filled with talented, hard-driving students, as many as 12 percent were known to flunk out in the first year. Students outside McNamara's study group marveled, not without envy, at his prowess. Every Saturday evening ten-to-twenty-page papers were due—to be deposited in a metal box known as "the slot" in the hall of Baker Library, from which they were collected precisely at nine o'clock. Just before that witching hour, a crowd of students would assemble by the slot to cheer latecomers racing down the corridor with papers raised in triumph. According to other students interviewed by Hendrickson, no one ever witnessed McNamara sprinting across the finish line.[6] The end of the first semester found him the top student in the entering class—which prompted Berkeley's President Sproul to send him "heartiest congratulations. While none of us is surprised, it pleases us nonetheless. Mrs. Sproul and Marion join me in kindest personal regards and best wishes."[7] Sproul's kindness reflected not only his respect for McNamara but the fact that Bob had stayed in touch even after graduating. Learning in the fall of 1937 that a young Berkeley radical who was a Golden Bear had insulted Sproul at a meeting of the Order, McNamara wrote: "I want to mention a matter which is very close to my heart. . . . Having heard of the insulting and intolerant remarks made by one of the Fellows at the first meeting of the Order this semester, I was not surprised at your decision to refrain from attending future meetings."[8]

Given his almost instantaneous success at HBS, McNamara's explanation of why he chose business is surprising. "Because," he recalled fifty-five years later, "I wanted an advanced degree. . . . I didn't know what I wanted to do, so I went to business school."[9] With McNamara's eventual rise to the top of the Ford Motor Company, one might suspect his choice of HBS was more focused than he admitted, that he wanted to build on his college economics major to make a lucrative career in business. In fact, he claimed it was the intellectual challenge as much as the prospect of financial rewards that motivated him in the beginning. After graduating from HBS in 1939, he tried his hand at accounting at the Price Waterhouse office in San Francisco, but by midyear he found he was "bored as hell" and returned to HBS in the fall of 1940 as an instructor on the faculty.[10]

In some ways, he didn't fit in. Most of the HBS faculty regarded the three of their colleagues who anonymously supported FDR against Wendell Willkie in a 1940 straw poll as "fools." McNamara backed FDR anyway. When one senior professor said he'd heard that a contemporary of McNamara's was teaching "a pretty lively class," the younger colleague knew that was meant as criticism. But the very next year, at the age of twenty-five, McNamara became, he later bragged, the youngest assistant professor at Harvard.[11]

Did this success go to his head? "He liked to be in the spotlight," a Harvard classmate recalled.[12] "Bob did not tolerate fools lightly," remembered another one. "He was the most aloof man I ever met," said another.[13] The need for business to do more than pursue profits, to be socially responsible by serving the wider community, was a theme to which he kept returning. And the woman he eventually chose to be his wife and married in 1940 personified the warmer side of his character that he was trying to cultivate. Margaret McKinstry Craig, he recalled, "brought balance, strength and joy to my life. She complemented me in every way that mattered. Marg was born wise; she was warm, open, gentle, extroverted and beloved by all. Without her I would have been diminished."[14]

—————

MCNAMARA'S FAVORITE BUSINESS SCHOOL PROFESSORS, ESPECIALLY Ross G. Walker and Thomas W. Sanders, who taught accounting, and Edmund Learned, whose specialty was merchandising, "opened my eyes to American business," he later told a friend. "A whole new world of management techniques became clear to me."[15] The new approach he learned, which he later applied not only in business but to "nonprofits, or governmental or intergovernmental or international operations," was "to examine [a] problem, develop objectives, develop a plan to achieve the objectives, and then monitor performance in relation to achievement of those objectives, and on the basis of that monitoring, revise the plan if one was not achieving the objectives."[16]

Before the development of "control accounting," businesses operated with a more limited set of tools for decision-making, relying heavily on traditional accounting, intuition, and ad hoc methods. While these methods provided a foundation for business operations, the lack of detailed cost analysis, budgeting, and financial forecasting meant that businesses had fewer insights into their operations and were less equipped to make strategic decisions. The emergence of managerial accounting represented a revolutionary advancement, providing businesses with the tools to analyze operations more deeply, plan strategically, and optimize performance. The new process was called by various names: statistical control, financial control, control accounting, management control. Developed at the E. I. du Pont de Nemours Powder Company in the 1920s, it was used with great success to revive and sustain General Motors after it suffered huge losses early in the Depression. "GM was able to leap between the two world wars from a nearly bankrupt 12 percent share of the market to a 52 percent share and near-supremacy: the biggest company on earth."[17]

McNamara's aptitude for logic and statistics, plus his desire to control as much as he could of his own environment, made him a prime candidate to specialize on the new system. The fact that it was being perfected at Harvard Business School equipped him to emerge as one of its future champions. But what sort of room did this approach leave for business's social responsibility? One of his basic beliefs, McNamara later contended, was that "there was no contradiction between a soft heart and a hard head—that you could drive for profits and at the same time meet social responsibilities." Another was "that it *was* a responsibility of business executives to serve the society as well as their stockholders."[18] Could it be that this was part of the ethos that HBS's mostly conservative professors conveyed to their students, McNamara was later asked. "That's a good question," he replied. "I can't answer it really. I don't know—I think I came away from the Business School with that belief, certainly it's been my belief ever since. I don't know where I acquired it, except at the Business School, but I can't point to exactly where it came from there."[19]

To judge by what he wrote and said at the time, HBS's message on social responsibility was not entirely positive. At the end of his first month in Cambridge, he wrote to Berkeley president Sproul: "Although the policy of this school appears to be one of piling more work on the students than they can possibly do, the material is interesting and I heartily approve of the general atmosphere which the dean expressed very well when he said, 'It is no sin to make a profit.'"[20] But five months into his first term, in February 1938, he expressed doubts to Berkeley provost Deutsch: "Although the work here has proved very interesting, I sometimes think that the faculty places too much emphasis on the chase for the almighty dollar."[21] Two months later, he told Deutsch, "Our work here has continued to be most interesting, although I continue to question periodically the methods of teaching and the ends aimed at."[22] That same month he wrote to Berkeley friends who were now fledgling businessmen in San Francisco's North Beach neighborhood: "I am anxious to hear how both of you are progressing and how you feel about business in general. With little practical knowledge of it, the more & more I study the more I think it is a pretty mercenary sort of thing, affording one little opportunity to be of use to society in general and forcing one to subordinate broad social ends to one's own personal aims." Perhaps not coincidentally, in this same letter, McNamara mentions that he has been feeling melancholy.[23]

If chasing after profits on the one hand, and social responsibility on the other, constitute thesis and antithesis, McNamara thought he could reconcile them in a kind of synthesis. Professor Walker argued that by assisting a firm to avoid setbacks, financial control could help workers remain employed and thus benefit society. In his February letter to Provost Deutsch, McNamara coupled his lament about his professors' fondness for profits with this caveat: "However, perhaps this is necessary for the achievement of their aim of instilling in us a conception of the means by which the ethical and moral standards of business may be raised."[24] During an interview with Shapley fifty years later, he banged his left hand on the table, declaring that one of the main principles of his life was that "there needs to be *no conflict* between the goals of a large institution and those of society."[25]

But in the late thirties he was struggling to maintain that faith. One early indication was that, even after completing HBS, he still contemplated shifting to a medical career. To do so, he would have to complete undergraduate premed requirements and then embark on medical school. His aim, he later explained, would not have been to treat individual patients but to address what he called "societal health problems."[26] Will Goodwin later wrote that he had discussed Bob's plans with the dean of Johns Hopkins Medical School, who recommended McNamara accompany his application with a letter of recommendation from Berkeley president Sproul.[27]

In the meantime, while concentrating on his HBS courses and pondering the place of business in society, McNamara managed to have some fun. Stan Johnson, his Berkeley classmate who was now at Harvard Law, recalled their going out to dinner in Boston (McNamara particularly relished the lobster dinners, costing just a dollar, near Faneuil Hall), skiing in Vermont or in the Laurentian Mountains north of Montreal on Christmas vacations, and taking the train down to Baltimore on spring vacations to visit friends at Johns Hopkins (where Will Goodwin disguised them as interns and sneaked them into operating rooms).[28] During the summer of 1938, McNamara, Goodwin, Haas, and Hewitt drove back across the country to California in Haas's Plymouth, enjoying the delights of New Orleans, staying for several days in the "palatial southern home" of a Goodwin classmate in Jackson, Mississippi, and undertaking the invigorating hike down to the bottom of the Grand Canyon and the hard climb back up. "We walked down, and having sat at a desk all year, on the way up it was *deadly*," McNamara admitted but, of course, he was up to the challenge: "Anyhow, it was fun."[29]

MCNAMARA'S SECOND YEAR AT HARVARD, 1938–1939, WASN'T AS
much fun. His father died on November 4, 1938, at the age of seventy-six,
suffering from angina pectoris, bronchial pneumonia, and arteriosclero-
sis.[30] As a lapsed Catholic, Robert James was entitled neither to a funeral
mass nor a sacred burial place. His wife wanted a quick burial and didn't
want it to get in the way of her children's education. "Now we don't want to
disturb Bob," she told a friend who was helping with arrangements. "He's
in school, he has his hands full, it's so far away. . . . Bob can't do anything
about it anyway." Nor did Bob's sister make the funeral, although she was
much closer at the University of Colorado in Boulder. "Well, you see, my
mother just thought we shouldn't come home because it was November
and the weather was bad. . . . In later years, I saw it as a mistake."[31]

Nell McNamara's solicitude for her son in this case wasn't unusual.
In fact, she overwhelmed him with it during these Business School
years—to the point where he half rebelled against her. She wrote to him
practically every week while he was at Harvard. During the summer
of 1939, when he was traveling in Europe, she complained to his sister, who prompted Bob that "[Mother] has been waiting eleven days
now for a word from you and is very worried because no cards or anything. . . . You could write at least twice a week to us as I'm sure Hallie
[Booth, McNamara's Berkeley girlfriend] has received plenty of cards,
if not letters." Nell's long handwritten letters recounted at great length
details of her daily life and pressed for news about Bob's. They were full
of over-the-top praise, but also annoying, petty supervision of his daily
life. "Oh! I'm so proud of you," she wrote on March 3, 1939. "Last night
I shed tears for joy. To be the mother of a son like you would make any
woman rejoice. I truly have been blessed! Don't work too hard though,
Bob—be sure to eat well and have plenty of sunshine and exercise, or is
there any sunshine in Boston?" "Don't study too hard," she had urged
him on January 8. "Just remember you are expressing 'Divine Love' and
'Divine Intelligence' in all you do." (These terms recur often in Christian Science writings, which apparently interested Mrs. McNamara.)
Unlike her letters, which were written in beautiful, neat script, his were
"messy." But they were "always welcome. I never see them as anything

but perfect," she assured her son on March 9. Bob was so "wonderfully thoughtful of [his sister] Peg and me" that "I feel secure when you are with me," she added on April 23. With his final exams approaching in June, he was not to "worry about his grades. I know they are fine and even if they're not as high as in the past we won't worry about it as you have made enough A's in the past to carry you through life."

Nell's assiduous management extended to nearly all aspects of his life. "Bob, you left some towels and a washcloth here this summer. Do you want them?" (September 28, 1938). "Bob, *did you get your overcoat? I sincerely hope so.* You of course found the $100 check I put in the pocket of your Bank Book.... Also, get yourself a suit and a sport coat and I'll send you the money" (November 13, 1938). "I am enclosing a $3 check to buy yourself a nice Thanksgiving dinner. *Be sure* to do it, Bob" (November 18, 1938). "Be sure to get warm clothing and keep yourself warm at all times.... Never get your body chilled" (November 27, 1938). "Yes, it was nice of Mrs. Sherman to write you—*do* answer at once—*don't* neglect these social courtesies. They are fine, sincere friends" (December 2, 1938). "Hope you got your overcoat. *Do* keep warm!" (December 28, 1938).[32] "Try to eat the right kind of food in good, clean places. Do you sleep well at night?" (August 6, 1939).

These letters are painful to read. On the one hand, they fueled his ambition and modeled the kind of overbearing personality that McNamara himself later displayed when he micromanaged his subordinates at Ford and the Pentagon. On the other, his mother's infantilizing monitoring of his daily life sharpened his own need to buttress his sense of self-worth by gaining the approval of men like Berkeley president Sproul, Henry Ford II, and Presidents Kennedy and Johnson.

═══

MCNAMARA DID MAKE IT HOME AFTER HIS FATHER'S FUNERAL. Nell's letter of November 13, 1938, testifies to that: "Bob, it was sweet of you to come home. You'll never know what a comfort you were to Mother." And again a reference to his nearly godlike status: "Just know that you are expressing Divine Intelligence and Divine Love at all times."[33]

Hendrickson couldn't get McNamara to describe his feelings about the trip: "My memory regarding my trip home after my father's death is very hazy. While at Harvard I don't believe I realized Dad's death was imminent. Therefore, I believe you are probably correct: it would have been impossible for me to return home in time for the funeral. My main purpose in flying to California was to be with my mother."[34] Much later, McNamara's son Craig recalled, "I can't remember one time when Dad spoke to me about his father."[35]

Why was McNamara reluctant to discuss his father? Did that aloofness echo his father's remoteness from him? Did it reflect his general unwillingness to share personal feelings? Did he feel guilty about not attending the funeral? Whatever their source, his feelings (or the lack thereof) seem to have affected his academic performance when he returned to Cambridge. In order to graduate with honors, he had to excel on an oral examination conducted by three professors: Edmund Learned, Windsor Hosmer, and "Tiger" Lewis. "He didn't flunk," recalled Learned, "he just didn't do well. I couldn't get the committee to take into account the father's death."[36] "Some of us were terribly upset." Learned added later. "I have felt badly about it ever since. But one professor failed to make allowance for the death of [McNamara's] father. His work was generally splendid."[37]

Other factors, too, may have evoked McNamara's subpar performance. Former classmates of his suggested to Hendrickson that boredom and arrogance on McNamara's part were involved. Hendrickson learned from two former HBS faculty members that Professor Hosmer, who didn't like McNamara, asked him a question McNamara didn't like. When his answer failed to satisfy Hosmer, the latter asked: "You want to try again?"

"Nope," McNamara replied.

"Excuse me, would you like to try again?"

"Nope."

After the exam ended and McNamara left the room, Hosmer threw down a pencil and exclaimed: "That's it. The guy is arrogant."[38] Learned had anticipated that McNamara would get a "high distinction" on the examination, which would help him win an appointment to the faculty. But a "high pass" was all McNamara got.[39]

Harvard classmate Robert McVie had another theory. He was confirming to Hendrickson how far ahead of his classmates McNamara was when he suddenly added, "But not the second year. Because he had this girl back in California who began to stiffen up from arthritis and this was bothering him a lot."[40] The girl in California was Hallie Booth, one of the two striking coeds (Annalee was the other) whom McNamara had dated in high school and in college. Hallie was working for the telephone company, Annalee for the government, both in San Francisco, and they often had lunch together. Hallie told Annalee a lot about "the guys she said she had 'acquired,'" but didn't say much about McNamara. When she confided to Annalee that she was engaged to be married, her friend "didn't think it was Bob." Annalee assumed (perhaps wrongly) that Hallie would have told her if Bob was the man, so it must have been a year later that Hallie and Bob "got so serious." But in the meantime, Hallie's health had deteriorated, probably, thought Bob's medical school friend, Will Goodwin, the result of rheumatoid arthritis.[41] She had already began to limp a little in the fall of 1937, and her illness became more obvious as the year went on. During her time in San Francisco, she was limping more and more, Whitmore said. According to Annalee, Hallie had already broken one admirer's heart in high school, "a wonderful boy who was a football player and worshipped Hallie." After she broke up with John Britton during their senior year, he was "depressed for so many years," Annalee recalled. "John's life was ruined.... He changed entirely, people said. It just almost wrecked his life when Hallie left him."[42] Could it be that McNamara, whom one might have expected to be immune to lovesickness, underwent a similar ordeal as Hallie's health deteriorated? Not yet, as it turned out, for he was still dreaming of her during his trip to Europe in the summer of 1939 and dating her when he returned to San Francisco to work at Price Waterhouse that fall.

During the fall of 1938, before his father died, Nell had sensed that her son was depressed. "Bob, Daddy and I didn't think your last letter was cheerful. What's the matter? You don't mean to say you're giving up after the wonderful record you've made in the last *fifteen years*? Be *cheerful*, Bob! Be *happy*! You should go to church and read the Bible regularly—

you'll be surprised how this helps. I am sure you say your prayers every night. You have had such a successful life that each day you should offer up a prayer of thanks to God, our Heavenly Father."[43]

That same autumn, when Bob was at HBS, Hallie talked a lot about him with Gwynn Quigley, who thought she was the "nicest girl you'd ever meet." "He must have been corresponding with her," Quigley concluded. "I think that she rather expected to marry him. I remember seeing her at his father's funeral. We went over to the grave site and she was there. And Bob wasn't because his mother didn't want him there. [Hallie] talked a lot about Bob."[44]

During the summer of 1939, which McNamara spent touring Europe with friends, he talked endlessly to one of them about Hallie. "I remember all that summer, Bob writing to her, talking about her, wanting to marry her," another friend said.[45] Bob's letters from Boston, reflecting his penchant for quantitative thinking, had included his projection of what their budget would be "when we're married."[46] Hallie's sister Jean later insisted that Hallie and Bob "were engaged, though not formal or a public announcement, but she definitely had something of his, a ring from his fraternity maybe." Jean recalled double-dating: she, her future husband, Bob Mitchell, and Hallie and Bob McNamara. Jean even remembered Bob Mitchell telling an off-color joke about "the 'pee' in the swimming pool being silent." Jean didn't get it, insisting there was no letter *p* in the word *swimming*, while "the color was hugely rising in Bob McNamara."

"She loved Bob," Hallie's sister continued, "but not enough to marry him, that's what I think."[47] Perhaps Hallie worried about her own health. By the fall of 1939, when McNamara took up his job at Price Waterhouse, she was not only limping, her hands were bent, she needed help cutting her food, tennis (she had once been a champion) was beyond her, and, as a Christian Scientist, she wasn't getting the medical help she needed.[48]

Or perhaps McNamara's mother kiboshed the whole thing. During 1938–1939, Nell continually asked her son how Hallie was doing. Her questions were seemingly sympathetic, but their frequency (she asked at least ten times in letters to her son) suggests Nell was worried. "When one has *health* in this world," she wrote her son in the fall of 1938, "you should be *happy*, as the older you get the more you will realize that *health* is your most prized possession."[49] Nell reportedly told friends, "I don't want Bob marrying that girl."[50] Gwynn Quigley heard her warn many times against marrying anybody who doesn't have good health.[51] It's not clear when she delivered that sobering warning to her son. But it's possible the double blow of Hallie's illness and Nell's attitude toward her were already on McNamara's mind when he flubbed his oral exam at HBS.

The European tour in the summer of 1939 proved to be a frantic but welcome distraction. McNamara and six friends bought a secondhand 1936 Ford station wagon in New York and shipped it with them on the Italian liner, the *Vulcania*, on which they traveled third-class. Landing in Italy, they stacked suitcases in the back and drove through Switzerland, Germany, the Netherlands, Norway, Sweden, and back to Germany. Their adventures would have shocked McNamara's mother: swimming naked in the Mediterranean, smuggling discount German marks across borders (hidden inside the car's taillight covers) to finance their trip, plus a visit to a girlie club in Paris where one of the gang, Bob McVie, remembered McNamara with an "exquisite bare-breasted tart named Monique, swaying on Bob's lap, having a saucy old time. He's holding her rather delicately at the waist. His eyes are closed and he's swaying with the music." McNamara did penance for this sin; he "kept us up to pace on the cathedrals and monuments," another traveler recalled.[52]

Revealingly, McNamara himself chose to stress his retrospective "embarrassment" that he had not digested all the signs that Europe was on the verge of war: the Nazis' persecution of Jews in Germany, the 1937 Anschluss with Austria, the 1938 annexation of the Sudetenland followed by the takeover of the rest of Czechoslovakia. He was in Europe just when Hitler was about to launch his attack on Poland. He actually heard Hitler speak at a rally in Germany, and he was on Unter den Linden in Berlin when the Nazis struck on September 1, but "I did not recognize the imminence of war." Of course, McNamara continued, "we weren't fluent in languages," but "I am positive we were not as sensitive as we should have been—and I say this to my embarrassment—to the imminence of conflict."[53] This admission was clearly an understatement. Such innocence was stunning: his blindness was almost willful, especially for a future chief of the American war machine.

McNamara and Rich Hodgson planned to return home on another Italian liner a few days later. Since their tickets to San Francisco (via the Panama Canal) were already purchased, they figured they needed only enough money to pay the railroad fare from Berlin to Genoa, plus a couple of extra dollars. So when the ship's crossing was canceled due to the outbreak of war, they were reduced to subsistence living (in a room over a bar) for more than a week until they were able to cadge passage on a Dollar Line ship whose bosun remembered McNamara (and perhaps his Piedmont neighbor's father who owned the Dollar Line) from his merchant seaman days while in college. McNamara and his friend worked their way to New York as waiters (while owing half fare) for fourteen hours a day, from early morning to ten at night, and then borrowed money to buy coach fares on the train across the country, living on chocolate bars the last couple of days on the train.[54]

———

THE PRICE WATERHOUSE JOB WAS WAITING IN SAN FRANCISCO. According to McNamara, the firm was "*the* leading public accounting firm in the world, without any questions. Far ahead of anybody else."[55] The partner in charge of its Boston office had noticed McNamara at HBS more than a year earlier and, wanting to recruit him after graduation, hired him for part of the summer of 1938 in New York. That in itself was "quite unusual," McNamara bragged fifty years later, because the summer was a slow period and "normally they don't hire anybody then. But I had the highest grades of the first year Harvard Business School class and therefore I was given this employment." While in New York, McNamara worked under an account manager who helped probe a famous McKesson-Robbins scandal in which that healthcare company, having listed phony assets on its balance sheet, was required to undergo a Price Waterhouse audit. McNamara found the case, in which the CEO "carried on an amazing embezzlement of funds," to be "just fantastic"; the SEC report on the case read like a "mystery novel." Having proved himself in New York,

McNamara was offered a position in Boston the next year but got the firm to assign him to San Francisco instead.[56]

If working for a powerful firm on a sensational case was "fantastic," McNamara's San Francisco job wasn't. He served as a junior accountant "checking the accounting records of the company clients we were handling and determining whether they properly reflected the activities of the operation."[57] His salary was above average, about $40 a week or $165 per month (adding up to about $3,500 a year, more than the 1940 average of $1,368).[58] He spent much of his workdays, except for a half hour for lunch, running adding-machine tapes. During lunch he occasionally dropped by Dick Quigley's insurance office in the Mills Tower, where they would "chew the fat" for a while, as Quigley put it. Quigley felt they still had "a very pleasant relationship," but the ambitious McNamara would eventually lose interest in his old family friend. Years later, when McNamara was with Ford, Quigley asked him to say hello to his son who was visiting Michigan. "I never heard from him and he never saw him," Quigley recalled. Added Gwynn Quigley: "I think his sudden rise to fame was more than he could handle. We went to his mother's memorial service [she died at the end of 1964]. Dick had known him since birth. You know, [McNamara] said, 'How do you do?' and that was it. That's not the way to greet friends."[59] Other old pals like Wally Haas and Vernon Goodin remained close, but Haas became a senior executive at Levi Strauss and Goodin a prominent San Francisco lawyer. Perhaps McNamara viewed his friendship with Quigley as transactional and disposable.

As for Price Waterhouse, "I was bored as hell with public accounting," McNamara recalled.[60] "He hated that job," his sister Peggy told Hendrickson.[61] In addition, his relationship with Hallie was ending. By 1940, her hands were gnarled, she limped badly, and her shoulders were stiff. She still loved Bob's manners, his solicitude, and his courtliness, recalled her sister Jean, but not enough to marry him. He proposed, and she declined.[62] Hallie died not long after. The fact that McNamara proposed to her despite her illness speaks very well of him. And it's not surprising that, at about this time, McNamara informed his mother that he was considering applying to medical school. "My mother was furious," his sister Peggy recalled. Nell told him to get serious, that there would be no money to pay his med school tuition.[63]

McNamara did get serious—about Margy Craig, whom he had first met at Berkeley. She was originally from Seattle, but her family had moved to Alameda, south of Oakland, when she was a child. Her father was western regional manager for an insurance company, her mother a homemaker. Her parents could afford to send her to Berkeley, where she lived on campus. (McNamara confessed to an interviewer in 2004 that he didn't realize that most girls didn't go to college in those days because most of his female friends at Piedmont High did.)[64] McNamara initially met her during his first week at Berkeley in August 1933. He encountered her in student government activities and she dated several friends of his. Margy and McNamara had double-dated (she with his friend Vern Goodin, who later was best man at their wedding) when they were undergraduates, and had gone skiing once at Yosemite and once at the Sierra Club at Norden Summit.[65] But McNamara contended to an interviewer in 1995 that he and Margy had dated more often between 1937 and 1939, as if anxious to airbrush Hallie Booth out of his life retrospectively.[66]

Margy wasn't a gorgeous knockout like Hallie, nor as intellectual as Annalee Whitmore. She was small and (to put it mildly) vivacious, known as a fun-loving cutup. According to Shapley, she first caught McNamara's eye at a party "when one of the boys hoisted her, laughing and kicking, onto his shoulders." Margy had been a member of Torch and Shield, a society formed by senior women to rival Golden Bear, and worked on community projects at the campus Y. She majored in science and physical education at Berkeley and was teaching phys ed and biology at San Rafael High School when she and McNamara began dating seriously in early 1940. "We all liked her," remembered Will Goodwin.[67] It was a good thing Bob didn't marry either Hallie or Annalee, Mary Jo Goodwin would recall. As a high-powered journalist, Annalee would have been as "driven" as McNamara himself was. Whereas Margy was "just right" for him, a "different person," much more informal and even "Christlike" in the sacrifices she would make for him, who made him into a different person as a result of being married to her.[68]

Margy and Bob spent much of the spring of 1940 together—at Edy's on Shattuck Avenue for ice cream, at the movies at Grand Lake, skiing at Lassen Park, on picnics that Margy made sure featured Bob's favorite kippered herring—she later nicknamed him "Kip."[69] (Among her own nicknames in high school had been "Cutup" and "Muggs.") By midsummer, if not before, he was in love. "I had always hoped," he wrote to her in July, "that when love comes it would come this way—so complete and strong that nothing else seems to matter." He wanted to get married in August and then cruise with her on their honeymoon. He was hoping the ship would "sink near a desert island so that I can spend all the next fifty years looking at you 24 hours a day and feeling just as unbelievably happy as I do now."[70]

Actually, the honeymoon cruise would take them to New York on the way to Boston. For in the meantime, Harvard Business School reentered the picture. HBS's Dean Donham asked McNamara to return to Harvard. The partner in charge of Price Waterhouse's San Francisco office "was aghast" when he heard about Harvard's offer, McNamara recalled, "because they thought I'd done well during that year. He said it was a serious mistake for me to leave Price Waterhouse because there was every reason to believe that I'd be made a partner at a relatively young age." McNamara "disagreed with his judgment of the relative merits of the two positions," he recalled coolly, "so I left."[71]

Before that, however, there were two obstacles to be overcome: Would Margy agree to marry him and move to Cambridge with him? Would her father give his permission? He first asked her father (Margy was out of touch while traveling in the East), who demanded to know: "What are you going to finance a marriage with?" McNamara proudly cited his salary: it was "going to be raised from $1500 to $1800 a year." To which his future father-in-law retorted, "Young man, you come back and talk to me a year from now. You're in no position to provide for my daughter."[72] And Nell McNamara expressed similar sentiments. In a letter to Margy dated July 21, 1940, she wrote: "I feel Bob is not financially ready to start married life but, since you both are so willing to 'budget along,' I am sure you'll manage! With you at his side Bob is bound to go ahead very fast."[73]

Margy's sister Kay helped to overcome her father's resistance, but it remained to track down Margy herself. He reached her in a pay phone booth at the YWCA in Baltimore and popped the question: Would she marry him? She would.[74]

The wedding took place on August 13, 1940, in Alameda, the wedding reception at Pier 35 in San Francisco where the couple was about to board a liner to New York. McNamara's mother, elegantly attired with a black veil across her face, had been telling neighbors for several weeks, "The president of Harvard just won't leave Bob alone. He's made a special trip out here to see him. I guess Bob's going to have to leave his great job at Price Waterhouse." Of course, Nell's account wasn't true. Harvard's president hadn't visited. The HBS dean made the job offer, and not in person.[75]

———

IN BOSTON, THE NEWLYWEDS LIVED IN FELTON HALL, AN OLD building in Cambridge that had been turned into a rooming house. They had but one room, a bathroom, and no kitchen. "You had to wash the dishes in the bathtub," McNamara remembered, "but we were very happy there." After a few months, Margy became pregnant and they moved into a faculty apartment directly opposite his office on the HBS campus. "I could look out my office window, and when [our] kitchen window was steaming up, I knew it was time to go home." After their daughter—"Little Margy," they called her—was born, they needed more space, so they moved again to one of two apartments (previously used as an art gallery) in a two-story house on Brattle Street across from the president of Radcliffe's house. McNamara's deal with Radcliffe was that he would pay to repaint the apartment (when they moved in it was battleship gray from top to bottom) and in return Radcliffe would pay the rent.[76]

McNamara taught accounting and financial management or control, specifically "long-term planning in business in financial terms." In this scheme of things, "statistics were a tool to utilize in translating the plans into monitorable, quantitative measures."[77] By now, this approach was sacred to McNamara, but how did it go over with his students? He recalled them as "very intelligent" but spiced things up to get their full attention.

One trick he used, HBS legend has it, was to deploy a ready supply of jokes—and to keep track of them on a chart that listed dates on one axis, and jokes he had used along the other, with student responses recorded in squares on the grid. Another device was to emphasize the emotional conflicts in the business case studies he was analyzing. He would "create a tense situation at times just to dramatize a point. . . . You really have to move people to want to understand more than they did when they came into the room. Sometimes—I won't call it tricks—I focus on . . . strained relations between two people, or some slight exaggeration of a point, or framing it in an emotional way. As a teaching device [it] is useful."[78]

Charts with axes and grids, strained personal relations, emotions running high—two decades later at the Pentagon, these would be realities rather than teaching devices. But for the moment they energized McNamara's classes. "A very good teacher," remembered Professor Learned. "He organized his work well." "Rather inspiring, really," was Donald David's assessment. "He was able to give students confidence."[79] "A hell of a teacher," recalled McNamara's junior colleague Eugene Zuckert.[80]

The McNamaras' marriage was flourishing and their social life was, too, which helped to keep him in a good mood in the classroom. Myles Mace, another young HBS instructor, regarded McNamara as a good man with a wonderful wife, and Mace remembered happy outings that the McNamaras took with him and his wife—to a "marvelous restaurant outside Boston, over near Concord, called Hartwell Farms." "They'd give us an absolutely superbly cooked bowl of chicken soup, all that you could eat for 65 cents"—especially great because "you have to remember we didn't have much money." Bob was "a heavy eater and loved to eat."[81]

McNamara and other junior faculty got together to play poker while their wives prepared dinner in the next room. Everyone loved Margy for her freshness and good cheer and, as Hendrickson notes, "they didn't dislike" her husband.[82] "He was fun," recalled Eugene Zuckert, but "he had limited capacity for fun. He was a much harder worker than we were, even then. We were all in awe of McNamara because he was so damned bright." McNamara was a "very intense guy. We [other young faculty] were much more relaxed. We had a lot more fun. But McNamara was 90%

business. When he had fun, he had fun, but he was always intense, always
wound up." Zuckert recalled going up to the McNamaras' apartment after
a party: "A bunch of us came up there and McNamara was in there working. He'd had about nine drinks but he was still in there working."[83]

A somewhat more senior marketing teacher named Harry Hansen said,
"You could never really get close to Bob, put your feet up with him." But,
he added, "that power, that ambitiousness, that clawing and arrogance—
you never saw any of that around here with Bob, really." In the summer of
1941, the McNamaras and Hansens rented a cabin together on Whitton
Pond near the White Mountains of New Hampshire. Hansen preserved
photos of McNamara in his swimsuit chomping on a hot dog by a lake,
and of Margy, although quite pregnant, doing a cannonball leap into the
water. Hansen was four years senior to McNamara, but there was no tension between them. "It was easy," Hansen remembered. Not so several
decades later, when Hansen invited McNamara to attend a celebration
of his fifty years at HBS. McNamara declined without explaining why.[84]

Several others at HBS were shocked by the contrast between the
McNamara they had known in Cambridge and the Washington version they knew or heard about later on. McNamara's former professor of
accounting Thomas Sanders remembered him as compassionate, interested
in and sensitive to his students.[85] One of those students vividly recalled
McNamara's "sensitivity to and patience for those who didn't get [finan-
cial] control right off."[86] Another student who benefited from McNamara's
extra care and attention wrote to thank him nearly six decades later:

Dear Mr. McNamara,

It's been many, many years since our Harvard Business School days
but, off and on, memories of you have crossed my mind more times
than I can count. . . . I really mean this—and I have told many of
my friends that nothing you've said or done in your very illustrious
career will ever diminish my opinion of you or the regard in which
you are held by my family. . . . I do want you to know that I will
always be in your debt for being one of those who provided the inspi-

ration for me to try at all times to rise above the commonplace.... I was struggling at HBS with three low passes and two unsatisfactories. You were one of the people who turned me around in short order so that I was able to graduate with Distinction.[87]

McNamara's skill and comfort at teaching, along with the sweet energy of his new wife, softened the harder edges of his character and allowed him to show his gentler side to more than a small circle of close friends. His personality was not "nearly as warm" as his wife's, he told an interviewer many years later, "not nearly as outgoing," so she "helped me to some degree." He "never became as warm and outgoing" as his wife, but he became "more so than I would be without her." She "shaped my life," he continued, "probably not as much as it needed to be shaped," but she "moved it much more in directions that it needed to be moved in than it would have been without her and it was that influence that was so very very important." "She probably increased the warmth of my personality," he added, reaching for a technical term that would summarize the bottom line, "but it never became optimal."[88]

McNamara "absolutely loved" his new life in Cambridge. In return for a much-needed grant that Harvard gave it, the Boston Symphony performed a private series of concerts for Harvard faculty members in Memorial Hall. With Serge Koussevitsky conducting, McNamara remembered, it felt as if it was "your private orchestra. It was absolutely magnificent." When the Charles River froze during the winters, "we would skate on the river. It was a lovely life—interesting associations, satisfying, intellectually focused work." Many years later, McNamara overflowed with nostalgia. His time at Harvard was "just heaven on earth." The "happiest days of our lives were at Harvard." He was "going to make my life" there. He was "going to be a professor at Harvard." "It was a delightful life and I had every intention of pursuing it. I was taking a graduate course and pursuing a doctor's degree.... I had every intention of obtaining my doctoral degree and staying at the school forever."[89]

He might well have ended up happier had he done so.

CHAPTER FOUR

Waging War by the Numbers

Bob and Margy McNamara were still living in a faculty apartment on the HBS campus on Sunday, December 7, 1941, when the Japanese launched their surprise attack on Pearl Harbor. Three hundred fifty-three Japanese aircraft damaged six battleships and destroyed two, damaged three destroyers, destroyed or damaged 328 aircraft, killed 2,403 Americans, and wounded 1,178.[1]

McNamara was home when he heard the terrible news. He and Margy immediately pounded on the door of neighbors living across the hall on the third floor, Jack MacLane (who was also teaching at HBS) and his wife Patti, and all of them huddled in shock, pondering where this would lead.[2]

Where World War II led McNamara during the next four years was from Cambridge to Washington to England to Kansas to India to the South Pacific to Ohio and back to Washington. During that time he helped streamline operations of the United States Army Air Forces in Europe and the Pacific, rising in the process from a civilian instructor to lieutenant colonel with a Legion of Merit award. He proved himself invaluable to four leading American generals as well as to the assistant secretary of war, Robert Lovett; and during the last weeks of the conflict he ended up directing "the largest single organization of computers in the world, other than the U.S. Census," in charge of the Statistical Control System of the Air Technical Service Command.[3]

McNamara's wartime experience offered him the chance to pursue his dream of contributing to the overall welfare of his country and the world. As he later described his role, it sounds very technical and not very grand: to examine "the availability and level of training and effectiveness of personnel and matériel—aircraft and people—in relation to the objective: target destruction." "You had to know," he continued, "what your inventories were in order to compare what they were with what they ought to be; and in order to determine what they ought to be, you had to have some knowledge of the potential draw on those, which meant knowledge of the number of airplanes to be serviced, rates of utilization of those aircraft, and the relationship between the rates of utilization and the requirement for spare parts or service operations."[4] But his Legion of Merit award reads in part: "Through a brilliant series of statistical planning and initiation of action, [Lieutenant Colonel McNamara] made possible the greatly increased striking power of the Twentieth Air Force which brought about the final blow that ended Japanese resistance"—not the A-bomb but the massive firebombing of Japanese cities.[5]

McNamara's wartime experience changed his life. It vaulted him from the academic and accounting world, where he was turning into a star, to the heights of industry at the Ford Motor Company, and then to the top of the federal government commanding the American defense establishment. But, in fact, what McNamara originally wanted to do after the war was simply to return to teaching at Harvard Business School. Indeed, he would have done just that had his wife not come down in 1945 with a bad case of polio that required him to earn more money for her medical care than a professor's salary would provide.

Margy, too, wanted to return to Harvard after the war. Her husband could well have ended up leading its business school or perhaps—who knows? —even the university as whole (if Harvard hadn't preferred until then to select its presidents from the sciences, social sciences, and humanities rather than the business school). Would such a career have satisfied his ambition? Probably not. In that sense, he made the right choice for himself. But if his wartime experience pointed him toward the path he ended up following, it also undermined his ability to cope with the challenges awaiting him at Ford and the Pentagon. His exposure to hardboiled generals strengthened his determination to exercise command while concealing his own weaknesses. It hardened his heart to the horrors of war. But his role in preparing the firebombing of Tokyo, which incinerated an estimated 100,000 civilians, created an unacknowledged reservoir of guilt that deepened and eventually overflowed during and after the Vietnam War.

═══

IN THE EARLY AFTERMATH OF PEARL HARBOR, MCNAMARA WORried about being stranded at a school that would be a backwater at a time of national mobilization. His fellow HBS graduate-turned-instructor Myles Mace, who later served in the military with McNamara in England before returning to the HBS faculty, remembered their feeling of restlessness. McNamara tried to enlist in the navy but was turned down because of poor eyesight.[6] (He encouraged his sister Peggy to take up flying, used his connections in California to get her into flight school, and encouraged her to join the Women's Army Corps.)[7] But then, in the spring of 1942, the war came to him—in the person of Lt. Charles Bates ("Tex") Thornton, who was sent up from Washington by Assistant Secretary of War Robert A. Lovett and Gen. H. H. ("Hap") Arnold, commander of Army Air Forces.

Lovett was the blueblood son of the chairman of the Union Pacific Railroad, educated at Yale (where he was a member of Skull and Bones) and trained in law and business at Harvard. He became a naval aviator in World War One, then a prominent New York investment banker, and later served as undersecretary of state (1947–1949), deputy secretary of defense (1950–1951), and defense secretary (1951–1953). Lovett understood, McNamara recalled, "how crucial the flow of information is to good management. But the air corps he had inherited was tiny, gung ho, and so informal that he had almost no data with which to plan and control operations."[8] Even before Pearl Harbor, Lovett had assigned Thornton to ascertain what resources the Army Air Corps possessed and where they might be required. They knew enough about Harvard's pioneering statistical control program to conclude that it could help bring order to the air force.

By now, HBS faculty had created the field of "managerial accounting." In 1941, HBS established an Industrial Administrator degree and a new Management Controls course that would form the foundation of the Army Air Force's Statistical School. The premise of this approach, David Halberstam later wrote, "was that this vast new mechanized war was as much about the production and allocation of resources as it was about combat bravery, and the best brains should be applied to that challenge."[9] Between 1920 and 1939, 190 military officers had earned an MBA degree at Harvard, which had learned to pursue military contracts as a way to sustain itself during difficult economic times and so pressed its candidacy to establish a "stat school" for the Pentagon.[10]

Robert Lovett, who kept track of McNamara's rise in the military during the war and afterward at Ford and recommended him as defense secretary in 1960, shared with him a series of personal traits: both had a distinctly intellectual bent (Lovett loved to read Kant and socialize with famous New York writers); both relished coping with complex numerical calculations and marshaling reams of statistics and factual evidence to backstop their arguments; both seemed what Lovett biographers called "a little boy-scoutish"; both were "doers" rather than compromisers and consensus builders.[11]

Compared to Lovett, "Tex" Thornton was a country boy—born in Knox County, Texas, he showed entrepreneurial flair by buying up to forty acres of land at age fourteen with income from odd jobs; he attended Texas Tech but dropped out and enrolled at George Washington University at night; he worked as a "junior statistical clerk" and then as a statistician at the US Housing Authority; he got a commercial science degree in 1937 and joined the army before the war.[12] When Lovett sent Thornton to HBS in early May 1942 to recruit professors to help with the war effort, he was a charismatic twenty-eight-year-old with a cheerleading smile. Thornton had a "vision," McNamara remembered; he was "ambitious, a salesman, and a man who thinks big, generates enthusiasm, and enjoys winning."[13] He obviously had a knack for numbers and was adept at painting "verbal pictures," Mace recalled. Thornton smoked cigarettes in a holder that he waved about à la Franklin Roosevelt.[14] In addition, he had impressed Lovett and others in Washington as a "goer." "Whenever they had asked 'Mr. Thornton' for answers, they got a minimum of dialogue and a maximum of action."[15]

When the war began in Europe, the Air Corps had fewer than 1,500 planes and 500 pilots. In 1940, President Roosevelt called for the production of 50,000 planes per year, compared with fewer than 6,000 in 1939. By the end of the war, Thornton would be a full colonel in charge of sixty-six Statistical Control units with 3,000 officers and 15,000 service personnel around the world. The statistical control system, McNamara later explained, recorded "things like the status of planes (ready for combat, repairable, out of action), the condition of the men (types of training, casualties, replacement needs), and the state of operations (number of missions flown, types of mission, targets attacked, degree of success, losses of men and equipment, and so on). By assembling such reports, commanders could get an up-to-date picture of the operations—and shortcomings—of American airpower all over the world."[16] Bomb damage assessment was particularly hard to calculate. It depended on aerial photography carried out by photo reconnaissance units flying modified bombers, which were often thwarted by weather conditions and the difficulty of measuring damage obscured by fires and smoke on the ground.

Thornton's assignment in visiting Harvard, he told his hosts, was "to see if we can't work out a plan to teach Air Force officer candidates to be statistical-control officers."[17] The idea was to bring such candidates to Cambridge to learn statistical control and then deploy them at American air bases. HBS received the contract awarding Harvard the stat school on May 8, 1942. Thornton wanted the school underway in a few weeks. Before then its Harvard professors must come down to Washington. Harvard's stat controllers didn't need much convincing. "When?" he was asked. "Tonight," he replied. That night, a delegation led by McNamara's faculty admirer Professor Edmund Learned left Boston by train at eleven, arriving at seven the next morning.[18]

McNamara was a perfect fit for Thornton. He had the analytical flair that Thornton, a charmer and promoter, did not. McNamara was full of ideas but knew how to subordinate his own thinking to Thornton's. "Whatever Tex decided was final," concluded a chronicler of his career. Foreshadowing his role in the Vietnam War under President Johnson, McNamara "accepted it and carried the order out, never looking back, always the loyal soldier."[19] On his first and later trips to Washington, McNamara helped prepare the Army Air Forces Statistical Control Officers School that opened for business at Harvard on June 8. "He did it well," his HBS dean recalled. "He came back with the situation all tied up in a neat package; there were no loose ends."[20] While in Washington, McNamara and Mace also drew up regulations requiring every squadron to track the state of their planes on a daily basis. "We ... worked in the Munitions Building," located on Constitution Avenue on the National Mall, Mace recalled. "We sat down with pads of paper. I wrote one reg, Bob another." They learned "how parts were numbered" and "how to make an airplane inventory system—on the wing. We were unafraid to try."[21] Their report allowed the Army Air Force to decide "how to allocate airplanes and crews, how to distribute equipment, plan training schedules and the movement of troops. It mandated a daily inventory of the number, disposition, location and use of all aircraft—down to type, model and serial number."[22]

The HBS stat school's first class consisted of 165 officer candidates, many of whom knew the military better than their Harvard mentors. The latter, Mace remembered, taught by "the seat of our pants."[23] For a while, McNamara and his colleagues were content with their role. But by the end of 1942, McNamara and Mace wanted more. "Do we want to sit out the war teaching OCS guys," Mace remembered asking, "or do we want to get in? Do we want to spend the war at Soldiers Field in Boston or are we going to try to get into uniform?"[24]

Into uniform it was—although, McNamara later emphasized, he had two draft deferments (for teaching airmen at Harvard and because he had a one-year-old child), that could have spared him military service.[25] But becoming an officer would require serving overseas, Thornton informed them, since the War Department was no longer offering direct commissions to officers at home. Thornton arranged for McNamara and Mace to become special consultants to the Eighth Air Force, based in England. They would have to leave their families behind, but his Harvard dean was so sure of McNamara's value to HBS that he promised to preserve McNamara's position while he was away and even paid the premium for $10,000 worth of life insurance covering the transatlantic flight. (According to McNamara, the same plane he flew on crashed on a subsequent flight to Lisbon.)[26]

═══

MCNAMARA AND MACE FLEW A PAN AM CLIPPER FIRST CLASS TO England on February 2, 1943, with a stop in Bermuda, refueling in the Azores, and then overnight flights to Lisbon and on to England. They slept in luxury on the plane in full-length beds and dined on what Mace recalled as "superb" meals.[27] But the living in the UK wasn't so easy. During the worst of the blitz, London had endured nightly bombing with the population taking shelter in deeply dug tube stations. The bombing had eased in the summer of 1941, but just after McNamara and Mace arrived, one of the worst civil disasters occurred when a large crowd seeking to take shelter in the Bethnal Green tube station panicked and stampeded, leaving 173 people crushed to death.[28] The two Yanks lived in Teddington, not far from the Eighth Air Force's headquarters in Bushy Park, the second largest of London's royal parks, just north of Hampton Court Palace in the borough of Richmond-on-Thames. They shared a room in a house owned by the Bealey family (mother, father, son, and daughter), which had a big crack in the ceiling opened by a German bomb that had landed nearby. "It was cold as hell," Mace remembered. It was February and March and "there was no heat in the house." The bathroom tub had a small water heater next to it that, for one shilling, would provide enough hot water for a "very shallow bath." One night when McNamara and Mace heard local antiaircraft guns firing at German planes, they went out to watch, but were quickly hustled inside by their landlady lest they be hit by flying shrapnel.[29] Like the long-ago incident in Shanghai, when young seaman McNamara had to be hurried inside while taking pictures of an attacking plane, the London episode confirmed that his fascination with war could render him oblivious to personal danger.

Their modest office at Bushy Park, where McNamara and Mace sat on opposite sides of a single table, was in a temporary building, but they had a much larger room for Statistical Control people just down the hall from the Eighth Air Force's tough commanding general, Ira C. Eaker, who had once informed his English hosts, "We won't do much talking until we've done more fighting."[30] McNamara and Mace rode their bikes two or three miles to work. Mace ate breakfast in the mess hall (usually powdered eggs and Spam), while McNamara "would go directly to the office. He never ate breakfast."[31] The two men worked seven days a week, but the officers they supervised were also stretched to the limit and resented being hounded by their Harvard tutors. After three weeks as "special consultants," McNamara and Mace requested military commissions as captains so they could outrank their students, but the personnel chief would make them only second lieutenants. Before appealing to General Eaker, McNamara slicked back his black hair while Mace "combed my graying hair forward." Eaker insisted they pass an "indoctrination test" (on military protocol and customs) and gave them two weeks to study for it. They returned just two days later, passed the test, and were commissioned temporary captains as of March 12, 1943.

That wasn't good enough, however, as evidenced by a spat later that month in which McNamara exhibited his determination to command rather than be commanded. Dusty Porterfield was a former stat control student at HBS who had been commissioned a captain before McNamara and Mace and thought he outranked them.

"Captain McNamara, I'm your superior officer," snapped Porterfield. "I'm of a mind to rack you back."

"I don't give a damn who you think you're superior to," growled McNamara.[32] Porterfield later refused to sign on at the Ford Motor Company after the war when he learned that McNamara would be part of the group working there.

Mace had to step between them. Thornton arrived in England to settle things down. Professor Learned wrote from Cambridge to his prize
pupil: "I feel from word I have had . . . that you have been working too
hard and I think you should make some definite plans to relax before
you collapse. If you become too tired, your relationships with other men
will become strained, and in a military organization you cannot afford
to snap at superiors, no matter how sincere your objectives are nor how
distressing they may be."[33]

While in England, however, McNamara still could be mild mannered,
at least with his friends. He was "brilliant, personable, friendly," Mace
later insisted. "With that full head of black hair combed back," he looked
"formidable." "When he has a serious, straight look on his face," he looked
"more formidable than he is. But if you know him and he knows you, you
know he's not formidable—forbidding. He's not a cold person." He was
"an exciting person to be with"—"not given to much idle talk, although
when he wants to have idle talk socially, he's an active participant. He
didn't shun it, but he didn't waste much time on idle talk."[34] In all the time
they were together, Mace "never once saw a drop in [McNamara's] energy
level. Bob could never be devious, circuitous. There were no half-truths."[35]

====

MCNAMARA'S EXTENDED ABSENCE DURING THE WAR PUT A TRE-
mendous burden on his wife. She had to raise Little Margy on her own
and then, after his stint in the States, another daughter, named Kathleen,
was born on July 22, 1944. Not to mention his mother, who helped to
take care of Little Margy for a while in California but then became a
burden herself. It was "a Godawful life" for his wife, McNamara recalled.
"She was helping to take care of her mother" as well. But as he did so often,
McNamara managed to develop two opposite convictions—that what
was so awful, also was wonderful—along with the stress that accompanied such cognitive dissonance. "We thought it was great," he continued,
"that was what you did. We didn't have any regrets, we didn't feel we were
doing anything unusual."[36] Whether Margy herself actually shared the
upbeat optimism he attributed to her is unclear. And McNamara himself

didn't always sound that way at the time. On March 26, 1943, just a few weeks into his English exile, he wrote Margy: "This period will always be rather a nightmare to me. . . . Marg. . . . I don't think that if we had the decision to make over again we would decide differently. Even now I'm not sure what we are fighting for, but I'm quite certain that it's the duty of every young man not only to be in the army but to serve where most needed, which in almost every case means foreign service. . . . I can't help but think I would feel like a slacker if we had taken any other course."[37]

To comfort himself and his wife, McNamara filled his letters to her, which he tried to write almost every day, with passionate declarations of love for her and Little Margy. If further proof is needed that a man who later seemed cold and forbidding was capable of strong sentiment and deep emotion, this is it: "I can never tell you how much I miss you and our little one. People who are perfectly fitted for each other can never be even passably happy when apart. There hasn't been a day since I've been here that I've been able to put you and home out of my mind for even a minute."[38]

August 13, 1943: "I've loved you every moment of the last three years and continue to consider myself the luckiest man in all the world."[39]

September 1, 1943: McNamara was "dreaming" of when he could "return to you and Little Marg. The subject is constantly in my thoughts my darling and I'm just living for that day." "A thousand hugs and kisses my lover," he wrote. "You are in my thoughts every moment of every day and I won't really be alive again until I am in your arms."[40]

April 22, 1944: "I want to tell you how much I love you, how frequently I think of you throughout my waking hours, . . . how much your ever-present enthusiasm, your sparkling zest for life, your love of people enriches and broadens my life. Don't ever lose those qualities, my darling—having one in the family who has a tendency to allow the day's cares to act as a damper is more than enough."[41]

July 26, 1944: Celebrating baby Kathleen's birth: "She must be a darling, my sweetheart. Give her a big hug and kiss for her daddy, and tell little Marg that I would gladly give ten years of my life to be able to give her one sweet kiss."[42]

Margy's letters to Bob were almost as passionate. On March 13, 1943, she imagined that once they were together again, "Let's never get out of bed for a month. You know it's like being blended together and then pushed apart, leaving only fragments of ourselves to go on separately." A few days later, she described the wonderful, quiet life she dreamed they would some-day share—so starkly different from the tragedy-mixed-with-triumph, for their family as well as their country, that awaited them in Washington: "All my life is for you and where you are. Perhaps someday we can be on a hill in a sunny place and just live and enjoy life. I hope that someday after this mess is over, that we can find our spot and just live for each other and you won't have to be under pressure when you work—just to have a little 2X4 [a lean-to] in the mountains and a bungalow on a hill."[43]

DID MCNAMARA MISS HIS MOTHER? TO JUDGE BY HER COMPLAINTS that he wasn't writing to her, it would seem not. "I haven't heard from Bob in weeks," she complained to Margy on July 30, 1943. "It's so hard to write when I don't hear. I think I'm the only mother whose son hasn't time to write to her. . . . My heart is broken—he seems to have walked out of my life, and why? 'What have I done to deserve this?' I keep saying to myself during my sleepless nights. . . . Everyone who knows us knows that no mother ever loved a son more—and now that I am alone and need his love he has put himself out of my life." She made up things to tell her friends who assumed she heard from him weekly. Could Margy help to "change the relationship between Bob and me?" In the meantime, his wife must never tell Bob about his mother's despair nor how "I make believe . . . I hear from him and misplaced his letters" so that she couldn't read them to others.[44]

It would not be strange if McNamara had grown irritated with his mother's constant intrusions into his life, with her steady drumbeat of uber-extravagant praise, plus annoying monitoring of his behavior. And to make matters worse, to judge by his wife's letters to him, Claranel had recruited Margy to press him to respond to his mother's missives.

March 13, 1943: "Your mom is a little worried about her paying so much rent, $60 per month, and I thought it would be nice to start giving her $10 a month and $20 just as soon as we can. She has done so much and we should have done it long ago."

March 18, 1943: "Say young man, if you don't write your mother P.D.Q. [pretty damn quick] things will happen. Use the time you'd write me some nite real soon. And this is serious I want to let you know ... and I'm getting embarrassed. Please sweet do."

March 19, 1943: "She isn't very well Kip and feels it terribly when you don't write."

April 20, 1943: "While I think of it, your sweet Mama has only had ONE letter from you to date. Nuf said."

May 3, 1943: "Mother M seems to be feeling better these days. For a while she was depressed."

June 26, 1943: "Are you getting your Mom's mail regularly? ... Do write to her Mlove she looks forward to them so, even if you skip writing me one nite."

Perhaps in response to Margy's entreaties, McNamara's own letters to Margy sounded positively warm about his mother. He even encouraged her to move east to be nearer to his family. Nell couldn't do so in the near future, but Margy could report that "a wonderful letter from Mom came 5 days ago. She seemed much more cheerful and happy."[45]

McNamara's mother may have exaggerated his inattention in order to "guilt-trip" him and his wife. Margy may have shamed her husband into paying more heed to his mother than he really wanted to. But McNamara's conscience may have trumped his annoyance and prompted him to behave like the good Eagle Scout he had once trained to be.

AFTER NINE MONTHS IN ENGLAND, MCNAMARA WAS ASSIGNED TO the Fifty-Eighth Bomb Wing in Salina, Kansas, which was being equipped with a new "Superfortress" bomber, the B-29. The move offered him the chance to reunite with his family, who met him in New York and drove out to Kansas with him in a 1940 convertible. By now Little Margy was almost two, and since the car was overloaded, she rode for a while atop her potty chair, which her father quietly abandoned by a curb in Allentown, Pennsylvania.[46]

The B-29, a four-engined propeller-driven heavy bomber, was one of the largest aircraft to fly in World War II; it had space for roughly eleven crew members. An unmodified B-29 could carry as much as 20,000 pounds in bombs over short distances. At long range (the B-29 could fly 3,250 miles without refueling) and high altitude, this maximum dropped to 5,000 pounds. The B-29 was a high-priority project because the B-17, which until then had been the primary strategic bomber, wasn't suited for the Pacific Theater, which required a bigger plane that could carry a larger load for more than 3,000 miles. The B-29s would be based in India, from which they would fly to forward bases in China for refueling, then on to bomb Japan, and then back to China and India. Befitting its importance, the new bomb wing would not be under the control of the China-Burma-India theater headed by the British general Lord Mountbatten, but directly responsible to Gen. Hap Arnold, chief of the US Army Air Forces in Washington.

The new planes were slated to fly to India in early 1944, but, McNamara remembered, "everything was behind schedule. We didn't get the first airplanes until February. They were just totally brand-new." The planes "required considerable skill in handling. The engines were newly designed and they had a very U-shaped curve in fuel consumption. You had to learn how to run the damned things so that you had low consumption and high efficiency." Wright Aeronautics made the engines. Apparently, they were poorly designed for the B-29's needs in the tropics. McNamara began collecting information on the planes' "life between overhauls." He discovered "many, many engines that had to be overhauled with less than 100 hours on them." Engines were so inefficient that "we literally flew the aircraft from Kansas to India with a spare engine in the bomb bay so that if we had to change engines en route, that could be done." The planes flew via Brazil to Ascension Island in the Atlantic and then across Africa and the Middle East to India. "The net of the whole thing," McNamara continued, "was that it was a disaster. We had planes scattered from Kansas to India."[47]

For his high-quality work on this high-priority project, McNamara was promoted to major and sent to India in April 1944. In view of the checkered record of the B-29s, he flew on a lesser plane. Once there, he confronted the challenge posed by the Himalayan mountain range. Before the B-29s arrived, he recalled, the Transport Command that had been resupplying forces in China "were losing a hell of a lot of aircraft," C-46s, whose ceiling of 17,000 feet was 2,000 feet below the height of the mountain peaks they circumnavigated. "The weather was Godawful and we were losing crews." "You carried currency so that if you bailed out, you could pay the tribes to get [you] the hell out of there." The B-29s had a ceiling in the twenty thousands, but because of the high rate at which they consumed fuel, McNamara concluded, "the net of the whole damned thing was that we couldn't build up enough fuel in China for a long time to accomplish anything. And it never did accomplish anything." As a result, Gen. Kenneth "K. B." Wolfe, who was in command when McNamara arrived, was replaced by Gen. LaVerne G. "Blondie" Saunders, a former all-American football star at West Point turned combat commander. Saunders was replaced by Gen. Curtis LeMay, an even tougher commanding officer who, according to McNamara, "looked the place over and said, hell, he'd never be able to do anything from India; therefore get the thing out of India and move it to the Pacific, the Marianas," where McNamara eventually joined him.[48]

LeMay, who was McNamara's boss in the South Pacific, was later his nemesis during the Cuban missile crisis in 1962. As described in a biography that lauds him as "America's most innovative . . . commander," he was "dark, brooding and forbidding. He rarely smiled, he spoke even less, and when he did, his words seemed to come out in a snarl. Women seated next to him at dinner said he could sit through an entire meal and not utter a single syllable. Surly, tactless, and with a lifeless, moist cigar constantly locked between his teeth, he was the prototype of the brutal, inhuman militarist" whom most people found "frightening."[49]

McNamara remembered LeMay as "tough and brutal." "I never heard him say more than two words in sequence. It was basically, 'Yes, No, Yep, That's all, or to hell with it.' That's all he said." Whereas other generals talked about how many planes they had and how many bombs they dropped, LeMay cared only about destroying targets. That's why McNamara advised LeMay, "You haven't accomplished a damn thing with the B-29's in India and China. You ought to get them out of there into some place where you can accomplish and kill more—destroy more targets." "I didn't say kill more people," McNamara corrected his own account.[50]

Before being replaced, General Wolfe taught McNamara a key lesson about suppressing his doubts and taking charge. McNamara had noticed that planes supplying fuel to China were transporting far more lubricating oil than was needed "to balance the fuel stocks." When he reported this to Wolfe, the latter growled, "Why the hell don't you *do* something about it?"

"Look, I'm only a statistical control officer," McNamara replied. "I might make a mistake in judgment."

"Goddammit, do it! Get it done. You know it ought to be done. Do it! All I ask is that you be right 51 percent of the time."

McNamara always remembered that, he recalled. "Because he was *so* right in the sense of freeing yourself up from fear of errors. Be careful you don't make any errors you can possibly avoid, but don't let the risk of failure or the risk of error stand in the way of taking action. I've always remembered that, and he was the one who taught it to me."[51]

General Wolfe taught McNamara another lesson. While in India, McNamara was stationed at Kharagur, outside Calcutta. Perhaps his main memory, he recalled, was "it was *hot as hell*" and that "a substantial percentage of the command was always unavailable for duty" with diarrhea and malaria. Moreover, since "everything was in short supply," the former Eagle Scout had to "steal" (that is, "liberate," he corrected himself) pads of paper from Wolfe's desk: "I'd go in with a folder and sit down at his desk and try to get myself in a position so I could drop the folder on top of a pad he usually had there. Then when I got up to leave, I'd just scoop up the folder and the pad." Until Wolfe caught him at it: "Say, Bob, I've been watching you. I see what you do. Now, Goddamit, if you need paper, just ask and I'll get it for you."[52]

McNamara had previously touched down in poor countries during ocean voyages—in Panama in 1935, in China and the Philippines in 1937. But this hardly prepared him for Calcutta where, after a major famine in 1944, "there were about 10,000 dead bodies on the streets at any one time and 100,000 people sleeping on the streets." When he walked around the city at night, "there were forms on the street—you didn't know if they were dead or alive; it was just the most Godawful mess you can imagine . . . it was a ghastly experience."[53]

Given the pressure of his job and the harsh living conditions, McNamara missed his family all the more. As had been his habit throughout his life, he managed to lose himself in his work. But he found time every day to write more warm, loving letters to his wife.

April 25, 1944: I miss you terribly my darling, and think of you every minute of the day. Kisses in your pillow my sweet. All my love.

April 26, 1944: My dearest one—Another banner day with two letters from you my darling, written on the 11th and 12th of April. Gosh, but it is wonderful to receive your letters, Marg—they change one's entire outlook on life and make no matter how black a day a happy one.

Undated: How I miss you my sweetheart. You are in my thoughts every minute of the day. Nothing seems the same without you. The room is colder in the morning, the bed is more uncomfortable, dinner just something one attends to stay alive, all have changed just because you are not beside me. This morning I was lying in bed awake at 6 o'clock and would have given a million dollars to have felt you soft and warm beside me and to have heard little Marg [indecipherable word] to jump in beside us.[54]

Passionate, sentimental declarations. "Black days." "A tendency to allow the day's cares to act as a damper." McNamara's deep, up-and-down emotions, so invisible in public as to seem entirely absent, continued to churn under the surface. But whether feeling melancholy or not, McNamara's work was outstanding as usual. Professor Learned, still keeping track of his prize pupil, judged it to be "spectacular" and "entirely new." "The best logistics report the Air Force ever received was originated by him in China," concluded Learned.[55] Several months after being made a major, McNamara was promoted to lieutenant colonel.

═══

NEXT STOP: WASHINGTON IN THE FALL OF 1944. ANOTHER HIGH-priority assignment, this time as stat control officer for the Twentieth Air Force under Gen. Lauris Norstad, the youngest general in the air force. McNamara's office, in Pentagon Room 4D1053, was down the corridor from Lovett and Thornton, and not far from Suite 3E880, which would become the office of the secretary of defense when that position was created in 1947.[56] The now-four-member McNamara family was united again in a small apartment in Arlington, Virginia. But soon duty summoned him to the South Pacific.

While McNamara's stint in Guam didn't last long, it put him at the command center for the firebombing air attacks on Tokyo: "I was at LeMay's headquarters on Guam at the time President Roosevelt died [on April 12, 1945]," he remembered in a 1992 interview. "I'd been there a few weeks and stayed a short time thereafter, maybe a month or two."[57] Only one of the three books about McNamara's life published before 1996, whose authors had extensive access to him, mentions his time in Guam at all; Shapley gives it one sentence.[58] His own memoirs, published in 1995, give it exactly two words: "the Pacific," in a listing of places he served during the war.[59]

His time at Guam deserves greater attention. McNamara's analysis of American bombing campaigns confirmed that the optimum altitude for aerial bombardment was 7,000 feet rather than the higher altitude that pilots preferred. His work helped General LeMay to perfect the massive firebombing of Japanese cities, a brutal tactic that McNamara favored at the time. "I was part of a mechanism that, in a sense, recommended it," he said years later. "I was not a flying officer, I was a staff officer, but I analyzed bombing and bombing operations and how to make them more efficient, i.e. not more efficient in a sense of killing more," although that's exactly what they did, "but more efficient in weakening the adversary."[60]

That euphemism softened McNamara's recollection. While working with LeMay, he greatly admired him for directing the savage firebombing campaign. "LeMay was without any question the most outstanding combat commander I observed or was associated with in the Air Force" because "he conceived of his responsibility exactly" as McNamara understood it, namely, "target destruction."[61] LeMay "thought in terms of results," McNamara explained, and that led him to move the B-29s from India/China to the Marianas. Not only that, he ordered that they attack at 7,000 feet rather than 29,000 so that, McNamara added, they could accomplish "a hell of a lot."[62]

The planes that had preceded the B-29s in Europe, B-17s and B-24s that flew at 17,000 feet, had been missing their targets because of intervening cloud layers and their vulnerability to enemy aircraft and air defense. Flying in at lower altitudes would enhance bombing accuracy but render bombers more vulnerable. The average loss rate of planes in the Eighth Air Force in Europe was 4 percent, McNamara recalled, "a *hell* of a high attrition rate." And that led to a high abort rate, as high as 20 percent, of planes that turned back before reaching their targets. Pilots who failed to get to targets often claimed "electrical appliance chutes failed or mechanical failure, or whatever it was."[63] But when McNamara probed deeper he found that "the real cause of a high percentage of aborts was fear on the part of the crews" who "knew the 4 percent casualty rate and just didn't want to go to the target." McNamara reported what he had learned to LeMay, who insisted on attacking from 7,000 feet. LeMay issued the following order: "Every plane which takes off will go to the target or the crew will be court-martialed, and I am going to be in the lead aircraft."[64] McNamara remembered taking part in a briefing session in Guam in March 1945 after a firebombing raid over Tokyo at which one B-29 crew commander complained, "Some Goddamned fool took this airplane that can fly at high altitude and ordered us to go in at 7,000, and I lost my wingman. I'd like to know who that son-of-a-bitch was."[65]

McNamara happened to be sitting next to LeMay. "He knew, having been in the lead airplane himself, exactly what that young man had been facing. He got up and gave a very sensitively stated—sympathetic but clear—answer. He said, in effect, 'Well, our job is to destroy targets and the proper measure you should give, captain, of relative losses at high level and low level is not per sortie, but per target destroyed. So, per unit of destruction, you're way ahead.'"[66]

"Units of destruction"—besides steel mills and other hard targets, air force historians concluded that the Twentieth's Air Force's incendiary raid on Tokyo on the night of March 9, 1945, killed an estimated 100,000 people and left over a million homeless (more than some estimates of the number killed the day of the atomic bombing of Hiroshima), and that in the next five months American firebombing destroyed or gravely damaged more than sixty Japanese cities.[67] LeMay summarized the result this way: "Sixteen hundred and sixty-five tons of incendiary bombs went hissing down upon that city, and hot drafts from the resulting furnace tossed some of our aircraft two thousand feet above their original altitude. We burned up nearly sixteen square miles of Tokyo"—producing what Gen. Thomas Power, who led the attack, described as "more casualties than in any other military action in the history of the world."[68]

McNamara did not invent incendiary bombs or decide on their use. A small team of scientists designed, produced, and tested a unique firebomb, the M-69, especially suited for incinerating Japanese cities. General Arnold, who had initially resisted doing so, eventually authorized their use, and LeMay sent them against Tokyo on the night of March 9.[69] But years later, LeMay recalled that McNamara coaxed 30 percent more flying time out of his B-29 bombers by applying operations analysis to calculate the numbers of crews and planes and to reschedule them more efficiently than other members of LeMay's staff could.[70] After the war, LeMay admitted, "If we'd lost the war, we'd all have been prosecuted as war criminals."[71] At least one historian, having noted that McNamara helped "kill hundreds of thousands of civilians," described him as seemingly "impervious to the human cost of his work."[72] Perhaps he seemed so at the time. But fifty years later, in the film *The Fog of War*, he agreed with LeMay: "He'd say, and I'd say we were behaving like war criminals." In a single night, he recalled grim-faced, with tears in his eyes, "we burned to death 100,000 civilians in Tokyo: men, women and children."[73]

McNamara never told his son about this when Craig was growing up. In fact, McNamara told him only one story "about this period of his life, his actual military service"—about how after one of his flights over the Hump from India into China, he saw hundreds of Chinese peasants pulling a steamroller over a rough dirt landing strip. As they did so, one peasant slipped and was crushed to death. It was apparently on that trip that McNamara purchased a small statue that he kept for years on his desk in Washington. As Craig describes it, "a small infant climbs on the Buddha's warm, round belly. The infant's eyes are wide, gazing up in an adoring and joyful expression. The babe's mouth is open as if in the middle of a gurgling laugh. The Buddha's mouth, lined with ivory teeth, returns the laugh." Craig wondered why his father kept this statue: "Did Dad see himself in the omnipotence of the Buddha's great, smooth head? Did he feel the joy of the infant climbing the curves of the Buddha's belly, possibly wondering if this would be his experience with his own son? I wonder why that story from his brief time in China—briefly miraculous, suddenly tragic—was the only one he told me."[74]

———

ON JULY 22, 1945, MCNAMARA TOOK UP HIS LAST WARTIME ASSIGN-ment at the Air Technical Service Command at Wright Field in Ohio, headquarters of statistical control for all US Air Force planes around the world. With the war over in Europe, Lovett and Thornton needed him to oversee the process of cutting back aircraft production on a predictable timetable. According to an official Pentagon summary, having previously "organized, directed and operated statistical control system in the 8th and 20th Air Forces," he now "directed Statistical Control system of ATSC

[Air Technical Service Command] supervising directly 1700 employees and having direct or technical supervision of over 5,000 employees."[75]

Housing was scarce at Wright Field. The McNamara family, with their two little girls in tow, squeezed into a two-bedroom apartment in Springfield, not far from the base, which they shared with his executive officer, Leonard Cling, and his wife and two babies.[76] But soon after they arrived in Dayton, a double tragedy of a quite personal sort struck. McNamara fell sick with what looked like malaria but turned out to be polio. Admitted to the military hospital at the base, McNamara initially seemed sick enough to need a replacement in his new job. But when Charles Bosworth arrived to take over, expecting to find McNamara paralyzed, he found him hard at work in bed, scrutinizing reports and issuing orders. "Oh, I'm fine, fine," McNamara assured Bosworth. Bosworth had assumed he would take command, but McNamara remained in control from his hospital perch, giving Bosworth assignments to carry out at the office. And within six weeks, McNamara was out of the hospital.[77]

McNamara's case of polio was mild.[78] His wife's was not. She was on a local bus when she felt sick. She got off and threw up into a paper bag. Finding her way to a local hospital, she was diagnosed with a severe case of polio (her lower body was soon paralyzed, along with her entire right side) that the military hospital could not handle. McNamara was well enough to try to get her transferred. Thornton tried to get her into the Army-Navy Hospital in Hot Springs, Arkansas, but they weren't taking civilians. For the time being, the Cling family took care of Little Margy and Kathy until McNamara could find another apartment and another babysitter. But when the new sitter turned out to be a Christian Scientist who would not take Kathleen to the doctor for sores that had appeared on her backside, McNamara appealed to his relatives. His sister Peggy arrived from Murfreesboro, Tennessee, where her husband was in the army; he then joined her to lend a hand. Several months later, in December 1945, after McNamara arranged for his wife to be moved to a rehabilitation center in Baltimore, and himself to be transferred to the Pentagon, he took Little Margy to live with his mother in Oakland (or rather, halfway, to Lincoln, Nebraska, where Peggy and her husband took her and her suitcase with clothes and dolls on to California), and Kathleen to Margy's parents, who were living in Toronto.[79] That meant the girls were separated, living with grandparents they hardly knew, and didn't see their mother for months after not seeing their father while he was overseas.[80]

Asked by Hendrickson about his illness many years later, McNamara preferred to talk about his wife's, weeping as he did so—how she refused to accept that she might never walk again, how she fought back heroically, how in a nearly full-body cast in Baltimore Children's Hospital she encouraged paralyzed children all around her, reassuring them, entertaining them, ordering candy and other goodies for them.[81] "The doctor said she'd never lift an arm or a leg off the bed again," McNamara remembered, "that she'd be a permanent invalid."[82] "Everything seemed so dark," recalled Vern Goodin and his wife Marion.[83] All told, Margy spent four months in the Ohio hospital and five more in Baltimore, but "she had an extremely strong will," marveled her husband. "She just was determined to recover."[84] "She was so warm and so lovely and so kind," he added in another interview, "that many didn't know that she had such a streak of steel in her."[85]

How do polio survivors' ordeals affect their outlook on life? Some survivors, experts told Hendrickson, "end up tight, rigid, emotionally constrained." If you are that way to begin with, you can become more so, or you can be more "reflective, spiritual, softer, appreciative of the subtler things." Some who have beaten polio become "overstriving" once they recover. But what if you're overstriving already? "If you're young you get wiped out physically," said the director of the Michigan Medical Center's postpolio clinic. "So if you survive, you count on using your mind, you're not sure whether your body can be counted on from there on out. You live with a certain amount of hidden dread." On the other hand, added a Michigan medical colleague, "if you've won a war and you've triumphed over polio, wouldn't this really tend to give you a confidence and a hubris? There's a physical hubris, I've noticed, a physical need for postpolio patients to push themselves beyond the average threshold of pain."[86]

Margy McNamara, her husband remembered, "began to ski within a year of getting out of the hospital. I had to ski absolutely adjacent to her because when she fell on the snow there was no way for her to get up because of the weakness in her knees." The first summer, or perhaps the second, after she got out of the hospital, they went on a three-day hike in Yosemite in the high-country camps, starting at Tuolumne Meadows, then up to Vogelsang Camp, then to Merced Lake Camp, and finally down through Little Yosemite into Yosemite Valley. "It was almost torture for her," McNamara recalled. "The first day was about six miles. She wasn't carrying a backpack but she was really in pain." He insisted "that's what she wanted to do."[87] Or was she seeking to please him?

McNamara didn't like to talk about his own polio experience. But one wonders whether his own and his wife's didn't intensify his determination to keep challenging himself with feats of physical exertion virtually to the end of his life. And whether their experience didn't sharpen both sides of his character—the tireless, rigid striving to do well and do good at the same time, and his mostly hidden capacity for dread and emotional pain, which would later mount along with all his remarkable achievements.

CHAPTER FIVE

Power Steering

When World War II ended, the Ford Motor Company was a mess. Even before the war, Ford struggled to compete with its main rivals. With less than 19 percent of total prewar sales, Ford regularly trailed General Motors and Chrysler. Yet, during the war, Ford became the country's third-largest defense contractor (behind GM and Curtiss-Wright, the aircraft manufacturer), producing jeeps, armored cars, troop carriers, trucks, and tanks—thanks to the fact that it mass-produced vehicles, unlike many companies.[1] After the war, however, when GM embarked on a carefully prepared return to peacetime production, Ford, which had not planned ahead, faced a mammoth task of reconversion. According to a history of the company, "death, resignations, and discharges had torn the managerial fabric of the firm full of gaps and tatters." Reconversion "demanded great expenditures for machine tools, factory remodeling and new plants. Scarcities of essential materials, government controls of purchasing and selling prices and the honest but disruptive disagreement of executives on policies represented hurdles which would prove difficult to clear."[2] Ford boasted forty-eight factories in twenty-three countries, with a workforce of 150,000, but it was losing more than $2 million a week, because, as Walter Hayes, a Henry Ford II biographer, put it, "nobody knew how much it cost to build a car or anything else for that matter."[3]

Henry Ford I had refused to modernize the company he founded. "Because the old man had hated banks and borrowing, there was no line of credit to draw on as the cash neared zero."[4] When Henry's son Edsel died in 1943, his own son, Henry II, was released from the navy to take over the company, but he was hardly prepared to do so. Henry II had a patrician's education at the Hotchkiss School and Yale but failed to make the most of it. "I flunked in engineering," he recalled, and when "the other guys said sociology was a snap course" and "I figured that was for me, I flunked it, too."[5] Henry II was expelled from Yale for plagiarizing another student's paper. Of the several hundred top Ford executives in 1945, only a handful had college degrees.[6]

Ford needed a man like McNamara, and McNamara seemed to thrive at Ford. He rose steadily to the top of the company; he claimed he loved his work; he and his wife chose to live in Ann Arbor, home of the University of Michigan, which offered many of the same cultural and intellectual rewards as Cambridge. But the same Ford years had a downside that loomed larger as time went on. He produced profits for the company and won admirers both in and outside it. But his brilliance and the stern and abrasive habits of command he had observed in the military and cultivated in himself alienated many of his colleagues.

The challenges he faced at Ford paled in comparison with those that would confront him in the Vietnam War. But the stress he had felt since childhood was now sharpened and deepened, he recalled, by his nonconformity amid the corporate culture of Ford during the 1950s.[7] This stress had become almost second nature to him. He had learned to compartmentalize the two sides of his personality—his soaring ambition and hard-edged management/leadership persona conflicting with his softer, emotional side. That two-sidedness was already fracturing at Ford. McNamara's public relations man at Ford, Holmes Brown, described him as a "Puritan in Babylon."[8] To be true to the "values we wanted to instill in our children," McNamara recalled, he played the role of "a maverick" at Ford. "That's why we moved to Ann Arbor... into a university environment as opposed to the social environment of Grosse Pointe or Bloomfield Hills where the other executives lived." "That's why I didn't contribute to the Republican party when I was an executive at Ford, it's why we didn't accept Henry Ford [II]'s invitation to the marriage of one of their children."[9] Henry Ford "would tolerate my eccentricities," McNamara recalled, but others deeply resented them.[10]

===

THE SAME CHARISMATIC TEXAN WHO SWEPT MCNAMARA OUT OF HBS and into the war resettled him at Ford. Tex Thornton's claims that statistical controllers like McNamara improved Army Air Corps operations were supported by a later study that concluded that "'balance sheet warriors' enabled the U.S. Army Air Forces to become the best-equipped, best-trained and best-informed military force the world had ever seen."[11] So Thornton recruited his nine brightest and most accomplished acolytes and offered them as a ten-man team to a series of companies including U.S. Steel, Eastman Kodak, Nash Motor, and Arthur D. Little. But he zeroed in on Ford, according to McNamara, after Thornton "simply read in *Life Magazine* that Henry Ford II had been called out of the Navy when his father died in 1943 and had gone back to Ford Motor Company without any real preparation." "That's the man that needs me and my associates!" Thornton said. He wrote to Henry Ford II, McNamara remembered, saying: "'You need me. I can deliver ten outstanding young men to you, and we will come out and help you run the company.' It sounds absurd, but that's exactly what happened, and Ford agreed to it."[12]

Actually, McNamara's initial response to Thornton's proposal was: "To hell with it, Tex. I'm not going to be part of it. I'm going back to Harvard, that's what Marg and I want to do. I'm going to spend my life there. Harvard's been marvelous to me in the war, they paid my [retirement insurance premiums] all the time I was there, both their portion of it and mine ... and the dean at Harvard says I can teach any course I want to in the Graduate School of Business. It's a tremendous offer. I'm doing it."[13] McNamara had returned to Cambridge to talk to HBS Dean Donald David, who assured him that if he took a break of two or three years at

Ford, such business experience would actually strengthen McNamara as a scholar and teacher, which would qualify him to return to HBS at the even higher rank of full professor. "You've got to come back," David insisted. "We can make it possible for you to do so financially." But McNamara's desire to return to Harvard was blunted by Margy's continued need for expensive medical care as she recovered from polio. How could he pay Margy's huge hospital bills on an assistant professor's salary of $4,500? "I couldn't conceive of how that could be done," he recalled.[14] Thornton was also persuasive. The McNamaras were broke. "Look, Bob," Thornton argued, "you've got a sick wife."[15] He continued, "You owe it to her."[16]

McNamara insisted that the group meet with Henry Ford II before making a final decision. The team arrived in Detroit on November 7, 1945. McNamara and Charlie Bosworth drove up in McNamara's weather-beaten Ford Model A Roadster. When McNamara started at Ford on January 28, 1946, he recalled, "they never had a certified financial statement, never, in the history of the company." They had decided they needed certified statements, balance sheets, and profit and loss statements and hired an outside company, but the company "worked a year and gave up."[17]

Not long after starting work at Ford, McNamara described the company's dismal management situation to his mentor, Edmund Learned, who had led Harvard Business School's engagement with the Army Air Force and its Statistical Control unit. "In many ways it reminds me of those early days in the Air Force when there was no information on which to base decisions, no organization pattern, and when it seemed as if everyone was running around like chickens with their heads cut off. The extent of decay which existed throughout the organization defies description. Although a complete new layer of top executive talent has been brought in since the first of this year, it will be months, if not years, before its influence can extend down through the echelons. Channels of communication are poor, controls are lacking, organization is nonexistent, planning is unheard of, and the personnel problem is serious beyond belief."[18]

Once Henry II took over at Ford, his longtime public relations adviser Ted Mecke recalled, he showed himself to be assertive, opinionated, and intolerant of those he regarded as dullards. He knew he desperately needed Thornton's team.[19] As McNamara remembered it, Ford wanted to surround himself with a team distinctly loyal to him and the new company he wanted to build rather than to the old company he had inherited.[20] "We were all talking to him," Thornton team member Arjay Miller remembered, and Ford said, " 'Well, just write down your name, how much money you want, and when you can come to work.' Tex put his name down first at $12,000. Then he put McNamara down for $11,000."[21] The team signed their contracts in November 1945 and began work at Ford in January 1946.

Although Ford wasn't McNamara's first choice, he immediately struck Robert Dunham, the Ford executive who organized their visit to Dearborn (and then a six-week training program for them), as "really the smart one of the group, which later turned out to be the fact. He asked the searching questions. He seemed to absorb information very easily and quickly. It was obvious that he was forming opinions. He just struck me as the one who should be the leader instead of Thornton."[22] Arjay Miller quickly grasped that McNamara was "clearly the ranking person under Tex."[23] In fact, Miller later learned, McNamara was "the first" of the men Thornton recruited because he regarded him as "the outstanding guy of the whole 3,000" he had supervised during the war.[24]

Even before they could get to work, however, the Thornton team ran into resistance. John Bugas was a former FBI agent whom Henry Ford hired to protect his grandchildren from a potential replay of the kidnapping and murder of the twenty-month-old son of world-famous aviator Charles Lindbergh in the spring of 1932. Bugas was one of the old-guard top executives at Ford. Feeling threatened by the Thornton team, especially by their as yet vague job mandate, he counseled Henry Ford II to hesitate before hiring them, saying, "Well, Mr. Ford, if you subsequently feel you want to employ these people . . . ," only to have Ford snap, "John, stop giving me this 'if stuff.' I am going to hire these men and that's all I want to hear about it."[25]

Bugas still insisted on subjecting them to three days of IQ and psychological tests that they suspected were designed to discredit them. But since their higher education was virtually unique among company executives, they welcomed the challenge. For an entire day they took tests of "ability and practical judgment, achievement exams challenging their knowledge of current social problems, science and mathematics, psychological profiles and mental stability exams," and tests that ranked them "against the general population on such factors as masculinity and depression." In addition, a Ford psychologist conducted individual interviews with the men. Measured against the general population, the group "ranked above the ninetieth percentile in general mental ability, practical judgment, business practice, cooperation, self-reliance, objectivity and masculinity."[26] Probing the degree of masculinity, one of the questions was whether the test taker would rather be a coal miner or a florist. Knowing that if he answered "florist" he would seem effeminate, McNamara answered: "coal miner."

"We just *killed* those tests," Arjay Miller recalled, citing scores that were said to be the best ever recorded in the history of the exams.[27] McNamara wrote to his wife that he and two others got "higher marks on the judgment section of the test than had ever been made by anyone else who had ever taken that test at Ford."[28] According to the official test results, he was one of the top four in all but three measures, and of those top four, he was "#1." His scores put him in the 100th percentile of test-takers for "total mental level." His interviewer noticed "a tendency toward hyperactivity," which might "account for [his] relatively lower ranking in the group in [emotional] stability." McNamara also "displayed an unusual ability for self-analysis," prefiguring the later self-scrutiny that led to such torment about his role in the Vietnam War.[29] Interestingly, Thornton himself scored "lower than 50 percent of the group in ability and knowledge, in the middle of the group in adjustment, and at the top in leadership qualities."[30]

Even after acing these tests, the Thornton team faced more obstacles; they were required to punch time clocks and wear badges until they rebelled and refused to do so. During their first weeks on the job, McNamara and his colleagues roamed Ford's various plants and shops, peppering supervisors with questions, jotting down answers, imagining ways to improve performance, earning the nickname "Quiz Kids," after the hotshot underage stars of a popular radio show. After a while, the label that stuck to the cocky newcomers was "Whiz Kids." Although Henry II believed in his new crew, he also brought in two experienced car industry executives to help him run the whole show, Ernest Breech and Lewis Crusoe, who had both worked at General Motors. Many years later, Bob Dunham recalled in a letter to Thornton, McNamara, and other "Whiz Kids" that Breech had almost immediately tried to get rid of Thornton, "saying there wasn't room for both of you, adding that one day you would thank him." Thornton's and the others' first reaction was "that everybody would leave," but "cooler heads prevailed."[31]

The challenge that faced all the new executives was immense. Before the war, the automobile industry had been the single largest component of American industry, but during the war, production of cars for civilians had virtually ceased and some three and one half million passenger cars had been junked—so that pent-up demand was estimated to be from five to nine million new cars. On August 15, 1945, Henry Ford II estimated his company could produce between 75,000 and 85,000 passenger cars, as well as 50,000 trucks, by Christmas, which amounted to a yearly rate of about 250,000. Before the war it had often exceeded that in a month, but by the end of 1945 Ford had managed to turn out only 34,439 cars. The most popular Ford had required 87 man-hours to construct in 1941, but 128 in 1945.[32]

Henry Ford I had played a foundational role in creating the automobile industry. His triumph in designing and mass-producing the Model T had been transformational. But by 1945 his stodginess and biases were visible even in the shape and layout of the main Ford office building. "The worldwide headquarters of Ford was four stories high," McNamara later sneered, "relatively small, glass partitions from the waist up on every floor so Henry Ford, Sr., could sit down in the office in the corner of the southwest wing and look across the whole first floor and make sure nobody was smoking. And they'd taken the doors off the johns and the second and third and fourth floors were the same way exactly."[33]

During McNamara's first eight months on the job, the company lost nearly $55 million, "which in those days was a lot of money," McNamara recalled.[34] (Equivalent in 2024 dollars: $926,979,670.) All told, Ford's after-tax profits during 1946 amounted to just $2,000, but they reached $64.8 million in 1947, and nearly three times that in 1949. By 1954, Ford's new car registrations barely lost out to Chevrolet, 1,400,440 to 1,417,453, although GM's luxury divisions (Pontiac, Buick, Oldsmobile, and Cadillac) far outpaced Ford's Lincoln and Mercury brands.[35] McNamara's first assignments were as assistant director and then director of the Ford planning office, where he supervised several subdepartments: programming (production and sales), organization (structure of the company), and financial planning (projections of income and asset management). Three years later he was promoted to comptroller, responsible for all accounting and related financial planning. In 1952, he became assistant general manager (under Crusoe) of the company's main division (the Ford division) with the understanding that he would succeed Crusoe when the latter moved up to become group vice president of all three car divisions (Ford, Lincoln, and Mercury). As general manager, McNamara supervised styling, car design, engineering, procurement, management of assembly-line operations, and sales, including advertising. Next stop: group vice president in charge of all car divisions (the three just mentioned, plus Edsel).[36] Last stop: president of the whole company, the first who was not a member of the Ford family, for just a few short weeks in late 1960 before president-elect John Kennedy recruited him to be secretary of defense.

Given the company's successes as he rose in the ranks, his sense of satisfaction was not surprising. In the transcript of a long 1992 interview, his enthusiasm practically leaps off the page. He was "fascinated by serving as an executive in a complex enterprise" operating worldwide with well over 100,000 employees, especially doing so "at a relatively young age and also in a company that was going through a very dramatic and in a sense, traumatic, transition period." He "enjoyed" both the intellectual and the personal or political challenge—"the intellectual complexity in the sense of trying to decide what to do in a free market, and particularly the intellectual challenge of taking a company that hadn't made a profit in twenty years and bringing it back. It was fascinating to just think about how one could turn this around. And then, having conceived how this could be done, *getting it done.*" To a "young person it was a heavy responsibility and a very challenging one. So I enjoyed it very much. And beyond that, I enjoyed very much the people I associated with— particularly the people I went out there with. It was very exciting. And for a young person at the time, I was paid well, so it was satisfying financially."[37]

Even his physical environment at work eventually proved pleasing. In 1956, Ford opened its new twelve-story, glass-enclosed World Headquarters, designed by a Chicago firm, Skidmore, Owings and Merrill, that created other symbols of triumphal postwar modernism, in which eleventh-floor executives were entitled to a potted plant and a Monet reproduction and twelfth-floor suites came with a sofa and a conversation area. Not surprisingly, however, McNamara claimed "the most interesting aspect of my work at Ford was seeking to advance societal interests and stockholder interests simultaneously." Too idealistic? Not really, since "an objective of U.S. executives should be to do just that"—even though "if you wrote to the top 500 CEOs in the country and asked, 'To whom do you consider you're responsible?,' if it was a secret unsigned statement they would say stockholders—or maybe not even that."[38] Moreover, McNamara confessed in a 1988 interview that he himself believed "you have to know who you work for. In the automobile industry, and this may sound boy-scoutish, but I would go home and think how had I advanced the value for stockholders today."[39]

Of course, what stockholders (and CEOs) generally want most are "increased profits, increased stock value and increased market share," all of which McNamara helped produce.[40] In 1947, Ford showed a profit of $64,800,000 (after tax deductions), in 1948, of $96,000,000, and in 1949, $177,265,000.[41] But McNamara was particularly proud of Ford's societal contributions achieved under his supervision. One was "safety"— "the responsibility of the industry to reduce accidents and/or fatalities and injuries from accidents."[42]

The automobile industry hadn't entirely ignored safety. As early as 1928, shatterproof glass became standard equipment on the Ford Model A cars, while General Motors installed shatterproof windshields on 1930 Cadillac models. But in general, carmakers counted on modern styling to attract buyers even when streamlining conflicted with safety. On the contrary, McNamara thought that safety features could actually increase sales. "The '56 Chevy had a new style and the V-8 engine," recalled Holmes Brown. "We knew this a year in advance and knew we were in trouble. So we went back to our car and wondered what we could do. We didn't have much in the way of options so we decided to sell safety. It was a last chance decision and an expedient one."[43]

McNamara prized safety for its own sake. Long before Ralph Nader made auto safety a prominent national issue. McNamara got Ford to financially support research on safety at Cornell University. But the heart of McNamara's program was Ford's 1956 campaign for a new five-part "Lifeguard" system, including as standard features a deep-dish steering wheel that gave way in a crash and safety latches to keep doors shut despite impact. Front seatbelts, a padded instrument panel and sun visors, and crash-resistant rearview mirrors were optional. The ad campaign for this package was unprecedented. At no time in automobile advertising history, a later study concluded, "had the general theme of safety been advertised or funded as a major selling point."[44]

Even as McNamara championed safety, he recalled, there remained "tremendous opposition" in the industry, which (a) didn't think it was responsible for safety, (b) didn't think it could reduce accidents anyway, and (c) "didn't think it was compatible with selling cars and therefore shouldn't be done even if we were responsible or even if we could make an impact."[45]

Opposition to the safety campaign within Ford expressed itself in many ways. When McNamara installed safety belts in a thousand or so cars of the Ford division corporate fleet, company executives didn't bother to fasten them. When a company driver who picked him up at the Dallas airport on the way to a meeting of dealers noticed McNamara fastening his belt, the driver asked, "What's the matter? Don't you trust my driving?" When Chevrolet outsold Ford by 190,000 cars in 1956, Henry Ford II complained to a reporter, "McNamara is selling safety, but Chevrolet is selling cars."[46]

McNamara defended himself. In May 1955, while making the case for safety as a Ford priority, he hailed nonconformity in a speech prepared for the University of Alabama commencement: "In any corporation, and we are no exception, there is a certain inertia, a tendency to discourage fresh thought and innovation. . . . It takes a degree of moral courage to withstand that pressure."[47] One of his Ford bosses saw the advance text and insisted this passage be deleted. "Damn it," McNamara growled to friends. "I'm making more money for them than they've ever had made before. Why can't they leave me alone?" When it turned out that the veto applied only to the printed text and not to the actual speech, a colleague remembered, "He went down there and when he got to the part . . . he said it so goddamn loud you could hear him in Detroit."[48] Alabama senator Lister Hill arranged to print the Alabama commencement address in an appendix to the *Congressional Record* as (in his view, not necessarily McNamara's) "a thought-provoking reaffirmation of the value of individualism in preserving our American freedoms and furthering our economic progress."[49] In a statement read for McNamara to a congressional hearing on automobile seat belts in August 1957, he announced that Ford "intends to continue the promotion of safety through education of the public regarding the use of seat belts and will continue to develop new safety features to reduce accidents and crash injuries."[50]

Lee Iacocca went to work at Ford in 1946; he was named vice president and general manager of the Ford division about the time McNamara left for the Pentagon in 1960, and served as Ford president before becoming Chrysler's famous CEO. He described McNamara's values as "markedly different from those of his fellow auto executives at Ford and elsewhere" and recalled that McNamara "had almost lost his job because . . . of the safety campaign."[51] According to another account, "McNamara suddenly came down with the flu. He went to Florida for a long vacation. His career hung by a thread. He later returned and came up with a successful sales year in 1957 (minus the 'Lifeguard safety' package.)"[52]

Another McNamara emphasis at Ford, designed both to sell cars and serve society, was "quality," that is, trying "to engineer into the vehicle long life and high quality and low maintenance" and "improving gas consumption, gasoline mileage, fuel efficiency, in effect." To which, McNamara recalled, his sales executives retorted, "'Bob, you just shouldn't do this. You're going to have the petroleum industry down on your ears.'" Gas station attendants would urge customers to buy other brands. "Oh hell, I just don't believe it," was McNamara's response. A petroleum industry committee did indeed call him and "basically threatened Ford Motor Company if we moved in that direction," but "we moved in that direction anyhow."[53]

Cheaper cars were another McNamara goal, exemplified by the extremely profitable new car, the Falcon, which Ford introduced, he said, despite objections that "there wouldn't be any market" for it.[54] One Ford executive mocked the Falcon, sneering, "super low cost, zero personality," but it sold more than 400,000 the first year and more than one million within two years.[55] By the same token, McNamara regretted the company's canceling a new small car, the Cardinal, which he was developing before he left Ford, as a result of which, he claimed, the company was years late in competing with German and Japanese models in the small-car market.[56]

———

MCNAMARA FOUGHT THE GOOD FIGHT FOR HIS BELIEFS IN A SETting that ensured he would lose as often as he won. But beyond the controversies, some of which he recognized, he either didn't notice others or repressed them so as to convince himself as well as the wider world that he had lived happily, if not ever after, at Ford.

One of the drawbacks was the insulated, isolated life of most Ford executives. When McNamara first arrived at Ford, he rented a Ford-subsidized apartment in Dearborn, a complex close to the Ford plant that residents dubbed "the Ford Foundation." Most top Ford officials, including most of the Thornton team, eventually secluded themselves in the upper-class Detroit suburbs of Grosse Pointe and Bloomfield Hills. "If you belong to the Bloomfield Hills Country Club," one of his colleagues remarked, "sooner or later you're going to meet almost every executive of General Motors" as well.[57] But Holmes Brown, McNamara's public relations man, questioned even that degree of outside intermingling, claiming, "You never saw anybody with General Motors." Rather, you spent almost all your time with people in your Ford division, with whom you worked every day. All the Ford kids went to the same private schools, Brown continued, and there was a "pecking order" among the wives, who wore the same coats as if it were "a uniform," just as the men wore the same sorts of suits.[58]

"We didn't want our children to grow up in that atmosphere," McNamara remembered. "Detroit was a very materialistic town . . . a 'company town' in the true meaning of the term," and "we wanted to bring our children up in a university environment."[59] "We didn't want them to think of themselves as children of rich people," he added.[60] How his bosses felt about his choosing to live in Ann Arbor isn't entirely clear. He attributed some of the stress he felt at Ford to their negative reaction. But he later would say, "Henry Ford II and I had an unwritten contract. If I produced profits for the company, I could live any damned way I pleased."[61]

One thing the McNamaras did enjoy in Dearborn was weekly socializing with other Thornton team members in each other's apartments. At their first get-together in Bob and Margy's apartment, which lacked furniture except for Bob's Harvard chair and beds for themselves and their daughters, they sat on packing crates and consumed a potluck supper. Margy, although still recuperating from polio, nonetheless managed to be a warm, cheerful hostess. Later they celebrated a set of promotions by staging a mock press conference recorded in photos that their son Robert Craig McNamara, born in 1950 and known as Craig, later preserved. "They reenacted a radio studio together," Craig reported, "complete with microphone sets, wigs, and makeup. These are some of the only pictures I have where my father isn't sporting his signature, severe hairdo." And the hijinks continued after the McNamaras moved to Ann Arbor, in the form of elaborate Halloween parties for which the McNamaras dressed up as Charles Addams characters: Margy as Morticia and Bob as Lurch. Years later, Craig McNamara's parents looked to him in black-and-white photos of these parties as "more unguarded and natural than during the Washington days, when Mom went through a frumpy phase and Dad aged a hundred years."[62]

Ann Arbor, a small city of roughly 47,000, was also a company town, but the company was the University of Michigan. Founded in 1817 by the old Michigan Territory, twenty years before the territory became a state, UM had grown into one of the nation's top universities, with 33,000–34,000 students. "You had all types of people" who lived there, recalled Eugene Power, a local friend of the McNamaras, but "essentially [it was a] kind of an intellectual community."[63] In 1948, the McNamaras bought a lot and built a house on Kenilworth Avenue on the outskirts of the city and settled there early in 1949. Later they moved to 410 Highland Road, just above the arboretum and near the campus. This neighborhood featured spacious homes favored by senior faculty members. The McNamaras' shaded fieldstone house, with two chimneys, dormer windows, and leaded panes, cost about $50,000, a substantial sum at the time, but less than a showier Bloomfield Hills mansion.[64] "It was a lovely, lovely spot," McNamara remembered, "physically beautiful. Lovely old elm trees."[65]

Before Craig McNamara was born, Margy McNamara had a "therapeutic abortion" because her knees remained weak from polio. "The doctors said she couldn't carry the extra weight," her husband recalled. He also remembered that he and his wife didn't discuss this intimate family issue "adequately. I don't mean we didn't discuss it, but I don't think I understood it fully or discussed it fully." The problem, he added, "wasn't hers, the problem was mine. I'm just very unwilling to share my thoughts. It wasn't that I was unwilling to share with her or the children, I just don't share my thoughts period."[66]

McNamara claims he spent more time at home while at Ford than he would later in Washington: He didn't "arrive at the office at seven and stay until seven, and I frequently didn't work on Saturday" as he did at the Pentagon. He was working only "moderately hard," he said.[67] Actually, according to Robert Dunham, the Ford official who had guided the Thornton team around Ford when they first arrived there and who chose to live a block away from the McNamaras in Ann Arbor, McNamara "used to run out of the house with a glass of orange juice [whether mixed with a raw egg as his mother had taught him is not recorded] in his hand at 6:30 in the morning. He'd be at work by 7, wouldn't get home 'til maybe 7 o'clock at night and never minded it—never felt put upon. He often worked weekends."[68] Whether Margy McNamara felt put upon isn't clear.

McNamara insisted he was "quite busy just playing the role of father," although "in that period the male did not perform the functions that at least my son and sons-in-law do today [in 1992] in relation to children."[69] He assigned his children to do necessary yard work on Saturdays while he was in Dearborn, but he also made sure that family vacations (often joined by old friends from California) lived up to his rigorous standards: climbing and skiing in the High Sierras or Teton Range after he meticulously scrutinized topography maps and plotted out routes that posed demanding personal challenges, especially for himself. Golf, on the other hand, turned out to be too much for McNamara. Having decided to take it up, he characteristically consulted at great length with a golf pro, took numerous lessons, and bought books. Dunham remembered that "he had seven or eight books on golf." But "none of this helped him. He wasn't any better at the end of the season than when he took it up. So in true Bob McNamara fashion, he threw golf out, got rid of his equipment, and never tried to play it again. Because he couldn't excel going about it the way he did. He thought that in four months of playing this game diligently you should do very well. He didn't know that people play twenty years and don't do very well."[70] He did, however, progress at tennis, which he later played with fierce determination in Washington.[71]

McNamara made the most of his access to the university itself: he recalled getting to know faculty members "in anthropology, economics and other wide-ranging disciplines," occasionally lecturing to graduate students, and dining once a month with a circle of male friends, including the university president, Harlan Hatcher, state Democratic Party leader Neil Staebler, and Warren Huff, a prominent cattleman and farmer.[72] According to one club member, Eugene Power, "there was no set format. We appraised, discussed and examined the economic conditions of the country. I think we talked about the automobile industry. We talked about the situation with Germany—it was just after the war, relatively. We were all interested in a lot of foreign affairs and national affairs. It was a very interesting group."[73]

As happened before, McNamara showed himself to be more personable when relaxing with friends than he did at work. One university professor, who was awed by McNamara's "trigger-fast perceptivity," regarded him as "really a triple-threat man: a highly skilled industrial executive, he has an intellectually questing mind, and he is a person [who is] naturally extremely able in dealing with people."[74] McNamara's friend described him as "a very sympathetic and tolerant person. Both he and his wife were. Bob was just a great guy."[75]

McNamara also involved himself in community affairs, conspicuously supporting liberal causes that were not necessarily Henry Ford's favorites. He backed a move to tear down dilapidated housing and contributed money to build replacement projects. He became an elder of the First Presbyterian Church, where he and Margy signed a "covenant of open occupancy" designed to combat racial discrimination in real estate sales. Part of Highland Road had once had a racially restrictive covenant, but not where the McNamaras lived. Their neighborhood was not segregated by the time they moved in, and they fought to keep it that way by signing the covenant. McNamara backed both Democratic senator Philip Hart and Republican Paul Bagwell's unsuccessful campaign for governor, and let it be known that he voted for John F. Kennedy for president in 1960. He supported the National Association for the Advancement of Colored People and the American Civil Liberties Union.[76]

As a member of the Citizens for Michigan Committee, headed by American Motors chief George Romney, McNamara characteristically pressed for a meticulous, systematic study of taxes, starting by defining objectives and then canvassing alternative schemes. "No matter how well he prepares something," noted an American Motors vice president, "he has to be sure it's perfect. If there is some weakness, or something that can't be quickly documented, that thing seems to leap at Bob."[77] But club member Power saw him as less perfectionist and more flexible. He was, as Power put it, a "liberal Republican" or a "Democratic Republican." He was "liberal" and "practical."[78]

Margy McNamara was impressive in her own way. Not long after the McNamaras moved to Ann Arbor, she was driving a station wagon full of children to Detroit when a Ford test car (identifiable by a bicycle wheel attached in the rear to register the car's speed) rocketed past her on a stretch of four-lane highway near the Westland Factory. Specially constructed to serve the factory that built bombers during the war, the highway now served as a test track to check high-speed braking. Margy's husband learned about this during a lunch for top Ford executives to which younger officials like him were occasionally invited. He was sitting silently, observing the rule that junior executives "spoke when spoken to," when the dour (and apparently anti-Irish) vice president for engineering said, "McNamara, is that your name? That's an odd name. You live in Ann Arbor, don't you? Well, it's amazing. There must be several McNamaras there because I got a letter from a woman named McNamara and she just gave me unshirted hell because she complained we were exposing accidental risk and death to individuals on the highway between Dearborn and Ann Arbor. . . . If I ever see her I'm going to give her a piece of my mind."

"So I went home and said, 'Sweetheart, what in hell did you do?' Well, she said, 'Bob, you know very well. Your company is endangering the lives of thousands of people. . . . And I told him to stop it or I'd report them to the state.'"[79]

Margy didn't play golf either—unlike most of the corporate wives—nor did she bowl with them weekly at the Bloomfield Center's fourteen-lane bowling alley. She was a member of the local UN group and the League of Women Voters. Before 1957, Ford dealers' wives had been treated to entertainments like "a fashion show and a speech from a female impersonator, who marked the climax of the proceedings by triumphantly flinging his wig in the air." But when her turn came to put on a show, Mrs. McNamara gave wives a tour of the new University of Michigan cyclotron.[80]

"She was a lovely, lovely person," Dunham remembered. "She was outgoing, friendly, and she had a great sense of social responsibility. She worked hard for causes. And not causes like antiabortion or things like that. She got around here in the town more. Because she was active in so many circles, she got to know many, many people in Ann Arbor. I don't mean big people at the university or anything, just people. She was a lovely woman and a wonderful wife for him. Compassionate, understanding, sympathetic."[81] No wonder Margy looked back on her family's time in Ann Arbor as "wonderful years."[82]

Margy was also a wonderful mother. Craig, plagued by dyslexia, struggled with his schoolwork. Many were the nights when his mother tried to help him with his homework. "We would sit in the den just off their bedroom," Craig recalled, "and I would cry as I struggled." To Craig, his mother "was the essence of Mother Nature, embodying lifegiving and nurturing qualities. Her sense of comfort rubbed off on Dad too." Craig's handicap, which made for such a glaring contrast with his brilliant father, contributed to the distance between them. But his mother, too, he suspected, may have also "thought I'd become a doctor, surgeon, or some kind of scientist." For she tried to foster in him her fascination with animals, which traced back to her own favorite biology lab class at Berkeley. One sign of that was that she attended Halloween parties with a live rat or a small alligator in her vinyl purse. Another was that she took Craig down to a local Ann Arbor slaughterhouse where she collected cow lungs, brains, and eyeballs to instruct Craig in "the science of dissection."[83]

Possibly at his mother's urging, more likely at his father's initiative, Craig also learned what he calls "several innocuous, yet unbreakable rules," some of which McNamara had learned from his own parents: "No gum chewing, tuck in your shirt, never say *damn* [which his father inserted in virtually every other sentence away from home], look people in the eye, be a good Scout, don't tell lies, wake up early, no need for a bathrobe, don't join country clubs, golf is a waste of time, work hard, never quit." That last one, adds Craig, "was literally the opposite of what we needed to do in Vietnam."[84]

════

IN ADDITION TO HIS ACCOMPLISHMENTS AT FORD AND THE PLEA-sures of life in Ann Arbor, McNamara enjoyed the respect of many of his Ford colleagues. Tex Thornton himself, who clashed with old-timers Breech and Crusoe, was fired by Henry II, and went on to a stellar career as founder and CEO of Litton Industries, blessed McNamara as his successor at Ford. He was "willing to step up and make the hard decisions," Arjay Miller remembered. McNamara "*likes* to make tough decisions." That was one reason, Miller continued, why "Henry Ford was awed by

McNamara. He liked his take-charge style and his performance," and "it wasn't just talk; Bob was making a hell of a lot of money" for the Ford division. According to Miller, who himself became Ford president in 1963, Henry Ford "would fall in and out of love with people. But his love affair with Bob," like John Kennedy's and Lyndon Johnson's later on, was "continuous and strong from the start."[85]

Bob Dunham had been a tough FBI agent in Detroit before joining Ford as a personnel specialist. He didn't deem himself an intellectual match for McNamara, but after McNamara convinced him to move to Ann Arbor, he considered himself one of McNamara's closest friends.[86] He "was very, very thorough," remembered Dunham. "He wasn't one to appoint a task force or committee and then forget about them. If he appointed a group to study a project or a problem, he gave them a timetable and they had to be back with an answer. He wanted clear, concise answers. He didn't want 'if' or 'might be.'" He "had an air of leadership about him. You always had the feeling, even if it was in rough times, that he was aware of what was going on and he had a program and he was going to follow through," which "really inspired" his fellow managers to think, "'we've got a firm hand on the tiller here, and I'm going to do my part, and we're going to come out of this.'" Those same managers judged that McNamara "had a real product sense," a "sense of style, performance of the automobile and of its public appeal. . . . It was not something that he brought to Ford; he just acquired this in his rise through the management hierarchy."

But although McNamara was "a dollars-and-cents guy: he was in business to make a profit," Dunham could see his heart was softer than it seemed. Once, in the late '50s, when McNamara was group vice president in charge of the three car divisions, the truck division, and engineering, sales slowed to the point that some five hundred engineers were slated to be laid off on December 1. Considering that "a hell of a Christmas present for their families," Dunham, in charge of salaried personnel, proposed that the unpleasant deed be done after Christmas.

"Well," McNamara asked, "what do you figure it would cost if we did it in January instead of in December?" Dunham: "A million, a million and a half." To which McNamara replied: "Tell them to wait until January."[87]

McNamara's reputation as an executive who cared about average employees may have even expanded into urban legend. In an interview from 1992, Myles Mace, McNamara's sidekick during the war who rejoined him at Ford, recalled an instance of his goodwill that was probably implausible. Mace said McNamara was bothered that "when we have a model change at Ford, we lay off all of the employees and the only people who are there are the people who are installing the new equipment to build the new models." According to Mace, McNamara said, "You know, that's just not right. They don't get paid when they're laid off. You know, that's not their fault. They're there prepared to work. It doesn't seem equitable. We get paid—all the others get paid who are staying there—but they don't. That's just wrong."[88] But automotive industry historian Daniel Clark denies that this occurred with any regularity and explains that work disruptions during model changeovers "usually coincided with summer vacation, which meant that there was no particular hardship for those who had to make way for the changeover crews." Employment instability in the automotive industry at this time was the product of automation that McNamara championed and encouraged. Clark suggests that McNamara was "out of touch with what actually was going on inside Ford plants."[89]

Lee Iacocca considered McNamara:

[O]ne of the smartest men I've ever met, with a phenomenal IQ and a steel-trap mind. He was a mental giant. With his amazing capacity to absorb facts, he also retained everything he learned. But McNamara knew more than the actual facts—he also knew the hypothetical ones. When you talked to him, you realized that he had already played out in his head the relevant details for every conceivable option and scenario. He taught me never to make a major decision without having a choice of at least vanilla or chocolate. And if more than a hundred million dollars were at stake, it was a good idea to have strawberry, too. When it came to spending large amounts of money, McNamara calculated the consequence of every possible decision. Unlike anyone else I've met, he could carry

a dozen plans in his head and could spin out all the facts and figures
without ever consulting his notes.[90]

David Halberstam's best-known (and highly unflattering) portrait
of McNamara is included in his devastating book about the Vietnam
War, *The Best and the Brightest*. But in *The Reckoning*, a study of the Ford
Motor Company in crisis, Halberstam concludes: "Before the Whiz Kids
arrived, waste and petty profiteering were a way of life at Ford. McNamara
did more than cleanse the company, he purified it. . . . No company in the
country needed discipline as the Ford Motor Company did, or benefited
from it more. Under McNamara, for the first time in more than twenty-
five years, the company always knew where it was, how much it was spending and how much it was making, and it could project both costs and
earnings. Soon, it could readily tell where its faults were."[91]

━━━

SO MUCH FOR MCNAMARA'S VIRTUES. HIS VICES MAY HAVE OUT-
numbered them. Some of the criticism he received reflected institutional
rivalries: the old guard's ethos glorified mechanics, not numerical wizards; the tensions between finance and manufacturing transcended personalities.[92] But some of his former employees nursed bitter grievances
against him, and even those who admired McNamara recognized serious
shortcomings.

Iacocca regarded McNamara's arrival at Ford as "one of the best things that
ever happened to the company," but his leaving was "also one of the best things
that ever happened." McNamara's high standards for personal integrity, cultivated since childhood, "sometimes drove [Iacocca] crazy": "McNamara used
to say that the boss had to be more Catholic than the Pope—and as clean as
a hound's tooth. He preached a certain aloofness, and he practiced what he
preached. He was never one of the boys." Iacocca saw McNamara as "a conflicted man, torn between his need to show an ever greater profit and his private preference for small utilitarian cars." According to Halberstam, Iacocca
respected McNamara as an efficiency expert, but not as a "car man." He particularly hated McNamara's prize progeny, the utilitarian Falcon, which, as

Iacocca's deputy Hal Sprelich put it, was a car that looked like McNamara himself: "He had those granny glasses and he made a granny car."[93]

Norman Krandall was an assistant product planning manager for the Ford division when McNamara was group VP in the 1950s. Later, after McNamara left for Washington, he became director of market research and manager of the factory that made the Falcon. Known himself as "something of a maverick,"[94] Krandall described McNamara as "a man who had to prevail," who had "loaded up" a discussion so that it could come out only one way—"his way." According to Krandall, what McNamara was always "telegraphing, as far as I could see, was 'I really know the answer, but I want to let you guys wallow through in your own stupid way.'" When someone really disagreed with him, "he'd look at them as if they weren't there," or "he'd sit there, and just drum his fingers on the desktop, so tight, so rigid, and it was such a severe test for him just to be tolerating this other point of view."[95]

Krandall was so bitter about McNamara that one may be tempted to discount his recollection. But in an interview with Hendrickson, he ventured a psychological interpretation that echoes others' views—that McNamara's harsh, cold exterior compensated for deeper stresses underneath; that the surface harshness was "hiding the doubter from the world," that McNamara's mask expressed not only pride, power, and ego, but "fear," that is, the "embarrassment/pain of yielding."[96]

Leo C. Beebe, who directed Ford's motor sports program, thought McNamara "took too much for granted"; he thought "people were more like him than they were." "If you're very, very bright," Beebe continued sarcastically, "isn't it difficult to imagine what it's like to be dumb and slow?" "It's hard to know exactly how people tick if you don't have empathy."[97]

Dunham, despite his admiration for McNamara, admitted his boss was "more of a numbers man than a people man." He regretted that McNamara was so "suspicious." "For instance—and I'm sure he'd deny this today if you asked him about it—but every time he met with Henry Ford, he would go back to his office and write copious notes about what he said and what Henry Ford said to protect himself." Ford could be "a very mercurial individual," Dunham admitted, but given his obvious and continuing devotion to McNamara (in contrast to his later fear that Iacocca was gunning for Ford's own job), McNamara's suspiciousness seemed excessive. "This is ultra-simplistic," Dunham added, "but Bob's the kind of guy who, walking down the street, meets a friend who says, 'Good morning, Bob.' Bob replies and goes on and wonders, 'Did he really mean that?' "[98]

Arjay Miller's wife Frances thought McNamara's ambition sometimes blinded him to other people and things: "When he came to Ford . . . he had five-year plans for his life. He talked to me sometimes; we spent a lot of time socializing. He was a dedicated kind of a person in many ways. He was so dedicated that his peripheral vision was not always great."[99] McNamara's secretary, Virginia Gerrity, liked working for him, but only up to a point: "If he wanted a chair, it should be there, if he wanted a piece of paper it should be there."[100] "He was not an easy person," according to Arjay Miller. "He had his own friends and he made them his own way." He was "not an easy socializer. A lot of people were afraid of Bob. That complicated it. He was a tough guy. So he got a reputation—no small talk. He didn't socialize as easily with women as he did with men. . . . I have a very smart wife. A lot of men would be more comfortable around her than Bob would be."[101] But in fact, when it came to deeper, more personal connections, it was with women that Bob shared his hidden emotions— including with Frances Miller herself. He spent a lot of time talking to her, she remembered, and once, early on, said to her, " 'If it wasn't for Margy and the children, I would go back to medical school.' " "He told me that!" she marveled. What it symbolized to her was his continuing dedication to "the higher public good," even higher, that is, than producing better, cheaper, safer cars.[102] What it also signified was McNamara's subterranean unhappiness with himself.

Part of the problem was that McNamara was so damn smart. "Even when you knew he was wrong," said one of his underlings, "he would plow you under."[103] Peter Collier and David Horowitz report that McNamara "stunned listeners with his critical acumen. He prepared for Executive Committee meetings as if cramming for Ph. D. orals, poring over minutes of previous meetings to see who had said what and arming himself with arguments for the coming debate."[104]

Another problem, which was to plague him during the Vietnam War, was that he resisted changing his mind. "Bob *hated* to change the course of action after he got going on something," recalled Arjay Miller. "I heard him say one time, 'After I make up my mind, I don't have time to go back and keep going through it all again.'" Speaking in 1992, with the history of McNamara's management of the Vietnam War in mind, Frances Miller confessed, "I want Bob to do a *mea culpa*." To which her husband quickly responded, "He never will. Bob can't say, 'I was wrong.'"[105] The fact that McNamara eventually confessed he was "terribly wrong" about Vietnam shows Miller was wrong, but that it took him nearly three decades to do so also shows Frances Miller was right.

McNamara's sense of moral rectitude undergirded his stubbornness. During the Whiz Kids' first Christmas at Ford, the company's advertising agency presented them with gifts. All but one of them gratefully accepted them. McNamara reprimanded the agency and returned his gift.[106] Once, when the McNamara family was planning a skiing vacation in Colorado, Iacocca offered to obtain a company car, install a ski rack on it, and have it left for McNamara at the Denver airport. But McNamara "wouldn't hear of it. He insisted that we rent him a car from Hertz, pay extra for the ski rack, and send him the bill. He resolutely refused to use a company car on his vacation, even though we loaned out hundreds of courtesy cars every weekend to other VIPs."[107] The same pattern repeated itself on a skiing vacation in Europe, where he rejected a company car waiting for him at the airport in Switzerland, rented another car instead, and drove away, leaving the regional Ford rep who had made the arrangements fearing for his own future. Actually, Robert Lacey reports, "there was method in this mortification, for when the spurned Swiss executive shadowed McNamara out to the Hertz parking lot, he was horrified to crane around a corner and see his boss getting into an Opel station wagon—a General Motors car." Not surprisingly, McNamara "came home with some well-tested ideas about the product requirements for the station-wagon version of his beloved Falcon."[108]

A "Puritan in Babylon" though he was, McNamara deigned to drive luxury Ford cars (Lincolns or Continentals) on his daily commute to work from Ann Arbor, a thirty-eight-mile trip that took about forty-five minutes each way. The drive struck colleagues living closer to head-quarters as a steep price to pay for his strange Ann Arbor affectation.[109] But McNamara's own children noticed the contradiction. They insisted, when their mother ferried them to school and back, that she drop them off a couple of blocks away from the school entrance so their luxury cars couldn't be spotted.[110]

Over time, McNamara's flaws seemed to some of his colleagues to be expanding, as if he were being corrupted by his growing power and author-ity. At meetings chaired by Henry Ford or Ernest Breech, McNamara had a habit of keeping a "low profile through most of the meeting," but then, after "everyone else had pretty much shown his cards," he would "swoop in with a dazzling point-by-point summary (usually enumerating the points by counting on the fingers of his right hand—he once counted to six—demonstrating the inherent conflicts and gridlock) . . . and then would lay out his proposed plan of action." In the beginning, his "clear and positive words were always welcomed," remembered Will Scott, who joined the Ford Finance Staff in 1948 and became the Ford division's product planning manager in 1956. But "as Bob got stronger and stronger, the counsel he got was less and less sincere." Scott remembered a meeting where "feelings ran high" and "most committee members were strongly opposed to what Bob wanted to do." Scott therefore "took it upon myself to suggest that [McNamara] poll the members at the table, not just ask for comments." But when McNamara took the advice, "all of the participants supported his plan with enthusiasm."[111]

Deborah Shapley collected several other accounts of McNamara's growing imperiousness. "He could be generous toward men . . . whom he liked. But he habitually treated everyone else like adversaries to be bul-lied or manipulated." He was particularly rough on car dealers, whom he regarded as "weak and corrupt. In his mind they were missing out on a $170 million market in servicing the millions of new Fords around the country. The number of Fords on the road had increased as postwar sales grew, but Ford dealers' income from repairs stayed level."[112]

McNamara had lofty standards for design, too. Asked by a designer which of several designs he liked, he pointed at one but added, " 'That one, but it doesn't move me like the stained-glass windows of Notre Dame.' " After McNamara left the room, the designer growled to one of his colleagues, " 'Shit, man! These guys who buy their cars never heard of Notre Dame. They just want something that looks as if it's laying down rubber and going ninety while it's standing still.' "[113]

Ford's fancy, ill-fated Edsel model, introduced in 1957, was one of the greatest, if not the greatest, flops in American automotive history. Designed to give Ford another brand to compete with General Motors and Chrysler cars like Buick, Oldsmobile, Dodge, and DeSoto, and named after Henry Ford I's son, the Edsel bombed. Its first buyers discovered "oil leaks, sticking hoods, trunks that wouldn't open and push buttons that couldn't be budged with a hammer." Expected to sell 200,000 cars in its first year (1957–1958), after two years it had sold only 109,466, and Ford had lost around $350 million. Production was halted at the end of 1959.[114]

McNamara didn't like the Edsel on either aesthetic or utilitarian grounds and opposed the plan, but felt he had to go along with it. As group vice president, he had to take responsibility for it. But as it began to fail, he raged against it with an intensity that belied his image as cold and calculating. He summoned those responsible for the Edsel ad campaign and stormed around the room glaring at advertisements they had posted on the wall. At one point, Shapley reports, "he climbed up on the leather-covered chairs along the wall and began tearing off the ads and waving them as examples of what the men had done wrong. The ad men, their careers already ruined, sat meekly, while McNamara stomped along the chair seats in his wet boots."[115] Recalled Edsel's publicity manager: "It looked like a band of vandals had just left the room." Said another witness: It was "the most incredible performance by a Ford executive I'd ever seen."[116]

Rare though it was, this outburst confirmed that powerful emotions churned just beneath McNamara's surface. There was another indication of McNamara's internal tension, if you knew where to look for it. When his face was grim and humorless, his associates who glanced under the table "could see his hands gathering the fabric of his trousers in bunches.

The more impatient he became and the more likely he would explode, the more intensely he would tug on his pants, raising them higher and higher until he pulled them up to his knees."[117] "Let me tell you," he later told Shapley, "the Ford Motor Company was stressful. . . . Stress is self-stress, there's no doubt about that."[118]

Another sign that no one except Margy McNamara noticed at the time was that in the late 1950s, long before the Vietnam War, McNamara began suffering from bruxism—the habit, often caused by stress, of grinding, gnashing, and clenching his teeth. His nightly struggles with the condition disrupted Margy's sleep for nearly a year. He described the sustained ordeal in detail: "I went to a doctor in New York because my dentist in Ann Arbor said there were only three doctors in the entire country at that time that could treat it. . . . what they do is they cut the top of your tooth off and they drill a channel in the part that remains and then they put an apparatus on your head and they connect it on to a metal thing and they fix them all so that when you grind, you spread the stress across all of your bone structure. Otherwise, you actually erode the bone structure. It was damned expensive. It was extraordinarily painful. I wouldn't do it again for anything. . . . It was a hell of a mess because the dentist in Ann Arbor started by saying, 'well the thing to do is to wear a rubber thing to put in your mouth so that you grind on rubber.' Well, I bit through that in a few nights." That same dentist "prescribed this thing that was made out of a, like a rubber tire, it was a very tough rubber. And in three or four months I bit through that."[119]

Yet another sign of stress that Dunham picked up reflected the disconnect between McNamara's hard head and softer heart. As the impression solidified at Ford that McNamara was "cold and not outwardly sympathetic to people," Dunham slowly reached another conclusion—that "the air that he put out that led people to think he was cold was protection for himself. He didn't want to be thought of as a pushover. Yet underneath, as far as people were concerned, he was a pushover. Except he fought it all the time."[120] Like his father who tried to project strength by erecting a wall against emotions, including those of his hyperemotional wife? Wherever it came from, it made McNamara almost impenetrable, even to someone like Tex Thornton, who, when he tried to praise Bob's virtues, ended up illustrating why they seemed so overpowering.

"The picture that some colleagues, acquaintances and even friends draw of McNamara," Thornton said in a background interview with *Time* magazine, is "one of cold, almost ruthless business efficiency, a man seemingly devoid of humor, warmth or human frailty." Not so, according to Thornton. "Bob is very sincere—a warm, dedicated individual with very high principles . . . who wouldn't dream of being unfaithful to his wife." And his standards for his business conduct are "no less rigid." "You can disagree with him freely. But the odds are that he's going to be right." "He's tolerant of people—as long as someone is working hard and if their motivations are the same as his." An example: an associate who makes his case and then says, " 'Don't you agree, Bob?' Bob said, 'No.' " "He didn't get angry," but in the end, he had the other fellow convinced. "It's true that working for Bob is a chore, because you can't loaf. If you ask me, the only people who've been critical of him have been the fellows who have been over their heads in their jobs and have been looking for excuses to blame someone else for their failures." McNamara will "take a drink, but I've never seen him tight or even come close to it." He's a man of "complete integrity. He wouldn't tell you a lie if it meant his life, his mother's, or his grandmother's. A man like Bob just couldn't get up and play the role of politician."[121]

These last two claims, in particular, would be sorely tested.

————

WHEN MCNAMARA BECAME PRESIDENT OF FORD ON NOVEMBER 9, 1960, it appeared to Henry Ford II that his dream of "professional, assured, sophisticated management" operating under his control had been achieved. When McNamara defected fifty-one days later to become US defense secretary, Henry Ford was devastated. In a public statement issued by the Ford board, he wrote: "I know of no one in America better qualified to take over the post of Defense Secretary than Bob McNamara . . . the gain—measured in the national interest—will make it easier for Ford Motor to sustain the loss of his leaving."[122] Privately, he moaned, "This may be one of the worst days of my life." McNamara was "the first president outside the family. After all those years of training, he's leaving. I can't believe it. Now what do I do?"[123] But many others in the company were relieved. And seven years later, when Henry Ford was informed that his former protégé might be interested in leaving the Pentagon if he were invited back to Ford, he reacted ironically. "I don't know that we could find a place *worthy* of him," Ford said. McNamara had been away from the car business for a long time. "I could make him president of the Ford Foundation," Ford added, "but then it wouldn't be the Ford Foundation any longer; it would be the McNamara Foundation."[124]

SECTION II

In the Wheelhouse

=◆=

1961–1968

CHAPTER SIX

Potomac Fever

On the morning of Thursday, December 8, 1960, early in his second month as president of Ford, McNamara left Ann Arbor before dawn as usual, stopped by the company's mammoth River Rouge Plant, and arrived at his office on the twelfth floor of the Ford headquarters building, known as the Glass House, at about 10:30. His secretary, Virginia Marshall, had left a list of phone messages on his desk. His habit was to "direct her to force me to return every call that came in—including complaints—so without looking at the list, I handed it back and said, 'Start down it.'" About half an hour later she announced, "Mr. Robert Kennedy is on the line." McNamara "knew who he was," he later recalled, "but had never met or talked to him."

"The President-elect would be grateful if you would meet with our brother-in-law, Sarge Shriver," said Kennedy.

McNamara suggested the following Tuesday.

"No, no," Kennedy replied, "he wants to see you today."

McNamara pointed out it was almost 11:00 A.M.

"You set the time and he'll be there," said Kennedy.

When Shriver arrived at four o'clock, he quickly got to the point: "I'm authorized by President-elect Kennedy to offer you the position of secretary of the treasury."

"You're out of your mind," responded McNamara. "I'm not qualified for that." In that case, Shriver continued, "I'm authorized to say that Jack Kennedy wishes you to serve as secretary of defense."

"This is absurd!" McNamara objected. "I'm not qualified."

"Well, the President-elect at least hopes you will give him the courtesy of agreeing to meet with him tomorrow in Washington."

"Well, I can hardly refuse that."[1]

McNamara's doubts about the defense job were real. "What do I know about the application of force," he worried, "and what do I know about the strategy required to defend the West against what was a generally accepted threat . . . [and] the force structure necessary to effectively counter the threat?"[2]

Kennedy wanted McNamara in his cabinet because so many discerning people vouched for him. Robert Lovett, the former Truman defense secretary who had been following (and promoting) McNamara's career ever since the war, was a key recommender after turning down the defense job himself due to ill health. He had first spotted McNamara at Statistical Control during the war and told friends that he thought McNamara was "the pick of the litter."[3] Another recommender, according to McNamara, was Harvard economist and Kennedy adviser John Kenneth Galbraith, who had once interviewed McNamara in Detroit for a book he was writing.[4] Kennedy liked the idea of including a liberal Republican in his cabinet (McNamara contends that he had frequently been reported to be a Republican because, when he first registered to vote in California at age twenty-one, he had done so as a Republican "for no other reason than that my father was"[5]), but Michigan Democratic Party boss Neil Staebler, a member of McNamara's Ann Arbor political discussion group, praised him, as did Jack Conway of the United Auto Workers.

Harris Wofford, one of Kennedy's main recruiters, got McNamara's name from Adam Yarmolinsky, who had interviewed McNamara twice in the '50s, in Ann Arbor and Dearborn, once while working on a civil liberties project for the Fund for the Republic when he heard McNamara was a member of the American Civil Liberties Union. He interviewed McNamara another time when Yarmolinsky was advising the Ford Foundation on whether they should start a program on automobile safety. They decided not to because the Foundation was too associated in the public mind with the Ford Motor Company. Yarmolinsky found McNamara to be "tremendously energetic" and "an original thinker, someone who goes against the grain," an intellectual who read books like *The Phenomenon of Man* by the religious philosopher Teilhard de Chardin. Kennedy liked surrounding himself with intellectuals. McNamara's limited military experience didn't count for much: "The cult of the outsider was already beginning," recalled Yarmolinsky. "New frontiersmen were supposedly a breath of fresh air."[6]

On his way to Washington the next morning on a Ford Company plane, McNamara stopped in New York to talk to Henry Ford II and to Ford Company director Sidney Weinberg. He told Ford about the Kennedy offer and that he was not going to accept it. Weinberg, who had risen from being a janitor to become Goldman Sachs CEO, concurred: "Don't touch it!"[7] McNamara had an appointment with Kennedy in the afternoon, but before that at the Pentagon with Thomas Gates, then secretary of defense, whom he knew from the board of directors of the Scott Paper Company. Mentioning Kennedy's job offer, McNamara repeated that he didn't feel qualified, so he wanted to have another name to suggest in case Kennedy asked for one. He wanted to recommend Gates and came away thinking Gates would agree to stay on in the Pentagon.

Kennedy lived on N Street in Georgetown. Since the street was crowded with newspaper, television, and radio reporters, the Secret Service took McNamara down the back alley and through a back door. McNamara repeated that he wasn't qualified to be defense secretary. Kennedy responded, "Well, you know, there isn't any school for presidents either." Kennedy said he had examined McNamara's record and "I believe that you would be well qualified to serve in my cabinet."

"I just don't think so," McNamara insisted.

"Well, would you be willing to at least agree to think about it for a day or two, and then perhaps we can meet again on Monday?"

During the meeting, McNamara cheekily asked Kennedy if he had actually written *Profiles in Courage*, a best-selling book published in 1956 in which then-Senator John Kennedy recounted courageous, politically unpopular actions by eight United States senators. Kennedy had been awarded a Pulitzer Prize for the book, but rumors immediately circulated that someone else had written it, possibly Arthur Krock, a well-known *New York Times* reporter and columnist.

Ted Sorensen said in 2008 that he had written the first draft of most chapters. "I am not sure precisely how he answered," McNamara later recalled about his initial encounter with Kennedy. "But I came away with the firm conclusion that the book represented Kennedy's thinking, even if many of the words were written by Ted."[8]

McNamara flew home that afternoon. Over the weekend he talked with his family and Ford colleagues he trusted. One consideration was that his lofty Ford salary of $410,000 (worth many millions in today's dollars), plus huge unexercised stock options, would plummet to $25,000 a year. "The children cared not a whit," he wrote in his memoirs, although it turned out that his daughter Kathleen hated to leave her high school friends in Ann Arbor behind, and "Marg wanted only what I wanted."[9] His "family was not, nor was I, attracted by wealth and money.... One couldn't balance one's responsibility to a private corporation or one's personal welfare against the opportunity and responsibility to serve one's nation"—provided "there was a chance of doing it successfully," which depended on whether he could "surround myself with highly qualified individuals who knew a lot more about government, politics, security and defense management than I did."[10]

McNamara decided he would accept the job if Kennedy agreed to two conditions. First, McNamara could "staff the Defense Department's upper echelons with the ablest individuals in the nation—regardless of party affiliation—to offset my own inexperience."[11] Second, he wished to inform Kennedy he wanted to avoid Washington social life, much as he had done in Detroit by living in Ann Arbor. "I was to be a working Secretary as opposed to what I called a 'socializing' Secretary," McNamara recalled.[12] But he worried that "the President might not fully understand what I'm saying, or I might forget what he said, or I might misunderstand him." McNamara wanted the guarantee in writing, but "after all, one does not negotiate a contract with a president-elect."

Then "suddenly, it hit me." As he and his family conferred in Ann Arbor, it was snowing slightly. "Why don't I call the president-elect," he thought, "tell him the weather will delay my return to Washington for a day or two and say that, in the meantime, I'll send a letter explaining my position?" When McNamara reached Kennedy on the phone in Palm Beach, the president-elect said he couldn't get back to Washington until Tuesday anyway.[13] So McNamara decided to take the letter with him to Washington. It did not include a reference to his role in Washington's social life. Contrary to a later description of it by Roswell Gilpatric, who served as McNamara's top Pentagon deputy, it also did not include a spot at the bottom where Kennedy could apply his signature above the words "Agreed to and accepted by John F. Kennedy."[14] Given McNamara's own recollection about raising the social life issue with Kennedy, it seems likely that he did so in conversation with Kennedy.

Shapley provides a different version. She says McNamara told her he lied to Kennedy to try to avoid meeting him again, implying that he still planned to stay at Ford. She contends there was no snowstorm, so he could have flown to Washington on Monday, and that McNamara's "bald misstatement—to the president-elect no less—showed his penchant for tactically useful fibs."[15] Indeed, there were snow flurries but no snowstorm in Detroit that would have prevented McNamara from going to Washington.

On Tuesday, McNamara again entered Kennedy's house through the back door. This time Bobby Kennedy was there, too. Both brothers seated themselves on a loveseat with McNamara in a chair opposite them. He explained that when he thought he would miss the meeting, he had written the president-elect a letter that he now took out of his pocket. "Perhaps the quickest thing to do would be to give you that," he told Kennedy. "You can read it and we can talk about it." The president-elect read the letter, didn't say anything, and passed it to his brother, who read it and returned it to JFK.

"What do you think?" John Kennedy asked his brother.

"I think it's great," Bobby replied.

"So do I," declared the president-elect. "Let's announce it."

Kennedy took out a yellow pad and wrote a statement. He and McNamara then walked out onto the front stoop of the house where he announced to the assembled journalists his choice to be secretary of defense. That was how Margy and the McNamara children learned they would be moving to Washington. As for the "contract letter" that McNamara had prepared for the president-elect's signature, he once asked Kennedy what he had done with it. "Oh," the president said, "I just laughed and later on I threw it away."[16]

═══

UNTIL MCNAMARA BECAME US SECRETARY OF DEFENSE IN JANUARY 1961, he had met and mastered nearly every major challenge in his life—from the first grade through the Ford Motor Company. But the Vietnam War, of which he became the main American manager, mastered him—with devastating consequences not only for his country and the world but for himself and his family. One might therefore see his arrival in the Pentagon as the fateful fulcrum in his life. Not so, according to his longtime friend and colleague Arjay Miller, who met McNamara in 1946 and was close to him for the rest of his life. "Until 1963," said Miller in 2014, "up until he was forty-seven, all the signals came up green. He was a great student, married his college sweetheart, had a good assignment at Harvard, was very successful when he went into the war and at Ford. And for the first years of the 1960s he was almost the most powerful guy in Washington. The next four years were years of transition."[17]

Miller was right. McNamara conquered Washington fast and furiously, quickly taking charge of the American military establishment, developing a crucial voice in foreign as well as defense policy, and becoming the key member of President Kennedy's cabinet. Vietnam seemed a secondary issue in the first months of the Kennedy administration, "a sideshow during much of this time," McNamara called it four decades later.[18] In the beginning, most observers in and out of the administration thought a small contingent of American military advisers would suffice to help the Saigon government put down Vietcong rebels. By 1963, McNamara understood that the Communist challenge in Vietnam was much more serious, but even so, he foresaw an end to the war by 1965. Either Communist rebels would be defeated or the United States could withdraw its advisers anyway, claiming that the war had always been South Vietnam's to win and that if South Vietnam had not done so it was Saigon's fault, not Washington's. In that sense, McNamara mastered Washington, too, for three years, and thought he had mastered Vietnam as well.

Recalling those years four decades later, McNamara referred several times to "the president and me" as if the two of them were in control. "You said at one point in retrospect," an interviewer interjected, "that you were the third most powerful person in the US government." "I don't think I said that," McNamara objected, "but it may have been true."[19] McNamara's Pentagon deputy Roswell Gilpatric described the Kennedy-McNamara relationship as "a mutual admiration society. Kennedy singled out McNamara as the first among equals."[20] Robert Kennedy later said his brother thought "most highly" of McNamara, "more than any other cabinet member," especially after a crisis like Cuba "when you can see what can happen to the country and how much depends on a particular individual."

As President Kennedy grew impatient over time with Secretary of State Dean Rusk, he talked of putting McNamara in that post. According to Robert Kennedy, the president actually "thought of moving in the direction that would get the [1968 presidential] nomination for Bob McNamara" to make sure the country was "placed in the best possible hands." So persuasive was McNamara, recalled Bobby, that he actually "frightens me a little."[21] McNamara himself later described the day he was sworn in as defense secretary as, "except for my marriage, after that point, it was the most momentous day of my life. I was so proud to be sworn in. It was just magnificent."[22] As for his relationship with Kennedy, "I loved that man," he recalled at one point.[23] On another occasion, he said, "I admired him and loved working for him." He also said, "I benefited from, appreciated the opportunity to serve the nation" along with President Kennedy and his two brothers. "It was a delight."[24]

After watching John Kennedy and Robert McNamara work together, Ted Sorensen, the longtime Kennedy aide and speechwriter, observed: "The two men forged a close personal as well as official relationship. They reinforced each other in reasserting civilian control over the military. Both put in long, hard hours. Both preferred precise decisions to prolonged attempts to please everyone. In eleven years with Kennedy, I never saw him develop admiration and personal regard for another man as quickly as he did with Robert McNamara, enabling the McNamaras to be excepted from the general Kennedy rule of keeping official and social friendships separate. Repeatedly, publicly and privately, the president praised his defense secretary in glowing terms."[25] Joining the Kennedy administration also gave McNamara an opportunity to befriend Jacqueline Kennedy. The forbidding defense secretary and the elegant, stylish, softspoken First Lady soon developed an improbable friendship that deepened into a warmly affectionate relationship.

Given McNamara's rapid rise and early success in President Kennedy's inner circle, it seems strange in retrospect that he felt quite insecure at first. McNamara cites various incidents to show "I had hay in my hair." But these episodes also show a kind of clueless self-confidence. Soon after he arrived in Washington, the press reported that Franklin D. Roosevelt Jr. was to be named secretary of the navy. "I was so green I didn't pay any attention to it," McNamara recalled. His impression was that "Roosevelt wasn't qualified, therefore I wouldn't nominate him, therefore he wasn't going to be secretary of the navy." It never occurred to him that "FDR, Jr., wanting to follow in his father's footsteps, had arranged this with President-elect Kennedy, and he or one of his friends leaked it to the press to set it in concrete." In any event, a week later, when McNamara had yet to propose anyone else for the job, Kennedy himself suggested Roosevelt.

"I have heard his name mentioned," McNamara said, "but he's a playboy and totally unqualified."

"Well, have you met him?" asked Kennedy. "Don't you think you should do so before coming to a final judgment?"

After meeting Roosevelt, McNamara called Kennedy. "What do you think?" the president-elect asked with what McNamara remembered as "great anticipation in his voice."

"I think he's a playboy and totally unqualified for the job," McNamara repeated. After a long pause, Kennedy asked whether McNamara had taken note of the West Virginia primary. McNamara knew Kennedy's victory there had silenced doubts that a Catholic couldn't win the presidency, but didn't know what Kennedy now told him—that "Franklin Roosevelt Jr. played a major role in my victory."

"Well," McNamara insisted, "he's still not qualified to be secretary of the navy."

After a long silence that McNamara thought "would never end," Kennedy sighed and said, "I guess I'll have to take care of him some other way." Roosevelt was later appointed undersecretary of commerce, and McNamara went on to propose John B. Connally Jr. of Texas for navy secretary, but not before again demonstrating his naivete. When he mentioned Connally to Kennedy, the president-elect said, "Well, that's interesting. It's not a name I would have thought of. But there are two men here who probably know Connally better than I do. Tell them our views, get theirs and then I'll come back on the line."

The two were Vice President-elect Lyndon Johnson and Speaker of the House of Representatives Sam Rayburn. "I was so green," McNamara recalled, "I did not realize that Kennedy was playing a joke." Since Johnson and Rayburn were Texans, and "as close to Connally as his own father," their endorsement wasn't in doubt. When Kennedy came back on the phone, he said, "Bob, I am delighted." Confessed McNamara in his memoirs: "It wasn't until afterward that I figured it out."[26]

In one case, at least, the selection of an undersecretary of the navy, McNamara bowed to Kennedy's insistence that an unqualified buddy, Red Fay, get the job. Fay had served in the navy at the same time as Kennedy, and the two men had met while recuperating from Japanese attacks on their PT boats. Fay had become a Kennedy sidekick after the war. To deal with Fay's lack of qualifications, McNamara and Roswell Gilpatric, the new deputy defense secretary, structured the navy's civilian management in a way that sidelined Fay.[27]

Still another sign of McNamara's political inexperience concerned the alleged "missile gap" in Moscow's favor for which Kennedy had successfully blamed the Republicans during his presidential campaign. The charge that Moscow possessed far more intercontinental missiles capable of striking the United States than Washington had rockets capable of reaching the USSR derived from an air force intelligence report that had been leaked to the Democrats. But since the CIA's classified estimate, based on the initial flights of a highly secret new American satellite reconnaissance system that had photographed Soviet missile bases in 1960, was more reassuring, McNamara was determined, upon taking office, to settle the dispute and to close the gap if, indeed, it existed. He and Gilpatric spent several weeks scrutinizing the data and concluded: "There was a gap—but it was in our favor!"[28]

That conclusion was stunning. It revealed not only that a key plank in the Democratic campaign platform was bogus but that the alleged nuclear imbalance of power, which Moscow was counting on to expand its world influence and which Washington had feared was eroding its own, could now have the opposite effect. In October 1961, the administration would officially reveal the truth (in a speech by Gilpatric) that helped prompt Nikita Khrushchev to send intermediate range missiles to Cuba. But on February 6, 1961, when McNamara held his first meeting with the Pentagon press corps, what he and Gilpatric had discovered was still top secret, as were the spy satellite operations that revealed the truth.

Arthur Sylvester, McNamara's assistant secretary for public affairs, had urged him to meet the press: "Bob, you haven't met the Pentagon press yet, and you have to do that." McNamara replied that he "knew nothing about the Washington press and was totally unprepared to meet them," but Sylvester praised them as "a fine bunch" who would "treat you well." Actually, McNamara wrote later, "they were sharks, as they themselves would have admitted."

McNamara thought the meeting was "off-the-record," meaning that it could not be cited. In fact, it was "on background," permitting the press to report what they heard without attributing it directly to McNamara.

The first question concerned the missile gap. McNamara replied that if one existed it was in our favor.

"My God," McNamara remembered. The newsmen "damn near broke the door down to get out!" The next morning's *New York Times* ran the story on page one. Senate Minority Leader Everett Dirksen (R-IL) called for McNamara to resign.

"God almighty!" McNamara recalled. "I remember going to see Kennedy: 'Mr. President, I came down here to help you and all I've done is stimulate demands for your resignation. I'm fully prepared to resign.'"

"Oh, come on, Bob. Forget it. We're in a helluva mess, but we all put our foot in our mouth once in a while. Just forget it. It'll blow over." It eventually did, McNamara admitted, but he never forgot "the generous way he forgave my stupidity."

Kennedy's understanding response to McNamara's mistakes won his undying respect, loyalty, and affection. His willingness to have McNamara appoint aides regardless of political affiliation was "magnificent." Kennedy's acquiescence in Roosevelt's nonappointment was "one of the reasons I loved him." The missile gap mess? "Another reason I loved him." "It still amazes me," McNamara wrote in his 1995 memoir, "that my naivete never seemed to annoy President Kennedy."[29]

═══

IF MCNAMARA'S HALTING ACCEPTANCE OF KENNEDY'S OFFER AND some of his initial steps as defense secretary revealed his inexperience and naivete, Kennedy and the other members of the president's inner circle of national security aides possessed just the sort of knowledge and savvy that McNamara lacked. Despite Kennedy's striking youth (he was but forty-four when he assumed office), he was not only a Washington veteran but had broad exposure to world politics. His national security adviser, McGeorge Bundy, two years younger than Kennedy, had been Harvard's dean of the faculty and had collaborated with his family friend Henry Stimson, a former secretary of state (under President Hoover) and Roosevelt's secretary of war, on Stimson's memoirs. Dean Rusk, born in

1909, rose from poverty with the help of a Rhodes Scholarship and wartime service in Asia to become a top State Department official, serving as deputy undersecretary for Dean Acheson, and assistant secretary for Far Eastern affairs during the Korean War. Who would have predicted that McNamara would emerge as the star of the Kennedy cabinet and primary manager of the Vietnam War? But JFK proved to be not only the perfect patron for McNamara but a personal friend as well, while Bundy and Rusk not only welcomed McNamara as their close partner but turned out to lack key skills that he possessed.

Kennedy's family background propelled him toward a career in politics and foreign affairs. His father, Joseph P. Kennedy, accumulated great wealth and power in Boston, Washington, and London. Having made an initial fortune in the 1920s, he got out of the stock market before the 1929 crash, vastly increased his wealth during the Great Depression by investing in Hollywood, shipping, and real estate, served as chairman of the US Securities and Exchange Commission (1934–1935), and was appointed US ambassador to Britain in 1938. As an Irish Catholic, he was excluded from Boston's WASP elite, but dreamed of seeing his elder son Joe make it all the way to the White House. After Joe was killed during the war, his father hitched his hopes to John. Jack Kennedy attended Choate and Harvard, but without great academic success until, alarmed by the deteriorating world situation, he buckled down and wrote his 1939 Harvard senior thesis on "Appeasement at Munich: The Inevitable Result of the Slowness of Conversion of British Democracy from a Disarmament to Rearmament Policy."

Kennedy biographer (and Harvard historian) Fredrik Logevall, who read Kennedy's notes from his Harvard classes, concluded that Kennedy "delved deeply into the twentieth-century 'isms'—communism, socialism, fascism, capitalism, nationalism, totalitarianism." According to Logevall, who has supervised plenty of senior theses at Cornell and Harvard, Kennedy argues with "clinical detachment" that "dictatorships by their nature have an easier time than democracies do in mobilizing resources." "Not every undergraduate thesis can truly be called an original contribution to knowledge," but Kennedy's "fit the bill."[30] John Kennedy's aggressively

pushy father and other Kennedy "family connections" offered him access
to prominent, influential people. At an age when McNamara was finding
his way at Harvard Business School, Kennedy hobnobbed with leading
lights of politics and society in Boston, Washington, and New York as well
as overseas. Media luminaries like *The New York Times*' Arthur Krock and
Clare Booth, wife of Henry Luce, the founder of *Time* and *Life* magazines,
and an influential journalist in her own right, helped him along.

Kennedy was worldly, in the literal sense of the word. With the help
of his father, he traveled all over Europe, both West and East (including
Moscow), the Middle East, and Latin America before he was twenty-four,
meeting both English royalty and the pope, and writing up his impressions in well-informed commentaries. One from Jerusalem Logevall
deems especially "subtle and penetrating," showing Kennedy's "growing
maturity as a thinker—and no doubt, his many years of accumulated
knowledge as a reader of history and international affairs."[31] In 1940, at
the age of twenty-three, Kennedy turned his Harvard thesis into what
became a best-selling book, *While England Slept*.

By 1939, while Kennedy was still an undergraduate, his travels
amounted, Logevall says, to "the kind of exposure and training that no
future president since John Quincy Adams had enjoyed at so young an
age. And the experience left its mark, cultivating in him an intensified
passion for foreign policy and world affairs that he never abandoned, and
completing his transition to adulthood."[32] By 1945, following his visit to
defeated Germany, the now twenty-eight-year-old "Kennedy could legit-
imately claim to be as well versed on the issues as were many journalists who crowded into Potsdam [where Kennedy hung out during the
Big Three summit], and arguably more informed than Truman."[33] Not
to mention his visit to Indochina with his brother Bobby in 1951, where
they were greeted at the airport by Bao Dai, the former emperor whom the
French had installed as a token head of state. There the brothers derived
the impression, to which JFK would return in 1963, that the key to defeating Communism in Southeast Asia was "to get the Asians themselves to
assume the burden of the struggle. As long as it's a conflict between native
communists and western imperialists, success will be impossible."[34]

Kennedy served in the House of Representatives from 1947 to 1953, and then as US senator until he was elected president in 1960. By that time he made himself into an intellectual as well as a politician—not interested in ideas for their own sake but in order to understand and operate in the world.

Kennedy's pre-presidential experience was the kind McNamara would have wished for if he had known he was going to end up as secretary of defense. In addition, the two men shared some personal characteristics. Kennedy managed to keep up with his endlessly energetic family, seemed tireless when engaged in a pressing task, and often, reports Ted Sorensen, radiated a "restless energy"—although JFK was plagued by ill health throughout his life.[35] Like McNamara, he was "reluctant to reveal his innermost feelings."[36] Neither man was noted for his empathy, at least in the public performance of his job. Each could be his own "most exacting critic,"[37] but both were masters at "compartmentalizing,"[38] including putting aside inner doubts so as to get on with their important work. If McNamara's cold image concealed an emotional nature, Kennedy, according to Logevall, was "a romantic underneath his cool exterior."[39] Both men could and did dump former friends who were no longer useful to them.[40] Neither was inclined to include associates and staff in their social lives. Both put a high priority on loyalty and prided themselves on making "hardheaded judgments."[41] Both loved to read widely, and their taste extended to poetry.

Similarities like these would help to create a mutual admiration society between Kennedy and McNamara. But the two differed in important ways, as well. Whereas Kennedy's family, particularly his hard-driving father, boosted his rise shamelessly and successfully, McNamara's success (despite his mother's pushiness) was mostly self-made—a contrast in social class that made Kennedy's unexpected embrace all the more gratifying to McNamara. There were times when Kennedy was so ill that he was practically immobilized, and other times when he was entirely distracted by his continual womanizing, an activity at which he was a past master, even after he married. McNamara's energy never seemed to flag, and he was deeply devoted to his wife.

If Kennedy was sophisticated and intellectual, McGeorge Bundy was even more so. His Boston Brahmin family was a far more natural fit with the Eastern Establishment than Kennedy's Catholic clan and almost as well-heeled (especially after Bundy married wealthy Mary Buckminster Lothrop). Bundy had a more idyllic childhood than Kennedy, who was often ill. His education at Groton (rather than Choate) and Yale (where he was a Skull-and-Bonesman) was even more exclusive than Kennedy's, and his intellectual credentials more impressive: a coveted Society of Fellows postgraduate appointment at Harvard (free room, board, and books, annual stipend, freedom to pursue any course of study in his own way, privileged access to faculty members); appointment to the Harvard faculty and a grant of tenure in government without having taken any undergraduate or graduate courses in that field; and elevation to dean of the Harvard faculty in 1953 at the age of thirty-four. Bundy's wartime experience (particularly as a young aide to Rear Adm. Alan R. Kirk, commander of allied amphibious forces for the Sicily and Normandy invasions) didn't include combat heroism like Kennedy's, but it put him in touch with top British and American civilian and military officials. His role as a public intellectual after the war included ghostwriting Henry Stimson's memoirs, editing a book of Secretary of State Dean Acheson's speeches, and serving on a State Department disarmament panel with Robert Oppenheimer, the architect of the first atomic bomb, and in a Council on Foreign Relations study group with Dwight Eisenhower, George Kennan, Allen Dulles, and Richard Bissell. By 1960, even while living in Cambridge, Bundy, too, had become a Washington insider.

While he was Harvard's dean of the faculty, Bundy met Kennedy, who served on the university's Board of Overseers. "There was no mistaking that they liked each other immensely," reports Bundy biographer Kai Bird. "Kennedy jokingly told his (and Bundy's) childhood friend, *Newsweek* bureau chief Ben Bradlee, 'I only hope he [Bundy] leaves a few residual functions to me. . . . You can't beat brains. . . . He does a tremendous amount of work. And he doesn't fold or get rattled when they're sniping at him.' Temperamentally, Bundy and Kennedy were cast from the same impatient mold. A Harvard professor who knew both men said of Bundy, 'He pays no attention to what the other fellow may think. He's as cold as ice and snippy about everything. He and Jack are two of a kind.' "[42]

Prior to Bundy's appointment, the president's national security adviser had carried out the unglamorous staff function of executive secretary of the National Security Council created by the National Security Act of 1947. With Kennedy's support, Bundy vastly expanded his role to become the president's main foreign policy adviser, eclipsing Secretary of State Dean Rusk but not McNamara.

Dean Rusk's background was far humbler than Kennedy's and Bundy's and more so than even McNamara's. Born in 1909 to a poor farming family in Cherokee County, Georgia, he remembered going barefoot in the summer and "living on pork, killing the hogs with a 38-pistol right after the first hard freeze, to keep the meat fresh and the flies down." He didn't remember eating the pigs' ears, tail, and feet, but as his sister Margaret said, 'We ate everything but the squeal'—fatback, crackling, chitlings, bacon, smoked ham, liver mush—which was liver, kidney and heart all ground up," plus "hog brains scrambled with eggs [which] were a real treat."[43]

According to his son Richard, who finally got his taciturn father to dictate his memoirs, Rusk "never got over how a freckle-faced boy from Cherokee County, Georgia became an American secretary of state." His rise was indeed spectacular—from Davidson College, to Oxford on a Rhodes Scholarship, to professor of government and international relations at Mills College, to World War II adviser to Gen. Joseph Stillwell in the China-Burma-India theater, to the State Department, to president of the Rockefeller Foundation. But Rusk always insisted that the "roll of the dice best explains what happened to me," that "accident, chance, happenstance" are what moved him ahead, that "in tracing my journey one should not try to find rare talents and special qualities because whatever ability I had was shared by millions of others."[44]

Such modesty became Rusk, but it also explains his failure to lead the State Department more vigorously and to advise Kennedy more incisively. One reason Kennedy came to rely on McNamara for advice about the political situation in Saigon, recalled Bundy, was "he knew that he could not get an answer if he called the Secretary of State and he could get one if he called Secretary of Defense." Rusk once complained to Bundy that he found it "very hard to give his candid and full advice to the President when there is a large mob of other people in the room." But in Bundy's view, "the President does not find that he gets that much more from the Secretary when they are alone together."[45] Or as Dean Acheson once put it when people complained that it was hard to decipher what Rusk was thinking: "Did it ever occur to you that he wasn't thinking?"[46]

Kennedy had "such high hopes for Rusk in the beginning," Jackie Kennedy remembered, "and he liked him personally. . . . Jack used to come home nights and say, 'Goddamn it, Bundy and I get more done in one day in the White House than they do in six months in the State Department.'" Sending an order to Rusk in the State Department, JFK complained to his wife, was "like dropping it in the dead letter box." At one point, Mrs. Kennedy continued, Kennedy "was sort of toying with the idea of putting McNamara in there. . . . he wanted someone in there, you know, almost like McNamara or Bobby.[47]

═══

HAVING BEEN SELECTED AS DEFENSE SECRETARY, MCNAMARA quickly began selecting his own Pentagon associates. He flew back to Michigan the same day that Kennedy announced his appointment, packed his clothes that night, and returned to Washington the next morning. With "no residence, no office, no secretary, no staff," he occupied a Ford Motor Company suite at the Shoreham Hotel and began drawing up a list of people who "might meet my standards of intelligence, education and experience." Armed with a deck of 3×5 index cards, he telephoned people to get recommendations (Lovett, Galbraith, Tex Thornton, John J. McCloy, a lawyer/banker sometimes known as the "chairman of the Eastern Establishment," and others) and then contacted candidates themselves.[48]

The result of McNamara's search for Pentagon talent, he later boasted, was "the most qualified group of associates of any cabinet officer in the history of the country. It was a magnificent group, all at one moment

in time." Several of his appointees later achieved cabinet status themselves: Harold Brown (secretary of defense under Jimmy Carter), Joseph
Califano (Lyndon Johnson's secretary of health, education, and welfare), John Connally (Nixon's treasury secretary), Paul Nitze (Johnson's
deputy defense secretary), and Cyrus Vance (Carter's secretary of state).
McNamara didn't hesitate, he said, to hire "people with more experience
than I had and perhaps with more ability than I had." He didn't know
any of them beforehand, with the exception of Eugene Zuckert, whom he
chose to be secretary of the air force.[49]

McNamara's other condition for accepting his new job—that he
would distance himself from Washington socializing—was reflected in
his choice of where to live: *not* in Georgetown, the lovely old area of the
capital with cobblestone streets and charming houses inhabited by the
political elite. As Gregg Herken points out in his book, *The Georgetown
Set*, the "formal dinner party" was a "hoary old tradition in the nation's
capital . . . where the sole industry was politics, and where elections made
impermanence a fact of life."[50] According to Herken, "the most sought-
after and exclusive invitation was to one of Joe Alsop's Sunday night suppers, a cocktails-and-dinner ritual that . . . became a tradition and fixture
in postwar Georgetown." Alsop, a famous conservative newspaper columnist who in his spare time was an erudite connoisseur of fine art, raised
fine (and not so fine) dining to an art form. "Less formal than the capital's
prewar soirees, the suppers were an occasion for a close coterie of those
Alsop called his 'tribal friends' and assorted guests to get together when
their maids and cooks had the night off." Alsop called them "zoo parties"
since, in addition to his Georgetown pals, guests usually included a couple
of leading senators, foreign ambassadors, a Supreme Court justice or two,
and some up-and-coming young member of the current administration.

As *Washington Post* publisher Katharine Graham put it: "Within
Washington there's a nucleus of people who know each other and enjoy
each other's company and see each other no matter what's happening
politically or who is in or out of power."[51] Phil Graham, Katharine's husband and *Post* publisher from 1946 to 1963, toasted Georgetown this way
at a party celebrating the two hundredth anniversary of Georgetown's

founding: "In other cities people go to parties primarily to have fun. In Georgetown, people who have fun aren't getting much work done. That's because parties in Georgetown aren't really parties in the true sense of the word. They're business after hours, a form of government by invitation."[52]

Soon after arriving in the capital, the McNamaras rented a house on Kalorama Circle. Kalorama wasn't nearly as far geographically and culturally from Georgetown as Ann Arbor had been from Grosse Pointe; it was just across Rock Creek Park from Georgetown, but its residents were more likely to be corporate types than New Deal Democrats who congregated in Georgetown. Later, McNamara bought a house at 2412 Tracy Place, not far from Kalorama Circle. In the meantime, however, the Kennedy connection drew him into their social circle. Three nights before the new president's inauguration, McNamara showed up at the Georgetown home of Kennedy's sister Jean, and her husband, Steve Smith. The glittering gathering at the Smith home at Thirty-First and O Streets, NW, an early signal that the Kennedy clan intended to set a lively new standard for Washington socializing, included a host of incoming administration officials and Hollywood celebrities who dined, drank, and danced under a heated tent. McNamara strolled in moments after Milton Berle and Jimmy Durante, star comedians of the era. Frank Sinatra, the most famous pop singer in the country, also joined the crowd.[53] Soon, McNamara would become a frequent guest at White House dinner dances and at seminars and spirited Kennedy family gatherings at Hickory Hill, Robert Kennedy's rambling northern Virginia estate. He gamely participated in raucous touch football games with the Kennedy clan on the lawns at Hickory Hill, and his son, Craig, started hanging out at the Hickory Hill swimming pool with various Kennedy cousins and the children of administration officials.[54]

The McNamaras also encountered Hickory Hill through a series of seminars that Bobby and Ethel Kennedy asked Harvard-professor-turned-Kennedy-adviser Arthur M. Schlesinger Jr. to organize there in 1961. Inspired by seminars they had encountered in Aspen, Colorado, that summer, the Kennedys wanted to expose administration leaders to "the world of ideas beyond government." The first seminar took place on

November 27. Lecturers ranged from the British philosopher Isaiah Berlin to the cartoonist Al Capp to the ecologist Rachel Carson. "Students" included Bob and Margy McNamara, Averell and Marie Harriman, Treasury Secretary Douglas Dillon, and United States Information Agency chief Edward R. Murrow. The group met every month or so (except for summers) with sessions, accompanied by dinner and drinks, occasionally held at other homes. President Kennedy rarely attended, but Attorney General Kennedy could be counted on to interrogate the speakers. "You had the feeling that if you were shabby on any important point," recalled John Kenneth Galbraith, "you could pretty well count on Bobby to come in and press you on it." Alice Roosevelt Longworth, Theodore Roosevelt's oldest child, who had a cynical view of Washington after decades of observing its denizens, said the seminars "sound rather precious, but there was nothing precious about these lectures. It was all sorts of fun."[55]

Margy McNamara didn't adjust as quickly as her husband did to the Washington whirl. "People in Washington think I'm stupid," she confessed to her old friend Mary Jo Goodwin. McNamara's wife did in fact strike Washingtonians as naive. One day their next-door neighbor noticed Margy clambering over her car clutching car wax and rags. Why was she doing this? Betty Eisenstein asked. We're going to the White House, Margy answered brightly. They're so innocent, thought Eisenstein. And when the McNamaras began to accept invitations to parties, they struck their hosts as almost provincial. "Bob and Margy were so straight," one hostess recalled. "I don't think they had ever been exposed to witty conversation before," was the suave columnist Joseph Alsop's verdict.[56] Alsop had "no doubts about [McNamara's] remarkable powers of mind," but with "his earnestness and his puritanical side, he struck me as a bit priggish."

But as the months passed, McNamara and his wife became regular guests at Georgetown dinner parties, including the exclusive Sunday suppers hosted by Joseph and Susan Mary Alsop at their home at 2720 Dumbarton Avenue in Georgetown. It took President Kennedy to make the match—when Kennedy suggested Alsop invite McNamara to a quiet breakfast at Dumbarton Avenue. But the occasion backfired thanks to a "beautiful but loud-spoken toucan" that lived in the Alsops' garden room where the two men breakfasted. Joe and Bob were "beginning to become friends," Alsop recalled, "and on the verge of discussing what in Washington is called 'substance,' when the toucan, strategically positioned at the secretary's back, gave a deafening shriek and, with unerring aim, spat at least half of a well-chewed banana onto McNamara's bald spot."

Despite this incident, Alsop "came to admire McNamara more and more," to the point that "before his downfall in Vietnam, I used to think of McNamara as the best defense minister the Western world had known since Louvois, who effectively invented the profession for Louis XIV and was largely responsible for the French army's domination of seventeenth-century Europe."[57] Teenager Bill Patten (Susan Mary's son and Joe's stepson), who sometimes acted as bartender, remembers McNamara stopping by for a "quick businesslike lunch" in the early days of the Kennedy administration, but lingering longer, "nursing martinis," on later occasions. Patten's memoir contains a photo of McNamara seated comfortably in "Joe's chair" at the Alsops' Dumbarton Avenue home.[58]

Was the Georgetown social scene, and the Kennedys' penchant for partying, contagious, or did McNamara make a calculated decision to drop his aloof posture to ingratiate himself with the president, his family, and various Georgetown potentates? Probably a combination. At least one Pentagon colleague, Paul Nitze, found McNamara's peripatetic socializing distasteful and self-aggrandizing. Nitze's grandson, Nicholas Thompson, reported that Nitze "did not go to parties at the Kennedy compound on Cape Cod or let Robert Kennedy's children throw him into their pool in Virginia—and he thought rather less of the people, like Robert McNamara, who did." Years later, talking about the Kennedys, Nitze said, "I knew them all, and from time to time went to these things, but you know [my wife and I] don't like to become parts of somebody else's group."[59]

While their parents socialized, the McNamara children[60] struggled to adjust to the move from Michigan. By now Little Margy was attending Stanford. But as the result of a hearing problem that developed in childhood and led her parents to place her in a lab school, she was falling behind in math. Her father's attitude, she remembers, was that "every problem had an answer or a solution." He was always "certain there was a way out" and had told the children, "You can do it." When she seemed stumped by a problem, he would say, "Try again. If you stall, I'll try to help." His attitude was, "if you're in a hole, get out. If we got sick on a vacation, we just soldiered on." Margy remembers her father waking her up early every morning. "Time to get up," he would say, pulling the covers off her bed. Once when she felt very sick, he reassured her, "You'll feel better at school." It turned out she had measles.

Margy's father always "encouraged and supported me," she remembered. But what support could he offer when she was at Stanford and he was three thousand miles away in Washington and overwhelmed with work? The answer came one day when, upon returning to her dorm room, she was stunned to find her father waiting for her. He had taken a late-night flight to California and wanted to help. "There were no recriminations," she remembers. "He just asked what the problems were and how I was seeking to solve them, and he made some suggestions." What this showed, Margy said, was "his concern, his caring, his empathy."

Kathy McNamara, however, torn from high school in Ann Arbor in the middle of her junior year, was unhappy with her move to Sidwell Friends School in Washington. Dyslexic eleven-year-old Craig continued the sometimes tearful tutoring sessions with his mother that had begun in Ann Arbor. And while Kathy and Craig worried their mother, they saw less and less of their father, who left for work before seven every morning, six days a week (including Saturdays), after gulping down his customary breakfast of a glass of orange juice mixed with a raw egg. He didn't return until after seven-thirty in the evening. Not to mention his many trips to Europe and (after the Vietnam War gained momentum) once a month to Hawaii to meet with military commanders. As Shapley points out, this pattern (of a household run by the mother with a largely absent father) repeated the pattern of McNamara's own childhood—with additional tension stemming from McNamara's exalted rank. That rank, with its everyday exposure to secrets of all sorts, led him to compartmentalize his life, strictly segregating his work and home lives. According to Shapley, "the children learned not to ask about his work—he was terribly important; he was much smarter than they and knew so much more about the world. If he avoided discussing his work with them, who were they to insist?"[61] "My father never shared his real life with us," Craig said later.[62]

The Tracy Place house itself contributed to this separation. The living room, dining room, and small library where McNamara often buried himself in reading were separate from the front hall and the stairs leading up to the children's rooms. The children occasionally got their own meals and could come and go without entering the public rooms or the library where their father spent most of his evenings. The children recall many convivial family dinners together and enjoyable family vacations: ski trips over Christmas to the Colorado Rockies or California's Sierra Nevada range, summer trips to a cabin in Michigan, camping with old friends in California. But even on these trips, McNamara managed to separate himself from his family at times, while at the same time dominating planning for the trips. He and other men in the group would reserve for themselves the toughest terrain, as if to prove their endurance against nature. Before each trip, he would calculate exactly how much of what kind of food and drink to take into the wild, how much each adult and child should lug in his or her backpack, and then, shortly before departure, he would scour the supermarket checking to see if the sizes and weights of what was available fit his meticulously prepared plans.

Over the years, McNamara's devotion to the mountains inspired numerous family excursions through the Colorado high country in winter and summer and the construction of spartan backcountry huts where McNamara family and friends would gather for holidays. As he grew older, McNamara would hire porters to carry supplies ahead. Curt Strand, an Aspen friend who accompanied McNamara on many of these outings, recalled how much McNamara loved the vigorous hiking or cross-country skiing required to reach the shelters and how McNamara joined in parlor games like charades. "It was a McNamara favorite," Strand said. "He enjoyed doing it." McNamara never talked about work, Strand reported. The series of huts, sponsored by the 10th Mountain Division, thanks largely to McNamara's lobbying, eventually extended from Aspen to Vail and became favored destinations for backcountry enthusiasts who could score a reservation through the association that took over management of the huts. Perched near or above the tree line, spartanly furnished, they came with breathtaking views of the mountains. One hut was eventually named for McNamara, another for Margy McNamara. Visitors to this day will find McNamara family memorabilia at the two McNamara-named huts, including daily handwritten records of family activities and the names of family members and friends who joined McNamara on his mountain forays.[63]

Yet for all of McNamara's physical prowess, he was oddly self-conscious as he learned to play tennis at Margy's behest as they got settled in Washington. She found a skillful and charming instructor in Allie Ritzenberg, who was just establishing a tennis club centered on the courts of the St. Albans School, an elite private academy located in a leafy Northwest DC neighborhood near Washington Cathedral. The club attracted a who's who of Washington power brokers, including top Kennedy administration officials and newspaper reporters and columnists. After Margy signed up for lessons, she persuaded her husband to take up the game. He insisted on scheduling his lessons before other members showed up. "He was embarrassed to play where he could be seen," Ritzenberg recalled. How interesting. The powerful, cocky secretary of defense evidently did not wish anyone to see him mishitting a tennis ball or standing helpless as a crosscourt or down-the-line zinger streaked beyond his reach.

The tennis sessions with Ritzenberg were revealing in another way. Once the two men agreed on a twice-a-week early morning routine, McNamara unfailingly showed up exactly two minutes before the appointed time of 7:00 a.m. on Tuesdays and Thursdays, well before other members arrived. (As his proficiency at tennis improved, he eventually overcame his aversion to being seen on the court.) Ritzenberg could recall only two times during McNamara's tenure as defense secretary when he was late or unexpectedly absent. On the day he did not appear, a Pentagon aide arrived later to apologize, informing Ritzenberg that something unfolding at the Bay of Pigs in Cuba had prevented McNamara from appearing. McNamara maintained the same routine for forty years.[64]

═══

THE LONG, INTENSE WORKDAYS THAT MCNAMARA LOGGED, AND the immense pressure he put on himself to excel, were now coupled with a very active social life that often, but not always, included his wife. For a man known around the Pentagon as a relentless, humorless taskmaster, McNamara seemed virtually unrecognizable on the party circuit, mingling casually with journalists, fellow government officials, and vivacious Georgetown hostesses. His appearance in Washington newspaper gossip and social columns must have astounded his Pentagon colleagues. On February 9, 1962, a little over a year after taking office, McNamara made headlines by dancing the twist with Jackie Kennedy at a White House party. The moment was chronicled by society writer Betty Beale. Declaring that "The Twist has truly arrived," Beale reported: "Anyone who still had any misgivings about the current dance craze simply hasn't seen it done the way Mrs. Kennedy, who looked lovely in a long white satin sheath, and Secretary McNamara, frequently called 'the brain' of the cabinet, performed it. It was rhythmic, fun and peppy, and more restrained than the good old Charleston which doesn't seem to shock anyone." Jackie partied and danced until 3 the next morning. The president, who disappeared at least once during the night for an assignation with Mary Meyer (the sister of Toni Bradlee, wife of the prominent *Washington Post* reporter and editor Ben Bradlee) in the family quarters upstairs, stayed at the party until 4:30 a.m., when the band finally quit.[65]

A few days after the gala, the First Lady sent McNamara a lighthearted valentine collage she had pasted together showing the two of them doing the twist, their faces superimposed over photos of bodies doing the twist. The four-page collage featured snippets of news coverage about the dance, including Drew Pearson's account in his "The Washington Merry-Go-Round" column in *The Washington Post*. "Bob McNamara proved to be the most agile of the Cabinet twisters," Pearson reported.[66] Jackie had the collage delivered by hand in a White House envelope, simply addressed to "The Secretary of Defense."[67] Around the same time, Jackie playfully wrote to McNamara, apparently enclosing a few photos of them dancing together. She jokingly asked McNamara if they would have to invoke executive privilege if Senator Strom Thurmond ever saw the photos.[68] Thurmond was a staunch conservative from South Carolina who had run unsuccessfully for president in 1948 as a Dixiecrat opponent of desegregation.

Jackie's early 1962 missives to McNamara seem inspired by an amiable friendship that had developed between them by that time. How it got started and grew quickly is not fully evident in historical records, their own writings and oral histories, and the recollections of friends and associates, but some clues are available. Ben Bradlee, a close friend of the Kennedys who later served as executive editor of *The Washington Post*, recalled an evening at the Kennedy White House when the president told him that Jackie thought McNamara was attractive and had told him that "Men can't understand his sex appeal."[69] Jackie's sister, Lee Radziwill, thought Jackie warmed to McNamara because "he was very quick and very affectionate."[70]

Roswell Gilpatric, who worked closely with McNamara as deputy defense secretary and developed his own warm relationship with Jackie, detected the affection between McNamara and the First Lady. "Jackie thought he was a great asset at a party," Gilpatrick recalled.[71] As for McNamara's attitude, McNamara said of Jackie, "She was flirtatious," though primarily interested in his ideas. Gilpatric reported that McNamara would get "incandescent" when dancing with Jackie.[72] Years later, McNamara confided to two people collaborating with him on a book that he had stayed overnight with Jackie at her family home in Newport, Rhode Island, while he was defense secretary and Margy was traveling. "I was, am close to Jackie. I am very fond of her. But I don't think that has to be part of the book," McNamara said.[73]

Jacqueline Bouvier grew up in a family with aristocratic pretensions but not enough money, and with a philandering, alcoholic father. Barbara Leaming, one of her biographers, reported that Jackie's paternal grandfather had privately printed a fraudulent family history asserting that the Bouviers were descended from French nobility. Jackie seems to have forgiven her father's "compulsive womanizing,"[74] but welcomed the wealth that came, after her parents' divorce, with her stepfather, investment banker and Standard Oil heir Hugh D. Auchincloss Jr. Schooled at Miss Porter's to attract a wealthy husband and become an attractive, obedient wife, Jackie aspired to more than that. As a Vassar undergraduate, she ventured to postwar Paris in 1949 for a year abroad in a Smith College program. While there, she studied French history and lived in spartan, freezing quarters with a French widow who had participated with her husband in the Resistance. The husband had been killed during the war. Jackie studied at the Sorbonne during the day. On some evenings, acting more like a young socialite, she would head to the Ritz Hotel.

She traveled to Vienna, a war-torn city under the divided control of the four victorious World War II nations—Britain, France, the Soviet Union, and the United States. An encounter with armed Soviet troops frightened her, generating vivid memories of her few days in the Austrian capital. The time abroad gave her a taste of European life and culture and left her determined not to settle for a humdrum domestic life with a dull but affluent husband. Hoping to return to Paris, she applied successfully for a *Vogue* magazine yearlong internship that would put her in New York and Paris, each for six months. In response to an application question about three historical figures she would like to have known, a worldly Jackie selected authors Charles Baudelaire and Oscar Wilde, and Sergei Diaghilev, a Russian arts benefactor and impresario who founded the Ballets Russes. She reported to the *Vogue* offices in New York in 1951 after completing her undergraduate degree in French literature at George Washington University but dropped the internship after the first day, apparently discouraged by a senior editor who advised her to head to Washington to find a husband.[75]

With an assist from Arthur Krock, a family friend who happened to be the Washington bureau chief of *The New York Times*, she landed a job at the *Washington Times-Herald*. Frank Waldrop, the executive editor, soon promoted her to serve as the "Inquiring Photographer" columnist. The assignment: roam the capital with an unwieldy Graflex camera asking people a question and taking their picture. She showed a flair for the job, driving around in a black Mercury convertible with a red interior that she called Zelda, questioning and snapping photos of baseball players, truck drivers, and other assorted folk. Waldrop, impressed by her moxie, renamed the column "Inquiring Camera Girl" and gave her a byline.[76]

By this time, her active social life included a short-lived engagement to John Husted, a New York stockbroker, and a growing relationship with John Kennedy. He seemed in no rush to propose to her as he spent time with a number of other women, but he eventually asked her to marry him after winning election to the Senate in 1952 as a Democrat from Massachusetts. They wed on September 12, 1953, in St. Mary's Roman Catholic Church in Newport. The life they shared proved to be far more exciting than the times she might have experienced with some of the eligible men she had dated, but her marriage was in many ways difficult.

She found Jack to be "unbelievably heavenly" on their honeymoon in Acapulco—until in the middle of it, after huddling with his wartime buddy Red Fay, he sent her back east alone. In the early years of her marriage, reports Leaming, "she had to learn how to navigate life with a man who was often absent, frequently ill, and perpetually unfaithful," to "live among people [including in his family] who . . . fond of the young wife though they professed to be, could always be expected to put Jack's interests first," to "face the reality" that "although she had been brought in to help her husband politically," he and his counselors had begun to "wonder whether she might be doing him more harm than good."[77]

Jack was wonderful with their children when, despite losing two of them to miscarriages, Jackie was able to have Caroline and John Jr. But his frenetic life as a political star left her alone with them often. And as a philanderer, he was in a class with his own father and with "Black Jack" Bouvier. Prior to the wedding, Jack's boyhood friend, Lem Billings, whispered to Jackie about her husband-to-be's sexual habits, but according to Lem, Jackie didn't expect "the humiliation she would suffer when she found herself stranded at parties while Jack would suddenly disappear with a pretty young girl."[78] Even as Jackie was nursing Jack back to health after a back operation so fraught that it led a priest to administer last rites, Jack was seeking to arrange a rendezvous with a Swedish beauty

McNamara as an Eagle Scout.

McNamara at Ford Motor Company, January 1, 1955.

President-elect Kennedy and McNamara outside JFK's Georgetown home where Kennedy announced McNamara's appointment as Secretary of Defense, December 12, 1960.

With President Kennedy walking toward a pier to board a boat at Hyannis Port, Massachusetts, July 8, 1961.

In his office at the Pentagon, November 8, 1962.

Skiing enthusiast McNamara before starting a downhill run in Aspen, Colorado, December 31, 1962.

With Robert F. Kennedy.

With Secretary of State Dean Rusk.

At his desk at the Pentagon, March 28, 1963.

Between US Air Force chief of staff Curtis LeMay (left), under whom McNamara served in World War II and with whom he clashed during the Cuban missile crisis and in Vietnam, and General Maxwell Taylor, chairman of the Joint Chiefs of Staff, April 10, 1963.

Conferring with President Lyndon B. Johnson in the White House in 1963.

South Vietnamese General Cao showing McNamara captured enemy weapons (William Bundy in white shirt, left) at Ca Mau, December 1963.

During a TV interview (by
Harry Reasoner) in his
Pentagon office,
December 12, 1963.

With South Vietnamese premier General Nguyen Khanh during a tour of the Mekong River, March 1, 1964.

Greeting South Vietnamese children in the Mekong River Delta village of Hoa Hao, March 9, 1964.

Veteran mountain climber McNamara in Switzerland, August 19, 1964.

Pointing out to American journalists where two American destroyers were reportedly attacked in the Tonkin Gulf on August 2 and 4, 1964. In fact, the August 2 attack did occur but the August 4 attack did not.

Getting a firsthand report on frontline action from Lieutenant Van Buren Wake Jr.; General William Westmoreland is at right, July 20, 1965.

(Gunilla von Post) whom he had met only once before.[79] And this, according to Leaming, was followed by more of the same: "Frolicking with other young women (JFK had a fondness for threesomes) in Jackie's own bed in the White House family quarters while she was at Glen Ora, the couple's rented country house in Virginia," and embarking on "an affair with a recent Miss Porter's graduate, Mimi Beardsley, whom he met when she came to the White House to interview Jackie's White House social secretary, Letitia Baldrige." It wasn't "that he cheated on her," remembered a Secret Service agent assigned to guard Jackie, "but that everybody knew about it, and then she's got to appear with him."[80] Not to mention his fling with Marilyn Monroe, plus, as Leaming puts it, "the sex parties, the mistresses, the prostitutes, the procurers and the drugs that were regular features of his private life."[81]

══

JACKIE'S EXUBERANT HANDWRITTEN NOTES AND LETTERS TO McNamara as the Kennedy presidency unfolded reveal a deepening relationship, possibly fueled by a sense that McNamara offered a stable, supportive refuge from her husband's predatory sexual pursuits. The tone moves from her saucy February 1962 note about doing the twist, and the valentine collage about it that she sent him, to a profound admiration for McNamara's role during the October 1962 Cuban missile crisis. On October 25, as the crisis was culminating, she sent a heartfelt handwritten note to him saying she knew he must be fatigued. Acknowledging that she was struggling to find words to express her feelings, she told McNamara she was proud of him and thankful that he had been present during deliberations about the crisis. Worried that her letter might sound stuffy and saccharine, she wrote, "Please know that this is not said as Jack's wife—but just as a plain person." Her impression that she knew what was happening during the crisis, she reported, had been upended by early morning calls to her husband and her discovery of Secretary of State Rusk dozing by the desk of a presidential aide with one hand numbly planted in a cactus plant. Calling herself "the girl in the driveway" because security considerations prevented her from being just another person in the street sending a letter to the defense secretary, Jackie told McNamara seriously not to laugh at her note—and to know how much she admired him and how she was grateful to God that he was there.[82]

When Valentine's Day arrived in February 1963, McNamara crafted a handmade card for Jackie. She quickly replied with a White House card on which she drew a heart with an arrow through it and described McNamara's note as the "most marvelous" valentine she had ever received. Saying she might put his card in a future Kennedy museum, she told McNamara that his "jolly" note was "quite fantastic." She mischeviously said that Godfrey McHugh, President Kennedy's military aide, had received an unsigned valentine card and thought it was from McNamara.[83]

By this point, McNamara was clearly enthralled by the spirited partying of the Kennedys. Margy McNamara as well. "We [are] still in the happy image of last nites [sic] delightful evening, such a wonderful time," Margy wrote to the First Lady in mid-March. "For one who hardly ever used to dance, R.S is making up for lost time. And loves every minute of it.

"Someone I was dancing with said, 'What is it that makes all these New Frontier people such good dancers?' . . . my answer to that 'It's our leader of course!'" She added a smiling face to the note after the exclamation point.

Margy continued, "Kip and I can't thank the Kennedys enough for changing our lives—as he said the other nite how will we ever get 'unused' to all this stimulation & challenge! He loves every minute of it with all the problems included—Don't believe what you read in the Papers! Need I tell you!"[84]

On April 24, Jackie penned a seven-page note to McNamara and Margy, thanking them effusively for giving the president and Jackie a striking early engraving of Mount Vernon, George Washington's home on the Potomac, that Jackie and the White House curator had long talked of acquiring for the executive mansion and she had hoped to give Kennedy as a birthday gift. Avidly describing her and her husband's delight upon finding the gift package wrapped in gold paper when they returned home, she told the McNamaras the president exclaimed, "That's incredible." Adapting language from Shakespeare's *Henry V,* she told McNamara he stood out among Kennedy cabinet members, whom she described as "we often unhappy band of brothers" toiling in difficult times. He was the most "unforgettable," she said, adding that she did not care if all the other cabinet members saw what she was writing about McNamara.[85]

On June 26, 1963, President Kennedy delivered a memorable speech in West Berlin. Standing on a platform overlooking the Berlin Wall and a huge crowd assembled at the site, he declared, "Ich bin ein Berliner" ("I am a Berliner"). Jackie, who was pregnant, had not accompanied him; she was in Washington and planned to leave the capital the next day for the Kennedy compound in Hyannis, Massachusetts, where she would stay until giving birth. (The baby, Patrick, died a day after he was born.) McNamara, whose wife Margy was in Ann Arbor visiting friends from Ford, joined Jackie in the family quarters of the White House to watch a replay of the speech on television. "She and I were talking about his speaking," McNamara recalled, alluding to Kennedy's delivery of the Berlin address. Jackie was proud of how much his public speaking skills had improved over the years.[86] That evening, McNamara and Jackie met for dinner at Salle du Bois, a swank Georgetown restaurant. The next day, before departing the White House, Jackie dispatched a note to McNamara, telling him she loved a book he had apparently given her the day before and the time they had spent together. She enclosed a "battered" copy of *The Lotus and the Robot* by Arthur Koestler, an exploration of Eastern mysticism, and told McNamara that his humility reminded her of George Romney, the Republican governor of Michigan. She looked forward to "a long exchange" of religious books with McNamara, and ended with a lighthearted postscript, asking McNamara to let her be the first to know when he was "humbled" enough to admit he had a "sense of style."[87]

Koestler was the best-selling author of *Darkness at Noon*, a denunciation of totalitarianism published in 1940. Jackie's interest in *The Lotus and the Robot* bespeaks an interest in spiritual insights that might be gained from studying religious customs in India and Japan, where Koestler had traveled. It is hard to know what to make of Jackie's decision to send her "battered" copy to McNamara and allude to his humility. Had the two of them talked about the book at dinner? Might their interest in it reflect curiosity about Asian beliefs and mysticism, ways of looking at the world that differed from Western beliefs and faith in science? McNamara had lived briefly in India during World War II. Jackie's reference to Governor Romney, a Mormon, could have been inspired by his custom of holding open office hours one morning a week for citizens who wanted to meet him. Or she might have been thinking of the prayerful, if inherently political, public fast he had conducted in February 1962 as he pondered whether to run for governor. It is unclear if she was serious about exchanging religious books with McNamara.

Was Margy McNamara alarmed by her husband's deep friendship with Jackie? For that matter, did Jackie find it awkward to spend time alone with McNamara while maintaining a cordial relationship with Margy? And did McNamara feel any remorse about growing close to Jackie? No definitive answer is available to these questions. There is one hint that Margy was concerned about the time her husband was devoting to Jackie. While Roswell Gilpatric thought Margy was perfectly comfortable with her husband seeing Jackie and even encouraged it, the June 26 dinner at Salle du Bois elicited a different reaction from her. She was in Ann Arbor that evening, dining with Bob Dunham and his wife. As the evening advanced, Margy repeatedly tried without success to reach her husband, becoming "visibly bothered," Dunham recalled. She finally reached him after midnight, learning he had been dining out with Jackie at a tony Georgetown restaurant. "Well I reached him!" she emphatically told the Dunhams and did not seem happy about it.[88]

How John Kennedy felt about the growing friendship between his wife and McNamara is also unclear, or even whether he knew a close bond was developing. As for Jackie, the attraction she felt for McNamara may have reflected her life with a womanizing husband. The notion that Jackie Kennedy and Robert McNamara would, over time, forge a deep and trusting relationship seemed implausible at the time, and still does today. The public persona each presented made the idea seem fanciful. Jackie's public image revolved around her beauty, elegance, love of literature and the arts, flair for fashion, and quiet, even shy demeanor. Though she was well aware of her husband's compulsive philandering and the many young women in his orbit, some of whom he unabashedly invited to the White House for quick sexual encounters in the family quarters upstairs, Jackie looked to be the model of a devoted, faithful spouse.

McNamara was clearly deeply in love with his wife and would often proclaim his devotion to her to friends and strangers. As defense secretary, he immersed himself in work, traveled constantly, and struck colleagues as cold, brilliant, and intimidating. Yet, as friends of each knew, Jackie and McNamara were far more multifaceted than that. Richard Goodwin, who got to know Jackie while working as a Kennedy campaign aide in 1960 and saw a good deal of her during and after the Kennedy administration as a White House speechwriter, witnessed the multidimensional Jackie. Doris Kearns Goodwin described her husband's depiction of Jackie this way: "She worked ferociously hard, advocating for the things she cared about with a sweetness that had a powerful edge. The breathy voice and saccharine manner that is so often depicted barely coincided with the disarmingly honest, funny, sarcastic, bookish, chain-smoking buddy" Goodwin knew.[89] The traits that Jackie and McNamara had displayed before becoming public figures, and in private gatherings once they stepped into the limelight, matched up surprisingly well. They liked to dance, shared a love of poetry, and were drawn to literature and dramas about the mysterious depths of friendship and love. McNamara over the years maintained a collection of favorite poems that he shared with women he admired. It included works by Emily Brontë, T. S. Eliot, Robert Frost, Rudyard Kipling, Dylan Thomas, and William Butler Yeats. Both he and Jackie seemed to yearn for companionship outside their marriages, even intimacy, if more of the soul than the body. Unlike many of the men in the Kennedy administration and family, including the president, McNamara radiated respect for women and an interest in their lives and intellectual pursuits. He could be a sensitive companion with them, a sympathetic listener. Over time, these qualities, and apparently the sex appeal that Jackie noted, drew a number of women to him.

For Jackie, an offstage friendship with McNamara may have offered an escape from the glare of the White House and the intensity of the Kennedy clan and its preoccupation with politics and competitive sports. The relationship was also transactional at times, as she sought his assistance as defense secretary on a number of matters. Here was a confident, powerful, and reliable man, yet in her company a surprisingly vulnerable and empathetic figure who could be trusted to keep secrets and favored some of the same books and music that she did. A more stable homebody than her husband, he was determined to be an intellectual; a dedicated reader; he seemed to her to be compassionate about other people's suffering; strong and decisive, brilliant but not a show-off, capable of sweetness and sorrow.

For McNamara, the friendship with Jackie must have been exciting as well as satisfying. Her attention surely flattered him. Arthur Schlesinger, who knew her well, said of Jackie: "Why besides being so astonishingly beautiful and intelligent is Jackie so fascinating? Because of the impression she gives of total, exclusive and absorbed concentration on oneself, as if she felt she were talking to the most fascinating person in the room. One knows it is simply her way, but it is irresistible all the same."[90] How scintillating for a straight-arrow auto executive from a humble background to find himself a close friend of the First Lady of the United States. "Jackie was much brighter, with a broader intellect than people have given her credit for," McNamara said.[91] Perhaps he felt sorry for her due to the president's serial philandering. He knew Kennedy was unfaithful, though later said he was unaware of the extent.[92] When Lyndon Johnson became president, McNamara periodically quizzed Jackie about Kennedy family political intentions and reported what he learned to Johnson.

The softer side of McNamara that Jackie saw and admired was absent in his abrasive management of the Pentagon as he assumed command there and bent the Defense Department and its top generals and admirals to his demanding determination to put them firmly under civilian control. Nor were his gentler qualities much apparent as he started to address America's role in South Vietnam. So thoroughly did McNamara compartmentalize his life that only he knew over time how much his effort to hide his emotions was leading to unimaginable and unmanageable levels of stress.

CHAPTER SEVEN

Storming the Pentagon

When McNamara took over the Defense Department, Kennedy ordered him to conduct a complete review of defense policy and Pentagon organization and gave him thirty days to do so. McNamara understood his mandate to include eliminating waste and inefficiency, providing "'active, imaginative and decisive leadership,'" and ending "'the passive practice of simply refereeing the disputes of traditional and partisan factions [namely, the separate branches of the military]' that had occurred under President Eisenhower's defense secretaries."[1]

Actually, the "passive practice" McNamara undertook to eliminate had plagued the American military establishment much longer than that. When World War II ended, the military services (the army with its air force and the navy, including the Marine Corps), were still independent entities, often competing for funding. The National Security Act of 1947 brought them together in a "National Military Establishment" and established a secretary of defense to provide "general direction, authority and control," to "establish general programs and policies," and to "formulate and determine the budget estimates for submission to the Bureau of the Budget."[2] But the first two defense secretaries failed to tame the competing services. James Forrestal, suffering from mental illness, died trying, throwing himself from a sixteenth-floor window of the Bethesda Naval Medical Center in May 1949. Louis Johnson was fired the next year when the Korean War rendered irrelevant the budget restrictions he had tried to impose at President Truman's behest. Eisenhower's three defense secretaries (Charles Wilson, Neil McElroy, and Thomas Gates) failed, too, despite amendments to the 1947 Act intended to strengthen their authority and the Defense Reorganization Act of 1958, which specified that the three services were "under the direction, authority and control of the Secretary of Defense." Despite McElroy's objections, the 1958 Act preserved the right of the services and the Joint Chiefs of Staff to make their own recommendations and express independent opinions to Congress—where legislators were all too ready to provide support, especially for defense spending in their districts.[3]

What needed changing in the Pentagon was illustrated by how the service chiefs responded when McNamara asked them how the defense budget inherited from the Eisenhower administration should be altered: They asked for what Eisenhower had denied them. "Do they think I'm a fool?" McNamara snorted to an associate. "Don't they have ideas?" Advised to increase production of Polaris nuclear submarines (the kind that could launch nuclear-armed ballistic missiles at the Soviet Union), McNamara asked how many were needed. Seven, he was told. Why seven? he asked. Because that's the number that the House Appropriations Committee chairman, George Mahon, wanted. "That's a hell of a way to build a program," McNamara retorted. "It's not logical."[4]

The logical way to build a program, as McNamara saw it, was to introduce the "Planning-Programming-Budgeting System" (PPBS). This system, recommended by the Rand Corporation's Charles Hitch, who soon became the Pentagon's comptroller, reminded McNamara of the management accounting he had learned at Harvard and applied at Ford. PPBS grouped weapons programs that had the same aim but had been managed separately (such as the navy's submarine-launched ballistic missiles and the air force's manned bombers) in "program packages"—to more rationally compare their advantages, disadvantages, and costs. It also thwarted the old Pentagon tactic (nicknamed "the edge of the wedge") by which separate services started pet weapons systems small and in isolation from competing systems, counting on them to grow in the absence of objections from the Pentagon's civilian leaders.

Other innovations helped McNamara consolidate control over the services. The Joint Chiefs of Staff now reported to him rather than directly to the president, enabling the White House to receive one clear Pentagon position rather than several clashing views.[5] Early on, McNamara circulated a list of ninety-six basic questions (dubbed the "Ninety-six Trombones" by Pentagon wags), such as "Why does the navy need a new class of aircraft carriers?" and "What is the basic security policy of the United States?" He demanded answers from the Joint Chiefs and others in six weeks. "We are telescoping a lifetime of work," he said.[6]

"This place is a jungle," McNamara reportedly complained.[7] But he "had no patience," he recalled later, "with the myth that the Defense Department could not be managed. It was an extraordinarily large organization, but the notion that it was some sort of ungovernable force was absurd. I had spent fifteen years as a manager identifying problems and forcing organizations—often against their will—to think deeply about alternative courses of actions and their consequences. My team and I were determined to guide the department in such a way as to achieve the objective the president had set: security for the nation at the lowest possible cost."[8] Dismissing the notion that his experience at Ford might not have prepared him to manage the Pentagon, he told *Time* magazine, which put him on its cover in April 1961, "I hate to say this. After all, I came from a company of pretty good size. And when you get up to this size, much greater size doesn't mean very much."[9] His command of detail astounded and intimidated military leaders. At an early briefing by generals and admirals in Honolulu, McNamara impatiently sat through an extended slide show packed with data. When slide number 297 was projected, he instructed briefers to go back to slide 11 and told them to put the two slides side by side on the screen. "I knew it," he declared. "There's something wrong with 297. It doesn't agree with slide eleven."[10]

The results of McNamara's radical reforms were impressive. As *Time* reported two years into his tenure as defense secretary:

McNamara has presided over a fundamental reorganization of the armed services to increase efficiency and save money. Where top Pentagon officials formerly had to wade through as many as eleven separate—and often conflicting—intelligence reports from the services daily, they now get a single, four page summary from the unified Defense Intelligence Agency. Millions of dollars have been saved on items ranging from belt buckles to bloomers by the creation of a single Defense Supply Agency. Instead of the charming, old-fashioned practice of trying to cut up the defense budget pie more or less equally among the services, McNamara now budgets by function, cutting across service lines to provide funds for Strategic Retaliatory Forces, Continental Air and Missile Defense Forces, General Purpose Forces, Airlift and Sealift Forces, Reserve and National Guard Forces. Over anguished protests, he is pushing ahead with a reorganization of the National Guard and Army Reserve, including the elimination of 1,850 units. He has ordered nearly 100 military installations shut down, including many overseas.[11]

As McNamara and his team of civilian aides reordered Pentagon policy making and budget-setting practices, the military brass grew alarmed. "McNamara's critics are legion," *Time* reported. "They can be found in the Pentagon, the Congress and in foreign capitals. His love of computers, and his own computerlike mind, have led to the bitter quip that IBM really stands for "I, Bob McNamara." A top general complained to *Time*: "He's one of the most egotistical persons I know. It never dawns on him that he might get more help from the military. He doesn't take our advice." *Time* added that "another military official contends that he has 'tremendous intellectual arrogance.'" A former civilian aide told the magazine, "He will listen, but unless the discussion is in line with his preconceived ideas, he listens very impatiently. He constantly gives the impression of preferring to be rapid rather than right." *Time* also reported that an admiral who was critical of McNamara's monopoly of Pentagon authority said: "The concentration of detailed decisions at the top tends to build the idea of the indispensable man at the top. And it tends to destroy the initiative of people down below."[12]

H. R. McMaster (army-general-turned-historian-turned–Donald Trump's–national security adviser) reported that McNamara's "autocratic style and the condescending attitude of his young civilian assistants deeply disturbed the Joint Chiefs and other military officers in the Pentagon." The military viewed McNamara's staff as "adversaries," with differences between the two sides extending to "new management techniques, the military budget, and weapons procurement." Military men nicknamed McNamara's young staffers "happy little hot dogs." Air Force Chief of Staff Curtis LeMay (for whom McNamara had worked during the war and with whom he would soon joust over issues ranging from Cuba to Vietnam) recalled McNamara's "Whiz Kids" as "the most egotistical people that I ever saw in my life. They had no faith in the military; they had no respect for the military at all. They felt that the Harvard Business School method of solving problems would solve any problem in the world.... They were better than all the rest of us; otherwise they wouldn't have gotten their superior education, as they saw it."[13]

As word spread of McNamara's ruthlessness toward Pentagon generals, men who had known him at Harvard Business School were surprised. Professor Learned, who so admired McNamara at Harvard, wondered where the alleged arrogance and condescension came from, especially since he didn't believe it marked McNamara's behavior at Ford. So something must have "got out of kilter" at the Defense Department.[14] HBS grad Alfred Dickinson, who had read all the horror stories about Defense Secretary McNamara, concluded that "people change."[15] Another former friend of McNamara, Jim Wright, who worked with McNamara at the Ford Motor Company, put it this way (as paraphrased by Hendrickson): "My God, what have they done to our Bob McNamara?"[16]

Paul Ignatius, one of McNamara's "Whiz Kids" who later served as assistant defense secretary and secretary of the navy, recalled that his boss "took the Pentagon by storm."[17] One way he did it, according to Roswell Gilpatric, was that he "did make very quick decisions." The military, Gilpatric explained, "has certain ways of doing things. McNamara wasn't going to take the time and he didn't have the patience to go through all these motions.... I think the pride, the *amour propre* of some of these generals was offended by the fact that instead of reading the papers or turning them over to a staff and then coming down with a memorandum two or three days later, he'd just write out and give them an answer right off the bat."[18]

It took all McNamara's immense energy and self-assurance to tame the Pentagon. "It never bothered me," he remembered, "that I overruled the majority of the chiefs, or even occasionally the unanimous recommendations of the chiefs. It didn't bother me in the slightest."[19] President Kennedy was grateful that his man at the Pentagon could handle problems that, according to JFK, were "so complicated and so technical that only a handful of people can understand them," problems that forced ordinary people to rely on "outdated and meaningless slogans."[20]

——

MCNAMARA ALSO ADDRESSED HIMSELF TO FOREIGN POLICY. "I believed," he recounted in a 1975 oral history interview, "that there must be a definite integration of defense policies and programs with State Department policies. Military strategy must be a derivative of foreign policy. Force structure is a derivative of military strategy. Budgets are a derivative of force structures. So, in a very real sense, a defense budget, in all of its detail, is a function of the foreign policy of the nation."[21]

In theory, McNamara could have left it to the president and secretary of state to define that policy. But several circumstances and considerations led him into a direct role in foreign policy making. One was the weakness of Secretary of State Dean Rusk. Whether or not Kennedy deliberately picked a pallid secretary of state so as to emphasize his own central role in foreign policy, the effect was to offer a bigger voice to McNamara, who was equipped by ambition and personality to take it. Outwardly, McNamara deferred to Rusk, but with a "little State Department" of his own in the form of the Pentagon's International Security Affairs office (headed at first by foreign policy veteran Paul Nitze), he moved quickly into the breach. Following Kennedy's bruising Vienna summit with Khrushchev in June 1961, during which the Soviet leader reignited the dormant Berlin crisis, the president asked Rusk to prepare a white paper on Washington's options on Berlin. When the State Department took weeks to produce the paper, McNamara's leadership of a special Berlin Task Force took on greater importance.[22]

The size of the American military arsenal, particularly its nuclear component, and the strategy for using it (or threatening to use it) were, as Trewhitt points out, "something approaching the ultimate intellectual exercise" for a man like McNamara, "part pragmatic, part theoretical. To one who thrived on challenge, this was challenge supreme with infinite stakes."[23] Once the "missile gap" turned out to be a missile myth, the question became how many intercontinental rockets the US really needed. At the time, Moscow had but a handful of ICBMs and it didn't launch a crash program to build more until the late 1970s. But as McNamara later pointed out, the Pentagon rule was not to guess at Soviet intentions but to examine their capabilities and to assume (in a "worst case scenario") that they would obtain as many rockets as they could. That helps explain why at least one air force general proposed building 10,000 Minuteman ICBMs, and the air force formally requested 3,000. But another alleged advantage of such a massively superior force was that it could back up the long-standing American threat to respond to an overwhelming Soviet invasion of Western Europe with a nuclear strike against the USSR. The lesser but still substantial force that McNamara recommended ("merely" 1,200 ICBMs) reflected the pressure he was under from the air force, but also Kennedy's fear that responding to a Soviet conventional attack in Europe with an all-out nuclear assault on the USSR would result in mutual annihilation.

The new administration preferred a "flexible response" capability that required fewer missiles but more conventional weapons that would allow it to fight a conventional war in Europe. On the assumption that a nuclear war might occur despite all-out efforts to avoid it, McNamara for a time also argued for a "counterforce" nuclear strategy, namely, for targeting Soviet forces rather than cities in the hope of limiting damage if Moscow did the same. But deep down McNamara believed something he could never publicly admit lest it vitiate the whole theory of nuclear deterrence, namely, that any kind of nuclear war, no matter how limited, would be a total disaster for mankind—hence his advocacy later in life for the abolition of nuclear weapons.

His thinking about nuclear weapons deeply impressed Daniel Ellsberg, at the time a young defense analyst at the Rand Corporation who later became famous as a Vietnam War critic and leaker of the Pentagon Papers to *The New York Times* and other news organizations. After a private 1961 meeting with McNamara—McNamara had read some of Ellsberg's Rand papers and invited him to lunch at the Pentagon—Ellsberg recalled: "I left the secretary's suite thinking that Robert McNamara was someone worthy of my greatest loyalty and trust. He had, as I saw it, the right perspective on the greatest dangers in the world and the power and determination to reduce them."[24]

If the size of the American ICBM force was clearly a Defense Department issue, the plan that Kennedy inherited from Eisenhower for Cuban exiles to invade the island and topple Fidel Castro's regime was not. The Joint Chiefs of Staff muted their doubts about the CIA scheme because it wasn't their operation. "You couldn't expect us, any one at the Chiefs' level, to say this plan is no damn good, you ought to call it off," recalled JCS chairman Lyman Lemnitzer several decades later. "The responsibility was not ours."[25] Nor did McNamara, Rusk, or National Security Adviser McGeorge Bundy oppose the plan although they all had reservations about it. "I just didn't understand it very well," McNamara remembered. "I was in no position to have an independent judgment on the strength of the exile force, and I had no real basis for appraising how Castro would react and what his capabilities would be."[26] "I let myself become a passive bystander."[27] To Richard Bissell, the CIA official formally in charge of the Bay of Pigs operation who took part in White House discussions of the plan, McNamara seemed "diffident about voicing opinions on strictly military matters in the presence of the Joint Chiefs, which is understandable. He was a civilian; he had no recent military experience . . . and none at high levels of command."[28]

The failure of the Bay of Pigs invasion by some 1,400 Cuban exiles, which was crushed by Castro's forces on April 17, 1961, triggered another burst of self-reproach by McNamara—as well as his tendency to blame himself for bad results for which he was not fully or even mainly responsible. He shared, he later confessed, "the responsibility for proceeding with what I can only call a serious error of judgment," and he insisted on telling Kennedy so even after the president went on TV to accept full fault himself. "I knew where I was at the time the decision was made," he told Kennedy. "I was at that table and nineteen out of twenty people said, 'Go ahead.' I am fully prepared to say I was one of those and to say it publicly." (The only dissenter was Arkansas senator J. William Fulbright.)

"Bob," Kennedy replied, "I was president. I made the decision. I must accept the responsibility." Said McNamara many years later: "I admire him immensely for that."[29] He added, "I made up my mind not to let him down again."[30]

The Bay of Pigs failure had "such a traumatic effect on everybody," McNamara's deputy Gilpatric recalled. "It was bound to shake up any assurance we had in just carrying forward with existing programs or concepts.... As far as McNamara was concerned, he became so disenchanted with the military advice he got that he insisted on examining basic data himself"—a lesson he applied in the Cuban missile crisis of October 1962.[31]

When an American U-2 surveillance plane discovered the intermediate-range missiles Nikita Khrushchev had secretly installed in Cuba, American-Soviet tensions rapidly escalated over the next two weeks as the two sides drew perilously close to nuclear war. McNamara later said he never went home during the crisis, sleeping instead at the Pentagon.[32] Kennedy and his men initially interpreted the missiles as a mortal military threat. Their first instinct was to eliminate them in a surgical strike followed by an invasion of the island. McNamara began to prepare a plan (together with Joint Chiefs of Staff chairman Maxwell Taylor) for attacking the missile sites and invading Cuba, but he quickly became a voice for caution, along with Robert Kennedy. Given Washington's overwhelming advantage in intercontinental missiles, McNamara minimized the importance of Moscow's intermediate-range rockets. When McGeorge Bundy asked him at a meeting of the National Security Council's Executive Committee to estimate "the strategic impact on the United States" of the missiles, that is, "how gravely" they changed "the strategic balance," McNamara replied he had asked the Chiefs that and their answer was "substantially." His own personal view, he added, was "not at all." When Curtis LeMay and other generals advocated bombing the missile sites, McNamara argued instead for a naval quarantine of the island as less likely to escalate into a nuclear war. LeMay sneered, directly to Kennedy, that a blockade, which itself would "lead right into war," was "almost as bad as the appeasement at Munich."[33]

According to Gilpatric, McNamara "was very articulate. He dominated the [White House] discussions [during the crisis]. . . . McNamara did most of the talking."[34] And he shouted down Adm. George W. Anderson, the chief of naval operations, who tried to keep McNamara from interfering in the navy's conduct of the blockade. Anderson was prepared to fire on the first Soviet ship that challenged the quarantine. When McNamara demanded to know why, Anderson waved a copy of the navy regulations manual, saying, "It's all in there."

"I don't give a damn what John Paul Jones would have done. I want to know what you are going to do now."[35]

After the blockade was imposed—President Kennedy chose to call it a "quarantine" when he announced the action to the nation because "blockade" implied an act of war—several days of high tension played out at sea. Probably the most dangerous moment occurred on October 27, when a US Navy destroyer dropped depth charges on a Soviet submarine, ordering it to surface. The sub's captain, Valentin Savitsky, took that as an attack, panicked, and prepared to launch a nuclear torpedo that could have sunk the USS *Randolph*, a nearby American aircraft carrier. But Savitsky was overruled by the sub brigade's chief of staff, Vasily Arkhipov, who happened to be on board and recognized that the American ship was trying to force the submarine to the surface and photograph it.[36] The US Navy intercepted Soviet ships, and Soviet leader Nikita Khrushchev sent contradictory messages to Kennedy, one militant, the other seeming to open the door to a diplomatic resolution. During this phase of the crisis, McNamara took a more aggressive stance in meetings as he and military commanders pushed ahead with preparations for air strikes and an invasion if the crisis was not soon resolved. Audio recordings of the White House meetings capture the shift in McNamara's attitude as the mobilization of American military forces gathered speed. As defense secretary, he was responsible for readying the military to go to war and refining attack plans. Differing historical interpretations of his performance during the crisis rest to some extent on how much to read into his presentations about combat plans in the final days of the showdown and whether he was advocating them or simply presenting them to Kennedy.[37]

McNamara's description of how he felt at the peak of the crisis on Saturday evening, October 27, has often been quoted: "I wondered if I'd ever see another Saturday night." When the Soviets agreed the next day to dismantle their missiles, McNamara's mood (described by his aide Adam Yarmolinsky) was "exaltation."[38] The crisis confirmed his determination to trust his own judgment more than that of his generals. It also strengthened Kennedy's trust in McNamara.

McNamara's relations with Congress later became strained. He had to "sort of restrain himself because his IQ was so much higher," Gilpatric recalled. "He had to be careful not to appear to be playing down to the politicians on the Hill. But during the three years I was with him [1961–1963] he had very good relations with the people on the Hill." In February 1961, Carl Vinson of the House Armed Services Committee asked McNamara, "How much is enough? Now, will you be in a position to tell the committee, then, from your study, what we need in the field of missiles, aircraft and vessels?"

"Yes sir," answered McNamara.

"You will be able to tell us what we need?" Vinson asked, amazed.

"Yes sir," repeated McNamara.

"And hardware?" another committee member broke in.

"Yes sir," McNamara pledged.[39]

=

THE PARADOX OF VIETNAM WAS THAT ALTHOUGH THE KENNEDY administration knew almost nothing about the country, the Cold War axioms that underlay its broader foreign policy virtually required that it join the war there. Paul Kattenburg, deputy director of the State Department's Southeast Asia Affairs office, captured the degree of ignorance about Vietnam after attending a 1963 policy meeting with McNamara, Rusk, Bundy, General Maxwell Taylor, and William Colby, a CIA officer handling agency operations in South Vietnam: "I listened for about an hour or an hour and a half to this conversation before I was asked to say anything . . . and they looked to me absolutely helpless, the whole group of them. There was not a single person there that knew what he was talking about. . . . They were all great men. It was appalling to watch. I didn't have the feeling that any of them . . . really knew . . . Vietnam. They didn't know the past. They had forgotten history. They simply didn't understand the identification of nationalism and Communism, and the more the meeting went on, the more I sat there and thought, 'God, we're walking into a major disaster.' "[40]

Kennedy and company knew, of course, that Vietnam had been a French colony until the Japanese occupied it in World War II, that the French had taken control again after the war only to be forced out shortly after a losing a decisive 1954 battle to Vietnamese Communists at Dien Bien Phu, and that the country had been formally divided between the Communist North and non-Communist South at the Geneva conference in 1954. They knew that the Eisenhower administration had backed Saigon with military aid and advisers against Communist guerrilla forces in the south known as Vietcong that were supported and armed by North Vietnam. On the day before Kennedy's inauguration, Eisenhower personally warned him and McNamara that if Vietnam's neighbor Laos fell to its own Communist rebels, "in the long run we will lose all of Southeast Asia."

"That was his belief," McNamara declared forty years later. "It was our belief. That was part of the cold war in our minds." "There was a cold war twenty-four hours a day three hundred and sixty-five days a year; for seven years as secretary of defense, I lived the cold war. We felt we were under immense pressure from the Communist bloc, China and the Russians, to yield freedom." During "my seven years as secretary we came within a hairsbreadth of war with the Soviet Union on three different occasions."[41]

This was Washington's long-standing Cold War consensus—that

Communism must be contained, not only in Europe, which George F. Kennan primarily had in mind when he propounded his famous containment doctrine in 1947, but in Asia too, especially after Communists seized control of China in 1949 and North Korea invaded South Korea in 1950. Like Eisenhower, Kennedy and his advisers accepted the "domino theory" that the loss of even one Southeast Asia country could lead to the fall of all the rest and eventually threaten Japan. On January 6, 1961, Khrushchev endorsed "wars of national liberation" as both "inevitable" and "sacred." According to Arthur Schlesinger, "the bellicose confidence" that surged through Khrushchev's speech, "especially the declared faith in victory through rebellion, subversion and guerrilla warfare," alarmed Kennedy. Ignoring a warning from former American ambassador to Moscow Llewellyn Thompson that the speech expressed only one side of the complicated Khrushchev, Kennedy answered back in his State of the Union address on January 30: "We must never be lulled into believing that either power [the Soviet Union or Communist China] has yielded its ambitions for world domination—ambitions which they forcefully restated only a short time ago. On the contrary, our task is to convince them that aggression and subversion will not be profitable routes to pursue these ends."[42]

Ten years earlier, even before he was elected senator, John Kennedy and his brother Bobby had visited Vietnam. In 1954 the young senator from Massachusetts opposed aiding the French at Dien Bien Phu: "To pour money, *materiel*, and men into the jungles of Indochina without at least a remote prospect of victory would be dangerously futile and self-destructive." But, speaking to a lobby group called the American Friends of Vietnam in 1956, he described Vietnam as "the cornerstone of the Free World in Southeast Asia" as a "test of American responsibility and determination." "This is our offspring. We cannot abandon it."[43]

By the time he became president, Kennedy was "deeply interested in Vietnam," recalled McGeorge Bundy, and "inclined from the first to believe that the United States should do more there and do it better."[44] Several international crises in 1961 strengthened that view, especially the Bay of Pigs fiasco and the fiery summit in June during which Khrushchev bullied and browbeat Kennedy. "Roughest thing in my life," the president told *New York Times* columnist James Reston afterward. "I think he did it because of the Bay of Pigs. I think he thought that anyone who was so young and inexperienced as to get into that mess could be taken. And anyone who got into it and didn't see it through had no guts. So he just beat the hell out of me. So I've got a terrible problem. If he thinks I'm inexperienced and have no guts, until we remove those ideas, we won't get anywhere with him. So we have to act."[45]

Vietnam was one place to act. Prompted by increasing Vietcong attacks and shrinking support for his government, South Vietnamese president Ngo Dinh Diem asked Washington for more assistance. In response, Kennedy sent Gen. Maxwell Taylor, at the time his special military representative, and Deputy National Security Adviser Walt Rostow to Saigon to evaluate the situation. A photo of the two men in Saigon resting on a bench in tennis whites before or after playing tennis during their visit seemed aptly to capture Washington's misperceptions about Vietnam. Fred Dutton, a Kennedy family aide and friend, later said the two men looked like "old French courtiers."[46]

Their report, delivered in Washington on November 3, 1961, urged sending more military advisers and even a limited number of combat troops, and McNamara's first instinct was to agree. In a November 8 memorandum to the president, McNamara urged "the dispatch of substantial U.S. forces, along with a willingness to bring the war to North Vietnam," adding that even if such action were to "trigger Chinese intervention," some "six divisions" (205,000 men) "would suffice without diverting resources from Berlin."[47] On November 15, after digesting the report of the Maxwell Taylor/Walt Rostow mission, Kennedy signaled his disinclination to dispatch combat troops to Vietnam, a view that McNamara quickly made his own. It would not be the last time he seemed to tailor his views about Vietnam to align them with his president's. Eugene M. Zuckert, an astute observer of McNamara who had first met him at Harvard Business School and later became air force secretary, pointedly said McNamara was "never more vigorous in defending a position than the one his boss had told him to take which he really didn't believe in, and he always overcompensated to make sure that his boss's position was the one that prevailed."[48]

McNamara later denied he had switched his position on Vietnam to fall in line with Kennedy. "As soon as I sent the memo to the White House," he recalled in his memoirs, "I started worrying that we had been too hasty in our advice to the President. For the next couple of days, I dug deeper into the Vietnam problem. The more I probed, the more the complexity of the situation and the uncertainties of our ability to deal with it by military means became apparent. I realized that seconding the Taylor-Rostow memo had been a bad idea."[49]

The Taylor-Rostow proposal reactivated Kennedy's allergy to sending American soldiers to fight Asian wars. "The troops will march in; the bands will play; the crowds will cheer," he told Schlesinger, "and in four days everyone will have forgotten. It's like taking a drink. The effect wears off and you have to take another."[50] Kennedy refused to send troops. Yet, "precisely *because* Kennedy refused the combat troop request," historian Brian VanDeMark points out, "he felt compelled to grant the request for more American advisers," who increased over the next two years from 948 in November 1961 to 2,646 in January 1962 to 11,300 at the end of that year, to 16,732 in October 1963, the month before Kennedy's assassination.[51]

Asked many years later about Kennedy's motives for beginning this increase in 1961, McNamara cited "the nearly unanimous view of his advisers that without such assistance South Vietnam would be lost and with it all of Southeast Asia." But also the "damage to the alliance and [Kennedy's] domestic political position," which "would be less if he tried to help the Vietnamese help themselves and they proved incapable of doing so than it would be if he failed to make such an effort."[52]

McNamara's own view of Kennedy's decision was "ambivalent," he recalled. "I stressed the action recommended in the Taylor report might well be insufficient" and that "in all probability, U.S. troops, planes and resources would have to be supplied in additional quantities at a later date." What McNamara did not do, he later confessed, was "insist that we present the president with an exhaustive analysis of the pros and cons of the alternatives we faced and urge him to participate in a full debate on the merits of each of the alternatives before a decision was made."[53]

Had intervention in Vietnam been fully examined, it is far from clear that critical factors would have been considered. The complexities of Vietnam were more daunting than McNamara realized and inadequately appreciated by the Kennedy team, as Paul Kattenburg had seen. Washington's preoccupation with the Communist threat blinded McNamara, Rusk, Bundy, and others to the pivotal role that nationalism played in Ho Chi Minh's determination to reunite Vietnam. American officials, by and large, failed to appreciate the long history of hostility between Vietnam and China, mistakenly viewing the Communist world as a monolithic threat. The Saigon government was corrupt, authoritarian, and lacked popular support. Opposition to it was multifaceted, not simply an invading army. Opponents included a large Buddhist community, the guerrilla warriors supported by North Vietnam, and regular North Vietnamese troops. Combating an insurgency would require a more nuanced strategy than countering an enemy army on the battlefield. A large number of enemy combatants, the Vietcong, were South Vietnamese, living among fellow citizens in hamlets and cities across South Vietnam. They could easily melt into the local population, making them hard to identify and attack. They used guerrilla tactics, ambushing South Vietnamese forces, staging surprise assaults on bases and encampments, setting lethal traps in the jungle, and vanishing as quickly as they materialized.

This was not a set of challenges familiar to the Pentagon. Nor was Vietnam's topography conducive to the kind of military campaign American commanders had been trained to wage. Much of South Vietnam's terrain was clogged with thick jungle vegetation that impeded visibility and movement. The landscape was largely unsuitable for mechanized ground warfare with tanks and artillery, a staple of previous American warfighting tactics. Any US combat forces sent to Vietnam would have to rely on mobile strike tactics with infantry delivered by helicopter to battle sites, fierce firefights in the jungle and rice paddies, and bombing strikes against enemy targets in South and North

Vietnam. Given the elusiveness of enemy forces, there would surely be a strong temptation to use defoliants and incendiary compounds to clear the jungle canopy that hid them (which Washington did). It was not hard to imagine that American troops, impatient with the lethal attacks by enemy forces that disappeared into civilian populations, would become frustrated and end up conducting mistaken or wanton attacks on civilians. (Indeed, in July 1965, CBS News correspondent Morley Safer and a South Vietnamese cameraman recorded disturbing images of American marines setting the small hamlet of Cam Ne ablaze as elderly residents watched in horror. In March 1968, United States Army forces killed hundreds of civilians, including women and children, in the hamlet of My Lai. The atrocities were not publicly disclosed until November 1969, when journalist Seymour Hersh reported them in the Dispatch News Service, a small independent news organization.)

Despite the unconventional military challenges that the United States faced in Vietnam, most civilian and military leaders in Washington assumed that overwhelming American firepower, if applied, could eventually defeat the Vietcong and North Vietnamese forces in South Vietnam, and that punishing air strikes against targets in North Vietnam, including Hanoi, would break the will of Ho Chi Minh and his fellow leaders. These tactics might have worked had Kennedy or Johnson been willing to send a million American combat troops to Vietnam, invade North Vietnam, and reduce Hanoi to ruins. In the end, Johnson and McNamara settled on a tempered strategy that underestimated the nationalist zeal that motivated North Vietnamese leaders to keep fighting and that was tragically destined to end in stalemate or a US defeat—after the loss of tens of thousands of American troops and far more Vietnamese in South and North Vietnam.

Despite the complexities inherent in Vietnam, it was about this same time that McNamara offered to be Kennedy's main Vietnam manager. "He felt very sure of himself," Gilpatric remembered, and he also felt "a very heavy responsibility because he knew the President's reluctance about the whole operation."[54] The additional irony is that he was even less qualified to manage Vietnam than he had been to be secretary of defense.

His main skills were administration and management. If he had excelled in the Cuban missile crisis, that was because, as he later said, it was "a relatively simple problem," with a restricted number of players and a limited time frame—as compared to the "complexities of rampant nationalism, perhaps supported by Communist aggression in Vietnam."[55] Not only had he never been to Vietnam, he was ill-equipped to understand its history, culture, and politics. Moreover, his own personality would undermine him as well, especially the premium he placed on winning, his determination never to give up, and his tendency to blame himself when the outcome wasn't what he wished.

═══

VIETNAM WASN'T YET THE ADMINISTRATION'S MAIN FOCUS IN 1962; it was concentrating on relations with the Soviet Union, climaxing in the Cuban crisis. But McNamara's first trip to Saigon in May revealed him to be ripe for the kinds of misperceptions and misunderstandings that would plague him throughout the war. The briefing he received from American military men in Saigon didn't satisfy him. "He didn't like men in uniform with pointers reading off things," Gilpatric noted. "He wanted to ask his own questions and he wanted un-stereotyped answers."[56] But when the US commander in Vietnam, General Paul Harkins, buried him in statistics and maps showing how well the South Vietnamese army was doing, McNamara was impressed. He insisted on touring the country by helicopter, dropping into military posts, provincial and district headquarters, and rural villages, but he failed to understand that South Vietnamese officials' cultural code required them to keep negative information to themselves while telling McNamara what they assumed he wanted to hear. McNamara didn't stay long in Vietnam (merely forty-eight hours), but felt he acquired "a good feel" for conditions there. Asked by a reporter if he might feel differently had he spent more time there, he replied, "Absolutely not," that had he stayed longer, his impressions would have been "reinforced" several times over. When another reporter, Neil Sheehan, wondered how such a smart man could be optimistic so soon, McNamara retorted, "Every quantitative measurement we have shows that we're winning this war."[57]

Sheehan was one of several journalists (David Halberstam was another) who knew the war wasn't going as well as McNamara thought. They dubbed Harkins's daily briefings as "the Five O-clock Follies" and nicknamed him "General Blimp," after a fatuous, corpulent British cartoon character named Colonel Blimp. Young American diplomats like Richard Holbrooke and Anthony Lake, who were stationed in the provinces, also could see how ineffective the South Vietnamese regime was. But McNamara could foresee a time when the Saigon regime would no longer need American advisory support, and he told Harkins to prepare a withdrawal plan. The plan, presented to McNamara in July, called for reducing American advisers from 7,500 to 1,600 and estimated that would take "one year from the time that we are able to get [South Vietnamese forces] fully operational and really pressing the VC in all areas." McNamara, not wanting to be overly optimistic, set 1965 as the year when American advisers could finally leave Vietnam.[58]

Despite McNamara's optimism, Kennedy sensed trouble and asked Senate Majority Leader Mike Mansfield, who had served as a marine in the Philippines and China in the 1920s and taught Asian history at the University of Montana, to check out the situation in Vietnam. Mansfield's conclusion, which he conveyed to Kennedy the day after Christmas in Palm Beach, was that the South Vietnamese were far from ready to defeat the Vietcong. In fact, that would require "a truly massive commitment of American military personnel and other resources—in short, going to war fully ourselves against the guerrillas—and the establishment of some form of neocolonial rule in South Vietnam." After the meeting, Kennedy told his aide Kenny O'Donnell, "I got angry with myself because I found myself agreeing with [Mansfield]." Several months later, after Mansfield repeated his view at a congressional leadership breakfast, Kennedy privately confessed that although he wanted to withdraw from Vietnam, "I can't do it until 1965—after I'm reelected." As he put it to O'Donnell, "In 1965, I'll become one of the most unpopular Presidents in history. I'll be damned everywhere as a Communist appeaser. But I don't care. If I tried to pull out completely now from Vietnam, we would have another Joe McCarthy red scare on our hands, but I can do it after I'm reelected. So we had better make damned sure that I *am* reelected."[59]

The year 1963 sharpened the contradictions Kennedy and McNamara were facing. The fact that the Diem regime was brutalizing its Buddhist opponents and suffering major military defeats made it seem ever less deserving of American support, but less likely to survive without it. On the morning of June 11, Quang Duc, a sixty-six-year-old Buddhist monk, set himself ablaze in a busy Saigon intersection to protest the Diem regime's repression of Buddhists. Malcolm Browne, an Associated Press correspondent who had been alerted in advance about the protest, took photographs of the shocking scene that appeared on front pages and news broadcasts around the world the next day. The event shocked Washington. "No news picture in history has generated so much emotion around the world as that one," recalled Henry Cabot Lodge, a Massachustetts Republican who served as a US senator and was Richard Nixon's running mate in the 1960 presidential election.[60] Kennedy appointed him as ambassador to South Vietnam not long after Quang Duc's suicide.

That summer, Rusk reported the feeling in Congress "that we're up to our hips in the mud out there," but, said Kennedy, "they'll be madder if South Vietnam goes down the drain."[61] On September 2, Kennedy told CBS News anchorman Walter Cronkite in a taped TV interview, "In the final analysis, it is their war. They are the ones who have to win it or lose it. We can help them, we can give them equipment, we can send our men out there as advisers, but they have to win it, the people of Vietnam, against the Communists." But in the same interview Kennedy insisted, "I don't agree with those who say we should withdraw. That would be a great mistake.... This is a very important struggle even though it is far away."[62]

What this and other similar Kennedy statements show is that Kennedy had two incompatible convictions—that it wasn't America's job to save South Vietnam, but that we couldn't afford not to do so—which he continued to hold until he was assassinated. On the morning of September 23, just before McNamara and General Taylor embarked on another

trip to Vietnam, the president asked them, "If the situation there continues to unwind, then what the hell do we do?" "We'll have to take some
rather desperate measures," he continued, "because we're going to bear
responsibility six months from now." And, in the meantime, "we're beginning to lose." McNamara tried to reassure him. "We have plans for withdrawal of our forces when military success warrants it." "We hope that
before the end of the year we can be withdrawing military personnel if
the military situation improves."[63]

By this time, the Defense Department was using herbicides and defoliants in a limited way to clear terrain in South Vietnam. As early as late
1961, McNamara had endorsed a testing program, proposed by the Joint
Chiefs, and Kennedy had approved it. Both men eventually approved use
of the chemicals beyond testing in a program codenamed OPERATION
RANCH HAND. McNamara ordered that American involvement be
masked so that the aerial spraying missions would appear to be conducted
by the South Vietnamese government. On January 11, 1962, the South
Vietnamese government announced the program. "The chemicals will
be supplied by the United States at the request of the Vietnamese Government. The Government emphasized that neither of the two chemicals
is toxic, and that neither will harm wildlife, domestic animals, human
beings, or the soil. There will be little, if any, effect on plants outside the
sprayed strip."[64]

Over the ensuing years, the United States made extensive use of defoliants, including widespread use by American forces of Agent Orange,
a particularly toxic chemical. The United States Veterans Administration, citing an independent study by the Institute of Medicine, said in
2009: "Between January 1965 and April 1970, an estimated 2.6 million
military personnel who served in Vietnam were potentially exposed to
sprayed Agent Orange."[65] The number of Vietnamese was much higher.
As a result, many Americans and Vietnamese developed serious health
problems. McNamara would later say, "I'm not certain I had anything
to do with its use. And if I did, I didn't know enough about toxicity to
know whether it would or wouldn't kill people, innocent people. And I
certainly didn't know anything about whether it was legal or illegal."[66]

The use of napalm, a highly flammable incendiary substance made by the Dow Chemical Company, began in South Vietnam in 1965.

———

THERE HAS BEEN A SPIRITED DEBATE AMONG HISTORIANS AND others about whether Kennedy would have withdrawn from Vietnam had he lived. What seems clear is that McNamara believed he would have done so. Thirty years later he concluded it was "highly probable that, had President Kennedy lived, he would have pulled us out of Vietnam. He would have concluded that the South Vietnamese were incapable of defending themselves, and that Saigon's grave political weakness made it unwise" to send "U.S. combat troops on a large scale." He would have accepted even the loss of Southeast Asia to Communism because the South Vietnamese had failed to do their part and because fighting on in Vietnam would "ultimately lead to the same result, while exacting a terrible price in blood."[67] Looking back, McNamara said, "The burden of proof is on those of us who stayed . . . why the hell."[68]

What did McNamara think at the time? On September 23, 1963, he and Taylor flew to Vietnam to gather more information. Their impression was mixed: although there was some progress in the war effort, the Diem regime was flailing. The report they prepared on the way home recommended that "a program be established to train Vietnamese so that essential functions now performed by U.S. military personnel can be carried out by Vietnamese by the end of 1965," and that "in accordance with the program to progressively train Vietnamese to take over military functions, the Defense Department should announce in the very near future presently prepared plans to withdraw 1000 U.S. military personnel by the end of 1963." On October 2, McNamara told Kennedy, "We need a way to get out of Vietnam and this is a way of doing it. To leave forces here when they're not needed I think is wasteful and complicates both their problem and ours."[69]

At a National Security Council meeting to discuss the McNamara-Taylor report on the evening of October 2, Kennedy seemed satisfied: "We've pretty much got our policy now," he said. But when he left the room, McGeorge Bundy, with whom he had privately discussed the report, noted that the president wasn't sure that US advisers could accomplish their job by the end of 1965. Especially since the American goal remained, as Bundy summarized Kennedy's view, "to win the war."[70]

Less than a month later, on November 1, an event occurred in Saigon that dramatically complicated the task of winning the war. With Washington's backing, a group of South Vietnamese generals seized power in a coup that resulted in the bloody murder of President Diem and his brother Ngo Dinh Nhu. The brothers' repression of Buddhists had come to seem to Washington an insuperable obstacle to Saigon's war effort. But the generals who took their place, themselves to be ousted later in another of a continuing series of coups, proved corrupt and ineffective.

On November 21, 1963, the day before his own assassination, Kennedy told his aide Michael Forrestal, "I want to start a complete and very profound review of how we got into this country, what we thought we were doing and what we now think we can do. . . . I even want to think about whether or not we should be there."[71] In other words, the basic conundrum he had faced and McNamara would continue to face was still far from resolved: how to withdraw from a war that had to be won but wasn't going to be won anytime soon. Clark Clifford, a longtime confidant of Democratic presidents including Kennedy, said years later that Kennedy would never have dispatched ground combat troops to Vietnam. With the benefit of hindsight, he told the editors of his memoir, "In judging matters of this kind [Kennedy] was a real cold fish." Clifford said "he could be totally objective . . . under the façade of charm and attractiveness. . . . He was cold, calculating and penetrating." He imagined Kennedy would have said, "I'm not willing to take the chance. I don't like what I see ahead. I'm suspicious of the people who are involved. I just don't think I ought to accept the representations of the military with full faith and credit extended. . . . I'm just going to get more deeply involved in what is a stinking mess."[72]

McNamara's public and private life in 1961 and 1962 did not prepare him for the Vietnam crucible to come. The public power he accumulated made

him the obvious candidate to direct the Vietnam War. But the arrogance
he displayed and the resentment it provoked help explain why he bore so
much of the blame when the war went disastrously awry. His distance
from his family reduced the loving support that he would so badly need
to survive. The assassination of Kennedy brought McNamara and Jackie
Kennedy together in ways that tightened their bond and helped sustain
both through the difficult years that followed the tragic events of November 22, 1963.

CHAPTER EIGHT

Assassination and Aftermath

Early on the afternoon of November 22, 1963, at 1:40 p.m. to be precise, the Pentagon Command Center pulled McNamara out of a meeting with McGeorge Bundy and several other officials to inform him, as he recalled, "that a CIA agent had reported that the president had been shot and killed." He later said that he had never tracked down the origin of the report "but it was minutes ahead of anyone else." McNamara immediately called the Secret Service, which told him Kennedy had been shot but the agency knew nothing more. He tried unsuccessfully to reach Robert Kennedy, then stepped back into the meeting room to let Bundy and the others know what he had learned. The meeting quickly ended. It was 1:55 p.m. "There was still no indication that the president had been killed," other than the Command Center information that had been passed on to him, McNamara said. The Secret Service confirmed the death to McNamara roughly ten minutes later.[1]

In the following minutes, McNamara instructed the Joint Chiefs to place American military forces around the world on alert, not knowing whether the attack was part of a wider plot against the United States or how the assassination might affect America's foreign relations. In several phone calls, McNamara and Attorney General Robert Kennedy agreed that they and Gen. Maxwell Taylor, chairman of the Joint Chiefs, should go by helicopter to Andrews Air Force Base outside the capital to await the arrival of Air Force One carrying Kennedy's body, his wife, and the new president of the United States, Lyndon B. Johnson, who had taken the oath of office aboard the plane before it left Dallas.[2]

When McNamara, Kennedy, and General Taylor got to the base, Robert Kennedy made clear he wanted some moments alone. So did McNamara. "I stood in a shadow by myself for 15–20 minutes," he recalled.[3] After Air Force One landed, Robert Kennedy urged McNamara to go aboard. He declined. "It so clearly seemed a moment of intimacy and privacy for a family in shock and sorrow," he later recalled.[4] Robert Kennedy brushed past Johnson to reach Jackie. As the passengers disembarked, McNamara directed his attention to Johnson. In Shapley's description, McNamara rushed straight through the crowd to the new president, "his gleaming, straight-combed hair is unmistakable even from behind. The crowd parts without a jostle to let him through. McNamara seizes Johnson's hand, clasping it so firmly and long that the gesture looks rehearsed. He turns and hugs Lady Bird Johnson and moves with the new presidential couple off to stage right. He is assisting and deferential, smooth, obedient, and custodial—a physical symbol of confidence and continuity."[5]

At Johnson's request, McNamara, McGeorge Bundy, and Under Secretary of State George Ball joined the new president as he flew by helicopter to the White House. Johnson made clear to the men that he wanted them to stay on in his administration. Asked by Johnson if there were any important defense matters pending, McNamara informed him about the location and disposition of American military forces around the world.[6]

After returning home for a brief, mournful dinner with Margy, McNamara headed for Bethesda Naval Hospital at Jackie's request, conveyed by Robert Kennedy over the phone, to join her while the autopsy of the president was conducted. Family and friends were gathering in a suite on the seventeenth floor of the hospital, including Robert and Ethel Kennedy, Jackie's mother, Janet Lee Bouvier Auchincloss, Ben and Toni Bradlee, Kennedy's sister Jean Smith, and others. Traumatized and consumed by the day's events—when the lethal bullet shattered Kennedy's head, blood and brain matter splattered Jackie, seated next to the president in a pink suit—Jackie recounted the harrowing moments over and over again to various guests. McNamara listened patiently for hours, seated on the floor of the kitchen next to Jackie, who was perched on a high stool. "I got to the hospital at 7:45 p.m., and she talked for the entire time until we left for the White House, arriving there at 4:25 a.m."[7]

"She was in that suit with the bloody skirt and blood all over her stockings," McNamara said. "I felt I had to be calm for her and listen to her . . . I was concentrating entirely upon her, because she needed me and I felt, the hell with the others, let them take care of themselves." During the night, he made an extraordinary offer to Jackie, telling her that he would, if she wished, buy for her the Georgetown house where she and Kennedy had lived before moving to the White House.[8]

It seems inconceivable that the shocking death of Kennedy and McNamara's long night at Jackie's side as she recounted the gruesome scene in Dallas did not shake him to his core. He later confided to Joseph Alsop that he never got over the loss of Kennedy. "The Washington landscape seemed to me to be littered with male widows," Alsop observed.[9]

Ben Bradlee was impressed by Robert Kennedy and McNamara as the somber night progressed. He described McNamara as "the second towering figure" in the suite. "No subterfuge, no special smiles. The naked strength. A man without guile."[10] As dawn came, McNamara accompanied Kennedy's body to the White House. With a number of Kennedy family members and aides, he viewed the corpse in an open casket, peering at the grotesque, partly reconstructed head prepared by morticians, and agreed with recommendations that the casket be closed for the funeral and burial ceremonies that lay ahead.

Arthur Schlesinger, who had also stared in disbelief at the open casket, drove McNamara home. The two sat for a while in Schlesinger's car outside McNamara's house, talking about Johnson and what manner of president he would be. "McNamara did not know him and was uncertain whether the relationship would work," Schlesinger recalled.[11]

Some Kennedy family members favored burial in Kennedy's home state of Massachusetts. McNamara made the case for Arlington National

Cemetery, across the Potomac in northern Virginia, saying Kennedy had been president of the United States, not Massachusetts. To buttress his position, he walked through the cemetery the next morning looking for an appropriate burial site. As rain fell, McNamara and the cemetery super-intendent stopped atop a gentle hill that rises from the river to the Custis-Lee Mansion. "I could see across Memorial Bridge and to the Lincoln Memorial in the distance, even in the increasing fog," he recalled. " 'This is the place,' I said quietly."[12] A Park Service ranger told him later in the day that when President Kennedy had toured the cemetery a few weeks earlier, he had come to the same spot, telling the ranger "this was the most beautiful sight in Washington." Jackie visited the site with McNamara the afternoon of November 23, immediately approving the choice.[13]

On Saturday evening, November 24, grieving Kennedy family and friends gathered at the White House for an informal dinner. The group included McNamara and his wife, Margy, two Kennedy sisters, Patri-cia Lawford and Eunice Shriver, and their husbands. Treasury Secre-tary Douglas Dillon recalled the scene, including a surreal moment involving McNamara: "Everybody was trying not to talk about what happened, and we succeeded quite well. It was not serious. It was really gay. I know that sounds awful, but it wasn't. There was some horseplay. You know that Ethel wears a wig when she doesn't have time to do her hair. Well she was wearing one, and it was snatched off her head and passed around and placed on various heads. President Kennedy would have enjoyed that. It even perched for a moment on the head of Bob McNamara."[14]

A week after the assassination, as Jackie was preparing to move out of the White House, she sent a gift to McNamara—the Chippendale-style black leather armchair he sat in during cabinet meetings at the White House. The custom then, sometimes continued to this day, is that sec-retaries of state and defense flank the president at the cabinet table. In a note to McNamara, she said she wanted to give him something "special of Jack's" that would be meaningful to McNamara and that her late husband would have wanted McNamara to have. After going through Kennedy's things, many of which she described as of little value and difficult for anyone but her to understand, she said she had settled on the cabinet chair. Telling McNamara he was the only cabinet member to get such a gift, she thanked him for all he had done to "help Jack's name shine so brightly."[15]

In early December, the McNamaras sent Jackie two painted portraits of President Kennedy, hoping she would choose one as a gift. She declined in a December 11 letter addressed to Margy, saying she could not bear to look at depictions of her late husband in which his face was visible. The only photo she had on hand at her temporary quarters in Georgetown—Averell Harriman had vacated his home so she could stay there—showed Kennedy with his back turned. She described a moment that evening when her son, John, licking a lollipop, encountered the picture of his father, kissed it, and "said goodnight Daddy."

Jackie suggested that the McNamaras donate the portrait she liked most to the future Kennedy Library, where it would hang in a place of honor from the Kennedy cabinet member "who gave the most (as much as Jack's own brother Bobby gave)." She went on to ask if McNamara would "watch out" for John as he grew up, assisting him if he failed exams, offering advice about his life. Acknowledging that McNamara really could not be John's companion—"the Secretary of Defense would look rather ridiculous trotting around with a 3 year old"—she appealed to McNamara to keep an eye on John in the years ahead, perhaps taking him on a helicopter trip along with his own son, Craig. "He still doesn't realize Jack is gone," she said, and speaks of his father as if he would step through the door at any moment. In closing, she told McNamara she wanted John to benefit from the influence and example of men "so he will grow to be all his father wanted." She added that she she did not want him "to be ruined" by growing up only in the company of women.[16]

McNamara's ministrations to Jackie were rewarded in early December with a flattering note from Ben Bradlee, who had watched him console Jackie and was familiar with the defense secretary's pivotal role in the Kennedy presidency. Bradlee suggested that he was willing to help McNamara, as Phil Graham, the publisher of *The Washington Post*, had done before ending his own life in August 1963.

Dear Bob:

I have taken too long to tell you what you must already know . . . that
your presence and strength have meant and mean so much to Jackie,
and that your continued presence and strength in the administration mean so much to us all as Americans.

John Kennedy admired no man more than you—and your family, too, and how proud you must be of that.

If I can ever help you, as a pale substitute for Phil, or as your
friend, I know you will tell me.

As ever,

Ben[17]

=====

THE SHOCKING TRANSITION FROM THE KENNEDY PRESIDENCY TO
the Johnson presidency jolted McNamara in ways that directly and indirectly, consciously and probably subconsciously, impacted his handling of
the Vietnam War. It may help explain his increasingly conflicted views
about the war and about Lyndon Johnson. In an instant, the assassination eliminated the president who had vaulted him to global prominence
and graciously forgiven him for his mistakes, a dynamic young leader
whom McNamara greatly respected, trusted, even loved. Into the Oval
Office stepped a coarse, moody, politically astute dealmaker with whom
McNamara had little personal rapport but needed to please to keep his
job. Kennedy had plenty of flaws, and Johnson's leadership skills on legislative affairs with Congress, honed during his years as Senate majority leader, far eclipsed Kennedy's. But for McNamara, the change was
wrenching. All the more so because he had grown so close to the Kennedy
family, especially Jackie, now suddenly a grieving widow, and Robert,
now the mourning brother of the president whose murder immediately
made Bobby a prospective heir to the presidency and a threat to Johnson.
"The Kennedys and I had started as strangers but had grown very close,"
McNamara later said. "Unlike many subsequent administrations, they

drew in some of their associates, transforming them from colleagues to friends. We could laugh with one another. And we could cry with one another. It had been that way with me, and that made the president's death even more devastating."[18]

It was as if fate had thrown McNamara simultaneously into the arms of all three of them—Lyndon Johnson, Jackie Kennedy, and Robert Kennedy. As the months and years passed, he struggled to manage these volatile, crosscutting relationships. For a man already consumed at times by stress, the psychic and emotional toll of operating in the inner circle of the Johnson White House and directing the Vietnam War while consoling and confiding in Jackie and Robert Kennedy, who opposed the widening of the war, must have been tremendous. McNamara's close connections to other members of the Kennedy clan can only have added to the strain as he commiserated with and offered advice to numerous Kennedys, including Rose, the slain president's mother, Senator Edward Kennedy, and others. They made clear their devotion to him in a steady stream of cordial correspondence as he joined Johnson's inner circle.

The challenge and stress for McNamara were compounded by his own changing attitude toward the war. In the summer of 1965, when the president made the fateful decision to send combat troops to Vietnam, McNamara was a fierce advocate of doing so. "Our national honor is at stake," he insisted, according to the memoirs of Clark Clifford, who succeeded him as defense secretary in 1968. "Our withdrawal would start further probing by the Communists. We would lose all of Southeast Asia."[19] "Laos, Cambodia, Thailand, Burma, surely affect Malaysia. In 2–3 years Communist domination would stop there, but the ripple effect would be great—Japan, India. We would have to give up some bases. Ayub [President Ayub Khan of Pakistan] would move closer to China. Greece, Turkey would move to neutralist position. Communist agitation would increase in Africa."[20]

But just a few months later, according to McNamara's closest aide at the Pentagon, John McNaughton (writing in his diary in March 1966), McNamara was thinking of "leaving his post" at the Pentagon. Recently McNamara had told him: "We've made mistakes in Vietnam. . . . I've made mistakes. But the mistakes I've made are not the ones they say I've made." "The fact is," McNaughton continued, "he believes we never should have gotten into a combat role out there." And on April 8: "Bob, in an unguarded moment said, 'I want to give the order to get our troops out of there so bad that I can hardly stand it.' "[21]

McNamara's abrupt loss of hope that the war could be won is stunning. But it's equally stunning that he had any hope to lose, that after he and Kennedy had begun a drawdown of American advisers in 1963 designed to end the war two years later, McNamara would argue so strongly in July 1965 for escalation. How can we explain, first, McNamara's complicity in escalating the war, and then, his startling disenchantment with it? How, asked George Ball, the undersecretary of state, who had opposed escalation, could McNamara have seen the same flaws that Ball thought doomed the American war effort and yet argue so powerfully for intensifying it? Knowing that Ball was inclined to disagree with his proposals in front of the president, McNamara made a habit of visiting Ball privately before larger-group meetings. In these meetings, according to Ball, the defense secretary "would appear to be quite sympathetic," and McNamara would indicate that he and Ball "were fundamentally in agreement." Shortly thereafter, according to Ball, they would meet with Johnson, and McNamara would "shoot me down in flames with all these new statistics I hadn't heard before. He tried to give the impression I didn't know what I was talking about."[22] It wasn't that McNamara was being dishonest, Ball said. "It wasn't deliberate. If anything, he's a very honest man. It reflected his own schizophrenia."[23]

Schizophrenia in the medical sense of the term (disabling hallucinations and delusions) it was not. Rather, McNamara was deeply torn between wanting to win in Vietnam and wanting to withdraw from it. When he finally spoke publicly about the war nearly two decades after leaving the Pentagon, he blamed himself for not forcing the Kennedy and Johnson administrations to confront and debate the hardest questions: whether the war was worth fighting in the first place, whether it could ever be won at a cost Americans would be willing to pay, whether withdrawing from it would in fact "lose" most of Asia and trigger fatal political consequences at home. But this kind of self-criticism reveals something else about McNamara himself.

> "In retrospect," he confessed in an interview, "it is impossible for me to understand why I, as an executive who, even at that time, had more than twenty years in managing large organizations, and who understood one of the responsibilities of a manager was to be skeptical of all major arguments presented to me, and who therefore forced considerations of hard questions . . . and when he couldn't get satisfactory answers made it his responsibility to research and analyze the issue . . . I can't understand why with that background I accepted with respect to this perhaps most important single decision made in several years with respect to Vietnam [the July 1965 decision to send ground troops], why I failed to probe the underlying assumptions."[24]

Nor could he remember thirty-five years later exactly when he had concluded that the war was unwinnable militarily: "It was clear to me by some date in 1965, I believe, perhaps mid-65, certainly later in '65 . . . it was clear to me that we were not going to achieve our objective in Vietnam, in the terms that we initially had established it and at the cost we had initially estimated."[25]

McNamara's sudden shift in thinking about Vietnam was accompanied by intense emotional agitation. Buffeted by family strains, including objections to the war by his children and the anxieties of his wife, plus a growing antiwar movement in the nation, his fierce determination to compartmentalize his life—to keep personal and professional endeavors totally separate—slowly disintegrated. One Pentagon reporter later recalled a McNamara moment that seemed to capture McNamara's personality and reveal the molten person hidden under the frosty persona. Jon Rinehart, a *Time* correspondent, was interviewing the defense secretary when McNamara started talking joyfully about his days as a seaman. "Suddenly there was this warm human being in front of me," Rinehart recalled. Then, like flicking a light switch, the impersonal McNamara abruptly reappeared. "Zam, suddenly he was right back to where he always was."[26]

At the same time, Johnson was subject to periods of hyperactivity followed by immobilizing depression, all recounted by Lady Bird in a detailed and candid diary that she maintained.[27] George Reedy, who worked for Johnson as a press aide for more than a decade, including as White House press secretary from March 19, 1964, to July 8, 1965, was convinced that Johnson was manic-depressive, the term at the time for a psychological condition now known as bipolar disorder. "When he was pleased with himself, the phrase 'walking on air' really applied to him," Reedy recalled. "There would be kind of a glow, and he wouldn't see anything or anybody. He would just see his dreams. But you would get the feeling of a man whose feet were not touching the earth. I saw this several times. It always worried me, because I knew it was going to be followed by a fit of depression. I've talked to some doctors since then and described the process precisely to them, and they've all told me there's no question that he was a manic-depressive. Whenever he had a manic phase, you could be certain it would be followed by extreme depression."[28] Reedy added, "He was up-down, up-down. It was a constant with him. And usually the further up he went, the further down he went, too."[29]

Johnson also began to show signs of paranoia and alarming conduct. His press secretary Bill Moyers and speechwriter Richard Goodwin became so concerned about Johnson that they privately consulted psychiatrists. How much McNamara knew of Johnson's mood swings and paranoia, and attempted to cater to them, is unclear. Was McNamara's role in serving Johnson not unlike Lady Bird's? Was he, like her, tenacious, tireless, and patient, aware of Johnson's weaknesses as well as his strengths, loyal and protective even as his boss's moods shifted and sagged? As Lady Bird's biographer noted, only Johnson's wife knew "the full mixture of Johnson's private insecurities: his rage, his stunted ego, the deep valleys of his depressions, his hypersexuality."[30] But to the extent that McNamara saw, or sensed, Johnson's growing despair and even recognized it as akin to his own, perhaps that rendered him, paradoxically, both more determined to break away and less willing to hurt LBJ by doing so with a howl of protest.

Whatever McNamara's conscious or subconscious impulses, there seems to be no question that the critical decisions taken in mid-1965 to escalate American military operations in Vietnam were driven by two psychologically troubled men.

===

LYNDON JOHNSON WAS AN EXCEEDINGLY COMPLICATED PERSON. TO understand his character, one must trace it taking shape during his life, beginning with a nightmare he had many times as a boy. In the dream, as cited by Lady Bird Johnson's biographer, Jan Jarboe Russell, "he is a boy of fifteen seated alone in a small cage in front of a stone bench piled high with dark books. As he bent down to pick up the books, an old lady—a hag—with a mirror in her hand walked in front of the cage. It was then that he caught sight of himself in the mirror and found he had been transformed into an old man twisted and bent with long silver hair and skin with dark blotches. He pleaded with the old woman to let him out, but she turned and walked away." Each time he "awoke drenched in sweat and muttering, 'I must get away.'" According to Russell, the dream showed "how caged he felt by his father's financial failures and his mother's unhappiness," as well his mother's warning: "'Do what I say or you'll amount to nothing, like your father!'" All his life, Russell concludes, Johnson "wanted out of his cage, but he never made it, which fueled his sense of inner desperation"—until "twisted by the failure of the Vietnam War and the chaos of civil unrest, his hair long and speckled with brown spots on his flesh," he died, "having become his [own] worst nightmare."[31]

One need not buy wholesale this interpretation of Johnson's dream to see intimations of it recurring in Johnson's life. He grew up in hard-scrabble Texas Hill Country. From his early years he aspired to rise much higher, and he certainly did, but LBJ felt he had been deprived in his youth, especially compared to the well-to-do, highly educated Eastern elite with whom he worked at the top of the Kennedy administration (especially

JFK himself) and whom he kept on when he succeeded Kennedy. He was convinced that Eastern intellectuals hated him: "The men of ideas think little of me, they despise me." Even though Johnson remarked on another occasion, "my daddy always told me that if I brushed up against the grindstone of life, I'd come away with far more polish than I could ever get at Harvard and Yale. I wanted to believe him but somehow I never could."[32]

Johnson's daddy himself, too, dreamed of making it big. He succeeded for a time, first in business and then in politics. According to his son, Sam Johnson was one of the three most successful businessmen in the area, and he stood out in the Texas legislature as a tall, charismatic man who carried a long-barreled six-shooter on his hip and campaigned for populist causes. As a boy, Lyndon adored his father and was entranced by his success. As LBJ later told Doris Kearns Goodwin, "I loved going with my father to the legislature. I would sit in the gallery for hours watching all the activity on the floor and then would wander around the halls trying to figure out what was going on. The only thing I loved more was going with him on the trail during his campaigns for reelection. . . . Christ, sometimes, I wished it could go on forever."[33]

Sam Johnson overreached in what Texans called "real-estatin," went broke, and had to drop out of the legislature and take a two-dollar-a-day job as a part-time game warden to make a dent in his $40,000 debt. That made him not a model for his son but a figure of ridicule, his formerly respected family becoming, Robert Caro reports, "the laughingstock of the town."[34]

Johnson's mother, Rebekah, better educated than her husband, graduated from Baylor University and taught elocution in Fredericksburg while stringing for the Austin, Texas, newspaper. She was, her son Sam Jr. wrote, "probably the best educated woman in the whole county," as ethereal, Caro adds, as Johnson women were earthy, while her husband was the "opposite—loud and boisterous, impatient and cursed with a fierce temper." Their marriage, according to Lyndon's cousin Ava, was a "misfit," but she wanted to make the best of it because "she loved him. And he loved her. Oh, he adored her. He worshipped the ground she walked on."[35]

Reduced to poverty and burdened by debt, Lyndon's mother turned away from her husband and invested her hopes in her son. "Everything was competition for Lyndon," cousin Ava recalled. "He had to win." A friend of Lyndon's regarded him as a "natural born leader," but "if he didn't lead, he didn't care much about playing." Added another boy: "Lyndon wasn't worth a darn as a pitcher, but if we didn't let him pitch, he'd take his ball [the only one available] and go home. So, yeah, we let him pitch."[36] Lyndon remembered that his mother's love for him made him feel "big and important. It made me believe that I could do anything in the whole world."[37] One day during recess at school, his teacher recalled, "All of a sudden, Lyndon looked up at the blue sky and said, 'Someday, I'm going to be President of the United States.' We hadn't been talking about politics or the presidency or anything like that. He just came out with it."[38]

While Johnson's mother conditioned her love on his success, his father's fate underlined the terrible cost of failure. But something else he inherited from his parents complicated his efforts to succeed: both of them suffered from "disabling depressions," in his father's case following upon his manic rise in business and politics.[39]

Lyndon resisted learning in school and didn't do his homework, leading his father to shout angrily at his wife, "That boy of yours isn't worth a damn, Rebekah. He'll never amount to anything. He'll never amount to a Goddamned thing!"—a phrase that must have hurt even more later on when Lyndon's father, whom he had so idolized, sank to that depth himself.[40]

Lyndon's college experience set the pattern that characterized him as an adult. Southwest Texas State Teachers College at San Marcos wasn't an elite institution. It graduated its first class in 1927, the year that Johnson enrolled. Only one of its professors had a doctorate and several faculty members had no degree at all. "It was a poor boys' school," an alumnus said, "most of the kids were there because they couldn't afford to go elsewhere." Johnson was "one scared chicken," remembered Ava, who stood in line with him when he waited to register for college.[41] But before long, he took San Marcos by storm.

To his classmates Johnson seemed always in motion, "always in high gallop," "with long loping strides," "swinging them long arms, just walking like the seat of his britches was on fire," "clamoring for recognition." Students began referring to him as "Bull" Johnson. "Because he was so full of bullshit, manure." The *College Star*'s humor column defined "Bull" as "Greek philosophy in which Lyndon Johnson has an M.B. degree." "'Master of Bullshit'—that's what M.B. means. He was known as the biggest liar on the campus."[42]

Johnson "bulled" his way into leading roles in almost every college activity and group. But it helped that he could also be charming, persuasive, and warm. The proprietress of the boardinghouse where he lived recalled how he dominated conversation at the dinner table: "He'd just interrupt you—my God, his voice would just ride over you until you stopped. He monopolized the conversation from the time he came in until the time he left." But he also entertained his tablemates with colorful political tales and spot-on imitations of people they knew and of well-known Texas politicians. "Lyndon would drape that big arm around you and he'd get his mouth about an inch from yours and look you right in the eye," a classmate recalled. That could be intimidating, but another one remembered, "He was so warm and affectionate, he grabbed my mother and kissed her, and my sisters—my father said, 'That boy you brought down here—I thought he was going to kiss *me*.' "[43]

Johnson didn't kiss his teachers, but he sucked up to them shamelessly. As editor of the *College Star*, he flattered faculty members. Dean of Women Mary C. Bragdon was a merciless monitor of campus morals, but Johnson's newspaper hailed the cafeteria refreshments she provided after a literary society gathering as "the best part of the whole evening and the boys think she is one of the best sports on the hill." "Prexy" Cecil Eugene Evans, whose boring, pedantic speeches were infamous, emerged in a front-page student newspaper editorial as "great as an educator and as an executive," but "greatest as a man." Johnson attached notes to his written exams designed to butter up his graders. His English teacher, Mrs. V. S. Netterville, who was a devout Baptist, replied to one such note from her otherwise nonreligious flatterer as follows: "To have led you through your study of Robert Browning in such a way as to have strengthened your faith is the best reward I could ask for. . . . May God continue to bless you and keep you always a firm believer." President Evans was so impressed that he allowed Johnson, who was strapped for funds, to live rent-free above his garage and paid him double the usual wage to paint the apartment—four times in the course of one term.[44]

Despite all this hyperactivity, or rather, in alternation with it, Johnson was plagued at San Marcos by depression. "Normally, Lyndon was so outgoing, so bubbling, so loud," Ethel Davis remembered, "but sometimes he would turn quiet, and stay quiet all day, and when Lyndon was quiet like that, you see he was *really* down." Sometimes, Caro adds, those "down" periods were correlated with the absence of letters from Johnson's mother, to whom he wrote several times a week, and who generally wrote him almost every day. "Dearest Mother," he once wrote her, "You can't realize the difference in atmosphere after one of your sweet letters. I know of nothing so stimulating and inspiring to me as one of your encouraging and beautifully-written letters. . . . Mother, I love you so. Don't neglect me." To his father, who had told him: "You don't have enough sense to take a college education," Lyndon wrote nothing. "Damn, I wanted to show him!" he would recall. When he got respectable grades during his second term at college, he "took them home—they were on a little yellow card—and I threw them down in front of him and said, 'Does that look like I've got enough sense to take a college education?'"[45]

Johnson's warmth and capacity for empathy emerged more clearly during a year (1928–1929) he took off from college to teach in Cotulla, a small town 130 miles south of San Marcos, where his students were mostly poor Mexican Americans. He needed to make money to pay his San Marcos tuition. As the only male on a staff of four teachers, he was named principal at the age of twenty. But he set out to lift up the student body. He established extracurricular activities such as public speaking, debate, spelling bees, band, baseball, and a parent-teacher association. He encouraged children to think they could rise in life as he himself was intent on doing. Both students and teachers were said to be "crazy about him." "He put us to work," said one pupil, "but he was the kind of teacher you wanted to work for." "This may sound strange but a lot of us felt he was too good for us." Recalled another: "We wanted to take advantage of his being here. It was like a blessing from the clear sky."[46] But, far from his mother and his friends, Johnson was lonely. "Occasionally," reports Caro, "he would get very quiet and stay quiet, sometimes for days. People would see him wandering up the rise in back of town, a tall, skinny, awkward figure staring into those endless, empty distances."[47]

After graduating from San Marcos, Johnson served for a year as a speech and debate coach at a Houston high school, where he impressed his colleagues and students as "a steam engine in pants."[48] He was, in other words, a great success, but his first love, politics, soon beckoned. During his last semester at San Marcos, he got involved in a state Senate campaign and in the fall of 1931, he accepted an appointment as secretary to newly elected US congressman Richard Kleberg, who was also a member of the wealthy family that owned the massive King Ranch in south Texas. Since Kleberg wasn't that interested in legislating, he left Johnson largely in charge of his office. And Johnson charged into that vacuum.

To get to know other congressional aides who lived in overcrowded rooms at the Dodge Hotel and shared communal showers and toilets, he showered four times one day so as to meet several others living there. The next day he washed his face and brushed his teeth five times in the course of fifty minutes to meet his other neighbors. He was soon beating them all to work in the morning. He didn't stop for lunch (which he ate at his desk), and he stayed later than most of the others at night, calling people nearly nonstop and chortling with his secretary, Estelle Harbin, when he got what he wanted. "He had charm to burn," Harbin recalled. "Very soon he had a real pipeline to all the bureaus. And he wouldn't take no for an answer—he would pursue these things like it was life and death. And when he got something for somebody—when we could write and tell somebody that they could look forward to getting something—that was a real victory. He'd put down the phone—'*Stelle! Yay!*' He'd practically jump up and down."[49]

Johnson recruited former students of his in Houston to work with him in Washington. Recalled Gene Latimer: "He can be mean. He can make people cry. He can make you feel so bad you could go out and shoot yourself." But Latimer "had so much respect for the man. I don't know any other man I had so much respect for.... He can make you cry, he can make you laugh—he can do anything."[50] One of the things Johnson could do was humiliate another former Houston student, L. E. Jones, whose spotless attire (in starched dress shirts and double-breasted suits) signaled that, as a friend put it, "any kind of coarseness or crudeness just disgusted him." Johnson made him take dictation while Johnson sat on the toilet—a practice to which he would subject victims far more distinguished than Jones in the White House.[51]

But Johnson himself sometimes seemed victimized. In the absence of letters from his mother, said Estelle Harbin, "you could see him get quiet and homesick." Even when such letters came regularly, he could "get quiet." Lyndon "could get very low." "When he got real quiet, it was bad." She thought it was related to his "burning ambition to be somebody. He didn't know what he wanted to be, but he wanted to be *somebody*. He couldn't stand not being somebody—just could not *stand* it." That's why he could be hurt by an unintended insult. "He was very sensitive to the other person, and he was very sensitive himself. And he was very, very easily hurt." "Sometimes," Harbin added, "I felt very sorry for him."[52]

Claudia Alta Taylor, otherwise known as Lady Bird, or just Bird to her friends, didn't feel sorry for Johnson when they first met in 1934. "He was so dynamic and so insistent," she recalled. "He came on very strong and my first instinct was to withdraw."[53] Lady Bird was four years older than Johnson, from a wealthy family, better educated than he (with two degrees, in liberal arts and journalism, from the University of Texas at Austin), more widely traveled (having sailed from Galveston to New York City), and more interested in books and ideas. But she was shy, and was shocked on their first date when, after bombarding her with questions and boasting about his plans to become somebody, he proposed marriage to her. She wasn't ready, of course, but she saw in him, her biographer reports, "a man who was exactly where she wanted to be—powerfully situated in the middle of things."[54]

He could lift her up, but she also understood, with the help of a squall of letters he wrote her from Washington during the next few weeks, that she would have to stabilize him. The letters made clear, according to Betty

Boyd Caroli (author of a book about the Johnsons' marriage), who read them after they were released in 2013, that Johnson "was often sick, and he lived on a seesaw, with his moods shifting wildly from top-of-the-world, when he thought he could do anything, to very low, when he registered only doom and failure." One day he felt so "blue and depressed" that he came home from the office at 3:30 and went to bed. He doubted his "own perseverance, willpower and self-control" and regretted his "moodiness," especially his "always feeling blue" when he didn't hear from her. He wanted a woman "who loved me, would pet me, and be as affectionate as I am," someone "to nurse me" and "help me climb." In her replies to these letters, she assumed the cheerleading, enabling role she would play throughout their married life. After he announced in a letter, "For weeks I've only halfheartedly done anything," she ordered him to "Stop it! (That's a command!)" In contrast to Johnson, who wrote that he felt like a "little sick man," like a child "wanting to be with his mother," she rarely got sick. In fact, she was to discover she was stronger than her seemingly overpowering man.[55]

In 1935, Johnson was appointed head of the Texas branch of the National Youth Administration, which supported educational and job opportunities for young people, a position in which he honed his patented practice of both abusing and inspiring his staff simultaneously. Recalled Ernest Morgan, a young San Marcos graduate: "Listening to him, I heard every curse word I had ever heard, and some combinations I had *never* heard. God, he could rip a man up and down." As Caro points out, "not all the rage was real." Sometimes, "seemingly out of control," he would answer the phone with a voice that was "soft and calm, and if the caller was important, deferential."[56]

Having seen Washington close up, Johnson thirsted to return as a congressman in his own right, and he succeeded in 1937. Ed Clark had worked in other campaigns before, but remembered Johnson's as unique. "I never saw anyone campaign as hard as that," Clark recalled. "I never thought it was *possible* for anyone to work that hard."[57] He wasn't a great legislator; he didn't introduce much if any legislation. But he was a "political genius" in the sense, Caro reports, that he had the ability "to look at an organization and see in it political potentialities that no one else saw, to transform that organization into a political force, and to reap from that transformation personal advantage."[58] He looked at President Roosevelt, saw how he could be useful to FDR's campaigns, and turned the president's gratitude into invaluable support for his own.

Roosevelt backed Johnson's run for the US Senate in 1941, but to no avail. Texas governor "Pappy" O'Daniel's victory threw Johnson into another slough of despond; in fact, he first fell into it when a poll showed him trailing badly. The poll "made me feel mighty bad," Johnson recalled. "I know that my throat got bad on me, and I had to spend a few days in the hospital." Two weeks, actually, and although his aide John Connally blamed "pneumonia" and another labeled it "nervous exhaustion," Lady Bird said, "He was depressed, and it was bad."[59] But after new polling showed Johnson in the lead, Caro writes, Johnson's "mood soared upward to euphoria as fast as it had plummeted into depression five weeks before."[60]

The years 1941 to 1948 were the bleakest yet for LBJ, years of "hopelessness and despair," Caro writes, when "he came to the very verge of abandoning politics for a full-time business career."[61] Trapped in a job he had seen only as a stepping stone to bigger things, he pushed himself during the war into a role as an observer of a single Pacific bombing run, and then portrayed it as having been in combat. After the war, according to Caro, Johnson's "moods soared and sank, but when they sank now, they seemed to sink lower—and last longer." The prospect of running for the Senate in 1948 was daunting since he would have to give up his House seat. So, "at first," he later told Doris Kearns Goodwin, "I just could not bear the thought of losing everything."[62] In the end he ran and managed to defeat a popular governor, Coke Stevenson, by fair means and foul, and that put him in position to "master" the Senate as he had tamed lesser institutions before. (Caro's second volume, *Means of Ascent*, is devoted to this campaign.) For a Senate newcomer to swiftly become a dominating majority leader was miraculous. Looking back at her husband's time as a senator from 1948 to 1960, Lady Bird said, "Those were the happiest years of our lives."[63] But these years, too, were marked by more dramatic mood swings—from frenetic efforts to mobilize legislators to pass legislation, to a dinner party at which Russell Baker watched Johnson "chain smoking one cigarette on top of another and pouring down Scotch whiskey like a man who had a date with a firing squad,"[64] to periods of depression in 1955 and 1958.

Six months after his election as majority leader of the Senate in January 1955, Johnson suffered a massive heart attack, followed by an extended period of acute depression. Knowing that men in his family had died young, he had long dreaded such an event, and now that it had occurred, he feared it would end his political career. Caro said that once Johnson returned to his ranch from a prolonged and melancholy stay at the hospital after the heart episode, he "fell into a despair deeper than his despair in the hospital."[65] Depression is common among heart attack victims, but doctors told Johnson aides George Reedy and Walter Jenkins that Johnson's was particularly deep. "He felt," recalled Jenkins, "if he had any chance to be President or Vice President or something, that this had ended it. " Johnson remained in the hospital for five weeks (accompanied by Lady Bird, who went home only twice during that time), often so depressed that Jenkins feared "that he would kind of give up, maybe wouldn't make the effort to [recover]. I thought he would just say, 'This is it. I've had it.' "[66]

George Reedy thought LBJ was experiencing a midlife crisis: "He used to tell me that he saw his life as a race in three parts: the first third he had to rush to position himself for further advancement, the second he had to work like hell and accumulate power and money, and in the third he could relax."[67] The heart attack threatened to derail this sequence.

Three years later, his beloved mother's death at age seventy-eight, together with his own fiftieth birthday, reawakened his own fear of death, triggering what Reedy called "a pattern of conduct that indicated beyond doubt a desire to revert to childhood. He intermingled almost daily childish tantrums; threats of resignation . . . wild drinking bouts; a remarkably nonpaternal yen for young girls; and an almost frantic desire to be in the company of young people."[68]

By 1960, he had not only recovered but was seeking the Democratic nomination for president. He didn't get it, of course, and had to settle for being John F. Kennedy's running mate and serving as vice president. The pinnacle for Johnson was the presidency itself. The vice presidency under the young, virile John Kennedy seemed the end of the line. Instead of being exhilarated by the prospect of being one step away from the presidency, he experienced another bout of depression, marked, according to Reedy, by "the heaviest period of boozing" in his life, by his staff having "to lift him physically out of bed and pump his arms up and down to stimulate breathing and make him functional," and one night when, fortified by liquor, "he went on an incredible toot . . . wandered up and down the [hotel] corridors" and flopped into bed with one of his secretaries trying "to snuggle into her arms the same way a small child will snuggle into its mother's arms."[69] According to Reedy, Johnson drank more and more and spent entire days in bed at home staring at the ceiling. "He just couldn't accept anything short of being President. It was like a demon in him."[70]

What petrified Johnson about being vice president was that, given Kennedy's youth, by the time the presidency opened up again in 1968 Johnson himself would almost surely be too old and ill to achieve it. What's more, his vice presidency itself turned out be a miserable experience. Johnson tried to maintain his mastery of the Senate by preserving his powers and privileges there. "That's where I can do Jack Kennedy the most good," he told his aide Bobby Baker, since "all those Bostons and Harvards don't know any more about Capitol Hill than an old maid does about fucking."[71] But senators who had obeyed him as majority leader refused to let the executive branch encroach on their legislative turf. Kennedy counted on the trappings of power to keep Johnson happy, giving him a six-room suite of offices in the Executive Office Building next to the White House, inviting him to attend pre-press conference briefings, cabinet meetings, and National Security Council meetings as required by law. JFK told his aide Kenny O'Donnell, "You are dealing with a very insecure, sensitive man with a huge ego. I want you literally to kiss his ass from one end of Washington to the other."

But that, plus other assignments like goodwill trips to foreign countries, wasn't enough to keep Johnson happy. He knew the president's men despised him and secretly mocked him as "Uncle Cornpone" or "Rufus

Cornpone"—even as he thought of JFK as a "whippersnapper" who "never said a word of importance in the Senate" but still "managed to create the image of himself as shining intellectual, a youthful leader who would change the face of the country," as a "sonny boy," a "lightweight" who could use "a little gray in his hair."[72]

Johnson played only a minor role in the administration's deliberations on the Cuban missile crisis. Unlike top members of the administration like McNamara, he was almost never invited to take part in a seminar addressed by intellectual luminaries at Robert Kennedy's Hickory Hill estate. Wilbur Mills, chair of the House Ways and Means Committee, thought the president "had more or less shelved the Vice President... turned him out to pasture." Daniel Patrick Moynihan recalled looking in Johnson's eyes and thinking, "This is a bull castrated very late in life." Johnson's response was passive-aggressive; he mostly remained silent at cabinet meetings and spoke so softly that he could hardly be heard. His listeners suspected this was a tactic designed to make them pity him and respond to his distress—which old friends like Jim Rowe confirm Johnson had previously used to get what he wanted—but given how he was being treated, it was almost certainly more than just a tactic. In any case, it didn't get him the respect he craved.[73]

Kennedy's assassination catapulted Johnson into the presidency. But instead of feeling triumphant, he was often left feeling defeated and depressed by the overwhelming demands of the office and the prospect of failing to live up to them. In the summer of 1964, about to be nominated for his own full term as president but consumed by fear that the country wanted Bobby Kennedy, not him, as its leader, Johnson confessed his doubts to his trusted aide Walter Jenkins: "I don't think a white Southerner is the man to unite this nation in this hour. I don't know who is, and I don't even want the responsibilities.... I've had doubts about whether a man born where I was born, raised like I was raised, could ever satisfy the Northern Jews, Catholics and union people." "I do not believe, Walter, that I can physically and mentally... Goldwater's had a couple of nervous breakdowns, and I don't want to be in this place.... I do not believe I can physically and mentally carry the responsibilities of the bomb, and the world and the Nigras and the South, and so on and so forth."[74]

As late as August 26, 1964, with the Democratic convention in Atlantic City about to launch him toward a second term, Johnson confessed to Jenkins: "I don't see any reason I ought to seek the right to endure the anguish of being here. They think I want great power. What I want is great solace and a little love, that's all I want."[75]

Johnson did run for president, of course, and won in a landslide. But three days after his inauguration, he was hospitalized after a cold and cough triggered chest pains again. Lady Bird welcomed the several days he stayed in the hospital as "the Lord giving him an enforced rest."[76] But two months later, distressed by the situation in Vietnam, Johnson was looking forward to not running again in 1968. Too troubled to sleep, he would enter Lady Bird's adjoining bedroom and agonize about the war. "We can't get out," he complained, "and we can't finish it." On March 7, 1965, she confided to her diary her own discouragement ("I have been swimming upstream against a feeling of depression") and that "Lyndon lives in a cloud of troubles, with a few rays of light."[77]

GIVEN JOHNSON'S DEEP PSYCHOLOGICAL ISSUES AND INSECURITY, it is no wonder that he came to see the ultraefficient and seemingly superconfident McNamara as an invaluable lieutenant. But McNamara treasured Johnson's extravagant attention and approbation as confirmation of McNamara's own self-worth. From the outset of the Kennedy administration, Johnson had been impressed by "the fellow from Ford with the Stacomb on his hair." Presidential admiration only grew after Johnson took over. According to Lady Bird, "There is nobody he is more at home with, more fond of, more respectful of in this Administration than Bob McNamara." "If I got word that Bob had died or quit," Johnson confessed to his wife, "I don't believe I could go on with this job." According to Brian VanDeMark, "Every time McNamara was on a mission to Vietnam, noted Lady Bird, Lyndon spoke of how frightened he was: 'I lie awake until he gets back.'"[78]

In 1965, Johnson said of his defense secretary:

He is always prompt and always prepared. He does his homework.
He is an expert on economic matters, prices, strikes, taxes and other
things as well as defense. He is the strongest poverty and Head Start
man except for Shriver. He is the first one at work and the last one
to leave. When I wake up, the first one I call is McNamara. He is
there at seven every morning including Saturday. The only difference is that Saturday he wears a sport coat. He is the best utility
man. I would make him Secretary of State or Secretary of Transportation tomorrow—he is that qualified. He is smart, patriotic, works
hard. . . . And he always advises me where I'm wrong, although most
Cabinet officers do not. If I had my way he would play more, have
more personal friends, be a little more sentimental. He's like a jack-
hammer. He drills through granite rock until he's there. Limitations? One would be health. No human can take what he takes, he
drives too hard. He is too perfect. [Georgia Senator Richard] Russell
says he is too good, that he wishes he would stumble once.[79]

Typical of McNamara's winning performances was the occasion when
Johnson met with aides to talk about a possible railway strike. When the
president asked how much one of the union's complex wage-increase proposals would cost railroad management, McNamara did some lightning
calculations in his head and volunteered an answer within five seconds.
Five minutes later, after working the numbers on paper, Labor Department officials at the meeting confirmed McNamara's answer. "Thanks,
Bob," Johnson said.[80] Johnson even considered the defense secretary as a
possible running mate in the upcoming 1964 presidential election. Johnson showered McNamara with extravagant flattery. After McNamara
spent seven hours testifying before the House Armed Services Committee in January 1964, he spoke with Johnson about a range of national security issues, including Vietnam. Johnson told him, "Good God Almighty,
I salute you again. You're the most unbelievable man I know."[81] Three
months later: "I think that you're one of the strongest men in this country,

and I'm not just flattering you now. I'm just giving you my appraisal."[82] Three years later Johnson told an interviewer, "If you asked those boys in the cabinet to run through a buzz saw for their President, Bob McNamara would be the first to go through it."[83]

McNamara was not the only Kennedy man whom LBJ cultivated. He could tell how the others felt without Kennedy from "the looks on their faces and the sound of their voices." Suddenly "they were outsiders just as I had been for almost three years, outsiders on the inside." So he was determined "to keep them informed, determined to keep them busy. I constantly requested their advice and asked for their help." He "honored his staff," as Kearns put it, with "benevolent intimacies," such as "personal intimacy, access to the presidential office, power for themselves."[84]

But some of the Kennedy men were easier to win over than others. Rusk, according to Johnson aide Harry McPherson, was "easier to win and more genuinely won because he had been treated not too elegantly by the Kennedys." Bundy, just the kind of upper-class Harvard man who Johnson assumed despised him, was a bigger challenge. McNamara, Harvard-connected but of more humble origins, needed to be wooed, but was entirely gettable. Johnson telephoned McNamara repeatedly at the Pentagon, at home at night, and when the McNamaras were vacationing in Aspen. Craig McNamara remembers that Johnson often called on Sundays, his father's one day with his family, ordering the family to abandon the hamburgers they were grilling and hurry to the White House for lunch. Or he would suddenly summon them to Camp David for the weekend. Johnson was particularly fascinated by McNamara's mastery of statistics. Presidential aide Jack Valenti recalled meetings where Johnson asked McNamara some challenging economic question. When McNamara answered without skipping a beat, the president then met "the eyes of the other men around the long, polished table with an expression of pleasure and pride [that Valenti] took to mean: Isn't he amazing? And he is *mine*."[85]

So dazzled was Johnson with his defense secretary's brilliance that he not only relied on him to run the Pentagon and the Vietnam War but almost anything else that struck the president's fancy, such as the nondefense program to develop a supersonic transport plane (SST) that otherwise was managed by the Federal Aviation Administration. No wonder FAA administrator Najeeb Halaby (who strongly favored the SST, whereas McNamara didn't) dubbed McNamara "executive vice-president of the United States."[86] In early August, as he was preparing for the Democratic convention, Johnson actually asked McNamara to fill precisely that expansive role. "I want you to think how you can do it without getting in their hair, and I know you're not looking for any more assignments. And I've overloaded you now, and I don't want you to have a breakdown. But I want you to think—this administration coming up—what you can do as my executive vice president to help me direct this Cabinet." McNamara said he doubted the job could be handled by a cabinet member, suggesting a White House official would be better suited, but he would think about it.[87] Johnson never elevated McNamara to the imagined post, though McNamara often got involved in government affairs far removed from the defense secretary's responsibilities.

But Johnson could also be brutal in his handling of aides, just as he had been when dealing with fellow senators. Johnson wanted "real loyalty" from his top associates: "I want someone who will kiss my ass in a Macy's window and stand up and say, 'Boy, wasn't that sweet!'" But that discouraged them from telling him unpleasant truths he needed to hear. Johnson was a masterly reader of other men—"of their strengths and weaknesses and hopes and fears," Caro remarks, "what it was that the man wanted—not what he said he wanted but what he *really* wanted—and what it was that the man feared, *really* feared."[88] Adds Doris Kearns Goodwin: LBJ "shaped a composite mental portrait of every Senator," including "how he liked his liquor, how he felt about his wife and family, and, most important, how he felt about himself."[89] Johnson failed in his effort to recruit congressional aide Bryce Harlow because Harlow knew "Lyndon would maneuver people into positions of dependency and vulnerability so he could do what he wanted with them."[90] Recalled Hubert Humphrey on the basis of personal experience: Johnson was like "a psychiatrist." He knew how "to appeal" to every senator's "vanity, to their needs, to their ambitions."[91]

Johnson subjected some Kennedy administration veterans to personal indignity—inviting them (badgering them, actually) to swim nude with him in the White House pool, holding conversations with them in the bathroom as he sat on the toilet, relishing the sight, he told Richard Goodwin, of McGeorge Bundy—"one of the delicate Kennedyites"—"who came into the bathroom with me and then found it utterly impossible to look at me as I sat on the toilet." Johnson went on, "You'd think he had never seen those parts of the body before. For there he was, standing as far away from me as he possibly could, keeping his back to me the whole time, trying to carry on a conversation. I could barely hear a word he said. I kept straining my ears and then finally asked him to come a little closer to me. Then began the most ludicrous scene I had ever witnessed. Instead of simply turning around and walking over to me, he kept his face away from me and walked backward, one rickety step at a time. For a moment there I thought he was going to run right into me. It certainly made me wonder how that man had made it so far in the world."[92]

Johnson's press secretary, Bill Moyers, later insisted he never saw Johnson bully McNamara the way he did other aides.[93] But former secretary of state Dean Acheson reportedly saw Johnson "squeeze [McNamara] like a lemon" at a meeting. And Bobby Kennedy was appalled that after a long session at which Johnson browbeat his cabinet members to testify to how they were lowering costs by "turning out lights and things," McNamara characterized the session as a "fine meeting." As Kennedy put it, Johnson was "able to eat people up, even people who were considered rather strong figures—I mean, as I saw, Mac Bundy or Bob McNamara. . . . They've just—nothing left of them."[94]

In a 1994 interview McNamara insisted, "Johnson knew he couldn't rule me, he knew goddam well that I would leave if we didn't develop a constructive relationship."[95] The fact that McNamara had made enough money at Ford to live on in Washington, and that he could have easily found other lucrative employment if he left the Pentagon, "allowed me to say things to [Kennedy and Johnson] that perhaps others without that—I'll call it—self confidence—would not have said. So I was able to say to Johnson, 'I think you're wrong.'" McNamara admitted how hard it was to do so—that "it takes a lot of guts, a lot of knowledge and a lot of honesty."[96] Perhaps so, but he didn't admit how often he himself failed to say directly what he knew Johnson didn't want to hear or how he tailored his views so they coincided with Johnson's.

McNamara was particularly vulnerable to Johnson's blend of rough tactics and blandishments because of his abiding need to excel and succeed. His efforts to cultivate Johnson and win his favor, especially during the first years of the Johnson administration, were evident in many of their conversations, as McNamara frequently flattered the president about his handling of press conferences and other matters. "Mr. President," he told Johnson five months after the Kennedy assassination, "I don't want to bother you but I just want to say that was a terrific performance. By far the best news conference to date. Just magnificent, I thought."[97] The day after Johnson overwhelmingly won election to a full term, McNamara called him to say it was "a tremendous accomplishment, Mr. President. I think—the newspaper reports and the columnists report that it's the greatest political achievement of this century."[98] McNamara was almost always deferential to Johnson, at times solicitous, even obsequious—not uncommon traits among presidential aides. He was quick to assure the president that he would carry out his wishes, whether accommodating powerful congressional committee chairmen about budgetary matters, postponing base closings, or ensuring that the Pentagon ordered sufficient amounts of beef in response to congressional pressure on Johnson from the beef industry. He rarely hesitated to respond to Johnson's requests for advice on all manner of issues, including international trade and the selection of ambassadors to the Soviet Union, not normally questions for the secretary of defense. It seems clear from dozens of these calls how much the two men admired one another and depended on each other—and how much McNamara wanted to please his boss and keep his job.

But Johnson's periodic opprobrium reminded McNamara of what he, too, could face if he fell short. Early in 1964, Johnson caustically reminded McNamara that Kennedy and McNamara at one time had favored withdrawing American forces from Vietnam. "I always thought it was foolish for you to make any statements about withdrawing," Johnson said. "I thought it was bad psychologically. But you and the President thought otherwise and I just sat silent." McNamara began to reply ("The problem is—") but Johnson cut him off: "How in hell does McNamara think, when he's losing a war, that he can pull men out of there?"[99]

McNamara needed to look no further than the example of Vice President Hubert Humphrey. After Humphrey urged Johnson to wind down the war in 1965, the president excluded him from Vietnam policy making deliberations for months—until the penitent vice president became an enthusiastic booster of Johnson's war policies.

Another reason for McNamara's loyalty to Johnson was his genuine admiration for LBJ—which was also useful to McNamara. Taking his cue from others in Kennedy's inner circle, he had kept his distance from Vice President Johnson. But McNamara had always supported efforts to help disadvantaged Americans, especially African Americans, and Johnson, he now learned, saw his role as "identifying differences" among Americans and then "reconciling them so the country could move forward toward a better life for all"—just what the nation needed most during "a period of growing racial unrest and persistent economic inequalities."[100] McNamara was present when Johnson "personally got that [Civil Rights] bill through a Senate that was absolutely opposed to it. He prevented this country from destroying itself. Could Kennedy have done that? I don't know."[101]

But if Johnson was a master of domestic politics, his changeable stance on Vietnam, quite possibly a by-product of his shifting personal moods, struck McNamara as dangerous for the country. In a December 1966 conversation with British journalist Henry Brandon, McNamara lamented that the president "is not decisive enough, not a strong leader. . . . He has difficulty making up his mind, he procrastinates, delays, and then misses too many opportunities. He is not imaginatively daring, though this is the time to be."[102] By the end of 1966, McNamara wanted his boss to push harder for negotiations that might end the war in Vietnam, but the same sense of Johnson's indecisiveness may have animated McNamara's push for escalation in the spring of 1965. Was McNamara's willingness to push Johnson limited by his determination to preserve his own position? His wife, Margy, thought so. In late 1966, she shared her thoughts with Brandon, who recalled, "She confirmed that Bob wants to get out of VN as quickly as possible. She said he still feels he must prove something, he is so concerned about himself that he will not stand up and defend and fight for others."[103] Or as John Kenneth Galbraith, a confidant of John Kennedy and friend of the McNamaras, described McNamara: "He is an organization man who, once a decision is taken, accepts and supports it. He does not fight, as some Cabinet members do, a guerrilla war within the Administration."[104]

In a 2001 interview, McNamara said, "I had tremendous affection and respect for Johnson." "He and I got along wonderfully well."[105] But on another occasion, in 1995, his description of Johnson was positively Shakespearean: "Lyndon Baines Johnson was one of the most complex, intelligent, and hardworking individuals I have ever known. He possessed a kaleidoscopic personality: by turns open and devious, loving and mean, compassionate and tough, gentle and cruel. He was a towering, powerful, paradoxical figure."[106]

That assessment was nowhere more fitting for Johnson than in his far-reaching decisions in 1965 to commit America to war in Vietnam, decisions that McNamara encouraged and abetted even as he came to doubt their wisdom.

CHAPTER NINE

Turning Points

As Johnson settled into the presidency in 1964, hoping to focus on domestic issues like civil rights and poverty, he was drawn inexorably into managing Cold War challenges, including the conflict in Vietnam. Inexperienced in national security policy, sidelined on defense matters during the Kennedy administration by a national security team that disdained his advice, he struggled to fashion a coherent approach to Vietnam. He often seemed of two minds about the conflict, eager to wield American power decisively to preserve the independence of South Vietnam, yet hesitant to send American troops into combat. He deeply feared becoming the first American president to lose a foreign war, and the political consequences that might follow. And he was convinced that defeat in Vietnam would lead to a wave of Communist conquests in Southeast Asia and beyond. At the same time, he could see that the government of South Vietnam was an unreliable partner lacking support among its own people and that winning a ground war in the jungles of Vietnam would be grueling. He understood from the outset that the maximum use of American power—invading North Vietnam, possibly using nuclear weapons—was untenable because it could lead to war with China or the Soviet Union.

His ambivalence showed. One day, he would tell aides to settle for nothing less than victory in Vietnam. Another day, he would confide with anguish to friends that the war was unwinnable militarily but he couldn't see a way out. He ordered American warplanes to bomb enemy targets in South Vietnam and North Vietnam, then told his wife he doubted his will to serve as commander in chief dispatching American boys in harm's way. As the weeks passed, Johnson tilted more and more toward war, abetted by McNamara, Rusk, and Bundy, all of whom shared his concern about the Communist threat and advised him to take military steps they deemed necessary to reverse what they saw as North Vietnamese aggression in South Vietnam. At each stage of escalation, Johnson and his men dug themselves deeper into the quicksand of Vietnam, navigating what they viewed as a middle course between the full use of American power and a humiliating retreat.

The turning points kept coming:

The August 1964 Gulf of Tonkin incident, when Johnson and McNamara assured the nation that American destroyers had come under unprovoked attack off the North Vietnamese coast even though they perceived that covert CIA-sponsored South Vietnamese operations might have provoked the incident. They also realized navy commanders were unsure if the attacks had actually occurred. Johnson nevertheless ordered retaliatory strikes and secured nearly unanimous congressional approval for a resolution that handed him open-ended power to use military force in Vietnam.

The February 1965 decision to unleash American warplanes against North Vietnamese targets after a North Vietnamese attack on an American base while Bundy was in South Vietnam, the beginning of the American air war against North Vietnam.

The fateful July 1965 decision to send tens of thousands of American combat troops to Vietnam, increasing the number of American ground forces in South Vietnam from tens of thousands of "advisers" to hundreds of thousands of combat troops, with more promised.

McNamara championed all these decisions. But over time he himself reached a personal turning point as he came to see that the war was unwinnable with the strategy Washington had set. By the fall of 1965 he started pushing for bombing pauses and diplomatic initiatives but acted inconsistently and weakly, as if frozen within a Johnson force field and his own irresolution. His quandary was exacerbated by his continuing relationships with Jackie and Bobby Kennedy and their rising pressure on him to deescalate the war. The closer he got to them, the greater grew his concerns about Vietnam. Johnson, well aware of McNamara's ties to the Kennedys, enlisted him to inform on them. He did so. He was walking a psychologically and emotionally treacherous tightrope.

——

JOHNSON'S INITIAL APPROACH TO THE VIETNAM WAR ECHOED JOHN Kennedy's ambivalence. Following his only trip to Vietnam as vice president in May 1961, he reported that if the battle against Communism were not "joined in Southeast Asia with strength and determination," the United States might as well "throw in the towel," "pull back our defenses to San Francisco," and watch "the vast Pacific become a Red Sea." But the dispatch of US troops to Vietnam was "not only not required" but "not desirable." After becoming president, aware of his own unfamiliarity with foreign policy, he implored Kennedy's troika of Rusk, McNamara, and Bundy to stay on after JFK's assassination.[1] (He also needed them to appeal to the Eastern Establishment, he later told Doris Kearns Goodwin, since "without them I would have lost my link to John Kennedy, and without that I would have had absolutely no chance of gaining support of the media, or the Easterners or the intellectuals."[2]) He thought he faced the same Vietnam conundrum that Kennedy encountered—that the war might not be winnable, but it had to be fought. Just two days after Kennedy's assassination, following Johnson's first meeting with his Vietnam advisers, he described Vietnam as "going to hell in a handbasket." Having told Ambassador Lodge "to go back and tell those generals in Saigon that Lyndon Johnson intends to stand by our word ... I want 'em to get off their butts and get out in those jungles and whip hell out of some Communists," Johnson felt like "I just grabbed a big juicy worm with a right sharp hook in the middle of it."[3]

McNamara noticed Johnson's "tone for action" in Vietnam at the meeting two days after Kennedy's death. According to CIA director John McCone's notes on the meeting, Johnson "was anxious to get along, win the war—he didn't want as much effort placed on social reforms" in Vietnam.[4] And McNamara never forgot it. Three decades later, he and Bundy recalled how the new president "really laid down the law on this first day." "There was no namby-pamby," Bundy remembered. It was "don't hold back, and don't let's not have any division on the team." Johnson's stern instruction was to "win the war."[5] "If you're going to kill a snake with a hoe," Johnson once told Hubert Humphrey, "you have to get it with one blow at the head."[6] But that tactic wouldn't work with North Vietnam backed by China and the USSR.

Less than a month after Kennedy's assassination, McNamara headed to South Vietnam to assess developments. He found the new post-Diem government "indecisive and drifting," the Vietcong taking over more of the countryside, the statistics on which he had based his earlier optimism "grossly in error." He informed Johnson: "The situation is very disturbing. Current trends, unless reversed in the next 2–3 months, will lead to neutralization at best and more likely to a Communist-controlled state." His conclusion: "We should watch the situation very carefully, running scared, hoping for the best, but preparing for more forceful moves if the situation does not show early signs of improvement."[7]

Senator Mansfield urged Johnson, as he had Kennedy, to avoid the tendency "to talk ourselves out on a limb with overstatements of our purpose and commitment only to discover in the end that there were no sufficient American interests to support with blood and treasure in a desperate final plunge." Mansfield recommended negotiating with the Communists to achieve neutralization and an American withdrawal. But McNamara, Bundy, and Rusk disagreed, telling Johnson that American security interests "unquestionably call for holding the line against further Communist gains."[8]

In early March 1964, Johnson reviewed Vietnam policy options with McNamara as the president looked for a viable strategy that would keep South Vietnam independent without sending American combat forces

there. He was also eager to keep the conflict from expanding during
an election year when he was seeking a full term as president. He told
McGeorge Bundy in March, "I just can't believe that we can't take 15,000
[*sic*] advisers and 200,000 people (South Vietnamese troops) and maintain the status quo for six months. I just believe we can do that, if we do
it right."[9] Johnson was also eager to come up with a way to talk publicly
about the war that would mollify rising concerns in the Senate about
his intentions. Senator Hugh Scott, a Pennsylvania Republican, had just
said, "The war, which we can neither win, lose, nor drop, is evidence of
an instability of ideas, a floating series of judgments, or a policy of nervous conciliation, which is extremely disturbing." *The New York Times*
summarized the Vietnam conundrum facing Johnson and McNamara
in early March:

> Mr. McNamara arrives in Saigon for his fourth visit this week. The
> situation there is as critical as it ever was. The war against the Com-
> munist guerrillas in South Vietnam is not going well. Secretary
> McNamara's journey is part of a fundamental reappraisal by the
> United States to determine what is wrong and what should be done
> next. The problem poses a serious dilemma for the Johnson Admin-
> istration. The choices open to it are difficult—whether to enlarge
> the war and therefore the United States' military commitment; or
> to pull out in a humiliating concession of defeat; or to continue on
> the present course at heavy cost in blood and treasure.[10]

In a phone call on March 2, Johnson asked McNamara to draft a brief
memo "with four-letter words and short sentences" that he could read,
study, and memorize for use when talking about Vietnam. He instructed
McNamara how to organize the memo, saying he favored a policy of training the South Vietnamese armed forces to fight the Vietcong rather than
sending US military forces to do the job.

> I'd like for you to say that there are several courses that could be
> followed. We could send our own divisions in there and our own

Marines in there, and they could start attacking the Vietcong, and the results that would likely flow from that.

We could come out of there and say we're willing to neutralize and let them neutralize South Vietnam and let the Commies take North Vietnam, and as soon as we get out, they could swallow up South Vietnam, and that would go.

Or we could pull out and say the hell with you, we're going to have Fortress America; we're going home. And that would mean that...here's what would happen in Thailand, and here's what would happen in the Philippines. And come on back and get us back to Honolulu.

Or we can say this is a Vietnamese war, and they've got 200,000 men, and they're untrained, and we've got to bring their morale up. They have nothing really to fight for because of the type of government they've had. We can put in socially conscious people and try to get them to improve their own government, and what the people get out of their own government, and we can train them how to fight, and 200,000 ultimately will be able to take care of these 25,000 [Vietcong forces].

And that after considering all of these, it seems that the latter offers the best alternative for America to follow. Now, if the latter has failed, then we have to make another decision. But at this point it has not failed, and in the last month X number of Vietcong were killed, and X number of South Vietnamese. Last year 20,000 [Vietcong] killed, to 5,000 [South Vietnamese]. While we have lost a total of 100 people, in one day in Korea, we lost 1,000, or whatever it is. And that, after all, this is it.

As the conversation continued, McNamara confessed he was pessimistic about Vietnam and the two men talked about immediate steps that could be taken to buttress Nguyen Khanh, the recently installed leader of South Vietnam. "Well, I do think, Mr. President, that it would be wise for you to say as little as possible. The frank answer is we don't know what's going on out there. The signs I see coming through the cables are disturbing signs: poor morale in Vietnamese forces, poor morale in the armed forces, disunity, tremendous amount of coup planning against [Nguyen] Khanh."[11]

McNamara departed for Vietnam four days later, after telling reporters that North Vietnam was increasing its support of Communist insurgents in South Vietnam. He described the situation in South Vietnam as "grave."[12]

McNamara's trip was less an attempt to weigh all Washington's options there and (at Johnson's urging) more of a barnstorming tour on behalf of the new Saigon leader, Nguyen Khanh. McNamara's effusive praise of Khanh and appearances with him seemed to reflect McNamara's ignorance about South Vietnam. Rufus Phillips, a CIA officer involved in efforts to persuade Vietcong fighters to defect, found it tone deaf. "I didn't know whether to cry or laugh," Phillips recalled. "If you understood anything about this contest, which was a contest for the loyalty of the Vietnamese people, you would understand the Vietnamese people were intensely nationalistic. And if you expect to have a government that's attracting support, it's got to be a government that stands on its own two feet, that, in effect, gains support even by publicly defying the Americans."[13] McNamara's post-trip report stipulated: "Even talking about a US withdrawal would undermine any chance of keeping a non-Communist government in South Vietnam." When a reporter noted that the conflict was being called "McNamara's war," the defense secretary snapped: "I don't object to it being called McNamara's war. I think it is a very important war and I am pleased to be identified with it and do whatever I can to win it."[14]

Johnson's qualms about Vietnam lingered. On May 27, he described the war to his old friend Georgia senator Richard Russell, as "the damn worst mess I ever saw . . . I don't see how we're ever going to get out of it . . . I just don't know what to do."

"It's a tragic situation," agreed Russell. "It's just one of the places where you can't win. Anything you do is wrong."

"Well, they'd impeach a President they thought would run out, wouldn't they?" Johnson asked. But the very thought of sending to Vietnam the "little old sergeant" with six kids who "works for me over at the [White House] . . . just makes the chills run up my back. . . . I just haven't got the nerve to do it, and I don't see any other way out of it."[15]

Or, as he put it to Bundy in a call later that day, "I'll tell you, the more—I just stayed awake last night thinking about this thing—the more I think of it, I don't know what in the hell . . . it looks like to me we're getting into another Korea. [Bundy acknowledges.] It just worries the hell out of me. I don't see what we can ever hope to get out of there with once we're committed. I believe the Chinese Communists are coming into it. I don't think that we can fight them 10,000 miles away from home and ever get anywhere on—in that area. I don't think it's worth fighting for, and I don't think we can get out. And it's just the biggest damn mess I ever saw."[16]

In the spring of 1964, Johnson authorized contingency planning by the military and ordered drafting of a congressional resolution to authorize expansion of the war if and when that became necessary. By that time, the Joint Chiefs of Staff had been pressing the president for months to start bombing North Vietnam—on the grounds, as General LeMay put it colloquially, that "we are swatting flies when we should be going after the manure pile." But he still hesitated to escalate, partly because the 1964 presidential election was looming. The Republican Party platform called for "carrying the war to North Vietnam" so as to avoid "Munich-like appeasement." Barry Goldwater would declare in his acceptance speech at the Republican convention that "failures infest the jungles of Vietnam," and charged the Johnson administration was "eager to deal with Communism in every coin known . . . even human freedom itself." In contrast with Goldwater, it was easy for Johnson to present himself as the "peace" candidate who wasn't going to "send American boys nine or ten thousand miles away from home to do what Asian boys ought to be doing for themselves." But on August 3, he told McNamara that Americans "want to be damned sure I don't pull 'em out and run," that "we sure ought to always leave the impression that if you shoot at us, you're gonna get hit."[17]

Sure enough, the North Vietnamese had reportedly shot at an American destroyer, the *Maddox*, the day before in the Tonkin Gulf. The attack was likely in response to US Navy electronic intelligence gathering missions, code-named De Soto patrols, or OPLAN 34A, CIA-sponsored South Vietnamese sabotage and propaganda missions against North Vietnam, and was probably launched by a local North Vietnamese commander rather than on orders from Hanoi. In one of their first conversations about the Tonkin Gulf matter on August 3, McNamara described the American operations to Johnson, noting that a North Vietnamese attack on the *Maddox* was probably in reaction to the American actions: "And Friday night, as you probably know, we had four TP [*sic*] boats from [South] Vietnam, manned by [South] Vietnamese or other nationals, attack two islands. And we expended, oh, a thousand rounds of ammunition of one kind or another against them. We probably shot up a radar station and a few other miscellaneous buildings. And following 24 hours after that with this destroyer in that same area undoubtedly led them to connect the two events."[18]

Moreover, what seemed like a second attack the next day on another destroyer, the *C. Turner Joy*, almost certainly did not occur at all. Doubts about the second attack were relayed to Washington through the navy chain of command. "Review of action makes many reported contacts and torpedoes fired appear doubtful," Capt. John J. Herrick, commander of the two navy ships in the Gulf of Tonkin, reported to the Pentagon's Pacific command in Hawaii on August 4. "Freak weather effects on radar and overeager sonarmen may have accounted for many reports. No actual visual sightings by *Maddox* suggest evaluation before any further action."[19] Subsequent messages from Herrick reaffirmed doubts about the second attack and raised questions concerning the accuracy of reports about the initial attack on the *Maddox*, though Herrick said he continued to believe that the first attack had happened. "The new information was a cold bath," Daniel Ellsberg recalled. At the time, he was the first person to receive Herrick's messages in the top civilian echelons of the Pentagon, where he had just started work as an assistant to John McNaughton, an assistant secretary of defense and McNamara's top Vietnam adviser.[20]

Johnson leaped at the opportunity to order American forces to retaliate after the reports of a second attack. In a nationally televised speech on August 4, he declared:

> My fellow Americans, as President, and Commander-in-Chief, it is my duty to the American people to report that renewed hostile actions against United States ships on the high seas in the Gulf of Tonkin have today required me to order the military forces of the United States to take action in reply. The initial attack on the destroyer *Maddox*, on August 2, was repeated today by a number of hostile vessels tracking two U.S. destroyers with torpedoes. The destroyers and supporting aircraft acted at once on the orders I gave after the initial act of aggression. We believe at least two of the attacking boats were sunk. There were no U.S. losses.[21]

Johnson later learned that American and South Vietnamese forces had provoked the confrontation. "It reminds me of the movies in Texas," he later said. "You're sitting next to a pretty girl, and you have your hand on her ankle, and nothing happens. And you move it up to her knee and nothing happens. And you move it up further and you're thinking about moving a bit more and all of a sudden you get slapped. I think we got slapped."[22]

American forces struck back at North Vietnamese naval bases and an oil storage depot. Johnson quickly submitted a draft resolution to Congress authorizing him "to take all necessary steps, including the use of armed force" to counter attacks against US forces and to "prevent further aggression" in Southeast Asia. The administration privately informed a handful of senators that American covert military and intelligence operations against North Vietnamese targets might have provoked the attacks. On August 7, the Senate passed the resolution 99–2; the House, 416–0. The resolution propelled the United States across a critical threshold toward an American war in Southeast Asia. Afterward, public opinion polling recorded 85 percent support of the Washington reprisal strikes, and support for Johnson's overall handling of Vietnam rose from 58 to 72 percent.[23] Ellsberg watched the sequence of events with amazement, realizing that some, if not all, of the naval engagements in the Gulf of Tonkin had likely been imagined by American Navy crews and that Johnson and McNamara, he believed, had deceived Congress and the American people.[24]

═══

THE FIRST DAY OF THE TONKIN GULF INCIDENT, AS IT HAPPENS, WAS also a day when McNamara's divided loyalties between Johnson and the Kennedys came into sharp relief.

As North Vietnamese and US warships were maneuvering in the Tonkin Gulf on August 1, Johnson and McNamara were talking on the phone about Jackie and Robert Kennedy. McNamara's relationship with Jackie had remained close as 1964 unfolded. A month before the Gulf of Tonkin incident, McNamara had sent Jackie a copy of *Barabbas* a 1950 novel by Pär Lagerkvist, a Swedish writer who was awarded the 1951 Nobel Prize in Literature. The book recounts the story of Barabbas, who was imprisoned in Jerusalem along with Jesus of Nazareth. According to the Old Testament, the crowd that gathered on the day the men were to be crucified voted to pardon Barabbas rather than Jesus. Why McNamara thought the novel would interest Jackie is unclear, though it depicts Barabbas as enduring a crisis of faith as he lives on after the crucifixion of Jesus. Perhaps McNamara saw Jackie's post-assassination life as a crisis of faith for her. His reference to it as "light summer reading" must have been in jest.

Jackie thanked McNamara for the novel and another book that she did not identify in a letter dated July 2, 1964, telling him, "You do take such care of me." Noting that he had described the Lagerkvist book as light summer reading, she promised him she would read it. She also referred to "your book"—she did not note the title or author—that McNamara had sent her, informing McNamara that she would have read it all but started on page 44, which she called the best place. She offered "inexpressable thanks" for all he had done for her over the winter following the assassination.[25]

It was now early August and Johnson feared that Jackie might oppose his presidential campaign. Two days earlier, anxious to eliminate Robert Kennedy from consideration as his running mate at the upcoming Democratic convention, Johnson had announced that he would not select anyone from the cabinet. The gambit, which also eliminated McNamara, was designed to sideline Robert Kennedy without publicly singling him out for exclusion.

Before his assassination, President Kennedy and his brother had seriously thought of replacing Johnson with McNamara as the Democratic candidate for vice president in the 1964 election. "As the days passed," RFK recalled, JFK "felt stronger and stronger that he [LBJ] shouldn't be president, and that we would have to move in some different direction." McNamara was "head and shoulders above everyone else," remembered Bobby. The president considered "trying to move in the direction that would . . . get the nomination for Bob McNamara."[26]

With many Democrats hoping that Johnson would choose RFK, Johnson blithely told Kennedy friend Kenneth O'Donnell (who of course informed Bobby): "I don't want history to say I was elected to this office because I had Bobby on the ticket with me. But I'll take him if I need him." LBJ's brother Sam Houston Johnson assumed LBJ never really considered RFK for two obvious reasons: "a) Lyndon hated Bobby. b) Bobby hated Lyndon."[27] Bobby wasn't that sure he wanted to be chosen anyway, but Johnson told three White House correspondents how RFK had taken the news: "When I got him to the Oval Office and told him it would be 'inadvisable' for him to be on the ticket as the vice-presidential nominee, his face changed, and he started to swallow. He looked sick. His Adam's apple bounded up and down like a yoyo." According to RFK biographer Larry Tye, Johnson illustrated his account for his listeners by letting out "a fat gulp."[28]

Tension between Johnson and Robert Kennedy dated back to the 1950s. Johnson had long been spreading the story of how his hero Franklin Roosevelt had dumped Bobby's father, Joe Kennedy, as ambassador to Britain for appeasing Hitler, and Bobby had long resented it. At their first meeting in 1952 in the Senate cafeteria (where Bobby was sitting with his new boss, Senator Joe McCarthy), he was the only one at the table not to get up to greet Johnson. "Bobby could really look hating and that was how he looked then," recalled an LBJ aide. "He didn't want to get up, but Johnson was kind of forcing him to."[29]

Three years later, Joe Kennedy offered to finance an LBJ campaign for president if Johnson would select Jack Kennedy as his running mate, but Johnson declined. That, according to Tommy Corcoran, the contact man between Joe and Johnson, "infuriated" Bobby, who considered it "unforgivably discourteous to turn down his father's generous offer." In 1959, JFK dispatched his brother to Texas to see whether Johnson was intending to run for president or, if not, whom he would support. But the mission deepened the divide when Johnson insisted Bobby take part in a deer hunt, provided him with a powerful shotgun instead of a standard rifle, watched while the gun's recoil staggered Bobby, and said, "Son, you've got to learn to handle a gun like a man." Meanwhile, Johnson took to calling Bobby names (such as "a snotnose" and "that little shitass") behind his back, and at the 1960 Democratic convention, he told Washington State delegates, "[I] never thought Hitler was right," whereas Joe Kennedy was a "Chamberlain umbrella man." When Johnson aide Bobby Baker encountered Kennedy in a convention hotel coffee shop, RFK "immediately grew so red in the face I thought he might have a stroke."[30]

For much of his time as vice president, Johnson fumed about being patronized by the Kennedys and resented that Robert Kennedy effectively outranked Johnson in influence and power. He often railed privately about "the Harvards" in the Kennedy administration, Johnson shorthand for the Eastern Establishment. During the Cuban missile crisis, RFK biographer Evan Thomas reports, Johnson was clearly outclassed by McNamara, who was "the clearest mind" in helping JFK see "the consequences of [a] precipitous reaction." McNamara later singled out the president's brother, in his introduction to RFK's published account of the crisis, for "a most extraordinary combination of energy and courage, compassion and wisdom."[31] According to Tye, "every time [RFK and LBJ] interacted during the Kennedy administration, their relationship suffered." Johnson was "invited to Hickory Hill parties at the last minute if at all," and when he was, he was seated at what Ethel Kennedy called "the losers' table." During one such gathering that Johnson did not attend, Bobby's friends presented him with a Lyndon Johnson voodoo doll and a set of pins. For his part, LBJ "blamed Bobby for displacing him as JFK's second-in-charge and never missed a chance to belittle the Attorney General."[32]

JFK's assassination deepened this mutual enmity. When Air Force One landed at Andrews Air Force Base, Bobby ignored Johnson as he rushed aboard to reach Jackie. Bobby thought Johnson had been hasty and disrespectful by taking the oath of office aboard Air Force One in Dallas next to a bloodstained Jackie rather than waiting for John Kennedy's body to be brought back to Washington. By the time Bobby arrived at the Oval Office the next morning to make sure his brother's papers were being removed, Johnson had already asked Kennedy's longtime secretary Evelyn Lincoln "to clear your things out of your office by [9:30] so my girls can come in."[33] When Johnson held his first cabinet meeting that afternoon, Kennedy arrived late, interrupting Johnson's opening speech. Some cabinet members rose to greet him, but Johnson did not. According to Tye, "Kennedy stared at [Johnson] with undisguised loathing." Johnson's expression didn't change, but he later told a cabinet member that Kennedy had deliberately arrived late to spoil the meeting.[34]

====

NOW, ON AUGUST 1, 1964, AS JOHNSON AND MCNAMARA TALKED BY phone, Johnson worried that Robert Kennedy might organize an insurgent drive for the vice presidential nomination at the convention in Atlantic City. Johnson hoped Kennedy would instead opt to run for a Senate seat in New York. He also feared that Jackie would not attend the convention, thereby signaling distress at Johnson's candidacy. Knowing that McNamara was close to both Robert and Jackie, Johnson pressed McNamara for information and insights about the Kennedys' intentions. He seemed at a loss about how to handle Jackie and whether she would encourage Robert to run for the Senate.

Now, they all tell me—and I don't want to overdo it; I want to do everything that a considerate, compassionate, understanding friend would do, without crawling and being irritating—but they tell me a big problem is Mrs. Kennedy. They say that she—Ken O'Donnell told me yesterday, he said, "Sixty percent of the trouble comes out of here. She's upset, and she hasn't got reconciled to being out of here.

And that she feels this about Bobby. And Bobby feels he kind of has an obligation to her."

. . . Now, what can I do about that? What should I do? I don't know what to do. [McNamara attempts to interject.] I went to see her. I called her. I write her. I get a warm, courteous, standoffish reception, and I—she says she can't come around the White House. She just has such memories of it. And I can't very well do much else, so I don't know what to do.

McNamara pushed back a bit, doubting the validity of O'Donnell's read on Jackie's disposition. He also defended Jackie, saying that he did not think she is "moving toward a big scene in Atlantic City." But in the same breath, McNamara employed his access to Jackie to his own advantage, and to Johnson's. First, he reassured Johnson that he did not think Jackie "has any antagonism toward you." Then he told Johnson that he planned to stay with Jackie Kennedy that night, and said he would report back "tomorrow or Monday" if he learned more.

> **President Johnson:** If you have to—if you have to covertly do it, why, we got to do it. I want you to be thinking on. And you don't know anything else?
>
> **McNamara:** No, and I'd appreciate it if you'd keep confidential my staying with Jackie tonight.
>
> **President Johnson:** I won't—nobody—
>
> **McNamara:** I don't want to find—I don't want to get it in a society column.
>
> **President Johnson:** Not a human, not a human. Don't worry about that.
>
> **McNamara:** And I'll tell you when I get back—
>
> **President Johnson:** Not a human, not a human.
>
> **McNamara:** —what I think about it.
>
> **President Johnson:** Not a human. OK. All right, bye.
>
> **McNamara:** Thank you, Mr. President—
>
> **President Johnson:** Bye.[35]

That night, as word reached the Pentagon about the naval clash in Tonkin Gulf, McNamara was out of touch with Jackie at her mother's house in Newport, Rhode Island. As a result, he missed the White House meeting the next morning. "Where the hell was I?" he grunted in an October 9, 1993, interview with Brian VanDeMark and the publisher and editor of the McNamara memoir, Peter Osnos. "I was at Newport with Jackie. She was at her mother's house, had stayed overnight. Marg was traveling, and I went up and stayed overnight Saturday with Jackie." "I'm not trying to hide anything," he told his interlocutors. "But I don't want Jackie to feel that I'm playing on a relationship with her. That's the reason I'm not telling it. I was, am close to Jackie. I'm very fond of her. But I don't think that has to be part of the book."[36]

A week later, Johnson, still anxious about Bobby Kennedy's political ambitions, pressed McNamara about whether Kennedy planned to run for the Senate in New York. "I think it's an excellent solution," McNamara told Johnson. "I've been pressing him to do that, and I keep reminding him Teddy [Edward] Kennedy was in favor of it, and I talked to Jackie [Kennedy] about it before she left and asked her to push him. I don't think you're going to have trouble at the [Democratic National] Convention from either one of them, but I surely hope he announces before the convention."[37]

———

ON NOVEMBER 3, 1964, JOHNSON WAS REELECTED PRESIDENT WITH 61 percent of the popular vote. Soon afterward, McNamara's former deputy Roswell Gilpatric (who had resumed his law practice in New York) said to McNamara that he, too, could now leave office. "He had fought hard for Lyndon," Gilpatric recalled, so McNamara had done his duty. But like the young man he had been at Berkeley who stayed on in Phi Gam even though he had chosen the wrong fraternity, McNamara told Gilpatric he couldn't leave office now—he had to "see the Vietnam thing through."[38]

On November 1, Chairman Earle Wheeler had told McNamara that the Joint Chiefs were so committed to enlarged bombing of North Vietnam that if Johnson rejected their proposal, most of them believed the

United States should pull out of South Vietnam. Theoretically, Wheeler's broaching of a withdrawal could have sparked just the sort of fuller debate on US options that McNamara later wished he had forced during the war. But although he resisted Wheeler's proposal (having in mind, he later recalled, what he learned in World War II about the limited usefulness of conventional bombing to defeat or demoralize an enemy), he wasn't ready to consider withdrawal. A month before, George Ball had produced a sixty-seven-page memorandum challenging the administration's assumptions about the war and urging a political settlement without more US military involvement. "McNamara, in particular, was absolutely horrified" by the memo, Ball recalled. "He treated it like a poisonous snake." According to Ball, "Rusk and Bundy were more tolerant ... than McNamara was. He really just regarded it as next to treason that this had been put on paper."[39] McNamara later said of the Ball memo, "He was basically, or so I interpreted it, proposing unconditional withdrawal. And unconditional withdrawal would not achieve his objectives."[40]

Rusk sat on the Ball memo, failing to pass it along to Johnson for months. Looking back years later, McNamara said, "Where the hell was Dean? Here's this guy who's [under] secretary of state, saying we ought to get out and the goddamned memo didn't even get to the president. And the view wasn't raised. What in the hell was he doing running the State Department like that?" McNamara said that while he disagreed with Ball's arguments, "I would have forwarded the memo to the President," and told him it came from my deputy and "he's totally wrong and here's why. But I want you to know that view exists. And we would have debated it.... Now, that was Dean. And I've got to say this in a way that brings out the truth about Dean and yet doesn't shaft him.... Dean should have brought it to the president. And by God, if he didn't ... I should have."[41]

The working group that Johnson created on November 2 to review all of Washington's options didn't include diplomatic negotiations or withdrawal at all. Instead, the group offered three options: (1) maintain the present course indefinitely with defeat the likely outcome, (2) launch an intensive bombing campaign against military targets in North Vietnam and Hanoi's supply lines to South Vietnam, (3) initiate the bombing campaign in a graduated way, rather than a sudden, sharp escalation, hoping that would not ignite a wider war that might draw China or the Soviet Union into the conflict.[42] McNamara didn't object.[43] After all the administration's hesitation in 1964 about what to do next, the workaholic defense secretary who devoted his vacations to challenging himself with feats of hiking, climbing, and skiing was impatient for action.

So, too, were the Joint Chiefs, but they distrusted McNamara, believing that he would never accept an all-out commitment of American combat forces needed to defeat North Vietnam. They were convinced, correctly, that McNamara—and Johnson—wanted to wage a midcourse war that would maintain military pressure on North Vietnam short of drawing China or the Soviet Union into the fight but sufficient to keep Hanoi from conquering South Vietnam. Years later, Army general H. R. McMaster, a thoughtful student of military history, critiqued the military leadership's acquiescence to the Johnson-McNamara approach in *Dereliction of Duty: Lyndon Johnson, Robert McNamara, the Joint Chiefs of Staff, and the Lies That Led to Vietnam*. McMaster argued that the Johnson-McNamara policies required selling "a strategy for Vietnam that appeared cheap and could be conducted with minimal public and Congressional attention." It demanded "carefully controlled and sharply limited military action" that was "reversible and therefore could be carried out at minimal risk and cost." It was premised on "precise control of the application of force in Vietnam," which in turn necessitated "tight control over military officers."[44]

McNamara, in McMaster's view, was the perfect man to direct this process. As a superrational manager, he could calculate the amount of violence needed to put "graduated pressure" on the Vietcong in South Vietnam and then on North Vietnam itself. During the Cuban missile crisis, he had seen traditional military advice as "irrelevant and even dangerous" and learned to regard military action not as the path to victory but "as a form of communication, the object of which was to affect the enemy's calculation of interests and dissuade him from a particular activity."[45] As the boss of the Pentagon, he was in the position to filter the advice the Chiefs gave to the president and shape what they were told about the president's thinking.

According to McMaster, the Chiefs saw the strategy of "graduated pressure" as "fundamentally flawed." "To the North Vietnamese," he continued, "military action, involving as it did attacks on their forces and bombing of their territory, was not simply a means of communication." Rather, it convinced Hanoi that Washington aimed to destroy North Vietnam, prompting the Communists to fight to the death and "creating a dynamic that defies systems-analysis quantification." The Chiefs thought McNamara "viewed the war as another business management problem that, he assumed, would ultimately succumb to his reasoned judgment and others' rational calculations." He and his "whiz kid" civilian assistants "thought they could predict with great precision what amount of force applied in Vietnam would achieve the results they desired and they believed they could control that force with great precision from halfway around the world." Military men, on the other hand, understood that graduated pressure "would not affect Hanoi's will sufficiently to convince the North to desist from its support of the South, and that such a strategy would probably lead to an escalation of the war." Nevertheless, "McNamara refused to consider the consequences of his recommendations and forged ahead, oblivious of the human and psychological complexities of the war."[46]

Although most members of the JCS favored an "all-out" strategy, they never got to present it in full to Kennedy or Johnson. That was partly due to interservice rivalry within the military itself. Instead of offering their best overall advice, reports McMaster, they presented "single-service remedies to a complex military problem, [which] prevented them from developing a comprehensive estimate of the situation or from thinking effectively about strategy."[47] But they were also hamstrung by White House efforts that limited both their ability to speak directly to Kennedy and Johnson and what they knew of the presidents' own thinking. One way the White House limited debate was by reducing the importance of the National Security Council (consisting of the president, vice president, and several cabinet members) and making decisions instead at "Tuesday Lunch" meetings attended only by the president, McNamara, Bundy, and Rusk. Another device, according to McMaster, was "to shift real planning away from the JCS to ad hoc com-

mittees composed principally of civilian analysts and attorneys, whose main
goal was to obtain a consensus consistent with the president's pursuit of a
middle ground between disengagement and war." In addition, "McNamara
and Johnson also placed conditions and qualifications on questions they
asked the Chiefs"—and used a pliable JCS chairman (Maxwell Taylor and
then Earle Wheeler) to get the answers they wanted. "When the Chiefs'
advice was not consistent with his own recommendations, McNamara, with
the aid of the chairman of the Joint Chiefs of Staff, lied in National Security Council meetings about the Chiefs' views." For example, McMaster
continues, McNamara promised the top American commanders in South
Vietnam that "winning" the war was his top priority while "conceal[ing]
from the military the limitations on the level of effort that the president was
willing to approve."[48] Brian VanDeMark, the Vietnam War historian at the
Naval Academy who assisted McNamara in preparing his memoirs, said, "I
have found no evidence to support such accusations."[49]

ON DECEMBER 5, 1964, THE STRESS AND VOLATILE EMOTIONS THAT
McNamara rigorously hid from public view burst into sight at a White
House ceremony where Army Capt. Roger Donlon was awarded the Medal
of Honor for bravery in Vietnam. It was the first such medal awarded
to a Vietnam combatant. Donlon had acted with great courage during a
five-hour firefight with North Vietnamese and Vietcong forces at a South
Vietnamese outpost near the border with Laos. Donlon and eleven fellow
Green Berets were technically just advisers—the United States had not
yet committed ground troops to battle in Vietnam.

As McNamara stepped to the podium in the East Room and started
reading the medal citation, journalist Douglas Kiker recounted, "his voice
faltered and grew husky and tears sprang to his eyes. He finished with
great difficulty and as the President stepped forward to pin the medal
around the hardrock, impassive young officer's neck, he was constrained
first to place his arm around his Defense Secretary's shoulder and give him
a hug." Kiker added, "Question: Exactly whom was McNamara weeping
for?" The implied answer: America and McNamara himself.[50]

At the end of December, Johnson seemed disinclined to order an air war against North Vietnam but, unexpectedly, opened the door for the introduction of American ground troops. "Every time I get a military recommendation it seems to me that it calls for largescale bombing," he cabled Ambassador Maxwell Taylor in Saigon. The cable continued:

> I have never felt that this war will be won from the air, and it seems to me that what is much more needed and would be more effective is a larger and stronger use of Rangers and Special Forces and Marines, or other appropriate military strength on the ground and on the scene. I am ready to look with great favor on that kind of increased American effort, directed at the guerrillas and aimed to stiffen the aggressiveness of Vietnamese military units up and down the line. Any recommendation that you or General Westmoreland make in this sense will have immediate attention from me, although I know that it may involve the acceptance of larger American sacrifice. We have been building our strength to fight this kind of war ever since 1961, and I myself am ready to substantially increase the number of Americans in Vietnam if it is necessary to provide this kind of fighting force against the Viet Cong.[51]

As 1965 began, Johnson continued to complain about the Kennedy crowd, telling McNamara on January 13 that Kennedy acolytes thought that Johnson was trying to blame JFK for the Vietnam War and that Johnson had dispatched John McCone, the CIA chief, to so inform the Senate Armed Services Committee. Clearly, he knew McNamara was part of the Georgetown set and had influence there.

Johnson told McNamara:

> They're [The Kennedy circle] out and they don't get consulted and they
>   don't feel that great power. And you could throw all three of them
>   on a scale at once and they wouldn't be eighty-nine pounds. But
>   they have these little parties out at Georgetown.... Bill Moyers

tells me . . . that they had a party last night. Joe Alsop called up, very excited, today and said that he and [Joseph] Kraft and [Rowland] Evans . . . and the Kennedy crowd decided that I had framed up to get [the] Armed Services [Committee] in the Senate to call McCone to put the Vietnam War on Kennedy's tomb. And that I had a conspiracy going on to show that it was Kennedy's immaturity and poor judgment that originally led us into this thing. . . . And that his execution of it had brought havoc to the country. And that McCone had gone up and done it. And that this was my game—to lay Vietnam off onto Kennedy's inexperience [and] immaturity. . . . McCone told me he . . . didn't mention Vietnam [during his Armed Services testimony]. . . . So I assumed, since McNamara was a part of the administration, that—

McNamara: And he is going to be tagged with the war in any case! [*laughs*]

Johnson: . . . That since he was a part of the administration, I had assumed that he didn't resent very much what I'd said or he would have said to me . . . that it wasn't true. . . . [I told Moyers] that I considered myself responsible for every decision made by Kennedy. . . . And whatever he did, I supported. And if they can find a more loyal man in this town to him or to his memory, I would like for them to produce him. . . .

McNamara: I think so, Mr. President. . . . I can maybe do something about this. I probably should have gone to that party last night. . . . I can get back into communication with those people and, I think, throw some light of realism onto whatever they are thinking about. Did I understand that Alsop called to report this?

Johnson: Called to report it to Bill [Moyers]. . . . Alsop's charging that I'm getting McCone to go up and lay the blame for Vietnam on Kennedy's tomb. Now, of course, I have never laid any blame on Kennedy. Have you ever heard me blame Kennedy for anything?

McNamara: No, no, absolutely not! . . . I have mentioned this to Jackie several times. I've been very impressed by your attitude on that as well as when the President was alive.[52]

═══

BY THIS TIME, MCNAMARA WAS DETERMINED TO GALVANIZE decision-making about the Vietnam War. He recalled that he and Bundy "were deeply frustrated by a year of doing nothing" and believed "that doing nothing would be worst of all."[53] So they proposed, in a joint memorandum to Johnson, stepped-up bombing of the North to create a "bargainable instrument" in future negotiations with Hanoi. Or, as McNamara put it to Johnson later, "I'm absolutely certain in my own mind that bombing represents ... something we'll give up in return for something they'll do—at some point."[54]

On January 27, the two men sent Johnson a two-page note, later dubbed the "Fork in the Road" memo, that laid out two divergent options for the president—a marked increase in American military involvement or a diplomatic drive to end the war. They opened by telling Johnson that "both of us are now pretty well convinced that our current policy can lead only to disastrous defeat." They then starkly laid out the two options: "The first is to use our military power in the Far East and to force a change in Communist policy. The second is to deploy all our resources along a track of negotiation, aimed at salvaging what little can be preserved with no major addition to our present military risk." Their recommendation: "Bob and I tend to favor the first course, but we believe that both should be carefully studied and that alternative programs should be argued out before you." The recommendation to study the options carefully reflected McNamara's view that major decisions should follow an exacting examination of policy proposals. But in this case, as in so many others involving the Vietnam War, careful consideration quickly gave way to exigent developments in Vietnam and escalatory American military actions.[55]

Later that morning, McNamara, Bundy, and Dean Rusk, who did not agree with the McNamara-Bundy proposal, discussed the memo with Johnson. Rusk opposed both escalation and withdrawal, fearing either option would prove problematic for Washington. He favored sticking with the current approach and figuring out how to make it successful.

Johnson was in a bad mood, according to his wife. If he had previously hesitated to expand the war to increase his chances of winning the election, his electoral victory left him inclined to escalate the fighting, not only to avoid losing the war but to thwart Republicans bent on revenge for their massive 1964 electoral defeat, and hawkish southern Democrats, as well. "If I don't go in now and they show later that I should have, then they'll be all over me in Congress. They won't be talking about my civil rights bill, or education or beautification." Instead, they would "push Vietnam up my ass every time. Vietnam. Vietnam. Vietnam. Right up my ass!"[56]

"This week's mood is not good," Lady Bird noted in her diary on January 29. "But how to fight it? I think, by work, activity, as soon as Lyndon is more physically able. It's sort of a slough of despond—what a lyrical writer whom I used to love called 'the Valley of the Black Pig.'"[57] In 1965, a year of critical decisions about escalating the Vietnam War, Johnson battled depression at various points. Robert Dallek, a Johnson biographer, captured the president's mood at times during 1965.

"'It was a pronounced, prolonged depression,' [Bill] Moyers adds. 'He would just go within himself, just disappear—morose, self-pitying, angry. . . . He was a tormented man,' who described himself to Moyers as in a Louisiana swamp 'that's pulling me down.' When he said it, Moyers remembers, 'he was lying in bed with the covers almost above his head.'"[58]

"Mrs. Johnson remembers the President's pain over the war. 'It was just a hell of a thorn stuck in his throat,' she told me. 'It wouldn't come up; it wouldn't go down. . . . It was just pure hell and did not have that reassuring, strong feeling that this is right, that he had when he was in a crunch with civil rights or poverty or education. It didn't have that: we'll make it through this one: Win or lose, it's the right thing to do. So, uncertainty . . . we had a rich dose of that. . . . True, you can "bear any burden, pay any price" if you're sure you're doing right. But if you do not know you're doing right—' she ended, and her voice trailed off."[59]

How Johnson's mental state affected his decision-making is impossible to know. But it must have played a role, perhaps propelling him toward escalation as a way to escape a war stalemate that seemed to defy easy resolution and greatly frustrated Johnson and McNamara. For both men, the war seemed a trap without an exit. As McNamara put it later, "There weren't any answers. That was the terrible thing."[60]

As 1965 unfurled, Johnson and McNamara, wrestling with their own internal demons, made turning point decisions about the war. They felt foiled by the morass in Vietnam and their inability to alter the equation there short of either a massive escalation, which could bring the Soviet Union or China into the war, or a withdrawal that they feared could open the way to sweeping Communist advances in Asia and beyond. Yet, unwilling to accept the increasingly unsustainable status quo for emotional, psychological, and political reasons, they struck out with ill-considered moves that set them on a tragic course. Within days of the delivery of the Fork in the Road memo, the relatively small American military intervention began to grow. As the months passed, Johnson and McNamara increased the number of American troops in Vietnam from 23,000 to 175,000, with at least another 100,000 planned for 1966. What had been a relatively small American military intervention halfway around the world turned into a full-fledged American war.

═══

ON FEBRUARY 7, 1965, WHILE BUNDY WAS IN SOUTH VIETNAM, THE Vietcong swarmed Camp Holloway, a Special Forces base near Pleiku in the Central Highlands, killing eight Americans and injuring more than a hundred. Due to the time difference between Washington and South Vietnam, Johnson was informed about the attack on the afternoon of February 6 in Washington. After meeting with top advisers, he ordered retaliatory air strikes on targets in North Vietnam. He was awakened repeatedly that night to take calls from the Pentagon updating him on the American air operations. A few days later, reflecting on his decision to send American airmen into combat, he startled Lady Bird by telling Vice President Humphrey something he had told her several times in private but never said to anyone else. "I'm not temperamentally equipped to be Commander-in-Chief. I'm too sentimental to give the orders."[61]

But give the order he did. When Bundy reported to Johnson and congressional leaders upon his return, Johnson announced that he was embarking on "further pressure" against Hanoi. He would begin an "extensive and costly" campaign that would bring "higher and more visible" American casualties, but Johnson deceptively assured congressional leaders that it could be undertaken "without escalating the war." On March 2, one hundred American bombers roared north to begin the sustained bombing campaign code-named ROLLING THUNDER. As historian Brian VanDeMark writes, "Johnson had committed America to direct participation in the war—something that Truman, Eisenhower and Kennedy had never done." As Bundy's aide Chester Cooper put it, "Once the bombers were sent north, there was no turning back."[62] Over the next three years, the air force, navy, and Marine Corps flew more than 300,000 attack sorties against targets in North Vietnam, dropping 864,000 tons of American bombs, more than the United States used in the Korean War or in American operations in the Pacific Theater during World War II.

McNamara supported ROLLING THUNDER, as did his high-level colleagues like Dean Rusk (who embraced "the risk of major escalation" because "negotiation as a cover for abandonment of Southeast Asia to the Communist North cannot be accepted") and former president Eisenhower at a meeting at the White House on February 17. After watching all this from his front-row seat at the Pentagon, Ellsberg later said, "Given my admiration for Robert McNamara, I could never understand why he wanted to set out on this path of provocation and escalation at all, however 'gradually.' It was steadily more perplexing and disturbing for me to know that he was among the strongest proponents of bombing the North."[63]

Looking back later at this and other 1965 decisions to vastly escalate American combat operations in Vietnam and dispatch hundreds of thousands of troops there, McNamara and Bundy lamented Johnson's failure to level with the American people about the commitments and potential costs. McNamara regretted that Johnson "refuse[d] to take the American people into his confidence"; he later condemned Johnson's "obscuring" the extent of the escalation as "an unwise and ultimately self-defeating course." But he understood that Johnson "wanted nothing to divert atten-

tion and resources from his cherished domestic reforms" and feared hard-
line pressure from both Republicans and Democrats "for greater—and far
riskier—military action that might trigger responses, especially nuclear,
by China and/or the Soviet Union."[64] Bundy noted to McNamara, "He
worked to hold on in Vietnam and legislate the Great Society in the same
year." Like McNamara, Bundy rued that Johnson "did not go to the country or the Congress for approval of what was in reality a decision to go to
war. Instead he sneaked the decision past the country at very great eventual cost to both the country and himself."[65]

Johnson later told Doris Kearns Goodwin, "I knew from the start that
I was bound to be crucified either way I moved. If I left the woman I really
loved—the Great Society—in order to get involved with that bitch of a
war on the other side of the world, then I would lose everything at home.
All my programs, all my hopes.... All my dreams. But if I left that war,
and let the Communists take over South Vietnam, then I would be seen
as a coward and my nation would be seen as an appeaser." Johnson added,
"I was determined to keep the war from shattering that dream, which
meant I simply had no choice but to keep my foreign policy in the wings. I
knew the Congress as well as I know Lady Bird, and I knew that the day it
exploded into a major debate on the war, that day would be the beginning
of the end of the Great Society."[66]

Bundy wondered why he and McNamara had not objected to Johnson's effort to mask the buildup in Vietnam. "We didn't like that or want
it, but we did not publicly break with him. I think we both have to think
through why not and explain it. I think I'd do it again, but I'll see when
I've thought it through even more."[67] But at the time, still painfully aware
of his own shortcomings as a politician, McNamara was learning from
the master—even to the point of imitating him by obscuring the abysmal
state of South Vietnam's politics and war effort as he observed it on his
regular trips to Saigon. "We have slowed the flow of men and materiel and
this has adversely affected the Viet Cong, although I don't wish to over-
emphasize the degree to which it has affected them so far," McNamara
told reporters in April, referring to the American bombing campaign.
That was an overly optimistic assessment.[68]

McNamara may also have been thinking about the fate of Vice President Humphrey, who was trampled by Johnson after daring to press the president to wind down the war. Humphrey, who participated in the first conversations about escalating the war in February, was troubled by the absence of dissent. "Presidential advisers too often simply try to anticipate the President's decision, telling him not what he ought to hear, but what they think he wants to hear," Humphrey recalled. "As the war went on, there was a clear tendency on the part of the men around Johnson to do that—all of them weary, frustrated with the duration of the struggle and the obvious lack of success. Until the 'A to Z' review, in 1968, I heard very little counsel from any of those genuinely close to the President that could in the most generous fashion be interpreted as opposition to further commitments of American power."[69]

Alarmed by the move to escalate in February 1965, perhaps partly influenced by Johnson's confessional comment about serving as commander in chief on February 11, Humphrey sent the president a prophetic memo on February 17 warning that "the sustainability of the Vietnam policies now being discussed [is] likely to profoundly affect the success of your administration" both at home and abroad. Taking into account Johnson's fear that losing Vietnam would provoke a right-wing backlash in the US, Humphrey reminded him that Goldwater's "trigger-happy bomber image" had already lost the GOP the 1964 election. Noting how many Johnson foreign and domestic policies could be "jeopardized by an escalation in Vietnam," Humphrey warned that "if we go north, [the American] people will find it increasingly hard to understand why we risk World War III by enlarging a war under terms we found unacceptable 12 years ago in Korea." Flattering the president, Humphrey said, "President Johnson is personally identified with, and greatly admired for, political ingenuity. He will be expected to put all his great political sense to work now for international political solutions."

Humphrey closed by reiterating his loyalty: "I intend to support the Administration whatever the President's decisions. But these are my views."[70]

Thomas Hughes, the State Department's intelligence chief and a former Senate aide to Humphrey, described Johnson's reaction: "All hell broke loose. Mac Bundy was called into the Oval Office to find an irate Johnson exclaiming: 'That vice president of mine promised me his loyalty, and just look at this! Well, Humphrey is to have nothing further to do with Vietnam—no meetings, no visitors, no speeches, nothing. I am appointing you his nursemaid for the foreseeable future on foreign policy.'" The result, Hughes continued, "was that Humphrey was cut out of all Vietnam meetings for several months. He paid for his return to Johnson's good graces only by becoming an exuberant supporter of the war—ironically in 1966 when the war had already gone so badly that even McNamara was privately defecting."[71]

Johnson's brutal treatment of Humphrey must have registered with McNamara, who was soon well aware that the vice president was no longer welcome at Vietnam policy-making discussions. Would the same fate have awaited McNamara had he openly challenged the growing chorus within the national security team to expand the war, launch an extensive bombing campaign in North Vietnam, and commit American ground troops to combat in South Vietnam? Perhaps not, given Johnson's high regard for McNamara and the fact that McNamara, unlike Humphrey, exuded strength and toughness. But the issue never came up in 1965 because McNamara, at least in Johnson's presence, remained among the most enthusiastic cheerleaders for expanding the war. Whatever doubts he had, and he did have some, and they grew through 1965, he kept very private.[72]

McNamara's thinking in 1965 may also have been influenced by the example of George Ball, the undersecretary of state, who openly and persistently favored winding down the war. In this case, Johnson's punishment was not to ostracize Ball but to ignore his advice. On October 5, 1964, Ball had produced the long memo calling for American disengagement from South Vietnam that McNamara had opposed. In the memo, Ball said, "once on the tiger's back, we cannot be sure of picking the place to dismount."[73]

In February 1965, as the administration moved toward bombing North Vietnam in retaliation for the Vietcong attack on Camp Holloway, Ball counseled waiting until after Soviet premier Alexei Kosygin had left Hanoi (as did Hubert Humphrey in the memo that enraged Johnson). But, Ball recalled:

> McNamara brushed these caveats aside. I was, he protested, trying to block our retaliatory raid, not merely postpone it (which, in fact, was true). There would never be a perfect moment to begin bombing; someone could always find an objection and time was of the essence. We had to show immediately that we were reacting to the Vietcong attack. It was the quintessential McNamara approach. Once he had made up his mind to go forward, he would push aside the most formidable impediment that might threaten to slow him down or deflect him from his determined course. So once again he carried the day.[74]

It was only on February 24, 1965, that Ball gave his October 5, 1964, memo to Bill Moyers, who passed it on to Johnson. LBJ read it carefully (he even remembered page numbers where Ball's various arguments were stated) and called a meeting to discuss it. Johnson challenged several of those arguments, but it was McNamara who "responded with a pyrotechnic display of facts and statistics to prove that I had overstated the difficulties we were now encountering, suggesting at least by nuance, that I was not only prejudiced but ill-informed." Rusk added "a passionate argument about the dangers" of not escalating. "I had made no converts," Ball concluded. "My hope to force systematic reexamination of our total situation had manifestly failed."[75]

LADY BIRD WORRIED ABOUT HER HUSBAND'S PSYCHOLOGICAL struggles, and her own, as the war weighed on them. "For quite some time I have been swimming upstream against the feeling of depression and relative inertia," she noted in her diary on March 7. "I flinch from activity and involvement, and yet I rust without it. Lyndon too lives in a cloud of troubles, with few rays of light. . . . In talking about the Viet Nam situation, Lyndon summed it up quite simply, 'I can't get out, I can't finish it with what I have got, so what the hell can I do?' "[76]

Determined to get help for the president, Lady Bird asked Johnson's longtime personal physician, James Cain, and J. Willis Hurst, Johnson's cardiologist, to examine Johnson. On March 13, she noted:

> My dear friends Jim Cain and Willis Hurst are house guests, and this morning they completed the purpose of their visit—an examination of Lyndon. Essentially everything is fine. All the basic organs and the functioning thereof, but there is this heavy load of tension and this fog of depression. If you're enjoying what you do you don't get tired, no matter how hard you work, and if it's frustrating and full of uncertainties you use up energies struggling against what you have to do. In a nutshell, their prescription is exercise, diet, and a break—that is, get off to sunshine and rest for a couple of days every two weeks or, at the very outside, once a month.[77]

Johnson's ugly attitude seeped into his management of US foreign policy. Annoyed that Pakistan and India were critical of the American bombing campaign in Vietnam, he canceled White House visits planned by Pakistan's president and India's prime minister. He then blamed "disloyal Kennedy people over at the State Department" for press criticism that he had offended two of Asia's most important nations. Hugh Sidey, a reporter at *Time* magazine, told Richard Goodwin, "there was increasing worry about the president around town. A fear that his personal eccentricities were now affecting policy."[78]

Goodwin recalled:

> It was during this period, in the spring of 1965, that I first noticed that Johnson's public mask was beginning to stiffen. In his public appearances the face seemed frozen, the once-gesturing arms held tightly to the side or grasping a podium. Protective devices proliferated—TelePrompTers, special rostrums, the careful excision of colorful or original language—all, at least in part, I now believe, designed to guard him from spontaneously voicing inner convictions that he knew, in that part of his mind still firmly in touch with real-

ity, would, if voiced, discredit him. "You know, Dick," Johnson once told me, "I never really dare let myself go because I don't know where I'll stop." I let the comment pass, not realizing the significance of his revelation, a glimpse at the protective shield so carefully constructed against threatening forces that he knew might overwhelm him.[79]

In mid-June, Johnson was infuriated when he learned from news accounts that McGeorge Bundy planned to debate about the Vietnam War with five prominent American professors who were critical of the war on a CBS News telecast hosted by the correspondent Eric Sevareid. The broadcast, titled "Vietnam Dialogue: Mr. Bundy and the Professors," aired live from Georgetown University in Washington, DC, on June 21. Johnson ordered Bill Moyers to tell Bundy that the president "would be pleased, mighty pleased, to accept his resignation." When Moyers seemed hesitant to relay the message, Johnson told him, "That's the trouble with all you fellows. You're in bed with the Kennedys."[80] Not long after the episode, Bundy got in touch with Harvard president Nathan Pusey, asking if there might be a place for him back at Harvard if he decided to leave the Johnson administration.[81]

As the weeks passed, punctuated by wild Johnson complaints that he was the target of a Communist conspiracy, Goodwin and Moyers grew increasingly alarmed. "During the summer of 1965 Bill Moyers and I met every few days to discuss the president's increasingly vehement and less rational outbursts," Goodwin recalled. "We agreed that Johnson was changing, that some invasive inward force was distorting his perceptions, gradually infiltrating his actions, infecting the entire process of presidential decision. Although we were reluctant to acknowledge the possibility of a continued decline, refused to acknowledge it, the signs of aberration were too obvious to be ignored or rationalized as typical Johnsonian exaggerations."[82]

Uncertain what to do, they considered informing McNamara about Johnson's erratic behavior and seeking his help. But they wondered if McNamara's vaulting ambition might lead him to use the information to advance his own interests. "It has been a wild and unbelievable week,"

Goodwin recalled, "dinner with Bill and his assistant and another long discussion of Johnson in which we agreed on his paranoid condition. I asked Bill if he thought I should talk to anyone before I left, perhaps to Bob McNamara, whose position might let him keep things from getting out of hand. Bill seemed to think that it might be a good idea, but made me promise to tell him first, before I did anything. I don't know if we can trust McNamara. He is intelligent and skilled, could understand our fears, but was also very ambitious and could let his ambition run away with him."

Moyers and Goodwin had good reason to worry about McNamara. His irrepressible ambition—and continuing effort to remain faithful to the Kennedys while informing on them—was vividly evident during a June 17 conversation with Johnson. As the call began, Johnson and McNamara talked about their frustrations with critics of the war.

President Johnson: Now, [George] McGovern says that "the war has taken a very dangerous new turn with the commitment of large land forces to a combat mission. These guerrillas have lived 20 years off the countryside. They have fought largely with captured weapons. Their strength is they're part of the people, the terrain which they fight. And how long will it take for some people to realize that bombing Hanoi or Peking will have little or no effect on the guerrilla forces fighting a thousand miles away in the jungle."

McNamara: Well, if bombing won't have any effect and the added men are undesirable, what in the hell do we do? Get out? I just spent two and a half hours with the foreign correspondents from France, Italy, England, Germany, Switzerland, and Israel. And when I finished, I took a half an hour to go around the table and say, "All right, now, I've told you my views; you tell me your views." And there wasn't a single one of them there that when pressed had any program other than the one we're following. The Frenchman was the only one who had any real criticism, and he said we weren't taking account of the experience of Frenchmen in South Vietnam. That's the only thing he had to say to it.

The conversation then turned to Jackie Kennedy, as Johnson worried aloud about losing the services of Goodwin, his chief speechwriter, who seemed inclined to quit. He and McNamara plotted how to enlist Jackie's help when McNamara traveled to New York to see Jackie, whose views Goodwin respected. Johnson urged McNamara to bring up the issue with an assist from a few predinner cocktails.

> **McNamara:** I just wanted to tell you, unless you see some reason not to, I'm planning to have dinner with Jackie [Kennedy] tonight in New York. I can do something on that front, if I can't on Bobby. I confess to failure on the latter, but I have been able to do a little on the other.
>
> **Johnson:** I sure hope so.... Confidentially ... after your second drink, when you think that you can have some influence, I would sure urge her to keep Dick Goodwin down here to help us. I think [he's] getting some encouragement to move ... away.

McNamara assures Johnson he will raise the issue with Jackie.[83]

Four days later, Johnson sought McNamara's help to persuade Robert Kennedy, who had been elected to the Senate from New York in 1964, to stop criticizing a $700 million defense appropriation awaiting Senate approval. McNamara was undoubtedly familiar with Kennedy's concerns about the war. Dun Gifford, an aide to Senator Edward Kennedy, saw Robert Kennedy around this time leaning forward in a private jet on the way to Hyannis, pressuring McNamara: "Now what the hell is going on out there?"[84] Johnson complained that Kennedy was making "snide remarks" about the bill in the Senate cloakroom because he was opposed to Vietnam War spending. When McNamara objected, saying, "I don't think now is the time," Johnson pressed the issue. "I just think we ought to talk to him about it, because this is where most of our real trouble is coming from."

Then, musing about Vietnam, Johnson went on:

> I don't believe they're *ever* going to quit. And I don't see ... that we have any ... plan for a victory—militarily or diplomatically.... You

and Dean [Rusk] have got to sit down and try to see if there's any people that we have in those departments that can give us any program or plan or hope. If not, we got to . . . have you . . . go out there and take one good look at it and say to these new people, "Now you changed the government about the last time. And this is it." Call the Buddhists and the Catholics and the generals and everybody together and say we're going to do our best. And be sure they're willing to let new troops come in. Be sure they're not going to resent them. If not, why, you-all can run over us and have a government of your own choosing. But we just can't take these changes all the time. . . . You . . . better talk to your military people. . . . Say . . . the President wants some kind of plan that gives us some hope of victory.[85]

Johnson and McNamara sounded determined to prevail in South Vietnam when they talked at the end of June. They agreed that "giving up" was not an option and that sending more American troops presented less of a risk than "walking out," in Johnson's words.[86]

In early July, Johnson privately described his anguish about Vietnam to Lady Bird. "Vietnam is getting worse day by day. I have the choice to go in with great casualty lists or get out with great disgrace. It's like being in an airplane, and I have to choose between crashing the plane or jumping out. I do not have a parachute."[87]

Johnson's emotional agitation was evident at a July 14 staff meeting when he repeated the comment he had made to Lady Bird. Richard Goodwin described the scene. "Johnson walked into a staff meeting, took a seat, listened for a while, and then told us, 'Don't let me interrupt. But there's one thing you ought to know. Vietnam is like being in a plane without a parachute, when all the engines go out. If you jump, you'll probably be killed, and if you stay in, you'll crash and probably burn. That's what it is.' Then, without waiting for a response, the tall, slumped figure rose and left the room."[88]

That night, McNamara headed to South Vietnam to consult with General Westmoreland. Before departing, he talked with Johnson by phone.

Their worries about the war were evident, as was their inclination to commit a large number of American combat troops, a step that McNamara urged be accompanied by a call-up of reserves. McNamara predicted that they could gain congressional support for these steps without stirring a divisive debate about the war. Johnson said, "We know, ourselves, on our own conscience, that when we asked for this Tonkin Gulf Resolution, we had no intention of committing this many ground troops. And we're doing so now and we know it's going to be bad, and the question [is]: do we just want to do it out on a limb by ourselves." After McNamara made the case for seeking congressional approval to call up the reserves, he admitted that he might be wrong. "I don't know that you want to go that far and I'm not pressing you to. It's my judgment you should. But my judgment may be in error here."[89]

While McNamara was in Vietnam, Premier Nguyễn Cao Kỳ gave him a stuffed tiger as a gift. Once back in the United States, McNamara presented it to Jackie Kennedy as a gift for Caroline and John Jr. when he visited her on Cape Cod. She soon made a watercolor drawing of the tiger and sent it to McNamara, writing on the back that the watercolor was imperfect but that she had done her best to capture it in the drawing. He had it framed.[90]

The next huge step in the acceleration of the American war effort came soon after McNamara returned from Vietnam on July 21, when Johnson decided to send tens of thousands of combat troops to Vietnam. His decision was preceded by meetings at the White House and Camp David at which McNamara forcefully supported that decision.

America's Vietnam commander Gen. William Westmoreland had recommended that the United States massively escalate the war by sending some 100,000 ground troops there by the end of the year, with many more to follow in 1966. On July 21, Johnson's advisers considered Westmoreland's plan in the White House Cabinet Room: McNamara, Rusk, Bundy, Joint Chiefs of Staff chairman Wheeler, McNamara's deputy Cyrus Vance, Under Secretary of State George Ball, Assistant Secretary of State for Far Eastern Affairs William Bundy, CIA director William Raborn and his deputy Richard Helms, former ambassador to Saigon

Henry Cabot Lodge, US Information Agency director Carl Rowan, and White House press secretary Bill Moyers. Longtime Johnson friend and counselor Clark Clifford also attended as Johnson's special guest. In May, Clifford had told Johnson in a letter: "I believe our ground forces in South Vietnam should be kept to a minimum consistent with the protection of our installations and property in that country. My concern is that a substantial buildup of U.S. ground troops would be construed by the Communists, and by the world, as a determination on our part to win the war on the ground. This could be a quagmire. It could turn into an open ended commitment on our part that would take more and more ground troops, without a realistic hope of ultimate victory."[91]

But the only person at the meeting to resist Westmoreland's proposal was Ball. "We can't win," he said. "The war will be long and protracted with heavy casualties. The most we can hope for is a messy conclusion. We must measure this long-term price against the short-term loss that will result from a withdrawal."

"But wouldn't all these countries—Korea, Thailand, Western Europe—say Uncle Sam is a paper tiger?" asked Johnson. "Would we lose credibility by breaking the word of three Presidents if we give up as you propose?"

"If we were helping a country with a stable, viable government," Ball answered, "it would be a vastly different story."

Although all Johnson's senior advisers rebutted Ball, McNamara ("with his usual precision and air of certainty," noted Clifford) took the lead, saying, "I feel that the risks of following my program have been vastly overstated by George Ball."[92]

The next day, the Joint Chiefs of Staff and the secretaries of the army, navy, and air force joined the discussion along with McNamara, Bundy, Vance, and Clifford. This time all participants endorsed escalation, except Clifford who, as the sole private citizen in the room, remained silent. Johnson himself seemed torn. Turning toward McNamara, he said, "Westmoreland's request means that we are in a new war. This is going off the diving board."

At this point, McNamara offered what Clifford called "the most extreme version of the domino theory I had ever heard." After the session, Johnson summoned Clifford to the small anteroom next to the Oval Office and asked his view. Clifford admitted he shared Ball's doubts, but in the meantime, he had learned from Bill Moyers that Johnson "had virtually made up his mind to support McNamara and Westmoreland," but the president wanted to hear the pro and con arguments again. So he invited McNamara and Clifford to Camp David to debate the issue one last time.[93]

On Saturday afternoon, July 24, 1965, McNamara, his wife Margy, and their fifteen-year-old son Craig helicoptered to the presidential retreat in the Catoctin Mountains outside Washington. Also on board were President Johnson's daughter Luci and her husband, Pat Nugent, and Clark Clifford and his wife, Marny. The passengers spent the twenty-five-minute flight from the White House making pleasant small talk. Upon arrival, they and other guests (Supreme Court Justice Arthur Goldberg, who was to be sworn in as US ambassador to the United Nations the next day; Indiana senator Birch Bayh and his wife; and Johnson aides Horace Busby and Jack Valenti) spent the rest of the afternoon relaxing on Camp David's lovely grounds and then dining with the president and First Lady. Lady Bird hoped that her husband would reach a final decision in this relaxed setting. McNamara did, too. "She'd seen time and again how the release of tension that comes with a difficult decision could ease Lyndon's torment, self-doubt and depression," Julia Sweig reported in her portrait of Lady Bird. McNamara had been torn, too, about what to do, but after months of presidential indecision, he wanted to settle on a decisive military strategy. That may explain the extra conviction with which he had recently been making the case for escalation.[94]

But the main business of the weekend for Johnson, McNamara, and Clifford was Vietnam. The president sat at the end of a rectangular dining room table in Camp David's Aspen Lodge on Sunday afternoon with McNamara to his right directly across the table from Clifford. Clifford said the following:

I hate this war. I do not believe we can win. If we send in 100,000 more men, the North Vietnamese will match us. If the North Viet-

namese run out of men, the Chinese will send in "volunteers." Russia
and China don't intend for us to win the war. If we "won," we could
face a long occupation with constant trouble. And if we don't win
after a big buildup, it will be a huge catastrophe. We could lose more
than 50,000 men in Vietnam. It will ruin us. Five years, 50,000 men
killed, hundreds of billions of dollars—it's just not for us.

Asked by Johnson to reply, McNamara (according to Clifford) said
"forcefully that he did not agree with my premises or my assessment of
the chances for success in Vietnam," and repeated arguments he had made
at the White House earlier in the week.

Johnson then adjourned the meeting without further debate. That evening the company returned to Washington, and the next day the larger
group of advisers reconvened at the White House to make more specific
plans for the coming buildup.[95]

Recognizing that ordering tens of thousands of ground troops to South
Vietnam would raise the financial cost of the war, McNamara urged the
president to seek a tax increase as the escalation unfolded. "I said to Johnson, in effect, 'That's going to be inflationary, we have to have a tax increase.'
And Johnson said, 'Where's your vote count?' I said, '. . . get your own damn
vote count.' He said, 'You get your ass up there and get your vote count.'
So, I make an effort and I get the vote count and I come back. Sure, I knew
when I recommended it would be difficult. But I said I would rather try and
fail than not at all. It's the right thing to do." LBJ responded: "That's what's
wrong with you, Bob, you don't know a goddamned thing about politics."[96]

Several days after the pivotal decision to commit ground troops,
McNamara lashed out at *The New York Times*, complaining about critical coverage of the war in a meeting with James Reston, the paper's Washington bureau chief. Reston recounted the heated meeting in a memo for
his records:

Saw R. S. McNamara at 5:30 and discussed with him whether a
stalemate in Vietnam would be in our interest or in the Communists.' He was worried about the prospect that this might be just

what they wanted, but felt confident that the U.S. could carry the burden of the war without being diverted from its greater foreign-policy and social objectives. He expected that there would be great pressure for some kind of mobilization [putting reserve forces on active duty] but that he was determined to resist.

McNamara was emotional, and almost violently critical of The Times in general and of [*Times* reporter] Hanson Baldwin in particular for their criticism of his politics.... I suggested that he was getting too excited about this but he was in no mood to be diverted from his wrath.[97]

=====

FAST FORWARD TO NOVEMBER 1965. JOHNSON'S DECISION TO SEND ground troops, fiercely defended by McNamara, had been taken four months before. Now came a personal turning point for McNamara, his conclusion that the war was unwinnable militarily.

Visiting South Vietnam on November 28–29, McNamara could see that Washington's buildup was already Americanizing the war and the economy, that the Vietcong were still gaining ground, that areas they controlled had been blasted by twenty-ton payloads dropped from mammoth B-52 bombers, leaving craters ten feet deep and twenty feet wide, and that American corpses in flag-draped aluminum caskets were being loaded into C-130 Hercules transport planes for their final trip home. From this trip, he told Johnson afterward, "came an understanding of the situation much more comprehensive than I had before." The situation was "much more critical than I had realized."[98]

So was the situation at home. Although opinion polls showed three-quarters of Americans still supporting Johnson on the war, protests were stirring on college campuses. McNamara's son Craig would eventually hang an American flag upside down in his bedroom at the McNamara home in silent protest, and once at college, would join public protests at Stanford and Berkeley. Johnson dismissed the college unrest to George Ball, saying, "George, don't pay attention to what those little shits on campuses do. The great beast is the reactionary elements in this country. Those are the people we have to fear."[99] On November 27, some 100,000 antiwar demonstrators marched in ninety cities, including 20,000 in Washington who staged a protest in front of the White House.

But the public protest that shook McNamara most involved just one man—and his infant daughter. Early on the evening of November 2, as Pentagon workers were heading home, a thirty-one-year-old Quaker named Norman Morrison, holding his infant daughter in his arms, drenched himself with kerosene and set himself on fire in a parking lot underneath McNamara's office window. As the flames consumed him, bystanders yelled, "Drop the child!" and he threw her toward them. How much of the horrifying scene McNamara witnessed is unclear. In some accounts, he first looked out his window as medics were covering the body in blankets. In another, McNamara watched the flames consume Morrison.[100]

He didn't yet know the full story—who the man was and whether his daughter had survived (she did)—but he was shattered. Years later he would barely discuss it with Shapley. Speaking in a low voice filled with emotion, he described what he had seen from the window as "awful." The suicide was "a personal tragedy for me," he added. "It was an outcry," he said in his memoirs, "against the killing that was destroying the lives of so many Vietnamese and American youth."[101] Morrison's belief, McNamara remembered in 2001, was "that human beings must stop killing other human beings, and that's a belief that I shared. I shared it then and I believe it even more strongly today."[102]

Columnist Art Buchwald, a McNamara friend, wrote that McNamara's witnessing of Morrison's self-immolation was "one of the darkest moments of his life."[103] In his memoir, McNamara wrote that he "reacted to the horror of his action by bottling up my emotions and avoided talking about them with anyone—even my family. I knew Marg and our three children shared many of Morrison's feelings about the war, as did the wives and children of several of my cabinet colleagues. And I believed I understood and shared some of his thoughts. There was much Marg and I and the children should have talked about, yet at moments like this I often turn inward instead—it is a grave weakness. The episode created tension at home that only deepened as dissent and criticism of the war continued to grow."[104] His mother's stern dictates and the uncommunicative habits they engendered in McNamara were painfully evident many decades later.

The direction of events at home and abroad "shook me," McNamara later said, "and altered my attitude perceptibly."[105] The first major combat between American and North Vietnamese forces in mid-November in the Ia Drang Valley near the border with Cambodia was a sobering event. The five-day firefight between two North Vietnamese regiments and elements of the First and Seventh Cavalry Divisions left 300 Americans and 1,300 North Vietnamese soldiers dead. The sense of an American victory was undercut by the realization that North Vietnam was moving far more forces into South Vietnam than the American military command in Saigon had estimated, meaning more American troops would be needed. General Westmoreland cabled Washington on November 23 with a revised request for additional forces: 200,000 more troops in 1966, twice the number he had asked for in July.

"The message came as a shattering blow," McNamara recalled. He had predicted in July that sending ground troops stood "a good chance of achieving an acceptable outcome within a reasonable time." Now he saw that he was clearly mistaken. During meetings with Westmoreland and other officials in Saigon in late November, McNamara described the American outlook in Vietnam as bleak. "The U.S. presence rested on a bowl of jelly," he later recalled. "Political instability had increased, pacification had stalled, South Vietnamese Army desertions had skyrocketed." Projections for increasing American forces meant there would be 400,000 American troops in South Vietnam by the end of 1966, with another 200,000 possibly to be added in 1967.[106] An American officer at one of McNamara's briefings in Saigon in November noticed, "Mr. McNamara is beginning to show the strain." When the defense secretary entered Bundy's West Wing office after returning from South Vietnam, Bundy's aide Chester Cooper thought "he looked different," "concerned and grave."[107]

On November 30, McNamara presented the president with two options: "to go now for a compromise solution" while holding "further deployments to a minimum," or to "stick with our stated objectives and with the war, and provide what it takes in men and materiel" combined with a gradually stepped-up bombing. If Johnson chose the second option, McNamara would argue for a three- or four-week bombing pause to "lay a foundation in the mind of the American public and in world opinion for such an enlarged phase of the war" and to give North Vietnam "a face-saving chance to stop the aggression."[108]

McNamara lobbied hard for the bombing pause, trying to overcome Johnson's skepticism and the opinion of JCS chairman Wheeler, who wanted more bombing, not less. During a December 17 meeting at the White House at which his top advisers debated a pause, Johnson implied that McNamara's original support for bombing had created the mess they were now in: "We are there now because of the bombing. We wouldn't be there without it." The next day, McNamara said that the chance of a military solution in Vietnam was no better than fifty-fifty.

"You mean that no matter what we do in the military field, you think there is no sure victory," Johnson asked.

"That's right," McNamara said in a low voice. "We have been too optimistic. I'm saying we may never find a military solution. We need to explore other means. Our military approach is an unlikely route to a successful conclusion."

Johnson later admitted to Rusk that what McNamara said "just shocked me and, furthermore, it shocked everybody at the table." Two months later, Rusk, who was usually polite, especially about his high-level colleagues, dismissed McNamara's judgment, saying, "frankly, Mr. President, Bob hasn't had much experience dealing with crises." Even Clark Clifford, who attended another meeting on December 18 at Johnson's invitation, opposed a bombing pause lest it fail, triggering pressure for another escalation of the war.[109]

Eventually, Johnson gave in and approved a brief bombing pause over Christmas. When he decided to extend it for just another day or two, McNamara, vacationing in Aspen, called the president, who was in Texas for the holidays, and asked to meet Johnson as soon as possible. During their talk at the Johnson Ranch the next day, Johnson agreed to an indefinite extension and renewed diplomatic efforts to see if Hanoi was ready to hold peace talks. "We sure backed into" the pause, McNamara told John McNaughton. "We worked it out at the ranch on Monday night."[110]

The pause ended at the end of January—it had lasted thirty-seven days but produced no diplomatic breakthrough. The North Vietnamese depicted it as a "trick"; the Joint Chiefs used it to push for resumed bombing. Johnson told Rusk at the end of the pause that "you and I both knew this thing wouldn't work to begin with" and was a "big mistake."[111]

While war tribulations were closing in on McNamara that fall, he found time to dash to Manhattan to attend a lavish dinner party hosted by Jackie Kennedy for John Kenneth Galbraith, the close Kennedy family friend who had served as ambassador to India during the first two years of the Kennedy administration. The evening turned out to be the occasion when Jackie, two years on from the assassination, now living in Manhattan, resumed socializing in public view. She and McNamara could be seen dancing the Frug, the latest fad, at the Sign of the Dove, the Upper East Side restaurant that was the site of the party.[112] William Walton, who was a painter and another Kennedy family favorite, squired her to the dinner, where she also danced with Galbraith and others.

As 1965 came to a close, McNamara seemed profoundly shaken by the colliding forces bearing down on him: the dichotomy between his developing private doubts about the war and his public support of it and role in escalating America's involvement; his silent agony over Norman Morrison's fiery suicide and his own family's opposition to the war and alienation from him; his strained efforts to serve Lyndon Johnson loyally while remaining faithful to Robert Kennedy and close to Jackie Kennedy. The stress burst into view at a New Year's Eve party in Georgetown when McNamara started weeping while talking about the war with Toni Bradlee. Her husband, Ben Bradlee, described the scene: "Tears were gushing down his cheeks. He was doing most of the talking. Toni was saying very little."[113] The scene was reminiscent of his teary performance at the Medal of Honor ceremony in early December 1964.

On January 6, 1966, Arthur M. Schlesinger Jr. hosted a private dinner in Georgetown for a small group of former Kennedy administration aides.

McNamara confessed he had concluded that the war could not be won militarily. His objective, therefore, had become "withdrawal with honor," but he did not know how to achieve it. Schlesinger noted in his journal that night that McNamara "seemed deeply oppressed and concerned at the prospect of indefinite escalation."[114]

McNamara's fitful, indecisive efforts in the months ahead to get Johnson to disengage from Vietnam would cost him his job and leave him an emotional wreck.

CHAPTER TEN

Equivocation

B y the fall of 1965, McNamara wanted the United States out of Vietnam and had thought of resigning. Yet he remained at his post for almost two and a half more years, continuing to manage the war until February 1968 when he finally stepped down, unsure of whether he resigned or was fired.

During those two years, roughly 18,000 more Americans died in Vietnam, along with countless Vietnamese. That's why, when McNamara confessed many years later that he had continued to direct the war even after he concluded it couldn't be won militarily, the animus against him only increased. "McNamara's war" was bad enough when he actually believed in it, many of his critics charged, but even worse when he did not.

Why did he stay on at the Pentagon? Did he push at White House meetings for a rapid withdrawal from Vietnam, only to be overruled? Did he try to limit American involvement while pressing for negotiations that might end the conflict? Did he alter the way he portrayed the war in public? How did his deepening doubts affect his relations with President Johnson, as well as with his colleagues in the government and the military?

McNamara waited nearly a quarter of a century to address those questions. And when he finally did, his answers seemed as strained as

he appeared to be at the time. He was "ahead of the [American] public in disaffection and a feeling that [the current strategy can't win] and
we've got to get out," he told an interviewer in December 1993.[1] What
"was in my mind at the time," he said, was to propose negotiations that
"would give [North Vietnam] something that came close to what they
ultimately had." By doing so, he added, "I would have saved 25,000 or
30,000 American lives, and I would not have had a situation any worse
than we had, ultimately."[2] What he wanted Johnson to do, he insisted,
was to "get us out."[3]

But he failed to make this case directly to the president, settling instead
for policy recommendations that would diminish the American combat
role and emphasize negotiations with North Vietnam to seek a political
settlement. He also failed to do what he prided himself on doing throughout his career: force full and open debate in the administration on what
was going wrong in the war and on alternatives to its current policy,
including withdrawal. Pressed by later interviewers to explain his reti-
cence, McNamara retreated to a contradictory confession of confusion
and impotence: "I didn't want to bomb Hanoi," he told his biographer
Deborah Shapley. "I didn't want to withdraw. I didn't have the answers.
All I knew was we were in a hell of a mess."[4] He might also have asked
himself why he stayed on as defense secretary despite his rising doubts,
and why he resisted entreaties from friends, including Robert Kennedy,
to resign with a howl of protest against a misguided and mismanaged war.
The answer, as with so much of McNamara's history, is multifaceted, laced
with his own misjudgments, misperceptions, and inability to reckon hon-
estly with his own limitations.

For starters, he thought his paramount duty as defense secretary was to
serve the president loyally, contrary to the oath that he and all other cabinet members took that made clear that their primary obligation was to
uphold and defend the Constitution of the United States. The oath makes
no mention of the president. He surely understood the meaning of the
oath but chose not to honor it or to assume, mistakenly, that his management of an ill-fated war was in service of the Constitution. When his son,
Craig, emotionally wounded by his father's long refusal to criticize the

war, demanded to know why, three decades later, McNamara answered with one word: "loyalty."[5] Edgar Boyles, an Aspen friend of McNamara and a fellow mountaineer, said he thought McNamara's refusal to turn against Johnson and the war was grounded in an old-fashioned sense of propriety common to McNamara's generation. "The propriety comes with a code of ethics of honor and what you don't say as well as what you do say," Boyles suggested. "If he was asked to do a job, he was going to do the job well."[6]

Robert McNamara also believed that by remaining at Johnson's side he could help prevent the president from approving the sharper escalation of the war recommended by the Joint Chiefs, a step McNamara feared would bring China or the Soviet Union into the fight and could lead to a global nuclear war. Seasoned by the Cuban missile crisis and the successful application of moderate rather than extreme force to achieve a Kremlin retreat, he thought his presence was essential to warding off the Joint Chiefs' aggressive recommendations. Jackie Kennedy's appeals to him to end the war, which reached a dramatic high point in 1966–1967, must also have weighed on him and may have motivated him to stick around to prevent the Joint Chiefs from prevailing and to pursue his own hopes of finding a diplomatic resolution to the war.

Yet paradoxically, at the same time, he still believed that defeat in Vietnam might lead to Communist advances throughout Southeast Asia, making him question whether the moderate course he recommended was sufficient, a doubt that also left him unwilling to break publicly with Johnson. Beyond that, he argued at the time and long afterward that airing any misgivings he had about the war would undermine the war effort and be seized on by Hanoi as a propaganda bonanza. His paralysis was compounded by his admiration for Johnson's domestic social and economic programs that McNamara embraced and sought to support. And, not least, McNamara still savored the power and responsibilities of his office and his marquee role in Washington.

All together, it was a recipe for inaction and a refusal to align his public declarations about the war, and his advice to Johnson about how to wage it, with his private views. McNamara could not bring himself to tell Johnson that the time had come, in Vermont senator George Aiken's memorable words, to declare victory and bring the troops home. McNamara's equivocal performance eventually unnerved McNamara himself and tormented him for the rest of his life.

═══

THROUGHOUT 1966 AND THE FIRST HALF OF 1967, MCNAMARA PLOTted with John McNaughton, his closest Pentagon aide, about how to disengage from Vietnam, how to persuade Johnson to cut his losses and push for a negotiated end to the war, and how to get peace talks started. They pressed for bombing pauses and tracked nascent diplomatic efforts initiated by a number of foreign governments, including Britain, the Soviet Union, and Poland. They encouraged Washington's own peacemaking overtures, which were handled primarily by Averell Harriman, the heir of a railroad fortune who had served as governor of New York, ambassador to Moscow, and in a variety of other senior posts under Democratic presidents beginning with Franklin Roosevelt. McNamara himself took charge of one initiative to open peace talks with Hanoi, engineered by Harvard professor Henry Kissinger, after Rusk dismissed it as a waste of time.

McNaughton, assistant secretary of defense for international security affairs, was a Rhodes scholar, a Harvard Law School graduate, and a navy veteran. A tall, ambitious man with a scholarly bent, McNaughton aspired to higher office, hoping someday to become deputy secretary of defense, even defense secretary. McNamara eventually appointed him navy secretary. On Vietnam issues, he was a pragmatist who recognized by 1966 that the United States was losing the war and should look for a way out.

Unbeknownst to McNamara, McNaughton recorded McNamara's every step, private thoughts, and emotional swings in a secret diary that he maintained from January 1, 1966, until days before his untimely death, at age forty-five, in a commercial airplane crash on July 19, 1967. He was to assume office as navy secretary two weeks later. The diary provides an intimate and revealing window into McNamara's growing distress about the war and his indecision about how hard to press Johnson to disengage. For all of McNamara's attempts to wind down the combat and seek a negotiated settlement, he never pushed directly for withdrawal from the war. McNamara's confidential recommendations to Johnson amounted to what might be called a "damage limitation" strategy: his prognosis for the war grew increasingly pessimistic; he opposed major escalations of it; but he acquiesced in lesser American troop buildups and extensions of the fighting.

====

BEGINNING IN JANUARY 1966, THE JOINT CHIEFS REQUESTED PERmission to bomb storage areas where North Vietnam kept supplies of petroleum, oil, and lubricants (POL), which were mainly delivered by Soviet tankers since the North had no oil supplies of its own. McNamara refused to support their proposal. On background, he told journalist Stanley Karnow and other reporters, "You cannot bomb an agrarian society into submission."[7] But later that spring he yielded and endorsed striking POL.

McGeorge Bundy shared McNamara's misgivings about the war. After a January 25 lunch with Bundy at his White House office, McNaughton noted in his diary that Bundy favored seeking a compromise outcome in Vietnam, an approach that Bundy said the top people in the Johnson administration, apart from Rusk, also favored. "He thinks we should pour effort into the nonmilitary side," McNaughton recorded in his diary.[8] But Bundy's days as national security adviser were numbered. Fatigued after five years in the post, and sensing correctly that Johnson had come to distrust him and his Kennedy connections, he departed the White House at the end of February to become president of the Ford Foundation. "The Ford offer was a godsend," Bundy later said, recalling that his relationship with Johnson had frayed. He confided to McNamara, "The problem was that I did not want to break publicly, so I needed a reason that would look good enough to most people, (if not you)."[9] John McCloy, chairman of the foundation, had approached McNamara about the post, but McNamara told him he was not interested.[10]

Bundy's exit deprived McNamara of a vital ally and friend in the White House. Walt Rostow, Bundy's successor, did not share McNamara's doubts about the war. In fact, he was a fierce defender of the war effort. "Mac Bundy's departure was a grievous loss," McNamara recalled. Rostow, in his view, was uncritical about the war. "Optimistic by nature, he tended to be skeptical of any report that failed to indicate we were making progress."[11] McNamara said of Rostow to John McNaughton, "He is full of ideas; the trouble is—so many of them are wrong."[12] Bundy was surprised by Johnson's choice. "I thought it would be someone closer to him culturally—maybe Moyers—and I thought that would be better for everyone and for the country."[13]

On January 29, McNamara, looking for ways to limit the war, was seized with the idea of building a barrier between North and South Vietnam that would prevent the infiltration of arms and troops from North Vietnam into South Vietnam. As he and McNaughton talked about the idea, McNamara grew increasingly excited. "Before long he was bouncing around the room," McNaughton reported. "He said, 'Give me $2 billion and I'll build a barrier no one can get through.'"[14] The concept seemed alluring because, unlike the bombing of North Vietnam, it might hamper North Vietnamese operations in South Vietnam with minimum bloodshed. McNamara, abetted by a group of eminent American scientists who studied and supported the erection of an electronic barrier, pursued the idea despite objections from American military commanders who thought a barrier would prove ineffective. The dubious project, dubbed "The McNamara Line," ultimately was criticized by a Pentagon historian. He called it "a metaphor for the secretary's arbitrary, highly personal, and aggressive management style that bypassed normal procedures and sometimes ignored experts to get things done. He had adopted an idea from civilian academics, forced a reluctant military to implement it, opted for technology over experience, launched the project quickly and with minimum coordination, rejected informed criticism, insisted available forces sufficed for the effort, and poured millions of dollars into a system that proceeded by fits and starts."[15]

By April, McNamara's concerns about the war shot through his conversations with McNaughton. On April 4, the two men pondered how Washington could disengage. McNaughton described their discussion:

Today I went on record with Bob recommending that we use the semi-anarchy in Vietnam as a foundation for disengagement. I spent six hours yesterday at home on the subject and it is clear to me that the ground beneath us is mush out there; the war cannot be won without a political base in South Vietnam and the base is not and will not be there. Since the big issue is US reputation, the time to disengage is when the blame is on someone else—in this case on the Vietnamese, whose total incapacity to behave themselves should amount to at least a minimum justification for our dumping them.

The problem, of course, is how. Could Dean Rusk swallow it? Could Cabot Lodge? How would we minimize the damage—especially since the military government in Saigon is totally polarized both anti-Buddhist (Tri Quang) and anti-Vietcong?

Bob wouldn't hint his state of mind, but he did disclose sympathy for a Buddhist government, which Lodge reported would make a deal with the VC! Also he has repeatedly agreed with me that our increased deployments each time were hoped (by him and me) to provide strength from which a <u>compromise</u> could be struck; each time Rusk kept the US eye on the VC total capitulation![16]

Two days later, McNamara and McNaughton returned to the question of whether the ineffective leadership and infighting in the Saigon government would produce a situation in which, as McNaughton put it, "no one would blame us for washing our hands of the situation." McNaughton recounted their conversation: "Bob said he favored putting on the pressure while negotiating. I said I did too, but that we are not disciplined enough to pull it off; the sights stay too high as the force goes in. He was thinking of talking to the President about it, maybe suggesting that [Ambassador] Lodge be told to try out [South Vietnamese president] Thi[eu] on the subject of an accommodation with "nationalist VC." McNaughton added, "Apparently Ken Galbraith called the President to advise him to take this opportunity to get out of Vietnam."[17]

On April 8, after McNaughton repeated to McNamara the notion that internecine strife in Saigon might "provide us about as good an excuse as we could find to disengage," McNamara startled him by declaring that he wanted to pull American troops out of South Vietnam so urgently he could "hardly stand it.' "[18]

As April came to a close, McNaughton updated the thinking about Vietnam in his diary:

> Things have bogged down re South Vietnam. The "Ball" working group came up with a C+ paper offering three courses of action: A= more of the same; B= push the South Vietnamese to talk to the VC; and C= grab (or create) an excuse to exit. Rusk pushed for a "modified A" (allowing for some "probes" of the VC); Bob pushed for a "hard B" (really the same as Rusk's route). Lodge will be here May 9. Some of the thoughts will be tried out on him. Frankly, no one sees a decent way out of this one. The popular thing to say now is that the political juvenilism we see in Saigon is but a part of "growing up." I suspect, though, that the next time they get themselves into an internecine flap, we might just elect to leave them scrapping as they go over the waterfall. (Except, somehow, nothing ever flows in the direction and at the speed one expects out there.)[19]

While McNamara and McNaughton were ruminating about how to end the conflict, Johnson was digging in on the war, complaining bitterly to Tom Wicker of *The New York Times* about antiwar sentiment at home and the *Times'* coverage of the war. In a seventy-five-minute private meeting with Wicker at the White House on April 25, he used a football analogy to describe his frustration with war critics, imagining a team driving toward a touchdown. "We are trying to get down the field and it is bad enough that the other team is playing rough, kicking and gouging. But it gets really tough when your own fans and the trombone player from your own band come out on the field and hit you from behind, too." Bill Moyers told Wicker that Johnson was angered by a *Times* story a few days earlier that reported that mismatching bomb components had led to ordnance shortages limiting American bombing sorties in South Vietnam.

Johnson acidly told Wicker that he, Johnson, would be happier to see the war end than Arthur Hays Sulzberger, the publisher of the *Times*.[20]

In May, McNamara gave two public speeches that clashed with his image as a cold-blooded warrior and obliquely implied that he was disillusioned with the Vietnam War. At Carnegie Musical Hall in Pittsburgh, he spoke at his daughter Kathleen's commencement at Chatham University as Vietnam War protestors picketed outside. His presence and fear of disruption had forced the school to move its commencement off campus. He noted the anxiety that society "has fallen victim to bureaucratic tyranny of technology and autocracy." He cited a sign carried at Berkeley that read, "I am a human being; do not fold, bend or mutilate," and added, this is "a sentiment we can all emphatically agree with."[21] Quoting numerous poets and philosophers in a long address, McNamara sounded more like a college English professor extolling the humanities than a secretary of defense.

In Montreal on May 18, in a speech to the American Society of Newspaper Editors that McNaughton helped draft, he debunked the idea that military force was the main instrument of US foreign policy. "We still tend to conceive of national security almost solely as a state of armed readiness," he warned. "We are still haunted by this concept of military hardware." But the real key to security was the "character" of the country's "relationships with the world," the "fund of compatible beliefs" and "shared ideas" of the sort that bound the United States and Canada together. It almost sounded as if he were repudiating the Vietnam War. As for less developed nations, "security is not military force—though it may involve it. Security is not traditional military activity—though it may encompass it. Security is development. Without development there can be no security."[22]

It was a startling speech by an American defense secretary. But its relationship to McNamara's private thoughts about Vietnam was clear to those familiar with them. The same day McNamara delivered the speech, McNaughton met in Washington with Averell Harriman. McNamara had made clear to both men that he wanted to end the war.

"I had a good talk with Averell Harriman tonight from 5–6:15 in his office," McNaughton noted in his diary. "He thinks we should be 'talking' with the VC and with the North Vietnamese. He thinks our bargaining position is not too good, but it won't hurt to talk. He reported that Bob had told him we should offer to pull out of SVN [South Vietnam] if the DRV [North Vietnam] would. Averell pointed out that the Communists didn't abide by the Laos deal 'for one minute,' but maybe there's something there. He said Bob said he'd go for a coalition government. Averell thinks we could get the Russians to try quietly to work out a deal. He rejected the idea of a 'public' third-party appeal to which the US could with honor accede."[23]

McNamara had not cleared the Montreal speech in advance with the president. "It caused all kinds of hell in Washington," he recalled. "It upset the President immensely, but it was true."[24] Although McNamara had no inkling yet that the next stop in his career would be as president of the World Bank, his words clearly implied that he would be more comfortable promoting economic development than managing war. Vice President Humphrey, ostracized by Johnson a year earlier because he had dared to propose a withdrawal from Vietnam, sent a supportive note to McNamara, perhaps sensing a kindred spirit. "That was an excellent speech at Montreal. The press reports were good, but the substance of what you had to say was much needed and I predict will have a most favorable reaction."[25]

The press did, indeed, take notice. Columnist Mary McGrory wrote that "the real Robert McNamara, lofty and far-ranging and liberal beyond any dogmas," had "stood up" in Montreal.[26] According to *New York Times* columnist James Reston, McNamara was "reaching beyond the draft, beyond the Pentagon, beyond administration policy, beyond the present, even beyond the concept of sovereign nation states." Reston went on: "He is searching for a unifying principle between power and principle, between the restless, defiant generation on the campuses and the harassed and distracted policymakers in Washington." Reston added, "McNamara will probably not last long enough here to see much progress toward his ideals. He is not the symbol but the critic of Pentagon power. He has fought too many battles against the military interests, the commercial interests, and the political interests—the generals, who want more guns and planes, the manufacturers who make the guns and planes, and the politicians and communities who benefit from the manufacture of guns and planes—to be popular or even to endure."[27]

Journalists like McGrory and Reston had learned that McNamara was disenchanted with the war. But other critics of his Vietnam policy had not—witness the reaction of students at Amherst College at their commencement that spring. As McNamara rose to receive an honorary degree, twenty students walked out (although all but one made sure to receive their diplomas from college president Calvin Plimpton before departing), while twenty others wore white armbands. Most of the class of 270 and several hundred relatives and friends gave McNamara a standing ovation. Plimpton said of McNamara that in "a position of incredible responsibility, in a situation of unimaginable difficulty, and to an unrecognized war of inexplicable dimensions, you have brought a dedicated devotion which inspires admiration for your efforts and awe for your courage." But the former Berkeley and Harvard Business School standout who was being honored was pained to note that it was Amherst honors graduates, more than nonhonors seniors, who wore armbands and walked out.[28]

On June 28, as one of General Westmoreland's search-and-destroy missions was being launched in Vietnam, McNamara blurted out to Johnson in a phone conversation, "It scares me to see what we're doing there—taking 6,000 U.S. soldiers and God knows how many airplanes and helicopters and firepower and going after a bunch of half-starved beggars—2,000 at most, and probably less than that."[29]

That same summer, McNamara asked the CIA, which he regarded as more objective than the military itself, for a no-holds-barred assessment of how the war was going. According to its 250-page report, US bombing couldn't stop the North from supplying the Vietcong with reinforcements, China and the USSR could replace supplies that the American bombing destroyed, and Hanoi was determined to continue the war indefinitely. McNamara summoned the CIA analyst who had written it, a man who had worked on Vietnam for seventeen years and had lived there for the last two, and asked his advice. George Allen replied he would halt the bombing and the buildup of American troops and would negotiate a ceasefire with Hanoi. But wouldn't that result in Communist control of the South? asked McNamara. It would, Allen replied, but so would the war if it continued. But McNamara questioned how the US could give up after sacrificing so many lives and so much money and insisting that American prestige depended on winning the war.[30]

During the summer of 1966, Westmoreland requested still more troops, a 50 percent increase over those already there, which would bring the total to 543,000 by the end of 1967. In response, McNamara demanded "a detailed line-by-line analysis for these requirements to determine that each is truly essential for carrying out the war plan," and he refused to yield when the Chiefs resisted any "reduction in the requirements submitted." Instead, McNamara pressed Johnson to establish "a ceiling on force levels. I don't think we ought to . . . say we're going to go higher and higher—up to 600,000, 700,000—whatever it takes. . . . Somewhere between 500,000 and 600,000 ought to be the ceiling." In September 1966, McNamara also advised halting the bombing in the North, so as to encourage peace talks with Hanoi.[31]

If Johnson read McNamara's advice to be a sign of disillusionment with the war and disenchantment with Johnson, the president, conveniently, had an opportunity to draw McNamara closer when McNamara's eldest child, Margy, was married to Barry Carter, a former Stanford classmate. The Johnsons attended the September 1 wedding at the Bethlehem Chapel at the National Cathedral—Senators Robert Kennedy and Edward Kennedy were seated just behind them—and joined the McNamara family for a reception at their home on Tracy Place. In the hierarchical world of Washington, which McNamara well understood, the presence of the president and First Lady elevated the event and publicly underscored how much Johnson valued McNamara. Lady Bird thought it was a wonderful occasion. "There is nobody in the Government that I admire more than Margy and Bob with their wholesomeness, their intelligence, tough devotion to their jobs, and their sense of fun."[32]

After another trip to Vietnam in October, McNamara told Johnson he saw "no reasonable way to bring the war to an end soon." Pacification had "gone backward," "full security exists nowhere," and even behind American lines in the countryside "the enemy almost completely controls the night." His October 14 memo to the president insisted that the war "must be fought and won by the Vietnamese themselves." "We have known this from the beginning," he continued. "But the discouraging truth is that, as was the case in 1961 and 1963 and 1965, we have not found the formula, the catalyst, for training and inspiring them into effective action."[33] As Brian VanDeMark notes, "these words reflected a return in McNamara's thinking to his position during the Kennedy years. But in the interim the die had been cast, in considerable measure through his efforts."[34] McNaughton, who drafted McNamara's memo to Johnson, summed up the bottom line: "Find a way out." He noted he had told McNamara that the war "would destroy him and prevent LBJ's reelection."[35]

McNamara's public comments about the war in October conflicted with the private doubts he expressed to Johnson. Daniel Ellsberg, who traveled with McNamara on the October trip, was shaken by the gap between McNamara's private views and what he told reporters upon landing at Andrews Air Force Base outside Washington. As their plane was approaching Washington, Ellsberg recalled, McNamara had told Robert Komer, a White House aide, that he thought American-led pacification efforts in South Vietnam had made no progress over the past year. When Ellsberg confirmed McNamara's assessment, McNamara declared, "That proves what I am saying. We've put more than a hundred thousand more troops into the country over the last year, and there's been no improvement. Things aren't any better at all. That means the underlying situation is really worse. Isn't that right?"[36]

Moments later, after landing, he blithely told a swarm of reporters who greeted him at the airfield that the war was going quite well:

> Approximately a year ago when I returned from a similar trip I reported that the situation had deteriorated substantially in the previous year. Today I can tell you that military progress in the past 12 months has exceeded our expectations. The Viet Cong have been unable to mount the monsoon offensive that they had planned for the period June through October of this year, an offensive designed to cut the country in half at its narrow waist. The military pressure

which the South Vietnamese and Free World forces have brought against them has prevented them from mounting that offensive and has inflicted heavy casualties on them. Similarly, the attacks on their lines of communication from North Vietnam to South Vietnam have forced them to shift their lines of communication away from the Ho Chi Minh trail through the Demilitarized Zone in an attempt to shorten them and avoid the very heavy losses that they previously had been sustaining. I think they will be equally unsuccessful in avoiding those losses in their present route.

He went on to note that the South Vietnamese economy had "measurably improved." His one cautionary note: "The effort to pacify the countryside and bring security to hamlets had been "less than satisfactory" and would require increased attention.[37]

A month later, another McNamara memo to Johnson rebutted the Chiefs' contention that the military situation had "improved substantially over the past year," and that bombing of the North should be intensified.[38] In his view, "further large increases in US forces do not appear to be the answer."[39] Faint hopes around this time about a secret Polish-Italian peacemaking effort dissolved when Johnson approved additional aerial bombardment of targets in North Vietnam. The historian James Hershberg, drawing on Communist archives from the period, argued in a 2012 book that the initiative was much more promising than depicted at the time and that Hanoi had agreed to open direct talks with Washington before the effort collapsed.[40]

WHILE GRAPPLING WITH THE JOINT CHIEFS ABOUT VIETNAM, McNamara dealt with a very different conflict closer to home—resolving a dispute between Jackie Kennedy and the Army Corps of Engineers about the landscaping of a permanent John Kennedy gravesite under construction at Arlington Cemetery. It would replace the temporary site selected immediately after the assassination.

By mid-1966, McNamara was making a habit of visiting Jackie in New

York and dining with her at La Caravelle, an upscale French restaurant, when his wife, Margy, was traveling. "When Marg would go out of town, I frequently went up to New York," he recalled. Their encounters happened roughly once a month, McNamara later told Bob Woodward.[41] In May, he headed to Manhattan on a commercial flight, without a security detail, as was his custom when traveling within the United States. New York taxi drivers were on strike. McNamara hopped onto a bus that was headed uptown from his room at the River House on East Fifty-Second Street. Jackie lived at Fifth Avenue and Eighty-Fifth Street. As he exited the bus, unrecognized, he later insisted, he was jostled by passengers in front and behind him. He soon realized they had stolen his wallet. Without cash or credit cards, he had no way to pay for dinner. "So here I am, picking up Jackie for dinner," he recalled, "and I think, *What in the hell to do?*" He was rescued by George Woods, the president of the World Bank, who happened to be seated at a nearby table at La Caravelle and slipped McNamara some cash.[42]

Jackie's mood that summer may have accounted for the frequency of their Manhattan dinners and her desire for friendly company. In mid-July, responding to a letter from Dick Goodwin, she wrote to him from Hawaii, where she had gone to unwind from the incessant pressure in New York. She told Goodwin about the people who had "found peace out here." She named Robert Louis Stevenson, Jack London, Mark Twain, and Paul Gauguin, and said she had read their memoirs. She talked about how she dreamed of living in Argentina, Spain, and Hawaii because they offered fresh thoughts and a new life. She told Goodwin she lacked the strength to return to the old world because of "memories that drag you down" and you "struggle against despair." She went on to inform Goodwin that she had given up smoking and drinking while in Hawaii. She closed by musing about how some cultures managed when life was unbearable by avoiding it. Not a bad idea, she said. Telling Goodwin he was the only person she would say that to, she wrote, "as you are kind of a lost soul too."[43]

Whether McNamara and Jackie talked about the Kennedy gravesite landscape plan at La Caravelle is not known but seems likely. She was convinced by mid-1966 that the plan, designed by her close friend and garden designer, Bunny Mellon, the wife of Paul Mellon, a philanthropist and art collector, was being undermined by the Corps of Engineers and that a "disaster" was inevitable. Her hopes that Senator Robert Kennedy could intervene on her behalf were dashed in her view when Kennedy failed to persuade William Manchester to stop publication and serialization of his book about the Kennedy assassination, *The Death of a President*, a book that Jackie had commissioned and cooperated with but grew wary of over time.

Convinced that the Corps of Engineers was mangling Mellon's design and that Robert Kennedy would be unable to help, she turned to McNamara. He quickly resolved the clash in favor of the Mellon design. Jackie was ecstatic. In a September 14 letter, she thanked him "with all my heart," telling him how important resolution of the problem was for her, how she felt peaceful and optimistic for the first time in months. She had not known how to change the disaster or if it could be averted, she said.[44]

As the last obstacles to the Mellon plan dissolved that fall, Jackie dispatched a letter of effusive thanks and affection to McNamara on November 9. The letter made plain how deeply she admired him. She opened with a playful tone, quoting from a letter that Bunny Mellon had dropped off at Jackie's home that evening. Telling McNamara she was unsure whether she or Bunny loved him the most, Jackie said Bunny "will be my Cyrano" because she stated her feelings about McNamara more effectively than Jackie could. Several paragraphs from Bunny's letter followed that described McNamara's role in nudging the Corps of Engineers to set aside the "ponderous" design plans that Bunny and Jackie opposed. Bunny's relief was clear, as was Jackie's. Jackie appealed to McNamara to understand his value as a person. "If I could give you one thing—I tried so to give it to Jack in his black moments—but I think maybe men can never accept it—it is to know that it is that about yourself that matters." She zestfully told McNamara, "Bunny + I are Vox Populi—even if you think we can't stand peas under our mattresses." Jackie closed by assuring McNamara "there was never anyone like you."[45]

Their relationship seemed to grow even closer in late 1966 and 1967. In a fall 1966 letter that outlined his wish that he and Margy be buried at Arlington National Cemetery adjacent to the Kennedy gravesite, he talked of Jackie's "beauty, intelligence, grace and wit."[46] Jackie, increasingly disturbed by the war and convinced that McNamara desperately wanted to end it, implored him to do so when they met at her Fifth Avenue apartment in New York one evening while Margy McNamara was traveling. (The date of this encounter was not recorded but appears to be in late 1966 or the first months of 1967.) Unlike so many Americans who saw McNamara as the callous architect of the war, Jackie viewed him as an ardent opponent. Her intuition about him was right, up to a point. But Jackie's faith in McNamara seemed to go beyond the private doubts about the war that he shared with her and others at the time. Rather, it seemed grounded in a naive perception of him as a heroic figure battling against the belligerent military brass and a cruel president to end the suffering in Vietnam. And it seemed to draw on her steadfast sense of him as a sensitive, isolated, emotionally troubled figure with whom she had forged an intimate bond during the Kennedy presidency and whom she had come to see as her protector after the assassination.

McNamara described their encounter at Jackie's apartment overlooking Central Park:

> At one point during my long process of growing doubt about the wisdom of our course, Jackie—this dear friend whom I admired enormously—erupted in fury and tears and directed her wrath at me. I was so overwhelmed by her feelings that I still remember every detail of the incident.
>
> Marg was traveling, so I had gone to New York to dine with Jackie. After dinner, we sat on a couch in the small library of her Manhattan apartment discussing the work of Chilean poet and Nobel Prize winner Gabriela Mistral. Both [of] us were especially fond of her poem "Prayer." It is a plea to God to grant forgiveness to the man Mistral loved, who had committed suicide. She writes, "You say he was cruel? You forget I loved him ever.... To love (as YOU well understand) is a bitter task."
>
> Jackie was indeed a glamorous woman. But she was also extremely sensitive. Whether her emotions were triggered by the poem or by something I said, I do not know. She had grown very depressed by,

and very critical of, the war. In any event, she became so tense that she could hardly speak. She suddenly exploded. She turned and began, literally, to beat on my chest, demanding that I "do something to stop the slaughter!"[47]

In another recounting of the incident, he put it this way: "She was just obsessed with the killing that was going on. She was sitting here and I was sitting here and, hell, she didn't have to talk to me about it. I was as obsessed about it as she was. I was getting annoyed and I couldn't do anything, and she saw that I wasn't doing anything."[48]

He described Mistral and her poem (included in McNamara's poetry album), and his encounter with Jackie to Errol Morris this way:

She fell in love with a lowly construction worker—I think he was a worker on the railroad. And ultimately, he committed suicide, and he was a Catholic. And she knew that God would not allow a Catholic who had [committed] suicide into heaven. And therefore, the poem is a prayer to God to admit this man, this poor man, this man who had tried to do good in life, into heaven. It's a very moving poem. But the point of it is that Jackie was moved by it, and I was moved by it.[49]

One wonders if the poem resonated with McNamara because he saw himself as a person who had tried to do good in his life but was now unlikely to be admitted to heaven because of his leading role in the Vietnam War.

Historical records do not precisely record the ramifications of this potent encounter with Jackie, but it must have increased both McNamara's determination to wind down the war and his anguish about his failure to do so. His words graphically captured his predicament, one largely of his own making. Like Jackie, he was "obsessed" with the killing. Yet, as he said, "I couldn't do anything." And perhaps most stinging, given his personal regard for Jackie, "She saw that I wasn't doing anything." As the months passed after this encounter, McNamara repeatedly urged Johnson to seek a negotiated settlement with North Vietnam.

═══

ON NOVEMBER 6, 1966, MCNAMARA TRAVELED TO HARVARD FOR what he imagined would be a day of vigorous but peaceful dialogue with students and a private meeting with Harvard professors, many of whom he knew. The visit quickly turned into a chaotic confrontation with antiwar protestors and ended with a startlingly confessional session with faculty members, including Henry Kissinger. To the surprise of the faculty members, McNamara firmly aligned himself with dovish war critics. It was a performance that would have infuriated Lyndon Johnson, had he heard about it, which he apparently did not, and would have delighted Jackie Kennedy. Whether she heard about it is unknown.

The day was to begin with an off-the-record seminar with a small group of star students. McNamara, apparently convinced that he could handle any protests on his own, traveled to Cambridge without a security team. Barney Frank, later a liberal Democratic congressman from Massachusetts, was then a Harvard graduate student deputized by the Institute of Politics to organize seminars with distinguished speakers. But radical students, some of them members of the still-fledgling Students for a Democratic Society, heard McNamara was coming and demanded a public accounting from him. To avoid a confrontation, Frank arranged for a decoy car to pick up a "false McNamara" at the seminar at Quincy House and drive him to a class Henry Kissinger was teaching on another part of the campus. But demonstrators detected the ploy and surrounded the real McNamara's car.

At that point, recalled McNamara, "all hell broke loose. Students pressed in around the car and started rocking it." When the driver panicked and started driving into the crowd McNamara stopped him, got out, and climbed onto the car's hood. When he told the crowd, which now numbered in the hundreds, that he himself had taken part in demonstrations when he was a student at Berkeley, they responded with catcalls and more pushing and shoving. To which he responded: "I must say there was one difference between you and me. I was both tougher than you and more courteous. I was tougher then and I'm tougher today."

Whether McNamara was taunting his tormentors or quaking in fear of mob violence, or both (one of the SDS organizers later said he noticed McNamara trembling, his pant legs shaking), they took it as a challenge. Guarded by a flying wedge of policemen, he fled into a steam tunnel used to supply food to nearby Leverett House, emerged near Eliot House on Boylston Street, talked to Kissinger's class, and then dined with Harvard faculty friends.[50]

The McNamara who faced the faculty group was entirely unlike public depictions of the man. Graham Allison, a Harvard graduate student at the time who went on to serve as dean of Harvard's Kennedy School of Government and an assistant secretary of defense for policy and plans, took notes during the faculty meeting. His summary memo presented a portrait of the defense secretary that John McNaughton would have recognized but that the American people would have found startling:

> Two images dominate most Cambridge observers' conception of the Secretary of Defense. Both spring from his standard public appearance: the televised press conference on the progress of the war. First, there is the McNamara of "McNamara's War," a harsh, hawklike, hardchinned man symbolized by his cool, dispassionate citation of facts and figures concerning the number of North Vietnamese bridges, PT boats, and gallons of oil destroyed by the latest American attack. Second, there is the McNamara of "McNamara's Revolution": an intelligent, IBMish model of rationality symbolized by his extraordinary capacity to generate and process facts from the number of bolts in a drawer at Fort Leavenworth to the number of megatons required to insure unacceptable damage. The first seems immoral, the second inhuman.
>
> Nothing was more striking about The Secretary's recent visit than the gap between these images and the man. His forthright statements of his own—as opposed to the government's—views concerning Vietnam, the lesson of Cuba II [the Cuban missile crisis], and the role of force in relations among superpowers today revealed the most dovish principal in the government. The depth of his feeling towards the

"unfit" and the Negro, a willingness to laugh at his own errors, the stuff of his gut reactions from his justification of intervention in the Dominican Republic to his reflex in the mob scene—such characteristics unveiled a profoundly sensitive, subtle, and humane personality.[51]

When the discussion turned to Vietnam, McNamara told the professors, "I don't know of a single square mile of Vietnam that has been pacified. Many military men disagree with me on this, but no one has yet identified that square mile. When they try, I tell them that I'm going to get in a jeep—without a battalion escort—and ride through that area. Though some of them might like to see me try, none of them will let me. They wouldn't ride through the area unescorted either."

Asked about his controversial speech in Montreal earlier in the year, McNamara doubled down on his sense of guilt—confessing not only his failure to alter the course of the Vietnam War but the maladroit way he had questioned the overall contribution of the military to buttress US security. On the eve of his Montreal speech, he admitted,

I got so goddamn frustrated that I had to have some release. Otherwise, I would have had to get out of the government then. The remarks were weak and somewhat childish. That's a hell of a way to manage the Department of Defense, but I was frustrated.

My job is to train, equip, and inspire men to risk their lives. In that perspective, Montreal was an immature act. My responsibility is not to build my image but to manage a department. In those terms, Montreal was a luxury. You don't inspire men to obey commands by casting doubt on a central doctrine of their reason for being; that is, that security equals military power.

Perhaps the speech inspired some of you fellows, but that's not my job. That no one else was saying it helps explain my frustration, but you can't excuse childishness.[52]

It is doubtful that President Johnson learned of McNamara's sacrilegious comments at Harvard, but by this time he knew enough of

McNamara's doubts that he started to distance himself from his defense secretary. McNaughton detected the change. On December 11, he noted: "I notice a diminution of power, of influence, in McNamara's hands. This is mainly because the President is in political trouble, I think. But for whatever reason, I sense less harmony between the two men. . . . Now I sense that the President is on the 'hard' side of Bob—e.g., on Vietnam, in Europe, regarding Anti-Ballistic missiles, etc. Bob (and I) is much less effective if the President is really trusting the Chiefs, for example."[53]

A few days later, McNaughton took stock of Vietnam developments:

> We returned to find that the bombing of North Vietnam is being construed by everyone as having escalated. The government is apparently trying to deny it, saying the targets are not new, etc. But the fact is that there has been noticeable escalation. Bob McN. told me this noon that "there are few things that I fight hard with the President, but this will be one of them. The Cuba missile crisis was one, but it turned out the President agreed with me [blockade vs bombing and invasion]; the ABM is another. I'll carry out his decision, but I'm going to fight this one hard." He wants to tone down the bombing. (He believes that the targets hit are not worth the cost on men and equipment, that it is depriving us of international support, and it is frustrating negotiations—which he sees as the only way out of this war.)[54]

As 1967 began, McNamara worried that Johnson, seeking a decisive step in Vietnam, was ready to expand bombing targets in North Vietnam. McNaughton noted: "Bob reports that the President is getting itchy. He wants to act more decisively. Apparently he right now favors strikes at the cement and steel plants and at the thermal power plant grid. Rusk & McNamara are opposed and holding him back. Bob said to me 'It's insane to make those strikes with these things in the wind.' These things are numerous hints that Hanoi & the VC want to talk. They want us to stop bombing first."[55]

Just a few weeks later, McNamara and McNaughton thought efforts to open negotiations with Hanoi looked promising. Harold Wilson, the

British prime minister and a critic of the war, was meeting in London with Alexei Kosygin, the Soviet premier. Chester Cooper, an American diplomat assigned to help encourage peace talks, was in London to monitor the Wilson-Kosygin talks. Poland had offered to help broker negotiations, and Henry Kissinger, then teaching at Harvard, was trying to play a behind-the-scenes role to get peace talks started.

McNamara and McNaughton remained upbeat the next day:

> We definitely are in a new phase in Vietnam. Our reports from London emphasize that Kosygin spent most of his time talking about China—about how they had gone wild, mad—about how the US didn't appreciate what a threat China is, not only to SVN but to all of Asia (!). K apparently let on that he wanted US and UK to stick together.
>
> We have resumed our bombing of NVN. Our deal—last communicated—was that we would stop bombing if NVN certified (?) that it <u>had</u> stopped all infiltration and supply (including resupply) and once we had time to confirm NVN's stoppage, we would stop augmenting (not rotating) our forces. We got no answer from NVN, but we have reason to believe that K passed the word onto Hanoi and that the Soviets are <u>in</u> this thing, trying to bring Hanoi around to a reasonable position.
>
> Bob ventured a hint at optimism this afternoon. He sees a possibility of ending the war this year. He even thinks our side might "win the peace"—but he is really assuming an enemy withdrawal without a commensurate simultaneous US withdrawal.
>
> We'll see. Ho obviously has <u>his</u> problems, including his hawks to deal with.[56]

McNamara's optimism was doubtless genuine, but by this point his influence with Johnson was receding, the prospect of peace talks with Hanoi was still remote, and he was unraveling emotionally.

CHAPTER ELEVEN

Meltdown

As McNamara's anguish over the war deepened in 1967, abetted by his own family's distress and the strong antiwar sentiments of his dear friends Jackie and Robert Kennedy, he found it increasingly difficult to sustain his dual role as a public defender and private critic of the American role in Vietnam. "Bobby had grown to be one of my best friends," he recalled. "When I first met him, he had seemed a rough, tough character who believed that in politics the end justifies the means. But during the eight years I knew him, he grew thirty years in terms of his values and his understanding of the world."[1] McNamara had sensed the depth of their friendship the night of the Kennedy assassination when the two men traveled together to Andrews Air Force Base when Air Force One returned from Dallas with John Kennedy's body. He recalled, "We bonded because we had shared values, number one, and a shared sense of loyalty to the president. Bobby knew that I was loyal to the president. And he also, in a sense, knew that I was loyal to him."[2]

By mid-1967, he and Robert Kennedy were talking at least once a week, according to Kennedy aide Peter Edelman, and the defense secretary was giving the senator "figures, classified material, or at least, you know, unreleased material."[3] Edelman remembered that RFK would often begin his

remarks about the war by saying, "Well, Bob McNamara told me . . ."
Richard Goodwin recalled that "McNamara gave Kennedy copies of his
memos to Johnson. . . . He sent them to Bob *before* Johnson." (McNamara
denied this, writes Thomas.[4])

By 1967, Schlesinger reports, Johnson had become "driven, irascible,
inflamed by wild suspicions." According to Chester Bowles, former undersecretary of state and then ambassador to India, "half his time together
[with LBJ] was taken up by almost paranoiac references to Bobby Kennedy, Wayne Morse, Bill Fulbright and others." When *Newsweek* reported
that Kennedy had detected a North Vietnamese "peace feeler" while visiting Paris, a story that Johnson figured Kennedy had slipped to the magazine, Johnson erupted. "The war will be over this year," he told Kennedy,
"and when it is, I'll destroy you and every one of your dove friends. You'll
be dead politically in six months."[5]

Henry Kissinger, helping McNamara at the time to promote Vietnam
negotiations, described Johnson pressuring McNamara in the summer of
1967: "How can I hit them in the nuts? Tell me how I can hit them in the
nuts." By this time, Johnson later told Doris Kearns Goodwin, "The Kennedys began pushing [McNamara] harder and harder. Every day Bobby
would call McNamara, telling him how the war was terrible and immoral
and that he had to leave. Two months before he left he felt he was a murderer and didn't know how to extricate himself. I never felt like a murderer, that's the difference."[6]

According to Evan Thomas, McNamara and Kennedy did their
talking about Vietnam "privately, not in their offices or over the phone
but while out walking at Hickory Hill. Kennedy feared LBJ was bugging
him." Years later, when interviewed by Thomas, McNamara was "still cir-
cumspect discussing his private talks with RFK in the fall and winter of
1965–1966." "We talked often," recalled McNamara. "We talked about
a lot of things. I recall that he was increasingly doubtful that we could
win the war militarily. That coincided with my feelings." How much
of what McNamara knew about the war and administration policy did
he tell Kennedy? "With Bob I would not have failed to tell the truth,"
McNamara answered. "I'm not sure how much truth. He knew I was in a

difficult position. I loved them both. He [Kennedy] didn't want to make it any harder than it was. We steered away from anything like that. He knew I was determined to be loyal to both, and he didn't want to make it too difficult for me." Did McNamara influence Kennedy's view of the war? "I don't have any doubt about it," was McNamara's answer.[7]

McNamara assured Deborah Shapley that he was careful never to speak against Johnson or the war at Hickory Hill or anywhere else. "We met frequently at his home or my office or whatever, and it never bothered me. I recognized Johnson probably knew about it and wondered whether I was in effect being disloyal to Johnson. I wasn't being disloyal to Johnson, but it was clear to me that Johnson might think so. But that didn't stop me."[8]

The stress of straddling the Johnson-Kennedy divide became ever greater as the months passed. Their disagreements played out politely but plainly during weekly policy-making lunches that Johnson hosted on Tuesdays at the White House with McNamara, Rusk, and other top officials. McNamara often countered the president's hawkish outlook with more dovish views during the lunches, never breaking with Johnson but quietly arguing that escalation was inadvisable and would be ineffective. Johnson sensed McNamara's dissent, even as the defense secretary loyally carried out his duties, and began to distance himself from McNamara. In January 1967, Johnson hung up the phone on McNamara in the middle of a conversation for the first time. Before long, Johnson stopped calling McNamara on the latter's private phone.[9] By that summer, the president was looking for a gentle way to unload McNamara.

McNamara's family reflected the tension that surrounded him and gave him more cause for concern. He never discussed Vietnam, or politics in general, with his children, but if that was partly to insulate them from the turmoil, it had the effect of intensifying their worry. His eldest daughter, Margy, seemed most immune: at age twenty-six and shyer than her parents, she had shunned the limelight in school ("because of my name," she recalled), and she certainly avoided Vietnam protests. She had marched for civil rights in Selma, Alabama, in 1965, which greatly pleased her father. But that didn't convince her that everything was all right.[10]

Kathleen McNamara, three years younger than her sister and more of a rebel, broke with family norms on etiquette as well as politics. Working for Bobby Kennedy in 1966, she invited her friend Sam Brown, a young antiwar activist, to her parents' house for dinner. "There was a great effort on the part of all to maintain cordiality," Brown remembered. "But the arguments became bitter rather early. I was a proselytizer of a cause, and if I could have any influence on a man of McNamara's power I would try. We discussed the war at some considerable length and heat." As he was leaving, Brown said to McNamara, "Anyone who loves the mountains as much as you do can't be all bad."[11]

Craig McNamara, age seventeen in 1967, had struggled to live up to his father's ideals. Dyslexic, he stumbled in school with reading and with mathematics. His grades fell far below his father's, and he never became an Eagle Scout. While a student at St. Paul's School in New Hampshire, he saw a psychiatrist every week in Boston and learned about the Vietnam War's terrible cost at a 1966 teach-in at the school when Jonathan Mirsky, a Dartmouth professor and a war critic, addressed students. But when he called his father in Washington and asked for information on the war, he never received any.[12] How did his father first learn of Craig's opposition to the war? "Dad only noticed when he saw the American flag upside down on Craig's wall," Margy remembered.[13] When the McNamara family gathered at the Mountain Chalet Aspen in December, as they had for years during ski trips, they attended a Quaker-style meeting one evening organized by one of the families that joined them in Aspen every year. When the discussion turned to Vietnam, Craig recalled, "it was a difficult moment for my father." Craig concluded during the meeting, "We were on the wrong side."[14]

McNamara's wife Margy was the only one he confided in at home. How much he actually told her isn't clear, but she could see for herself the tension over the war between her husband and her children, and this, he later admitted, was "a hell of a problem inside my family. It tore my wife apart."[15] In 1966, she was tutoring in DC schools when she conceived of a program, "Reading Is Fundamental," that would supply free books to kids throughout the city. With the help of some well-connected friends and later support from the Ford Foundation, the program grew into a major undertaking, sending vans filled with books to schools around the city. Meanwhile, her husband was taking sleeping pills and grinding his teeth in his sleep, her friend Robert Kennedy was increasingly upset by the war, and she was feeling so ill that her doctor told her to slow down—which of course she didn't. When it turned out she had an ulcer that required surgery in 1967 ("Bob has all the problems, but I have the ulcer," she said; "Margy got my ulcer," he added), he began driving to Johns Hopkins University Hospital in Baltimore at night to see her, managing to return to his Pentagon office right on time the next morning, looking exhausted and often unshaven.[16]

Several McNamara associates noticed his deterioration. Henry Glass, special assistant to the secretary of defense, recalled that McNamara seemed headed for an emotional breakdown. Glass said that McNamara looked gaunt and that the Oxford dress shirts McNamara favored no longer fit crisply as he lost weight. "What I remember is how terribly loose around the neck they began to look," he said.[17] Timothy Stanley, deputy US representative to NATO, hosted Bob and Margy McNamara at his home in Brussels in the spring of 1967. "Bob presented the façade of the human machine," Stanley recalled. "I got beyond that and saw him reflecting doubts about the wisdom of our whole course in Vietnam." Margy told Stanley's wife that she wasn't sure how long her husband could hang on.[18] McNamara later said he used sleeping pills to help him deal with the casualty reports coming in from Vietnam.[19] William Brehm, a Pentagon colleague, watched in amazement one afternoon during a meeting in McNamara's office as the defense secretary dissolved in tears as he gazed upon the portrait of James Forrestal, an earlier Pentagon chief who had committed suicide. Brehm recalled that McNamara shuddered violently and cried as though he could never stop.[20]

AS 1967 BEGAN, JACKIE KENNEDY TURNED TO MCNAMARA FOR HELP arranging a visit to the twelfth-century temples at Angkor Wat in Cambodia. She had long dreamed of seeing the temples, and a visit to Southeast Asia may also have appealed to her as a way of duplicating a successful trip she had made as First Lady to India and Pakistan in 1962. Going to Cambodia would not be as easy. Cambodia's strongman leader, Prince Norodom Sihanouk, was an outspoken opponent of the Vietnam War. Indeed, the United States and Cambodia did not even have diplomatic relations in 1967.

Normally, a former First Lady seeking government assistance for a foreign trip would work with the White House or State Department. But Jackie, no fan of President Johnson or Dean Rusk, asked McNamara to handle the delicate diplomacy. He readily agreed and recruited Averell Harriman, ambassador at large and a primary player in America's fitful efforts to find a negotiated resolution to the war, to assist Jackie. Working through Australia's ambassador in Cambodia, Harriman and his staff were eventually able to arrange the visit in the fall.

On February 27, Jackie consulted with McNamara about a letter she planned to send to Sihanouk, a French speaker. She had drafted it—in French—with Andre Meyer, a French American investment banker who had long been a friend of the Kennedys. She told McNamara in a note that she had informed Sihanouk that she had long wanted to visit his country. Meyer, she said, had corrected her use of past participles and approved the letter. Noting that Meyer and she had talked of McNamara, she added she had been thinking of him "so much" in recent days and knew the times must be "so hard" for him. "You have been so brave for so long," she wrote.[21]

The reference to the hard times McNamara faced and his bravery may have been inspired by a *New York Times* story on February 25 in which he denied disagreeing with Dean Rusk about bombing North Vietnam. The *Times* article, in turn, was likely initiated in response to a newly published article in the *Atlantic* that reported that McNamara had opposed bombing. The *Atlantic* article, "The Education of Robert McNamara," was written by Douglas Kiker, the magazine's Washington columnist. It portrayed McNamara as a beleaguered and isolated figure who had turned against the Vietnam War, an instinctively innocent man struggling to survive in a viciously competitive town.

Recalling that McNamara worked as a counselor at a boys camp when he was growing up in northern California, Kiker said, "Young men who worked as counselors at boys camps possess a basic quality of innocence not usually associated with Secretaries of Defense. But Mr. McNamara remains a man of essentially innocent nature today. It is an innocence largely obscured by his achievement, his power, his energy, his intellect, his awesome ability, and his stern management manner. But there it is, it is pervasive, often it is charming. History may also show that it is dangerous."

"Mr. McNamara is not only the second most powerful man in Washington today. He is also the second most controversial. He inspires emotional response. His friends are as passionate in their defense and praise of him as his enemies are violent in their denunciation." Noting that McNamara had consistently misled the American people about the war, Kiker included a devastating bill of particulars that Peter Osnos later succinctly summarized: "In January 1962 McNamara described the situation in Vietnam as 'encouraging.' In September 1963 it was 'getting better and better.' In March 1964 it had 'significantly improved.' In May, 'excellent progress was being made.' By November 1965, the 'United States had stopped losing the war.' By July 1966, he was 'cautiously optimistic.'"[22]

Kiker reported, "It is just as well to share the matter bluntly: The American military establishment doesn't like Robert McNamara, never did like him, and never will like him."

Kiker smartly observed, "Can a Secretary of Defense who increasingly stands in isolated, philosophical objection to the policy decisions he must implement on the field of battle long endure?

"Doesn't it smack of a dangerous innocence—either that or an ultimate intellectual hypocrisy—on his part to assume he can?"[23]

As copies of the *Atlantic* piece started to circulate in Washington, another insightful story about McNamara appeared in *Parade*, the widely read weekly magazine tucked into the Sunday editions of many American newspapers. The *Parade* article, written by Lloyd Shearer, the magazine's most prominent reporter, appeared under the headline, "Will the Real Robert McNamara Please Stand Up?" Although a generally sympathetic portrait of McNamara, the story included unsparing criticism of the defense secretary as it explored his six-year tenure at the Pentagon. "As Defense Secretary, Robert McNamara was sailing full speed ahead until he ran into the Vietnam storm," Shearer wrote. "Since then he has been condemned, criticized, belittled, damned, lampooned, mocked, denounced, denigrated, castigated and vilified. He has become the target of Viet Cong assassins, the object of contumely by both hawks and doves, the disappointment of academicians who feel that, along with his phenomenal memory and wizardlike calculating ability, he somehow in his 50 years should have acquired enough wisdom in international affairs to find a quick answer to Vietnam."[24]

One of the articles, most likely the *Parade* piece, affected Jackie profoundly. She sent a passionately supportive letter to McNamara on March 7, two days after the Shearer story was published. It was an extraordinary letter that made clear how much McNamara meant to her, how close she felt to him, and how deeply she believed he was a force for peace, not war.

She felt "tears stinging my eyes" when she read the article, she told McNamara, and she recalled that her husband had said, "'One man can make a difference.'" McNamara, in her view, was making a vital difference by standing against the relentless power of the government and the military, trying his best to "stop the nightmare." How many people in the world, she wondered, owed their lives to him, and any sense of peace that they and their children enjoyed. History must understand that, she emphasized, promising that she would record it and "leave it buried somewhere for people to find when I am dead—and I will tell my children that about you." She told McNamara she understood how hard it was for him, assuring him, "I will never desert you." She promised to provide the support he needed when he could not help himself and when the forces arrayed against him tried to extinguish his spirit. Calling his travails "more complex than any dark hell Shakespeare ever looked into," she implored him not to let his critics reduce him to a question mark that would make him expendable. "I feel so close to you" in difficult times, she said, "because in my dark times you were always the one who helped me." Finally, she affirmed her faith and trust in him. "I wish I could change the world for you—the only thing I can do is tell you how much you mean to me."[25]

On March 12, McNaughton again sensed there might be a diplomatic way to exit Vietnam with some help from the Kremlin, which seemed interested in encouraging peace talks.

"There is some hope emerging. We may—if our bombing of the Steel mill and thermal power plants doesn't screw things up—be able to get some secret talks going without stopping the bombing. This thru the good offices of Moscow. And then the issue is what we talk about. The nut-cutting. Perhaps the time has come to force a faceup to what we'll settle for. Specifically, what role do we envisage for the VC in the South; the other issues probably can be surmounted."[26]

A month later, Jackie revisited her Cambodia plans in a letter to McNamara, seeking his help to persuade Sihanouk not to turn the visit into a media spectacle. "Otherwise it will just be a circus," she wrote. She wanted to limit press coverage to her arrival and departure and one formal government event. In addition, allowing Sihanouk's private photographer to take one photo of her with the prince at Angkor Wat would be fine, she said. That photo could be released for worldwide use.[27]

On April 18, McNamara's tenure as defense secretary unexpectedly reached a critical moment. During a two-hour lunch at the World Bank with its president, George Woods, McNamara learned that Woods's term would expire at the end of the year and that Woods thought McNamara should succeed him. "I expressed considerable interest," McNamara later recalled.[28] But he told Woods that he had rejected similarly appealing job possibilities, including the presidency of the Ford Foundation. "Hell George, I'm working for President Johnson in the middle of a war. I'm not about to leave, no way."[29] But McNamara was so taken with the idea that he and Margy stayed up until 4 a.m. discussing the possibility.[30] Despite McNamara's association with an unpopular war, numerous corporations, foundations, and universities were eager to talk to him about joining their ranks as a top executive or board member when he tired of serving as defense secretary.[31] McNamara reported the World Bank feeler to

Johnson three or four weeks later. The president seemed noncommittal. "Never once did I take the initiative to leave," McNamara recalled.[32] He left it to the president to raise the issue again if he wished. As the largest donor to the bank, the United States—specifically, the president of the United States—traditionally selected the bank president.

The fuse to McNamara's departure was lit.

=====

McNamara's misgivings about the war reached a pivotal point in May. He sent a pessimistic twenty-two-page, single-spaced memorandum to the president on May 19, 1967. "There appears to be no attractive course of action," was his grim conclusion. Continuation of Washington's current course would likely not persuade Hanoi to negotiate until at least after the American presidential election in 1968. Increasing US forces and actions against the North would likely lead to "a serious confrontation if not war, with China and Russia." Meanwhile, the American public "are convinced that somehow we should not have gotten in this deeply. All want the war ended and expect their President to end it. Successfully, or else." Given all this, the US had two options. "Course A" would give Westmoreland the 200,000 additional troops he wanted, which would require calling up the reserves and upping the defense budget by $10 billion. But this option "could lead to a major national disaster."

McNamara recommended "Course B": No more than 30,000 fresh troops for Westmoreland; no incursion into Laos and Cambodia; limiting bombing of North Vietnam to below 20 degrees north latitude, plus "periodic peace probes" offering a role in the South for members of the Vietcong. Course B "will not win the Vietnam war in a military sense in a short time," McNamara wrote, but it would "avoid the larger war" threatened by Course A. Course B would be part of "a sound military-political/pacification-diplomatic package that gets things moving toward a successful outcome of the war in a few years. More than that cannot be expected."[33]

Walt Rostow, the national security adviser, disagreed. In a memo to Johnson he said, "It appears a reaction against the JCS position as he understands it and projects it—a reaction that goes a bit too far. It is a strategy further towards the other end of the scale than the one I would recommend." As for McNamara's recommendation to limit bombing of North Vietnam, Rostow argued, "I would leave more room for bombing the Hanoi-Haiphong area."[34]

By the spring of 1967, the cost of the war in American lives had risen to a new high: 274 American soldiers were killed during the last week of March, bringing the total in the war so far to 8,560.[35] Despite sharply increased U.S. bombing, Communist troop strength in the South had grown from 204,000 to 278,000. With no prospect of ending the war, on June 17, McNamara commissioned a secret study (without telling Johnson, Rusk, or Rostow) about how the United States had gotten involved and managed the war. Later known as the "Pentagon Papers," McNamara wanted "an encyclopedic and objective" collection of primary documents "throwing light on the decision-making process so that lessons could be drawn" by future historians. Assigning the project to his military aide, Col. Robert Gard, and to John McNaughton, McNamara told them, "Tell your researchers not to hold back.... Let the chips fall where they may." McNaughton passed the project to his special assistant Morton Halperin, who assigned it to his deputy, Leslie Gelb, who recruited more than thirty researchers, including Daniel Ellsberg and Richard Holbrooke, who produced forty-seven volumes containing more than 7,000 pages and 2.5 million words, which weren't completed until 1969, by which time McNamara had left office.[36]

＝＝

AS MCNAMARA TRIED TO STEER JOHNSON TOWARD A DIPLOMATIC resolution of the war, his devotion to Jackie Kennedy played out openly at the May 27 christening of a new aircraft carrier named after President Kennedy. Thinking that he would deliver the keynote address at the ceremony at the shipbuilding yard in Newport News, Virginia, McNamara and his chief Pentagon speechwriter drafted an emotional tribute to Kennedy. The speech was shelved when Johnson decided to attend the christening and deliver his own remarks. But McNamara's protective concern about Jackie was evident when he cheekily defied the expected protocol of escorting Jackie and her two children to a postchristening reception hosted by Johnson, a prime opportunity for media coverage of Johnson and JFK's widow. After telling the president that Jackie would join him shortly, McNamara instead spirited her and Caroline and John Jr. to a helicopter that delivered them to a private jet for the flight to the Kennedy estate in Hyannis Port, Massachusetts. "I have reached the point where I cannot go through any more public functions," Jackie said. "Today was heartbreaking . . . and I cannot keep it up."[37] Shortly after the christening, Bobby Kennedy said to McNamara in a handwritten note, "You have carried the burden so well for so long. And for this we are all grateful—and I speak for my children and the others like them."[38]

On June 1, in a letter to Margy McNamara saying she could not accept a McNamara dinner invitation in Washington, Jackie described Robert McNamara's adroit handling of the postchristening scene at the Newport News shipyard. "What would we have done without Bob?" she wrote, marveling at how McNamara had told Johnson that she and McNamara would join him at the reception soon and then "whisked" her and her children to the helicopter. She was grateful for having been able to come and go so quickly at the christening. She had been in "a kind of a trance," she said, anticipating the event and seeing so many familiar people there.[39]

=====

BACK IN VIETNAM (FOR THE NINTH TRIP) IN EARLY JULY, THIS TIME with General Wheeler and Nicholas Katzenbach, the undersecretary of state, McNamara was pressed yet again for more troops. He seemed "unusually quiet and withdrawn." And when informed that the Saigon government couldn't supply those soldiers itself by lowering its draft age from twenty to eighteen as in the United States ("Psychologically, we hope they would accept this," commented one of Westmoreland's aides), McNamara burst out: "Let me just say this, general: psychologically, I cannot accept it. I am sick and tired of having problems in what the GVN [Government of South Vietnam] accept when American society is under the strain it is under today." McNamara's explosion "stunned everyone in the room accustomed to his normally restrained and methodical style."[40]

The outburst was likely related to stress about Margy's deteriorating health. On July 7, the day he left Washington to travel to Saigon, she was hospitalized because of an acute ulcer that required surgery. She would remain at Johns Hopkins Medical Center in Baltimore for more than a month. Cyrus Vance, his deputy and friend, had left office in late June. Around this time, McNamara told Colonel Gard that the "body count" of Communist dead that he and the military had used to gauge progress in the war was obviously misleading: "If the reports of enemy casualties are correct, we would have destroyed the North Vietnamese army two times over."[41]

On July 12, a day after returning from Vietnam, McNamara briefed Johnson about his visit. His report was a good deal more upbeat than the glum assessments he had shared privately over the past year with McNaughton, Harvard scholars, and Jackie Kennedy. When Johnson asked him, "Are we going to be able to win this goddamned war?" McNamara said he thought so. "For the first time Secretary McNamara said he felt that if we follow the same program we will win the war and end the fighting," the notetaker at the meeting recorded. Both McNamara and Wheeler assured Johnson that the war was not stalemated.[42]

At a lunch following the meeting, Johnson told McNamara he should tell the press about his visit to South Vietnam. The president, listing items that had come up at the earlier meeting, instructed McNamara to say that some additional American troops would be needed, that American forces deployed to South Vietnam should be better utilized, and that Washington would be asking a number of countries to commit their own troops to the war. Anxious to reassure Americans that Washington could manage the war effort without mobilizing reserve forces, he asked McNamara to say there was no reason to call up reserves to meet manpower requirements in South Vietnam. Lastly, he told McNamara to inform the press that there was no military stalemate in South Vietnam.[43]

McNamara dutifully did so that afternoon in a meeting with reporters at the White House, knowing full well that his comments clashed with his own pessimistic views. *The New York Times* front page the next morning carried a prominent headline, "McNamara Sees No Reserve Call for Vietnam War." The story began, "Defense Secretary Robert S. McNamara said today that 'some more' American troops would be needed in South Vietnam but not so many as to require a callup of reserves." At the time, the *Times* said, with 450,000 to 460,000 American troops in the war zone, just 30,000 short of the total authorized by Johnson, the army could provide only one more division with supporting units without needing to activate reserve units. McNamara "hinted" to reporters that various allies, including Australia, South Korea, the Philippines, and Thailand, would be asked to help fill the new manpower requirements. Channeling Johnson, McNamara assured the journalists that several hundred senior American and Vietnamese officers in South Vietnam considered reports of a stalemated war to be, "in their words, the most ridiculous statements they ever heard."[44]

In a separate story the same day that belied McNamara's comments and underscored the acute level of bloodshed in Vietnam, the *Times* reported that thirty-five soldiers in the Fourth Infantry Division had been killed and thirty-one wounded in a battle with North Vietnamese forces in the Central Highlands.[45]

The gap between McNamara's doubts about the war and the positive reports he gave to Johnson and the press smacked of hypocrisy. By his actions and words at this moment in July, McNamara seemed desperately to be trying to keep his job by reassuring Johnson that they were still on the same page. Looking back at it years later, McNamara unpersuasively defended his performance by saying, "The optimistic briefings I had received in Saigon had momentarily eased my longstanding doubts about the war's progress in the South."[46]

On July 19, McNamara was staggered by news that John McNaughton had been killed in a plane crash, along with his wife, Sally, and their eleven-year old son, Theodore. Their other son, Alex, eighteen at the time, was not on the flight. The McNaughtons were passengers aboard Piedmont Airlines flight 22, scheduled for a short hop from Asheville, North Carolina, to Roanoke, Virginia. Shortly after taking off at Asheville, the commercial jet collided with a twin-engine Cessna over Hendersonville, North Carolina. There were no survivors from either plane.

McNamara was informed about McNaughton's death in a call from his military aide while visiting Margy at Johns Hopkins Hospital. Back at his Pentagon office, McNamara *seemed* unperturbed by the death, carrying on business as usual, even playing squash. His chief speechwriter, John Maddux, later recalled that McNamara was laughing, acting as if nothing had happened. Maddux figured it was just the latest example of his tightly disciplined boss bottling up his emotions, refusing to show his feelings.[47] But a group of women journalists who met with McNamara that day noted a change in his demeanor compared to encounters in earlier years. "The strain of his job, his travels, and his wife's illness showed," one of the women wrote in a story about the meeting. "McNamara appeared thin, pale and tense. He did not speak like a man who knew all the answers."[48]

McNaughton's death came just as McNamara was managing a secret diplomatic effort to open peace talks with North Vietnam. The secret operation, code-named "Pennsylvania," started just days before McNaughton's plane went down, when Henry Kissinger cabled McNamara from Paris, where he was attending a meeting of the Pugwash Conference, a gathering of scholars, scientists, and government officials to discuss ways to prevent armed conflict. Kissinger reported that he had met Herbert Marcovich, a French scholar, who said he could help arrange direct contact between Washington and Hanoi as a first step toward peace talks. Another Frenchman, Raymond Aubrac, a longtime friend of Ho Chi Minh, offered to assist. McNamara informed McNaughton about the Kissinger message. "We've made a lot of abortive attempts to open negotiations with no results and this may prove to be another of those dead ends," he told McNaughton. "But why don't we explore it in ways that won't involve costs or risks?"[49]

When McNamara reported the development to Johnson and Rusk at lunch the next day, Rusk swatted away the idea. "Oh Bob, this is just another of those blind alleys that lead nowhere. We've been down them before. Forget it."[50] Unwilling to let it go, McNamara persuaded Johnson and Rusk to let him pursue it, even though it clearly fell into the State

Department's area of responsibility. McNamara energetically encouraged the initiative from his Pentagon office, gaining Johnson's approval to tell Kissinger that Marcovich and Aubrac could deliver a message to the North Vietnamese that the United States was willing to stop aerial and naval attacks on North Vietnam if the stoppage would lead promptly to productive peace talks. At a July 25 meeting with Johnson, McNamara, and other top aides, Rusk again dismissed reports that opening negotiations with Hanoi might be possible. Rusk reported that a number of diplomatic "probes" had proven futile. "There is nothing which indicates a serious change" in Hanoi's attitude, Rusk said.[51]

Two weeks later, at another White House meeting, subtle but unmistakable strains between Johnson and McNamara shot through the conversation when the discussion turned to a new set of North Vietnam bombing target recommendations from the Joint Chiefs and the Kissinger diplomatic initiative. Johnson, McNamara, Rusk, and Katzenbach all approved striking a thermal power plant in Hanoi. But McNamara was wary about hitting targets in a buffer zone in North Vietnam near the Chinese border, fearing an accidental intrusion into Chinese air space. Johnson agreed there was a danger but approved the bombing as long as it was executed carefully. As for the Chiefs' recommendation to widen the number of targets around Hanoi and the nearby port of Haiphong, McNamara advised restraint. He warned that additional bombing would cause civilian casualties, undermine diplomatic efforts to end the war, and fuel antiwar sentiment at home. Johnson disagreed, bluntly saying he was concerned they were not escalating enough to win. McNamara pushed back, telling Johnson that going after the new targets would not necessarily produce a win.

As the group talked through the pros and cons of several specific targets in and around Hanoi and Haiphong, including a critical bridge in Hanoi, Johnson grew impatient with McNamara, according to notes made at the meeting by Tom Johnson, a presidential aide:

> The President said he would authorize all targets except the cities
> and the buffer zone if General Wheeler can do it without going into
> China. The President said he would seriously consider taking out the

Hanoi bridge if it is so essential to transportation. The President said, "We have got to do something to win. We aren't doing much now." The President said Secretary McNamara should worry about the heat he has to take on the Hill about bombing limitations. The Secretary said he was not worried about the heat as long as he knew what we were doing is right. He questioned: "Does this help get it over?"[52]

Differences between McNamara and Johnson, and McNamara and Walt Rostow, sharpened when McNamara updated the group about the Kissinger diplomatic track involving the two Frenchmen. He reported that, according to Kissinger, the two men had received an encouraging response from North Vietnamese officials. Tom Johnson's notes detailed the discussion:

> These individuals were debriefed in Paris by Mr. Kisinger [sic], a consultant to the Department of State. They related that Hanoi was willing to negotiate after a cessation of the bombing, even a de facto cessation. They agreed to negotiate secretly on matters affecting North Vietnam without the Vietcong but said the VC must be represented on issues affecting South Vietnam. They said they recognized the need for U.S. troops to stay in Vietnam until after a political settlement. They recognize the need for a coalition government. Hanoi will not push for reunification until after a political settlement.
>
> The most important part of the memorandum, Rostow and McNamara said, was that Hanoi told the Frenchmen they would not take advantage of the bombing cessation.
>
> Secretary McNamara said it was the most interesting message on the matter of negotiations which we have ever had.
>
> The Secretary said there will be further discussions on the 16th. The President questioned about the reliability of the two men. Secretary McNamara said to his knowledge, they were completely reliable and that Kisinger is a tough, shrewd negotiator.
>
> The president said he saw no need until the facts become clearer to slow up the bombing. He said the moment they are willing, we cer-

tainly are ready to sit down. We will discontinue all bombing north of the 17th parallel if we know they will not take advantage of it.

But we will not quit until we have their assurance they will not take advantage of the bombing halt. If at the end of that time they take advantage of it, we will answer it with interest.

At this point, Johnson asked Rostow for his advice about the Joint Chiefs' proposed bombing targets. Rostow recommended striking the thermal power plant, the bridges, various transportation links, and other targets. Johnson again was dismissive about hesitating. "The President said—that propaganda about a stalemate has us wobbling now, that he was no longer worried about the stop-the-bombing pitch." The meeting ended with Rostow and McNamara arguing over the effectiveness of the American bombing. When Rostow said some reports showed that bombing was impeding North Vietnamese infiltration into South Vietnam by 50 percent, McNamara fired back that the number was closer to 1 percent and that diseases like malaria were a far greater obstacle to the North Vietnamese than the American bombing raids.[53]

The day after these testy exchanges at the White House, the Preparedness Investigating Subcommittee of the Senate Armed Services Committee confronted McNamara with the necessity to state his views in public. The result, he recalled, was "one of the most horrible experiences I have ever gone through."[54] He had once told his former Harvard Business School colleague Eugene Zuckert, now secretary of the air force, that "except for Dick Russell and a few others, most of those people are really stupid."[55] Even so, McNamara prepped for such hearings as if his reputation, not theirs, was on the line, imagining questions he would be asked, devoting hours to preparing for each hour in the witness chair, donning his familiar mask of cool, bloodless logic, not deigning to flatter or joke with his interrogators. They, in turn, regarded him as condescending and decided to precede his appearance with several days of testimony from generals and admirals boiling over with anger and frustration at the way he had prevented them from winning the war.

Adm. U. S. Grant Sharp, commander of air operations over Vietnam,

JCS Chairman Earle Wheeler, and air force and navy chiefs Gen. John McConnell and Adm. Thomas Moorer all argued strenuously for greatly expanded bombing of the North, including attacking Hanoi directly and mining Haiphong harbor. When McNamara testified several days later, his rebuttal was a classic example of his ability to mobilize facts and figures— but this time not to make the case for war but for limiting it. It was true that "the great bulk" of Hanoi's imports now entered through Haiphong— perhaps as much as 4,700 out of 5,800 tons per day—but only about 500 tons of military equipment came by sea. Even if Haiphong and other ports were closed, the North "would be able to import over 8,400 tons a day by rail, road and waterway." Even if road, rail, and the Red River waterway traffic could be reduced by 50 percent, Hanoi "could maintain roughly 70 percent of its current imports." In sum, there was "no basis to believe that any bombing campaign, short of one which had the population as its target, would by itself force Ho Chi Minh's regime into submission."

"I am terribly disappointed with your statement," sneered Strom Thurmond of South Carolina when McNamara finished. "I think it is a statement of placating the Communists. It is a statement of appeasing the Communists. It is a statement of no-win. It seems to me that if we follow what you have recommended, we ought to get out of Vietnam at once, because we have no chance to win, and I deeply regret that a man in your position is taking that position today."[56] Thurmond's advice to exit was rhetorical. As VanDeMark correctly points out, "McNamara's analysis pointed to the same policy verdict, but he could not bring himself to advocate withdrawal."[57]

Johnson was incensed by McNamara's performance. His defense secretary had not cleared his prepared congressional statement with the White House beforehand because he "knew [his statement] would infuriate Johnson," recalled Roswell Gilpatric. "It was just a question of how large the explosion would be and what the denouement would be." Johnson summoned McNamara to the White House and gave him hell. The harangue— anger, weeping, telling McNamara he had wrecked his presidency—raged on from 7 p.m. to 11 p.m. "I've been through a lot in my life, but never so completely drained as after that," McNamara told Gilpatric.[58] According to another aide, the president said afterward, "I forgot he had been president of Ford for only one week."[59] McGeorge Bundy once said of Johnson that "he would hear anything if he could hear it privately."[60] So it wasn't only what McNamara had said, but that he said it openly.

As the summer progressed, White House aide John Roche concluded McNamara was "disturbed" and near a "nervous breakdown." He noted, "McNamara was hanging on by his fingernails.... Oh God, he looked awful.... The heat was terrific. He was, I think, a very disturbed guy and I think the President was aware of this also." One day in August, Roche entered the Oval Office after Johnson had been talking on the phone to Margy McNamara, who was still hospitalized. "You know," said the president, McNamara "is a fine man, a wonderful man. He has given everything, just about everything, and you know, we just can't afford another Forrestal." In late August, James Reston told a friend, "Sally and I had lunch with Bob McNamara and his wife at Kay Graham's yesterday and he was obviously depressed and yet even in that small and intimate group, not really prepared to talk about Vietnam, which is of course the heart of our difficulties."[61]

McNamara's eagerness to move the Vietnam conflict from the battle-field to the bargaining table was vividly evident at a September 26 luncheon meeting with Johnson, Walt Rostow, Katzenbach, CIA director Richard Helms, and George Christian, the White House press secretary. McNamara and Katzenbach pressed Johnson to suspend bombing raids in North Vietnam to signal American restraint as North Vietnamese leaders weighed whether to embrace the Kissinger diplomatic overture led by the two Frenchmen. Johnson was torn, hoping diplomatic talks would materialize yet adamant about keeping military pressure on Hanoi to drive them to negotiate. Helms sided with Johnson. Rostow, like Johnson, was ambivalent but ultimately supported continued bombing.

McNamara summarized the situation, according to notes of the meeting:

On targets, the JCS recommends elimination of restrictions around Hanoi. They recommend a strike on Phuc Yen airbase, and they want restrike authority on targets previously hit inside the 10-mile circle. There are 25 targets which have been authorized but not struck. In my opinion, it would be harmful to the Paris talks if we were to intensify the bombing. It is unlikely that the military progress which they would produce would be great enough to change attitudes toward negotiations.

There have been two questions sent to Hanoi:

1. Do we understand that if we stop the bombing that within two days you will go to the conference table?
2. Will you talk to Kissinger if we hold the current level of bombing?

While there are these discussions I would recommend against additional bombing. We have enough targets for another week. On Phuc Yen, I see no great risk of the Soviets reacting at this time. I will not strongly recommend against the strike.

As the discussion proceeded, McNamara made an impassioned plea to Johnson to let the peace initiative continue. "The serious problem is that you must show the American people that you are willing to walk that last mile. You sent a good formula. No American President could expect you to do more. But we do not pay much for keeping this going." Johnson was dubious.

I think they are playing us for suckers. They have no more intention of talking than we have of surrendering. In my judgment everything you hit is important. It makes them hurt more. Relatively few men are holding down a lot of men. I think we should get them down and keep them down. We will give them an opportunity to speak and talk if they will. If we believe that we should bomb, then we should hit their bridges, their power plants, and other strategic targets outside the ones which we have ruled off-limits.

We get nothing in return for giving all we have got. But I guess a pause won't hurt because the weather is bad anyway. But I do want to get all the targets hit that we dare approve. Then we will make public the pause that Thieu had mentioned. If they do not talk we will have to go to more drastic steps. We are losing support in this country. The people just do not understand the war. But nobody can justify holding off for five weeks. We must look at this thing very carefully. I agree with Dick Helms. It makes no difference in their minds where we hit. Hanoi alone will not do it.

They still want permanent cessation, their four points, and what they have said. How do you wrap up the channel if it is getting us nowhere.[62]

As the lunch ended, Johnson instructed Katzenbach to prepare a paper explaining why the Kissinger effort should be extended.

McGeorge Bundy, reflecting years later on the abortive American diplomatic efforts to end the war, said, "LBJ never let anyone see his hole card on the question of acceptable peace terms." He added, "This way of stating it may be wrong—maybe he didn't have a hole card—no concession beyond the position of Dean Rusk, which as I remember it was simply that the North should get out of the South and leave it to the South and the U.S. to decide their own relations."[63]

═════

ON OCTOBER 21, AS PLANS FOR JACKIE'S THREE-DAY NOVEMBER VISIT to Cambodia were being finalized, McNamara and the Pentagon became the target of one of the largest antiwar protests of the Vietnam conflict. More than 20,000 demonstrators surged from the Lincoln Memorial over the Memorial Bridge to the Pentagon, bringing the antiwar movement to McNamara's doorstep. McNamara knew that defending the Pentagon, surrounded by open lawns and parking lots, would be impossible unless combat troops were employed and given orders to shoot protestors who tried to storm the building. He was determined to avoid a bloody confrontation. Combat soldiers from the Eighty-Second Airborne Division, ordered to Washington to defend the Pentagon, blocked the main entrance but were restricted by rules of engagement that prohibited the firing of their weapons. Protestors taunted the troops but remained peaceful, some placing flowers in the rifle barrels of soldiers, and the day ended without bloodshed or a shot being fired. Norman Mailer chronicled the events in *The Armies of the Night*, a blend of fiction and nonfiction that won a Pulitzer Prize for the author. As the protestors assembled, a photo-journalist recorded a striking photo of McNamara peering impassively out an open Pentagon window at the crowds below.

McNamara was offended by the uncouth behavior of some of the pro-testors and the disorderly way the demonstration was led. "Girls were rub-bing their naked breasts in the soldiers' faces," he later told Hendrickson. "They're spitting on them; they're taunting them. God, it was a mess." "They did it all wrong," the former Eagle Scout continued. "My God, if fifty thousand people had been disciplined and I had been the leader, I absolutely guarantee you I could have shut down the whole goddamn place. You see, they didn't set up proper procedures."[64]

Jackie saw the McNamara photo the next day and promptly dispatched an admiring letter on October 22 to McNamara about his role during the protest. It also talked about her fascination with the number 3 and a 1949 film, *The Third Man*, a noir depiction of postwar Vienna. The let-ter is revealing in several ways. It reaffirms her view of McNamara as a heroic figure, evidently reinforced by his successful efforts to secure a visa for her to visit Cambodia; it shows that she and McNamara exchanged favorite records and listened to them when together, a cozy custom that underscores the warmth of their relationship; and the letter's references to the film reflect a fascination with the occult and a compelling vision of McNamara that she perceived incongruously in the movie.

"Dear, Dear Bob," she wrote, "I am thinking so many kind thoughts of you tonight." Referring to the photo of McNamara watching the pro-test from his Pentagon window, she said, "I never saw anything so brave." She reported that she had played all his records that evening, thinking of the movie *The Third Man*, and the number 3, which she described as "a magic number." Urging him to keep a promise he had made to watch it, she told McNamara about her visit to Vienna while a student in Paris. She recalled being frightened by Russian soldiers patrolling the streets with machine guns. Returning to the movie, she struggled to explain its fascination for her, calling the film melancholy yet hopeful and somehow relevant to America in the 1960s. "Everything I have loved I want to share with you," she told McNamara. She joked that if McNamara viewed the film, he would fall in love with the female star, Alida Valli, making Jackie wonder why she was insisting that he see the film. She whimsically but mysteriously referred to secrets of Prince Sihanouk and Ho Chi Minh and ended the letter by calling McNamara the third man.[65]

Jackie's reference to 3 as a "magic number" in light of McNamara's handling of the Pentagon protest seems puzzling, unless she means that the date of the demonstration, October 21, could be translated into 3 by adding the 2 and 1 in 21. In the world of numerology, where the occult or esoteric meaning of numbers is pursued, 3 is regarded as an auspicious number. In March, she had sent him a very brief, cryptic note that just included a warm salutation and the number 3.[66] What was this fascination with the number 3 about?

Jackie's interest in the movie *The Third Man* may offer a window into how she saw McNamara and why she was so intrigued by him. On one level, unrelated to McNamara, the movie brought back frightening memories of her brief visit to Vienna while a student in Paris in 1949–1950. At the time, the four victorious powers of World War II—the United States, Britain, the Soviet Union, and France—still maintained military forces in the city, each nation patrolling separate quarters of the inner city area. But on another level, the film clearly made her think of McNamara. That might have been simply because one of the main characters, Harry Lime, played by Orson Welles, had deftly arranged a visa for an American buddy, Holly Martins, played by Joseph Cotten, to come to Vienna to work for him. This may have led Jackie to think of McNamara's role in getting a visa for her to visit Cambodia, a trip scheduled to begin just a few days after the march at the Pentagon. In the movie, Harry Lime is the third man. Her reference in the letter to the secrets that Sihanouk and Ho tell her—Prince Sihanouk and Ho Chi Minh, the North Vietnamese leader—must have been a playful riff about her upcoming visit to Southeast Asia.

But there seems to be more to it. Harry Lime is a complex character, admirable in his loyalty to friends, loathsome in the way he made a living.

He is a profound cynic. He makes money by stealing penicillin from military hospitals and selling it in diluted form on the black market, leading to the death of many innocent people. That Jackie would somehow equate him with McNamara seems puzzling. Yet the noir qualities of postwar Vienna, and the moral ambiguity of the screenplay by Graham Greene, clearly evoked contemporary America for Jackie in 1967.[67]

There is a scene in the movie that may have evoked the Vietnam War for her. Once Holly and Harry are reunited in Vienna—much of the movie revolves around Holly's efforts to investigate the falsely reported death of Harry, often impeded by Soviet officials in Vienna—the two ride a Ferris wheel.

As the Ferris wheel slowly turns, Lime opens the door of their cabin and invites Martins to gaze at the people far below—really, Lime says, "dots down there." Then he sneers: "Victims? Don't be melodramatic. Look down there. Look down there. Would you really feel any pity if one of those dots stop moving—forever? If I offered you twenty thousand for every dot that stops, would you really, old man, tell me to keep my money or would you calculate how many dots you could afford to spare?"

Lime continues: "Nobody thinks in terms of human beings. Governments don't, why should we?" But he's no atheist. Lime says, "Oh, I still do believe in God, old man. I believe in God and mercy and all that, but the dead are happier dead. They don't miss much here, poor devils."[68]

Did the scene, and Lime's cold-blooded description of "dots," bring to mind the victims of the Vietnam War, American and Vietnamese? McNamara was anything but a hardened killer to Jackie, but the Ferris wheel scene may have summoned Vietnam visions for her.

Jackie's lighthearted reference to Alida Valli bespeaks a flirtatious relationship with McNamara. Valli played the role of Anna Schmidt, Harry Lime's girlfriend, who also proves very alluring to Holly Martins.

═══

WHAT MCNAMARA MADE OF THE LETTER, OR WHETHER HE EVER got around to watching *The Third Man*, we do not know. But October 1967 proved to be a fateful month for McNamara. As he dealt with Jackie and her trip to Cambodia, and looked out upon the thousands of demonstrators massed beneath his Pentagon window, he was marshaling his ideas about ending the war. David K. E. Bruce, the American ambassador to Britain, got a glimpse of the war within McNamara when he visited Washington in October. Expressing his own opinion, as well as the unofficial view of the Labour government, that the US should tamp down the conflict and get out of Vietnam, Bruce wound up in a hot argument with McNamara. But when Bruce returned to London, McNamara called and said, "I just wanted you to know that I agree with everything you said. But in my position as defense secretary, I can't give any hint of that."[69]

On October 16, Johnson asked McNamara if he was still interested in the World Bank. McNamara told Johnson he remained interested in the job but would remain as defense secretary as long as the president wished. As McNamara later recalled, Johnson told him, "You deserve whatever you want from this government. My obligation is to help you and you can have whatever is within my power to bestow."[70] The job switch would serve both men's interests. McNamara would be free of Vietnam and could devote his still considerable energies to uplifting the poor of the world. Johnson would be free of McNamara, confident that he was protecting his faithful counselor's health while insulating himself from criticism by McNamara, who would then be bound by World Bank rules from commenting on the domestic politics of any of the bank's member states.

By the end of the month, McNamara decided to make his doubts abundantly clear to Johnson, and in doing so, sealed his ouster. On November 1, he sent a decisive memo only to Johnson because its views "may be incompatible with your own." It condemned "the present course of action in Southeast Asia" as "dangerous, costly in lives and unsatisfactory to the American people," and warned that already approved increase of US combat forces would only increase the carnage on both sides, and would soon confront Johnson with demands for even more troops and more pressure to expand the war into Laos, Cambodia, and North Vietnam.[71] Specifically, McNamara proposed an indefinite suspension of the American bombing campaign in North Vietnam and stabilizing American forces in South Vietnam instead of increasing their number. This implied what McNamara had privately been thinking for two years—that the war could not be won at a price the country would be willing to pay, and that therefore the United States should get out—but even in what turned out to be a sort of farewell report to his boss, he was unable to say straight out what he deeply believed.

Johnson had always had his own doubts about whether the war could be won, but he was still determined to try. As late as March 15, 1967, the president put it this way: "If we were prepared to stay the course in Vietnam, we could help lay the cornerstone for a diverse and independent Asia. . . . But if we faltered, the forces of chaos would scent victory and decades of strife and aggression would stretch endlessly before us. . . . We will stay the course. . . . We must not—we shall not—we will not fail."[72] Johnson's comments during summer and fall meetings about the war continued to reflect a strong desire to win militarily.

Walt Rostow, the adamantly hawkish national security adviser, was alarmed by McNamara's memo and determined to oppose it. After conferring with Rusk, the military brass and others, but not McNamara or Katzenbach, who shared McNamara's views, Rostow drafted a memo for Johnson firmly rejecting McNamara's proposals to de-escalate the war. Rusk himself registered his disagreement with much of McNamara's position in a separate memo to Johnson.[73] Johnson approved the Rostow rejection and signed it.[74] By this point, McNamara later said, "Rusk lived on whiskey and aspirin."[75] In his Pentagon memoir, McNamara recalled the time earlier that year that a distraught Rusk asked McNamara to come urgently to his office. Once McNamara arrived, Rusk grabbed a bottle of whiskey in his desk and informed McNamara that he was going to resign. The reason: his daughter was going to marry a Black classmate at Stanford—a step, Rusk thought, that would be keenly embarrassing for him and Johnson because they were both white southerners. McNamara was stunned and urged Rusk to reconsider. He did.[76]

On November 8, McNamara and outgoing World Bank president George Woods shared a ride from the Pentagon to the White House, where McNamara had a luncheon date. Woods told him that the time to select a new World Bank president was imminent and that he would soon tell Treasury secretary Joseph Fowler, the US governor of the bank, to submit nominees. Unknown to McNamara, Fowler wanted the job himself. The treasury secretary told Johnson that the United States usually submitted three nominees. Johnson replied, "OK, it's McNamara, McNamara, McNamara."[77] Neither Johnson nor Fowler informed McNamara. On November 25, Rostow sent a top secret memorandum to Johnson, who was spending Thanksgiving at his Texas ranch, that American spy agencies had intercepted two foreign communications indicating that Washington had nominated McNamara to succeed Woods. Rostow warned Johnson that the news might "leak out of other capitals soon."[78]

On November 27, the *Financial Times* reported that McNamara would succeed Woods. McNamara was flabbergasted. He phoned Tom Johnson at the White House. "Tom, was I fired?" he demanded to know. "Tom, was I fired?" Johnson replied, "No. Mr. Secretary, President Johnson saw this opportunity at the World Bank, this opportunity to fulfill so many of your own dreams about hoping to make this world a better place."[79] Woods and a delegation of World Bank directors formally offered the job to McNamara at his Pentagon office.[80] He accepted. Johnson announced the appointment a day later. The White House said he would step down as defense secretary on February 29, 1968. Henry Glass, who talked with McNamara shortly before the announcement, recalled, "He was very down . . . I could see the guy was collapsing emotionally."[81]

By arranging for McNamara to become president of the World Bank, Johnson not only rid his cabinet of McNamara but silenced him on Vietnam—because, like other World Bank officials, its president was barred from interfering in the "political affairs" of member countries, including his own. The plum job may also have left McNamara so grateful that he felt any criticism of Johnson and the war would be a betrayal of his patron.

Katharine Graham, the *Washington Post* publisher and McNamara's social friend, was outraged. She called Bill Moyers, the former White House aide, in tears. "It's absolutely horrible how the president is treating Bob McNamara," she told Moyers. "It's the worst thing that ever happened in this town." James Reston at *The New York Times* had told her that Johnson had fired McNamara. The president, she said, is treating McNamara "like a janitor working for a subsidiary company." Graham warned Moyers that the *Post* was considering publishing an editorial commentary about the matter on its front page the next day. Printing an editorial on the front page would have been highly unusual, signaling the *Post*'s strong objections to the treatment of McNamara. Moyers quickly dispatched a note about the call to Tom Johnson at the White House.[82] The *Post* did publish an editorial the next day, in the customary place on the editorial page. It lauded McNamara's public service while mildly rebuking the White House for its handling of McNamara.[83]

Did McNamara quit or was he fired? When he told his "very close and dear friend" Katharine Graham that he wasn't sure, she snapped, "You're out of your mind, of course, you were fired." And in the end he had to agree: "The difference of point of view between Johnson and me was so great that we couldn't continue. Something had to give. And I suppose Kay is probably right. He eased me out. He loved me. He really did."[84]

According to *Newsweek*, the news landed in Washington "with the force of a string of Claymore mines exploding along Pennsylvania Avenue."[85] It hit McNamara with almost equal force. "It was the only time that I've known him," recalled Adam Yarmolinsky, "when he really seemed at a loss. He said, in effect, 'I don't know where I am.'"[86]

When the news broke, Robert Kennedy dashed over to the Pentagon. Just a month before, Kennedy had told Neil Sheehan of the *Times*, as Sheehan paraphrased in his notes, "there is a growing conflict between mcnamara the man and mcnamara the minister of defense." But Kennedy believed that McNamara would not resign. According to Sheehan's summary of their conversation (all lowercase), Kennedy said McNamara believed that "1. he is a good influence within the government in that he acts as a restraining influence. said mcnamara stopped the generals from getting 250,000 troops last spring and invading cambodia and laos and southern part of north Vietnam. Said generals wanted to do this and were convinced China would not intervene. mcnamara against and stopped it. 2. mcnamara feels a responsibility for the war because he's been there all along, mcnamara committed mistakes as did all of them and feels he cannot walk out on it now."[87]

Kennedy urged McNamara to decline the World Bank appointment but resign from the government with a howl of protest against the war—with "a hell of a bang," as Kennedy put it. The result would be to enroll McNamara fully in Kennedy's camp, but the defense secretary declined. He "wasn't ready," he recalled, "to do anything that wasn't in my opinion in the national interest." Given McNamara's hesitation, Kennedy pushed him instead simply to resign without condemning Johnson or the war—because RFK knew, according to Adam Walinsky, that "sooner or later he'd get" McNamara.[88] But McNamara held firm. Soon afterward, Schlesinger griped to Kennedy about McNamara's failure to stand up to Johnson. "Wouldn't any self-respecting man have his resignation on the President's desk [in] half an hour? Why did he fall in with LBJ's plan to silence him and cover everything up?" RFK remained silent but, according to Evan Thomas, "his mood grew bleaker. If a strong man like McNamara could not defy Johnson, how could he?"[89]

One reason McNamara stayed on (and on and on) despite the growing tension with Johnson was, as Kennedy told Neil Sheehan, that he thought he could still influence the president. Although he blasted McNamara's Senate testimony, Johnson took his advice rather than the Joint Chiefs'; he ultimately suspended bombing within a ten-mile radius of Hanoi as part of another McNamara effort to start talks with the North. The president gave a speech in San Antonio offering to halt bombing altogether not if Hanoi ended all infiltration into the South (the president's previous demand) but if it agreed "not to take advantage" of a cessation to increase supplies to the South.[90]

McNamara stayed on, he told an interviewer in 1994, "as long as the President wanted me to stay and as long as I felt I was still having an influence on him."[91] He was using that influence to prevent what he regarded as the worst possible outcome—an ever-expanding war that would likely result in ever-increasing casualties and a possible global conflict with China and Russia. Realizing that the United States could not win the war, he urged Johnson to end it through negotiations with the North Vietnamese.

"We should try to move to negotiations and by those negotiations develop a settlement that would permit us to disengage militarily without losing all of Southeast Asia. That was what I was trying to do," he recalled.[92]

Farther than that he could not go, he said, because he was only a "cabinet officer" who had no independent power, who had "no constituency" other than the president.[93] "I just felt that I was serving at the request of the president, who had been elected by the American people. And it was my responsibility to try to help him carry out the office as he believed was in the interest of our people."[94] Moreover, McNamara continued, he had not been absolutely sure he was right; after all, he had been "in a minority" among the president's advisers, both military and civilian, who seemed so certain of their views. On top of that, the man who had internalized so many of the commandments impressed on him by his parents, Sunday school teachers, and Boy Scout leaders, felt an obligation to be loyal to his commander in chief in the midst of a war—and to all those who had sacrificed so much while following his orders.[95]

McNamara's definition of loyalty, which he spelled out to a *Life* magazine writer shortly after exiting the Pentagon, departed radically from the loyalty to the United States Constitution that he and other senior American government officials pledged to honor when sworn into office, as he did on January 21, 1961. On that day, he promised, "I do solemnly swear (or affirm) that I will support and defend the Constitution of the United States against all enemies, foreign and domestic; that I will bear true faith and allegiance to the same; that I take this obligation freely, without any mental reservation or purpose of evasion; and that I will well and faithfully discharge the duties of the office on which I am about to enter. So help me God."[96]

The definition of loyalty he gave Brock Brower, the *Life* writer, made no mention of the Constitution. "Around Washington there is a concept of 'the higher loyalty,'" he told Brower, who reported that McNamara offered the thought with an edge of contempt. "I think it's a heretical concept, this idea that there's a duty to serve the nation above the duty to serve the President, and that you're justified in doing so. It will destroy democracy if it is followed. You have to subordinate yourself, a part of your views."[97]

McNamara elaborated on his view during the interview with Brower:

> To some degree, my view of loyalty is in the nature of a belief about how
> men move forward toward some objective. A group of people in any
> pursuit—a church or educational structure, for example—establishes
> an objective, and unless in effect each is loyal to the organization, the
> objective cannot be reached. If each begins to substitute his own judg-
> ment, you fragment and weaken the organization. It is far better to
> move together toward a reasonably acceptable goal than one just a few
> degrees off from it, on your own. That's how I would define loyalty. In
> the current situation, you have a President who was elected by the peo-
> ple, and I make it an absolute, fundamental rule that I am not going to
> shade my actions, either to protect myself or to try to move him.[98]

At the time, McNamara, like most of his colleagues in the Johnson
administration, also firmly believed that a North Vietnamese victory would
give powerful momentum to Communist goals of world domination. Most
of them accepted the domino theory of Soviet conquest that Dwight Eisenhower had outlined as president, namely that the loss of South Vietnam
and Laos would put all of Asia at risk of Communist domination. "I was
still obsessed with this Soviet threat," McNamara told Charlie Rose three
decades later in a television interview. "I believed that, in a sense, Eisenhower's statement in 1954 of the 'dominoes' and in 1961 to President Kennedy
and me that if we lost Laos and Vietnam, we'd lose all of Southeast Asia. If
we lost all of Southeast Asia, we were very likely to lose all of Asia, including
India. If we did that, the power of the communists against Western Europe
and against this nation would increase. Now, that was what appeared to be
at risk if we lost Vietnam." Ultimately, he feared, falling Southeast Asian
dominoes could lead to a catastrophic nuclear conflict with the Kremlin.[99]

McNamara eventually came to doubt the theory, but not until well
after he had exited the Pentagon. In 1995, in conjunction with the publication of his book about the Vietnam War, he said he had belatedly recognized that Ho Chi Minh, the North Vietnamese leader, like Josip Broz
Tito, the postwar nationalist leader of Yugoslavia, was a Communist but

remained defiantly independent of the Kremlin. "I believe today that Ho Chi Minh was not a follower of Stalin and Khrushchev, which I thought he was at the time," McNamara said. "He was a Tito. He was an Asian Tito. I believe the war in South Vietnam was not a war of foreign aggression. I believe it was a civil war. I believe that it was the power of nationalism that was at stake here. I believe that under those circumstances, no foreign army can substitute for the people of that country deciding the civil war themselves. It's impossible."[100]

He elaborated: "I tell you, I tell you, I would have fought like hell to stop the war and withdraw—take our losses and get out. And this, by the way, is one of the lessons. We're going to make mistakes. I mean, we the people, we the leaders, we're going to make mistakes, and for God's sakes, when you make a mistake and people are being killed and you know you've made a mistake, cut your losses and get out. Now, if I'd believed then what I've just told you, I would have fought to my death to get out, without any question. I didn't believe it. What I believed was half-right. We couldn't win it militarily. What I feared was if we didn't at least prevent communist control of Vietnam, we would endanger the security of the West, and I was trying to balance those."[101]

Another reason he often cited for not bolting from the administration to add his voice and weight to the antiwar movement was his concern that such a step would give "aid and comfort" to the enemy and quite possibly demoralize American troops in South Vietnam. He clung to this explanation after exiting the Pentagon in early 1968, even in the face of pleas from Robert Kennedy that McNamara act on his private disillusionment with the war and throw his support behind Kennedy's antiwar presidential campaign.

Ironically, by staying in office, McNamara may have thought he was honoring Jackie Kennedy's appeals to him to end the war, to use the humane qualities she saw in him as defense secretary to persuade Johnson to stem the bloodshed. As she had once implored him to do at her New York apartment, pounding on his chest for emphasis. And as she had more than once told him, "one man can make a difference." Though he sometimes spoke privately about his affection for Jackie, and her vehement appeals to him to stop the war, he never overtly connected her appeals to his decision to remain in office. Nor did she publicly say whether she thought his prolonged service as defense secretary advanced her goal of ending the conflict.

====

TWO DAYS BEFORE HIS FORMAL FAREWELL, MCNAMARA MET WITH other senior decision makers at the State Department to discuss General Westmoreland's request for 205,000 more troops. Looking tense and haggard, he voiced "grave doubts" about the request. In his view, the number that should be sent was "zero." Challenged by Walt Rostow, McNamara pointed out that the air force had dropped more bombs on South Vietnam in the last year than the Allies had dropped on Europe during the last year of World War II. The bombing was "destroying the countryside in the South." It was "making lasting enemies. And still the damned Air Force wants more!" According to another attendee: "There were tears in his eyes and his voice." McNamara was "full of rage and grief and almost disorientation." Turning to Clark Clifford, who was going to replace him as defense secretary, McNamara managed to say: "We simply have to end this thing. I just hope you can get hold of it. It is out of control." "McNamara was weeping," recalled another witness. "He was speaking in sobs . . . and he was shaking."[102]

The next morning, Johnson escorted McNamara into the White House's East Room to present him with the country's highest civilian honor, the Medal of Freedom. The room overflowed with the Washington elite: congressional leaders of both parties, Supreme Court justices, government colleagues, McNamara's family and friends. "If ever I have sensed emotion, it was there today," wrote Lady Bird Johnson in her diary that night. Margy McNamara and her three children stood before military service battle flags at the south end of the room. Under the glare of television lights, Johnson approached the podium and began to speak: "America is giving to the world, and if I may be very personal, I am giving to the world, the very best we have to win the most important war of all." McNamara, he continued, was "an intensely loyal, brilliant and good man." "That simple word 'good' almost undid me," wrote Lady Bird, "and it did not help to look around the room. There were stricken faces, and tight composure and frank tears."[103]

When it was McNamara's turn to speak, he received a standing ovation, but he was unable to utter a word. As his audience sat stunned, tears appeared in his eyes. He coughed and lifted his hand to his mouth. Finally, in a choked voice, he said, "Mr. President, I cannot find words to express what lies in my heart today. I think—I think I had better respond on another occasion."[104]

═══

A QUARTER OF A CENTURY LATER, WHEN MCNAMARA WAS COMPOSing his memoirs, he wrote down what he thought he would have said that day: "Today I end 1,558 days of the most intimate association with the most complex individual I have ever known. Many in this room believe Lyndon Johnson is crude, mean, vindictive, scheming, untruthful. Perhaps at times he has shown each of these characteristics. But he is much, much more. I believe that in the decades ahead, history will judge him to have done more—for example, through such legislation as the Civil Rights Act, the Voting Rights Act, and the Great Society legislation—to alert us all to our responsibility toward the poor, the disadvantaged, and the victims of racial prejudice than any other political leader of our time. But for Vietnam, a war which he inherited—and which admittedly neither he nor we managed wisely—we would have been much further along in solving those problems."[105]

This ex post facto farewell statement reveals that McNamara's presidential mentor had been a tormentor as well. But it barely touches the emotions that fed his erratic behavior between 1965 and 1968, that rendered him silent on February 29, and that he still couldn't fully reckon with a quarter of a century later.

"I've killed people—hundreds, thousands, tens of thousands—by my mistakes," he confessed in a December 14, 1993, conversation with Brian VanDeMark.[106] "I owe an explanation to those I killed," he added to VanDeMark and Peter Osnos on September 16, 1994.[107]

In another 1994 conversation, David Ginsburg, a veteran Washington lawyer whom Johnson appointed executive director of the Kerner Commission to evaluate the roots of urban riots in the late 1960s, argued that it was Johnson, not McNamara, who was mainly responsible for American sins in Vietnam. "I know the man," said Ginsburg. "He wanted certain results. He didn't want to lose the war. You know that." But McNamara demanded his full share of the blame: He could and should have persuaded Johnson otherwise. Excessive self-blame, Ginsburg pointed out, was the other side of the coin of arrogance. But McNamara plowed on.[108] In retrospect he wished he'd had less influence "because then I wouldn't have to be responsible. But I think the record . . . shows that it was I who was preparing the papers. The memos were determining Johnson's actions."[109]

It was true, McNamara told Bundy in 1994, that Johnson "thought every man had his price," and Johnson figured his price "must be to be nice to Marg," who at one point said to her husband, "If that man kisses me once again, I want you to resign from the cabinet."[110] But McNamara didn't have any price, he insisted. If Johnson told Margy how invaluable McNamara was, LBJ told Bundy's Boston Brahmin mother he "didn't know how he could do this impossible job if he didn't have his good right arm Mac Bundy"—which is how Bundy "heard him describe at least 20" other people.[111] But whether or not McNamara actually was invaluable, being told he was by the president of the United States never lost its allure.

Looking back at the period between 1965 and 1967, McNamara chastised himself for not telling Johnson, "Cut our losses. Get out. It's cheaper to get out. Let's find the cheapest way to."[112] He comforted himself with the thought that he had done what he promised both Kennedy and Johnson he would do: "I would be totally loyal but, as part of that, I would tell them what I believed, and finally, I would ultimately do what they decided and support what they decided, or I would leave."[113] But in fact he had not been totally candid with Johnson. He had conveyed his pessimism about bleak developments in Vietnam that made military victory unlikely and had pushed for negotiations to end the war, but had not pressed Johnson to "cut our losses. Get out."

Lyndon Johnson's cold-blooded last words about McNamara were telling. After his presidency ended, he vented to Doris Kearns Goodwin about McNamara and his association with the Kennedys. Goodwin, the wife of Richard Goodwin, the Johnson speechwriter, was doing research for a book about Johnson and his presidency. "McNamara's problem," Johnson told her, "was that he began to feel a division in his loyalties. He had always loved and admired the Kennedys; he was more their cup of tea, but he also admired and respected the Presidency. Then, when he came to work for me, I believed he developed a deep affection for me as well, not so deep as the one he held for the Kennedys but deep enough, combined with his feelings about the office itself, to keep him completely loyal for three long years." That would be 1964–1966, suggesting Johnson thought McNamara was disloyal in 1966 and 1967.

Johnson continued, referring dismissively to three Pentagon aides and John Kenneth Galbraith, the Harvard economist and former Kennedy ambassador to India:

Then he got surrounded by Paul Warnke, Adam Yarmolinsky, and Alain Enthoven; they excited him with their brilliance, all the same cup of tea, all came to the same conclusion after old man Galbraith. Then the Kennedys began pushing him harder and harder. Every day Bobby would call up McNamara, telling him that the war was terrible and immoral and he had to leave. Two months before he left he felt he was a murderer, and didn't know how to extricate himself. I never felt like a murderer, that's the difference. Someone had to call Hitler and someone had to call Ho. We can't let the Kennedys be peacemakers and us warmakers simply because they came from the Charles River.

After a while, the pressure got so great that Bob couldn't sleep at night. I was afraid he might have a nervous breakdown. I loved him and I didn't want to let him go, but he was just short of cracking and I felt it would be a damn unfair thing to force him to stay.[114]

Just weeks before Clark Clifford succeeded McNamara as defense secretary in early 1968, McNamara seemed to sum up his dyspeptic view of the job during a meeting with Johnson, Clifford, and other senior

national security officials. "This is what it is like on a typical day," he dryly
told his colleagues as the White House lunch meeting began. "We had an
inadvertent intrusion into Cambodia. We lost a B-52 with four H-bombs
aboard. We had an intelligence ship captured by the North Koreans."
Clifford deadpanned, "May I leave now?"[115] Indeed, an American spy
ship, the *Pueblo*, and its eighty-three crew members had been captured by
North Korea. And a B-52 carrying four hydrogen bombs had crashed in
the icy waters just off the United States Air Force Base in Thule, Green-
land. The bombs did not detonate, but the conventional explosives contained in three of the nuclear weapons exploded, rupturing them and
scattering highly radioactive debris in the area. The fourth bomb disappeared beneath the ice, never to be recovered. Five of the six crew members
aboard the B-52 were killed.

A week later, Vietcong and North Vietnamese forces launched a surprise multifront offensive in South Vietnam that coincided with Tet, the
Vietnamese New Year. The attacks, dubbed the Tet Offensive, caught
American and South Vietnamese forces unprepared. Initial victories,
including seizing control of several South Vietnamese cities, soon gave
way to South Vietnamese and American counterattacks, and the offensive
failed to ignite a popular uprising against the South Vietnamese government that Hanoi had expected. But Americans at home watching news
reports from South Vietnam were staggered by the North Vietnamese
operations and the undeniable perception that years of American bloodshed on the battlefields of Vietnam had brought so little security there.

In his last weeks as defense secretary, McNamara persisted in advising Johnson to limit the bombing of North Vietnam. Johnson was not
inclined to agree and privately vented about McNamara on February 5 to
a *Washington Star* reporter. "When McNamara leaves, why he becomes
a hero! He was the goddamnnest screwball as long as he's in there."[116]
At a White House meeting the next day, Wheeler requested permission
from the president to lighten bombing restrictions around Hanoi and
Haiphong, proposing to narrow the no-bombing circle around both cities
from a five-mile diameter to three and a half miles. McNamara told Johnson, according to meeting notes, "Any attack of this type is very expensive

both in the number of U.S. aircraft lost and in civilian destruction. I do not recommend this. The military effect is small and our night time attack capability is small. Civilian casualties will be high. In my judgment, the price is high and the gain is low. The military commanders will dispute all the points I have made except air craft loss."

Wheeler replied:

I do not think the effects on the civilian population will be that high. As you know, they have an excellent warning system and most of them go to shelters and tunnels. From that standpoint, civilian loss could be lower than it is in other areas. We have had nothing like this civilian destruction that took place in World War II and Korea. But the targets which are there are military targets of military value. Frankly, this (civilian casualties which might result) does not bother me when I compare it with the organized death and butchery by the North Vietnamese and the Viet Cong during the last two weeks in South Vietnam. All of this relates to the matter of pressure.

When Johnson reminded everyone that McNamara had said that "the loss was not worth the gain," Wheeler erupted:

I am fed up to the teeth with the activities of the North Vietnamese and the Viet Cong. We apply rigid restrictions to ourselves and try to operate in a humanitarian manner with concern for civilians at all times. They apply a double standard. Look at what they did in South Vietnam last week. In addition, they place their munitions inside of populated areas because they think they are safe there. In fact they place their Sams [Surface-to-Air Missiles] in civilian buildings to fire at our aircraft. We showed during the good weather period that our campaign of bombing cut off Hanoi and Haiphong from each other and from the rest of the country. Photo reconnaissance showed that their air supplies were stacked all over and their turn around time for ships was very lengthy. That turn around time has now been reduced and the ships are able to unload much more quickly.

The meeting notes recorded Johnson's decision in a few simple words that unintentionally but aptly captured how far McNamara's influence had waned since his first triumphant years as defense secretary. "The President approved the removal of the five-mile limit, agreed to strike the fourteen authorized targets. After these targets are hit, the question of granting permission of armed reconnaissance will be raised again."[117]

As he packed up his papers and prepared to vacate the defense secretary's spacious office, McNamara was a tormented man. But he wouldn't admit it. He was neither physically nor mentally impaired, he insisted in his memoirs and in interviews in the 1990s. But he told VanDeMark that he took sleeping pills.[118] He did not feel guilt, only regret. The Vietnam War was tragic, but he was not himself a tragic figure. But "history's judgment," one of McNamara's interviewers politely reminded him in 1994, was that "you were in a state of heightened emotion and anxiety." "It may be, but it was not my judgment." McNamara retorted. "To hell with history. . . . I just get emotional at the wrong times."[119]

McNamara's last day as defense secretary was February 29, 1968. There would be new challenges at the World Bank, most better suited to his instincts and managerial skills. But the psychic wounds of Vietnam lingered, intensifying over time.

SECTION III

AFTERMATH

=◆=

1968–2009

CHAPTER TWELVE

Swords to Plowshares

McNamara's appointment as World Bank president looked like a convenient escape from the Vietnam crucible into a much more congenial environment. It offered the chance he had dreamed of as a youth when he told his friend Will Goodwin that he wanted to help people "on a big scale, on a worldwide scale."[1] At last he could apply his celebrated data-processing and managerial skills not to firebombing Japanese civilians, not to selling cars with humongous tail fins, not to fighting an unwinnable war in Southeast Asian jungles, but to pursuing the great and noble goal of lifting the lives of the global poor. For the first time in his career, he was mostly his own boss. He was ultimately answerable to the more than one hundred countries that were members of the Bank, but most of them were far away, and he no longer had Curtis LeMay, or Henry Ford II, or John Kennedy, or Lyndon Johnson, looming over him.

In fact, McNamara recalled twenty years later, "The Bank was, to me, the most satisfying adventure—and it was an adventure—the most satisfying adventure of my life."[2] His wife told one of his assistants, not once but several times, that the job was "the most rewarding thing Bob has ever had."[3] And she loved his new job herself since it brought the chance, in fact, the obligation, to travel with him on his overseas missions for the bank.[4] But how did this tormented man manage the transition to another huge, overwhelming job? Did his tireless work habits and unceasing global travels amount to an effort to redeem himself for the guilt he felt over Vietnam? Moreover, running the World Bank itself presented problems similar to those that plagued him earlier in his career. The great goal he pursued, of eliminating what he called "absolute poverty," seemed unattainable.[5] He faced resistance, both within and outside the World Bank, including from his own government in Washington. His personal style of managing the Bank created resentment as it did at Ford and in the Pentagon. The two sides of McNamara's personality continued to manifest themselves. According to his closest aides at the Bank, he was "very demanding" and "impatient," and so "intellectually dominating in exchanges with his associates" that "some people, in awe of him, went mute or did not speak their mind." But he could also be "a most delightful and charming individual" with "a great sense of humor," particularly "in private gatherings" and "during trips abroad when there would be opportunities to relax at the end of a field day, often in the private homes of the local resident representative of the World Bank, feeling totally free to express himself." Even in Washington, he was often "amiable and a good, informal listener," a "man of passion, a man with great sensitivities and emotions—as controlled as they may have been—a man driven by an exceptionally strong sense of purpose and empathy."[6]

The ghosts of Vietnam continued to haunt McNamara at the Bank, both publicly and privately. Public protests greeted him in Calcutta in 1968 and Copenhagen in 1970. Margy McNamara's ulcers returned and she developed cancer and died before he stepped down at the Bank, while his relations with his children, especially Craig, whom he needed more than ever as his wife faded away, remained tense.

Jackie Kennedy's presence in his life lightened the emotional burden for McNamara as he started his service at the Bank. Their relationship reached a high point in the fall of 1968, just before she married Aristotle Onassis, a Greek shipping tycoon. But once wed, Jackie pulled away, despite repeated efforts by McNamara to stay actively engaged with her. McNamara eventually turned for companionship to Joan Braden, a married woman in Washington, while Margy was failing, and then made no secret of his affair with Braden in the years that followed Margy's death in 1981. McNamara also remained close to Robert Kennedy, who entered the 1968 presidential race following Lyndon Johnson's withdrawal after almost losing the New Hampshire primary to Senator Eugene McCarthy, a war critic. McNamara openly endorsed Kennedy, violating the World Bank's neutrality code of conduct.

=====

THE WORLD BANK, ITS NAME SHORT FOR THE INTERNATIONAL Bank for Reconstruction and Development, was created after World War II in response to what the victors understood to have been economic conditions that helped cause the conflict. The Bank's sister institution, the International Monetary Fund, formed at the same time, would prevent a renewal of the currency wars of the 1930s. The Bank itself would provide funds for postwar reconstruction, relief, and economic recovery. Member countries would supply startup capital, but the Bank would raise funds for long-term low-interest loans to governments by selling its own bonds. The Bank's Articles of Agreement allowed it to finance only clearly defined projects rather than provide general subsidies for recipients. Initial postwar subventions to West European countries were reconstruction loans; the Bank's later loans to developing countries, like a $13.5 million loan to Chile in 1948 for construction of hydroelectric dams, were intended to foster industrialization and economic growth by building infrastructure such as power plants, ports, and highways. As the country that contributed the most money to the Bank, the United States had the most power over it.

The Bank's presidency was reserved for Americans; McNamara's predecessors were Eugene Meyer, former chairman of the Federal Reserve, owner of *The Washington Post*, and father of McNamara's dear friend Katharine Graham, who inherited *The Post* from her father; John J. McCloy; former Chase National Bank executive Eugene Black; and another banker, George Woods. Many of its staffers came from the agencies of West European governments that had managed their former colonies. Although the Bank's Board of Executive Directors representing the member states formally sanctioned loans, the president "had full authority over staffing decisions and borrowing and lending negotiations." But the president, like the Bank's other officers, was barred from interfering in the "political affairs" of members, including his own country's.[7]

By the time McNamara took over as Bank president in April 1968, it was lending about $1 billion a year. But its staff and their culture were in many ways unchanged since its founding. Its 767 staff members were mostly American and British, with a few from Western Europe and only one high-level officer, a Pakistani, from a developing country. Lower-level staffers from the former colonies, Deborah Shapley reports, were "overwhelmingly anglicized, often seen in blazers. Meetings of the Oxford-Cambridge Society were announced in the Bank's newsletter. The place had the air of a boarding school such as Eton." William Clark, a former aide to British prime minister Anthony Eden and a veteran Bank officer who became a close adviser to McNamara, described the pace of work at the Bank as one of "leisurely perfectionism."[8]

Perfectionism could have been McNamara's middle name, but not of the leisurely sort. He arrived early on the morning of his first day, April 1, 1968, at the Bank's shiny building at 1818 H Street NW in Washington. His office, an immense space on the twelfth floor flooded with light, was as grand as the defense secretary's office at the Pentagon, but with more modern decor; his enormous desk boasted a black leather top and a carved wood border, and his private dining room, covered with a pink tablecloth, was nestled next door. That first morning, McNamara burst into the small office of the president's special assistant and reached out to shake Rainer Steckhan's hand. The young German, who had been George Woods's assistant, wasn't used to such informality and directness from his boss.[9] Many bank staffers were already leery of McNamara. "He came with the reputation of the war in Vietnam," recalled Olivier Lafourcade, the young Frenchman who became McNamara's last special assistant, and of being "a hardheaded numbers guy. The expectations were lukewarm, to put it mildly."[10]

Although he was expected to be a hard-driving boss, and eventually became one, McNamara started slowly. He kept Steckhan on for some time before hiring Leif Christoffersen, a Norwegian, to replace him. McNamara introduced himself to the Bank President's Council, consisting of senior managers who met weekly to advise him on policy and procedural issues, as "a new boy who needs to learn" about the Bank. But he went about learning, reports William Clark, with "a driving sense of mission." He "gorged himself on statistics of past Bank lending and was surprised to find how small and patchy the effort had been compared with the obvious need"—"no recent loans to critical areas such as Indonesia or Egypt, nor to the great majority of the very poorest countries in Africa." "Why was the lending for this fiscal year going to be below a billion dollars?" McNamara wanted to know "Why were so many needy member countries neglected by the Bank?"[11] He asked council members to present him with "a list of all projects or programs that [they] would wish to see the Bank carry out if there were no financial constraints" on its ability to lend or on developing countries' capacity to borrow.[12]

What McNamara himself wished the Bank to carry out was nothing less than a world war on poverty, on what he called "absolute poverty," on the plight of "hundreds of millions," of "one-third to one-half of two billion people" in the developing world who "suffer from hunger or malnutrition," where "twenty to twenty-five percent of their children die before their fifth birthdays," where "the life expectancy of the average person is twenty years less than in the affluent world," and where "eight hundred million of them are illiterate." To help the poorest of the poor, roughly the bottom 40 percent of the world's population, to attain "a reasonable standard of living" would require the Bank to raise much more money than it ever had, to take advantage of scientific and technological changes, such as the Green Revolution (in which high-yield cereal grains, expanded irrigation, and modern agricultural management techniques drastically increased food production), to turn itself into not just a bank but the world's leading development agency. If it did so, he told Senegalese officials in 1969, poverty could be "abolish[ed] from the earth by the year 2000." Still in a utopian mood, he told an interviewer in 1971 that "a Marshall Plan for the world" would not only rescue poor countries but help to create political stability, prevent wars, and increase markets for products advanced countries wanted to sell.[13]

The core of McNamara's case for the Bank was as much moral as economic. As he put it in his 1973 annual Bank/IMF meeting speech in Nairobi, the first time the meeting had ever been held in Africa: "All of the great religions teach the value of each human life. In a way that was never true in the past, we now have the power to create a decent life for all men and women. Should we not make the moral precept our guide to action? . . . You and I—and all of us in the international community— share that responsibility."[14]

"The speech was a happy, almost a triumphal occasion," William Clark remembered.[15] According to Shapley, "the cheering and applause from rows of people, many in bright African dress—and the Nairobi speech itself—were perhaps McNamara's finest hour."[16]

═══

AS MCNAMARA WAS SETTLING INTO THE JOB IN 1968, ROBERT KENnedy was campaigning for president. With Johnson out of the race for the Democratic nomination after Eugene McCarthy's surprisingly strong second-place finish in the New Hampshire primary, Kennedy was surging. In April, McNamara agreed to tape a TV statement hailing RFK's role in resolving the Cuban missile crisis. At a time "of the most intense strain I have ever operated under, [Kennedy] remained calm and cool, firm but restrained, never nettled and never rattled."[17] McNamara recalled RFK's reaction to this endorsement: "He knew damned well it was wrong for me to do it, but he also knew I would do it," McNamara remembered.[18] And others considered it wrong, too. Since McNamara was now an international civil servant who was obligated to stay out of American politics, *The New York Times* reproved him: his statement "displayed poor judgment and poorer taste"; it shook, "if it does not destroy, confidence in his sense of the political proprieties."[19] Sharp as such criticism was, McNamara, hyper-self-critical as always, exaggerated it: "All hell broke loose," he remembered. "I was almost forced out of the Bank. . . . I got myself in the

Goddamned mess. He was killed ten days or two weeks later, and I'm so pleased I did it."[20]

On June 6, moments after celebrating his victory in the California primary, Robert Kennedy was assassinated as he walked through the basement of the Ambassador Hotel in Los Angeles. McNamara was in West Germany. He and Margy caught the first plane to New York, arriving about the same time as the plane carrying Bobby's body arrived from California. They attended the memorial service at St. Patrick's Cathedral, and at Ethel Kennedy's invitation, joined her on the train taking the body to Washington on June 8, 1968, a trip scheduled to take four hours. But it took more than eight, McNamara recalled, teary-eyed in the film *The Fog of War*, because thousands of mourners lined the tracks.[21]

Following Kennedy's death, McNamara's friends worried about his mood and his increased intake of martinis. Margy telephoned his old friend Wally Haas and his wife in California and urged them to visit the McNamaras in Washington because Bob needed them. For a long time, portraits of John Kennedy and McNamara commanded the second-floor hall of the McNamara home at Tracy Place, while photos of RFK covered the walls of Margy McNamara's study.[22]

Throughout 1968, McNamara remained in touch with Jackie Kennedy. The gap between her contemptuous view of Lyndon Johnson and her continuing devotion to McNamara was apparent at the memorial service at St. Patrick's Cathedral. As the service ended, Johnson and Lady Bird stopped along the front row of pews to offer condolences to Ethel Kennedy and other Kennedy family members, including Jackie. She barely acknowledged their presence. Lady Bird vividly recalled the encounter: "And then I found myself in front of Mrs. Jacqueline Kennedy. I called her name and put out my hand. . . . She looked at me as though from a great distance, as though I were an apparition. I felt extreme hostility. Was it because I was alive? At last, without a flicker of expression, she extended her hand very slightly. I took it with some murmured word of sorrow and walked on quickly. It was somehow shocking. Never in any contact with her before had I experienced this."[23]

Jackie's visceral opposition to the Vietnam War must have been a factor in her cold reaction to the Johnsons. The scene makes one wonder how she could hold the president responsible for the killing in Vietnam while remaining enthralled by the defense secretary who was a primary architect and manager of the war. The answer must have rested on the deep affection she had developed for McNamara since their first meeting in 1961 and the frequent accounts he gave her about his own opposition to the war even as he prosecuted it with grim determination.

In July, she sought McNamara's counsel about the slow progress toward establishing the John F. Kennedy Presidential Library at Harvard. He had recently been appointed to the library board. She drafted a long, dishy letter about her concerns that would have rocked Harvard and a number of its leading scholars had it been made public at the time. "Dearest Bob," the letter began, "What would I do without you? I think as I write this letter—we appeal to you when we are drowning—and you save us," and Jackie went on to complain that the library was becoming "the deadest place in the world." She railed against various Harvard professors involved in the project, especially Richard Neustadt, who had advised her husband before and during Kennedy's time as president. She vented about various luminaries on the library board, including Robert Lovett, Averell Harriman, and Douglas Dillon, all of whom she thought were "old and don't want to rock the boat." She continued, "I am going to make such a fuss—or do something so Machiavellian—once you tell me which is the best way to deal with those people." Recalling that the Kennedys had given Harvard $20 million and thirteen acres of land, she dismissed the university's newly named Kennedy School as "dismal." She ended, "So you see my state of mind—but don't worry I am calm . . . I send you a big hug—and all my love—dear dear Bob—Jackie."[24]

Two months later, McNamara's devotion to Jackie was unmistakable at the commissioning of the aircraft carrier named for JFK. With Lyndon Johnson, now a lame-duck president, not planning to attend, McNamara dusted off the text of the speech he had planned to give at the ship's christening a year earlier but had been forced to set aside when Johnson decided to deliver the keynote address. McNamara's address, inspired by Pericles's funeral oration about fallen Athenian soldiers during the Peloponnesian War, was an emotional, moving ode to John Kennedy and his leadership, written in a poetic cadence. It is easy to see why he could not deliver the remarks in the presence of Johnson a year earlier; McNamara, returning to the Newport News shipyard, declared his boundless devotion to John Kennedy. McNamara choked back tears as he read it.

There are men whose very course across the sea of history alters the course of other men.

There are men in history who sail by so noble a heading that other men—looking on—fix their compass to the same course, and follow afterwards.

And so it is with us.

For though brief was his voyage, we who knew him will never again be the same men.

And it is thus not only for us few, but for multitudes of others the globe around.

For they—as we—saw in him the embodiment of a new hope— that reason and civility, and sanity, might prevail, that the rigidities of extremism might give way to the realities of accommodation.

He spoke of Jackie with equal reverence and affection. His words, delivered to the hundreds of men and women who had assembled for the ceremony, seemed intended for an audience of one—Jackie.

He journeyed not alone.

There stood by his side another.

She stands here today.

And like this great ship, she stands with a quiet, inner strength.

Her warmth, her grace and her beauty were his immense pride— and, through every setback and suffering, his enduring consolation.

Her presence at his side did not merely add to his achievement; it multiplied it many times over.

This ship is honored by his name; it is graced by her presence.[25]

McNamara could barely contain his tears as he ended the speech. He lurched awkwardly from the lectern to a chair next to it where he had been seated before speaking, abruptly crossed his legs, and sat motionless, a man clearly straining to keep his composure.[26] Jackie was profoundly moved by McNamara's comments. Late that night, back at her mother's home in Newport, Rhode Island, as everyone there slept, she wrote one of the most emotional of her many letters to McNamara over the years. Describing her fellow guests at the house as "moved, rocked, shattered" by his remarks, she compared her family members to the aristocratc White Russians who had settled in Paris after fleeing the Bolshevik Revolution in their homeland. The White Russians, she said, lived in a state of despair but found defiance and laughter at music-filled nighttime parties. The thought reminded her of her brother-in-law Ted Kennedy, sailing off Cape Cod that summer, "his lips cracked with red wine" as he took Bobby Kennedy's son and her son, John Jr., to sea. "It is Celtic," she lamented. "We will all be annihilated in the end." Telling McNamara that his speech at the commissioning ceremony was "more beautiful" than Pericles's funeral oration, she assured him he would wind up in Hades alongside Pericles and John Kennedy. "I love you—for what you are—and for what you suffer—and for all you are to me, my dear Bob."[27]

Within weeks, she would marry Aristotle Onassis. But it seemed at Newport News that it was Robert McNamara whom she truly loved. That they adored one another seems clear. That they often spent time together in intimate settings like Jackie's Manhattan apartment is evident. As for the physical extent of their friendship, unaddressed in her letters to him and the accounts of their contemporaries, the historical record is opaque.

On March 6, 1969, now married to Onassis, she spotted a story in *The New York Times* chronicling an intense debate within the Johnson administration in early 1968 about whether to escalate or de-escalate the American military's role in Vietnam. She wrote to McNamara, reminding him that he had read Ibsen's *The Master Builder* to her during their times together. She called him the Master Builder "for stopping the war," something that she said the whole world would eventually say of him. She assured him that "false" history might be written about him but no one could erase what the future "will always owe to you."[28]

Henrik Ibsen's *The Master Builder* is about an architect who aspires to greatness. He is obsessed with his work and inspired by a fire that burns down his wife's childhood home, although that leads to his children's death and his wife's depression. He seeks out a younger woman to whom he confesses his sins and who tries to reassure him, but he is killed when he falls from a high tower in what may have been suicide. The full set of parallels with McNamara himself couldn't have been apparent to him yet, but Jackie may have sensed them, as well as those to her late husband and her own life.

A few months later, McNamara joined a coterie of Kennedy family friends and advisers on Martha's Vineyard to strategize about how to defend Ted Kennedy, and salvage his political career, after the senator drove off a bridge on Chappaquiddick Island in mid-July after attending a party of young Kennedy aides known as the "Boiler Room Girls." Kennedy, a married man, escaped from his submerged car, but his twenty-nine-year-old companion, Mary Jo Kopechne, drowned. McNamara's effort to help Senator Kennedy, inappropriate for the president of the World Bank, reflected his closeness to the Kennedy family. "It was such a comfort to have Bob with me at the Cape during that difficult period and I shall never forget it," Kennedy wrote to Robert and Margy McNamara two months after the incident.[29]

Ted Kennedy's reverence for McNamara extended well beyond his role after Chappaquiddick. McNamara's papers, housed at the Library of Congress and other archives, include numerous letters and notes from Kennedy seeking his advice on topics ranging from family trust investments to international relations. "As you know," Kennedy wrote in 1970, "I value highly your friendship which has always been present, especially in the most difficult days. I would like to think that your greatest help to me is the continuing feeling I have that I can rely on you for guidance and counsel as I did my brothers."[30] Indeed, McNamara's papers are filled with warm and appreciative letters from many members of the Kennedy clan to the McNamaras, including the family matriarch, Rose Kennedy, Caroline Kennedy, Ethel Kennedy, Sargent Shriver, and others. The correspondence makes abundantly clear that Robert McNamara remained a revered figure for the family despite his leading role in Vietnam. It also shows a tight bond between the family and Margy McNamara, who kept up her own correspondence with many Kennedys over the years.[31]

MCNAMARA WAS FIRST AND FOREMOST A MANAGER, AND HE quickly put his managerial acumen to work at the World Bank. According to Nathaniel M. McKitterick, a policy adviser at the Bank in the late 1950s, "McNamara threw himself into the day-to-day management of the Bank with the tremendous energy he brings to everything he does." When he arrived at the Bank, it lacked a central accounting system, did not make state-of-the-art projections of its future operations or maintain complete records of its operations, and failed to standardize the information it did keep across all its departments. In McNamara's universe these were cardinal sins. One way he reformed the system was to introduce "country program papers" that employed a detailed, sector-by-sector statistical analysis of the country's economy to prepare a five-year lending plan. Another innovation was an "'annual country allocation exercise' [that] drew on these five-year plans to set targets for the Bank staff of each country and each sector within each country." McNamara consolidated his control over the Bank by reducing the role of the board of directors; "the more important the issue the fewer people who should be involved," he had once said at the Pentagon. He ordered Bank officials to lobby the foreign ministries (in addition to the finance ministries and central banks) of wealthy nations and to cultivate a broader range of investors for its bonds in Western Europe, Japan, the Middle East, and emerging markets.[32]

By 1981, the Bank was lending $12 billion a year to a broader range of recipients for a more diverse set of projects. But old-school staffers felt he was "slighting growth in order to pursue redistribution." Many resisted his effort to establish a system for estimating "the social rate of return" of Bank projects. His program for "integrated rural development," a way of tying together provision of credits, construction of irrigation systems, and establishment of education and training centers, struck Bank old-timers as "basically nonsense...much too utopian."[33] According to Christoffersen, himself an ardent supporter of most of McNamara's innovations, "many old-timers felt we should stick to what we were supposed to do—to work on relationships between countries north and south, not what income distribution was within countries." By now, Christoffersen continued in a 2019 interview, McNamara's approach has been "adopted by the entire international system," but "many board members didn't like it and senior bank management didn't like it."[34]

McNamara also put some colleagues off by seeming so sure of himself. "He knew exactly what he wanted," remembers Lafourcade. "He would have stacks of paper on his desk. He would obviously not read all of it, but he knew exactly what was on the table that he needed to look at to support his way of thinking. He would say 'Give me options. Give me options.' So you would present him with four or five options and he would say, 'I like the sixth one'"—presumably the one he constructed for himself. In contrast, McNamara's successor, A. W. Clausen, provided with options by his staff, would ask, "How do I know how to decide? You should tell me which one I should choose, and I will tell you yes or no, but don't give me a choice."[35]

According to Clark, McNamara's penchant for quantitative thinking, so questionable in Vietnam, meant that he tended to "numerify" problems so as to simplify them even though they weren't so straightforward.[36] By the same token, recalled Montague Yudelman, the Bank's director for agriculture and rural development, presenting issues to McNamara in numerical terms grabbed his attention. When Yudelman reported the International Labor Organization's estimate of the number of people in developing countries who would be coming on the job market in the next ten years, McNamara "just came to life. It was a light going on. It was the most vivid example I think I'd ever seen of something triggering a bell in a man's head and the man just springs to life. 'My God,' RSM said, 'why, that's five times the size of the United States military and twenty-four times the size of the Ford Motor Company.'"[37]

According to Clark, his boss tended "to treat those around him like machines, at least until 8 P.M. because that's how *he* is."[38] But Christoffersen remembered McNamara was "kind" to colleagues—"if he felt you were trustworthy. I can't recall his ever lashing out, whereas there were World Bank presidents after him who would trash their vice presidents in senior meetings. McNamara never did that. He would say, 'Charlie, could you and I have a meeting in my office later today?'" "He would never chastise or degrade people in front of other people." But, on the other hand, "many people were perhaps inhibited; they didn't really want to get in an argument with him because he was so fast—such a fast thinker that maybe they wouldn't do well. Much better if they could talk to him in private, so to speak." Harking back to his Berkeley habit of being kind to people less accomplished than he was, McNamara was particularly "courteous with his secretaries," according to Lafourcade, "with the lowest-ranking people—not warm, but absolutely considerate." When someone asked a question that wasn't totally clear, he would "rephrase the question, thus giving time to the guy to think through" what he wanted to say. But when a vice president said "something stupid," then McNamara "could be ruthless," never "insulting, never personal," but making a "sharp substantive rebuttal."

McNamara could also be painfully aloof. "His door was normally closed," Lafourcade recalls. "He wasn't comfortable in large staff meetings," remembers Christoffersen. "He wasn't comfortable having small talk with people at a Christmas party. He would do it if necessary, but he was much better in small groups." Christoffersen wished his boss, who was such a "great manager" in the sense of "breaking new ground, pioneering, learning, testing, experimenting and as a master of budget analysis," had been "better socially in taking the initiative himself to open up to people below him." Eugene Black had practiced the "walking-down-the-corridor" style of management, spending a half a day once a month dropping in on subordinates to find out what they were doing and what problems they faced. But, Christoffersen observed, "McNamara couldn't do that."[39]

McNamara's relations with the US government also created problems for him. According to Clark, his boss "irritated many important leaders in the Nixon administration. They had thought that, as an American, McNamara should be responsive to policy nudges, but over and over again he proved to be un-nudgeable," for example, when he resisted Washington's call for a cutoff in Bank aid to Chile after [the radical Socialist] Salvador Allende came to power in 1970. As a result, Clark reports, "American support for a second [five-year] term for McNamara [in 1973] was belated and grudging."[40] (On the other hand, Secretary of State Henry Kissinger, who reportedly urged McNamara's reappointment on President Nixon, had a remarkably mixed relationship with McNamara, centering around their conduct of the Vietnam War.)[41] Meanwhile, however, McNamara's concentration on Washington caused further resentment inside the Bank. According to Clark, "one wise European executive director" grumbled that "the trouble with McNamara is that he is an insider fighting desperately to keep this Bank outside Washington politics"—but that took "what seemed to many on the Bank staff an inordinate share of time. To the three-quarters of the Bank staff who were not American, it often seemed that all their President cared about was getting American support, and that he was not very successful either on the Hill or with the administration."[42]

═══

DESPITE THE PROBLEMS AND CHALLENGES HE FACED AT THE WORLD Bank, McNamara "blossomed" there, according to Christoffersen.[43] Barbara Ward, the British author whose championing of foreign aid inspired much of McNamara's thinking, described him to William Clark in 1976 as "a deeply wounded man."[44] But if so, his stint at the Bank was a time of healing. His assistant Lafourcade could sense "the scars" behind the façade, although "the emotions of a highly emotional person were subdued, controlled." Many have seen McNamara's stewardship of the Bank as his way of "repenting" for his Vietnam sins. But if he was atoning for the past, he was also building the future. It was as if, said Lafourcade, McNamara thought that he may have been misguided before, but "now I have a good cause and I put all my energy into it."[45] That energy overflowed so plentifully that it has been described as a kind of "hyperactivity" that kept McNamara from thinking about Vietnam. Patrick Sharma, author of a book about McNamara's leadership of the World Bank, says its "primary motivation was to keep [McNamara] busy."[46] But that sort of exertion had always been a part of his makeup. As he had throughout his career, McNamara got to work early (around 7:55) and left late (7:05), but not as early and late at the Bank as he had at the Pentagon. He jogged up the twelve flights to his office at the Bank two steps at a time, and once in Mexico City (altitude: 7,382 feet) when McNamara and his party couldn't all fit into a small elevator from the fortieth to the fiftieth floor, he challenged Christoffersen to run up the remaining stairs.[47] These feats continued his pattern of racing his friends up and down mountains in Colorado and the High Sierras.[48]

McNamara's visits to countries to which the Bank was lending were frequent and hectic. But the man who had worked his way to Asia on freighters when he was young loved seeing the world, and the world, although initially put off by his record in Vietnam, came to respect him—not only because he came bearing large financial gifts to developing countries but because he was so deeply committed to helping them and so obviously enjoying his exposure to them, not just to their capitals but to villages, the countryside, and the people who lived there. According to Shapley, the man who had relished the California landscape as a boy, and who kept returning to California and Colorado mountains all his life, treasured "the expanses of southern Africa, the jewellike islands of Indonesia, the tiered green terraces of the Punjab set against stunning mountain backdrops."[49]

═══

ANOTHER REASON MCNAMARA LOVED HIS WORLD BANK JOB, HE often said, was that his wife did, too—and vice versa: she did because he did. One of the Bank's traditions, he recalled, was that "the wife of the president of the Bank travels with him everywhere" to show people in developing countries that both men and women in the developed world had "a strong interest" in their activity. This was, he added, "one of the most delightful things. I was married to the loveliest human being in the

entire world. And whatever I did, in effect, reflected her values."[50] According to William Clark, Margy was delighted to be sharing her husband's
life after the years in which he buried himself at the Pentagon.

During the day, while he was inspecting dams and agricultural stations and meeting with finance ministers and local bankers, she would
undertake her own tours, and then in the evening the McNamaras and
Clark would reunite for dinners.[51] "She was incredible," Christoffersen
recalled. "She had the social graces he didn't have and she was very funny,
she was lighthearted and he absolutely adored her."[52] She was "a formidable woman," remembered Lafourcade, "nice, friendly, sweet, very determined"; with "a legitimacy of her own, which partly derived from having
established the Reading Is Fundamental program in the poor districts of
Washington. She was always considered to be a very good influence on
the conscience of Mr. Bob McNamara." And besides being "committed,
dedicated and very attentive," she had "a more practical sense of reality at
the field level" and special "empathy with the realities of poor people."[53]

Yet while extolling Margy's virtues, and telling people how much he
loved her, McNamara remained good friends with Jackie Kennedy. Their
correspondence had slowed to a trickle during her marriage to Onassis.
But they remained in touch and in late October 1975, seven months after
Onassis's death, McNamara and Jackie got together in New York. He
told her about his World Bank work and they talked about alleviating the
suffering of the world's poorest people. Within a few days, he prepared
to send her a copy of a letter he had dispatched to Léopold Senghor, the
president of Senegal. McNamara had met with Senghor not long before
at a meeting of the World Bank's governing board. Moved by comments
Senghor made at a meeting a year earlier, McNamara alluded to them at
the end of his address to the governors. "When I was last in Africa, President Senghor gave me a small volume of his poetry. Reading it again yesterday afternoon, I was struck by one line in particular. In a moving and
beautiful passage, Senghor asks the questions: 'Who would give back the
memory of life to the man whose hopes were smashed?' Is not the answer,
'All of us in this room?' Is that not the task that brings us together? Can
we not, during these five days, take the initial steps toward action which

will bring back the memory of life to the hundreds of millions of our fellow men whose hopes have been smashed? I hope so."

McNamara added in his letter to Senghor, "As is characteristic of a poet, you have compressed into a single line a profound comment on life. It is I who should thank you for the use of it."

In his copy of the letter to Jackie, McNamara inserted by hand some personal comments to her in the margins. At the top of the page he wrote: "Jackie, Friday evening we were talking of the 'absolute poor' in the developing countries, those seven or eight hundred million human beings whose nutritional, health, and literacy levels are so low as to leave them living, literally, on the margin between life and death. I mentioned that I quoted to the penny-pinching finance ministers a line from Senghor to try to move them emotionally to deal more effectively with the problem. This is it. I hope you like it."

At the bottom of the page, he added a few words that clearly show how much he loved her: "As I was leaving you, I fear I revealed, unintentionally, how much I miss you and how deep my love for you remains—perhaps it was because your smile was never more beautiful."[54] It is unclear if McNamara sent these handwritten words to Jackie or thought better of doing so and just sent her a clean copy of his letter to President Senghor.

She responded a few days later with a brief note thanking him for his "beautiful letter," and saying everyone living through his time would take note of it and remember it and him, making no reference to his handwritten comments about their recent meeting and his ardent show of affection for her.[55] Jackie's muted response implied that the days when she looked to him for support and protection, and returned his overtures with effusive expressions of affection, were over.

━━━

ONE TERRIBLE REALITY OF POOR PEOPLE, ESPECIALLY IN THE SAHEL region of central Africa, was riverblindness (onchocerciasis), a disease transmitted by small black flies that live near rivers but can travel up to five hundred kilometers on prevailing winds. The flies plant microscopic worm larvae in humans they bite, which migrate through the body, triggering excruciating itching and, when they reach the eyes, permanent blindness. The disease was discovered by European scientists in the late nineteenth century and recognized as a terrible problem but was still not being addressed seriously a hundred years later. In the late 1960s, United States Agency for International Development (AID) public health officials asked the World Bank to lead an all-out attack on the disease, arguing that it undermined agriculture and slowed economic development, but the Bank declined on the grounds that public health was not its bailiwick.

Enter McNamara. Not only was he shifting the Bank's focus to poverty and economic development, and its beneficiaries from nation-states to disadvantaged population groups, but he had established a new sector at the Bank on Population, Health and Nutrition. During a March 1972 trip to Upper Volta, he chartered a plane to take him and his wife to a village in which 75 percent of the residents were infected with onchocerciasis, and one in seven were already blind.[56] The sight of eight adults staggering along holding on to a pole, being led by a child at the other end of the pole, was devastating. McNamara remembered seeing "children holding broomsticks in one hand. At the other end was an adult blind with onchocerciasis. The onchocerciasis blinded him—prevented him from doing anything, being productive. But it didn't kill him. So for the rest of his life he's led around by a child."[57]

"Margaret was particularly affected by this," remembered David Bell, former head of USAID.[58] One month later, McNamara chaired a meeting in London with heads of three UN agencies in addition to the World Bank, which led to the formation and financing of the Onchocerciasis Control Program with "regionally coordinated operations across seven countries in the Sahel, several of which were barely on speaking terms, to cover an area of 660,00 square kilometers, slightly larger than France."[59]

━━━

ALTHOUGH MCNAMARA'S MOVE TO THE WORLD BANK ALLOWED his previous Washington experience to recede, he couldn't escape the Vietnam War. Oddly enough, it caught up with him most dramatically in an incident that almost ended his life, on the ferry to Martha's Vineyard in September 1972.[60] He was enjoying a drink in the lunchroom of the MV *Islander* on a rainy evening when a short bearded stranger approached him to say there was a phone call for McNamara. "Please follow me," said the man, who led him onto the deck just outside the pilot house. The stranger was an artist who had once lived on the island, a Vietnam vet who was enraged when he saw McNamara "starting his long, privileged weekend on the Vineyard, stretched out against the counter like that, talking loud, laughing, obviously enjoying himself a great deal . . . as if he owned the lousy steamship authority or something." The two men entered the narrow walkway around the pilot house, where a four-foot railing was the only thing between them and the sea. "I didn't say a word," the stranger recalled, not "here's to Rolling Thunder, sir, or this one's for the Gulf of Tonkin, you lying sack of crap. Nope, nothing like that. I just grabbed him. I got him by the belt and shirt collar, right below the throat. I had him over, too. He was halfway over the side. He would have gone [in] another couple of seconds. He was just hanging there in the dark, clawing for the railing. I remember he screamed, 'Oh, my God, no.'" They were at the back of the boat, "so there was a good chance he was going to be sucked underneath, and in that case, the propeller probably would have gotten him if he hadn't drowned first."

People poured out of the lunchroom and the members of the crew rescued McNamara, pulling his attacker off him and restraining him. By the time the boat arrived, the stranger had escaped, helped by a member of the crew. But McNamara wasn't going to press charges anyway. He wanted the case dropped.[61]

The Vietnam War pursued him in other, somewhat less dramatic ways. World Bank aide Christoffersen remembers that "heads of state, prime ministers and finance ministers all tried to grill him in private moments about his previous job," but he "wouldn't have anything to do with that."[62] Late in 1968, he was greeted in Calcutta by a mob swarming the streets, burning buses, wielding a banner condemning "McNamara Yanqui," and burning an effigy of Uncle Sam who, in addition to his blue pants and red-and-white-striped jacket, boasted dark straight hair and wore glasses.[63] Two years later, Copenhagen authorities set up barricades to prevent demonstrators from storming the World Bank–IMF annual meetings.[64] The study McNamara had commissioned on Vietnam, formally titled "United States–Vietnam Relations, 1945–1967," but later christened "The Pentagon Papers," also came back to haunt him. Finished in January 1969, eighteen months after McNamara had launched the project, one of the fifteen sets of its forty-seven volumes was delivered to McNamara at the Bank by Leslie Gelb, who had supervised the study. McNamara had commissioned only a collection of documents, but Gelb and the thirty-six writers who assisted him (including mostly military men but also civilians Daniel Ellsberg and Richard Holbrooke) had added their own summaries and analyses. Gelb and an accompanying military officer set the boxes on a table in McNamara's office and extracted from them a bound volume with a light blue cover. McNamara glanced at it, pushed it back to Gelb, and told him to take it back to the Pentagon.[65] Years later, in 1989, McNamara told Bob Woodward that he had "never read" the Pentagon Papers.[66]

This extraordinary episode shows how averse McNamara was to reliving the war. But he couldn't avoid doing so. Ellsberg took it upon himself (risking prison) to sneak out a copy of the Pentagon Papers and deliver it to *The New York Times*. The *Times* assigned Neil Sheehan and other reporters to read through the volumes, choose excerpts from them and write interpretive articles about them, and then published the results, including some sharp criticism of McNamara himself. One column, by Sanche de Gramont, a journalist who also wrote under the name Ted Morgan, compared McNamara to Hitler's architect/minister of armaments Albert Speer.[67] McNamara refused to respond publicly to such accusations, saying, "I cannot be president of the World Bank and defend my record as Secretary of Defense." He appeared unruffled at the Bank as he recounted the study's origins to the President's Council the day after the *Times* series began to appear. But a friend told journalist Henry Trewhitt, "I was worried about him during most of the first week, and I was not alone." And that summer, when McNamara came down with shingles, his daughter Kathy remarked, "It wasn't the World Bank that gave him the Shingles."[68]

David Halberstam's bestseller *The Best and the Brightest*, which appeared soon after the Pentagon Papers, continued the assault on

McNamara, depicting George Ball as the hero who had warned that the Vietnam War would turn into a nightmare and McNamara as a "fool."[69] But several years later, McNamara insisted he had come close to resigning from the Bank in the summer of 1968 when he and Bundy learned that Hubert Humphrey was to meet with the president on a Saturday in August before the Democratic party nominating convention. They believed that Humphrey, about to be nominated for president, "was going to state at the convention if he were President, he would move away from the President's program in Vietnam," so they conveyed to Humphrey that if he would say that to the president in this meeting in August, that "we would publicly state we supported him and urged him to take such a public position." In that case, McNamara continued, he would have had to resign from the bank. But "typical of Johnson," McNamara remembered, he made Humphrey wait an hour, during which "Humphrey lost his nerve." This was "a terrible error on Humphrey's part not to have publicly broken with [Johnson]," but no more terrible than McNamara's own failure to do so.[70]

After Nixon defeated Humphrey in 1968, McNamara quietly tried to convey lessons he had gleaned from Vietnam in advice he gave to Henry Kissinger. In 1965, upon returning from a trip to Vietnam, Kissinger had found McNamara "tortured by the emerging inconclusiveness of the war." Two years later, when Kissinger was trying to negotiate a halt to the bombing through two French intermediaries, McNamara telephoned "after every contact with the North Vietnamese." Beginning in 1969, by which time McNamara had been denounced as a warmonger for several years, he "missed no opportunity," Kissinger recalled, "to press on to me courses of action that those who were vilifying him would have warmly embraced."[71] Kissinger was capable of mocking McNamara's weakness, as he did much later to a writer who told him he had just interviewed McNamara. "'Boohoo, boohoo,' Kissinger said, pretending to cry and rub his eyes. 'He's still beating his breast, right? Still feeling guilty?'" Kissinger spoke in a "mocking, singsong voice and patted his heart for emphasis," reported Jon Lee Anderson.[72] He boasted of his own strength in comparison: "I bet McNamara was less strong than I was. I love McNamara. He's a wonderful man."[73] But the two men did sympathize with each other. "I don't want

With President Johnson in the White House Cabinet Room.

With President Johnson, March 1967.

With Jacqueline Kennedy and John F. Kennedy Jr., on their way to the christening of the aircraft carrier USS *John F. Kennedy* in Newport News, Virginia, on May 27, 1967.

Watching from a Pentagon window as thousands demonstrate against the Vietnam War on October 21, 1967.

President Johnson and McNamara, showing their fatigue on February 7, 1968, just days after the beginning of the Tet Offensive.

McNamara and his family (left to right: his wife, Margaret Craig McNamara, and children, Craig, Margy, and Kathleen) with President and Lady Bird Johnson at the White House, February 28, 1968, when Johnson awarded McNamara the Medal of Freedom.

Arriving at the World Bank on his first day as president of the bank, May 1968.

With his son, Craig, at Craig's California farm, 1970s.

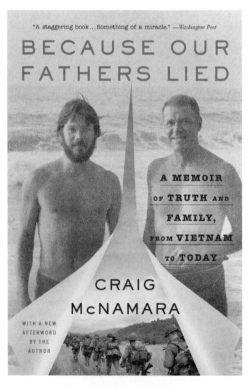

"A staggering book...Something of a miracle." —*Washington Post*

BECAUSE OUR FATHERS LIED

A MEMOIR OF TRUTH AND FAMILY, FROM VIETNAM TO TODAY

CRAIG McNAMARA

WITH A NEW AFTERWORD BY THE AUTHOR

The front cover of the paperback edition of
Craig McNamara's 2022 book.

Robert McNamara and his wife, Marg, at their Aspen, Colorado, home, circa 1975.

As World Bank president at the site of a bank-supported project on the outskirts of Lima, Peru, March 12, 1976.

With Joan Braden at a book launch party at the Manhattan home of Happy Rockefeller, March 25, 1982.

With *Washington Post* publisher
Katharine Graham at the Washington
Opera, January 22, 1982.

With his former North Vietnamese rival and chief of the North Vietnam army, General
Vo Nguyen Giap, at the Critical Oral History Conference in Hanoi, Vietnam,
November 9, 1995.

At the Critical Oral History Conference on the Cuban missile crisis in Havana, Cuba, 2002. Director of the private National Security Archive in Washington, Thomas Blanton, is to McNamara's left. At right is Arthur M. Schlesinger Jr.

With Craig McNamara at Craig's California home, circa 2007.

With his second wife, Diana McNamara, at dinner late in life. He asked her to show it to friends to disprove assertions that he never laughed.

With the weight of the world and his struggles with it showing on his face, 1984.

you to feel lonely," McNamara wrote to Kissinger after the appearance of Seymour Hersh's slashing book *The Price of Power: Kissinger in the Nixon White House*. "Misery does love company," Kissinger replied.[74] *Washington Post* publisher Katharine Graham hosted dinners during the Vietnam War so that the two of them could "commiserate about their war woes."[75] And the overall assessment of McNamara in Kissinger's memoirs captures the essence of the man as we have come to understand him:

> [T]hough an outstanding Secretary of Defense, McNamara proved an unfortunate choice for managing a war. . . . Above all, McNamara did not have his heart in the assignment. He had wanted to relate the awesome power of our nation to humane ends; he had no stomach for an endless war; he suffered from a deep feeling of guilt for having acquiesced in the decisions that made it both inevitable and inconclusive. . . . I found him tortured by the emerging inconclusiveness of the war; he was torn between his doubts and his sense of duty, between his analysis and his loyalties. He knew he would be able to restore many valued friendships by a dramatic gesture of protest, but he thought it was wrong to speak out when he considered himself partially responsible and thought he could promote his convictions more effectively in office than outside. . . . He suffered cruelly but never showed it.[76]

═══

OF ALL THE LEGACIES OF THE PAST THAT HAUNTED MCNAMARA, perhaps the most painful were those in his own family. By the end of the 1970s, his daughter Margy, who had seemed least wounded by Vietnam-related tensions, was divorced. Kathleen, who had opposed the war, defied her parents on dress, and allied with her brother in arguments with their father, was now pursuing a forestry degree at Yale. Asked by a Yale professor whether she was related to Robert McNamara, she replied, "He's my uncle."[77] Craig McNamara had finished St. Paul's, but despite his mediocre grades, had been admitted to Stanford, perhaps, he thought, benefiting from his father's name and his sister having attended Stanford, but now he was determined to escape "Washington, New England and the entire East Coast."[78]

When Craig arrived in 1969, the Bay Area was aflame with antiwar fervor. With his father stonily silent about the war, Craig decided to speak out himself. At a wild Berkeley demonstration, Craig at first tried to discourage rioters from smashing windows, but ended up joining in the destruction. Before long he became a follower of Stanford's firebrand English professor Bruce Franklin. During another demonstration, Craig tried to address fellow demonstrators but failed as an orator. Plagued by self-doubt, he craved his father's approbation even as he openly broke with him. "I was against the war, against authority, and against my father, but I still identified with him." Later, in Mexico City, while standing in a plaza, he felt "like an egg. My body was a shell. Somewhere at the center there was supposed to be a yolk."[79] A friend of one of the McNamara children compared Craig's situation to being a child of Hitler's aide Albert Speer.[80]

In 1970, Craig expected to be drafted for military service. Thanks to his ulcers and his history of psychotherapy, plus some help from his sister Margy's then-husband Barry Carter, a reserve officer who helped prepare his file, Craig was classified 4-F. After that, in the spring of 1971, in the middle of his sophomore year, he dropped out of Stanford and headed to South America on a motorcycle.

Craig traveled with two friends, a few maps, and no Spanish. He would not return to the States for two and a half years. His aim was to ride all the way to Tierra del Fuego, at the southernmost tip of the continent.[81] Despite several crashes and fierce rainstorms, he and his friends made it to Mexico City on Craig's birthday, which passed without contact with his parents, who didn't know where he was.[82] Onward to Guatemala on his motorcycle, via Honduras, El Salvador, Nicaragua, and Costa Rica, then on a fishing trawler and a freighter to Cartagena, Colombia, and by bike to Bogotá. At that point Craig split with his fellow travelers and headed solo toward Chile, feeling increasingly lonely, spending weeks without meeting anyone who spoke English.[83] Once in Santiago, where leftist president Salvador Allende was hosting Fidel Castro, Craig listened intently as Castro addressed a huge rally and cheered the Cuban leader. His days in Santiago revived Craig, but also presented him with a dilemma. It turned out Robert McNamara was also in the city, attending a UN session on trade and development. His father didn't know Craig was there, but would he have contacted him had he known? His mother would have, Craig assumed, if she were there. Craig decided not to seek out his father.[84]

Craig spent the next year and a half on Easter Island, one of the most remote inhabited islands in the world. There he worked with a crew restoring the moai statues, farmed, and lived in a cave for months.[85] By this time, his mother, whom he had called from the only phone available and to whom he was writing, was writing back, sending him care packages (which took three to six months to arrive) containing Hershey chocolate bars with almonds and Stim-u-Dents for cleaning his teeth, and she even came all the way to visit him for a week.[86] He felt "some joy" when she said, in parting, "You can come home anytime. We'll be ready."[87] Craig still hadn't heard from his father. But by this time, Craig recalled, his mom was "suffering so painfully from duodenal ulcers" that he realized, "I have to go home. I may lose my mother. She may die. And so I went home and indeed she was really in difficult shape."[88]

Craig returned home in the summer of 1973. "Things got a little better," he recalled—"for a time."[89] Berkeley police had arrested three men who were plotting to kidnap and assassinate Robert McNamara at his home in Snowmass, Colorado, and blow his house to bits. And now his father wanted Craig to testify to a judge as to the accuracy of the plotters' description of the McNamaras and their home. "I could not bring myself to testify," Craig remembered. "In my place, my aunt Katie (my mother's only sibling) went to court to vouch that the descriptions were correct."[90] Soon after that, while he was driving with his parents to Colorado, Margy started to moan softly from pain. Despite the fact that she had recently undergone another operation for ulcers, they were acting up again. "Dad became quiet," Craig recalled, "which was his way during times like this. He clutched his hands together, a protective gesture and a sign of being at a loss."[91]

McNamara wasn't at a loss on the subject of sustainable agriculture, which had become a focus for the World Bank, but he never asked his

son what Craig had learned about that or about the lives of subsistence
farmers in South America. Craig returned to Mexico for most of 1973
and 1974 to pursue those interests. He studied agriculture at the University of California at Davis (graduating in 1976), and then set out to find
"an agricultural apprenticeship" as a prelude to trying to buy a farm. At
this point, he recalls, "Dad sent many letters to his friends and colleagues,
trying to help me get an apprenticeship. I don't think I was aware of Dad's
letters at the time, but I recently discovered a large packet of them in my
office. They always included my resume. What strikes me about them is
the sheer extent of Dad's network and his willingness to use it." Nothing
came from these contacts, but "reading those letters now reminds me that
Dad was behind me. At least, he was behind my career. He didn't have a
clue how to address the turmoil he had caused me, but he was definitely
willing to help my career."[92]

After Craig settled down as a walnut farmer in California, his father
(according to Christoffersen) "seemed very pleased to see his son and was
proud of showing him around the Bank and telling us he was a farmer
doing amazing things."[93] Kathleen applied for a forestry job at the World
Bank in 1983, two years after her father left the Bank, and joined the Bank
in 1984. But despite these signs of reconciliation, some strains persisted,
and it wasn't the workaholic, peripatetic McNamara but rather Margy
who bore the main burden of family tension.

While her husband was at the Bank, Margy McNamara continued
to expand and manage her Reading Is Fundamental program. Having
taught high school in California, she had checked out elementary schools
when they first came to Washington and found that many children in
the sixth grade, with single parents on welfare, no fathers around, and
no printed matter—not a single book, magazine, or newspaper around—
could barely read. "I'm going to do something about it," she told her husband. He was "so busy," he recalled, that "I didn't pay any attention." So
she decided, with the permission of teachers, to provide free books in
schools, raised money with the help of Anne Richardson (wife of cabinet
member Elliot Richardson), President Johnson's daughter Lynda Robb,
and George H. W. Bush's wife, Barbara, and started Reading Is Funda-

mental.[94] By 1980, it had a full-time staff in Washington that was help-ing 3 million children at 13,000 sites in fifty states, distributing some 11 million books that year, for a total of 35 million books in 15 years. While traveling with McNamara, she kept track of RIF, bombarding its staff with her own letters from around the world, talking up its successes to leaders she met, and stimulating others in their countries to request more information about it.

Back at the Bank, she tried to make up for her husband's aloofness by forming an organization of Bank employee spouses (mostly wives). In con-trast to McNamara's forbidding formality, she was informal and warm. On top of all this, she worried about her children. "She would always ask about me," her daughter Margy remembers. "I never thought to ask her how she felt." "My mother was the essential ingredient, who always helped me," recalls Craig, "even in the darkest times, when I was very frustrated in my communication with Dad, she would say, 'Dad supports you even though he didn't show it at the moment.' It was those times with Mom that kept me going."[95]

Margy kept herself going on daunting treks with her husband and their friends. Meeting such challenges was nothing new to her; at age forty-eight, after having polio, she had rappelled 120 feet in the Teton Range. In 1973, she reached the base camp of Mount Everest at 16,000 feet. William Clark recalled climbing an Egyptian pyramid or a Mayan ruin (he wasn't sure which), with Bob racing up 200 or so stairs, Margy lagging behind, and Clark himself, who limped as a result of a war wound, bringing up the rear—until suddenly Bob stopped: "Oh, am I going too fast? It's not too far, is it?" After that, Clark says, McNamara was "very slow and very solic-itous, all the way down."[96] In 1980, by which time Margy was seriously ill, she insisted on joining a hiking trip in Nepal. Severe chest pains she felt in Aspen in February prompted her to return to Washington, where tests showed she had cancer and that her prognosis was grim. According to Ruth Graves, the RIF executive director who was with Margy when she got the bad news, Mrs. McNamara "accepted it instantly." But her husband did not. He continued traveling for the Bank.[97]

Craig and his wife-to-be, Julie, with financial help from his father, bought a walnut farm in Winters, California, in the fall of 1980. That Thanksgiving, they held their first family gathering at the farm. Craig's mother flew in from Washington, but by this time doctors said that mesothelioma, which she may have contracted from asbestos in the first Ann Arbor home she and McNamara had lived in, left her with only about eleven months to live. Her husband did not accompany her to California.

Craig hoisted his mother onto a tractor and drove her around the farm, the hair of her wig blowing slightly in the wind.[98] Back in Washington, President Jimmy Carter planned to award Margy the Medal of Freedom for her work in literacy education in a White House ceremony on January 16, 1981, a few days before he left office. By that time her husband knew she was dying, so he brought her home from Georgetown Hospital, set up a hospital room in the house, rented hospital furniture, and hired twenty-four-hour nursing help. He planned to attend the White House ceremony and bring back the medal and recount everything that happened. But she insisted on going along. By that time she weighed merely eighty-five pounds. "She was being fed intravenously," her husband remembered, "she had taped tubes stuck all over, she was taking a hundred and twenty cc's of a drug that helped to sedate her," but she insisted, 'I'm going.' I said, 'My God, you can't go.' She said, 'I'm going.'"

Still serving as World Bank president, McNamara used a seven-passenger Bank limousine to ferry Margy in a wheelchair, plus Craig and a nurse, to the White House. As they drove down Connecticut Avenue, Margy asked, "Why is the camel going with us?" She was hallucinating.[99]

Craig stayed on at Tracy Place for his mother's last weeks, listening while his father phoned all his contacts in medicine seeking any sort of treatment that could save his wife. With time running out, Margy turned toward Craig and said, "Don't do as I have done. Don't give everything to others so you leave nothing for yourself. Just remember to give to yourself."[100]

Margy McNamara died early in the morning of February 3, nineteen days after President Carter had awarded her the Presidential Medal of Freedom. Her husband had appointments that day with visiting Jordanians and at the State Department, and he kept them both. The Jordanians would have understood if he had canceled their meeting. At the State Department he apologized for being late.[101]

"She died because of Vietnam," McNamara later insisted, "or at least her deep trauma associated with it."[102] He arranged a big memorial service at Washington's National Cathedral in which he wanted to include a reading of Ecclesiastes 3: "To everything there is a season, and time to every purpose under the heaven. A time to be born and a time to die. A time to plant and time to pluck up that which is planted. A time to kill and time to heal." But he insisted on editing the Bible! "Damn it," he said: "There does not have to be a time to kill and certainly not at Marg's service!"[103]

In a 1995 interview, when asked whether his wife had been his adviser, McNamara replied that her role had been "much more fundamental than that. She shaped my life, probably not as much as it needed to be shaped, . . . but she moved it much more in directions that it needed to be moved than it would have been without her. And of course she had a tremendous influence on our children, far more than I did. Partially because at the time, fathers didn't play as important a role in relations to the children as they do today. . . . But also because I was very very busy both at Ford and Defense, she was the backbone of the family."[104]

In her eulogy, Margy's friend Lydia Katzenbach spoke of Margy's "quiet sense of destiny in her life." "She truly believed that people were good, that something could be done to alter misfortune, deprivation, to release the life forces, to turn an ugly detour back in the right direction. She was pure in her enjoyments and enthusiasms. She was thankful and felt lucky. First, and for all time, most important to Marg was her love and gratitude for her beloved husband, Bob. For he spread out the world and handed it to her. He took those bright blue shining eyes around the world, letting them meet and take in and shine on the most lowly and the most mighty. While she deeply wished to encourage the possibilities in others, she would not have changed her life."[105]

Craig reached out to put his arms around his father at the service, but according to Shapley, his father "shook him off, and sat there alone and sobbed."[106]

CHAPTER THIRTEEN

Hindsight and Foresight

On September 30, 1980, Robert McNamara spoke at an annual meeting of the Bank and the International Monetary Fund for the last time.[1] In attendance were some 3,000 members of the international finance and economic development community: prime ministers, ministers of finance, international civil servants, and others. "Everybody was there," recalled McNamara's assistant at the Bank, Olivier Lafourcade. "He could barely finish his speech. He was silent for almost a minute—drinking water, emotional; he was not in tears, but he was choking. You can imagine the impression created on 3,000 people."[2]

Superficially, the scene resembled, on a larger scale, the day McNamara choked up when President Johnson awarded him the Presidential Medal of Freedom at the White House in February 1968. But this time was very different. Instead of a paralyzing mix of pride and guilt over his role as defense secretary, he felt a deep sense of accomplishment. After presiding over the carnage in Vietnam, he had tried to lift up millions of the world's poorest people. "We do not see their faces, we do not know their names, we cannot count their number. But they are there. And their lives have been touched by us. And ours by them."[3]

Absent the responsibilities and pressures of another big assignment

when he retired from the bank in June 1981, and without his close companion of four decades, who had died five months earlier, what would he
do with the rest of his life? Looking back in 2001, he recalled throwing
himself into "dozens of research projects involving both academic specialists and practitioners in the issues that have continued to concern me,"
such as reduction of world poverty, the risk of great power conflict, and
the danger of nuclear war.[4] But that description doesn't do full justice to
McNamara's main preoccupation in his last years. With a kind of manic
intensity, he now reassessed his role at the Pentagon, noting his successes,
including his role in the 1962 Cuban missile crisis, but paying much more
attention to his failures in Vietnam, while drawing lessons for himself,
his country, and the world. He traveled and worked at a frantic pace that
belied his advanced years, as if propelled by a determination to exorcize
his demons. Roswell Gilpatric, his former Pentagon deputy, described
him as the Flying Dutchman, invoking Richard Wagner's opera of the
same name that features the ghost captain of a ship who is doomed to sail
on endlessly without ever making port. "He just can't be still. He doesn't
want to have a moment of his waking hours idle so he'll have to dwell on
something," Gilpatric said.[5] McNamara's peripatetic life seemed conso-
nant with a dictum attributed to Theodore Roosevelt: "Black care rarely
sits behind a rider whose pace is fast enough."

The extent to which McNamara went to reexamine himself and his
career, and the pain he felt in doing so, kept cropping up in unexpected
places and in ways that shocked the people he was with. In the late 1980s,
for example, when he was in Moscow, he encountered former MIT president Jerome Weisner, who had served as President Kennedy's science advi-
sor, and Rose Styron, representing Amnesty International. Together they
visited Soviet physicist-turned-dissident-turned-Supreme-Soviet-deputy
Andrei Sakharov, whom Weisner was inviting to the United States. The
Kremlin had forcibly removed Sakharov from Moscow in 1980 and placed
him under house arrest in Gorky, a city closed to foreigners, until 1986,
when Mikhail Gorbachev freed him. Later that evening at dinner with
Weisner and Styron, she recalls, "Suddenly McNamara started to cry and
went on crying wordlessly. Finally he began telling us how moved he was

by Sakharov, 'that great moral man,' and how bad he felt about his own less-than-noble role in the Vietnam War."[6]

In 1984, McNamara broke his long public silence about Vietnam— not by defending his own role in the war, not by blaming others, but in defense of Gen. William Westmoreland, with whom he had so often clashed during the conflict. Westmoreland had sued CBS for claim- ing Westmoreland's overly optimistic reports on the war had deceived McNamara and President Johnson. Like the boy scout he had once been, McNamara swore in court that his former opponent had not deceived his civilian bosses.[7]

Some of the impetus for McNamara's extended self-examination came from outside. Between 1987 and 1992 two scholars, James Blight and janet Lang (she does not use a capital J in her name), pioneers in the field of critical oral history at Harvard's Kennedy School of Government and Brown University's Center for Foreign Policy Development, organized a series of five critical oral history conferences on the Cuban missile crisis (held in Hawks Cay, Florida; Cambridge, Massachusetts; Moscow, Anti- gua, and Havana), and then another series on Vietnam in Vietnam. They recruited McNamara as a key participant. At these conferences he talked more than he had before about his time as secretary of defense. The writer Deborah Shapley published a biography, *Power and Promise: The Life and Times of Robert McNamara*, in 1993. McNamara had cooperated with Shapley, but was disappointed in the result. He confided to McGeorge Bundy, "I confess that the Shapley book—which I have glanced at, but haven't yet read—left me in a state of deep depression." He added, "If and when you decide to write—or speak out—on Vietnam, I may try to bring myself to do the same."[8] He did, at long last, write his own memoirs, pub- lished in 1995, devoted mostly to his Pentagon years and particularly to the Vietnam War.

The critical reaction to his memoirs was, to put it gently, mixed. His willingness to confess that the war in Vietnam was "wrong, terribly wrong," prompted some critics to insist he was even more "evil" than thay had thought since, it turned out, he had continued to send thousands more Americans and Vietnamese to their deaths even after he concluded the war was unwinnable. Between 1995 and 2003, McNamara joined with Blight and Lang in organizing critical oral history conferences in Vietnam where, for the first time, he confronted face-to-face Vietnamese leaders who had managed the war from Hanoi. Then, in 2003, he was the focus of a powerful documentary film, Errol Morris's *The Fog of War*, which amounted to his most revealing attempt yet at self-explanation.

On most of these occasions McNamara tried, not always successfully, to steer clear of his deepest feelings and emotions in public, just as he had throughout his career, although he eventually sought out the personal psychological sources of his own shortcomings in sessions with a Johns Hopkins psychiatrist. But when he highlighted his failures and challenged his former adversaries (in Vietnam, Russia, and Cuba) to do likewise, that too was an expression of his character. Aspiring since childhood to excel at everything he tackled in life, only to stumble and be brought low by Vietnam, he now searched for retrospective mastery over what had eluded him and why. He was trained to hold himself to the highest ethical standards, but having failed to do so, he tried to understand where and how he and others had fallen short.

In all these undertakings, he kept coming back to the mortal danger of a nuclear war, to how he had fought to prevent the Cuban crisis and then the Vietnam War from escalating into one, and how he was now campaigning to eliminate nukes—as if those efforts absolved him, well, *almost* absolved him, of his sins. But as Blight and Lang, who worked closely with him for more than twenty years on both the Cuba and Vietnam conferences and the books that emerged from them, concluded: "Nothing would ever absolve him, not even 'almost.' He knew this in his bones. The only thing he could do now was to work to make things better for the next generation. The scales would never balance, but he could put good stuff on that other scale."[9]

Blight and Lang had first met McNamara in 1984 at a Harvard-sponsored conference on "Avoiding Nuclear War." Their affectionate nickname for him, "Maximum Bob" (after a character in an Elmore Leonard crime novel), captured his personality as they came to know it: "the intensity, the take-no-prisoners demeanor, and the messianic zeal with which he delivered his message." They came to think of him as the "Jeremiah" of the nuclear age, "a stooped octogenarian, left shoulder drooping far below the level of his right (Bob was left handed), wearing his tattered Burberry raincoat, carrying his ancient travel bag through some airport, on his way to some place to scare the hell out of yet another audience." No matter what the audience—"defense experts, teachers, retirees, military officers, students, you name it . . . his volcanic personality, his amazing command of facts and figures, the quickness of his mind, even into his eighties, meant that Bob's agenda would be *the* agenda." In *The Fog of War*, McNamara wore "his 'official' interview outfit: blue blazer, white shirt and blue tie," but "in person Bob would usually remove his blazer . . . would then roll up his sleeves . . . all the way past his elbows, creating fewer restrictions on his left arm, which was his gesturing and pounding arm. He would lean forward, ready to come straight at you with high-volume recollections of the [Cuban] crisis, references to research on the crisis, and admonitions to abolish nuclear weapons before they abolish us."[10]

═══

"CRITICAL ORAL HISTORY," AS BLIGHT AND LANG CALL THE research method that they and McNamara adopted in the Cuba and Vietnam conferences, differs from conventional oral history in which people simply recount their stories. Critical oral history begins with meetings attended by both scholars and former policymakers for which all prepare by studying hundreds of pages of declassified primary documents and secondary accounts. The idea is to ensure that recollections presented at the conferences are conveyed "within the constraints of the facts (such as they are known)." In other words, policymakers' accounts "must answer to three judges: the documentary record, the expertise of specialists in the field, and the recollections of those who lived through the event in positions of official responsibility."[11]

Planning for the Cuban conferences began shortly after the "Avoiding Nuclear War" conference in Big Sky, Montana, in July 1984. Despite its ominous subject, Big Sky participants had politely debated various estimates of nuclear risk until, toward the end of the first day, McNamara (in Blight and Lang's paraphrase) exploded: "You people don't know what you're talking about. You are talking about some presumed level of risk, at this moment, in the comfort of this isolated conference center, while we all sip our coffee and eat our cookies. Some say the risk is high; most say it is low; everyone seems to think it is in any case manageable. But ladies and gentlemen, this conversation is insane in the light of what I know about the Cuban missile crisis. Together with the Russians, we came very close to destroying our societies and probably all of human civilization with it."[12]

That was not the conventional view of the crisis. On the contrary, it had generally been viewed as an example of masterly, if improvised, crisis management in which the US and the USSR found themselves in a tense confrontation but managed to step back and settle it without a war. McNamara had not felt so sanguine at the time. He remembered Saturday night, October 27, 1962, the day before the crisis eased, as "a perfectly beautiful night, as fall nights are in Washington. I walked out of the President's Oval Office, and as I walked out, I thought I might never live to see another Saturday night."[13] Now, a quarter of a century later, he was determined to prove that the world had been a whisker away from nuclear war—while adding that Vietnam hadn't been far from the brink either.

Throughout the Cold War, Washington had counted on the threat of nuclear weapons to deter their own use, that is, on the threat of US nuclear retaliation to deter a Soviet nuclear first strike, or even a Soviet attack on Western Europe with conventional weapons. But McNamara recalled at Hawk's Cay that "people in the Pentagon were even talking about a first strike" in March 1961, which looked more tempting once the alleged "missile gap" in Moscow's favor was discovered to be, in fact, massively in America's. When he examined the military's master nuclear war plan (the "Single Integrated Operational Plan," known as SIOP) in 1961, he discovered it contained four retaliatory options, but also a first-strike plan, which Gen. Curtis LeMay, McNamara's World War II boss in the Marianas and now air force chief of staff, talked about implementing "if the Russians ever back us into a corner."

Neither McNamara himself, nor Kennedy, he insisted at Hawk's Cay, "*ever* thought that we would launch a first-strike under *any* circumstances.

Putting moral issues aside," he continued, "there was no reasonable chance that we could get away with a first strike unscathed." To admit that publicly would destroy deterrence, so they "didn't tell the military," and "the Soviets, of course, had no way of knowing this." But the military continued to believe, as Harvard defense expert Graham Allison put it at Hawk's Cay, that Washington's huge superiority in the number of missiles and bombers gave it "a 'reasonable' prospect" of " 'getting them all' [i.e., Soviet missiles and planes capable of striking the US] in a first strike."[14] That was one reason why LeMay and other generals insisted that the Soviet missiles in Cuba, which reduced the American advantage, made for a dangerous shift in the balance of power. But McNamara had cited that same American superiority to contend in 1962 that Soviet missiles in Cuba would *not* significantly alter the nuclear balance.

Emboldened by the American advantage, McNamara recalled, hawkish Kennedy advisers like LeMay pressed for a sudden air strike to take out the Soviet missiles, followed by an all-out invasion of Cuba. But McNamara feared Moscow would respond to such an attack with a strike of its own against NATO ally Turkey, where the US had stationed rockets, or West Berlin. Another hawk, Paul Nitze, dismissed that possibility in his post-conference interview. He had counted on Washington's nuclear superiority to deter Moscow, as had Douglas Dillon, who said after Hawk's Cay: "I am frankly flabbergasted at this notion that the nuclear balance made no difference in the missile crisis. Of course, it made a huge, decisive difference"—it gave Washington the assurance that if it did indeed attack Cuba, Moscow would not in fact respond by attacking Turkey or Berlin.[15]

Obviously, all these possibilities (How would the Soviets respond to an American attack on Cuba? How would the Americans respond to the Soviet response?) were uncertain. But that was exactly the point McNamara insisted on in his post–Hawk's Cay interview with Blight. He wasn't asserting there had been "a high probability" of massive conventional warfare or nuclear warfare, but rather that "when one is pursuing a new and in fact unprecedented course of action, one should recognize the uncertainty, the fallibility, the risk of an error of judgment and where that risk takes you. To me, while the risk might have been small—I think it was small—an error in judgment could have been disastrous, and that's why I thought we had to act with extreme caution."[16]

McNamara feared in 1962 and still did in 1987 that "in a crisis people may act impulsively and they may preempt," meaning strike first with nuclear weapons. Not that the US would have done so: "No way that was *ever* going to happen, and I want that to be absolutely clear. No. We worried about a *Soviet* preemptive strike." McNamara knew that sounded:

> [N]onsensical, because, rationally, a Soviet first strike, and our retaliation, would have resulted—or could have—in their complete obliteration. But if I put myself in the Soviets' shoes in those days and in that crisis, and if I look around and see U.S. forces on alert, and if for some reason I become convinced that the U.S. is going to strike, well then . . . maybe I strike first in an attempt to use my few forces before they are destroyed. I don't know. My point is that you don't want a situation to arise in which there is the slightest chance of this happening.[17]

Putting himself in his "opponent's shoes" was something McNamara did again and again as he reassessed Cuba and Vietnam. He was always the first to do so, Lang remembers, astounding his former adversaries and sometimes prompting them to do likewise. His doing so, he contended, had been "very influential in my decisions relating to Vietnam." McNamara still wasn't discussing Vietnam publicly, he admitted in a 1987 interview, but, "on this general point about low-probability, highly adverse consequences, it is relevant." Right-wing critics charged he had been "afraid to use all the force at his command and that is why we failed to win the war in Vietnam." What was wrong with that, he insisted, was the same thing that was wrong with striking Cuba during the missile crisis. "I mean, if you just say the hell with it, let's go all out, bomb them—Cubans or Vietnamese—into oblivion, look what you are doing. You are practically requiring the Soviets, or in certain circumstances the Chinese, to retaliate militarily. And then what happens? I'll tell you what: we're in a major war between nuclear powers. Anything might happen."[18]

═══

THE NEXT CUBAN CONFERENCE, IN CAMBRIDGE, MASSACHUSETTS, on October 11–12, 1987, included three Soviet participants: Sergo Mikoyan, son of Khrushchev's closest Kremlin ally, Anastas Mikoyan, and himself a specialist on Latin America; Fyodor Burlatsky, a newspaper columnist and sometimes speechwriter for Khrushchev; plus Georgy Shakhnazarov, a leading political adviser to Mikhail Gorbachev.[19] Like Kennedy and his advisers in 1961, the Americans at Hawk's Cay had surmised that Khrushchev sent missiles to Cuba to rectify the nuclear imbalance that had been in Washington's favor, and to pressure Kennedy to yield in Berlin. But what emerged from the Cambridge conference was the key role that Cuba itself played in the crisis. The Soviet delegation insisted Khrushchev's main motivation was to protect Cuba from an American invasion following the Cuban exiles' failed incursion at the Bay of Pigs a year earlier. McNamara swore that no such invasion had been coming— despite Washington's covert actions designed to destabilize the Castro regime and even assassinate Castro himself. That, plus Washington's mistaken assumption that Khrushchev would never send missiles to Cuba, convinced McNamara that the whole crisis was a product of misperception and misjudgment on both sides.

But what disturbed him even more was that, according to Mikoyan supported by Shakhnazarov, Moscow worried that "somebody in the United States might think that a seventeen-to-one [nuclear] superiority would mean that a first strike was possible."[20] And that, according to McNamara's fearful logic, might have led Moscow itself to think of striking first. Which led McNamara to formulate what he dubbed "McNamara's Law": "In this nuclear age, it is not possible to predict with a high degree of certainty what the effects of the use of military force will be because of the risks of accident, misperception, miscalculation and inadvertence."[21]

The Moscow conference (January 27–29, 1989) included three former Soviet officials who had played leading roles in the Cuban crisis—Foreign Minister Andrei Gromyko, Ambassador to the US Anatoly Dobrynin, and Ambassador to Cuba Aleksandr Alekseyev—as well as a Cuban delegation that included Jorge Risquet, a member of the Cuban Communist politburo; Army commander Sergio del Valle; and Fidel Castro's long-time revolutionary comrade Emilio Aragones.[22] The Russians revealed that Soviet nuclear inferiority in October 1962 was even greater than the Americans knew: Moscow had only twenty intercontinental rockets capable of reaching the US rather than the seventy-five estimated by American intelligence analysts. The Antigua conference, in January 1991, prepared the way for the Havana meeting (January 9–12, 1992), attended by Castro himself. By that time, Castro's aides had briefed him on McNamara's passion and intensity, his determination to admit mistakes, and his pressure on the Cubans and Russians to confess theirs, too. When the two men first met, Castro looked ready for battle in "green fatigues, highly polished combat boots," and what appeared to Blight and Lang to be a bulletproof vest, while McNamara wore his usual conference outfit: "a short-sleeve blue polo shirt, khaki pants and New Balance running shoes." When Castro arrived, all the other participants rose from their seats. He walked around the table greeting them, starting with the Russians and ending with the US delegation. Face-to-face with McNamara, Castro stared at his erstwhile nemesis for a long time, until McNamara blurted out, "Robert McNamara, sir!" After a tense silence, Castro smiled broadly, stuck out his right hand, and exclaimed (through his interpreter), "So, Mr. McNamara, we meet at last."[23] As this conference proceeded, both McNamara and Castro took detailed notes as each other spoke.

The most dramatic moment in all the Cuba conferences occurred when Soviet general Anatoly Gribkov, who had helped plan and organize the secret deployment of missiles to Cuba, addressed the Havana gathering. "A thick-necked, humorless, prickly military man right out of Soviet central casting" (as described by Blight and Lang), he revealed that in addition to rockets capable of hitting the US, Moscow had secretly delivered short-range tactical nuclear weapons usable against invading Americans, and had delegated authority to use them to its commander in Cuba, Gen. Issa Pliyev. Washington knew about the medium-range missiles, but not about the short-range weapons.[24]

Blight and Lang describe McNamara's reaction to Gribkov's revelation: He "grimaces with astonishment and fumbles with his earphone,

striving to hear the translation more clearly. McNamara realizes that if
the United States had invaded Cuba, as many felt would be necessary
had Khrushchev not agreed to remove the missiles, thousands of American soldiers might have been killed on Cuban beaches by Soviet tactical nuclear weapons." Fearful as he had been during the crisis itself,
McNamara now realized: "We greatly underestimated the danger. It was
far more severe than I thought." If the US forces massed in Florida had
attacked Cuba, "as many in the U.S. government—military and civilian
alike—were recommending to the president on the 27th and 28th, we
don't need to speculate what would have happened. . . . no one should
believe that a U.S. force could have been attacked by tactical nuclear warheads without responding with nuclear warheads. And where would it
have ended? In utter disaster."[25]

Castro himself shared that view, but as a committed revolutionary, he
was prepared to die for the cause. "If the commanders were authorized
to use tactical nuclear weapons," he told the conference, "it goes without
saying that in the event of an invasion we would have had a nuclear war."
That's why, on Friday night, October 26, 1962, he had dictated a letter to
Khrushchev seeming to urge the Soviet leader to strike first so as not to
be struck first as the USSR had been by Hitler on June 22, 1941—a plea
that Khrushchev saw as terrifying.[26]

After the conference, over drinks at the Hotel Comodoro, McNamara
confessed to Blight and Lang that he had been thinking obsessively about
the worst-case scenario ever since Gribkov's revelation. If the US had invaded
Cuba, and if the Russians had repulsed the invasion with tactical nuclear weapons, and if the Russians had "nuked" the American base at Guantánamo and
moved to cut off West Berlin, and if the US had used tactical "nukes" to resist
numerically superior Russian and East German forces, then—choking with
horror, McNamara could barely finish the sequence—both sides, attempting
to preempt the other, could have destroyed the world.[27]

A week after the Havana conference, addressing the National Press
Club in Washington, McNamara championed his new cause: "To prevent
the destruction of nations, we have no choice but to abolish nuclear weapons as swiftly and safely as possible."[28]

Ten years after that, at another Havana conference on the fortieth anniversary of the Cuban crisis, sponsored by the Cuban government and the National Security Archive, a private organization in Washington that gathers declassified documents on foreign affairs, Castro urged McNamara to return again in 2012 to mark the crisis's fiftieth anniversary. McNamara replied, "I will not be in Havana, I will be in hell," and walked out of the room.[29]

═══

DEBORAH SHAPLEY'S BIOGRAPHY CAME OUT IN 1993. IT IS A COMprehensive, well-researched book in which Shapley tries to present a balanced portrait of McNamara, documenting both his virtues and shortcomings. But according to his secretary at the time, Jeanne Moore, McNamara was "finding the reading of this book very difficult indeed."[30] Letters from friends and former colleagues tried to comfort McNamara. President Kennedy's brother-in-law Sargent Shriver reminded him that it wasn't he, but JFK and LBJ, who decided "what was to be done or not done in Vietnam."[31] But the most emotional message and most meaningful to him came from Jackie Kennedy on February 24. By this time, their relationship had cooled. Her letters to him, while still cordial, had grown shorter over the years and were clearly sent as courteous responses to many missives from him as he tried to stay in touch. But in light of the Shapley book and McNamara's dark reaction to it, word of which must have reached her, Jackie penned a brief but heartfelt letter to him, reminiscent of letters from years earlier. She told him never to doubt that he was respected, admired, and loved, a special figure in American history. She reminded him of Eleanor Roosevelt's comment that no one could humiliate her without her consent. "You will always be my shining knight," she wrote.[32]

To which McNamara replied the next day: "You are a dear. You knew how depressed I was so you wrote me a note—warm, sensitive, moving— like none I have ever received before. I will treasure it and [the quotation from Mrs. Roosevelt] until the end of my days. My spirits are soaring. With love, Bob."[33]

Fifteen months later, Mrs. Kennedy died at her Manhattan apartment overlooking Central Park at age sixty-four after battling non-Hodgkin's lymphoma. McNamara, who had returned from a visit to Africa the night before, spoke with emotion about her in an interview with CBS News, his voice wavering as he recalled the time when she battered his chest as she pleaded with him to end the killing in Vietnam. "I am a very emotional person," he later said about the interview, "and I am moved to tears very readily, to tell you the truth and, when that happens, my voice begins to break and I try very hard to stop it."[34] William Bundy sent McNamara his condolences when Jackie died, perceptively saying, "I had long sensed how devoted you were to her and how much she meant to you."[35] The *Los Angeles Times'* obituary about Jackie, alluding to her relationship with McNamara without elaborating, referred to McNamara as a "more appropriate suitor" than Aristotle Onassis.[36]

Whether Jackie's undying faith in him encouraged McNamara at last to write an account of his own life and career is unknown. But in the meantime, a young historian who had worked as a research assistant for Clark Clifford when McNamara's Pentagon successor wrote his memoir, had embarked on a McNamara biography, which soon turned into a collaboration with McNamara on the latter's own memoir.

Beginning in 1991, Brian VanDeMark had interviewed McNamara many times, as well as friends and colleagues from throughout his life, but, as VanDeMark recalled, "the one topic he steadfastly refused to discuss was the one that mattered most and was the most sensitive for him—Vietnam." The publication of Shapley's book changed the situation. McNamara asked VanDeMark to read it and a week later received him in an office next to the Willard Hotel, just east of the White House on Pennsylvania Avenue. "Sitting at a large oak desk, wearing a worn oxford-cloth shirt and khakis, [McNamara] turned his lean, tightly coiled six-foot frame and intense hazel eyes toward me and asked in a clear forceful voice, his body language carefully controlled, 'What is your opinion of Shapley's book?' " Sensing McNamara didn't like the book, but believing correctly that he would respect an honest answer, VanDeMark praised it as "a fundamentally good book"—and then offered to drop his own biography project and help McNamara write his own memoir. McNamara agreed and a long, painful process began, guided by Peter Osnos, the editor. Over time, he was persuaded by Osnos that the memoir should be primarily about the Vietnam War rather than a traditional autobiography. McNamara "struggled," VanDeMark recalled, "as he approached the most sensitive and painful of topics, his speech slowing, thick with emotion. At times, he began to tear up almost out of panic, overwhelmed with shame. At one point, he halted altogether, incapacitated by perplexity and despondency.... At last, McNamara brought himself to ask, 'Do you think 58,000 Americans died in vain?' He labored to get each word out and wept in humiliation when he finished."[37]

In October 1988, in interviews with Bob Woodward, McNamara had briefly broached the subject of Vietnam. Woodward described the scene as they talked: "'Vietnam,' the word kind of comes out of his mouth like a giant two-syllable spark.... He then wipes his whole face with his hand as if he is eradicating the memory or waking up. It is a strange movement." McNamara told Woodward: "'I say never go into a room you can't get out of. Before each operation there should be a paper on how to get out. And if you can't get out, don't do it. A paper should say it, put the bounds on the risk. That's your job, force people to do it. Force them.' He stands up. He has to go, go to a dinner party next door. Starts racing around the room, picking up a paper here, a list, checking a schedule, a book. His small briefcase. Yes, this is important. We'll talk more. He'll help. He's going skiing in three weeks, looking forward to it. Has to get ready etc. But call again etc. (Note: a man on the verge of talking much more, almost on the verge of confession if there is one to be made.)"[38]

"This is a book I never planned to write" is the first sentence of McNamara's memoir. "Although pressed repeatedly for over a quarter of a century to add my views on Vietnam to the public record," he wrote, "I hesitated for fear that I might appear self-serving, defensive, or vindictive, which I wished to avoid at all costs," and also "because it is hard to face one's own mistakes." Why write now? Because although his colleagues in the Kennedy and Johnson administrations were "an exceptional group: young, vigorous, intelligent, well-meaning, patriotic servants of the

United States," "we were wrong, terribly wrong. We owe it to future generations to explain why."[39]

McNamara's more than three-hundred-page memoir devotes a mere twenty-five pages to "My Journey to Washington" from his birth in 1916 to the Kennedy administration's inauguration on January 20, 1961, and none to his post-Pentagon years. The focus of *In Retrospect*, named in its subtitle, is *The Tragedy and Lessons of Vietnam*. Those lessons not only catalog McNamara's and his colleagues' fateful errors in Vietnam, they prove eerily relevant to the later American military interventions in Iraq and Afghanistan.[40]

Unlike many American leaders at the end of the twentieth century and early years of the twenty-first, McNamara supplanted hubris with humility in thinking about defense policy. He enumerated warfighting principles derived from the misperceptions and miscalculations that he belatedly recognized had bedeviled Washington's management of the Vietnam War. He erased omniscience and omnipotence from the war calculus that had guided him as defense secretary, the sense among McNamara and his Johnson administration colleagues that Washington knew what was best for Vietnam and that American military might would prevail against a ragtag adversary. McNamara also banished the cocky notion that Washington's righteous ideological convictions could be applied in a distant place and culture that bore little resemblance to the United States and American history. Instead, he pointed to the importance of nationalism as a galvanizing force in nations determined to shed any vestige of colonial interference in their affairs, a factor that he had completely missed in his assessment of North Vietnam and its leader, Ho Chi Minh. He talked in his book about avoiding the dangerous miscalculation of taking the United States to war without candidly informing the American people and Congress about the potential human and financial costs. And he acknowledged that war inevitably produces unforeseen and unpredictable challenges that cannot easily be managed. All good advice for American leaders today.

His diagnosis was shamefully late in coming, but it was astute and offered a road map for future American wars that should have been studied and incorporated into Washington's military engagements in the post–Cold War era. American power never seemed greater than in the years after the 1991 disintegration of the Soviet Union. But as new threats developed, American leaders for the most part—with the notable exception of George H. W. Bush—failed to appreciate the limits of American power and continued to overestimate what military force alone could achieve. The rise of Islamic fundamentalist terrorism presented challenges that could only be effectively addressed through a combination of military, political, and economic action and an appreciation of the principles that McNamara described in his Vietnam lesson. Sadly, they were largely ignored in the American response to the terror attacks of September 11, 2001.

The tragedy McNamara depicts was also peculiarly personal, but despite all the evidence of his deep anguish, he stubbornly resisted Shapley's conclusion that he was what he called "a tragic figure," a "tragic man" with a "tragic life." "The hell with that stuff," McNamara told Peter Osnos, who was helping him edit his memoirs. If "Vietnam was a tragedy," and he "was associated with it," he went on, "then I must either feel a sense of regret or guilt or both." But "I think it's more regret than guilt. . . . I owe an explanation to those whom I killed. I don't put it quite as bluntly as that. But that's correct, that's what I mean to say, and that's the way it'll be read. I owe an explanation to them and I must answer the question, did they die in vain. And I say, no, they didn't."[41]

He never told Johnson to cut his losses and get out of Vietnam. Virtually no one else did either—not McGeorge Bundy, not Nicholas Katzenbach, not Hubert Humphrey (who tried but quickly retreated when shunned by LBJ), and not Chester Cooper, Bundy's deputy for Vietnam, who told Blight and Lang he had once been prepared to do so at a cabinet meeting but suddenly found himself saying, "Yes, President."[42] The only exceptions were George Ball, who had explicit permission to play devil's advocate; Richard Helms, CIA director, who wrote a strong memo to Johnson arguing that the US could withdraw from Vietnam without permanently damaging relations with allies, but never heard back from the president; and Clark Clifford, to whom Johnson listened only when almost all seemed lost in 1968.

What was different about McNamara was that he tortured himself trying to explain his own behavior and eventually confessed in public to doing so. In the late 1970s, James Thomson, a former Bundy aide at the National Security Council and later curator of the Nieman Foundation for Journalism at Harvard, invited Bundy to dinner and allowed a well-lubricated young guest to challenge Bundy: "You really fucked up [in Vietnam] didn't you?" To which, according to Thomson, Bundy replied, "Yes I did, and I'm not going to spend the rest of my life feeling guilty about it"—exactly what McNamara did.[43] In 1993, almost certainly influenced by McNamara's reassessment of his role in Vietnam, Bundy mused about writing about Vietnam himself. "I think I am going to conclude that there was no way of getting a good result, so we shouldn't have tried by U.S. force in '65—and second, that JFK would have understood that and acted accordingly. There would still have been costs and troubles—but less."[44] Eventually, in 1995 Bundy started to write an account of his own role in Vietnam, including his sins as well as his achievements, but he never finished before he died a year later.[45]

Why did McNamara champion the critical July 1965 decision to send ground troops to Vietnam? Why hadn't he forced "a knockdown, drag-out debate over the loose assumptions, unasked questions, and thin analyses underlying our military strategy in Vietnam?" "I doubt I will ever fully understand why I did not do so here," McNamara confessed in his memoir.[46] Johnson learned, McNamara insisted, "that I would deal straight with him, telling him what I believed rather than what I thought he wanted to hear."[47] But he concealed his growing sense—as early as the fall of 1965—that the United States would find it very difficult, if not impossible, to win in Vietnam. "What in hell was I doing for two years?" (1966–1967), he asks in his memoirs, when he failed to "mobilize people" in the administration to convince Johnson? Had Johnson bullied him into silence? Wasn't Johnson a bully? Osnos asked him. "Well I wouldn't say that," answered McNamara. "But it's a fact," countered Osnos. "That's right," McNamara agreed with him. But "I won't want to say that. . . . Lady Bird's still alive. I can't say that."[48] McNamara's verdict in his memoirs is: "He could be a bully, but he was never that way with me."[49] "I really don't know what I think about Johnson," he added in a March 1994 interview. "I am beginning to think I know what I think about myself."[50]

Lacunae like this help to explain the fiercely hostile reaction to McNamara's memoirs from many critics. In the words of David Halberstam, who reviewed the book for the *Los Angeles Times*:

> This is a shallow, mechanistic, immensely disappointing book. . . . Had it been published 25 years ago while the battle itself and the debate over it was still raging—had McNamara come forth then and said, as he does here, that what had come to be known as "McNamara's War" was "wrong, terribly wrong," it would have been an extremely valuable part of the ongoing debate; indeed, it might have ended the debate then and there. A secretary of defense of his seeming certitude who came forward and said that he had been mistaken in his earlier estimates and that the war could not be won would have been the most powerful of witnesses and would be now a revered American instead of one of our most divided and haunted of men. Sadly, the inner strength to do that, to put loyalty to country and to a larger truth above a narrow bureaucratic loyalty to a President and failed policy, was not within his powers.[51]

An unsigned *New York Times* editorial written by Howell Raines on April 12, 1995, said, "Mr. McNamara wants us to know" that he, too, realized by 1967 that "the war had to be stopped to avoid 'a major national disaster,'" but he "wants us to grant that his delicate sense of protocol excused him from any obligation to join the national debate over whether American troops should continue to die at the rate of hundreds a week in a war he knew to be futile. . . . His regret cannot be huge enough to balance the books for our dead soldiers. The ghosts of those unlived lives circle close around Mr. McNamara. Surely, he must in every quiet and prosperous moment hear the ceaseless whispers of those poor boys in the infantry, dying in the tall grass, platoon by platoon for no purpose. What he took from them cannot be repaid by primetime apology and stale tears three decades later."[52]

Painful as this *j'accuse* was, McNamara had almost certainly accused himself of the same sin. Perhaps that's why he reprinted Raines's indictment in an appendix to the paperback edition of his memoirs. (David Halberstam bluntly rejected McNamara's request to include a copy of Halberstam's scathing review in the *Los Angeles Times*. "I want no part of being in your book," Halberstam told McNamara.[53]) And why he devoted so much of his last years to improving the future when he could not undo the past. Writing later, theologian Robert McAfee Brown honored McNamara's apology for "having set a pattern virtually unknown in our nation's public life," but sensed that McNamara's "punishment is covert, self-inflicted and lacerating to a degree that no one else can ever measure."[54] In an April 1995 interview with Jonathan Alter in *Newsweek*, McNamara confessed to "such an emotional feeling" when he visited the Vietnam memorial in Washington, but quickly added, "I'm not going to discuss those feelings."[55]

On April 18, when Arthur Schlesinger Jr. called him, McNamara seemed "undaunted and in a fighting mood," but not so a few days later when he appeared at the Council on Foreign Relations at a session over which Schlesinger presided. Schlesinger recorded in his diary:

> He gives the impression now . . . of a man so wound up that he is almost out of control. He talks in his usual logical, forceful, clearcut way, but he can't stop talking. I finally had to cut his remarks off, and he then overanswered every question. The questions were courteous but surprisingly tough. One man who had served two years in Vietnam said that, when he came back, he felt he had a moral obligation to speak out against the war; "Why, Mr. Secretary, did you not feel the same obligation?" Bob's answer is pathetic. He draws a phony distinction between the obligations of a cabinet officer in a parliamentary system, where, as elected officials, their obligation is to their constituents, and in a presidential system, where, as appointed officials, their obligation is to the President. He also invokes the phony aid-and-comfort-to-the-enemy argument as another excuse for silence. Knowing Bob, the quintessential organization man, I can

understand why it has taken so long for him to speak out. He does not help himself by advancing these unconvincing rationalizations.

I could see the faces of Mac Bundy, Ted Sorensen, Ros Gilpatric and others fall as Bob rambled militantly and emotionally along. At the end, he started to read a letter sent him by the widow of a Quaker who had doused himself with gasoline and burned himself to death in front of the Pentagon twenty years ago. The letter pleaded for reconciliation and healing. Bob was about to break into tears, could not go on and gave the letter to me to read. Then he left. [56]

According to Blight and Lang, McNamara "often carried the letter from Anne Morrison Welch in his suit coat pocket."[57] In it, Morrison's widow expressed her thanks for "the honesty and forthrightness" of McNamara's memoir and for his "courage and openness."[58]

Six years later, at the age of eighty-five, McNamara claimed that he had by now learned the political skills he had lacked in the sixties. McNamara had admitted back then that he was not cut out to be a politician. But from time to time, he confessed that he was tempted to become one. On September 18, 1968, he told journalist Henry Brandon that he had "immense admiration" for elected officials: "I think in a sense it's the highest form of political activity because it's the means of translating the diverse interests of our people into some movement toward a common goal. It's a very, very intricate process and requires skill of the highest type. I think if I had my life to live over again I might well want to pursue that course."[59] More than three decades later, he claimed that he had by now learned the political skills that enabled President Johnson to go so far in "eliminating racism." "I think today I understand more about it than I did then. I think today I'd be more capable perhaps of achieving congressional approval of the Voting Rights Act and the other civil rights legislation."[60]

═══

IT WAS WHILE MCNAMARA WAS WRITING HIS MEMOIR, HE recalled, that he began "to wonder whether a process could be initiated with the Vietnamese" that might answer questions like these: Would China have intervened militarily, as it had in Korea, if the US had attempted to invade and occupy North Vietnam? Were any of his attempts to establish a ceasefire and move to negotiations between 1966 and 1968 taken seriously in Hanoi, and if so, why did they fail?[61]

McNamara asked Leslie Gelb, president of the Council on Foreign Relations, to see whether former Vietnamese officials and scholars would be willing to meet with their American counterparts. As was the case in the Cuban crisis, McNamara strongly suspected that "mutual misperception, misunderstanding and misjudgment by leaders in Washington and Hanoi" had resulted in "missed opportunities" to end the war or even avoid it entirely. He wanted to know whether, "if each side had known the truth about the other's reality," the outcome might have been "less tragic."[62] Impressed by McNamara's personal involvement, the Vietnamese agreed to cooperate, but when McNamara's exploratory trip to Hanoi in November 1995 sparked sharp criticism by Council on Foreign Relations members, the Council dropped out, leaving the project to be sponsored by Brown University's Thomas J. Watson Institute, which had worked with the Council from the beginning.

Over the next two years, James Blight, Watson Institute director Thomas Biersteker, Vassar College Vietnam expert Robert Brigham, National Security Archive research director Malcolm Byrne, and George Washington University Cold War historian James Hershberg gathered documents, wrote papers, and in various combinations made six working trips to Hanoi. After that, a bigger meeting in Hanoi was held on June 20–23, 1997, attended by McNamara; former US attorney general and deputy secretary of state Nicholas Katzenbach; former US deputy national security adviser Francis Bator; National Security Council Vietnam expert Chet Cooper; two former US generals, William Y. Smith and Dale Vesser; and several American scholars. The Vietnamese delegation was headed by Nguyen Co Thach, deputy foreign minister throughout the war (later foreign minister), and included retired four-star general, former defense minister of North Vietnam, and Hanoi's principal planner of the war, Vo Nguyen Giap (who did not attend key meetings in 1995 and 1997, but who met with McNamara one-on-one), along with other diplomats and military men.[63] Following these meetings, and a February 1998 meeting in Hanoi that McNamara did not attend, a final session was held in Bellagio, Italy, on July 27–31, 1998, at which McNamara and a group of scholars and journalists reviewed an early version of the manuscript of his and Blight's book about the project, *Argument Without End: In Search of Answers to the Vietnam Tragedy*.[64]

Outside the formal conference room, McNamara's presence in Hanoi on his first, exploratory trip created a sensation. The official welcome at the airport was unexpectedly warm. The kids who crowded around on the streets wanted to practice the foreign language they were studying in school, not French or Russian, but English: "Hello. I am fine. How are you? I'm fine. Goodbye"—followed by "giggling, waves and thrown kisses." Journalists who came from all over Asia competed to get as close to the Americans as Vietnamese security would allow. Jim Blight, who kept track, marveled at the fact that "the former secretary of defense had come to Hanoi to discuss a war in which 3.2 million Vietnamese had died and from which somewhere between 400,000 and 800,000 remain missing, and he is greeted not just cordially but warmly by old adversaries and young people with no memory of the war."[65]

The warm official welcome, it must be admitted, probably also reflected Hanoi's interest in improving US-Vietnam relations in light of tensions with China. The mood during the substantive exchanges at the exploratory meeting in 1995 and at the full conference two years later was more mixed. McNamara confessed on June 20, 1997, as he had at the Cuban conferences, that Washington had been partly to blame for the other side's conviction that the US was bent on their destruction. "If I had been a Vietnamese communist in January 1961, when the Kennedy administration came into office, I might well have believed, as I judge they did, that the United States' goal in Southeast Asia was to destroy the Hanoi government and its ally the NLF [National Liberation Front in South Vietnam]—that the US was an implacable enemy whose goal, in some fashion, was victory over their country." "However," he continued, "if I had been a Vietnamese communist and held those views I would have been totally mistaken."[66] But Nguyen Co Thach disagreed: "The Vietnamese mindset—our assessment of the U.S.—was essentially correct. Essentially correct. That is all."[67]

McNamara told General Giap in November 1995, "Hanoi and Washington may each have been mistaken, have misunderstood each other" in the Tonkin Gulf episode. But General Giap responded: "I don't believe we misunderstood you; you were the enemy; you wished to defeat us—to destroy us. So we were forced to fight you."

McNamara pressed on. "Were we—was I, was Kennedy, was Johnson—a 'neo-imperialist' in the sense that you are using the word?" "I would say, *absolutely not*!" To which Giap retorted, "Excuse me, but we *correctly* understood you."[68]

These and other similar exchanges were polite, but fierce. McNamara looked his age—thinning hair, age spots on his face, bony fingers jabbing the air as he shouted at his interlocutors. They, in turn, gave as good as they got. When asked in June 1997 why the North's huge loss of life didn't force them to negotiate, a Vietnamese diplomat snapped: "You listen to me! Our land was devastated and our people died. Vietnam would not accept the peace of the slave."[69] But other Vietnamese participants spoke more freely during breaks in the conferences, at small tables during lunches, when, for example, Cooper pressed them in February 1998 to explain why the North Vietnamese had seemed slavish servants of Moscow and Beijing (reinforcing the American image of a monolithic Communist camp trying to conquer South Vietnam) rather than signaling their own tensions with its Communist allies. "Why didn't you come to us and say, 'Look, don't believe the Chinese and Soviet propaganda. It doesn't apply to us. We assure you that we are anxious to pursue an independent policy. We think we should have some discussions about who is the true enemy of whom. Let's talk about this and get things cleared up.' "[70] Vietnamese historian Luu Doan Huynh seemed to agree. Referring to 1954, he said, "we wanted direct, bilateral Vietnam-U.S. talks so we could speak for ourselves and act in our own interests. But, you know, we could not say this openly because that would jeopardize the support given to North Vietnam by the USSR and China."[71] At one point after World War II, when the Vietnamese thought they might have to choose between French and Chinese occupation forces, Ho chastised advisers who preferred the Chinese: "You fools. The last time the Chinese came they stayed for one thousand years. As for me, I prefer to smell French shit for five years than Chinese shit for the rest of my life."[72]

Throughout these meetings McNamara kept in particularly close touch with Bob Brigham, drawing on the latter's expertise to understand what Vietnamese participants were saying and not saying. "I had never met someone who was as curious about his own role" in Vietnam, Brigham recalled. "He took notes like a freshman" when others "talked about the war." He "really wanted to get to the bottom of things. He really thought there were answers to everything, in a historical sense, not a military sense." Most of all he wanted to know why Hanoi had not responded to all his efforts to start negotiations that might end the war. " 'Why didn't they do this? Why didn't they do that? Did they understand this? Didn't they understand that? Did they understand when I moved chess piece A that . . . ?' "[73] According to Brigham, "Bob was upset that he 'didn't do better,' 'know more,' 'understand their mindset,' during the Americanization of the war in 1965."[74] Which traces back to his sense that smart as he was, he wasn't smart enough. Lesser humans, knowing their own limitations and being more reconciled to them, or having repressed an awareness of them, were not so self-condemnatory.

Brigham and Blight had invited McGeorge Bundy to take part in the conferences; Brigham had prepared a long talk on what Western historians had learned about the internal divisions and political intrigue that had shaped Hanoi's war policies. But two minutes into this presentation, Bundy stopped him and said, "I don't need to know this. It's really about Russia, China and the United States and [the Vietnamese] were just a pawn." Whereas McNamara spent what seemed like endless hours pressing Brigham for more information about the Vietnamese, often while taking long walks around Hanoi, sometimes in the dead of night in their hotel. "We often had adjoining rooms at these conferences," Brigham recalled, "and he would bang on my door at all hours of the night, stressed out about everything, about an answer to a question today, about what somebody said during these meetings," even extending to the current condition of Vietnam. "The most intense conversation I ever saw him have," remembered Brigham, "was with the prime minister of Vietnam when they were talking about poverty"—about McNamara's time at the World Bank and what Vietnam was doing to reduce poverty.[75]

Although they defended their cause and their conduct vigorously, Vietnamese officials confirmed McNamara's suspicions that mutual misperceptions had intensified the war, for example, after the brazen North Vietnamese attack on Americans at the Pleiku air base in February 1965 that provoked Washington to start bombing the North. Assuming that Hanoi knew that McGeorge Bundy was in Vietnam at the time, Washington took the attack as a direct, intolerable challenge. But a Vietnamese general involved in the Pleiku attack insisted Hanoi didn't know Bundy was there and that a local commander, not Hanoi, had ordered the assault. Chet Cooper had written the angry report on the Pleiku attack that Bundy later would present to LBJ. Cooper's voice now cracked upon learning that the Vietnamese did not know that Bundy was in the country, let alone at Pleiku, and later, alone with Blight and Lang, Cooper cried.[76]

Revelations like these allowed McNamara to conclude that the war could have been avoided or ended much sooner had the two sides understood each other better and communicated more candidly at the highest level. But the conferences also confirmed McNamara's contention, as had the Cuban conferences, that avoiding a nuclear confrontation had been a close call. McNamara recalled that the Joint Chiefs, "who at various times favored a U.S. invasion of North Vietnam, stated it might lead to war with Russia and China, in which case the United States might be forced to use nuclear weapons."[77] Brigham later wrote that "new material from the Communist archives suggests that China never would have allowed an American invasion of North Vietnam to go unanswered." According to Luu Doan Huynh, "The Americans thought the Chinese were bluffing. The Chinese wanted you to know they weren't bluffing."[78] To McNamara, who had fought throughout the war to prevent the American military from provoking a direct clash with the Chinese and/or Russians, this was a kind of vindication.

And yet, in *Argument Without End* he rejected another sort of vindication. Harvard historian Ernest May had written that "given the assumptions generally shared by Americans in the 1960s, it seems probable that any collection of men or women would have decided as did members of the Kennedy and Johnson administrations."[79] Or as May put it about McNamara's own recollections, they were "a little like a memoir by a Crusader who cannot remember why he particularly cared about the fate of Jerusalem."[80] But McNamara took that as a challenge, as if May were saying that "leaders of these two administrations, myself included," had been "pushed along, like leaves before the wind, by forces no one could have resisted."[81]

May's point was that McNamara had been too critical of himself. But McNamara refused to be absolved. "Leaders are supposed to lead, to resist pressures or 'forces' of this sort, to understand more fully than others the range of options and the implications of choosing such options." Roosevelt had done so when he convinced the American people to help allies fight the Nazis, and Kennedy likewise in resisting pressure to bomb Soviet missile sites in Cuba. "And I believe this is what President Johnson and his associates, including myself, should have done to resist the pressure ... toward a military solution to the problem of Vietnam."[82]

In 2001, a few days before he turned eighty-five, McNamara published yet another book, coauthored with James Blight, *Wilson's Ghost: Reducing the Risk of Conflict, Killing, and Catastrophe in the 21st Century. Wilson's Ghost's* warning, as conjured by the authors, was to remember "the blindness and folly" that led nations into World War One, "a disaster theretofore without compare in world history," and to beware the temptation to believe an alleged "balance of power" could maintain the peace without a strong international organization.[83] In the twentieth century, McNamara said, 160 million people, of whom as many as 100 million may have been civilians, were killed in two world wars, by Stalin's and Mao's mass murders and other mass violence, including the Vietnam War.[84] More than 5 million worldwide, he and Blight reported, had been killed in the first five years after the fall of the Berlin Wall, and at that rate, the twenty-first century's toll might amount to as many as 300 million.[85] Deeming the most likely sources of twenty-first-century carnage to be great power conflict, communal killing, and nuclear catastrophe, they proposed three "imperatives" to reduce the killing. The "moral imperative" would establish as a major goal of US foreign policy, and indeed of foreign policies across the globe, the avoidance of such carnage. The "multilateral imperative" would demand that the United States "will not apply its economic, political or military power unilaterally, other than in the unlikely circumstances of a defense of the continental United States, Hawaii and Alaska."[86] The third was the "empathy imperative."[87]

Like McNamara's lessons of Vietnam, his prescriptions for the future may be debated. The fact that the American failures he identified in Vietnam recurred in Iraq and Afghanistan, with the correlation so precise as to be uncanny, suggests his successors in charge of American foreign policy have not learned those lessons. That McNamara himself learned and accepted them testifies to his transformation from a "realist" who ran the Vietnam War into an idealistic crusader for world peace. At the same time, he rejected the cold, calculating persona he cultivated before and during the war and revealed the softer, more emotional side of himself. After watching *The Fog of War*, American journalist Sidney Schanberg, who had covered the Vietnam War, concluded: "McNamara is a tormented being" who is "crying out for forgiveness but unable to get the words out." He has "put himself on trial, seeking acquittal and absolution. Yet he cannot bring himself to say the ultimate word: that he bore personal responsibility. Maybe he hasn't taken the first step, which is to forgive himself."[88]

═══

ERROL MORRIS'S FILM *THE FOG OF WAR* IS A KIND OF AUTOBIOGRAPHical documentary in which McNamara, speaking directly into the camera, narrates his life with occasional questions from the unseen Morris and flashes of newsreel footage and family photos. He talks raptly and urgently, like a preacher, but sprinkles in frequent "damn its," "helluvas," and "my Gods" that his mother had begged him to avoid. He laughs at himself but from time to time seems about to weep. He reminds *New Yorker* writer Roger Angell of an old man "stand[ing] in our path with the bony finger and crazy agenda of a street saint."[89] He confesses his short-comings (or at least some of them), but still boasts of achievements.

At the age of eighty-five, says McNamara, he is "drawing conclusions about himself." Some people, he says, "think I'm a son-of-a-bitch." And he seems to agree. On an earlier occasion, at Brown, he addressed a large crowd in the university's biggest auditorium, after which he invited comments from people lined up at microphones in the aisles. One potential questioner, a Vietnam vet wearing a jacket with the insignia of his Marine unit that fought at Hue, kept hesitating to speak until the Q&A ended, but then suddenly ran up to the stage and yelled McNamara was a "son-of-a-bitch" responsible for the deaths of his buddies. Security rushed in, but McNamara shooed them away. Seating himself on the edge of the stage with his legs dangling over it, he said, "Let's talk. Let's start with something we can agree on: 'I am a son-of-a-bitch.'" At that, the audience started to file back in to hear McNamara and the veteran talk about the tragedy that so many of the marine's buddies and many others died and that they should work to prevent that from happening again.[90]

"In that single night in 1945," McNamara says in *The Fog of War*, his eyes filling with tears, "we burned to death 100,000 Japanese civilians in Tokyo—men, women and children."[91] He and General LeMay, he admits, "were behaving as war criminals."[92] McNamara didn't give the order to obliterate Tokyo, he insists. But, he admits, "I was part of the mechanism that in a sense recommended it. I analyzed bombing operations and how to make them more efficient"—efficient, he explains, shifting from confessional to bureaucratic language, defined as "minimizing loss of [air crews] per target of destruction." The general lesson he wants to teach is that "Proportionality Should Be a Guideline in War"[93]—but he can't help saying that the Tokyo bombing was "not proportional in the minds of *some people*."[94]

McNamara winces as he reveals Americans dropped two or three times as many bombs on Vietnam as were dropped on Western Europe in all of World War II. He cites calculations that while 58,000 Americans died in Vietnam, about 3 million Vietnamese perished, which as a percentage of the overall population would be the equivalent of 27 million in the

United States.[95] He is still tormented by Norman Morrison's fiery suicide beneath his Pentagon office window, but insists that he and Morrison were both "sensitive human beings" struggling with how to react to the war, and that "I believe I shared" many of Morrison's values.[96] McNamara deeply regrets the Vietnam War's impact on his own family. "My wife probably got ulcers from it, may have even ultimately died from the stress. My son got ulcers. It was very traumatic." But, he quickly adds, his eyes wet and his voice rising as if seeking to convince himself, "they were some of the best years of our life and all members of my family benefited from it. It was terrific."[97]

The horror of war—its brutality, the way it leads good men to do evil, the fog in which it envelops all involved in it—is the terrible message McNamara wants to convey. That nature of war helps him explain why he failed despite his best intentions. He feels "very sorry" for all the errors he has made, but also "very proud" of what he accomplished.[98]

The film flashes back to some of his proudest moments. On the stoop of President-elect Kennedy's Georgetown home in January 1961, JFK is announcing that McNamara has just accepted his invitation to become secretary of defense. Journalists on the steps wear heavy coats and hats against the cold, but Kennedy and McNamara, brimming with youth and strength, are coatless. McNamara, trying to look humble but obviously deeply gratified, keeps sneaking looks at Kennedy as if to make sure this is really happening to him. Another clip shows him arriving at the Pentagon, probably on his first day in office, striding forward almost jauntily with a broad self-satisfied smile on his face. In yet another, he enters a Defense Department conference room where his generals and admirals (several of whom must hate his guts for the reforms he is forcing on them) are waiting for him respectfully; all rise as he enters and takes his seat at the table.

Schanberg notes McNamara says "compulsively at every turn" in the film "how smart he is, and how at every stage of his life he rose above the rest," but speculates these "badges of success that McNamara clings to are crutches that hold him up in a time of darkness."[99] Not only hold him up, one wants to add, but prevent him from fully confessing how far he has fallen.

Reflecting on the film more than two decades later, Blight and Lang said McNamara was "twisting on a rack that he himself is operating." It was as if he was saying: "It was horrible; it was wonderful. It was the best of times; it was the worst of times. I was at the zenith of my power and influence; I was making members of my family crack under the pressure. I had a responsibility to my president; I had a responsibility to my family. I failed on both counts."[100]

At the very end of the film, Morris asks McNamara why he didn't speak out against the war after he left the Pentagon. "I'm not going to say any more than I have," McNamara replies. "These are the kinds of questions that get me into trouble." Morris presses on: "Do you feel in any way responsible for the war?" "I don't want to go any further with this discussion," is McNamara's nonanswer. Morris asks whether McNamara feels "damned if you do and [damned] if you don't." McNamara replies: "Yeah, that's right. And I'd rather be damned if I don't."[101] He is not being flippant. He is confessing he is damned one way or another.

═══

ON APRIL 27, 2005, BLIGHT AND LANG SAT IN THEIR OFFICE AT Brown University's Watson Institute with McNamara. Although now eighty-eight, he agreed to give one last public talk about the Cuban missile crisis. When they arrived at Starr auditorium, the hall was full and people were standing on the sidewalk, some of them shouting "war criminal" at the speaker. McNamara smiled grimly: "I'm already on record agreeing with them, you know," he told his hosts. On the way to the stage, obviously shaky on his feet but refusing to use a cane, McNamara almost fell into a group of undergraduates—at which point the crowd broke into applause. Having reached the stage, McNamara, Blight, and Brown historian Abbott Gleason seated themselves at a table where McNamara slung his blazer over the back of his chair. Dressed in his usual white shirt, sleeves rolled up, khaki pants, gray New Balance shoes, he looked, according to Blight and Lang, like "the world's oldest living preppie." He and they had agreed on the format: after an introduction by Gleason, McNamara would talk about the findings of the Cuban crisis conferences. But suddenly, as Gleason was speaking, McNamara whispered to Blight: "I can't remember what I was going to say—something about nuclear weapons, right? Anyway, you have to give the presentation, not me. . . . I'm all done. Now it's up to you to carry on." For a moment, McNamara "stares glassy-eyed, straight ahead, into space." Then he interrupted Gleason to explain that he wanted Blight to do the speaking since this was, after all, Brown, where Blight and Lang worked.

Blight scrambled to collect his thoughts and started speaking. Fifteen minutes into his improvised remarks, McNamara interrupted to add "a point of clarification" that turned into a forty-minute oration blending horror story ("we nearly blew up the world in October 1962"), a call to arms, or rather to abolish them ("get off your butts and abolish nuclear weapons before they abolish you"), and Camelot name-dropping ("President told me this, Bobby said that, Jackie took me aside").

Finally, McNamara subsided. "Jim, I'm sorry to have interrupted," he apologized, "but I had something I wanted to add." The audience, mostly students young enough to be McNamara's grandchildren, who viewed him as a kind of phenomenon, exploded in laughter, and rose to their feet, cheering and clapping. Later, after dinner, while walking to the inn where he was staying, McNamara tripped on the wet pavement and fell hard. Blight and Lang helped him up, then up several flights of stairs to his room, where they made sure his alarm was set so he could be picked up at 5:30 a.m. by the car that would take him to the airport. (He did make his plane.) They bade him good night. He replied "in barely more than a whisper: 'That was fun. A good one to go out on.' "[102]

CHAPTER FOURTEEN

Lonely Widower Seeks Companionship

"After my mom died in 1981," Craig McNamara remembers, "the boards of Dutch Shell Oil, Bank of America, *The Washington Post*, and the Rockefeller Foundation wined and dined Dad, flying him all over the world to consult on the cutting issues of the time. His confidants were Jackie Kennedy, Kay Graham, Ted Kennedy, and President Bill Clinton. The firm Corning Glass gave him a handsome corner office in Washington" (to which he always took the stairs rather than the elevator) with a full-time secretary, where he kept a mammoth globe from the World Bank.[1] According to Craig, "Each and every one of his friends, in and out of government, appreciated his loyalty to them. Though he never bragged about his captainship of global intelligentsia and [world] trade, I know that he liked it. He often told me how much he enjoyed flying from Boston to London to attend meetings, because he could see Martha's Vineyard out the window of the plane."[2] But his hyperactivity was also a way of fighting off loneliness. James Blight and janet Lang could see that he was "fighting to remain optimistic even as he plowed ever more deeply into his personal heart of darkness."[3]

McNamara didn't confess his innermost thoughts to Blight and Lang, nor to his children. Nor is it clear how much he had revealed even to his wife. Shortly before she died, McNamara recalled, "she was insistent that I remarry. I was just as insistent that I wouldn't—and I didn't, at least for 23 years."[4] McNamara, who had always opened up more to women than to men, desperately needed female companionship. The problem was that the women to whom he was attracted and who were attracted to him were high-powered people whose own complex lives circumscribed their relationships with him. But he acted as if that were no permanent obstacle, courting them with the same drive and intensity that had marked his pursuit of many of his goals in life.

═══

AFTER MARGY DIED, MCNAMARA NEEDED HIS CHILDREN, AND THEY needed him more, but their relations with him were still strained. He continued to support them financially, but that, too, could be fraught. He was probably closest to his daughter Margy, who reminded friends of her mother and whose second husband, Bob Pastor, had been a member of the National Security Council staff under President Carter and who worked closely with McNamara in preparing the Havana conference on the Cuban crisis. Margy spoke lovingly of her father then and still does, but in 2006, Margy wrote to her father: "I look forward to hearing from you, wish it wasn't about money."[5] He sometimes interrogated Kathleen about her financial issues. As for his son, Craig, their path to a full reconciliation was particularly uneven, though their love for each other survived periods of estrangement and grew stronger in later years.

The first time McNamara visited his son's California walnut farm, which Craig and Julie, soon to be his wife, bought in 1980, was for Craig's wedding in 1982. But "other than his presence, he didn't contribute much to the ceremony," Craig recalled. Moreover, Craig continued, Julie soon "felt marginalized by my father . . . continually hurt by his absence from the farm, from our lives, and from her life more specifically." McNamara supported his son and daughter-in-law financially, but, Craig said, "he placed a boundary around his personal life." Craig had hoped that becoming a grandfather would bring his father closer, "but his pattern of absence continued." When his father telephoned, it was "to talk about the production of the farm." Most of the calls came before 5 a.m. California time, McNamara seemingly oblivious to the three-hour time difference between his Washington, DC, home and Craig's farm. His cost-conscious father chose the early hour, Craig recalled, because daytime long-distance phone rates increased at 8 a.m. Eastern time. Sometimes "all he wanted was big data." His repeated "requests for spreadsheets, financial balances, and rate of return" reminded Craig of "the misleading statistics that had so doomed his [father's] wartime strategy." Or the senior McNamara would call when he needed help. "Being a lifelong incompetent at household tasks, and with Mom no longer around, Dad used to call Julie and have her recite instructions about operating the washing machine, the dishwasher, or the coffee maker, writing everything down while she spoke into the phone."[6] When he was on his own, McNamara made do with a jar of instant coffee in his kitchen—"no coffeemaker," add Blight and Lang, "nothing he had to plug in and turn on."[7]

Frequent hiking trips into the mountains brought Craig and his father closer. They were both happy when Bob McNamara succeeded in getting spartan huts, one named for his late wife and suitable year-round for shelter during long treks in summer or winter, built on National Forest land at high altitude between Aspen and Vail. He often joked that he had difficulty getting a reservation since they usually got booked early.[8] McNamara was "so loving" when he and Craig were together in the mountains, Craig recalled, "and the walnuts I'd grown were in his hands. We had a bond with nature that came from the beauty of those surroundings. But that did not replace the missing pieces. Eating walnuts with him on the trail reminded me that he had not visited the orchards for a very long time.

"'When do you think you might get out again, Dad?'

"'I'm not sure, Craigie. How's it looking?'

"We had perfected the paradox of our relationship," Craig remembered. "We were so close on trips to the mountains, and his absence wounded me deeply during all the other times. Each hiking or skiing trip repaired the hurt a little, and then the emotional scabs would break open."[9]

In 2003, McNamara invited his son to the Telluride Film Festival in Colorado to see *The Fog of War*. Craig hadn't been invited to Havana or Hanoi for the Cuban and Vietnam oral history conferences and had felt deeply hurt: "Maybe Dad didn't think a dirt-covered walnut farmer ought to be in the room with all those distinguished statesmen." So he was touched when he sensed in his father's voice "a need to have me with him in Telluride," which would be "a vulnerable position for him; he'd be even more exposed than in the pages of his memoir."[10] According to Blight and Lang, Craig's not being invited to Havana or Hanoi "had absolutely nothing to do" with Craig's being a "dirt-covered walnut farmer." Rather, they contend, McNamara wanted to protect Craig and his daughters from the ever-present risk of protests against him.[11] But Craig's interpretation of his father's motivation deepened the gulf between them.

In the time leading up to Telluride, McNamara called his son more often than usual, including twice on the day Craig flew to the festival. Craig thought his father was "anxious." Over dinner, McNamara seemed "in a very good mood. He wanted me to update him on the farm and to talk about the kids." But when they talked about *The Fog of War*, Craig "could tell he was nervous. He and I both remembered the huge blowback from *In Retrospect*. 'It's good to have you here, Craigie,' he told me. He knew I loved him."[12] But even though Telluride was a "home game," Blight and Lang remember McNamara worried that the reaction to *The Fog of War* would repeat the conclusion of several reviews of the film: "Errol is a genius and I'm a son-of-a-bitch."[13]

For the rest of their time in Telluride, Craig's father was "absent again." After dinner the first night, they didn't speak for the next twenty-four hours. Craig wasn't sure why his father "decided to exclude me after the first night, or if it was even conscious." He guessed his father "felt himself at the center of his own story during the festival. I was a supporting player, to be called upon only if needed. He wanted to receive any praise that would come, and he wanted to absorb any of the pain. For a person who had always been so singularly driven, ambitious, and self-centered, the distinction between the positive and negative effects of all this attention might not have been very clear."[14]

Some months later, Robert McNamara was interviewed (along with *The Fog of War* filmmaker Errol Morris) at Berkeley. This occasion, too, was fraught—given McNamara's memories of his undergraduate years there, plus his knowledge that he might have been strung up had he appeared there during the Vietnam War. Craig, his wife, and their children, Sean, Emily, and Graham, joined his father at a reception hosted by the chancellor and sat in the front row of a theater filled with an audience of nearly 3,000. Remembering wild antiwar demonstrations at Berkeley that he himself had attended, Craig imagined having to defend his father from a new wave of attackers. "When Dad came out onstage, the auditorium fell silent. The possibility of confrontation—the awkwardness and the silent threat—was in the air like electricity before a thunderstorm."[15]

During the conversation that followed the film, the moderator, Mark Danner, pressed McNamara on whether the lessons he drew from Vietnam applied to Iraq, which American military forces had invaded not long before the film festival. But in a throwback to the 1960s, McNamara refused to comment, citing the risk that could pose to American soldiers in the field, adding that former cabinet members shouldn't comment on the jobs current cabinet members are doing. Then, suddenly, he shouted at Danner: "We human beings killed 160 million other human beings in the 20th century. Is that what we want in this century? I don't think so!"

When Danner asked how he had dealt with reporters during difficult Pentagon press conferences, McNamara said, "Don't answer the question they asked. Answer the question you wish they'd asked."[16]

Don't all politicians avoid answering questions in this way? But McNamara's oldest friends swore that he couldn't tell a lie. So Craig asked himself: "Tell a lie?" He remembered his father telling him "Don't tell lies" when he was a kid. "I'm sure that I passed on to my own children the same lesson. How could someone as intelligent as Dad fail to see the contradiction?"

When McNamara "felt like he was done with an interview," Craig continues, "he was done." In true Bob McNamara style, he packed up his briefcase mid-question and walked off the Berkeley stage "without answering the last question," but "to thunderous applause."[17]

AT ONE POINT IN DESCRIBING DINNER WITH HIS FATHER AT TELLU-
ride, Craig noted: "He was with his girlfriend, who later became his second wife."[18] Diana Masieri was not McNamara's first girlfriend in the
years after he left the Pentagon. That seems to have been Joan Braden, a
married woman at the time. "In some ways I have, since Marg McNamara
died, taken the place of a wife to Robert McNamara," she claimed in
a book published in 1989, adding, "You'll notice I don't say I've taken
Marg's place."[19]

Joan Ridley Braden was born in Indianapolis in 1922 and raised in the
small Indiana town of Anderson. After majoring in economics at North-
western and finding a job at the Pentagon during the war, she worked
for Nelson Rockefeller, then assistant secretary of state for Latin American affairs, until 1951. In 1949 she married Tom Braden, a dashing Dartmouth graduate who had enlisted in the British Army before the United
States entered World War II. He served in the Office of Strategic Services
(predecessor to the Central Intelligence Agency) during the war, wrote a
book about the OSS with Stewart Alsop afterward, and then signed on
as CIA director Allen Dulles's personal assistant while living in Georgetown, where he joined Joseph Alsop and other members of "the Georgetown set." Tom left the CIA in 1954 and moved with Joan to California,
where he bought the small Oceanside newspaper, *The Blade-Tribune*,
with the help of a $100,000 loan from Nelson Rockefeller. Returning to
Washington in 1969, he became a newspaper columnist and radio and
television commentator while writing a book, *Eight Is Enough*, about his
family, which by now included eight children. Joan Braden worked on
John F. Kennedy's presidential campaign in 1960 and Robert Kennedy's
1968 campaign, and in 1976 became the State Department's coordinator
for consumer affairs.[20]

Joan had known McNamara "for as long as we've been in Washington," she told Paul Hendrickson, "or, at least since we moved back here the
second time, [in] 1969."[21] "Marg invited Tom and me to Bob's 60th birthday" in 1976, Joan wrote later, "where I got up the nerve to ask him about

riverblindness in Upper Volta, a country from which I'd just returned."
He was "a walking encyclopedia.... Standing in the center of the room at
that birthday party, he answered my questions for a full ten minutes." She
remembered saying to Tom as they left that party, "Robert McNamara
is the squarest man I've ever met." He was "so absorbed" in the course
of his lecture on river blindness "that if someone had dropped a drink
onto his lap in the middle of his lecture, he might have paid no more
attention... than you or I might give to the momentary annoyance of a
passing fly."[22]

At the State Department, Braden recalled, "I was desperately trying to
become an instant expert on trade and commodities," so she "thought of
Bob McNamara," called him, asked him to have lunch, and ended up getting "a lot of information, a lot of arguments, and a lot of lunches." At the
first lunch, he treated Joan "as a student who had to learn a lot of things
quickly." He brought a notebook to his small private dining room, with
a table suitable for no more than four, at the World Bank, and ended the
lunch after "precisely one hour." McNamara jotted down dates, names,
and questions that needed answers. After the third or fourth lunch, as
she was getting ready to leave, Braden remarked that her host "had eaten
all the pickles." "I like pickles, too," she said. When he looked at her with
"surprise and embarrassment," she noticed for the first time that "his eyes
were not at all the steely eyes which I had read about, but were in fact
very large eyes, compassionate eyes, warm eyes and brown. And then he
blushed. I think it was the first time he thought of me not merely as a
recipient of information, but as a person who might or might not like
pickles.... Quite suddenly, he didn't seem square. We had been friends
in a business sort of way. Now we were in a human way."[23]

However, Braden continues, "friendship between a woman who is
married and man who is not involves problems, and the first of these is
that some people look askance—in particular, women look askance."[24]
She and Bob had seen a lot of each other ("for lunch and things") when
Margy was still alive, and Margy had reportedly told her, "I'm happy
because you've made Bob happy."[25] Although Margy had urged him to
remarry after she died, McNamara told Shapley, "I had forty years of mar-

riage with one of God's loveliest creatures. There's nothing more I can have from marriage than I already have had."[26]After Margy died, Braden saw McNamara a lot more. Soon, she was sharing his friendships, and had "never known a man whose friends love him more dearly or of whom it could be said that the friends of his youth are the friends of his maturity. I've never known a man of higher intelligence nor any man who cared more deeply about other people or felt a greater obligation to put his best effort to helping mankind."[27]

In a 1987 interview, Braden admitted that her relationship with McNamara was "romantic," but insisted that it was "never romantic while his wife was living."[28] But they did not hide their intimacy at a dinner party at a time when Margy was very ill. Sally Quinn, the longtime *Washington Post* reporter, recalled seeing McNamara and Braden embracing at a dinner hosted by Jessica Hobby Catto, a Washington socialite. "I was shocked," Quinn said, "It was so inappropriate. Everyone knew Margy was very sick, she was forced to spend time lying on the McNamara dining table to ease her back pain. Yet, there were McNamara and Braden making out on the dance floor. It must have been so humiliating for Margy."[29]

In her 1989 book, *Just Enough Rope*, Braden wrote, "I suppose if a man is single (Marg McNamara died in 1981), if he is intelligent, if he is versed in economics, arms control, population growth, underdeveloped countries, developed countries, banking, and business, and if he has enough money to travel widely and nearly all the time; if in addition he's physically fit (Bob McNamara runs a mile every day and always takes the stairs two at a time), if he can ski, backpack, play tennis, swim, sail, owns a house in Aspen, Colorado, a house on Martha's Vineyard, and a house in Washington, D.C.—if, in addition to all these, he loves poetry and knows a lot of it by heart, he attracts the attention of a certain number of women who are divorced or whose husbands have died and wouldn't mind going along. And I'm the one who gets to go."[30]

She and Bob traveled together to the Netherlands, France, Russia, Greece, and Africa. "We go wherever he has board meetings or seminars or speeches that interest me. In short, I have more fun with Bob

McNamara than I do with anyone else in the world, sometimes, but not always, excepting my husband."

The "trouble with husbands," Braden observed, was that they too often speak of "mutual problems, family problems, children problems [especially one might add when there were eight of them], financial problems, housekeeping problems" and that "after a certain number of years, husbands tend to treat their wives as they treat their wallets or their easy chairs." They don't notice "anything about the easy chair except if suddenly it should disappear, go, not be there at all."[31]

Another of McNamara's virtues was that Joan was *not* married to him "so I am never cast in the role of the easy chair." He greeted her "with genuine pleasure," held her chair in restaurants, didn't complain about the number of bags she took on trips abroad, didn't object when she corrected him in conversation with the Queen of the Netherlands, noticed her new dresses or sweaters. And "the best part" was that when she got home, her husband Tom "greets me with genuine pleasure, takes me out to dinner, holds my chair before waiters can get to it, notices what I am wearing, is attentive to what I have done, what I have learned, whom I have seen, what they said and what I think about it."[32]

The only trouble with this idyllic panorama was that Joan Braden's adventures in life had also featured (to quote Maureen Dowd's short *New York Times* review of *Just Enough Rope*) "a shower scene with Nelson Rockefeller, a bedroom scene with Bobby Kennedy, a toe-tingling lunch with Kirk Douglas and an account of Frank Sinatra singing 'High Hopes' without his toupee."[33]

What did McNamara himself think of all this? "Look," he told Paul Hendrickson, "I know the whole Goddamn town's full of rumors, but the truth is there are only three people on earth who know what's going on and that's me, Joan and Tom Braden. . . . It's a very peculiar thing, I know. Look, she has these children and loves her husband very much and she's not about to leave him for me or any other man, and beyond that, I wouldn't marry her anyway because I'm not a homewrecker. She occasionally travels with me, you know. We never travel as Mr. and Mrs.

McNamara. We travel as Robert McNamara and Joan Braden. But she's a lovely girl. Beyond that, I love her company."[34]

In this same interview, McNamara told the story of how one evening upon his return from Europe on the Concorde, he took Joan out to dinner and brought her home at 10:30. Joan invited him in to see her daughter Susan, adding that Tom wanted to say hello, too.[35] "That's the kind of thing it is," McNamara said. "It's completely open between the three of us."[36]

Joan claimed she never saw McNamara or any other man without Tom's knowing about it. She and Tom had been married for thirty-five years, she told Hendrickson, and "when he walks into a room, he is still the handsomest man I've ever seen." Tom wanted her "to learn and to discover." He was "proud for me to be anywhere I'm learning something, whatever that something might be." Before she accompanied McNamara to South Africa, she worried about what Tom would think, but "Joanie," he said, "if I had a chance to go to South Africa do you think I wouldn't go? Go! Have a good time." She wouldn't have gone, she insisted, if it weren't OK with Tom. Of all the people she'd ever known, Tom was "the most secure." It "would never even occur to Tom to be jealous. All he cares about is that I love him."[37]

Tom's own version? "I long ago decided I don't give a damn what Washington is saying," he told Hendrickson. "I don't care what people are saying about me or my wife except in a professional sense. The kind of gossip you're referring to is uninformed. Gossip about my wife and some other man is always uninformed. Years ago, I used to hear it about Joanie and Nelson Rockefeller. I presume they enjoy each other's company. I mean, if it's balls, it's balls. On the other hand, if I thought my wife was seeing another man purely for secret lust, then I might say, 'Stay out of that one.' But if you're asking me about living with the morals of the twentieth century, then, of course, people see each other. I like McNamara fine. I'm not palsy with McNamara. We don't go places together. But he's fine."[38]

Joan insisted she felt the same way about Tom. "If he were going to Paris with a 30-year-old brainless beauty, I would not like it, not a bit. But if it were a woman of substance, say Anne Armstrong or Sandra Day

O'Connor, whether he went to bed with her or not, I would not try to stop him." "I make an enormous distinction between 'love' and 'in love,' and the only man I've ever been 'in love' with is Tom."[39]

Tom did blow up when Joan dared tell a reporter that she had found a trip with McNamara to Victoria Falls on the Zimbabwe/Zambia border "romantic." "Goddam it, Joanie," Tom blazed, "you've got everybody in town talking and how do you think I come out of this? I look like a cuckold or a fool. You look like an adulteress, and the only guy who isn't embarrassed is Bob McNamara."

Tom "subsided," Joan wrote, and insisted he didn't want to "run our lives . . . according to the way other people might say we should run them," but rather "the way we want to run them."

"So, it was reaffirmed," Joan concluded—the "never-quite-spoken original compact of our marriage." As to whether she was "keeping Bob McNamara from getting married, it worries me. What would I do without him?"[40]

═══

KATHARINE GRAHAM WAS VERY DIFFERENT. HER FAMILY WAS MUCH wealthier and more prominent than Joan Braden's. She grew up feeling shy and insecure, but ended up a press baroness. As head of *The Washington Post* and its media empire (and a member in good standing of "the Georgetown set"), she, of course, got to know Bob McNamara.

Wally Haas (1916–1995), who had been McNamara's classmate at Berkeley and remained his dear friend, introduced him and Margy to Graham, who was his cousin, and her husband Phil, and that led to "a strong friendship" that Graham described in her 1997 book as continuing "to this day."[41] When Phil Graham, whose brilliance and charisma had lifted him to the top leadership of the *Post*, became so ill in 1963 with bipolar disorder that he had to be hospitalized, Bob insisted on visiting him—"so typical of Bob," Katharine Graham recalled, "who was working at the Defense Department at a feverish pitch, to conclude that that was the best approach and to take time on a Saturday afternoon to drive an hour to Chestnut Lodge" in Rockville, Maryland. McNamara said to

Phil, "Goddamn you, get out of here, come down and help us. We need you."[42] (According to Blight and Lang, the phrase "Goddamn you," which McNamara's mother had banished from their home, was a sign of "deep friendship" for her son.)[43] And when Phil objected that "no one would accept him, Bob assured him that [Phil] knew more about the Defense Department than almost anyone"—partially "because he thought that's what Phil needed to hear, but more because it was basically true."[44] When Katharine Graham needed to hire someone to be president of the *Post* and didn't know whom, she "turned to my friend Bob McNamara," who recommended Paul Ignatius, who had been his secretary of the navy.[45] When *The New York Times* was agonizing about whether to publish the Pentagon Papers in the face of the Nixon administration's demand to censor them, McNamara urged publication and then celebrated at a birthday dinner for Mrs. Graham at Joe Alsop's house.[46] When she listed at the end of her book some of her "deepest friendships [that] began with an administration person . . . but grew over time into relationships whose core had nothing to do with politics or work," the first name on her list was Bob McNamara.[47]

Katharine Graham's book, *Personal History: A Memoir*, reveals how much the issues they cared most about overlapped. Although their fathers were poles apart in financial and social status, Robert James McNamara and Eugene Meyer were both "remote and strange" men (Graham's description of her father)[48] who were not close to many people. Kay Graham, like McNamara, was intellectually curious (she reports reading *War and Peace* during one summer vacation), but her mother, like McNamara's, "demanded perfection" and was ready to do battle with Vassar authorities who didn't share her high opinion of her daughter's performance on an assigned paper.[49] When they first met, Phil Graham impressed his future wife with characteristics she later encountered in McNamara: Phil was "bright, issue-oriented, hardworking," plus "he wanted to do public service and to deal with societal problems."[50] The Grahams socialized with John and Jackie Kennedy before the McNamaras did; after being invited by Joe Alsop to dine with the Kennedys as early as 1958, Phil Graham worked with JFK on his campaign, helping to draft his candidacy statement and to broker his invitation to Lyndon Johnson to run as his vice president. And Phil was even closer to LBJ, who cultivated Phil as the rising star of the *Post* by inviting the Grahams to the LBJ ranch in Texas in 1956.[51]

The night of Kennedy's 1960 election, the Grahams congratulated themselves that Phil had "helped bring about the election of our friend as the next president of the United States, and another, even closer friend as his vice-president."[52] Which allowed them to observe close-up the behaviors of both Kennedy and Johnson. That included McNamara's closeness to Kennedy, and the brief consideration Johnson gave to choosing McNamara as his vice presidential nominee in 1964.[53] Johnson's escalation of the Vietnam War greatly worried Katharine Graham, as did LBJ's brutal treatment of his aide Jack Valenti. Johnson "suddenly turned on Jack and laid him out savagely" in Graham's presence, she recalled, "the unpleasantness exacerbated by being delivered in front of a relative stranger. It was quite callous and inhuman, something I have never witnessed before or since."[54]

Katharine Graham took over the *Post* after her husband committed suicide in 1963, and she needed advice about how to run a large corporate enterprise. Who could be more helpful than the former president of the Ford Motor Company? Did Katharine Graham ever get wind of Johnson's manic depression, which resembled her husband's? If so, did she ever discuss the resemblance with McNamara? Did she ever mention to him a story that Clayton Fritchey, deputy US ambassador to the United Nations, told her about his boss, Adlai Stevenson, with whom Katharine, her mother, and her own daughter all enjoyed "close friendships"? JFK once told Fritchey he didn't understand why women, including his wife, Jackie, liked and admired Stevenson so much, confessing that he didn't feel as comfortable with women as Adlai did. "What do you suppose it means?" Kennedy asked. "Look, I may not be the best-looking guy out there, but for God's sake, Adlai's half bald, he's got a paunch, he wears his clothes in a dumpy sort of way. What's he got that I haven't got?" Fritchey's response, Graham wrote, pointed to what Graham herself thought women saw in Stevenson: "While you both love women,

Adlai also likes them, and women know the difference. . . . He conveys the idea that they are intelligent and worth listening to. He cares about what they're saying and what they've done, and that's really very fetching." To which Kennedy's response was: "Well, I don't say you're wrong, but I'm not sure I can go to those lengths."[55]

Graham doesn't say so, but McNamara's attention to women resembled Stevenson's—which would also explain why she was so fond of McNamara. "Men who appeal to me," she wrote, were "strong, bright, tough and involved." But such men "would probably not accept my own active and absorbing life. Those men need more attention and emotional energy than I had left over at the end of any working day, and I wasn't looking for a prince consort. In fact, I wasn't looking at all." "When you've lived alone for a number of years," Graham continued, "I'm afraid that you begin to realize how hard it would be to accommodate to living with someone else, adjusting to or even indulging his desires and his life. It was clear to me that I was married to my job, and that I loved it."[56]

According to a close friend of hers, Kay Graham had a "big crush" on McNamara and "adored him."[57] But she also tried to keep a certain distance from him, at least in public. When the *Post* ran a story about his relationship with Joan Braden, she admitted: "That's the sort of thing they layer away from me, and something I *want* layered away from me."[58] Private gatherings were different. She hosted a book party for him in April 1995 at her Georgetown home after publication of *In Retrospect*. She warmly toasted "my close friend," saying, "Bob has been a valued and trusted friend for much of my life, as well as a wise counselor and a staunch supporter in some difficult times." She recalled that she and Phil Graham were not instantly drawn to McNamara. "I have to confess it took a meeting or two before we got beyond the rimless glasses and severe hair," she said. "And we didn't respond immediately to Bob's unique personality and brilliance." She went on to take note of his concern about social issues and his efforts "in bettering the world." Recalling how McNamara had found time in his hectic schedule as defense secretary to visit and offer encouragement to Phil Graham in his darkest hours and had rushed to Ted Kennedy's side after Chappaquiddick, she told her guests, "Most people also don't realize how caring Bob is about people." She extolled McNamara for writing *In Retrospect*. "He thought it was important to discuss what went wrong in Vietnam because it is pertinent to decisionmakers today. He also realized he's one of the few remaining people who could discuss this subject with accuracy and insight from the top—and with wisdom, in my view."[59]

After the appearance of *Argument Without End* in 1999, the book about the Hanoi oral history conferences that McNamara wrote with Blight, Brigham, and others, Graham hosted another large reception and then a smaller dinner to honor its publication. McNamara playfully told the guests that he was "very competitive" and compared his performance as an athlete, corporate executive, and book author with Graham's record. In tennis, he said, "She beat me every time. Finally, she said to [me], 'why don't you find someone else to play with?' It absolutely humiliated me." He lauded her management of the Washington Post Company, noting that the company's stock price had increased far more during her time as CEO than Ford stock had risen under his leadership. As for their record as authors, his memoirs had sold 450,000 copies, he declared, but "no matter what happens on sales, Kay won the Pulitzer and I didn't get anywhere close. So in all three arenas she knocked the hell out of me." Everyone including Graham laughed, but Blight recalled, it was "Bob—the striver, still (and always) striving."[60]

Perhaps after he read a draft of Graham's autobiography, McNamara wrote her: "Our interview, in connection with your book, brought a flood of memories extending back 30 years. You must have sensed how important your friendship has been to me in the past and how important it remains today." In another, undated letter related to a party that he attended, McNamara wrote to Graham: "I have already written to tell Meg (Greenfield) the party was a smashing success and to say how pleased I was 'to have made the cut.' Again, I want to add that you never looked more beautiful or radiant."[61]

According to Graham's son and her successor as publisher of the *Post*, Don Graham, McNamara wanted to marry his mother and may well have proposed marriage to her. "My mother thought he was too peripatetic, traveling all the time," Don recalled.[62] Kay Graham died in 2001.

PHYLLIS MAHAFFEY COORS, A FOURTH-GENERATION COLORADAN,
grew up on a small farm in Wheat Ridge, where her father had a sand and
gravel business. "We worked hard," she recalled, but "didn't have a lot of
money." She attended Pueblo Junior College, later called the University of
Southern Colorado and now Colorado State University (Pueblo), studying to be a teacher, but worked as a receptionist and switchboard operator
at the Coors Brewing Company before becoming secretary to the president of the company, Bill Coors, and then marrying him. She and her husband, like Joan and Tom Braden and Katharine and Phil Graham, knew
Bob and Margy McNamara. Bill Coors was on the board of the Aspen Ski
Company in the 1970s when the couple met fellow board member Bob
McNamara and his wife on the short plane ride from Denver to Aspen.
Two decades later, in 1994, after Phyllis and Bill had divorced, Bob and
Phyllis met again at an Aspen dinner party. Two days later, he invited her
to dinner at the Little Nell restaurant in Aspen. "It was a two-hour din-
ner," Phyllis remembered, "and we never stopped talking."[63]

If Colorado was a relatively "safe place" for McNamara, Aspen, a few
miles from Snowmass, where the McNamara family had so often vaca-
tioned, was the safest of all. McNamara was seventy-eight and Phyllis was
sixty-three. Once they started dating, McNamara and Coors attended the
Western Fantasy Ball in Denver, and every December, the Kennedy Center
Honors in Washington. They went skiing together, played tennis, hiked
in the Colorado mountains, and attended the Aspen Music Festival. Bob
suspected Phyllis was letting him beat her down the mountain and letting
him win at tennis. She impersonated his reaction: "No way, Phyl! Winning
is everything!" He challenged her to beat him "Six–Love." So she did—and
then "felt so ashamed of myself. A nice lady wouldn't do that."[64]

McNamara and Coors attended church together—her church when
they were in Golden, Colorado, the National Cathedral when they were
in Washington. "I do strongly believe in a supreme being," McNamara
told her, "and I do strongly believe there's something beyond us." "That's
one of the things I appreciate about Bob," Phyllis said. "It's one of the

many things that have brought us closer together." He also regularly sent her flowers and poetry.

They traveled together to Guatemala, Sicily, South Africa, as well as to California and Martha's Vineyard. And when he was overseas alone, he called her nearly every morning, setting his alarm to phone her at a reasonable hour. If his family didn't know where he was, they could find out from her. Sometimes Bob and Phyllis flew economy class. "You just learn to appreciate that you have food and roof over your head," said Phyllis. Added Bob: "She's developed a feeling for people who didn't"—referring to Phyllis's work with Volunteers of America and the Denver Foundation. It was like Margy's good volunteer work with Reading Is Fundamental, although on a much smaller scale.[65]

Despite his advancing age (or perhaps to avoid thinking about that), McNamara kept up his usual frantic pace. When he was in Hanoi, a photographer had to run to keep up with him, not just when McNamara went for a run.[66] "He goes so fast," Coors said. "It's one of the things I'm always giving him heck for. I finally sat down and said, 'I'm no longer going to run behind you. You either slow down or I'm out of here.'" When he used priority mail to send her press clippings about education, literacy, or AIDS in Africa, she insisted he switch to less speedy first-class stamps. "He's going to save the world," she commented. "I mean, he's going to die trying." She admired his efforts to address the world's problems, even though some of them were beyond her. She appreciated his sharing his personal memories of events from the Cuban missile crisis to Vietnam. "He's safe with me," she joked. "I forget so much."[67]

Coors was grateful to McNamara for rescuing her from loneliness after her divorce. "Boy, it was scary at first. And then to have Bob come into my life. He has been there for me ever since, in any and all situations." But she also taught him things about himself. "One of them," he said, "is to be more sensitive to people, including my children. I love them . . . but I have been a little shy and a little withdrawn from them. And I'd say she's softened me. And I'm deeply grateful for that."[68]

Many years later, Coors said in a 2019 interview that "what I loved [was] the inner Bob McNamara"—the kind of person, one could add, that his high school girlfriend, Annalee Whitmore, had so enjoyed being with. "He was thoughtful. He was fun to be with. He was always very considerate. He was just an extraordinary man." Bob "wanted to get married," Coors admitted, but "I didn't ever want to marry again . . . I was too selfish, I think. I just didn't want to be, but God love him, he was so loyal, so good. Anytime I needed anything, he was there."[69]

Despite Coors's refusal to marry him, painfully aware that courtship by someone his age could prevent her from finding a younger partner, McNamara struggled to keep her close. "My dearest one," he wrote her on April 15, 1997, "I was deeply distressed when you found it necessary to say—with great pain—'I love you, but it can't go on in this way.'" She had charged him with behaving as though they were married when he knew she could "never marry again—not you or any other man." "I do know that," McNamara insisted: "You have made that clear from the day of our first date. . . . I thought I have behaved accordingly. Clearly, I have been wrong. You have said, 'You are my best friend and my lover.' That is all I aspire to. Please, please help me to deserve those feelings."[70]

To deserve those feelings, McNamara had insisted Coors go out with at least two other men before she allowed him to escort her to the next Western Fantasy Ball. But that, he wrote, led her to "cry" and say he "did not" love her. In July 1997, he wrote her, "I not only love you, I adore you" and that he wanted "to remain her best friend and lover for the rest of my life. But I know that will not be possible unless you have other men in your life. So, Phyl, darling, please, please do as I say."[71]

By January 1998, Phyllis had taken McNamara's advice: another man had appeared in her life. Meanwhile, Phyllis had left a scarf in Bob's Washington apartment, and he now returned it to her with these words: "Joe will be putting on a full-court press and I need to be represented by at least a scarf."[72]

In December 1998, McNamara revealed how painful it had been to urge Coors to find another suitor: "I have stood naked before you in a way I have never related to any other human being," he wrote. "You have caused me to reexamine myself. And in the process you have taught me to be a kinder, gentler, more caring human being, both to my children and my friends." "How do I love thee? I never cease counting the ways. I believe we will be friends forever and ever—and even longer."[73]

By April 1999, McNamara knew he was no longer Phyllis's "#1 beau." That meant she was "doing what I have urged you to do for 3 years. I have no hope to, and I am not trying to, reinstate myself. But I do wish to be your friend forever."[74] In June, he urged her to act with another beau "as though you had never met me and as though you would never see me again."[75] But one month later he proposed another plan. Coors had told him, "You must let me get on with my life." So he offered "a plan" to "do just that"— that he "cancel all dates [with her] for the next two or three months, after which I hope you will let me see you occasionally," while in the meantime, "instead of calling you everyday or every other day, I will call you every two or three weeks."[76] In March 2000, he added yet another proposal that yoked together both his love and his enduring propensity for expressing himself numerically: "I suggest that we lunch together two hours each month either at the restaurant in the mall in Golden or at your house (I would fly in in the morning and out in the afternoon). My doctors say I will probably have an additional ten years so that means I would see you for a total of 240 hours during the remainder of my life—this should not intimidate anyone; you can point out I am 83 and live 1500 miles away."[77]

Coors seems to have accepted his offer, or at least some version of it. But their relationship still changed. Nine months later, in December 2000, Aspen's local newspaper reported that Bob and Phyl were still deeply attached to each other— as "best friends." "It's a friendship, not a romance, they insist," the author, John Ensslin, wrote. "Each dates others. But they've come to rely on each other's friendship. Not many weeks go by without one's calling the other."

Bob and Phyl continued to drift apart. But in 2006, she contributed a tribute to a ninetieth birthday album prepared for McNamara by his daughter Margy. Coors had reread the 2000 Aspen newspaper story in which McNamara had said, "Phyl has softened me and for that I am deeply grateful." Now she told him, "You certainly made me feel significant, it was an honor coming from a dear friend for whom I have always had high regard and esteem."[78]

One token of McNamara's regard was that he presented Coors with a copy of his poetry album, which constituted a kind of recapitulation in the form of poems, of emotions he had found so difficult to express himself in the course of his life.

Ambition: Kipling's "The Palace."
Tragedy: From Matthew Arnold's "Dover Beach":

Ah love, let us be true
To one another, for the world which seems
To lie before us like a land of dreams
So various, so beautiful, so new
Hath neither joy, nor love, nor light
Nor certitude, nor peace, nor help for pain . . .

Pride: From Rupert Brooke's "The Hill":

'We are the Earth's best, that learnt her lessons here.
Life is our cry. We have kept the faith!' we said.
'We shall go down with unreluctant tread
Rose-crowned into the darkness!' . . . Proud we were
And laughed, that had such brave, true things to say.
—And then suddenly you cried, and turned away.

Wisdom: From T. S. Eliot in "The Fourth Quartet"

And the end of all our exploring
Will be to arrive where we started
And know the place for the first time.

Truth: From Ralph Waldo Emerson, "Sacrifice"

Though love repine and reason chafe,
There came a voice without reply, —

'Tis man's perdition to be safe
When for the truth he ought to die.

Suffering: From Nikos Kazantzakis, "Report to Greco"

Listen to my life, grandfather, and if I fought with you,
if I fell wounded and allowed no one to know of my suffering, if
I never turned my back to my enemy: Give me your blessing!

Ignorance: From George Santayana, "O World"

Our knowledge is a torch of smoky pine
That lights the pathway but one step ahead
Across a void of mystery and dread.

═══

IN 2002, MCNAMARA ARRIVED AT THE NEW YORK CITY APARTMENT of Maria Cristina Vettore Austin, the Italian socialite better known as Cristina Ford, the former wife of McNamara's former boss, Henry Ford II, from whom she had been divorced since 1976. Cristina Ford was still dressing to go out to dinner with McNamara, so her friend Diana Masieri, a widowed Italian socialite, greeted McNamara at Cristina's apartment door. McNamara stared at her, Masieri recalls, and she was struck by his deep dark eyes. "I knew instantly that this was a man who needed to be loved," she recalled.[79] "When he looks at people," she said several years later, "you can tell he's really interested. He's interested in everything, everything. He doesn't stop at war or politics."[80] Ford announced that the three of them would dine together. For the next month, McNamara, who had asked Masieri for her phone number, called her every morning at her northern Virginia home at precisely 7 a.m.[81] Finally, after about thirty days of this, he said, "Would you go to the symphony with me?" And that's how their relationship started.[82]

Masieri was born in Aviano, Italy, and grew up in a well-to-do family. Masieri herself loved horseback riding, drove Maseratis in rally car races, and was an avid tennis player.[83] She had married an American veteran of the OSS and CIA, Ernest Byfield Jr., whose father was a wealthy Chicago hotelier and owner of an advertising agency from 1970 to 1981. Byfield Jr.'s mother owned the Glen Ora estate in Virginia that John and Jackie Kennedy rented during JFK's presidency.[84] In America, Diana was president of Creazzo Imports, a major importer of Italian wines,[85] and in the early '90s she started a travel company, International Home Rentals, for wealthy customers.[86]

McNamara didn't directly propose to Masieri. Instead he posed a series of hypothetical questions: "If we married ... I'm not proposing ... but when would we get married? What do you think about getting married in Assisi?" Unlike Joan Braden, Kay Graham, and Phyllis Coors, Masieri was ready to devote her life to McNamara. "Now I'm concentrating on Bob," she said. "I want to make him happy."[87]

McNamara and Masieri were married in Assisi on September 16, 2004. Like so much in McNamara's life from the Vietnam War onward, the marriage affected him in contradictory ways. Diana clearly loved him, gave him the warm companionship he craved, and cared for him as his health deteriorated, but she also grew wary of his children and eventually became antagonistic toward them. In steps they could not understand and that angered them after his death, she failed to inform them that she had arranged to have a McNamara memorial stone placed at Arlington National Cemetery. She also auctioned off much of the memorabilia and some of the personal correspondence he had left her. She later said that he told her late in life that he wanted a gravesite at Arlington, consistent with the request he had made in 1966.[88]

CHAPTER FIFTEEN

Twilight Years

During the 1990s and early 2000s, when McNamara was reexamining his career and trying to draw lessons from it, he began a long, slow process of decline that was mostly unseen by the world. Even for his children and grandchildren it was obscured by his relentless surface optimism, reflecting what Craig McNamara and his family came to label "the chipper gene." "One of my father's favorite catch phrases," Craig recalled, "was, 'It's a glorious day!'" He would say, "'It's a glorious day' constantly, regardless of what kind of day it was. The sentiment survived all the changes in our relationship. When my daughter Emily was just five or six years old, she picked up on it. She would parrot Dad by saying, 'It's a glorious day, sweetie!' She'd lower her voice and puff out her cheeks, her eyes taking in the grins of all within earshot."[1]

Craig saw the "chipper gene" as signaling a deeper decline. "I think Dad's mental health deteriorated starting in his sixties," he continued. "As I observed him over the last decades of his life, I realized that his glorious days were few and far between." Craig remembered one less than glorious day in 2001. They were dining out at a restaurant. When his father "sat down at the table, he seemed immediately agitated. He was coughing a lot, a symptom of diverticulitis of the esophagus, which he struggled with throughout his later years. The server greeted him politely, but Dad rushed him. 'Sir! Two chardonnays.' As we waited, he kept trying to get the server's attention. 'Sir. Sir!' He wanted to know when the wine was going to show up. I talked to him about farming, and I tried to lead him to a question about my children. It didn't work. When the wine came, he finally started to relax."[2]

In 1992, McNamara had moved out of the family house on Tracy Place into a duplex Watergate apartment with a bedroom, kitchen, and living room. A storage unit in the basement contained memorabilia, family objects, and dozens of honorary degrees that Craig had moved from Tracy Place. Craig, his sisters, and McNamara's grandchildren spent days filling a dumpster, but they were "clandestinely saving various artifacts" because it seemed that, as if seeking to jettison his former life, he "wanted to throw almost everything away."[3] Before he was offered an office by the Corning Glass Company, on whose board of directors he had served and whose former president and chairman, Amory Houghton, had been a friend, he had an office in the Willard Hotel. He trusted a Corning secretary, who began working for him part-time in 2001, to write his checks but, she recalls, he "didn't reach out." The office was about half an hour on foot from the Watergate, and McNamara walked to work and back every day except the weekend, when, in a sharp break with his lifelong habit, he did not go to work.[4]

For McNamara's eightieth birthday in 1996, his son planned a throwback outing with family and old friends and hired the same mountaineering outfit the McNamara family had used three decades before for pack trips through the Sierras. This time mules carried Bob McNamara's gear, while younger hikers toted their own. "Dad was still strong enough to hike" and "keep a good pace," Craig recalls, even though, before the hike, Bob McNamara's friend Ben Eiseman gave Bob a lift and drove his topheavy truck off the road and flipped over. Ben and Bob survived, and the stoic senior McNamara waved off the accident "except to mention that he'd almost been scalped by a piece of the car door that had bent inward." The outing culminated in a celebration at the Ahwahnee Hotel in Yosemite Valley.[5]

Six years later, when McNamara did his interviews for *The Fog of War*, Craig sensed that his father's "emotional shield of power and prestige were truly compromised." Bob McNamara was "nervous about opening himself up in the film," reported Blight and Lang, and "wanted to be in control." But "his interest in passing on lessons overwhelmed all other concerns."[6] Craig knew his dad was "on antidepressants." He recalled that "there was talk of suicide." But either because he repressed the bad news or didn't want to discuss it, Craig confessed years later that he couldn't remember now "if I heard about this from his friends, one of my sisters, or the doctor who was treating him."[7] McNamara's new wife heard it from Bob himself. "When I met him," Diana confirms, "he was suicidal." He was seeing a psychiatrist; he was "up and down"; he was "blaming himself for things that were going wrong—for everything in the house, too. If something was wrong, it was his fault because he thought that God gave him enough intelligence to understand these things and he was to blame if he didn't use his intelligence." He "never said what kind of suicide he would have committed," but said that he didn't do it because of the "stigma" that would attach to his family.[8]

McNamara had been seeing a psychiatrist since 2000, he told Diana, but he considered that another weakness that added to his sense of guilt. No one else was to know, especially his children. "Don't tell my children. Nobody must know because it's shameful to go to a psychiatrist." Diana accompanied him to the doctor's office three times. "Every time," she recalled, "Vietnam came out. Vietnam was the big heavy albatross around his neck. And he couldn't get rid of it. It was suffocating. It was killing him."[9] At the end of the third session, the psychiatrist invited Diana into the office and she reports he told McNamara: "I've done everything I could. Now take Diana. Diana is your best medicine. Stay with her and don't come here anymore."[10]

Not surprisingly, Diana claims credit for reviving her husband. But her account has the ring of truth. "He needed me because I'm emotional. I'm Italian and I laugh. He liked me because I was laughing. I was putting everything on a laugh. And when he was very sad, I was laughing and saying a joke."[11] The McNamaras spent much of their time in her large home in Middleburg, Virginia, inherited from her first husband. Friends of McNamara report he "hated" the house to which Diana often took him as he grew increasingly frail.[12] But the house is filled with photos, in many of which McNamara is indeed laughing. In one he and Diana are seated at the dinner table with glasses of wine in hand, she looking as if she had just recounted an amusing anecdote, he laughing with his hand resting softly on her shoulder. Before his wedding, McNamara had praised Diana to a reporter as "very warm, kind, very amusing."[13] In the first years after their marriage, McNamara told Blight and Lang, "She takes good care of me." In his last few years, Lang recalled, Diana became more of a caregiver. "Diana married one man and cared for another toward the end."[14]

Diana McNamara devoted herself to him. Since he could no longer play tennis and even walks and stairs were a challenge, she arranged for a physical trainer to work with him. She drove him everywhere—not in the economical Ford Focus that he had chosen to be the yearly company car that Ford still gave him, but in the Lincoln Continental that she preferred.[15] She also directly addressed his sadness, the attacks by critics that seemed at times to overwhelm him (especially those on his memoir, in which he had dared to chastise himself), and the harshest criticism of all, which he directed at himself. "What makes you think you are exempt from criticism?" she asked him in a letter that she said she wrote and handed to him.

> There will always be people who will love you and people who will, unfortunately, detest you.... Don't let criticism destroy your confidence and your self-esteem, and don't let praise make you haughty.... Above all, you MUST find your peace. I told you to look in the mirror every morning and say: "You have done your best. You have accomplished what the majority of men never even dream of accomplishing. You brought good things to many. There are more persons admiring you than otherwise. And this is because of the great mind, determination, and untiring work you have always done to make a happier world and a better society. Now is the time to make yourself a happier man. It is time for you to decide to sit back

and spend time with your children and grandchildren, giving them
your wisdom and your love."[16]

Ironically, over time Diana herself contributed to the distance between
McNamara and his children and grandchildren; family relations became
extremely bitter after his death. Craig was often in Washington to visit
his son Sean, a student at Georgetown, and he wanted to see his father.
But Diana "didn't get along with us," he remembered. "She sometimes discouraged us from visiting their apartment, even to the point of being rude
to my children. This remarriage created a distance between us in those
vulnerable years. It was a time when no one was very happy."[17] Diana's
recollection is different. She says that her husband resisted inviting his
children because he said they had not had a close relationship with him
as adults, an assertion that Craig said was "untrue."[18]

Meanwhile, Diana was trying to understand the man she had married.
McNamara often told her he felt "very sorry he could not show his emotions: 'I cannot do it. It's stronger than myself, stronger than my desire of
showing love, tenderness.'" He was "frozen," she continued, "and he knew
it and was upset." Deep inside, "there was a volcano going all the time, but
he couldn't show it."[19]

Diana traced this pattern back to McNamara's childhood—to the
father he told her had never showed his emotions, to the "very strict" household his mother managed. McNamara talked a lot about President Kennedy, marveling that JFK grew up in such a "rich family with everything
one could wish to have since he was a boy." Looking back, McNamara
kept repeating "he was very sorry that he did not [resign] when Jack died.
He said, 'I stayed there because I thought I could handle Johnson,'" but
instead, he told Diana, "Johnson handled me."[20]

This comment, in particular, suggests yet another reason McNamara
continued to prosecute the Vietnam War long after he concluded it was
unwinnable—not just to keep it from escalating into a nuclear confrontation with Russia and China, not just in a vain attempt to start negotiations
that could bring it to an end, not only out of loyalty to President Johnson
and to the presidency itself, not only because he hated to give up on any

undertaking he started, but because McNamara was "cocky," Diana said, because he "thought he was so powerful he could overpower Johnson."[21] And when he could not do so, she continued, he was "tormented"— because "he wanted to end the war and he didn't succeed in doing that. So he was blaming himself. He always thought, 'maybe I could have done this, [or] I could have done the other. I should have done this and not the other.' So you see—that torment."[22]

Johnson not only thwarted McNamara but, Diana correctly insists, he and Kennedy corrupted him. The McNamara who arrived in Washington in 1960 was a faithful, loyal husband, but both JFK and LBJ were shameless womanizers. McNamara was shocked at first, Diana contends, but he too learned to play the game. "I tell you," Diana said, "in the world where he was living, women were not nice. Women had very easy customs. They interchanged husbands. Sex was just an entertaining thing that you do because it's there. You know, you go and have breakfast and then you have a glass of wine and then you have sex. . . . And oh, it was awful when I met him. I once left him in the middle of the road one day, because I said, No, are you kidding me? Out! Out of the car! And then he slowly understood." "He was telling me, It's normal. Everybody does it. I said, Okay, I don't. You go back there, and I will stay here."

Diana was particularly outraged by McNamara's history with Joan Braden. "I attacked him. I said, Aren't you ashamed of yourself? And he was saying, like a child: Why should I be ashamed? Sex is nothing, poof. I always remember that: Poof, just nothing. Either he changed or I wouldn't have stayed with him."

Diana echoed the values that McNamara in his last year told her that his mother had preached. One of them was honesty: When he gave his word to do something, Diana recalled, he did it. "He would be adamant in saying 'I will be there at three.' But he was always there at five to three." Another was religion: "He was always reading the Bible."[23]

In 2006, when McNamara was ninety, he broke his neck. He was walking to his office when he tripped on a curb. His doctors said he could wear a collar that would hold his head and neck in position until the fracture healed, possibly for several months. Or they could operate. Diana opposed an operation, but McNamara insisted. "Do you want me to be in this collar forever? No, we operate."[24] An ambulance took him to Johns Hopkins for the operation. All told he spent two weeks in the hospital and then almost sixty days in a rehab facility. When he came down with pneumonia and was moved into intensive care, Diana insisted on sleeping nearby, even after hospital officials demanded she leave; she prevailed with some help from McNamara's psychiatrist. When Blight and Lang telephoned him he said, "Diana is taking care of me. She's my nurse."[25]

While in the hospital, McNamara was attached to a feeding tube (among other devices), which he hated. Before it could be removed he had to pass a swallowing test, but he failed at least two of them. As his depression deepened, janet Lang told him of studies showing that people often adapted to treatments they "couldn't live with." The next time she called him, he was rejoicing: "janet, you'll never guess what I'm doing. I'm sipping cold orange juice and it's the most wonderful juice I've ever tasted." After his release from the hospital, Blight and Lang were dining with Bob and Diana at their Watergate apartment when Bob started to slide off his chair at the dinner table. Blight and Lang rushed to hold him while Diana pushed his chair back under him. "He was weak and exhausted," Lang remembers. "He finished dinner and we guided him to the couch."[26]

In the summer of 2006, McNamara's family and friends gathered again at the Ahwahnee Hotel to celebrate his ninetieth birthday. After his medical ordeals, he was confined to a wheelchair, unable to undertake the traditional trek. But his daughter Margy prepared a birthday album with tributes to him from friends, Kennedy/Johnson colleagues, World Bank associates, former special assistants of his, people in world affairs, and others, sixty-two in all, whom she asked to recall some "memorable incident" involving him. Some of them recalled outings in nature: Old friend Ben Eiseman remembered using "horses, mules, donkeys, yaks, llamas, camels, sleds, dog teams, canoes, rubber rafts, kayaks, dories and all sorts of sail and motor boats, sleeping on airport floors, outdoors in sleeping bags on mountains or in verdant meadows by a stream" or sometimes in "yurts and sheep herders' huts, and emerging to read the stack of accumulated *New York Times* that had been forwarded and awaited us."

McNamara's longtime tennis coach Allie Ritzenberg recalled McNamara's rivals on the St. Albans School courts: McGeorge Bundy, Walt Rostow, Arthur Schlesinger, and JFK's personal physician, Janet Travell. Ted Sorensen remembered JFK had regarded McNamara as "the star of his cabinet"—except for RFK. Caroline Kennedy said McNamara had taught her and her little brother "long-jumping off the guest room beds" in their mother's Washington apartment. Eugene Rotberg, an investment banker: "You never took credit. Indeed, you blamed yourself for what you perceived to be failure. You admitted to mistakes—often where there were none." Montague Yudelman (World Bank): "You drove us crazy digging up numbers to measure the impact of bank loans on farmer productivity" in Africa. Daughter Margy Pastor: "In our sunlit living room in Ann Arbor, one could always hear music—swing, jazz, and the wonderful musicals of the 1950s. You and mom started purchasing art in Ann Arbor. . . . You introduced us to the love of color, line and form." Emily McNamara (Craig's daughter): "When you gain just a little more strength, maybe I will be able to spend time with you in Martha's Vineyard again."[27]

Many years later, Craig still wished his father "had been able to make a speech himself [at Ahwahnee] in order to confess his misgivings, errors in judgment, honest mistakes, and arrogance; or to express his love for his family."[28] By this time, Robert McNamara's short-term memory was failing. During a 2008 appearance at the Kennedy Library celebrating the career of Ted Sorensen, President Kennedy's speechwriter and aide, McNamara repeated himself several times within the span of a few minutes.[29]

During the three years that remained for McNamara after his ninetieth birthday, his son made many attempts, as Craig puts it, to "fuse our lives." One time, while sitting by his father's bed, he asked, "Are you comfortable?"

"Yes."

"Are you happy?"

"Very happy."

"Is there anything that you need? Is there anything I can do to make your life more relaxed?"

"Oh, no. Thanks, Craigie."

Pause.

"Would you tell me if you weren't comfortable and happy?"

"No."[30]

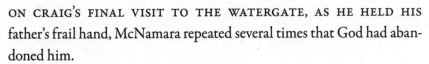

ON CRAIG'S FINAL VISIT TO THE WATERGATE, AS HE HELD HIS father's frail hand, McNamara repeated several times that God had abandoned him.

"No, Dad," Craig replied. "Let go of that. God is blessing you."

"I'm abandoned."

"No, Dad," Craig insisted. "God has not abandoned you. Dad, he is holding you in the palm of his hand. He is asking you to let go. He wants to welcome you to Heaven. He is ready for you."[31]

By this time, the tension between Diana McNamara and his children was so high that she took what Craig was saying to mean: "Dad, you better die, because we are ready for you to die. So go. Let yourself go. Die."[32]

McNamara died on July 6, 2009. "My father always told me that he wanted to be buried with my mother in the Rocky Mountains and at Martha's Vineyard," Craig recalled. "He didn't want a funeral."[33] When the then-defense secretary, Robert Gates, told his widow the Pentagon wanted to organize a formal memorial service, she informed him her husband had not wanted such a service.[34] So in September 2009, McNamara's extended family (including Margy and Kathleen with their families, and McNamara's nephew Rob with his) gathered on the Vineyard to inter his ashes along with those of his first wife. Among the poems they took turns reading, before placing Bob's and Marg's ashes in a quiet grove overlooking Oyster Pond, was their parents' favorite sonnet by Elizabeth Barrett Browning:

> *I love thee with a love I seemed to lose*
> *With my lost saints—I love thee with the breath,*
> *Smiles, tears, of all my life!—and, if God choose,*
> *I shall but love thee better after death.*[35]

It was a gathering that would have greatly pleased Bob.

But a year or so later, Craig learned from a friend who was visiting President Kennedy's Arlington Cemetery gravesite that a large pink gravestone had been erected nearby on which was inscribed:

ROBERT STRANGE MCNAMARA
1916–2009
SECRETARY OF DEFENSE
1961–1968

MARGARET CRAIG	DIANA MASIERI
1915–1981	1934–

"I never thought Dad wanted to be buried at Arlington," Craig contends. "I am sure that walking by the graves of Vietnam War soldiers—if he ever did—brought him tremendous sadness during his final years in D.C."[36] Whether he ever did walk there is unknown, but he did often visit the Vietnam War Memorial on the Washington mall—in the dark, at night, so that no one could see him staring at the names of so many for whose deaths he considered himself responsible.

"Though we never discussed it," Craig recalled, "I imagine his second wife must have arranged the plot [at Arlington] having saved some of his ashes. When I think about this now, I feel the weight of a price that has been continually paid in ongoing tragedy. In the fields of the dead, Robert McNamara is linked with the true human cost of decisions he later wished not to have made."[37]

Two more twists accompanied Robert McNamara's journey to the hereafter, one of them more farce than tragedy, the other, salting the family wounds of the McNamaras who remained. Bob McNamara died at 5:30 a.m. on July 6, 2009, in his Watergate apartment. His daughter Kathleen had done some research and suggested that Gawlers Funeral Home handle the cremation. But when Craig looked for Gawlers in the DC Yellow Pages in the darkened bedroom, his finger fell instead on Genesis, which advertised "Dignified and affordable direct cremation." After

Craig called them, a woman in her fifties arrived, "her demeanor kind and gentle," Craig recalls, followed by an elderly man, probably in his eighties, pushing a gurney "draped in a scarlet coverlet that looked as if it was from a bygone era." Since the old man was too frail to lift his father's body onto the gurney, Craig "gently lifted Dad up, holding him like a long babe in my arms. His body was stiff and slightly twisted, his mouth frozen open from his last breath. I could see the gold fillings in his teeth. I placed him on the antique gurney, covered him with the velvet blanket, and wheeled him out . . . into the alley where a 1970's-style hearse awaited. We placed him in the hearse. Like that, I said goodbye to the man whom I had known and loved for fifty-nine years. To the woman and the old man, I said something to the effect of, 'You'll take good care of my father, won't you?'"

When Craig reentered the apartment and reviewed the death certificate, he discovered it was filled out not by Gawlers but by Genesis. When he called Genesis, the woman who answered confirmed his error. "Oh no, Gawlers is much more expensive than we are. We are Genesis Funeral Home, and we saved you $7,000!"

"Dad, forever the Scotch thrift," Craig concluded, "would have loved this surprise."[38]

The second twist involved McNamara's possessions and personal effects. He had changed his will so as to bequeath these to Diana, should she choose to take them. She did, which she says prompted the children to threaten a suit until a settlement provided for an auction. Sales from the auction totaled $1,008,571.[39] She said that "a significant amount" of the proceeds was given to the children. Craig said her account was incorrect.[40]

On October 23, 2012, Craig reports, White House cabinet chairs that his father had occupied, "along with over 600 other pieces of personal memorabilia, were sold at a Sotheby's auction, timed to the 50th anniversary of the Cuban Missile Crisis." Sotheby's called the collection "The White House Years of Robert S. McNamara" and exhibited it for thirteen days prior to the sale, the same duration as the Cuban crisis itself. According to the auction catalog, the sale featured: "private papers and memorabilia from his tenure as Secretary of Defense, including his appointment from President Kennedy, extensive correspondence from Mrs. Kennedy, gifts from world leaders, and furnishings from his office and the Cabinet Room." It also included, Craig explained, material from his father's "California boyhood . . . handwritten letters; autographed photos of JFK, RFK, and LBJ; a cache of medals; Dad's Eagle Scout badge from 1933; his colorful Presidential Medal of Freedom; his official Secretary of Defense flag from the Pentagon; presidential signing pens and inaugural tokens; North Vietnamese propaganda; notes on *The Fog of War*; and volumes of political cartoons about him, warmly inscribed by the individual artists."[41] In addition, according to Craig: "our parents' love letters and telegrams from World War II; Dad's Giacometti sculpture; Picasso paintings and other art; scores of original letters; and many signed books from presidents, prime ministers, authors, and cartoonists."

Particularly important to Craig was "Dad's calendar from the Cuban Missile Crisis" (a small silver tile with the thirteen October 1962 days of the crisis engraved on it) that President Kennedy had given to his closest associates who had worked with him to resolve the crisis. Knowing how much the Cuban crisis calendar meant to Craig, his wife Julie and sister Margy set out to purchase it. The price listed in the catalog was $15,000 to $25,000, already above their ceiling. But they bid that much, only to see the price rise even higher.

"Do I hear $80,000?"

Too high, Craig thought, but they now offered $77,500.

"Sold—at $77,500!"

"There was no sense of celebration," Craig remembered. "no victory. Something that had been important in my life was returning, and I would be the steward of it, but it never should have been lost in the first place. I was fortunate that we had the collective means for this, but we shouldn't have had to bid on my memories. The auction left me feeling abandoned by him, even in his death." He hugged his wife and his sister. It was their earnings that "made this possible." The final bill, including Sotheby's commission, shipping, and insurance, came to over $100,000. "That was the price for reaching far into the past and reclaiming a memory of my father: sitting across from him, hugging him, kissing his cheek, smelling the Scotch he was drinking while he ran his fingers on that small silver tile."[42]

Instead of a funeral or memorial service, Bob McNamara asked that it simply be announced: "I leave this earth believing I have been blessed with a wife, children, and friends who have brought me love and happiness beyond compare—beyond anything I have ever dreamed possible. Heaven, for me, will be to remain in their hearts and memories as warm and close as we were in life. I will hope, as well, to see others continuing to pursue the objectives which I have sought (very imperfectly at times): to move the world toward peace among peoples and nations, and to accelerate economic and social programs for the least advantaged amongst us."[43]

It is true: More than any other political leader we can think of, Robert McNamara admitted his grave mistakes in the hope of helping others to do better than he did. But the final ironies of his life are that many who continued to pursue peace among peoples and nations and to help the least advantaged among us have been no more successful than he was, and that what has remained in the hearts and memories of his children may be warmer and closer than was the case during some periods of his life.

Epilogue

Perhaps the greatest irony of Robert McNamara's life is that the wise lessons he painfully distilled from his mismanagement of the Vietnam War late in his life went largely unnoticed and unattended by many of the American leaders who succeeded him. The price of ignominy is that valuable insights will be ignored or brushed aside when they come from a widely reviled figure. That is a pity, for the lessons that McNamara drew from America's defeat in Vietnam might have spared the United States ill-fated military interventions in Afghanistan and Iraq, or, at least, shaped them in ways more favorable to the United States.

McNamara outlined ten important points about committing American forces to combat in his 1993 book, *In Retrospect*, which was essentially a reexamination of the Vietnam War. The book drew lacerating criticism for McNamara's failure to apologize for the war, a reaction that threw him into depression. Coverage and commentary at the time focused largely on his recapitulation and critique of the decisions he had recommended, abetted, and in some cases, resisted. Many critics called his regrets too little, too late. Little attention was paid to the hard lessons he found amid the ruins of Lyndon Johnson's and his policies.

The self-defeating dynamics that McNamara identified have been characteristic of American defense policy over the past seven decades. They speak to a Washington mindset that tends to project American traditions and values on distant lands unsuited or hostile to democratic principles and governance. Each American military intervention or war since the Kennedy administration has come with distinct challenges and a unique blend of personalities at the White House, Pentagon, and State Department. In the case of Vietnam, the personality traits of Lyndon Johnson and Robert McNamara helped create a decision-making crucible in which Washington's flawed inclinations were constantly reinforced and intensified. The result was the most lethal and disastrous American war of the last seven decades.

McNamara's takeaways were simple and straightforward: Don't engage in mirror-imaging the enemy, assuming it operates in ways similar to America; do not fail to understand the power of nationalism as a force driving nations to free themselves from external interference in their affairs; be familiar with the history, culture, and politics of the people you are supporting or attacking and their leaders; recognize the limits of modern military technology; explain your intentions to Congress and the American people and level with them about the advantages and disadvantages of large-scale military actions you plan to take; secure the support of Congress and the American people; recognize that neither the American people nor their national leaders are omniscient; understand that in international affairs there may be problems for which there are no wise solutions; operate abroad with the active participation of multinational forces; organize the executive branch to deal with a range of complex issues associated with the use of military force, including the loss of life that comes with the use of force.

When his cautionary prescriptions were followed, albeit as refreshed and reformulated by Gen. Colin Powell and embraced by President George H. W. Bush, they led to an effective and largely successful American military campaign in 1991 to liberate Kuwait from the clutches of Saddam Hussein, the Iraqi dictator. Many Americans came to admire General Powell, who later served as secretary of state under President George W. Bush, for the guiding principles he enunciated for America's military offensive to push Iraqi forces out of oil-rich Kuwait, which they had invaded in 1991. As the general who broadly directed the American operations—Army General Norman Schwarzkopf directly commanded American and allied forces—Powell insisted that the United States attack with overwhelming force, that it have a plan in mind to end the war before it launched military action, and that Congress and the American people understand and support the engagement. President Bush shared these views and made them the centerpiece of his overall management of American diplomacy and military operations at the time.

These and other McNamara lessons were not applied, or were inadequately considered, when Washington reacted to the September 11, 2001, terror attacks in New York and Washington. The initial 2001 military intervention in Afghanistan was limited in scope, with American intelligence operatives and Pentagon combat forces quickly defeating Taliban forces that controlled much of the country and forcing Osama bin Laden, the mastermind of the September 11 attacks, to flee Afghanistan with his fellow terrorists. But without a clear understanding of Afghan history and culture, Washington also lacked a long-term plan for managing the conflict and stabilizing Afghanistan. When George W. Bush decided to turn American firepower on Iraq, military resources were diverted from Afghanistan. American neglect contributed to the slow demise of the American-backed central government in Kabul, perhaps an inevitable outcome under any circumstance in a country historically dominated by tribal factions. But the failure of four presidents—George W. Bush, Barack Obama, Donald Trump, and Joe Biden—to develop a coherent and practical plan for ending America's war in Afghanistan led to a seemingly endless seventeen-year conflict. The abrupt and chaotic evacuation of American forces in 2021 was a fiasco that heartbreakingly demonstrated the wisdom of Powell's admonition never to start a war without a plan to end it. It was a point McNamara had made to Bob Woodward when they talked in 1988 and McNamara said, "Never go into a war you can't get out of."[1] In 2007, he told Woodward, "I don't believe we ever should have gone into Iraq."[2]

The 2003 American invasion and subsequent occupation of Iraq were egregious examples of taking the United States to war without adequately understanding the history, culture, and politics of the target nation. There was a stunning degree of cultural ignorance inherent in Washington's mishandling of Iraq after American forces rolled into Baghdad and Saddam Hussein was removed as the Iraqi leader. Iraqi military forces were quickly disbanded, leaving a security vacuum in Iraq, and sectarian tensions between Sunni and Shiite populations that had long been suppressed by Saddam Hussein's brutal rule erupted. The resulting civil conflict and violent insurgency produced prolonged instability, forcing the American civilian occupiers of Iraq to shelter within a fortified area in Baghdad known as the Green Zone. Defense Secretary Donald Rumseld famously said of the anarchy that beset Iraq after the invasion, "Stuff happens," revealing a degree of arrogance and ignorance about Iraq that matched McNamara's pronouncements about Vietnam.

American mirror-imaging was rampant in Iraq as well, as the Bush administration dispatched people to Iraq to help build a democracy there. They came determined to remake Iraq in the image of America, down to establishing zip codes. The Americans were well-intentioned, just as the Americans in South Vietnam had been. But like their forebears in Vietnam, they had little understanding of the history and culture of the country they thought they were saving.

McNamara's repeated jeremiads about the danger of nuclear war also went largely unheeded. His passionate outbursts about the bomb as he grew older seemed nearly crazed at times, but fundamentally, he was right. And still is, as Russia, China, and the United States modernize their nuclear arsenals and continue to depend on them as the ultimate deterrent to a military attack. As tensions in Europe rose after the unprovoked 2022 Russian invasion of Ukraine and Vladimir Putin repeatedly threatened to use nuclear weapons, the prospect of a nuclear exchange no longer seemed so remote. Once begun, a nuclear volley will be difficult to limit or stop, exactly the fear that gripped McNamara and John Kennedy during the Cuban missile crisis, and McNamara and Lyndon Johnson during the Vietnam War.

President Biden's response to the Russian invasion of Ukraine reflected some McNamarian lessons, even though one doubts Biden directly consulted them. Biden knew enough about Russian and Ukrainian nationalism to fear the former and count on the latter. Well aware of the limits of military power, he contained the scope and range of weapons provided to Kiev. The Biden administration was careful to consult with Congress, which financed the provision of arms to Ukraine, and to recruit public opinion to pressure Congress—even though support for aid to Ukraine ebbed over time. And it galvanized multinational support through NATO. Is there, in fact, a good solution to the Ukrainian crisis? If neither side is strong enough to win the war and yet both sides refuse to settle it, will the upshot prove McNamara right that sometimes international problems have no good outcomes? If so, Biden's opposition to Ukraine's efforts to attack Russia itself, or to commit American forces to combat in Ukraine, bespoke a sensible fear of escalation to a Russian-American confrontation that could ultimately involve nuclear weapons.

McNamara proved to be a fatally flawed figure to lecture his successors in Washington about the risks inherent in taking America to war and to warn them about how quickly a flashpoint with Russia or China could escalate into a nuclear war. He was radioactive. In 2007, two years before he died, he lamented that his book had gone unread or been ignored by George W. Bush and his aides. "They haven't read it. And that's a damn shame. At one point I thought that I would propose that every president and every major secretary, State, Defense in particular, and every chairman of the Joint Chiefs, be required to state whether they had read the book or not. Because that's what it was written for."[3] He had actually sent an inscribed copy shortly after publication to William J. Perry in April 1995 while Perry was serving as defense secretary under President Bill Clinton. The inscription read: "To Bill, In the hope that this book will help you avoid some of our mistakes. With admiration, Bob." Perry read it, though the United States was not at war on his watch.[4] Jackie Kennedy had correctly diagnosed McNamara's problem years before when he told the Senate Foreign Relations Committee in December 1990 that the United States should not use military force to evict Iraqi forces from Kuwait. After the hearing, she said, "I love Bob, but on matters like this he is still working out his guilt about Vietnam."[5]

In the end, his legacy, despite his strenuous efforts to reclaim his reputation and explain himself, could not escape his calamitous role in the Vietnam War.

ACKNOWLEDGMENTS

This book would not have been possible without the generous support of Mimi Haas and Steve and Roberta Denning. Over the decades, a number of Haas family members intersected with Robert McNamara, including Walter (Wally) Haas, McNamara's Berkeley and Harvard Business School classmate. Walter's brother, Peter, also befriended McNamara at Berkeley. Mimi Haas, Peter's widow, generously provided research funding for this book with donations to Stanford's Center for International Security and Cooperation, as did Steve and Roberta Denning, who enthusiastically supported the project. Arjay Miller and Alain Enthoven, who worked with McNamara at different points in his career, provided additional research funding and met for interviews with Philip Taubman. All respected our independence as authors and honored our stipulation that they never, directly or indirectly, seek to influence the content of the book.

During the course of the project, Craig McNamara gave the authors access to family papers and photographs, opened doors to family members and friends in California; Washington, DC; Massachusetts; Colorado; and elsewhere, and offered insights about his father and mother. His sister Margy Pastor talked about her father with William Taubman.

Diana McNamara, Robert McNamara's second wife, invited the

authors to her homes in Washington, DC, and northern Virginia and opened to them the extensive collection of papers and other materials that Robert McNamara left in her care. These proved invaluable, including correspondence between McNamara family members across several generations and letters sent to McNamara by Jacqueline Kennedy. Diana helped launch the project more than a decade ago by offering access to these materials and encouraging the authors to do a book. Her support was essential.

Deborah Shapley and Paul Hendrickson, authors of excellent books about Robert McNamara that were published in 1993 and 1996, respectively, kindly agreed to meet with William Taubman and permit copying and use of their research materials, including interview transcripts and unpublished notes. Their research opened critical new windows into McNamara's life. We also thank Paul and his wife, Ceil, and Deborah, for their warm hospitality during visits to their homes and archives. Brian VanDeMark, a Naval Academy professor and historian of the Vietnam War who assisted McNamara with his 1995 book, *In Retrospect: The Tragedy and Lessons of Vietnam*, shared invaluable transcripts of his interviews with McNamara and relatives and friends of McNamara. His groundbreaking research proved indispensable to our book.

Peter Osnos, who covered the Vietnam War for *The Washington Post*, helped to pave the way for our book. He skillfully coaxed McNamara to do *In Retrospect* as a Vietnam-focused book rather than a lifetime memoir. Its publication in 1995 reignited national debate about McNamara and the war. Peter helped assemble materials used in the book and edited the manuscript at Times Books. Like Brian VanDeMark, Peter generously made available transcripts of his conversations with McNamara. Peter's latest insightful take on the war, *LBJ and McNamara: The Vietnam Partnership Destined to Fail*, was published in 2024.

We are grateful for the cooperation of Errol Morris, whose Academy Award–winning documentary about McNamara, *The Fog of War*, brilliantly captured the turmoil McNamara experienced about the Vietnam War. Morris provided complete transcripts of his marathon interviews with McNamara. His colleagues, Skip Skinner and Fabiola Washburn, were very helpful. We are thankful to Alex McNaughton, who made available a copy of a secret diary written by his father, John McNaughton, while serving as McNamara's closest Pentagon adviser on the Vietnam War during 1966–1967. John McNaughton died in a commercial airplane crash in 1967 just days before he was to become navy secretary. Bob Woodward gave us transcripts of unpublished interviews he conducted with McNamara between 1982 and 2007. Other valuable private papers were provided by Phyllis Coors, a McNamara friend in the 1990s, and her son, Scott Coors.

Jim Blight and his wife janet Lang (who does not capitalize the first letter of her first name), pioneers in the field of critical oral history, also deserve our gratitude. They recruited McNamara to participate in oral history conferences on the Cuban missile crisis and on the Vietnam War, worked closely with him for twenty years pondering and publishing conference results, and critiqued our chapter covering those conferences.

We are grateful for discerning critiques of our draft manuscript provided by Gordon Barrass, Madeleine Blais, Ellen Blumenthal, Courtney Douglas, Joseph Ellis, David Kennedy, Craig McNamara, Kathleen McNamara, Margy Pastor, Peter Osnos, Scott Sagan, and Brian VanDeMark. Diana McNamara kindly read and critiqued portions of the manuscript. We thank the many friends and former colleagues of Robert McNamara who shared their memories of him in interviews with us.

This project benefited greatly from the work of a series of talented and dedicated research assistants based at Stanford. Gabby Levikow, a Stanford graduate, resourcefully conducted McNamara research at the Library of Congress and other sites while assisting Philip Taubman with his biography of George Shultz, *In the Nation's Service: The Life and Times of George P. Shultz*. Her good humor and high energy animated everything she did. Gabby later earned a law degree at Duke Law School.

Courtney Douglas, also a Stanford graduate, joined the project in 2020 at the height of the pandemic. Her plan to work at Stanford unexpectedly gave way to working from San Diego, her hometown. Though initially isolated from friends and Stanford colleagues, Courtney adjusted to a challenging new world and did a brilliant job delving into various facets of McNamara's life. She produced insightful research reports on a wide range of topics, including McNamara's numerous recorded conversations with Lyndon Johnson, McNamara's love of poetry, psychological studies of McNamara, and other issues. She found and copied vitally important papers in private collections, including those of Diana McNamara and Tex Thornton, a World War II and Ford colleague of McNamara. Tex's son, Chuck, opened Tex's archive for us, ably assisted by Bette Cook. Courtney did all this with grace, enthusiasm, and unstinting dedication as she handled endnotes for the Shultz book. Courtney went on to law studies at the University of Virginia, where she served as editor of the *Virginia Law Review*.

Matt Kristoffersen, a Yale graduate, came next. Just weeks before starting work, Matt broke his back in a fall from a second-story dorm room at Berkeley, where he had traveled to attend his brother's commencement. Unsure if he would ever walk again, Matt spent weeks struggling to recover at his home in Southern California. Miraculously, he slowly healed and started walking again that summer. Within six months, he was able to travel. During his two years as research assistant, Matt tackled a dizzying array of research tasks, including visits to the Library of Congress, Harvard University, the Kennedy Library, and Boston University Library. He produced terrific research reports on McNamara's role in the 1945 firebombing of Tokyo, the 1962 Cuban missile crisis, and the 1964 Gulf of Tonkin naval encounters between American and North Vietnamese forces, to name just a few. He also meticulously fact-checked and rechecked the manuscript, and assembled the endnotes and bibliography. All in all, it was a courageous and splendid performance. Matt is now a student at Harvard Law School.

Emily Schrader played a vital part-time research role while a Stanford undergraduate. Her smart, in-depth work on Jackie Kennedy's correspondence with McNamara was critical to assembling, organizing, and analyzing the letters and tracking their trajectory from the hand of Jackie Kennedy to McNamara, their preservation and eventual sale by Diana McNamara, and their ultimate location, some at the Stanford University Library. Anat Peled, while a Stanford undergraduate, did illuminating research about McNamara's student years at Berkeley and found the thread that led to the McNaughton diary. Anat, later a Rhodes scholar, went on to work as a reporter in Israel for the *Wall Street Journal*. Cameron Waltz contributed indispensable research at the LBJ Library in Austin. While a senior at the University of Texas at Austin, Cameron spent countless hours at the library reviewing documents involving or related to McNamara. He pulled together a voluminous set of papers, organized them effectively, and distilled key findings. Matyas Kisiday, working now as a research assistant for Philip Taubman on another book project, assisted us with a variety of steps involved in bringing the book to publication.

We are grateful for the support of Mark Lawrence, director of the LBJ Library, who recommended the hiring of Cameron and made the library's vast archives available to us. For their assistance at the LBJ Library, we thank staff members Jenna de Graffenried, Calvin Clites, Carrie Tallichet Smith, Allen Fisher, Alexis Percle, Scott Seeley, and Liza Talbot. Marc Selverstone at University of Virginia's Miller Center facilitated access to White House recordings of conversations between Lyndon Johnson and Robert McNamara.

At the John F. Kennedy Presidential Library, we thank Abigail Malangone, Savannah York, and Stacey Chandler. For their assistance at the Library of Congress, we thank Bruce Kirby, Patrick Kerwin, Lewis Wyman, Ryan Reft, Ernest J. Emrich, Edith Sandler, and Margaret McAleer, and at the National Archives, John Wilson.

We benefited from the assistance of library staff at a number of university libraries and wish to thank these staff members: Sean Noel and Jane Parr at Boston University Libraries, Howard Gotlieb Archival Research Center; Kimberly Springer at Columbia University's Rare Book and Manuscript Library; Jill Severn at the University of Georgia, Richard B. Russell Library for Political Research and Studies; Melissa Murphy, Heather Oswald, and Kate Neptune at Harvard Business School, Baker Library/ Bloomberg Center; Taylor Fisk Henning, Linda Stahnke Stepp, Katherine Majewski, and Brenda Brown at the University of Illinois Urbana-Champaign Archives; Jeremy Smith at the University of Massachusetts, Amherst Libraries; Kevin Salisbury and Sheon Montgomery at the Texas Tech Archives; Kathryn M. Neal at University of California, Berkeley,

Bancroft Library; Brenna Larson at Wesleyan University; Craig Wesley Carpenter at Michigan State University; Robert Goodspeed at the University of Michigan Taubman College of Architecture and Urban Planning; and Daniel Clark at Oakland University.

We also extend our thanks to Bill Roberts at the Berkeley Historical Society; Kathy Makas at the Benson Ford Research Center; Mark Truby at Ford Motor Company; and Ciera Casteel, Leslie Armbruster, and Ted Ryan at Ford Motor Company Archives. We are also grateful to Thomas Janes, whose Harvard undergraduate thesis about John McNaughton informed our work. Lisa Liu, a Stanford graduate, assisted us by creating typed versions of McNamara family handwritten letters. Gary Slaughter, who served on the USS *Cony* during the Cuban missile crisis, helped us understand weapons systems used by the navy during the crisis.

Philip Taubman benefited in numerous ways from the community of scholars and students at Stanford's Center for International Security and Cooperation. It has been his book-writing home since 2008. While he worked on the McNamara book, CISAC's codirectors, Scott Sagan and the late Rod Ewing, provided intellectual and logistical support. Andrea Gray and Kelly Remus, who served sequentially as CISAC associate director of administration and finance, helped manage the book budget and played key roles in the selection and hiring of research assistants. Tracy Hines, a tireless and devoted staff member, lent a hand in innumerable ways. Mike McFaul, the director of Stanford's Freeman Spogli Institute for International Studies, invigorated the project with his ideas and friendship, as did Condoleezza Rice, the director of the Hoover Institution.

William Taubman has been retired from the Amherst College faculty for some years but has continued to benefit from stimulating intellectual exchanges with former colleagues, one of whom, English professor David Sofield, helped us to assess Robert McNamara's taste in poetry. Our understanding of Lyndon Johnson, who was such a central figure in McNamara's career, draws on many sources, but particularly on the heroic labors of Johnson's multivolume biographer, Robert Caro.

As we have worked on the book, friends and colleagues have asked what it is like doing a book with one's brother. The answer, thankfully: easy and pleasurable. That may have something to do with our age difference—Phil is six-plus years younger, a gap that helped suppress sibling rivalry. That each of has enjoyed productive careers—Bill in the academy, Philip in journalism—may have played a role. We also happily discovered that our writing voices are quite similar.

We are indebted to John Glusman at W. W. Norton, whose deft editing improved the book in many ways. John's enthusiasm for the project from the outset has sustained and energized us. He seemed unfazed by having to deal with coauthors. Also at W. W. Norton, we thank Rivka Genesen for her copyright expertise, Gary Von Euer for his meticulous copyediting, Wickliffe Hallos for his assistance on innumerable matters, small and large, and Rachel Salzman and Kyle Radler for their work on book promotion and publicity. We also thank Sarah Russo and Isabella Nugent at Page One Media for their assistance with publicity. Melissa Flamson and Renae Horstman at With Permission ably assisted with photo and text permissions and credits. Kathy Robbins, our gifted and experienced literary agent, played an invaluable role at every step of the project. Philip Taubman is also grateful for more than four decades of Amanda Urban's friendship and book-writing wisdom.

In the end, book projects depend on family support. We are lucky to have that in abundance. Felicity Barringer, Philip's spouse of fifty-three years and a fellow journalist, is the anchor of his life. Their sons, Michael and Gregory, and their families, including grandchildren, never seem to lose faith in Philip's book projects, however long they may take. Although Bill couldn't have written his biographies of Khrushchev and Gorbachev without the help of his wife, Jane Taubman, retired professor of Russian at Amherst College, he didn't need her this time to help interview Russians. But she was the first reader of McNamara chapters Bill drafted, and for her loving support throughout, she was irreplaceable.

Philip Taubman
William Taubman
May 16, 2025

NOTES

INTRODUCTION

1. Anonymous secretary, interview by William Taubman, June 18, 2021.
2. Thomas Blanton, interview by William Taubman, September 7, 2021.
3. Diana McNamara, interview by William Taubman, June 18, 2021.
4. Barry Goldwater said he was an IBM computer with legs. Stephen Braun, "Robert S. McNamara Dies at 93; Architect of the Vietnam War," *Los Angeles Times*, July 7, 2009.
5. Russell Baker to David Halberstam, February 8, 1997, David Halberstam Papers, Boston University.
6. Arthur M. Schlesinger Jr., *Journals: 1952–2000* (New York: Penguin Publishing Group, 2007), 681–82.
7. Robert S. McNamara with Brian VanDeMark, *In Retrospect: The Tragedy and Lessons of Vietnam* (New York: Random House, 1995), xvi.
8. These books include *Secret Empire: Eisenhower, the CIA, and the Hidden Story of America's Space Espionage* (2004), *The Partnership: Five Cold Warriors and Their Quest to Ban the Bomb* (2012), and *In the Nation's Service: The Life and Times of George P. Shultz* (2023).
9. See *Khrushchev: The Man and His Era* (1990) and *Gorbachev: His Life and Times* (2017).
10. "M'Namara Agrees to Call It His War," *New York Times*, April 25, 1964.
11. McNamara, *In Retrospect*, 317.
12. Craig McNamara, email to Philip Taubman, January 15, 2025.
13. Gospel of Thomas, logion 70.

CHAPTER ONE: DRIVEN TO EXCEL

1. Deborah Shapley, *Promise and Power: The Life and Times of Robert McNamara* (Boston: Little, Brown, 1993), 11.
2. Quoted in Shapley, *Promise and Power*, 16; Richard Quigley, interview by Brian VanDeMark, August 3, 1992; Paul Hendrickson, *The Living and the Dead: Robert McNamara and Five Lives of a Lost War* (New York: Vintage Books, 1997), 49.
3. Craig McNamara, conversation with Philip Taubman, April 12, 2022.

4. Vern Goodin, interview by Brian VanDeMark, October 30, 1991.

5. Annalee Whitmore, interview by Brian VanDeMark, January 5, 1992.

6. Quoted in Lloyd Shearer, "Will the Real Robert McNamara Please Stand Up?" *Parade Magazine*, March 5, 1967, 10.

7. Quoted in John A. Byrne, *The Whiz Kids: The Founding Fathers of American Business—and the Legacy They Left Us* (New York: Currency, 1993), 47.

8. Hendrickson, *The Living and the Dead*, 54–55.

9. Hendrickson, *The Living and the Dead*, 55.

10. Paul Hendrickson, Robert Strange McNamara Family Files, Paul Hendrickson Archive, Family Documents folder, p. 9.

11. Shapley, *Promise and Power*, 5.

12. Shapley, *Promise and Power*, 3; Peggy Slaymaker, interview by Paul Hendrickson, August 25, 1985; Robert McNamara, interview by Brian VanDeMark, February 11, 1992.

13. Richard Quigley, interview by Brian VanDeMark, August 3, 1992.

14. Shapley, *Promise and Power*, 5.

15. Hendrickson, *The Living and the Dead*, 50, 63.

16. Richard Quigley, interview by Brian VanDeMark, August 3, 1992; Hendrickson, *The Living and the Dead*, 53.

17. Peggy Slaymaker, interview by Paul Hendrickson, November 19, 1985, Paul Hendrickson Archive, Family Documents folder; Hendrickson, *The Living and the Dead*, 52.

18. Shapley, *Promise and Power*, 5–6.

19. Robert McNamara, interview by Errol Morris, May 1–2, 2001.

20. Hendrickson, *The Living and the Dead*, 51.

21. Hendrickson, *The Living and the Dead*, 52.

22. Hendrickson, *The Living and the Dead*, 51–54.

23. Peggy Slaymaker, interview by Paul Hendrickson, November 19, 1985.

24. Hendrickson, *The Living and the Dead*, 52.

25. Richard Quigley, interview by Brian VanDeMark, August 3, 1992.

26. Hendrickson, *The Living and the Dead*, 50, 53.

27. Robert McNamara, interview by Brian VanDeMark, November 14, 1991.

28. Hendrickson, *The Living and the Dead*, 49.

29. Shapley, *Promise and Power*, 16–17.

30. Mary Jo Goodwin, interview by Paul Hendrickson, August 1, 1985, Hendrickson Collection, Childhood and Berkeley folder.

31. Richard Quigley, interview by Brian VanDeMark, August 3, 1992.

32. Estelle O'Brien, interview by Paul Hendrickson, date unknown, Hendrickson Collection, Childhood and Berkeley folder, California File 2.

33. Hendrickson, *The Living and the Dead*, 49.

34. Robert McNamara, interview by Errol Morris, May 1–2, 2001.

35. Robert McNamara, interview by Brian VanDeMark, November 14, 1991.

36. Robert McNamara, interview by Brian VanDeMark, November 14, 1991.

37. Robert McNamara, interview by Brian VanDeMark, November 21, 1991.

38. Robert McNamara, interview by Brian VanDeMark, November 21, 1991.

39. Hendrickson, *The Living and the Dead*, 58–59.

40. Hendrickson, *The Living and the Dead*, 56.

41. Joseph Cooper, interview by Paul Hendrickson, July 24, 1985, Hendrickson Collection, Childhood and Berkeley folder, California File 1; Peggy Slaymaker, interview by Paul Hendrickson, February 26, 1986; Phil Pierpont, interview by Paul Hendrickson, date unknown, Hendrickson Collection, Childhood and Berkeley folder, California File 5.

42. Richard Quigley and Gwynn Quigley, interview by Brian VanDeMark, August 3, 1992.

43. Peggy Slaymaker, interview by Brian VanDeMark, December 10, 1991.

44. Claranel McNamara, *The Record of Our Baby Boy*, quoted in Hendrickson, *The Living and the Dead*, 56–57.

45. Gwynn Quigley, interview by Brian VanDeMark, August 3, 1992.

46. Gwynn Quigley, interview by Brian VanDeMark, August 3, 1992.

47. Peggy Slaymaker, interview by Paul Hendrickson, August 28, 1985.

48. Vern Goodin, interview by Brian VanDeMark, October 30, 1991; Gwynn Quigley, interview by Brian VanDeMark, August 3, 1992; Joseph Cooper, interview by Paul Hendrickson, July 24, 1985, Hendrickson Collection, Childhood and Berkeley folder, California File 1.

49. Robert McNamara, interview by Brian VanDeMark, November 14, 1991.

50. William Taubman interview with Margy Pastor, October 10, 2019.

51. Robert McNamara, interview by Errol Morris, May 1–2, 2001; Robert McNamara, interview by Brian VanDeMark, November 14, 1991; Robert McNamara, interview by Brian VanDeMark, November 21, 1991.

52. Robert McNamara, interview by Brian VanDeMark, January 18, 1992.

53. Will Goodwin to Deborah Shapley, November 28, 1984, Deborah Shapley Archive—Figure File, Goodwin, Willard and Mary Jo.

54. Paul Hendrickson, email to William Taubman, June 17, 2021.

55. Robert McNamara, interview by Suzan Travis-Robyns, September 1, 2004, Robert S. McNamara Papers, Library of Congress, Box 2:132.

56. Craig McNamara, *Because Our Fathers Lied: A Memoir of Truth and Family, from Vietnam to Today* (New York: Little, Brown, 2022), 23–24.

57. Craig McNamara, conversation with Philip Taubman, April 12, 2022.

58. Henry Trewhitt, *McNamara: His Ordeal in the Pentagon* (New York: Harper & Row, 1971), 30.

59. Peggy Slaymaker, interview by Brian VanDeMark, December 10, 1991.

60. Robert McNamara, interview by Brian VanDeMark, November 14, 1991.

61. Robert McNamara, interview by Brian VanDeMark, November 14, 1991.

62. Peggy Slaymaker, interview by Paul Hendrickson, August 25, 1985.

63. Peggy Slaymaker, interview by Brian VanDeMark, December 10, 1991.

64. Robert McNamara, interview by Brian VanDeMark, November 14, 1991.

65. Trewhitt, *McNamara*, 28.

66. The spelling of this street differs in different sources, e.g., it is "Annerley" on McNamara's death certificate, but "Annerly" in Oakland Precinct No. 480 voter rolls for November 5, 1940.

67. Richard Quigley, interview by Brian VanDeMark, August 3, 1992.

68. Anonymous resident, interview by Matt Kristoffersen, November 16, 2022.

69. Robert McNamara, interview by Errol Morris, May 1–2, 2001.

70. Trewhitt, *McNamara*, 29.

71. Stanley Johnson, interview by Brian VanDeMark, January 3, 1992.

72. Peggy Slaymaker, interview by Brian VanDeMark, November 14, 1991.

73. Peggy Slaymaker, interview by Brian VanDeMark, December 10, 1991.

74. Robert McNamara, interview by Brian VanDeMark, November 21, 1991.

75. Annalee Whitmore, interview by Brian VanDeMark, January 5, 1992.

76. Joe McCarthy, "The Quest for Fame," *This Week*, February 14, 1965.

77. Anna Lee Guest, interview by Paul Hendrickson, August 1, 1985, Hendrickson Collection, Childhood and Berkeley folder, California File 2.

78. Trewhitt, *McNamara*, 29.

79. Anna Lee Guest, interview by Paul Hendrickson, August 1, 1985, Hendrickson Collection, Childhood and Berkeley folder, California File 2.

80. Trewhitt, *McNamara*, 30.

81. Annalee Whitmore, interview by Brian VanDeMark, January 5, 1992.

82. Annalee Whitmore, interview by Brian VanDeMark, January 5, 1992.

83. See *The Piedmont Highlander* masthead, 1932, and other documents in the Piedmont High School Archives.

84. Vernon Goodin, interview by Brian VanDeMark, October 30, 1991.

85. Anna Lee Guest, interview by Paul Hendrickson, August 1, 1985, Hendrickson Collection, Childhood and Berkeley folder, California File 2.

86. Richard and Gwynn Quigley, interview by Brian VanDeMark, August 3, 1992.

87. Trewhitt, *McNamara*, 29–30.
88. Hendrickson, *The Living and the Dead*, 62.
89. Trewhitt, *McNamara*, 30.
90. Craig McNamara, conversation with Philip Taubman, April 12, 2022.

CHAPTER TWO: GOLDEN BEAR

1. Robert McNamara, interview by Brian VanDeMark, November 14, 1991.
2. "Stanford Provides Means for Students to Borrow Tuition," *Stanford Daily*, July 21, 1932.
3. Annalee Whitmore, interview by Brian VanDeMark, January 5, 1992; Richard Quigley, interview by Brian VanDeMark, August 3, 1992; Shapley, *Promise and Power*, 3; Hendrickson, *The Living and the Dead*, 66; Robert McNamara, interview by Brian VanDeMark, November 21, 1991.
4. Fran Helmer, interview by Paul Hendrickson, August 1985, Hendrickson Collection, Childhood and Berkeley folder, California File 1.
5. Robert McNamara, interview by Errol Morris, May 1–2, 2001.
6. Shapley, *Promise and Power*, 14.
7. Hendrickson, *The Living and the Dead*, 68.
8. Robert McNamara, interview by Deborah Shapley, December 7, 1984, Shapley-McNamara File, 40.
9. Shapley, *Promise and Power*, 13.
10. Robert McNamara, interview by Brian VanDeMark, November 21, 1991.
11. Trewhitt, *McNamara*, 31.
12. Hendrickson, *The Living and the Dead*, 71. McNamara would later connect with fellow students of Davisson in Indonesia while he worked at the World Bank.
13. Robert McNamara, interview by Deborah Shapley, date unknown, Deborah Shapley Papers, Shapley-McNamara File.
14. John L. Simpson, interview by Suzanne B. Riess, 1978, transcript, "Activities in a Troubled World: War Relief, Banking, and Business," Bancroft Library, Regional Oral History Office, University of California, Berkeley, 18.
15. Joseph W. Cooper Jr., interview by Brian VanDeMark, January 19, 1992.
16. Henry Morse Stephens, quoted in "Order of the Golden Bear" website.
17. Quoted in Shapley, *Promise and Power*, 14.
18. Stan Johnson, interview by Brian VanDeMark, January 3, 1992; Hendrickson, *The Living and the Dead*, 72; Rudyard Kipling, "The Palace," 1922.
19. Hendrickson, *The Living and the Dead*, 72.
20. Shapley, *Promise and Power*, 16.
21. Hendrickson, *The Living and the Dead*, 72; Agnes Robb, interview by Paul Hendrickson, date unknown, Hendrickson Collection, Childhood and Berkeley folder, California File 3.
22. *San Francisco Chronicle*, November 11, 1936, March 26, 1937; Robert McNamara, Report regarding American Institutions exam, Bancroft Library, found in Paul Hendrickson Archive, Childhood and Berkeley folder, Berkeley Materials, part 2.
23. Trewhitt, *McNamara*, 32.
24. Shapley, *Promise and Power*, 17.
25. Hendrickson, *The Living and the Dead*, 69.
26. Carson Magill, interview by Brian VanDeMark, February 1, 1992.
27. The Y's Bear, October 23, 1936, and April 9, 1937, Harry Lees Kingman Papers, Box 6, folder 10, Bancroft Library, University of California, Berkeley.
28. Carson Magill, interview by Brian VanDeMark, February 1, 1992.
29. Hendrickson, *The Living and the Dead*, 69.
30. Carson Magill, interview by Paul Hendrickson, July 10, 1985, Hendrickson Collection, Childhood and Berkeley folder, California File 2.
31. Quoted in Hendrickson, *The Living and the Dead*, 70.
32. Hendrickson, *The Living and the Dead*, 69.

33. Robert McNamara, Harvard University Graduate School of Business Administration Application for Admission, February 14, 1937, McNamara Collection, Box 2:125, folder 6, Library of Congress.

34. Carson Magill, interview by Brian VanDeMark, February 1, 1992.

35. Ron Bradley, interview by Paul Hendrickson, date unknown, Hendrickson Collection, Childhood and Berkeley folder, Berkeley File 1.

36. Carson Magill, interview by Brian VanDeMark, February 1, 1992.

37. Hendrickson, *The Living and the Dead*, 70.

38. Carroll Ebright, quoted in Henry Trewhitt, *McNamara*, 32–33.

39. Robert McNamara, interview by Lydia Bronte, July 12, 1989.

40. Shapley, *Promise and Power*, 12.

41. Hendrickson, *The Living and the Dead*, 70–71; *Washington Post*, June 18, 1961.

42. Stan Johnson, quoted in Trewhitt, *McNamara*, 33.

43. Joseph Cooper, interview by Brian VanDeMark, January 19, 1992.

44. Stan Johnson, interview by Brian VanDeMark, January 3, 1992.

45. Robert McNamara, interview by Brian VanDeMark, November 21, 1991; Robert McNamara, *In Retrospect: The Tragedy and Lessons of Vietnam* (New York: Vintage Books, 1993), 5.

46. Robert McNamara, interview by Errol Morris, May 1–2, 2001; Shapley, *Promise and Power*, 18; Hendrickson, *The Living and the Dead*, 74.

47. Robert McNamara, interviews by Errol Morris, May 1–2 and December 11–12, 2001.

48. Trewhitt, *McNamara*, 34; Shapley, *Promise and Power*, 18–19; Hendrickson, *The Living and the Dead*, 73–74.

49. Joseph W. Cooper Jr., interview by Brian VanDeMark, January 19, 1992.

50. Vern Goodin, interview by Brian VanDeMark, October 30, 1991.

51. Vern Goodin, quoted in Hendrickson, *The Living and the Dead*, 73.

52. Stan Johnson, interview by Brian VanDeMark, January 3, 1992.

53. Joseph Cooper, interview by Brian VanDeMark, January 19, 1992.

54. Robert McNamara, interview by Errol Morris, May 1–2, 2001.

55. Robert McNamara, interview by Brian VanDeMark, November 21, 1991.

56. Robert McNamara, interview by Henry Brandon, 1969, Henry Brandon Papers, Library of Congress, Box 18, folder 3.

57. Quoted in Trewhitt, *McNamara*, 32.

58. University of California, *Blue and Gold* (Berkeley, 1933), 226.

59. Steven Finacom, "Berkeley, A Look Back: City Manager Choice, Compulsory ROTC Questioned in 1940," *Marin Independent Journal*, March 4, 2015.

60. McNamara, *In Retrospect*, 6.

61. Monroe Deutsch to Woodson Spurlock, November 14, 1936, Office of the President Records, 1914–1956, CU-5, Series 2, Box 1936:469–561, folder 445, 82, Scholarships, Bancroft Library, University of California, Berkeley.

62. Robert McNamara, interview by Brian VanDeMark, February 11, 1992.

63. Shapley, *Promise and Power*, 17; Hendrickson, *The Living and the Dead*, 73.

64. Hendrickson, *The Living and the Dead*, 73.

65. Paul Hendrickson, *The Living and the Dead*, 74.

CHAPTER THREE: "THE HAPPIEST DAYS OF OUR LIVES"

1. Robert McNamara, interview by Errol Morris, December 11–12, 2001.

2. "A Concrete Symbol," Baker Library Historical Collections, Harvard Business School.

3. Wally Haas, quoted in Hendrickson, *The Living and the Dead*, 87.

4. Edmund Learned, quoted in Hendrickson, *The Living and the Dead*, 86.

5. Robert McNamara, interview by Brian VanDeMark, February 11, 1992.

6. Hendrickson, *The Living and the Dead*, 87.

7. Robert Gordon Sproul to Robert McNamara, March 7, 1938, Deborah Shapley Archive, Harvard Business School Notes. Shapley indicates that this letter, which she transcribes in

the above file, is located in the University of California, Berkeley, archives. A search for the original copy of the letter proved unsuccessful.

8. Robert McNamara to Robert Gordon Sproul, October 16, 1937, Deborah Shapley Archive, Harvard Business School Notes. Shapley indicates that this letter, which she transcribes in the above file, is located in the University of California, Berkeley, archives. A search for the original copy of the letter proved unsuccessful.

9. Robert McNamara, interview by Brian VanDeMark, February 11, 1992.

10. Robert McNamara, interview by Brian VanDeMark, February 11, 1992.

11. Shapley, *Promise and Power*, 27; Eugene Zuckert, interview by Brian VanDeMark, October 29, 1992.

12. Byrne, *Whiz Kids*, 47.

13. Shapley, *Promise and Power*, 25.

14. McNamara, *In Retrospect*, 6.

15. Trewhitt, *McNamara*, 34.

16. Robert McNamara, interview by Brian VanDeMark, February 11, 1992.

17. Hendrickson, *The Living and the Dead*, 84.

18. Robert McNamara, interview by Brian VanDeMark, February 11, 1992.

19. Robert McNamara, interview by Brian VanDeMark, February 11, 1992.

20. Robert McNamara to Robert Sproul, October 16, 1937. Quoted in Hendrickson, *The Living and the Dead*, 87.

21. Robert McNamara to Monroe Deutsch, February 10, 1938. Quoted in Hendrickson, *The Living and the Dead*, 87.

22. Robert McNamara to Monroe Deutsch, April 27, 1938, Office of the President Records, 1914–1956, CU-5, Series 2, Box 1938, folder 61 (2–3), Bancroft Library, University of California, Berkeley.

23. Robert McNamara to Harry Barber and Joe Cooper, April 1938. Quoted in Hendrickson, *The Living and the Dead*, 88.

24. Robert McNamara to Monroe Deutsch, February 10, 1938. Quoted in Shapley, *Promise and Power*, 21.

25. Shapley, *Promise and Power*, 20, 24.

26. Robert McNamara, interview by Suzan Travis-Robyns, September 20–21, 1995, Robert S. McNamara Papers, Library of Congress, Box 2:132.

27. Will Goodwin to Robert McNamara, May 24, 1940, Diana McNamara Archive, Family Correspondence folder, Peggy McNamara Slaymaker File, Part I.

28. Stanley Johnson, interview by Brian VanDeMark, January 3, 1992; Hendrickson, *The Living and the Dead*, 87, 89.

29. Robert McNamara, interview by Brian VanDeMark, March 24, 1992; Hendrickson, *The Living and the Dead*, 89.

30. Robert James McNamara, death certificate, November 4, 1938, Hendrickson, *The Living and the Dead*, 89.

31. Hendrickson, *The Living and the Dead*, 90–91.

32. Nell McNamara to Robert McNamara, various dates, Diana McNamara Archive, Family Correspondence folder, Claranel McNamara File. Emphasis in originals.

33. Nell McNamara to Robert McNamara, November 13, 1938, Diana McNamara Archive, Family Correspondence folder, Claranel McNamara File.

34. Hendrickson, *The Living and the Dead*, 89–91.

35. Craig McNamara, *Because Our Fathers Lied*, 23.

36. Hendrickson, *The Living and the Dead*, 91.

37. Trewhitt, *McNamara*, 35.

38. Hendrickson, *The Living and the Dead*, 92.

39. Shapley, *Promise and Power*, 25.

40. Hendrickson, *The Living and the Dead*, 92.

41. Will Goodwin to Robert McNamara, November 1, 1938, Diana McNamara Archives, Fam-

ily Correspondence—Slaymaker, Peggy, Part 2; Annalee Whitmore, interview by Brian Van-DeMark, January 5, 1992.

42. Annalee Whitmore, interview by Brian VanDeMark, January 5, 1992.

43. Nell McNamara to Robert McNamara, October 24, 1938, Diana McNamara Archives, Family Correspondence folder, Claranel McNamara File.

44. Gwynn Quigley, interview by Brian VanDeMark, August 3, 1992.

45. Hendrickson, *The Living and the Dead*, 93.

46. Jean Booth Mitchell, interview by Paul Hendrickson, November 22, 1985, Paul Hendrickson Archive, California File 2.

47. Hendrickson, *The Living and the Dead*, 94.

48. Hendrickson, *The Living and the Dead*, 94.

49. Nell McNamara to Robert McNamara, October 24, 1938, Diana McNamara Archives, Family Correspondence folder, Claranel McNamara File.

50. Hendrickson, *The Living and the Dead*, 81.

51. Gwynn Quigley, interview with Brian VanDeMark, August 3, 1992.

52. Hendrickson, *The Living and the Dead*, 92–93.

53. Robert McNamara, interview by Brian VanDeMark, February 11, 1992.

54. Hendrickson, *The Living and the Dead*, 93; Robert McNamara, interview by Brian VanDeMark, February 11, 1992.

55. Robert McNamara, interview by Brian VanDeMark, March 24, 1992.

56. Robert McNamara, interview by Brian VanDeMark, February 11, 1992.

57. Robert McNamara, interview by Brian VanDeMark, March 24, 1992.

58. Price, Waterhouse & Co. to Robert McNamara, June 29, 1940, Diana McNamara Archive, Family Correspondence—Peggy Slaymaker folder. This comes out to about $3,500 per month in today's dollars, or roughly $42,000 per year.

59. Richard and Gwynn Quigley, interview by Brian VanDeMark, August 3, 1992.

60. Robert McNamara, interview by Brian VanDeMark, February 11, 1992.

61. Hendrickson, *The Living and the Dead*, 94.

62. Jean Booth Mitchell, interview by Paul Hendrickson, November 22, 1985, Paul Hendrickson Archive, Childhood and Berkeley folder, California File 2.

63. Hendrickson, *The Living and the Dead*, 94–95.

64. Robert McNamara, interview by Suzan Travis-Robyns, July 7, 2004, Robert S. McNamara Papers, Box 2:132, Library of Congress, 3.

65. Robert McNamara, interview by Brian VanDeMark, February 11, 1992.

66. Robert McNamara, interview by Suzan Travis-Robyns, September 20, 1995, McNamara Collection, Box 2:132, Library of Congress, 3.

67. Shapley, *Promise and Power*, 26.

68. Willard and Mary Jo Goodwin, interview by Deborah Shapley, December 15, 1985, Deborah Shapley Archive.

69. Hendrickson, *The Living and the Dead*, 95.

70. Robert McNamara to Margy Craig, July 1940, Diana McNamara Collection, Family Correspondence folder, Peggy Slaymaker File, 1.

71. Robert McNamara, interview by Brian VanDeMark, March 24, 1992.

72. Robert McNamara, interview by Brian VanDeMark, March 24, 1992.

73. Nell McNamara to Margy Craig, July 21, 1940, Diana McNamara Archive, Family Correspondence, Peggy Slaymaker File, part 1.

74. Robert McNamara, interview by Brian VanDeMark, February 11, 1992.

75. Hendrickson, *The Living and the Dead*, 77–79.

76. Robert McNamara, interview by Brian VanDeMark, March 24, 1992.

77. Robert McNamara, interview by Brian VanDeMark, March 24, 1992.

78. Shapley, *Promise and Power*, 28.

79. Trewhitt, *McNamara*, 36.

80. Eugene Zuckert, interview by Brian VanDeMark, October 29, 1992.

81. Myles Mace, interview by Paul Hendrickson, October 1985, Hendrickson Collection, Harvard Business School folder; Myles Mace, interview by Brian VanDeMark, September 5, 1992.
82. Hendrickson, *The Living and the Dead*, 97.
83. Eugene Zuckert, interview by Brian VanDeMark, October 29, 1992.
84. Hendrickson, *The Living and the Dead*, 97.
85. Thomas Sanders, interview by Paul Hendrickson, June 8, 1986, Paul Hendrickson Archive, Harvard Business School folder.
86. Hendrickson, *The Living and the Dead*, 97. Student quote as paraphrased by Hendrickson.
87. Philip William Orth to Robert McNamara, August 1, 1997, Diana McNamara Archive, General Correspondence folder, 1996–1997 File.
88. Robert McNamara, interview by Suzan Travis-Robyns, September 20, 1995, Robert S. McNamara Papers, Library of Congress, Box 2:132.
89. Robert McNamara, interview by Brian VanDeMark, March 24, 1992; Robert McNamara, interviews by Errol Morris, May 1–2 and December 11–12, 2001.

CHAPTER FOUR: WAGING WAR BY THE NUMBERS

1. "Remembering Pearl Harbor: A Pearl Harbor Fact Sheet," National WWII Museum, date unknown.
2. Robert McNamara, interview by Brian VanDeMark, March 24, 1992.
3. Robert McNamara, interview by Errol Morris, May 1–2, 2001.
4. Robert McNamara, interview by Brian VanDeMark, March 24, 1992.
5. "Citation for Legion of Merit," date unknown, Tex Thornton Archive, Other Materials Regarding McNamara folder.
6. Trewhitt, *McNamara*, 36.
7. Margaret McNamara Slaymaker, interviewer unknown, November 21, 1975, Columbia Center for Oral History, Columbia University.
8. McNamara, *In Retrospect*, 8.
9. David Halberstam, *The Reckoning* (New York: William Morrow, 1986), 205; Stephen A. Zeff, "The Contribution of the Harvard Business School to Management Control, 1908–1980," *Journal of Management Accounting Research* 20, Special Issue (2008): 175–208, 191.
10. David Lowell Hay, "Bomber Businessmen: The Army Air Forces and the Rise of Statistical Control, 1940–1945," PhD thesis, University of Notre Dame, 1994, 127.
11. Walter Isaacson and Evan Thomas, *The Wise Men: Six Friends and the World They Made* (New York: Simon & Schuster, 1986), 21, 108, 112, 193–94.
12. Byrne, *The Whiz Kids*, 25–29.
13. Quoted in Beirne Lay Jr., *Someone Has to Make It Happen: The Inside Story of Tex Thornton, the Man Who Built Litton Industries* (Englewood Cliffs, NJ: Prentice-Hall, 1969), 179.
14. Shapley, *Promise and Power*, 29.
15. Lay, *Someone Has to Make It Happen*, 57.
16. McNamara, *In Retrospect*, 8–9.
17. Hendrickson, *The Living and the Dead*, 98.
18. Hendrickson, *The Living and the Dead*, 99–100.
19. Byrne, *The Whiz Kids*, 45–46.
20. Trewhitt, *McNamara*, 37.
21. Hendrickson, *The Living and the Dead*, 100.
22. Byrne, *The Whiz Kids*, 49.
23. Shapley, *Promise and Power*, 30; Hendrickson, *The Living and the Dead*, 100.
24. Hendrickson, *The Living and the Dead*, 100.
25. Robert McNamara, interview by Errol Morris, May 1–2, 2001.
26. Hendrickson, *The Living and the Dead*, 100; Trewhitt, *McNamara*, 37; Robert McNamara, interview by Errol Morris, May 1–2, 2001.

27. Hendrickson, *The Living and the Dead*, 101; Myles Mace, interview by Brian VanDeMark, September 5, 1992.

28. James Beardon, *The Spellmount Guide to London in the Second World War* (New York: History Press, 2013), 166.

29. Myles Mace, interview by Brian VanDeMark, September 5, 1992.

30. John T. Correll, "The Third Musketeer," *Air Force Magazine*, December 2014.

31. Myles Mace, interview by Brian VanDeMark, September 5, 1992.

32. Hendrickson, *The Living and the Dead*, 101–2.

33. Shapley, *Promise and Power*, 33.

34. Myles Mace, interview by Brian VanDeMark, September 5, 1992.

35. Hendrickson, *The Living and the Dead*, 102.

36. Robert McNamara, interview by Errol Morris, May 1–2, 2001.

37. Robert McNamara to Margaret Craig McNamara, March 26, 1943, Diana McNamara Archive, Family Correspondence folder, McNamara, Robert to Margaret Craig McNamara, 1940s, Binder 2.

38. Robert McNamara to Margaret Craig McNamara, March 26, 1943, Diana McNamara Archive, Family Correspondence folder, McNamara, Robert to Margaret Craig McNamara, 1940s, Binder 2.

39. Robert McNamara to Margaret Craig McNamara, August 13, 1943, Diana McNamara Archive, Family Correspondence folder, McNamara, Robert to Margaret Craig McNamara, 1940s, Binder 2.

40. Robert McNamara to Margaret Craig McNamara, September 1, 1943, Diana McNamara Archive, Family Correspondence folder, McNamara, Robert to Margaret Craig McNamara, 1940s, Binder 2.

41. Robert McNamara to Margaret Craig McNamara, April 22, 1944?, Diana McNamara Archive, Family Correspondence folder, McNamara, Robert to Margaret Craig McNamara, 1940s, Binder 2.

42. Robert McNamara to Margaret Craig McNamara, July 26, 1944, Diana McNamara Archive, Family Correspondence folder, McNamara, Robert to Margaret Craig McNamara, 1940s, Binder 2.

43. Margaret Craig McNamara to Robert McNamara, March 13, 1943, Diana McNamara Archive, Family Correspondence folder, McNamara, Margaret Craig to Robert McNamara, 1943.

44. Claranel McNamara to Margaret Craig McNamara, July 30, 1943, Diana McNamara Archive, Family Correspondence folder, Slaymaker, Peggy, File, part 1.

45. Robert McNamara and Margaret Craig McNamara correspondence, various dates, Diana McNamara Archive, Family Correspondence folder.

46. Trewhitt, *McNamara*, 38.

47. Robert McNamara, interview by Brian VanDeMark, March 24, 1992.

48. Robert McNamara, interview by Brian VanDeMark, March 24, 1992.

49. Warren Kozak, *LeMay: The Life and Wars of General Curtis LeMay* (Washington, DC: Regnery Publishing, 2009), ix.

50. Robert McNamara, interview by Errol Morris, May 1–2, 2001; Robert McNamara, interview by Errol Morris, December 11–12, 2001.

51. Robert McNamara, interview by Brian VanDeMark, March 24, 1992.

52. Robert McNamara, interview by Brian VanDeMark, May 1, 1992.

53. Robert McNamara, interview by Brian VanDeMark, May 1, 1992.

54. Robert McNamara to Margaret Craig McNamara, various dates, Diana McNamara Archive, Family Correspondence folder.

55. Trewhitt, *McNamara*, 38.

56. Trewhitt, *McNamara*, 37.

57. Robert McNamara, interview by Brian VanDeMark, March 24, 1992.

58. Shapley, *Promise and Power*, 35.

59. McNamara, *In Retrospect*, 9.

60. Robert McNamara, interview by Errol Morris, May 1–2, 2001.

61. George M. Watson Jr. and Herman S. Wolk, "'Whiz Kid': Robert S. McNamara's World War II Service," *Air Power History* 50, no. 4 (Winter 2003): 4–15, 8.

62. Robert McNamara, interview by Brian VanDeMark, March 24, 1992.

63. Robert McNamara, interview by Brian VanDeMark, March 24, 1992.

64. Robert McNamara, interview by Brian VanDeMark, March 24, 1992.

65. Robert McNamara, interview by Brian VanDeMark, March 24, 1992.

66. Robert McNamara, interview by Brian VanDeMark, March 24, 1992.

67. E. Bartlett Kerr, *Flames over Tokyo: The U.S. Army Air Forces' Incendiary Campaign Against Japan, 1944–1945* (New York: Donald I. Fine, 1991), xi.

68. Curtis LeMay and MacKinlay Kantor, *Mission with LeMay: My Story* (New York: Double-day, 1965), 10.

69. Kerr, *Flames over Tokyo*, xii–xiii.

70. John Byrne, *Whiz Kids*, 50.

71. Robert McNamara, interview by Errol Morris, December 11–12, 2001; *The Fog of War*, 41:40.

72. Max Boot, *The Road Not Taken: Edward Lansdale and the American Tragedy in Vietnam* (New York: Liveright Publishing, 2018), 365.

73. *The Fog of War*, 40:40; James Blight and janet Lang, *The Fog of War: Lessons from the Life of Robert S. McNamara* (Lanham, MD: Rowman & Littlefield, 2005), 113.

74. Craig McNamara, *Because Our Fathers Lied*, 66.

75. Paul Hendrickson, *The Living and the Dead*, 103.

76. Robert McNamara, interview by Brian VanDeMark, March 24, 1992; Robert McNamara, interview by Suzan Travis-Robyns, September 20–21, 1995, Robert S. McNamara Papers, Library of Congress, Box 2:132.

77. Byrne, *Whiz Kids*, 174.

78. McNamara, *In Retrospect*, 9–10.

79. Shapley, *Promise and Power*, 37–38; Hendrickson, *The Living and the Dead*, 103–5; Trewhitt, *McNamara*, 39.

80. Robert McNamara, interview by Suzan Travis-Robyns, June 29, 2004, Robert S. McNamara Papers, Library of Congress, Box 2:132.

81. Hendrickson, *The Living and the Dead*, 104–5.

82. Robert McNamara, interview by Brian VanDeMark, May 1, 1992.

83. Hendrickson, *The Living and the Dead*, 105.

84. Robert McNamara, interview by Brian VanDeMark, May 1, 1992.

85. Robert McNamara, interview by Suzan Travis-Robyns, September 20–21, 1995.

86. Hendrickson, *The Living and the Dead*, 104.

87. Robert McNamara, interview by Brian VanDeMark, May 1, 1992.

CHAPTER FIVE: POWER STEERING

1. Robert Lacey, *Ford: The Men and the Machine* (Boston: Little, Brown, 1986), 390, 420; Review of Timothy J. O'Callaghan, *Ford in the Service of America: Mass Production for the Military During the World Wars* (Jefferson, NC: McFarland, 2009), in *Michigan Historical Review* 37, no. 1 (Spring 2011): 168.

2. Allan Nevins and Frank Ernest Hill, *Ford: Decline and Rebirth, 1933–1962* (New York: Charles Scribner's Sons, 1963), 294.

3. Walter Hayes, *Henry: A Life of Henry Ford II* (New York: Grove Weidenfeld, 1990), 6.

4. Shapley, *Promise and Power*, 45.

5. Hayes, *Henry*, 9.

6. Byrne, *Whiz Kids*, 100.

7. Brian VanDeMark, "Memorandum of Conversation with Robert S. McNamara," January 18, 1993.

8. David Halberstam, "Interview with Holmes Brown," date unknown, David Halberstam Collection, Boston University, Box 62, folder 11, 42.

9. Robert McNamara, interview by Suzan Travis-Robyns, September 20, 1995, Robert S. McNamara Papers, Library of Congress, Box 2:132; Robert McNamara, interview by Errol Morris, May 1–2, 2001.

10. Robert McNamara, interview by Errol Morris, December 11–12, 2001.

11. David Lowell Hay, "Bomber Businessmen: The Army Air Forces and the Rise of Statistical Control, 1940–1945," PhD diss., University of Notre Dame, 1994, 10.

12. Robert McNamara, interview by Lydia Bronte, July 12, 1989.

13. Robert McNamara, interview by Errol Morris, May 1–2, 2001.

14. Robert McNamara, interview by Lydia Bronte, July 12, 1989.

15. Arjay Miller, interview by Felicity Barringer and Philip Taubman, August 12, 2014.

16. Trewhitt, *McNamara*, 41.

17. Robert McNamara, interview by Errol Morris, December 11–12, 2001.

18. Robert McNamara to E. P. Learned, November 29, 1946, Robert S. McNamara Papers, Library of Congress, Box 2: 125, folder 4.

19. Ted Mecke, interview by David Halberstam, David Halberstam Collection, Boston University, Box 62, folder 19.

20. Robert McNamara, interview by Frank Ernest Hill, Mira Wilkins, and Henry Edmunds, January 8, 1960, Ford Motor Company Archives.

21. Arjay Miller, interview by Brian VanDeMark, August 7, 1992.

22. Robert Dunham, interview by Brian VanDeMark, June 24, 1992.

23. Arjay Miller, interview by Brian VanDeMark, August 7, 1992.

24. Arjay Miller, interview by Philip Taubman and Felicity Barringer, August 12, 2014.

25. Byrne, *Whiz Kids*, 20.

26. Byrne, *Whiz Kids*, 96–97.

27. Shapley, *Promise and Power*, 42.

28. Robert McNamara to Margaret Craig McNamara, February 1, 1946, Diana McNamara Archive, Family Correspondence folder, McNamara, Robert, letters to Margaret Craig McNamara, 1940s, File, Binder 1.

29. Robert McNamara Psychological Test, Tex Thornton Papers.

30. Charles Thornton Psychological Test, Tex Thornton Papers.

31. Robert Dunham to Robert McNamara, Arjay Miller, Joseph Lundy, James Wright, and Charles Thornton, July 29, 1977, Tex Thornton Papers.

32. Nevins, *Ford: Decline and Rebirth*, 298, 300.

33. Robert McNamara, interview by Errol Morris, December 11–12, 2001.

34. Robert McNamara, interview by Brian VanDeMark, May 1, 1992.

35. Lacey, *Ford*, 477–78.

36. Robert McNamara, interview by Brian VanDeMark, May 1, 1992.

37. Robert McNamara, interview by Brian VanDeMark, June 16, 1992.

38. Robert McNamara, interview by Brian VanDeMark, June 16, 1992.

39. Robert McNamara, interview by Bob Woodward, October 18, 1988.

40. Robert McNamara, interview by Brian VanDeMark, June 16, 1992.

41. Nevins and Hill, *Ford: Decline and Rebirth*, 342.

42. Robert McNamara, interview by Brian VanDeMark, June 16, 1992.

43. Holmes Brown, interview by David Halberstam, January 27, 1969, David Halberstam Collection, Boston University, Box 62, folder 11, 453–54.

44. Larry Ronan, "Seat Belts: 1949–1956," Lexington Technology Associates, April 1979, Prepared for the US Department of Transportation, 24.

45. Robert McNamara, interview by Brian VanDeMark, June 16, 1992.

46. Richard A. Johnson, "The Outsider: How Robert McNamara Changed the Automobile Industry," *Invention & Technology Magazine*, Summer 2007.

47. Robert McNamara, Commencement Speech at the University of Alabama (Tuscaloosa, May 29, 1955), Ford Motor Company Archives.

48. Holmes Brown, interview by David Halberstam, January 27, 1969, David Halberstam Collection, Boston University, Box 62, folder 11, 453; David Halberstam, *The Best and the Brightest* (New York: Random House, 1972), 239.

49. 84 Cong. Rec. A4326 (1955) (statement of Representative Hill).

50. "Hearings Before a Subcommittee of the Committee on Interstate and Foreign Commerce, House of Representatives, Eighty-Fifth Congress, First Session, on Crashworthiness of Automobile Seat Belts," April 30, August 5, 6, 7, and 8, 1957, 56.

51. Lee Iacocca with William Novak, *Iacocca: An Autobiography* (New York: Bantam Books, 1984), 296.

52. Michael R. Lemov, *Car Safety Wars: One Hundred Years of Technology, Politics, and Death* (Madison, NJ: Fairleigh Dickinson University Press, 2015), 62.

53. Robert McNamara, interview by Brian VanDeMark, June 16, 1992.

54. Robert McNamara, interview by Brian VanDeMark, June 16, 1992.

55. Paul Ingrassia, *Engines of Change: A History of the American Dream in Fifteen Cars* (New York: Simon & Schuster, 2012), 146; Douglas Brinkley, *Wheels for the World: Henry Ford, His Company, and a Century of Progress, 1903–2003* (New York: Viking Penguin, 2003), 597.

56. Robert McNamara, interview by Brian VanDeMark, June 16, 1992.

57. Trewhitt, *McNamara*, 51.

58. David Halberstam, "Interview with Holmes Brown," date unknown, David Halberstam Collection, Boston University, Box 62, folder 11, 38.

59. Robert McNamara, interview by Brian VanDeMark, May 1, 1992.

60. Robert McNamara, interview by Errol Morris, December 11–12, 2001.

61. Robert McNamara, Notes from Editorial Meeting with Peter Osnos, Geoff Schandler, Peter Petre, and Brian VanDeMark, September 16, 1994.

62. Craig McNamara, *Because Our Fathers Lied*, 42.

63. Eugene Power, interview by Brian VanDeMark, Spring 1992.

64. Trewhitt, *McNamara*, 51–52.

65. Robert McNamara, interview by Brian VanDeMark, May 1, 1992.

66. Robert McNamara, interview by Suzan Travis-Robyns, September 20–21, 1995, Robert S. McNamara Papers, Library of Congress, Box 2:132.

67. Robert McNamara, interview by Brian VanDeMark, May 1, 1992.

68. Robert Dunham, interview by Brian VanDeMark, June 24, 1992.

69. Robert McNamara, interview by Brian VanDeMark, May 1, 1992.

70. Robert Dunham, interview by Brian VanDeMark, June 24, 1992.

71. See, for example, Matt Schudel, "Allie Ritzenberg, Tennis Pro Who Took D.C.'s Elite to the Court, Dies at 100," *Washington Post*, December 2, 2018; and Barbara Gamarekian, "Power Anyone? Tennis Is 'In,'" *New York Times*, May 11, 1986.

72. Robert McNamara, interview by Brian VanDeMark, May 1, 1992; Trewhitt, *McNamara*, 52.

73. Eugene Power, interview by Brian VanDeMark, Spring 1992.

74. Trewhitt, *McNamara*, 52–53.

75. Eugene Power, interview by Brian VanDeMark, Spring 1992.

76. Trewhitt, *McNamara*, 54.

77. Trewhitt, *McNamara*, 53.

78. Eugene Power, interview by Brian VanDeMark, Spring 1992.

79. Robert McNamara, interview by Errol Morris, April 2, 2002.

80. Lacey, *Ford*, 498.

81. Robert Dunham, interview by Brian VanDeMark, June 24, 1992.

82. Trewhitt, *McNamara*, 52.

83. Craig McNamara, *Because Our Fathers Lied*, 43–44.

84. Craig McNamara, *Because Our Fathers Lied*, 64.

85. Arjay Miller, interview by Brian VanDeMark, August 7, 1992.

86. Robert Dunham, interview by Paul Hendrickson, date unknown, Paul Hendrickson Collection, Ford Motor Company folder, File 1.

87. Robert Dunham, interview by Brian VanDeMark, June 24, 1992.

88. Myles Mace, interview by Brian VanDeMark, September 5, 1992.
89. See Daniel Clark, *Disruption in Detroit: Autoworkers and the Elusive Postwar Boom* (Urbana: University of Illinois Press, 2018), 93, 172, 179. We are grateful for Daniel Clark's help in understanding McNamara's assessment of work precarity in the automotive industry. In an email, Clark told us: "There could have been some examples of this sort of thing happening with certain model changeovers. . . . In the postwar era, model changeovers generally did not take that long, a week or two tops, as opposed to the months-long processes during the pre-WWII era. The changeovers would have been accomplished by a combination of skilled workers and grunt workers, not necessarily the line workers who normally ran the machines in the department. . . . Plenty of workers lost their jobs during model change-overs or extended layoffs, but that was generally because of the automation that people like McNamara dearly wanted. It wasn't a temporary displacement during model changeover."
90. Iacocca, *Iacocca*, 42.
91. Halberstam, *The Reckoning*, 207.
92. Byrne, *Whiz Kids*, 100, 175.
93. Halberstam, *The Reckoning*, 207, 359, 365; Iacocca, *Iacocca*, 42.
94. Halberstam, *The Reckoning*, 573.
95. Norman Krandall, interviews by Paul Hendrickson, April 15 and October 28, 1986, Paul Hendrickson Collection, Ford Motor Company folder, File 1.
96. Norman Krandall, interviews by Paul Hendrickson, April 15 and October 28, 1986, Paul Hendrickson Collection, Ford Motor Company folder, File 1.
97. Leo C. Beebe, interview by Paul Hendrickson, October 11, 1984, Paul Hendrickson Collection, Ford Motor Company folder, File 1.
98. Robert Dunham, interview by Brian VanDeMark, June 24, 1992.
99. Frances Miller, interview by Brian VanDeMark, August 7, 1992.
100. Virginia Gerrity, interview by Paul Hendrickson, December 10, year unknown, Paul Hendrickson Collection, Ford Motor Company folder, File 2.
101. Arjay Miller, interview by Brian VanDeMark, August 7, 1992.
102. Frances Miller, interview by Brian VanDeMark, August 7, 1992.
103. Lacey, *Ford*, 491.
104. Peter Collier and David Horowitz, *The Fords: An American Epic* (New York: Summit Books, 1987), 248.
105. Arjay and Frances Miller, interview by Brian VanDeMark, August 7, 1992.
106. Byrne, *Whiz Kids*, 249.
107. Iacocca, *Iacocca*, 42.
108. Lacey, *Ford, the Men and the Machine*, 497–98.
109. Arjay and Frances Miller, interview by Brian VanDeMark, August 7, 1992.
110. Robert McNamara, interview by Lydia Bronte, July 12, 1989.
111. Will Scott, interview by Brian VanDeMark, June 23, 1992.
112. Shapley, *Promise and Power*, 64–65.
113. Collier and Horowitz, *The Fords*, 249.
114. John Brooks, *Business Adventures: Twelve Classic Tales from the World of Wall Street* (New York: Open Road, 2014), 17, 35.
115. Shapley, *Promise and Power*, 54–56.
116. Byrne, *Whiz Kids*, 339.
117. Byrne, *Whiz Kids*, 248.
118. Shapley, *Promise and Power*, 59.
119. Robert McNamara, interview by Suzan Travis-Robyns, September 20–21, 1995, Robert S. McNamara Papers, Library of Congress, Box 2:132.
120. Robert Dunham, interview by Brian VanDeMark, June 24, 1992.
121. Martin, L.A., to Nation—(Tuohy), Memorandum of Interview with Charles B. Thornton, February 26, 1962, Tex Thornton Papers, Other Materials folder.
122. Henry Ford II, Executive Communication, December 13, 1960, Ford Motor Company Archives.

123. Shapley, *Promise and Power*, 87; Collier and Horowitz, *The Fords*, 292.
124. Collier and Horowitz, *The Fords*, 337.

CHAPTER SIX: POTOMAC FEVER

1. This account draws on McNamara, *In Retrospect*, 13–21, Robert McNamara, interview by Errol Morris, May 1–2, 2001, and Robert McNamara, interview by Brian VanDeMark, July 10, 1992.
2. Peter L. W. Osnos, "JFK and McNamara, Part Three," *LBJ and McNamara: The Vietnam Partnership Destined to Fail*, Peter Osnos Platform on Substack, June 18, 2024.
3. Clark Clifford, interview by Paul Hendrickson, November 28, 1984, Paul Hendrickson Archive, Pentagon folder.
4. Robert McNamara, interview by Lydia Bronte, July 12, 1989.
5. McNamara, *In Retrospect*, 15.
6. Adam Yarmolinsky, interview by Brian VanDeMark, April 1, 1993; Shapley, *Promise and Power*, 82.
7. Robert McNamara, interview by Errol Morris, May 1–2, 2001.
8. This account of McNamara's first meeting with Kennedy draws on McNamara, *In Retrospect*, 13–21, and Robert McNamara, interview by Brian VanDeMark, July 10, 1992.
9. McNamara, *In Retrospect*, 16.
10. Robert McNamara, interview by Brian VanDeMark, July 10, 1992.
11. McNamara, *In Retrospect*, 16.
12. Robert McNamara, interview by Alfred Goldberg and Maurice Matloff, April 3, 1986, Oral History, JFK Presidential Library.
13. McNamara, *In Retrospect*, 16.
14. Roswell Gilpatric, interview by Brian VanDeMark, November 5, 1992.
15. Shapley, *Promise and Power*, 84–85.
16. Roswell Gilpatric, interview by Brian VanDeMark, November 5, 1992.
17. Arjay Miller, interview by Philip Taubman and Felicity Barringer, August 12, 2014.
18. Robert McNamara, interview by Errol Morris, May 1–2, 2001.
19. Robert McNamara, interview by Errol Morris, May 1–2, 2001.
20. Roswell Gilpatric, interview by Brian VanDeMark, November 5, 1992.
21. Shapley, *Promise and Power*, 270, 127.
22. Robert McNamara, interview by Errol Morris, May 1–2, 2001.
23. Robert McNamara, interview by Errol Morris, December 11–12, 2001.
24. Robert McNamara, interview by Errol Morris, May 1–2, 2001.
25. Ted Sorensen, *Kennedy: The Classic Biography* (London: Hodder and Stoughton, 1965), 269.
26. McNamara, *In Retrospect*, 18–19.
27. Douglas Martin, "Paul B. Fay Jr., Confidant of President Kennedy, Dies at 91," *New York Times*, September 29, 2009.
28. McNamara, *In Retrospect*, 20.
29. McNamara, *In Retrospect*, 20–21.
30. Fredrik Logevall, *JFK: Coming of Age in the American Century, 1917–1956* (New York: Random House, 2020), 253–55.
31. Logevall, *JFK*, 212.
32. Logevall, *JFK*, 226–27.
33. Logevall, *JFK*, 402.
34. Logevall, *JFK*, 494.
35. Sorensen, *Kennedy*, 12.
36. Logevall, *JFK*, 308.
37. Logevall, *JFK*, 412.
38. Logevall, *JFK*, 549.
39. Logevall, *JFK*, 453.
40. Logevall, *JFK*, 435.

41. Sorensen, *Kennedy*, 34.

42. Kai Bird, *The Color of Truth: McGeorge Bundy and William Bundy: Brothers in Arms* (New York: Simon & Schuster, 2000), 189–90.

43. Dean Rusk, *As I Saw It* (New York: Penguin Books, 1991), 17.

44. Rusk, *As I Saw It*, 29.

45. Gordon M. Goldstein, *Lessons in Disaster: McGeorge Bundy and the Path to War in Vietnam* (New York: Henry Holt , 2008), 81.

46. Bird, *The Color of Truth*, 275.

47. Jacqueline Kennedy Onassis, Arthur M. Schlesinger Jr., Michael R. Beschloss, and Caroline Kennedy, *Jacqueline Kennedy: Historic Conversations on Life with John F. Kennedy, Interviews with Arthur M. Schlesinger Jr.* (New York: Hyperion, 2011), 312–13.

48. McNamara, *In Retrospect*, 17.

49. Robert McNamara, interview by Brian VanDeMark, July 10, 1992.

50. Gregg Herken, *The Georgetown Set: Friends and Rivals in Cold War Washington* (New York: Vintage, 2014), 17–18.

51. Herken, *The Georgetown Set*, 19.

52. Herken, *The Georgetown Set*, 61.

53. Sally Bedell Smith, *Grace and Power: The Private World of the Kennedy White House* (New York: Random House, 2004), 52.

54. Kevin Healy, Letter to the Editor, *Sports Illustrated*, September 3, 1962; John Katzenbach, interview by William and Philip Taubman, April 1, 2017.

55. Arthur M. Schlesinger Jr., *Robert Kennedy and His Times* (Boston: Houghton Mifflin, 1978), 592–93; Larry Tye, *Bobby Kennedy: The Making of a Liberal Icon* (New York: Random House, 2016), 180.

56. Shapley, *Promise and Power*, 91–92.

57. Joseph Alsop, *I've Seen the Best of It: Memoirs* (New York: W. W. Norton, 1992), 440–42.

58. William S. Patten, *My Three Fathers: And the Elegant Deceptions of My Mother, Susan Mary Alsop* (New York: PublicAffairs, 2008), 224.

59. Nicholas Thompson, *The Hawk and the Dove: Paul Nitze, George Kennan, and the History of the Cold War* (New York: Henry Holt, 2009), 170, 192, 198–99.

60. William Taubman interview with Margy Pastor, October 10, 2019.

61. The above and below descriptions of the McNamara home and life rely on paraphrases and quotes from Shapley, *Promise and Power*, 138, and Craig McNamara, *Because Our Fathers Lied*, 42.

62. Craig McNamara, interview with Philip Taubman, May 5, 2024.

63. Curt Strand, interview by Philip Taubman, August 23, 2019.

64. Allie Ritzenberg, *Capital Tennis: A Memoir* (Washington, DC: Francis Press, 2004), 75–76.

65. Betty Beale, quoted in David Lawrence, "White House Accent on Youth," *Evening Star*, Washington, DC, February 20, 1962; Barbara Leaming, *Jacqueline Bouvier Kennedy Onassis: The Untold Story* (New York: St. Martin's Press, 2014), 115.

66. Drew Pearson, "They Twisted at the White House," *Washington Post*, February 17, 1962.

67. Jackie Kennedy to Robert McNamara, February 1962, University Archives Catalog.

68. Jackie Kennedy to Robert McNamara, February 13, 1962, Sotheby's Catalog, Lot #103.

69. Ben Bradlee, *Conversations with Kennedy* (New York: W. W. Norton, 1984), 223.

70. Smith, *Grace and Power*, 163.

71. Paul Hendrickson, Notes from Interview with Gilpatric, May 29, 1985, Paul Hendrickson Archive, Pentagon folder.

72. Smith, *Grace and Power*, 163.

73. Robert McNamara, interview by Brian VanDeMark and Peter Osnos, October 9, 1993.

74. Leaming, *Jacqueline Bouvier Kennedy Onassis*, 8.

75. Leaming, *Jacqueline Bouvier Kennedy Onassis*, 18–21.

76. Carl Sferrazza Anthony, *Camera Girl: The Coming of Age of Jackie Bouvier Kennedy* (New York: Simon & Schuster, 2023); Maureen Dowd, "Jackie on My Mind," *New York Times*, June 3, 2023.

77. Leaming, *Jacqueline Bouvier Kennedy Onassis*, 104.

78. Leaming, *Jacqueline Bouvier Kennedy Onassis*, 56–57.

79. Leaming, *Jacqueline Bouvier Kennedy Onassis*, 68–69.

80. Leaming, *Jacqueline Bouvier Kennedy Onassis*, 114–15.

81. Leaming, *Jacqueline Bouvier Kennedy Onassis*, 119.

82. Jackie Kennedy to Robert McNamara, October 25, 1962, Diana McNamara Archive.

83. Jackie Kennedy to Robert McNamara, date unknown, Sotheby's Lot #103 Catalog.

84. Margy McNamara to Jackie Kennedy, March 16, 1963, JFK Presidential Library, White House Social Files, Box 578.

85. Jackie Kennedy to Robert and Margy McNamara, April 24, 1963, Sotheby's Lot #16 Catalog.

86. Smith, *Grace and Power*, 382.

87. Jackie Kennedy to Robert McNamara, June 27, 1963, Sotheby's Lot #102.

88. Paul Hendrickson, Notes of Interview with Robert Dunham, December 14, 1984, Paul Hendrickson Archive, Ford I folder.

89. Doris Kearns Goodwin, *An Unfinished Love Story: A Personal History of the 1960s* (New York: Simon & Schuster, 2024), 262.

90. Arthur M. Schlesinger Jr., *Journals: 1952–2000* (New York: Penguin Books, 2007), 472.

91. Smith, *Grace and Power*, 163.

92. Smith, *Grace and Power*, 155–56.

CHAPTER SEVEN: STORMING THE PENTAGON

1. Robert McNamara, *The Essence of Security: Reflections in Office* (New York: Harper & Row, 1968), x, quoted in H. R. McMaster, *Dereliction of Duty: Johnson, McNamara, the Joint Chiefs of Staff, and the Lies That Led to Vietnam* (New York: HarperCollins, 1998), 17.

2. Trewhitt, *McNamara*, 60.

3. Aurélie Basha i Novosejt, *"I Made Mistakes": Robert McNamara's Vietnam War Policy, 1960–1968* (New York: Cambridge University Press, 2019), 28–29.

4. Shapley, *Promise and Power*, 99.

5. Novosejt, *"I Made Mistakes,"* 39.

6. Shapley, *Promise and Power*, 103.

7. Shapley, *Promise and Power*, 103.

8. McNamara, *In Retrospect*, 22–23.

9. "Defense: Action in the E Ring," *Time*, April 7, 1961.

10. Rufus Phillips, interview by Paul Hendrickson, February 6, 1986, Paul Hendrickson Archive, Pentagon folder.

11. "Defense: The Dilemma & the Design," *Time*, February 15, 1963.

12. "Defense: The Dilemma & the Design," *Time*, February 15, 1963.

13. McMaster, *Dereliction of Duty*, 19–20.

14. Edmund Learned, interview by Paul Hendrickson, November 1985, Hendrickson Collection, Harvard Business School folder.

15. Al Dickinson, interview by Paul Hendrickson, June 6, 1986, Hendrickson Collection, Harvard Business School folder.

16. Hendrickson, *The Living and the Dead*, 22.

17. Paul Ignatius, interview by Philip Taubman, October 21, 2019.

18. Roswell Gilpatric, interview by Brian VanDeMark, November 5, 1992.

19. Novosejt, *"I Made Mistakes,"* 39.

20. Shapley, *Promise and Power*, 104.

21. Novosejt, *"I Made Mistakes,"* 38–39.

22. Shapley, *Promise and Power*, 126; Trewhitt, *McNamara*, 101.

23. Trewhitt, *McNamara*, 109.

24. Daniel Ellsberg, *Secrets: A Memoir of Vietnam and the Pentagon Papers* (New York: Penguin Books, 2003), 60.

25. Quoted in Brian VanDeMark, *Road to Disaster: A New History of America's Descent into Vietnam* (Boston: Mariner, 2018), 25.

26. Robert McNamara, interview by Brian VanDeMark, September 8, 1992.
27. McNamara, *In Retrospect*, 26.
28. Quoted in VanDeMark, *Road to Disaster*, 28.
29. Robert McNamara, interview by Brian VanDeMark, September 8, 1992.
30. Osnos, "JFK and McNamara, Part Three."
31. Shapley, *Promise and Power*, 115.
32. Peter L. W. Osnos, "Early Decisions, Part Four," *LBJ and McNamara: The Vietnam Partnership Destined to Fail*, Peter Osnos Platform on Substack, June 25, 2024.
33. VanDeMark, *Road to Disaster*, 80.
34. Roswell Gilpatric, interview by Brian VanDeMark, November 5, 1992.
35. Shapley, *Promise and Power*, 177. The historical record of this McNamara comment is unclear. It has often been cited in accounts of the missile crisis. According to janet Lang, McNamara was amused to hear the line attributed to President Kennedy in a movie about the crisis. "That's my line," she recalled him saying. janet Lang, email message to the authors, January 15, 2025.
36. nsarchive.gwu.edu/briefing-book/cuba-cuban missile crisis/2022-120-27/cuban-missile-crisis-60-most-dangerous day.
37. See especially Sheldon Stern, *The Cuban Missile Crisis in American Memory: Myths Versus Reality* (Stanford, CA: Stanford University Press, 2012).
38. Shapley, *Promise and Power*, 181.
39. Shapley, *Promise and Power*, 102; see also Trewhitt, *McNamara*, 88.
40. Lawrence S. Kaplan, Ronald D. Landa, and Edward J. Drea, *The McNamara Ascendancy, 1961–1965*, vol. 5 of History of the Office of the Secretary of Defense (Washington, DC: Office of the Secretary of Defense, 2006), 291–92.
41. Robert McNamara, interview by Errol Morris, May 1–2, 2001.
42. Quoted in William Taubman, *Khrushchev: The Man and His Era* (New York: W. W. Norton, 2003), 487–88.
43. VanDeMark, *Road to Disaster*, 138–39.
44. McGeorge Bundy, Draft Manuscript on Vietnam, chap. 1, April 27, 1996, pp. 2 and 5, Personal Papers of McGeorge Bundy, Box 223, John F. Kennedy Library, quoted in VanDeMark, *Road to Disaster*, 133.
45. Halberstam, *The Best and the Brightest*, 76.
46. David Halberstam, Memorandum of Conversation with Fred Dutton, November 4, 1969, David Halberstam Papers, Howard Gotlieb Archival Research Center at Boston University, Box 56, folder 18.
47. Kaplan et al., *The McNamara Ascendancy*, 272–73.
48. Kaplan et al., *The McNamara Ascendancy*, 35, 49.
49. McNamara, *In Retrospect*, 38–39.
50. VanDeMark, *Road to Disaster*, 135.
51. VanDeMark, *Road to Disaster*, 135.
52. Robert McNamara, interview by Brian VanDeMark, July 12, 1993.
53. Robert McNamara, interview by Brian VanDeMark, July 12, 1993.
54. Quoted in VanDeMark, *Road to Disaster*, 137.
55. Robert McNamara, interview by Brian VanDeMark, July 12, 1993.
56. VanDeMark, *Road to Disaster*, 141.
57. Shapley, *Promise and Power*, 150–52.
58. VanDeMark, *Road to Disaster*, 141–48.
59. VanDeMark, *Road to Disaster*, 156–57.
60. Henry Cabot Lodge, Oral History, August 4, 1965, John F. Kennedy Presidential Library.
61. Tape Recording of Presidential Meeting, August 29, 1963, Noon, John F. Kennedy Presidential Library, courtesy of NARA.
62. VanDeMark, *Road to Disaster*, 170–72.
63. VanDeMark, *Road to Disaster*, 178–79.
64. William A. Buckingham Jr., *Operation Ranch Hand: The Air Force and Herbicides in South-*

east Asia, 1961–1971 (Washington, DC: Office of Air Force History, United States Air Force, 1982), 33.

65. Institute of Medicine, *Veterans and Agent Orange: Health Effects of Herbicides Used in Vietnam* (Washington, DC: National Academy Press, 1994), cited in Veterans Affairs Public Affairs, "VA Extends 'Agent Orange' Benefits to More Veterans," October 13, 2009.

66. Robert McNamara, interview by Errol Morris, December 11–12, 2001.

67. McNamara, *In Retrospect*, 96.

68. Osnos, "Early Decisions, Part Four."

69. VanDeMark, *Road to Disaster*, 182–83.

70. VanDeMark, *Road to Disaster*, 184.

71. Schlesinger, *Robert Kennedy*, 722.

72. Osnos, "Early Decisions, Part Four."

CHAPTER EIGHT: ASSASSINATION AND AFTERMATH

1. Robert McNamara, interview by William Manchester, May 25, 1964, William Manchester Papers, Wesleyan University.

2. Robert McNamara, interview by William Manchester, May 25, 1964.

3. Robert McNamara, interview by William Manchester, May 25, 1964.

4. McNamara, *In Retrospect*, 90.

5. Shapley, *Promise and Power*, 271–75.

6. Robert McNamara, interview by William Manchester, May 25, 1964.

7. Robert McNamara, interview by William Manchester, May 25, 1964.

8. Leaming, *Jacqueline Bouvier Kennedy Onassis*, 135, 197.

9. Smith, *Grace and Power*, 459.

10. Smith, *Grace and Power*, 443.

11. Arthur Schlesinger, interview by William Manchester, May 29, 1964, William Manchester Papers, Wesleyan University.

12. McNamara, *In Retrospect*, 90.

13. McNamara, *In Retrospect*, 91–92.

14. C. Douglas Dillon, interview by William Manchester, August 14, 1964. Manchester noted on a copy of the interview transcript that "future historians may find it hard to credit" the description of McNamara.

15. Jackie Kennedy to Robert McNamara, November 30, 1963, Sotheby's Catalog, Lot #20.

16. Jackie Kennedy to Robert McNamara, December 11, 1963, Sotheby's Catalog, Lot #21.

17. Ben Bradlee to Robert McNamara, December 10, 1963, Sotheby's Catalog, Lot #103.

18. Robert McNamara, *In Retrospect*, 90–91.

19. Clark Clifford with Richard Holbrooke, *Counsel to the President: A Memoir* (New York: Anchor Books, 1992), 411–13.

20. Shapley, *Promise and Power*, 345.

21. Unclassified Personal Diary of John T. McNaughton, January 1, 1966–April 22, 1967, transcribed by Asheley Smith, 2003, 15, 16, 19.

22. Shapley, *Promise and Power*, 332–33.

23. Shapley, *Promise and Power*, 333.

24. Robert McNamara, interview by Brian VanDeMark, November 3, 1993.

25. Robert McNamara, interview by Errol Morris, December 11–12, 2001.

26. John Rinehart, interview by Paul Hendrickson, July 31, unknown year, Paul Hendrickson Archive, Pentagon folder.

27. Lady Bird Johnson's diary entries are held at the LBJ Presidential Library.

28. George Reedy Oral History, LBJ Presidential Library, 8:66.

29. George Reedy Oral History, LBJ Presidential Library, 20:16.

30. Jan Jarboe Russell, *Lady Bird: A Biography of Mrs. Johnson* (New York: Scribner, 1999), 184.

31. Russell, *Lady Bird*, 100–101.

32. Doris Kearns Goodwin, *Lyndon Johnson and the American Dream* (New York: Harper & Row, 1976), 41–42.

33. Robert A. Caro, *The Years of Lyndon Johnson: The Path to Power* (New York: Alfred A. Knopf, 1982), 74–75.

34. Caro, *The Path to Power*, 97.

35. Caro, *The Path to Power*, 59–60.

36. Caro, *The Path to Power*, 71, 72.

37. Robert Dallek, *Lone Star Rising: Lyndon Johnson and His Times 1908–1960* (New York: Oxford University Press, 1991), 36.

38. Caro, *The Path to Power*, 100.

39. D. Jablow Hershman and Gerald Tolchin, *Power Beyond Reason: The Mental Collapse of Lyndon Johnson* (Fort Lee, NJ: Barricade Books, 2002), 26.

40. Caro, *The Path to Power*, 102.

41. Caro, *The Path to Power*, 142, 143.

42. Dallek, *Lone Star Rising*, 67; Caro, *The Path to Power*, 160.

43. Dallek, *Lone Star Rising*, 68–69.

44. Caro, *The Path to Power*, 149–52.

45. Caro, *The Path to Power*, 147–48.

46. Dallek, *Lone Star Rising*, 80.

47. Caro, *The Path to Power*, 172.

48. Dallek, *Lone Star Rising*, 89–90.

49. Dallek, *Lone Star Rising*, 96–97; Caro, *The Path to Power*, 225–26.

50. Caro, *The Path to Power*, 237.

51. Caro, *The Path to Power*, 238–39.

52. Caro, *The Path to Power*, 228–29.

53. Russell, *Lady Bird*, 92.

54. Russell, *Lady Bird*, 92.

55. Betty Boyd Caroli, *Lady Bird and Lyndon: The Hidden Story of a Marriage That Made a President* (New York: Simon & Schuster, 2015), 70–73.

56. Caro, *The Path to Power*, 352–53, 359.

57. Caro, *The Path to Power*, 425.

58. Caro, *The Path to Power*, 607.

59. Caro, *The Path to Power*, 704.

60. Caro, *The Path to Power*, 731.

61. Robert A. Caro, *The Years of Lyndon Johnson: Means of Ascent* (New York: Alfred A. Knopf, 1990), xxviii.

62. Caro, *Means of Ascent*, 139–40.

63. Robert A. Caro, *The Years of Lyndon Johnson: Master of the Senate* (New York: Alfred A. Knopf, 2002), 1040.

64. Caro, *Master of the Senate*, 617.

65. Caro, *Master of the Senate*, 635.

66. Caro, *Master of the Senate*, 626, 630.

67. Russell, *Lady Bird Johnson*, 168.

68. Dallek, *Lone Star Rising*, 537.

69. Robert Dallek, *Flawed Giant: Lyndon Johnson and His Times, 1961–1973* (New York: Oxford University Press, 1998), 4.

70. Russell, *Lady Bird Johnson*, 209–10.

71. Robert A. Caro, *The Years of Lyndon Johnson: The Passage of Power* (New York: Alfred A. Knopf, 2012), 165.

72. Dallek, *Flawed Giant*, 7, 9–10.

73. Caro, *The Passage of Power*, 181–82, 204.

74. Russell, *Lady Bird Johnson*, 244–45.

75. Russell, *Lady Bird Johnson*, 245.

76. Jussell, *Lady Bird Johnson*, 129.
77. Lady Bird Johnson, Diary Entry, March 7, 1965, LBJ Presidential Library.
78. VanDeMark, *Road to Disaster*, 211.
79. Kearns Goodwin, *Lyndon Johnson and the American Dream*, 177.
80. Neil Sheehan, "You Don't Know Where Johnson Ends and McNamara Begins," *New York Times Magazine*, October 22, 1967.
81. Lyndon Johnson to Robert McNamara, January 29, 1964, Miller Center.
82. Lyndon Johnson to Robert McNamara, April 14, 1964, Miller Center.
83. Halberstam, *The Best and the Brightest*, 434.
84. Kearns Goodwin, *Lyndon Johnson and the American Dream*, 175.
85. Shapley, *Promise and Power*, 277–78.
86. Shapley, *Promise and Power*, xi.
87. Lyndon Johnson and Robert McNamara, August 1, 1964, White House Recording.
88. Caro, *Master of the Senate*, 136.
89. Kearns Goodwin, *Lyndon Johnson and the American Dream*, 119.
90. Caro, *Master of the Senate*, 130.
91. Hubert Humphrey, *The Education of a Public Man: My Life and Politics* (Minneapolis: University of Minnesota Press, 1991), 116.
92. Richard N. Goodwin, *Remembering America: A Voice from the Sixties* (New York: Open Road Integrated Media, 2014), 380.
93. Bill Moyers, email message to the authors, August 23, 2021.
94. Shapley, *Promise and Power*, 278–79.
95. VanDeMark, *Road to Disaster*, 211.
96. Robert McNamara, interview by Errol Morris, December 11–12, 2001.
97. Robert McNamara, April 16, 1964, White House Recording.
98. Robert McNamara, November 5, 1964, White House Recording.
99. James Blight, janet Lang, and David Welch, *Vietnam If Kennedy Had Lived: Virtual JFK* (Lanham, MD: Rowman & Littlefield, 2009), 388n24.
100. McNamara, *In Retrospect*, 98.
101. Robert McNamara, interview by Errol Morris, May 1–2, 2001.
102. Henry Brandon, Notes after Conversation with Robert McNamara, December 21, 1966, Henry Brandon Papers, Library of Congress, Box 60, folder 4.
103. Henry Brandon, Notes after Conversation with Maggie [*sic*] McNamara, December 23, 1966, Henry Brandon Papers, Library of Congress, Box 60, folder 4.
104. Henry Brandon, *Anatomy of Error: The Inside Story of the Asian War on the Potomac, 1954–1969* (Boston: Gambit, 1970), 68.
105. Robert McNamara, interview by Errol Morris, December 11–12, 2001.
106. McNamara, *In Retrospect*, 98.

CHAPTER NINE: TURNING POINTS

1. VanDeMark, *Road to Disaster*, 214–16.
2. Kearns Goodwin, *Lyndon Johnson and the American Dream*, 178.
3. VanDeMark, *Road to Disaster*, 214–16.
4. Shapley, *Promise and Power*, 292.
5. McGeorge Bundy, interview by Robert McNamara and Brian VanDeMark, March 18, 1994.
6. Merle Miller, *Lyndon: An Oral Biography* (New York: Putnam, 1980), 166.
7. VanDeMark, *Road to Disaster*, 218–19.
8. VanDeMark, *Road to Disaster*, 219.
9. Peter L. W. Osnos, "The Accidental President, Part Six," *LBJ and McNamara: The Vietnam Partnership Destined to Fail*, Peter Osnos Platform on Substack, July 9, 2024; Caro, *The Passage of Power*.
10. "The War in South Vietnam—Three Aspects of an Increasingly Critical Battle," *New York Times*, March 1, 1964.

11. Lyndon Johnson and Robert McNamara, White House Recording, March 2, 1964, Miller Center.
12. Jack Raymond, "McNamara Says Hanoi Increases Help to Vietcong," *New York Times*, March 6, 1964.
13. Rufus Phillips, interview by Paul Hendrickson, February 6, 1986, Paul Hendrickson Archive, Pentagon folder.
14. McNamara, *In Retrospect*, 118.
15. Lyndon Johnson, White House Recording, May 27, 1964, LBJ Presidential Library.
16. Lyndon Johnson, White House Recording, May 27, 1964, LBJ Presidential Library.
17. VanDeMark, *Road to Disaster*, 242–43.
18. Lyndon Johnson and Robert McNamara, White House Recording, August 3, 1964.
19. John Herrick, "Cable Regarding Weather and Lack of Visual by Maddox," August 4, 1964, LBJ Presidential Library, National Security File, Country File, Vietnam, Box 228, folder 2.
20. Ellsberg, *Secrets*, 7–12.
21. Lyndon Johnson, Statement by the President, August 4, 1964, LBJ Presidential Library, Bill Moyers Papers, Box 132, folder 7, "Tonkin Gulf Attack."
22. Goldstein, *Lessons in Disaster*, 122.
23. VanDeMark, *Road to Disaster*, 239–49.
24. Ellsberg, *Secrets*, 7–20.
25. Jackie Kennedy to Robert McNamara, July 2, 1964, Diana McNamara Archive, Correspondence—Jackie Kennedy folder. Jackie's reference in the letter to "your book" and her decision to start reading it at page 44 does not specify which McNamara book she was referring to. As of July 1964, McNamara had not written or published a book of his own. Jackie's reference seems to have been to a book that McNamara liked and wanted her to read.
26. Jeff Shesol, *Mutual Contempt: Lyndon Johnson, Robert Kennedy, and the Feud That Defined a Decade* (New York: W. W. Norton, 1997), 111.
27. Arthur M. Schlesinger Jr., *Robert Kennedy and His Times* (Boston: Mariner Books, 2018), 650.
28. Tye, *Bobby Kennedy*, 303.
29. Tye, *Bobby Kennedy*, 115.
30. Tye, *Bobby Kennedy*, 105, 115–16.
31. Tye, *Bobby Kennedy*, 272; Evan Thomas, *Robert Kennedy: His Life* (New York: Simon & Schuster, 2000), 214.
32. Tye, *Bobby Kennedy*, 295.
33. Schlesinger, *Robert Kennedy*, 627.
34. Tye, *Bobby Kennedy*, 279; Schlesinger, *Robert Kennedy*, 627.
35. Lyndon Johnson and Robert McNamara, August 1, 1964, White House Recording, Miller Center.
36. Robert McNamara, interview by Brian VanDeMark and Peter Osnos, October 9, 1993.
37. Lyndon Johnson and Robert McNamara, White House Recording, August 9, 1964.
38. Shapley, *Promise and Power*, 288.
39. Shapley, *Promise and Power*, 309–13.
40. Robert McNamara, interview by Brian VanDeMark, September 20, 1993.
41. Peter L. W. Osnos, "The State Department, Part Seven," *LBJ and McNamara: The Vietnam Partnership Destined to Fail*, Peter Osnos Platform on Substack, July 16, 2024.
42. McNamara, *In Retrospect*, 162.
43. VanDeMark, *Road to Disaster*, 255–58.
44. McMaster, *Dereliction of Duty*, 94, 326.
45. McMaster, *Dereliction of Duty*, 326.
46. McMaster, *Dereliction of Duty*, 326–27.
47. McMaster, *Dereliction of Duty*, 327–28.
48. McMaster, *Dereliction of Duty*, 97, 327–30.
49. Brian VanDeMark, email to the authors, October 13, 2024.
50. Douglas Kiker, "The Education of Robert McNamara," *Atlantic Monthly*, March 1967.

51. President Johnson to Taylor, December 30, 1964, *Foreign Relations of the United States, 1964–1968*, 1:1057–59.

52. Michael Beschloss, *Reaching for Glory: Lyndon Johnson's Secret White House Tapes, 1964–1965* (New York: Simon & Schuster, 2002), 157–58.

53. Robert McNamara, interview by McGeorge Bundy and Brian VanDeMark, March 18, 1994.

54. Telephone Conversation Between President Johnson and Secretary of Defense McNamara, January 17, 1966, *Foreign Relations of the United States, 1964–1968*, vol. 4, Vietnam, 1966.

55. McGeorge Bundy, Memorandum for the President, "Basic Policy in Vietnam," January 27, 1965, LBJ Presidential Library, National Security File, Country File, Vietnam, "Volume 28," Box 13.

56. VanDeMark, *Road to Disaster*, 262–64.

57. Lady Bird Johnson, Diary Entry, January 29, 1965, LBJ Presidential Library.

58. Dallek, *Lone Star Rising*, 282.

59. Dallek, *Lone Star Rising*, 283.

60. Robert McNamara, interview by Suzan Travis-Robyns, September 21, 1995.

61. Lady Bird Johnson, Diary Entry, February 7, 1965, and February 11, 1965, LBJ Presidential Library.

62. VanDeMark, *Road to Disaster*, 268.

63. Ellsberg, *Secrets*, 57.

64. McNamara, *In Retrospect*, 172–74.

65. McGeorge Bundy to Robert McNamara, March 24, 1994, JFK Presidential Library, McGeorge Bundy Personal Papers, Box 189, folder 12.

66. Kearns Goodwin, *An Unfinished Love Story*, 247–49.

67. McGeorge Bundy to Robert McNamara, March 24, 1994, JFK Presidential Library, McGeorge Bundy Personal Papers, Box 189, folder 12.

68. "Excerpts from Transcript of McNamara's Report," *New York Times*, April 27, 1965.

69. Humphrey, *The Education of a Public*, 318–19.

70. Charles Garrettson III, *Hubert H. Humphrey: The Politics of Joy* (New Brunswick, NJ: Transaction Publishers, 1993), 323–26; Memorandum from Vice President Humphrey to President Johnson, February 17, 1965, *Foreign Relations of the United States, 1964–1968*, vol. 2, Vietnam, January–June 1965.

71. Thomas Hughes, *Perilous Encounters: The Cold War Collisions of Domestic and World Politics* (Xlibris, 2011), 159–60.

72. Even after Humphrey returned to the fold, Johnson continued the torture. In 1967, during a walk in Rock Creek Park with Hughes ("This is the only place I feel free to talk," said the vice president), he recounted how he and his wife had recently invited the Johnsons to dine in their new apartment. While Lady Bird and Muriel Humphrey were preparing steaks in the kitchen, Johnson suddenly said, "Hubert, I hear you make the best speeches in explaining our country's effort in Vietnam. From the reports I get, you are our greatest national resource for dealing with members of the public who do not seem to understand the need for a patriotic commitment to the defense of freedom in Southeast Asia."

"Oh, I just say the usual things," replied Humphrey, trying to make light of the issue. But Johnson wanted "to hear more." Humphrey quickly summarized some of his stock arguments, but that wasn't enough either. "Give me one of your actual speeches. You've made some of these speeches, I know. Now, come on, let me just hear you say it."

Humphrey stood up in his own living room and started to comply. At that point, Johnson arose and headed to the bathroom. "Keep talkin', Hubert," he said over his shoulder. "I'm listenin'." Carl Solberg, *Hubert Humphrey: A Biography* (New York: W. W. Norton, 1984), 301–2.

73. George Ball, Memorandum, October 5, 1964.

74. George Ball, *The Past Has Another Pattern* (New York: W. W. Norton, 1982), 390.

75. Ball, *The Past Has Another Pattern*, 390.

76. Lady Bird Johnson, Diary Entry, March 7, 1965, LBJ Presidential Library.

77. Lady Bird Johnson, Diary Entry, March 13, 1965.

78. Goodwin, *Remembering America*, 576–78.
79. Goodwin, *Remembering America*, 583–84.
80. Goodwin, *Remembering America*, 584–85.
81. A. J. Langguth, *Our Vietnam: The War, 1954–1975* (New York: Simon & Schuster, 2000), 366–69.
82. Goodwin, *Remembering America*, 597.
83. Robert McNamara and Lyndon Johnson, June 17, 1965, White House Recording.
84. Thomas, *Robert Kennedy*, 314.
85. Lyndon Johnson and Robert McNamara, June 21, 1965, White House Recording.
86. Lyndon Johnson and Robert McNamara, June 30, 1965, White House Recording.
87. Lady Bird Johnson, Diary Entry, July 8, 1965.
88. Goodwin, *Remembering America*, 589.
89. McNamara, *In Retrospect*, 200–201; Lyndon Johnson and Robert McNamara, July 2, 1965, White House Recording.
90. Jackie Kennedy to Robert McNamara, Summer 1965, Sotheby's Catalog, Lot 44; Leaming, *Jacqueline Bouvier Kennedy Onassis*, 199.
91. Clifford, *Counsel to the President*, 410.
92. Clifford, *Counsel to the President*, 411–13.
93. Clifford, *Counsel to the President*, 413–16.
94. Julia Sweig, *Lady Bird Johnson: Hiding in Plain Sight* (New York: Random House, 2021), 177.
95. Clifford, *Counsel to the President*, 418–20.
96. Osnos, "The Accidental President, Part Six."
97. James Reston, "Notes of conversations with several newsmakers," August 2, 1965, James Reston Papers, University of Illinois Archives.
98. VanDeMark, *Road to Disaster*, 315.
99. VanDeMark, *Road to Disaster*, 269.
100. This account comes from VanDeMark, *Road to Disaster*; Hendrickson, *The Living and the Dead*; and Shapley, *Promise and Power*. These sources differ in their narratives, but the authors have sought to establish the most accurate composite account possible.
101. Shapley, *Promise and Power*, 353–54; McNamara, *In Retrospect*, 216.
102. Robert McNamara, interview by Errol Morris, April 2, 2001.
103. Anne Morrison Welsh with Joyce Hollyday, *Held in the Light: Norman Morrison's Sacrifice for Peace and His Family's Journey of Healing* (Ossining, NY: Orbis Books, 2008), 96.
104. Robert McNamara, *In Retrospect*, 217.
105. McNamara, *In Retrospect*, 222.
106. McNamara, *In Retrospect*, 221–22.
107. VanDeMark, *Road to Disaster*, 316.
108. VanDeMark, *Road to Disaster*, 317.
109. VanDeMark, *Road to Disaster*, 318–21.
110. John McNaughton, Diary Entry, January 1, 1966.
111. VanDeMark, *Road to Disaster*, 322.
112. Barbara Leaming, *Jacqueline Bouvier Kennedy Onassis*, 202.
113. Bird, *The Color of Truth*, 345.
114. VanDeMark, *Road to Disaster*, 326–27. See also Schlesinger, *Robert Kennedy*, 734–35.

CHAPTER TEN: EQUIVOCATION

1. Robert McNamara, transcript of meeting with Peter Osnos and Brian VanDeMark, December 14, 1993.
2. Robert McNamara, interview by Peter Osnos and Brian VanDeMark, April 4, 1994.
3. Robert McNamara, transcript of editing meeting with Peter Osnos, Geoff Shandler, and Brian VanDeMark, July 19, 1994.
4. Shapley, *Promise and Power*, 460.
5. Craig McNamara, *Because Our Fathers Lied*, 32.

6. Edgar Boyles, interview by Philip Taubman, August 21, 2019.

7. Shapley, *Promise and Power*, 367.

8. John McNaughton, Diary Entry, January 25, 1966.

9. McGeorge Bundy to Robert McNamara, March 24, 1994, JFK Presidential Library, McGeorge Bundy Personal Papers, Box 189, folder 12.

10. Robert McNamara, Notes on Post-Defense Offers, Library of Congress, Robert S. McNamara Papers, Box 1:89, folder 5.

11. McNamara, *In Retrospect*, 235.

12. John McNaughton, Diary Entry, January 31, 1966.

13. McGeorge Bundy to Robert McNamara, March 24, 1994.

14. John McNaughton, Diary Entry, January 29, 1966.

15. Edward J. Drea, *Secretaries of Defense Historical Series*, vol. 6: *McNamara, Clifford, and the Burdens of Vietnam, 1965–1969* (Washington, DC: Historical Office, Office of the Secretary of Defense, 2011), 178.

16. John McNaughton, Diary Entry, April 4, 1966.

17. John McNaughton, Diary Entry, April 6, 1966.

18. John McNaughton, Diary Entry, April 8, 1966.

19. John McNaughton, Diary Entry, April 30, 1966.

20. Tom Wicker, Memorandum, "Conversation with President Johnson," April 25, 1966, University of Illinois Archives in Urbana-Champaign, James Reston Papers, Box 57.

21. Robert McNamara, "The Age of Protest" (speech, Chatham College, Pittsburgh, May 22, 1966), copied in 112 Cong. Rec. A3456 (1966) (statement of Representative Moorhead).

22. Robert McNamara, "Security in the Contemporary World" (speech, Montreal, May 18, 1966), copied in *The New York Times*, May 19, 1966.

23. John McNaughton, Diary Entry, May 18, 1966.

24. Robert McNamara, interview by Errol Morris, December 11–12, 2001.

25. Hubert Humphrey to Robert McNamara, May 19, 1966, James Cummins Bookseller, Catalog.

26. Mary McGrory in *The Washington Star*, May 19, 1966.

27. James Reston, "Washington: The Computer That Turned Philosopher," *New York Times*, May 22, 1966.

28. McNamara, *In Retrospect*, 253; *New York Times*, June 7, 1966; "McNamara's Return," *Amherst Magazine*, Summer 1987, 19–20; *Amherst Student*, June 2, 1966.

29. Telephone Conversation between President Johnson and Robert McNamara, June 28, 1966, Tape 10266 (WH606.06), Miller Center White House Recordings, quoted in Brian VanDeMark, *Road to Disaster*, 361.

30. VanDeMark, *Road to Disaster*, 361–63.

31. VanDeMark, *Road to Disaster*, 361–63.

32. Lady Bird Johnson, Diary Entry, September 1, 1966, LBJ Presidential Library.

33. Memorandum from Secretary of Defense McNamara to President Johnson, October 14, 1966, *Foreign Relations of the United States, 1964–1968*, vol. 4, Vietnam, 1966.

34. VanDeMark, *Road to Disaster*, 367.

35. John McNaughton, Diary Entry, October 18, 1966.

36. Ellsberg, *Secrets*, 142.

37. Robert McNamara, "Remarks to the Press Upon Return from Saigon, with General Wheeler," October 14, 1966, LBJ Presidential Library, Personal Papers of Robert S. McNamara (General) Public Statements, 1966, Volume 7.

38. Memorandum from the Joint Chiefs of Staff to Secretary of Defense McNamara, October 14, 1966, *Foreign Relations of the United States, 1964–1968*, vol. 4, Vietnam, 1966, quoted in VanDeMark, *Road to Disaster*, 368.

39. "Recommended FY 67 Southeast Asia Supplemental Appropriation," November 17, 1966, McNaughton Files, Paul Warnke Papers, LBJ Library, quoted in Brian VanDeMark, *Road to Disaster*, 368.

40. James G. Hershberg, *Marigold: The Lost Chance for Peace in Vietnam* (Stanford, CA: Stanford University Press, 2012), 695–731.

41. Robert McNamara, interview by Bob Woodward, August 7, 2007.
42. Robert McNamara, interview by Brian VanDeMark and Peter Osnos, July 19, 1994.
43. Kearns Goodwin, *An Unfinished Love Story*, 289–90.
44. Jackie Kennedy to Robert McNamara, September 14, 1966, Diana McNamara Archive.
45. Jackie Kennedy to Robert McNamara, November 9, 1966, Sotheby's Catalog.
46. Robert McNamara, letter "to be delivered at the time of my death to the then secretary of defense," October 4, 1966, Diana McNamara archive.
47. McNamara, *In Retrospect*, 257–58.
48. Robert McNamara, interview by Brian VanDeMark and Peter Osnos, July 19, 1994.
49. Robert McNamara, interview by Errol Morris, December 11–12, 2001.
50. Barney Frank, interview by William Taubman, August 2, 2019; McNamara, *In Retrospect*, 254–57; Shapley, *Promise and Power*, 376–77; Hendrickson, *The Living and the Dead*, 285–86.
51. Graham Allison, "Impressions of the Secretary of Defense," November 15, 1966, John F. Kennedy Presidential Library, Adam Yarmolinsky Papers, Box 53, Harvard Institute of Politics, McNamara Visit 1966 folder.
52. Allison, "Impressions of the Secretary of Defense."
53. John McNaughton, Diary Entry, December 11, 1966.
54. John McNaughton, Diary Entry, December 16, 1966.
55. John McNaughton, Diary Entry, January 27, 1967.
56. John McNaughton, Diary Entry, February 13, 1967.

CHAPTER ELEVEN: MELTDOWN

1. McNamara, *In Retrospect*, 257.
2. Peter L. W. Osnos, "When Everything Changed, Part Five," *LBJ and McNamara: The Vietnam Partnership Destined to Fail*, Peter Osnos Platform on Substack, July 2, 2024.
3. Tye, *Bobby Kennedy*, 37.
4. Thomas, *Robert Kennedy*, 314.
5. Peter L. W. Osnos, "Jackie, Bobby, LBJ, Bob: Friends and Foes, Part Fourteen," *LBJ and McNamara: The Vietnam Partnership Destined to Fail*, Peter Osnos Platform on Substack, September 3, 2024.
6. Schlesinger, *Robert Kennedy*, 741, 822.
7. Thomas, *Robert Kennedy*, 314.
8. Shapley, *Promise and Power*, 410.
9. Shapley, *Promise and Power*, 425.
10. Margy Pastor, interview by William Taubman, September 29, 2019; Shapley, *Promise and Power*, 380.
11. Shapley, *Promise and Power*, 379–80.
12. Craig McNamara, *Because Our Fathers Lied*, 6, 9.
13. Shapley, *Promise and Power*, 380–81; Margy Pastor, interview by William Taubman, September 29, 2019.
14. Craig McNamara, interview by Philip Taubman, May 5, 2024.
15. Brian VanDeMark, *Road to Disaster*, 410.
16. Shapley, *Promise and Power*, 380; VanDeMark, *Road to Disaster*, 403.
17. Paul Hendrickson, interview notes with Henry Glass, March 10, 1986, Paul Hendrickson Archive, Pentagon folder.
18. Shapley, *Promise and Power*, 406.
19. Saul Pett, "McNamara Estimate of Pentagon Career," *Washington Star*, February 4, 1968, copied in 114 Cong. Rec. 4638 (1968) (statement of Senator Hart).
20. Shapley, *Promise and Power*, 415.
21. Jackie Kennedy to Robert McNamara, February 27, 1968, Sotheby's Catalog, Lot #55.
22. Osnos, "Jackie, Bobby, LBJ, Bob: Friends and Foes, Part Fourteen."
23. Douglas Kiker, "The Education of Robert McNamara," *Atlantic Monthly*, March 1967.
24. Lloyd Shearer, "Will the Real Robert McNamara Please Stand Up?" *Parade*, March 5, 1967.

25. Jackie Kennedy to Robert McNamara, March 7, 1967, Sotheby's Catalog, Lot #54.
26. John McNaughton, Diary Entry, March 12, 1967.
27. Jackie Kennedy to Robert McNamara, April 15, 1967, Sotheby's Catalog, Lot #55.
28. McNamara, *In Retrospect*, 312.
29. Robert McNamara, interview by Errol Morris, December 11–12, 2001.
30. Trewhitt, *McNamara*, 238.
31. These organizations include Harvard University, Johns Hopkins University, the University of California, US Steel, Montgomery Ward, the Ford Foundation, and the Rockefeller Foundation. Robert S. McNamara Papers, Library of Congress, Box 1:89, folder 5.
32. Robert McNamara, transcript of editing meeting with Peter Osnos, Brian VanDeMark, and Geoff Shandler, July 19, 1994.
33. Draft Memorandum from Secretary of Defense McNamara to President Johnson, May 19, 1967, *Foreign Relations of the United States, 1964–1968*, vol. 5, Vietnam, 1967; Shapley, *Promise and Power*, 418–20.
34. Walt Rostow, Memorandum, May 20, 1967, LBJ Presidential Library, National Security File, Country File, Vietnam, Box 75, folder 1, 2 EE.
35. "274 US Deaths in Week's Combat Highest of War," *New York Times*, March 31, 1967.
36. VanDeMark, *Road to Disaster*, 383–85.
37. Leaming, *Jacqueline Bouvier Kennedy Onassis*, 226–27.
38. Bobby Kennedy to Robert McNamara, May 30, 1967, Guernsey's Catalog, Lot 392.
39. Jackie Kennedy to Margy McNamara, June 1, 1967, Diana McNamara Archive.
40. VanDeMark, *Road to Disaster*, 387–88.
41. VanDeMark, *Road to Disaster*, 385–87.
42. Tom Johnson, Notes of Meeting, July 12, 1967, *Foreign Relations of the United States, 1964–1968*, vol. 5, Vietnam, 1967.
43. Tom Johnson, Notes of Meeting: Tuesday Lunch Group, July 12, 1967, LBJ Presidential Library, Tom Johnson Personal Papers, Box 1.
44. Max Frankel, "McNamara Sees No Reserve Call for Vietnam War," *New York Times*, July 13, 1967.
45. "35 Americans Die in Vietnam Clash," *New York Times*, July 13, 1967.
46. McNamara, *In Retrospect*, 283.
47. Paul Hendrickson, Notes about Interview with John Maddux, November 7, 1986, Paul Hendrickson Archive.
48. "Ulcer Slows Pace of Mrs. McNamara," Washington News Service, August 4, 1967.
49. McNamara, *In Retrospect*, 296.
50. McNamara, *In Retrospect*, 296.
51. Tom Johnson, Notes of Meeting, Tuesday Luncheon, July 25, 1967, LBJ Presidential Library, Tom Johnson Personal Papers, Box 1.
52. Tom Johnson, Notes of Meeting, Tuesday Luncheon, August 8, 1967, LBJ Presidential Library, Tom Johnson Personal Papers, Box 1.
53. Tom Johnson, Notes of Meeting, Tuesday Luncheon, August 8, 1967, LBJ Presidential Library, Tom Johnson Personal Papers, Box 1. Emphasis in the original.
54. Robert McNamara, interview by Errol Morris, May 1–2, 2001.
55. Eugene Zuckert, interview by Brian VanDeMark, October 29, 1992.
56. Testimony of Robert McNamara, "Air War Against North Vietnam: Hearings Before the Preparedness Investigating Subcommittee of the Committee on Armed Services, United States Senate, Ninetieth Congress, First Session," August 25, 1967 (Washington, DC: US Government Printing Office, 1967); Brian VanDeMark, *Road to Disaster*, 391–400; Shapley, *Promise and Power*, 428–30.
57. VanDeMark, *The Road to Disaster*, 400.
58. Paul Hendrickson, Notes from Interview with Roswell Gilpatric, May 29, 1985, Paul Hendrickson Archive, Pentagon folder.
59. Byrne, *The Whiz Kids*, 458.

60. Quoted in VanDeMark, *Road to Disaster*, 402.

61. James Reston to Adam Yarmolinsky, August 28, 1967, JFK Library, Adam Yarmolinsky Papers, Box 271.

62. Tom Johnson, Notes of Meeting, Tuesday Luncheon, September 26, 1967.

63. McGeorge Bundy to Robert McNamara, March 24, 1994, JFK Library.

64. Paul Hendrickson, "McNamara: Specters of Vietnam," *Washington Post*, May 10, 1984.

65. Jackie Kennedy to Robert McNamara, October 1967, Sotheby's Catalog.

66. Jackie Kennedy to Robert McNamara, March 17, 1967, Sotheby's Catalog, Lot #54.

67. Jackie Kennedy to Robert McNamara, October 1967.

68. Carol Reed, dir., *The Third Man* (1949; London: British Lion Film Corporation).

69. Shapley, *Promise and Power*, 434–35.

70. McNamara, *In Retrospect*, 312.

71. Draft Memorandum from Secretary of Defense McNamara to President Johnson, November 1, 1967, *Foreign Relations of the United States, 1964–1968*, vol. 5, Vietnam, 1967.

72. Address before the Tennessee Legislature, March 15, 1967, *Public Papers of the Presidents, Lyndon B. Johnson, 1967* (Washington, DC: US Government Printing Office, 1968), 348–54; VanDeMark, *Road to Disaster*, 363.

73. Dean Rusk, Memorandum to the President, November 20, 1967, LBJ Presidential Library, National Security File, Files of Walt W. Rostow, Box 3, folder 18.

74. Lyndon Johnson, Memorandum, December 18, 1967, LBJ Presidential Library, National Security File, Files of Walt W. Rostow, Box 3, folder 19.

75. Osnos, "The State Department, Part Seven."

76. McNamara, *In Retrospect*, 282.

77. McNamara, *In Retrospect*, 312–13.

78. Walt Rostow, Memorandum to the President, November 25, 1967, LBJ Presidential Library, National Security File, Files of Walt W. Rostow, Box 14, folder 3.

79. Tom Johnson, interview by Philip Taubman and William Taubman, August 6, 2021.

80. McNamara, *In Retrospect*, 313.

81. Paul Hendrickson, interview notes with Henry Glass, March 10, 1986, Paul Hendrickson Archive, Pentagon folder.

82. Tom Johnson, Memorandum for the President, November 29, 1967, LBJ Presidential Library, White House Confidential File, FG 115, Box 27, folder 3.

83. "McNamara's Next Mission," *Washington Post*, November 30, 1967.

84. Robert McNamara, interview by Errol Morris, December 11–12, 2001.

85. Edward Kosner, "McNamara: Why Is He Leaving?" *Newsweek*, December 11, 1967.

86. Adam Yarmolinsky, interview by Brian VanDeMark, April 1, 1993.

87. Neil Sheehan, Notes from Interview with Bobby Kennedy, October 17, 1967, Library of Congress, Neil Sheehan Papers, Box 191, folder 4.

88. Shesol, *Mutual Contempt*, 393–94.

89. Thomas, *Robert Kennedy*, 350.

90. VanDeMark, *Road to Disaster*, 403–4.

91. Robert McNamara, interview by David Ginsburg and Brian VanDeMark, April 14, 1994.

92. Robert McNamara, interview by Charlie Rose, April 17, 1995.

93. McNamara, *In Retrospect*, 314.

94. Osnos, "JFK and McNamara, Part Three."

95. Robert McNamara, interview by Brian VanDeMark, January 14, 1993.

96. Brock Brower, "McNamara Seen Now, Full Length," *Life*, May 10, 1968.

97. Brower, "McNamara Seen Now, Full Length."

98. Brower, "McNamara Seen Now, Full Length."

99. Robert McNamara, interview by Charlie Rose, April 17, 1995.

100. Robert McNamara, interview by Charlie Rose, April 17, 1995.

101. Robert McNamara, interview by Charlie Rose, April 17, 1995.

102. VanDeMark, *Road to Disaster*, 451–52.

103. Lady Bird Johnson, Diary Entry, February 28, 1968, LBJ Presidential Library.

104. VanDeMark, *Road to Disaster*, 454.

105. McNamara, *In Retrospect*, 317.

106. VanDeMark, *Road to Disaster*, 425.

107. Robert McNamara, meeting with Brian VanDeMark and Peter Osnos, September 16, 1994. Osnos, a former *Washington Post* reporter, was the editor and publisher of McNamara's *In Retrospect*.

108. David Ginsburg, interview by Brian VanDeMark and Robert McNamara, April 14, 1994.

109. Robert McNamara, interview by Brain VanDeMark, Alfred Goldberg, and other O.S.D. historians, April 29, 1994.

110. Robert McNamara, interview by McGeorge Bundy and Brian VanDeMark, March 18, 1994.

111. McGeorge Bundy, interview by Robert McNamara and Brian VanDeMark, March 18, 1994.

112. Robert McNamara, interview by McGeorge Bundy and Brian VanDeMark, March 18, 1994.

113. Robert McNamara, transcript of meeting regarding *In Retrospect*, September 16, 1994.

114. Kearns Goodwin, *Lyndon Johnson and the American Dream*, 320–21.

115. Tom Johnson, Notes of Meeting, Tuesday Luncheon, January 23, 1968, LBJ Presidential Library, Tom Johnson Personal Papers, Box 2.

116. Peter L. W. Osnos, "The Break, Part Sixteen," *LBJ and McNamara: The Vietnam Partnership Destined to Fail*, Peter Osnos Platform on Substack, September 17, 2024.

117. Tom Johnson, Notes of Meeting, Tuesday Luncheon, February 6, 1967, LBJ Presidential Library, Tom Johnson Personal Papers, Box 2.

118. Brian VanDeMark, email to the authors, October 13, 2024.

119. Robert McNamara, transcript of editing meeting with Brian VanDeMark and Peter Osnos, July 19, 1994.

CHAPTER TWELVE: SWORDS TO PLOWSHARES

1. Hendrickson, *The Living and the Dead*, 74.

2. Robert McNamara, interview by Errol Morris, December 11–12, 2001.

3. Leif Christoffersen, interview by William Taubman, October 2, 2019.

4. Robert McNamara, interview by Suzan Travis-Robyns, September 20–21, 1995, Robert S. McNamara Papers, Library of Congress, Box 2:132.

5. Shapley, *Promise and Power*, 10.

6. Olivier Lafourcade et al., *Robert S. McNamara at the World Bank: In Retrospect* (Washington, DC: World Bank, 2021), 18, 5, 7, 60, 67.

7. Patrick Allen Sharma, *Robert McNamara's Other War: The World Bank and International Development* (Philadelphia: University of Pennsylvania Press, 2017), 16.

8. Shapley, *Promise and Power*, 477.

9. Shapley, *Promise and Power*, 464.

10. Olivier Lafourcade interview by William Taubman, September 28, 2019.

11. William Clark, "Robert McNamara at the World Bank," *Foreign Affairs* 60, no. 1 (Fall 1981): 167–84.

12. Sharma, *McNamara's Other War*, 27.

13. Sharma, *McNamara's Other War*, 55–57, 75.

14. Robert McNamara, "Address to the Board of Governors" (speech, Nairobi, Kenya, September 24, 1973), World Bank Group.

15. Clark, "Robert McNamara at the World Bank."

16. Shapley, *Promise and Power*, 512.

17. Robert McNamara, "Introduction," in Robert Kennedy, *13 Days: A Memoir of the Cuban Missile Crisis* (New York: W. W. Norton, 1969), 21.

18. Robert McNamara, interview by Brian VanDeMark and Peter Osnos, October 9, 1993.

19. "Indiscretion," *New York Times*, April 16, 1968.

20. Robert McNamara, interview by Brian VanDeMark and Peter Osnos, October 9, 1993.

21. Robert McNamara, interview by Errol Morris, April 2, 2002.

22. Shapley, *Promise and Power*, 474–75.

23. Lady Bird Johnson, Diary Entry, June 8, 1968, Lady Bird Johnson's White House Diary Collection, LBJ Presidential Library, quoted in *The Lady Bird Diaries*, directed by Dawn Porter (Trilogy Films and ABC News, 2023), 1:40:00.

24. Jackie Kennedy to Robert McNamara, July 16, 1968, Sotheby's Catalog, Lot #80.

25. Robert McNamara, USS JFK Commissioning Address (speech, Newport News, VA, September 7, 1968), World Bank Archives, Records of President Robert S. McNamara, USS JFK Kennedy commissioning address—Correspondence 01 folder.

26. His behavior is depicted in a video of the commissioning: HelmerReenberg, "September 7, 1968—Jacqueline Kennedy and Family at Commissioning of USS John F. Kennedy Carrier," YouTube, 1:59, September 7, 2015, https://www.youtube.com/watch?v=lOVrK0-_hZ4.

27. Jackie Kennedy to Robert McNamara, September 7 or 8, 1968, Sotheby's Catalog, Lot #81.

28. Jackie Kennedy to Robert McNamara, March 6, 1969, Robert Cohn Collection, Stanford University Libraries.

29. Edward Kennedy to Robert and Margy McNamara, September 13, 1969, Diana McNamara Archive, Topic File—the Kennedy Family folder.

30. Edward Kennedy to Robert and Margy McNamara, October 7, 1970, Diana McNamara Archive, Topic File—the Kennedy Family folder.

31. See Kennedy correspondence folders in the Robert S. McNamara Papers, Library of Congress, and the Diana McNamara Archive.

32. Nathaniel McKitterick, "The World Bank & the McNamara Legacy," *National Interest* No. 4 (Summer 1986), 45–52; Sharma, *McNamara's Other War*, 43–47.

33. Sharma, *McNamara's Other War*, 66–67.

34. Leif Christoffersen, interview by William Taubman, October 2, 2019.

35. Olivier Lafourcade, interview by William Taubman, September 28, 2019.

36. William Clark, interview by Paul Hendrickson, December 3, 1984, Hendrickson Collection, World Bank folder.

37. Montague Yudelman, interview by Paul Hendrickson, November 28, 1986, Hendrickson Collection, World Bank folder.

38. William Clark, interview by Paul Hendrickson, December 3, 1984, Hendrickson Collection, World Bank folder.

39. Leif Christoffersen, interview by William Taubman, October 2, 2019; Olivier Lafourcade, interview by William Taubman, September 28, 2019.

40. Clark, "McNamara at the World Bank."

41. See, e.g., Stephen Ambrose, *Nixon: Volume Two: The Triumph of a Politician, 1962–1972* (New York: Simon & Schuster, 1989), 508.

42. Clark, "McNamara at the World Bank," 176.

43. Leif Christoffersen, interview by William Taubman, October 2, 2019.

44. Sharma, *McNamara's Other War*, 169.

45. Olivier Lafourcade, interview by William Taubman, September 28, 2019.

46. Sharma, *McNamara's Other War*, 30.

47. Leif Christoffersen, interview by William Taubman, October 2, 2019.

48. Lafourcade et al., *Robert S. McNamara at the World Bank*, 67.

49. Shapley, *Promise and Power*, 526.

50. Robert McNamara, interview by Errol Morris, December 11–12, 2001.

51. Shapley, *Promise and Power*, 470.

52. Leif Christoffersen, interview by William Taubman, October 2, 2019.

53. Olivier Lafourcade interview by William Taubman, September 28, 2019.

54. Robert McNamara to Jackie Kennedy Onassis, late October 1975, written on Robert McNamara to Leopold Senghor, October 6, 1975, Sotheby's Catalog, Lot #84.

55. Jackie Kennedy Onassis to Robert McNamara, November 14, 1975, Sotheby's Catalog, Lot #84. The uncertainty about whether McNamara sent his handwritten comments to Jackie Kennedy is due to the inexact history of McNamara's letter. It is one of just a few pieces of correspondence from McNamara to Jackie that were found among his papers after his death.

That suggests that he may never have sent the handwritten comments to her. Or it is possible the personal version was returned to him by Caroline Kennedy after her mother's death, when she sent him the letters he had sent to her mother. In a cover letter to McNamara, Caroline suggested that he someday donate them to the Kennedy Library, except for letters that might violate her mother's determination to protect her privacy, which Caroline urged him to keep and eventually destroy.

56. Bruce Benton, *Riverblindness in Africa: Taming the Lion's Stare* (Baltimore: Johns Hopkins University Press, 2020), 2–22.
57. Robert McNamara, interview by Errol Morris, December 11–12, 2001.
58. Shapley, *Promise and Power*, 523–24.
59. Benton, *Riverblindness in Africa*, 24. On the results of the program as of 2020, see 201–25.
60. This account is based on Hendrickson, *The Living and the Dead*, 7–23.
61. This episode quotes from, paraphrases, and in large part relies on Hendrickson, *The Living and the Dead*, 7–13.
62. Leif Christoffersen, interview by William Taubman, October 2, 2019.
63. Shapley, *Promise and Power*, 476–77.
64. Sharma, *McNamara's Other War*, 73.
65. Shapley, *Promise and Power*, 485–86.
66. Robert McNamara, interview by Bob Woodward, August 2, 1989.
67. Sanche de Gramont, "McNamara as Speer," *New York Times*, July 1, 1971.
68. Shapley, *Promise and Power*, 489–90.
69. Halberstam, *The Best and the Brightest*, 250.
70. Robert McNamara, conversation with David Ginsburg and Brian VanDeMark, April 14, 1994.
71. Henry Kissinger, *White House Years* (Boston: Little, Brown), 296–97.
72. Jon Lee Anderson, "Does Henry Kissinger Have a Conscience?" *The New Yorker*, August 20, 2016.
73. Stephen Talbot, "The Day Henry Kissinger Cried," *Salon*, December 5, 2002.
74. Henry Kissinger and Robert McNamara Correspondence, Robert S. McNamara Papers, Library of Congress, Box 1:9, "Kissinger, Henry, 1982–1988" folder.
75. Walter Isaacson, *Kissinger: A Biography* (New York: Simon & Schuster, 1992), 582–83.
76. Kissinger, *The White House Years*, 295–97.
77. Shapley, *Promise and Power*, 556.
78. Craig McNamara, *Because Our Fathers Lied*, 81.
79. Craig McNamara, *Because Our Fathers Lied*, 101.
80. Shapley, *Promise and Power*, 482.
81. Craig McNamara, *Because Our Fathers Lied*, 96.
82. Craig McNamara, *Because Our Fathers Lied*, 99.
83. Craig McNamara, *Because Our Fathers Lied*, 106.
84. Craig McNamara, *Because Our Fathers Lied*, 112–17.
85. Craig McNamara, *Because Our Fathers Lied*, 126–27.
86. Craig McNamara, *Because Our Fathers Lied*, 130–31.
87. Craig McNamara, *Because Our Fathers Lied*, 133.
88. Craig McNamara, interview by Philip Taubman, April 12, 2022.
89. Craig McNamara, *Because Our Fathers Lied*, 144.
90. Craig McNamara, *Because Our Fathers Lied*, 148.
91. Craig McNamara, *Because Our Fathers Lied*, 149–50.
92. Craig McNamara, *Because Our Fathers Lied*, 165–66.
93. Leif Christoffersen, interview by William Taubman, October 2, 2019.
94. Robert McNamara, interview by Errol Morris, December 11–12, 2001.
95. Shapley, *Promise and Power*, 557.
96. William Clark, interview by Paul Hendrickson, December 3, 1984, Hendrickson Collection, World Bank folder.

97. Shapley, *Promise and Power*, 575.

98. Shapley, *Promise and Power*, 581; Craig McNamara, *Because Our Fathers Lied*, 171–73.

99. Robert McNamara, interview by Errol Morris, December 11–12, 2001.

100. Craig McNamara, *Because Our Fathers Lied*, 174.

101. Shapley, *Promise and Power*, 581–82.

102. Carl Bernstein, "On the Mistakes of War: Robert McNamara," *Time*, February 11, 1991.

103. James Blight and janet Lang, email message to the authors, November 10, 2022, and February 6, 2024.

104. Robert McNamara, interview by Suzan Travis-Robyns, September 29, 1995, Library of Congress, Robert S. McNamara Papers, Box 2:132.

105. Lydia Katzenbach, "Eulogy" (speech, Washington, DC, February 6, 1981), Robert S. McNamara Papers, Library of Congress, Box 2:133, folder 5: McNamara, Margaret Craig Tributes, 1993.

106. Shapley, *Promise and Power*, 582.

CHAPTER THIRTEEN: HINDSIGHT AND FORESIGHT

1. Robert McNamara, "Address to the Board of Governors" (speech, Washington, DC, September 30, 1980), World Bank Group.

2. Olivier Lafourcade, interview with William Taubman, September 28, 2019.

3. Robert McNamara, "Address to the Board of Governors" (speech, Washington, DC, September 30, 1980), World Bank Group.

4. Robert McNamara and James Blight, *Wilson's Ghost: Reducing the Risk of Conflict, Killing, and Catastrophe in the 21st Century* (New York: PublicAffairs, 2001), xiii.

5. Roswell Gilpatric, interview by Paul Hendrickson, May 29, 1985, Paul Hendrickson Archive, Pentagon folder.

6. Rose Styron, *Beyond This Harbor: Adventurous Tales of the Heart* (New York: Alfred A. Knopf, 2021), 189.

7. M. A. Farber, "McNamara Discusses War at CBS Libel Trial," *New York Times*, December 7, 1984.

8. Robert McNamara to McGeorge Bundy, January 14, 1993, Robert S. McNamara Papers, Library of Congress, Box 1:2, folder 11.

9. James Blight and janet Lang, email message to William Taubman, September 19, 2022.

10. James Blight and janet Lang, *Dark Beyond Darkness: The Cuban Missile Crisis as History, Warning, and Catalyst* (Lanham, MD: Rowman & Littlefield, 2018), 58–62.

11. James Blight and David Welch, *On the Brink: Americans and Soviets Reexamine the Cuban Missile Crisis* (New York: Hill & Wang, 1989), 6. Participants in the first Cuban conference, held in Hawk's Cay, March 5–8, 1987, included (in addition to McNamara and several historians and political scientists) George Ball, McGeorge Bundy, former Treasury secretary Douglas Dillon, and John Kennedy's close confidants and later biographers, Arthur M. Schlesinger Jr. and Theodore Sorensen, among others. Contributing interviews or statements after the conferences were Dean Rusk, General Maxwell Taylor, Paul Nitze, and McNamara himself. See Blight and Welch, *On the Brink*, 9–15.

12. Blight and Lang, *Dark Beyond Darkness*, 210n4.

13. Robert McNamara, in *Cold War*, episode 10, "Cuba 1958–1962," aired November 28, 1998, on CNN, 41:41.

14. Blight and Welch, *On the Brink*, 29–32.

15. Douglas Dillon, interview by James Blight and janet Lang, May 15, 1987, in Blight and Welch, *On the Brink*, 165.

16. Robert McNamara, interview by James Blight and David Welch, May 21, 1987, in Blight and Welch, *On the Brink*, 186.

17. Robert McNamara, interview by James Blight and David Welch, May 21, 1987, in Blight and Welch, *On the Brink*, 199–200.

18. Robert McNamara, interview by James Blight and David Welch, May 21, 1987, in James Blight and David Welch, *On the Brink*, 193–94.

19. Blight and Welch, *On the Brink*, 226.

20. Blight and Welch, *On the Brink*, 242, 258, 261.

21. Blight and Welch, *On the Brink*, 281.

22. James Blight and janet Lang, "Burden of Nuclear Responsibility: Reflections on the Critical Oral History of the Cuban Missile Crisis," *Peace and Conflict: Journal of Peace Psychology* 1, no. 3 (September 1995): 225–64, 248.

23. Blight and Lang, *Dark Beyond Darkness*, 66–67.

24. Blight and Lang, *Dark Beyond Darkness*, 67.

25. James Blight, Bruce J. Allyn, and David Welch, *Cuba on the Brink: Castro, the Missile Crisis, and the Soviet Collapse* (New York: Pantheon, 1993), 55–56, 378–79.

26. Blight, Allyn, and Welch, *Cuba on the Brink*, 111. For further details, see William Taubman, *Khrushchev*, 572–73.

27. Blight and Lang, *Dark Beyond Darkness*, 71–72.

28. Blight and Lang, *Dark Beyond Darkness*, 71–72.

29. Scott Sagan, interview by Matt Kristoffersen, November 21, 2022.

30. Jeanne Moore to Blanche Moore and an unknown recipient, January 10, 1993, Robert S. McNamara Papers, Library of Congress, Box 2:126, folder 6.

31. Sargent Shriver to Robert McNamara, June 21, 1993, Robert S. McNamara Papers, Library of Congress, Box 2:126, folder 6.

32. Jackie Kennedy to Robert McNamara, February 24, 1993, Robert S. McNamara Papers, Library of Congress, Box 2:126, folder 6.

33. Robert McNamara to Jackie Kennedy, February 25, 1993, Robert S. McNamara Papers, Library of Congress, Box 2:126, folder 6.

34. Robert McNamara, interview by Brian VanDeMark, Geoff Shandler, and Peter Osnos, July 19, 1994.

35. William Bundy to Robert McNamara, May 23, 1994, Robert S. McNamara Papers, Library of Congress, Box 1:2.

36. Geraldine Baum, "Jacqueline Onassis Dies; First Lady of 'Camelot' was 84," *Los Angeles Times*, May 20, 1994.

37. VanDeMark, *Road to Disaster*, xix–xxv.

38. Bob Woodward, Notes from Interview with Robert McNamara, October 18, 1988.

39. McNamara, *In Retrospect*, xix–xx.

40. McNamara, *In Retrospect*, 321–23.

41. Robert McNamara, Transcript from Meeting with Brian VanDeMark, Peter Osnos, Geoff Schandler, and Peter Petre, September 16, 1994.

42. James Blight and janet Lang, email message to the authors, September 19, 2022.

43. Jim Thomson, interview by Paul Hendrickson, March 12, 1985, Paul Hendrickson Archive, Pentagon folder.

44. McGeorge Bundy to Robert McNamara, January 10, 1993, Robert S. McNamara Papers, Library of Congress, Box 1:2, folder 11.

45. Gordon M. Goldstein, who assisted Bundy in this effort, recounts it, including fragments of what Bundy wrote, in his book, *Lessons in Disaster*.

46. McNamara, *In Retrospect*, 203.

47. McNamara, *In Retrospect*, 99.

48. Robert McNamara, Transcript from Meeting with Peter Osnos, Brian VanDeMark, and Geoff Shandler, July 18, 1994.

49. McNamara, *In Retrospect*, 99.

50. Robert McNamara, interview by McGeorge Bundy and Brian VanDeMark, March 18, 1994.

51. David Halberstam, "Dead Wrong: Robert McNamara Says He Miscalculated Our Chances in Vietnam, But What's Not in His Book Is as Telling as What Is," *Los Angeles Times*, April 16, 1995.

52. Howell Raines, "Mr. McNamara's War," *New York Times*, April 12, 1995.

53. David Halberstam to Robert McNamara, January 19, 1996, David Halberstam Archive, Box 9.

54. Robert McAfee Brown, letter to the editor, *New York Times*, April 13, 1995, quoted in Robert McNamara, *In Retrospect*, 38.

55. Jonathan Alter, "'I Sweated Blood at Night About It,'" *Newsweek*, April 16, 1995.

56. Arthur M. Schlesinger Jr., *Journals, 1951–2000* (New York: Penguin Press, 2007), 681–82.

57. Jim Blight and janet Lang, email message to the authors, February 6, 2024.

58. Anne Morrison Welch to Robert McNamara, April 10 and 12, 1995, Robert S. McNamara Papers, Library of Congress, Box 2:106, folder 5.

59. Robert McNamara, interview by Henry Brandon, September 18, 1968, Henry Brandon Papers, Library of Congress, Box 18, folder 3.

60. Robert McNamara, interview by Errol Morris, December 11–12, 2001.

61. Robert McNamara, James Blight, Robert Brigham, Thomas Bierkster, and Herbert Schandler, *Argument Without End: In Search of Answers to the Vietnam Tragedy* (New York: PublicAffairs, 1999), 11–12.

62. McNamara, et al., *Argument Without End*, 6.

63. McNamara, et al., *Argument Without End*, xiii–xxiii.

64. McNamara, et al., *Argument Without End*, 421.

65. James Blight, "Missed Opportunities: Former U.S. and Vietnamese Leaders Reexamine the Vietnam War (1961–1968)," November 28, 1995, Robert S. McNamara Papers, Library of Congress, Box 2:73, folder 6.

66. "Missed Opportunities," Transcript of Proceedings, June 20–23, 1997, Robert S. McNamara Papers, Library of Congress, Box 2:73, folder 3, 11–12.

67. "Missed Opportunities," Transcript of Proceedings, 19.

68. McNamara, et al., *Argument Without End*, 23–24.

69. Daisaku Higashi, "Missed Opportunities: Dialogue of Enemies in the Vietnam War," NHK Television, 43:50–45:32.

70. McNamara, et al., *Argument Without End*, 80.

71. McNamara, et al., *Argument Without End*, 88.

72. Stanley Karnow, *Vietnam: A History* (New York: Penguin Books, 1997), 112.

73. Bob Brigham, interview by Philip Taubman, September 23, 2022.

74. Bob Brigham, interview by Philip Taubman and William Taubman, August 23, 2022.

75. Bob Brigham, interview by Philip Taubman, September 23, 2022.

76. James Blight and janet Lang, email message to authors, September 19, 2022.

77. McNamara, et al., *Argument Without End*, 317.

78. Robert Brigham, "Three Alternative U.S. Strategies in Vietnam: A Reexamination Based on New Chinese and Vietnamese Sources," included in McNamara et al., *Argument Without End*, 411–12.

79. Ernest R. May, *"Lessons" of the Past: The Use and Misuse of History in American Foreign Policy* (New York: Oxford University Press, 1973), 120–21.

80. Ernest May, "Comments by Professor Ernest R. May at the John F. Kennedy School of Government, Harvard University, April 25, 1995," quoted in Fox Butterfield, "29 Years Later, McNamara Is Given Warmer Welcome," *New York Times*, April 27, 1995.

81. McNamara, et al., *Argument Without End*, 7.

82. McNamara, et al., *Argument Without End*, 7–8.

83. McNamara and Blight, *Wilson's Ghost*, 3.

84. McNamara and Blight, *Wilson's Ghost*, 22.

85. McNamara and Blight, *Wilson's Ghost*, 26–27.

86. McNamara and Blight, *Wilson's Ghost*, 218.

87. McNamara and Blight, *Wilson's Ghost*, 234.

88. Sydney Schanberg, "Soul on Ice," *American Prospect*, October 27, 2003, in James Blight and janet Lang, *The Fog of War: Lessons from the Life of Robert S. McNamara*, 201.

89. Roger Angell, "Late Review," *New Yorker*, January 11, 2004, quoted in Blight and Lang, *The Fog of War: Lessons from the Life of Robert S. McNamara*, 231.

90. James Blight and janet Lang, email message to the author, September 19, 2022.

91. *The Fog of War: Eleven Lessons from the Life of Robert S. McNamara*, directed by Errol Morris (2003; New York: Sony Pictures Classics), 35:04.
92. Morris, *The Fog of War*, 42:44.
93. Morris, *The Fog of War*, 39:34.
94. Morris, *The Fog of War*, 41:41 (emphasis added).
95. Robert McNamara, interview by Errol Morris, May 1–2, 2001.
96. Morris, *The Fog of War*, 1:25:47.
97. Morris, *The Fog of War*, 57:20.
98. Morris, *The Fog of War*, 1:39:15.
99. Schanberg, "Soul on Ice."
100. Jim Blight and janet Lang, email message to the authors, February 6, 2024.
101. Morris, *The Fog of War*, 1:42:40.
102. James Blight and janet Lang, *The Armageddon Letters: Kennedy/Khrushchev/Castro in the Cuban Missile Crisis* (Lanham, MD: Rowman & Littlefield, 2012), 3–6.

CHAPTER FOURTEEN: LONELY WIDOWER SEEKS COMPANIONSHIP

1. Craig McNamara, *Because Our Fathers Lied*, 33.
2. Craig McNamara, *Because Our Fathers Lied*, 33–34.
3. James Blight and janet Lang, "McNamara in Winter: The Quixotic Quest of an Unquiet American," *Proceedings of the American Philosophical Society* 160, no. 4 (December 2016): 426–35, 428.
4. Roxanne Roberts, "Wedding Bells for Robert McNamara," *Washington Post*, September 8, 2004.
5. Margaret Pastor, interview by William Taubman, October 2018; Margaret Pastor, email message to Robert McNamara via Diana McNamara, January 17, 2006, Diana McNamara Archive, Family Correspondence—McNamara, Robert, Margy Pastor, and Bob Pastor folder.
6. Craig McNamara, *Because Our Fathers Lied*, 174–77.
7. James Blight and janet Lang, email message to the authors, November 10, 2022.
8. James Blight and janet Lang, email message to the authors, February 6, 2024.
9. Craig McNamara, *Because Our Fathers Lied*, 180.
10. Craig McNamara, *Because Our Fathers Lied*, 196.
11. James Blight and janet Lang, email messages to the authors, November 10, 2022, February 6, 2024.
12. Craig McNamara, *Because Our Fathers Lied*, 197–98.
13. James Blight and janet Lang, email message to the authors, November 10, 2022.
14. Craig McNamara, *Because Our Fathers Lied*, 199.
15. Craig McNamara, *Because Our Fathers Lied*, 202–3.
16. Craig McNamara, *Because Our Fathers Lied*, 204.
17. Craig McNamara, *Because Our Fathers Lied*, 205.
18. Craig McNamara, *Because Our Fathers Lied*, 197.
19. Joan Braden, *Just Enough Rope: An Intimate Memoir* (New York: Villard Books, 1989), 235.
20. Eric Pace, "Joan Braden Is Dead at 77; Hostess to a Capital Elite," *New York Times*, September 1, 1999.
21. Joan Braden, interview with Paul Hendrickson, date unknown, Paul Hendrickson Archive, Later in McNamara's Life folder, McNamara and Women File, part II.
22. Braden, *Just Enough Rope*, 236–37.
23. Braden, *Just Enough Rope*, 237–38.
24. Braden, *Just Enough Rope*, 238–39.
25. Joan Braden, interviews by Paul Hendrickson, dates unknown, Paul Hendrickson Archive, Later in McNamara's Life folder, McNamara and Women File.
26. Shapley, *Promise and Power*, 594.
27. Braden, *Just Enough Rope*, 236.

28. Charles Trueheart, "Joan Braden's Book Proposal: Kiss and Sell?" *Washington Post*, September 8, 1987.

29. Sally Quinn, interview by Philip Taubman, March 25, 2024.

30. Braden, *Just Enough Rope*, 235–40.

31. Braden, *Just Enough Rope*, 239–40.

32. Braden, *Just Enough Rope*, 240–41.

33. Maureen Dowd, "In Short: Nonfiction," *New York Times*, December 31, 1989.

34. Hendrickson, *The Living and the Dead*, 365–66.

35. Hendrickson, *The Living and the Dead*, 367.

36. Robert McNamara, interview by Paul Hendrickson, April 18, 1984, Paul Hendrickson Archive, Later in Life folder, McNamara and Women File, Part II.

37. Joan Braden, interview by Paul Hendrickson, date unknown, Hendrickson Collection, Later in Life folder, McNamara and Women File, Part II.

38. Tom Braden, interview by Paul Hendrickson, date unknown, Paul Hendrickson Archive, Later in Life folder, McNamara and Women File, Part II.

39. Trueheart, "Joan Braden's Book Proposal."

40. Joan Braden, *Just Enough Rope*, 242–43.

41. Katharine Graham, *Personal History* (New York: Knopf, 2002), 275.

42. Graham, *Personal History*, 327–28.

43. James Blight and janet Lang, email message to the authors, November 10, 2022.

44. Graham, *Personal History*, 328.

45. Graham, *Personal History*, 412.

46. Graham, *Personal History*, 446.

47. Graham, *Personal History*, 616.

48. Graham, *Personal History*, 30.

49. Graham, *Personal History*, 32, 72–73.

50. Graham, *Personal History*, 111, 149.

51. Graham, *Personal History*, 236, 259.

52. Graham, *Personal History*, 270.

53. Graham, *Personal History*, 364.

54. Graham, *Personal History*, 368.

55. Graham, *Personal History*, 290–91.

56. Graham, *Personal History*, 615.

57. Carol Felsenthal, *Power, Privilege and the Post: The Katharine Graham Story* (New York: G. P. Putnam's Sons, 1993), 325.

58. Larry Van Dyne, "The Bottom Line on Katharine Graham: The Woman, the Newspaper, the Empire," *Washingtonian*, December 1985.

59. Katharine Graham, "McNamara Book Party," April 18, 1995, Robert S. McNamara Papers, Library of Congress, Box 1:7.

60. C-SPAN, "Argument Without End: Book Party," May 9, 1999; James Blight and janet Lang, email message to the authors, November 10, 2022.

61. Robert McNamara to Katharine Graham, date unknown, Diana McNamara Archive.

62. Don Graham, interview by Philip Taubman, October 21, 2019.

63. John C. Ensslin, "Getting Along Famously," *Denver Rocky Mountain News*, December 3, 2000.

64. Ensslin, "Getting Along Famously."

65. Ensslin, "Getting Along Famously."

66. James Blight and janet Lang, email message to the authors, November 10, 2022.

67. Ensslin, "Getting Along Famously."

68. Ensslin, "Getting Along Famously."

69. Phyllis Coors, interview by Philip Taubman, August 21, 2019.

70. Robert McNamara to Phyllis Coors, April 15, 1997.

71. Robert McNamara to Phyllis Coors, July 22, 1997.

72. Robert McNamara to Phyllis Coors, January 19, 1998.

73. Robert McNamara to Phyllis Coors, December 25, 1998.

74. Robert McNamara to Phyllis Coors, April 30, 1999.
75. Robert McNamara to Phyllis Coors, June 8, 1999.
76. Robert McNamara to Phyllis Coors, July 13, 1999.
77. Robert McNamara to Phyllis Coors, March 6, 2000.
78. Phyllis Coors, in Robert McNamara Birthday Album.
79. Diana McNamara, conversation with Philip Taubman, March 23, 2010.
80. Roberts, "Wedding Bells for Robert McNamara."
81. Diana McNamara, conversation with Philip Taubman, March 23, 2010.
82. Diana McNamara, conversation with Philip Taubman, March 23, 2010.
83. Paul Bradley, "Firm's Homey Touch Enriches Exotic Spots," *Richmond Times-Dispatch*, June 29, 1992.
84. Vicky Hoon, "Polo in Art," *Washington Life Magazine*, December 19, 2012.
85. Walter Fletcher, "Bergamesco," *Dog World*, February 1982.
86. Bradley, "Firm's Homey Touch."
87. Roberts, "Wedding Bells for Robert McNamara."
88. Diana McNamara letter to the aurthors, January 14, 2025; Robert McNamara letter, October 4, 1966, Diana McNamara archive.

CHAPTER FIFTEEN: TWILIGHT YEARS

1. Craig McNamara, *Because Our Fathers Lied*, 62.
2. Craig McNamara, *Because Our Fathers Lied*, 63.
3. Craig McNamara, *Because Our Fathers Lied*, 211–12.
4. Interview with former secretary by William Taubman, June 18, 2021.
5. Craig McNamara, *Because Our Fathers Lied*, 211.
6. James Blight and janet Lang, email message to the authors, February 6, 2024.
7. Craig McNamara, *Because Our Fathers Lied*, 210.
8. Diana McNamara, interview by William Taubman, October 3, 2019.
9. Diana McNamara, interview by William Taubman, June 18, 2021.
10. Diana McNamara, interview by William Taubman, October 3, 2019.
11. Diana McNamara, interview by William Taubman, October 3, 2019.
12. James Blight and janet Lang, email message to the authors, November 10, 2022.
13. Roberts, "Wedding Bells for Robert McNamara."
14. James Blight and janet Lang, email message to the authors, February 6, 2024.
15. James Blight and janet Lang, email message to the authors, November 10, 2022.
16. Diana McNamara to Robert McNamara, date unknown, letter shown to William Taubman.
17. Craig McNamara, *Because Our Fathers Lied*, prepublication version used with McNamara's permission.
18. Diana McNamara letter to the authors, January 14, 2025; Philip Taubman phone call with Craig McNamara, January 25, 2025.
19. Diana McNamara, interview by William Taubman, October 3, 2019.
20. Diana McNamara, interview by William Taubman, October 3, 2019.
21. Diana McNamara, interview by William Taubman, October 3, 2019.
22. Diana McNamara, interview by William Taubman, June 18, 2021.
23. Diana McNamara, interview by William Taubman, October 3, 2019.
24. Diana McNamara, interview by William Taubman, June 18, 2021.
25. James Blight and janet Lang, email message to the authors, February 6, 2024.
26. James Blight and janet Lang, email message to the authors, November 10, 2022.
27. "Glorious Sweetie," Emily McNamara, June 9, 2006, Robert McNamara Birthday Album, edited by Margaret Pastor.
28. Craig McNamara, *Because Our Fathers Lied*, 214.
29. "An Evening with Ted Sorensen," May 28, 2008, JFK Presidential Library.
30. Craig McNamara, *Because Our Fathers Lied*, 212–13.
31. Craig McNamara, *Because Our Fathers Lied*, 213.

32. Diana McNamara, interview by William Taubman, June 18, 2021.
33. Craig McNamara, *Because Our Fathers Lied*, 189.
34. Diana McNamara, interview by Philip Taubman, March 23, 2010.
35. Elizabeth Barrett Browning, "Sonnets from the Portuguese."
36. Craig McNamara, *Because Our Fathers Lied*, 218.
37. Craig McNamara, *Because Our Fathers Lied*, 218–19.
38. Craig McNamara, *Because Our Fathers Lied*, 214–16.
39. "McNamara's Effects sell for over $1M at NY Auction," Associated Press, October 23, 2012.
40. Diana McNamara letter of January 15, 2025; Philip Taubman phone conversation with Craig McNamara, January 15, 2025.
41. Craig McNamara, *Because Our Fathers Lied*, 224–25.
42. Craig McNamara, *Because Our Fathers Lied*, 225–27.
43. Robert McNamara, "Death Announcement," Robert S. McNamara Papers, Library of Congress, Box 2:130, folder 1: Death of McNamara, memorial message, 2009.

EPILOGUE

1. Bob Woodward, Notes from an Interview with Robert McNamara, October 18, 1988.
2. Bob Woodward, Notes from an Interview with Robert McNamara, August 7, 2007.
3. Bob Woodward, Notes from Interview with Robert McNamara, August 7, 2007.
4. William Perry interview with Philip Taubman, May, 25, 2024.
5. Schlesinger, *Journals*, 697.

BIBLIOGRAPHY

ARCHIVAL SOURCES

Bancroft Library, UC Berkeley, Berkeley, California
  Harry Lees Kingman Papers
  Office of the President Records
Columbia Center for Oral History, Columbia University, New York, New York
Department of Defense Historical Office, Washington, DC
Federal Bureau of Intelligence, Washington, DC
  "The Vault," FOIA Library Papers
Ford Motor Company Archives, Dearborn, Michigan
Harvard University, Cambridge, Massachusetts
  Baker Library Historical Collections
  Harvard College Office of the Dean Records
  Mary Steichen Calderone Papers
  Robert Anthony Papers
  Robert Manning Papers
Howard Gotlieb Archival Research Center, Boston University, Boston, Massachusetts
  David Halberstam Papers
John F. Kennedy Presidential Library, Boston, Massachusetts
  Adam Yarmolinsky Personal Papers
  Arthur Schlesinger Papers
  Jacqueline Kennedy Papers
  Jean Stein Personal Papers
  Kenneth O'Donnell Papers
  McGeorge Bundy Personal Papers
  Nicholas Katzenbach Personal Papers
  Robert Kennedy—Attorney General Papers
  Robert Kennedy Personal Papers
  Sargent Shriver Papers
  White House Social Files

LBJ Presidential Library, Austin, Texas
    Bill Moyers Personal Papers
    Files of McGeorge Bundy
    Files of Robert Komer
    Files of Walt Rostow
    George Ball Personal Papers
    Komer-Leonhart File
    McGeorge Bundy Personal Papers
    National Security File
    Office Files of the White House Aides
    Office of the President File
    Paul C. Warnke Personal Papers
    Post-Presidential File
    Robert S. McNamara Personal Papers
    Special Files
    Statements of Lyndon B. Johnson
    Tom Johnson Personal Papers
    Walt Rostow Personal Papers
    White House Central File
    White House Confidential File
    White House Famous Names File
    White House Social Files
    William Westmoreland Personal Papers
Library of Congress, Washington, DC
    Agnes Meyer Papers
    Art Buchwald Papers
    Bernard Schriever Papers
    Bill Mauldin Papers
    Carl Sagan Papers
    Daniel Schorr Papers
    Elliot Richardson Papers
    Henry Brandon Papers
    Herbert Block Papers
    Ina Ginsburg Papers
    Joseph & Stewart Alsop Papers
    Lawrence Spivak Papers
    L. Patrick Gray Papers
    Neil Sheehan Papers
    Noel Parrish Papers
    Paul Nitze Papers
    Philip Geyelin Papers
    Robert S. McNamara Papers
    Saul Pett Papers
    W. Averell Harriman Papers
New York Public Library, New York
    Arthur M. Schlesinger Jr. Papers
Russell Library, University of Georgia, Athens
    Dean Rusk Papers
University of Illinois, Urbana
    James Reston Papers
Wesleyan University, Middletown, Connecticut
    William Manchester Papers
World Bank Group Archives, Washington, DC

PRIVATE ARCHIVAL SOURCES

Deborah Shapley Archive
Diana McNamara Archive
Errol Morris Archive
Morrow Cater Archive
Paul Hendrickson Archive
Tex Thornton Archive

PERIODICALS

Air Force Magazine
The Amherst Student
Associated Press
The Atlantic Monthly
Blue and Gold
Denver Rocky Mountain News
Dog World
The Evening Star
Invention & Technology Magazine
Life
Los Angeles Times
Marin Independent Journal
Newsweek
The New Yorker
The New York Times
The New York Times Magazine
Parade Magazine
The Piedmont Highlander
Richmond Times-Dispatch
Salon
San Francisco Chronicle
Sports Illustrated
The Stanford Daily
This Week
Time
Washington Life Magazine
Washington News Service
The Washington Post
Washington Star

PUBLISHED DOCUMENTS AND PUBLISHED COLLECTIONS OF DOCUMENTS

Congressional Record
Foreign Relations of the United States
Public Papers of the Presidents, Lyndon B. Johnson. Washington, DC: US Government Printing Office, 1968
White House Recordings, Lyndon B. Johnson Presidential Library
White House Recordings, Miller Center, University of Virginia, Charlottesville

MEMOIRS

Alsop, Joseph. *I've Seen the Best of It: Memoirs.* New York: W. W. Norton, 1992.

Ball, George. *The Past Has Another Pattern.* New York: W. W. Norton, 1982.

Braden, Joan. *Just Enough Rope.* New York: Villard Books, 1989.

Bundy, McGeorge. *Danger and Survival.* New York: Random House, 1988.

Clifford, Clark, and Richard Holbrooke. *Counsel to the President: A Memoir.* New York: Anchor Books, 1992.

Ellsberg, Daniel. *Secrets: A Memoir of Vietnam and the Pentagon Papers.* New York: Penguin Books, 2003.

Goodwin, Doris Kearns. *An Unfinished Love Story: A Personal History of the 1960s.* New York: Simon & Schuster, 2024.

Goodwin, Richard. *Remembering America: A Voice from the Sixties.* New York: Open Road Integrated Media, 2014.

Graham, Katharine. *Personal History.* New York: Knopf, 2002.

Humphrey, Hubert. *The Education of a Public Man: My Life and Politics.* Minneapolis: University of Minnesota Press, 1991.

Iacocca, Lee, and William Novak. *Iacocca: An Autobiography.* New York: Bantam Books, 1984.

Kennedy, Robert. *13 Days: A Memoir of the Cuban Missile Crisis.* New York: W. W. Norton, 1969.

Kissinger, Henry. *White House Years.* Boston: Little, Brown, 1979.

LeMay, Curtis, and MacKinlay Kantor. *Mission with LeMay: My Story.* New York: Doubleday, 1965.

McNamara, Craig. *Because Our Fathers Lied.* New York: Little, Brown, 2022.

McNamara, Robert, and Brian VanDeMark. *In Retrospect: The Tragedy and Lessons of Vietnam.* New York: Random House, 1995.

O'Donnell, Kenneth, David Powers, and Joe McCarthy. *"Johnny, We Hardly Knew Ye": Memories of John Fitzgerald Kennedy.* New York: Little, Brown, 1972.

Patten, William. *My Three Fathers: And the Elegant Deceptions of My Mother, Susan Mary Alsop.* New York: PublicAffairs, 2008.

Ritzenberg, Allie. *Capital Tennis: A Memoir.* Francis Press, 2004.

Rusk, Dean. *As I Saw It.* New York: Penguin Books, 1991.

Welsh, Anne Morrison, with Joyce Hollyday. *Held in the Light: Norman Morrison's Sacrifice for Peace and His Family's Journey of Healing.* Ossining, NY: Orbis Books, 2008.

UNPUBLISHED MEMOIRS AND DIARIES

Johnson, Lady Bird. Audio and written diaries held at the LBJ Presidential Library.

McNaughton, John. *Unclassified Personal Diary of John T. McNaughton, January 1, 1966–April 22, 1967.* Transcribed by Asheley Smith. 2003.

AUTHORS' INTERVIEWS

Allison, Graham. May 31, 2023.

Anonymous resident. November 16, 2022.

Anonymous secretary. June 18, 2021.

Blanton, Thomas. September 7, 2021.

Blumenthal, Ellen. October 1, 2012.

Boyles, Edgar. August 21, 2019.

Boyles, Elizabeth. Multiple interviews in August 2019.

Brigham, Robert. Multiple interviews between August and September 2022.

Califano, Joseph. September 18, 2019.

Christoffersen, Leif. October 2, 2019.

Coors, Phyllis. August 21, 2019.

Craig, Gregory. July 1, 2019.

Ellsberg, Daniel. September 23, 2021.

Enthoven, Alain. May 4, 2017.

Fadiman, Anne. December 31, 2019.

Frank, Barney. August 2, 2019.

Galbraith, James. August 22, 2020.
Graham, Don. October 21, 2019.
Halperin, Mort. September 30, 2019.
Hendrickson, Paul. June 16, 2021.
Hughes, Thomas. November 20, 2019.
Ignatius, Paul. October 21, 2019.
Johnson, Tom. August 6, 2021.
Katzenbach, John. April 1, 2017.
Lafourcade, Olivier. September 28, 2019.
Lake, Tony. July 2, 2023.
Lord, Sterling. July 29, 2017.
McNamara, Craig. Multiple interviews between 2021 and 2024.
McNamara, Diana. Multiple interviews between 2010 and 2021.
Miller, Arjay. August 12, 2014.
Pastor, Margy. Multiple interviews between February and November 2019.
Patten, William. March 29, 2020.
Perry, William. May 25, 2024.
Pursley, Robert. December 5 2019.
Quinn, Sally. March 25, 2024.
Sagan, Scott. November 21, 2022.
Savranskaya, Svetlana. Multiple interviews between 2020 and 2024.
Shapley, Deborah. June 17, 2021.
Stevens, George, Jr. September 21, 2019.
Strand, Curt. August 23, 2019.
Styron, Rose. July 1, 2019.
VanDeMark, Brian. October 13, 2019.

CORRESPONDENCE, INCLUDING EMAIL

Messages to the Authors
Blight, James, and janet Lang. Multiple messages between 2020 and 2024.
Clark, Daniel. October 25, 2022.
Hendrickson, Paul. June 17, 2021.
McNamara, Craig. Multiple messages between 2021 and 2024.
McNamara, Diana. Multiple messages between 2021 and 2024.
Moyers, Bill. August 23, 2021.
VanDeMark, Brian. October 13, 2024.

OTHER INTERVIEWS

Beebe, Leo. Unpublished interview by Paul Hendrickson (October 11, 1984). Provided to the authors by Mr. Hendrickson.
Braden, Joan. Multiple unpublished interviews by Paul Hendrickson, dates unknown. Provided to the authors by Mr. Hendrickson.
Braden, Tom. Unpublished interview by Paul Hendrickson, date unknown. Provided to the authors by Mr. Hendrickson.
Bradley, Ron. Unpublished interview by Paul Hendrickson, date unknown. Provided to the authors by Mr. Hendrickson.
Brown, Holmes. Multiple unpublished interviews by David Halberstam between January 27, 1969, and an unknown date. Found in the David Halberstam Collection, Boston University.
Brown, Holmes. Unpublished interview by Paul Hendrickson, date unknown. Provided to the authors by Mr. Hendrickson.
Bundy, McGeorge. Unpublished interview by Robert McNamara and Brian VanDeMark (March 18, 1994). Provided to the authors by Mr. VanDeMark.

Clark, William. Unpublished interview by Paul Hendrickson (December 3, 1984). Provided to the authors by Mr. Hendrickson.

Clifford, Clark. Unpublished interview by Paul Hendrickson (November 28, 1984). Provided to the authors by Mr. Hendrickson.

Cooper, Joseph. Unpublished interview by Paul Hendrickson (July 24, 1985). Provided to the authors by Mr. Hendrickson.

Dickinson, Al. Unpublished interview by Paul Hendrickson (June 6, 1986). Provided to the authors by Mr. Hendrickson.

Dillon, C. Douglas. Unpublished interview by William Manchester (August 14, 1964). Found in the William Manchester Papers, Wesleyan University.

Dunham, Robert. Unpublished interview by Brian VanDeMark (June 24, 1992). Provided to the authors by Mr. VanDeMark.

Gerry, Virginia. Unpublished interview by Paul Hendrickson (December 10, year unknown). Provided to the authors by Mr. Hendrickson.

Gilpatric, Roswell. Unpublished interview by Brian VanDeMark (November 5, 1992). Provided to the authors by Mr. VanDeMark.

Ginsburg, David. Unpublished interview by Brian VanDeMark and Robert McNamara (April 14, 1994). Provided to the authors by Mr. VanDeMark.

Glass, Henry. Unpublished interview by Paul Hendrickson (March 10, 1986). Provided to the authors by Mr. Hendrickson.

Goodin, Vernon. Unpublished interview by Brian VanDeMark (October 30, 1991). Provided to the authors by Mr. VanDeMark.

Goodwin, Mary Jo. Unpublished interview by Paul Hendrickson (August 1, 1985). Provided to the authors by Mr. Hendrickson.

Goodwin, Mary Jo, and Willard Goodwin. Unpublished interview by Deborah Shapley (December 15, 1985). Provided to the authors by Mrs. Shapley.

Guest, Anna Lee. Unpublished interview by Paul Hendrickson (August 1, 1985). Provided to the authors by Mr. Hendrickson.

Helmer, Fran. Unpublished interview by Paul Hendrickson (August 1985). Provided to the authors by Mr. Hendrickson.

Johnson, Stanley. Unpublished interview by Brian VanDeMark (January 3, 1992). Provided to the authors by Mr. VanDeMark.

Kennedy, Robert. Unpublished interview by Neil Sheehan (October 17, 1967). Found in the Neil Sheehan Papers, Library of Congress.

Krandall, Norman. Multiple unpublished interviews by Paul Hendrickson between April and October 1986. Provided to the authors by Mr. Hendrickson.

Learned, Edmund. Unpublished interview by Paul Hendrickson (November 1985). Provided to the authors by Mr. Hendrickson.

Lodge, Henry Cabot. Oral history (August 4, 1965). Found in the John F. Kennedy Presidential Library.

Mace, Myles. Unpublished interview by Paul Hendrickson (October 1985). Provided to the authors by Mr. Hendrickson.

———. Unpublished interview by Brian VanDeMark (September 5, 1992). Provided to the authors by Mr. VanDeMark.

Maddux, John. Unpublished interview by Paul Hendrickson (November 7, 1986). Provided to the authors by Mr. Hendrickson.

Magill, Carson. Unpublished interview by Paul Hendrickson (July 10, 1985). Provided to the authors by Mr. Hendrickson.

———. Unpublished interview by Brian VanDeMark (February 1, 1992). Provided to the authors by Mr. VanDeMark.

McNamara, Craig. Interview by Morton Halperin (March 20, 2018). Provided to the authors by Mr. Halperin.

———. Council of Foreign Relations interview (June 3, 2022). Found on Council of Foreign Relations YouTube channel.

McNamara, Margaret Craig. Unpublished interview by Henry Brandon (December 23, 1966). Found in the Henry Brandon Papers, Library of Congress.

McNamara, Robert. Unpublished interview by Frank Ernest Hill, Mira Wilkins, and Henry Edmunds (January 8, 1950). Found in Ford Motor Company Archives.

———. Unpublished interview by William Manchester (May 25, 1964). Found in the William Manchester Papers, Wesleyan University.

———. Multiple unpublished interviews by Henry Brandon between 1966 and 1969. Found in the Henry Brandon Papers, Library of Congress.

———. Multiple unpublished interviews by Bob Woodward between 1982 and 2007. Provided to the authors by Mr. Woodward.

———. Unpublished interview by Paul Hendrickson (April 18, 1984). Provided to the authors by Mr. Hendrickson.

———. Multiple unpublished interviews by Deborah Shapley in 1984. Provided to the authors by Mrs. Shapley.

———. Unpublished interview by Alfred Goldberg and Maurice Matloff (April 3, 1986). Found in the JFK Presidential Library.

———. Unpublished interview by Lydia Bronte (July 12, 1989). Provided to the authors by Mr. VanDeMark.

———. Multiple unpublished interviews by Brian VanDeMark between 1991 and 1994. Provided to the authors by Mr. VanDeMark.

———. Multiple unpublished interviews by Suzan Travis-Robyns between 1994 and 2004. Found in the Robert S. McNamara Papers, Library of Congress.

———. Television interview by Charlie Rose (April 17, 1995). C-SPAN.

———. Multiple unpublished interviews by Errol Morris between 2001 and 2002. Provided to the authors by Mr. Morris.

Miller, Arjay, and Frances Miller. Unpublished interview by Brian VanDeMark (August 7, 1992). Provided to the authors by Mr. VanDeMark.

Mitchell, Jean Booth. Unpublished interview by Paul Hendrickson (November 22, 1985). Provided to the authors by Mr. Hendrickson.

O'Brien, Estelle. Unpublished interview by Paul Hendrickson. Date unknown. Provided to the authors by Mr. Hendrickson.

Phillips, Rufus. Unpublished interview by Paul Hendrickson (February 6, 1986). Provided to the authors by Mr. Hendrickson.

Power, Eugene. Unpublished interview by Brian VanDeMark (Spring 1992). Provided to the authors by Mr. VanDeMark.

Quigley, Richard, and Gwynn Quigley. Unpublished interview by Brian VanDeMark (August 3, 1992). Provided to the authors by Mr. VanDeMark.

Reedy, George. Oral histories. Found in the LBJ Presidential Library.

Rinehart, John. Unpublished interview by Paul Hendrickson (July 31, year unknown). Provided to the authors by Mr. Hendrickson.

Robb, Agnes. Unpublished interview by Paul Hendrickson, date unknown. Provided to the authors by Mr. Hendrickson.

Sanders, Thomas. Unpublished interview by Paul Hendrickson (June 8, 1986). Provided to the authors by Mr. Hendrickson.

Schlesinger, Arthur. Unpublished interview by William Manchester (May 29, 1964). Found in the William Manchester Papers, Wesleyan University.

Slaymaker, Peggy. Unpublished interview (November 21, 1975). Found in Columbia Center for Oral History, Columbia University.

———. Multiple unpublished interviews by Paul Hendrickson between 1985 and 1986. Provided to the authors by Mr. Hendrickson.

———. Unpublished interview by Brian VanDeMark (December 10, 1991). Provided to the authors by Mr. VanDeMark.

Thomson, Jim. Unpublished interview by Paul Hendrickson (March 12, 1985). Provided to the authors by Mr. Hendrickson.

Whitmore, Annalee. Unpublished interview by Brian VanDeMark (January 5, 1992). Provided to the authors by Mr. VanDeMark.

Yarmolinsky, Adam. Unpublished interview by Brian VanDeMark (April 1, 1993). Provided to the authors by Mr. VanDeMark.

Yudelman, Montague. Unpublished interview by Paul Hendrickson (November 28, 1986). Provided to the authors by Mr. Hendrickson.

Zuckert, Eugene. Unpublished interview by Brian VanDeMark (October 29, 1992). Provided to the authors by Mr. VanDeMark.

BOOKS

Alsop, Stewart. *The Center: People and Power in Political Washington*. New York: Popular Library, 1968.

Ambrose, Stephen. *Nixon: Volume Two: The Triumph of a Politician, 1962–1972*. New York: Simon & Schuster, 1989.

Anthony, Carl Sferrazza. *Camera Girl: The Coming of Age of Jackie Bouvier Kennedy*. New York: Simon & Schuster, 2023.

Basha i Novosejt, Aurélie. *"I Made Mistakes": Robert McNamara's Vietnam War Policy, 1960–1968*. New York: Cambridge University Press, 2019.

Beardon, James. *The Spellmount Guide to London in the Second World War*. New York: History Press, 2013.

Benton, Bruce. *Riverblindness in Africa: Taming the Lion's Stare*. Baltimore: Johns Hopkins University Press, 2020.

Beschloss, Michael. *Reaching for Glory: Lyndon Johnson's Secret White House Tapes, 1964–1965*. New York: Simon & Schuster, 2002.

Bird, Kai. *The Color of Truth: McGeorge Bundy and William Bundy, Brothers in Arms*. New York: Simon & Schuster, 2000.

Blight, James, Bruce Allyn, and David Welch. *Cuba on the Brink: Castro, the Missile Crisis, and the Soviet Collapse*. New York: Pantheon, 1993.

Blight, James, and janet Lang. *Dark Beyond Darkness*. Lanham, MD: Rowman & Littlefield, 2018.

———. *The Fog of War: Lessons from the Life of Robert S. McNamara*. Lanham, MD: Rowman & Littlefield, 2005.

Blight, James, janet Lang, and David Welch. *Vietnam If Kennedy Had Lived: Virtual JFK*. Lanham, MD: Rowman & Littlefield, 2009.

Blight, James, and David Welch. *On the Brink: Americans and Soviets Reexamine the Cuban Missile Crisis*. New York: Hill & Wang, 1989.

Boot, Max. *The Road Not Taken: Edward Lansdale and the American Tragedy in Vietnam*. New York: Liveright Publishing, 2018.

Bradlee, Ben. *Conversations with Kennedy*. New York: W. W. Norton, 1984.

Brandon, Henry. *Anatomy of Error: The Inside Story of the Asian War on the Potomac, 1954–1969*. Boston: Gambit, 1970.

Brinkley, Douglas. *Wheels for the World: Henry Ford, His Company, and a Century of Progress, 1903–2003*. New York: Viking Penguin, 2003.

Brooks, John. *Business Adventures: Twelve Classic Tales from the World of Wall Street*. New York: Open Road, 2014.

Buckingham, William, Jr. *Operation Ranch Hand: The Air Force and Herbicides in Southeast Asia, 1961–1971*. Washington, DC: Office of Air Force History, United States Air Force, 1982.

Byrne, John. *The Whiz Kids: The Founding Fathers of American Business—and the Legacy They Left Us*. New York: Currency, 1993.

Caro, Robert. *The Years of Lyndon Johnson: Master of the Senate*. New York: Alfred A. Knopf, 2002.

———. *The Years of Lyndon Johnson: Means of Ascent*. New York: Alfred A. Knopf, 1990.

———. *The Years of Lyndon Johnson: The Passage of Power*. New York: Alfred A. Knopf, 2012.

———. *The Years of Lyndon Johnson: The Path to Power*. New York: Alfred A. Knopf, 1982.

Caroli, Betty Boyd. *Lady Bird and Lyndon: The Hidden Story of a Marriage That Made a President.* New York: Simon & Schuster, 2015.

Clark, Daniel. *Disruption in Detroit: Autoworkers and the Elusive Postwar Boom.* Urbana: University of Illinois Press, 2018.

Collier, Peter, and David Horowitz. *The Fords: An American Epic.* New York: Summit Books, 1987.

Dallek, Robert. *Flawed Giant: Lyndon Johnson and His Times, 1961–1973.* New York: Oxford University Press, 1998.

———. *Lone Star Rising: Lyndon Johnson and His Times, 1908–1960.* New York: Oxford University Press, 1991.

Dobbs, Michael. *One Minute to Midnight: Kennedy, Khrushchev, and Castro on the Brink of Nuclear War.* New York: Alfred A. Knopf, 2008.

Drea, Edward. *Secretaries of Defense Historical Series, Volume VI: McNamara, Clifford, and the Burdens of Vietnam, 1965–1969.* Washington, DC: Historical Office, Office of the Secretary of Defense, 2011.

Felsenthal, Carol. *Power, Privilege, and the Post: The Katharine Graham Story.* New York: G. P. Putnam's Sons, 1993.

Garrettson, Charles. *Hubert H. Humphrey: The Politics of Joy.* New Brunswick, NJ: Transaction Publishers, 1993.

Goldstein, Gordon. *Lessons in Disaster: McGeorge Bundy and the Path to War in Vietnam.* New York: Henry Holt, 2008.

Goodwin, Doris Kearns. *Lyndon Johnson and the American Dream.* New York: Harper & Row, 1976.

Halberstam, David. *The Best and the Brightest.* New York: Random House, 1972.

———. *The Reckoning.* New York: William Morrow, 1986.

Hastings, Max. *Vietnam: An Epic History of a Tragic War.* Glasgow: William Collins, 2019.

Hayes, Walter. *Henry: A Life of Henry Ford II.* New York: Grove Weidenfeld, 1990.

Hendrickson, Paul. *The Living and the Dead: Robert McNamara and Five Lives of a Lost War.* New York: Vintage Books, 1997.

Herken, Gregg. *The Georgetown Set: Friends and Rivals in Cold War Washington.* New York: Vintage, 2014.

Hershberg, James G. *Marigold: The Lost Chance for Peace in Vietnam.* Stanford, CA: Stanford University Press, 2012.

Hershman, D. Jablow, and Gerald Tolchin. *Power Beyond Reason: The Mental Collapse of Lyndon Johnson.* Fort Lee, NJ: Barricade Books, 2002.

Hughes, Thomas. *Perilous Encounters: The Cold War Collisions of Domestic and World Politics.* Xlibris Corporation, 2011.

Ingrassia, Paul. *Engines of Change: A History of the American Dream in Fifteen Cars.* New York: Simon & Schuster, 2012.

Isaacson, Walter. *Kissinger: A Biography.* New York: Simon & Schuster, 1992.

Isaacson, Walter, and Evan Thomas. *The Wise Men: Six Friends and the World They Made.* New York: Simon & Schuster, 1986.

Kaplan, Fred. *The Wizards of Armageddon.* Stanford, CA: Stanford University Press, 1991.

Kaplan, Lawrence S., Ronald D. Landa, and Edward J. Drea. *The McNamara Ascendancy, 1961–1965, vol. 5 of History of the Office of the Secretary of Defense.* Washington, DC: Office of the Secretary of Defense, 2006.

Karnow, Stanley. *Vietnam: A History.* New York: Penguin Books, 1997.

Kaufmann, William. *The McNamara Strategy.* New York: Harper & Row, 1964.

Kerr, E. Bartlett. *Flames over Tokyo: The U.S. Army Air Forces' Incendiary Campaign Against Japan, 1944–1945.* New York: Donald I. Fine, 1991.

Kozak, Warren. *LeMay: The Life and Wars of General Curtis LeMay.* Washington, DC: Regnery Publishing, 2009.

Lacey, Robert. *Ford: The Men and the Machine.* Boston: Little, Brown, 1986.

Langguth, A. J. *Our Vietnam: The War, 1954–1975.* New York: Simon & Schuster, 2000.

Lankford, Nelson. *The Last American Aristocrat.* Boston: Little, Brown, 1996.

Lay, Beirne. *Someone Has to Make It Happen: The Inside Story of Tex Thornton, the Man Who Built Litton Industries.* Englewood Cliffs, NJ: Prentice-Hall, 1969.

Leaming, Barbara. *Jacqueline Bouvier Kennedy Onassis: The Untold Story.* New York: St. Martin's Press, 2014.

Lemov, Michael. *Car Safety Wars: One Hundred Years of Technology, Politics, and Death.* Madison, NJ: Fairleigh Dickinson University Press, 2015.

Logevall, Fredrik. *JFK: Coming of Age in the American Century, 1917–1956.* New York: Random House, 2020.

May, Ernest. *"Lessons" of the Past: The Use and Misuse of History in American Foreign Policy.* New York: Oxford University Press, 1973.

McMaster, H. R. *Dereliction of Duty: Lyndon Johnson, Robert McNamara, the Joint Chiefs of Staff, and the Lies That Led to Vietnam.* New York: HarperCollins, 1998.

McNamara, Robert. *Blundering into Disaster: Surviving the First Century of the Nuclear Age.* New York: Pantheon, 1986.

———. *The Essence of Security: Reflections in Office.* New York: Harper & Row, 1968.

McNamara, Robert, and James Blight. *Wilson's Ghost: Reducing the Risk of Conflict, Killing, and Catastrophe in the 21st Century.* New York: PublicAffairs, 2001.

McNamara, Robert, James Blight, Robert Brigham, Thomas Biersteker, and Col. Herbert Schandler. *Argument Without End: In Search of Answers to the Vietnam Tragedy.* New York: PublicAffairs, 1999.

Miller, Merle. *Lyndon: An Oral Biography.* New York: Putnam, 1980.

Nevins, Allan, and Frank Ernest Hill. *Ford: Decline and Rebirth, 1933–1962.* New York: Charles Scribner's Sons, 1963.

Onassis, Jacqueline Kennedy, Arthur M. Schlesinger Jr., Michael R. Beschloss, and Caroline Kennedy. *Jacqueline Kennedy: Historic Conversations on Life with John F. Kennedy.* New York: Hyperion, 2011.

Osnos, Peter. *LBJ and McNamara: The Vietnam Partnership Destined to Fail.* Rivertowns Books, 2024.

Patten, William. *My Three Fathers: And the Elegant Deceptions of My Mother, Susan Mary Alsop.* New York: PublicAffairs, 2008.

Russell, Jan Jarboe. *Lady Bird: A Biography of Mrs. Johnson.* New York: Scribner, 1999.

Schlesinger, Arthur M., Jr. *Journals: 1952–2000.* New York: Penguin Books, 2007.

———. *Robert Kennedy and His Times.* Boston: Houghton Mifflin, 1978.

———. *A Thousand Days: John F. Kennedy in the White House.* Boston: Houghton Mifflin, 1965.

Shapley, Deborah, *Promise and Power: The Life and Times of Robert McNamara.* Boston: Little, Brown, 1993.

Sharma, Patrick Allen. *Robert McNamara's Other War: The World Bank and International Development.* Philadelphia: University of Pennsylvania Press, 2017.

Shesol, Jeff. *Mutual Contempt: Lyndon Johnson, Robert Kennedy, and the Feud That Defined a Decade.* New York: W. W. Norton, 1997.

Sidney, Hugh. *A Very Personal Presidency: Lyndon Johnson in the White House.* New York: Atheneum, 1968.

Smith, Sally Bedell. *Grace and Power: The Private World of the Kennedy White House.* New York: Random House, 2004.

Solberg, Carl. *Hubert Humphrey: A Biography.* New York: W. W. Norton, 1984.

Sorensen, Ted. *Kennedy: The Classic Biography.* London: Hodder and Stoughton, 1965.

Stern, Sheldon. *The Cuban Missile Crisis in American Memory: Myths Versus Reality.* Stanford, CA: Stanford University Press, 2012.

Styron, Rose. *Beyond This Harbor: Adventurous Tales of the Heart.* New York: Alfred A. Knopf, 2021.

Sweig, Julia. *Lady Bird Johnson: Hiding in Plain Sight.* New York: Random House, 2021.

Taubman, William. *Khrushchev: The Man and His Era.* New York: W. W. Norton, 2003.

Thomas, Evan. *Robert Kennedy: His Life*. New York: Simon & Schuster, 2000.

Thompson, Nicholas. *The Hawk and the Dove: Paul Nitze, George Kennan, and the History of the Cold War*. New York: Henry Holt, 2009.

Trewhitt, Henry. *McNamara: His Ordeal in the Pentagon*. New York: Harper & Row, 1971.

Tye, Larry. *Bobby Kennedy: The Making of a Liberal Icon*. New York: Random House, 2016.

VanDeMark, Brian. *Road to Disaster: A New History of America's Descent into Vietnam*. Boston: Mariner, 2018.

ARTICLES

Blight, James, and janet Lang. "Burden of Nuclear Responsibility: Reflections on the Critical Oral History of the Cuban Missile Crisis." *Peace and Conflict: Journal of Peace Psychology* 1, no. 3 (September 1995): 225–64.

Blight, James, and janet Lang. "McNamara in Winter: The Quixotic Quest of an Unquiet American." *Proceedings of the American Philosophical Society* 160, no. 4 (December 2016): 426–35.

Clark, William. "Robert McNamara at the World Bank." *Foreign Affairs* 60, no. 1 (Fall 1981).

Hay, David Lowell. "Bomber Businessmen: The Army Air Forces and the Rise of Statistical Control, 1940–1945." PhD thesis, University of Notre Dame, 1994.

McKitterick, Nathaniel. "The World Bank & the McNamara Legacy." *National Interest* 4 (Summer 1986).

Ronan, Larry. "Seat Belts: 1949–1956." April 1979. Prepared for the US Department of Transportation.

Veterans Affairs Public Affairs. "VA Extends 'Agent Orange' Benefits to More Veterans." October 13, 2009.

Watson, George, Jr., and Herman S. Wolk. "'Whiz Kid': Robert S. McNamara's World War II Service." *Air Power History* 50, no. 4 (Winter 2003): 4–15, 8.

Zeff, Stephen. "The Contribution of the Harvard Business School to Management Control, 1908–1980." *Journal of Management Accounting Research* 20, Special Issue (2008): 175–208.

POEMS

Arnold, Matthew. "Dover Beach." 1867.

Brooke, Rupert. "The Hill." Date unknown.

Browning, Elizabeth Barrett. "Sonnets from the Portuguese." 1850.

Eliot, T. S. "The Fourth Quartet." 1941.

Emerson, Ralph Waldo. "Sacrifice." Date unknown.

Kazantzakis, Nikos. "Report to Greco." 1966.

Kipling, Rudyard. "The Palace." 1922.

Santayana, George. "O World." Date unknown.

Thomas, Dylan. "The Hand That Signed the Paper." 1936.

TELEVISION EPISODES AND FILMS

"Argument Without End: Book Party." Aired May 9, 1999. C-SPAN.

"Missed Opportunities: Dialogue of Enemies in the Vietnam War." NHK Television.

Burns, Ken, and Lynn Novick, dir. *The Vietnam War*. Aired September 17–28, 2017. PBS.

Mitchell, Pat, and Jeremy Isaacs, prod. *Cold War*. Episode 10, "Cuba: 1958–1962." Aired November 29, 1998. CNN.

Morris, Errol, dir. *The Fog of War*. 2003. Sony Pictures Classics.

Porter, Dawn, dir. *The Lady Bird Diaries*. 2023. Hulu.

Reed, Carol, dir. *The Third Man*. 1949. London, UK: British Lion Film Corporation.

AUCTION CATALOGS

Sotheby's, Robert S. McNamara Estate.
University Archives, Robert S. McNamara Estate.
James Cummins Bookseller, Hubert Humphrey Letters.
Guernsey's, Robert Kennedy Letters.

UNPUBLISHED MANUSCRIPTS AND ARTICLES

Pastor, Margy. Robert McNamara Ninetieth Birthday Album.
McNamara, Robert. "Selected Poems." Date Unknown.

UNPUBLISHED PROCEEDINGS OF CONFERENCES

Blight, James. "Missed Opportunities: Former U.S. and Vietnamese Leaders Reexamine the
    Vietnam War (1961–1968)." November 28, 1995. Robert S. McNamara Papers, Library
    of Congress.

CREDITS

ILLUSTRATION CREDITS

McNamara as an Eagle Scout: Photo by Claranel McNamara. Courtesy of Craig McNamara

McNamara at Ford Motor Company: Bettmann/Getty Images

President-elect Kennedy and McNamara outside JFK's Georgetown home: AP Photo/John Rous

With President Kennedy walking toward a pier: AP Photo/John Rous

In his office at the Pentagon: Leonard Mccombe/The LIFE Picture Collection/Shutterstock

Skiing enthusiast McNamara: AP Photo

With Robert F. Kennedy: VA005775, Vietnam Veterans Institute Collection, Vietnam Center and Sam Johnson Vietnam Archive, Texas Tech University

With Secretary of State Dean Rusk: VA021183, Larry Berman Collection (Personal Papers), Vietnam Center and Sam Johnson Vietnam Archive, Texas Tech University

At his desk at the Pentagon: AP Photo/Harvey Georges

Between US Air Force chief of staff Curtis LeMay (left) and General Maxwell Taylor, chairman of the Joint Chiefs of Staff: Keystone-France/Gamma-Rapho via Getty Images

Conferring with President Lyndon B. Johnson in the White House: Stan Wayman/The LIFE Picture Collection/Shutterstock

South Vietnamese General Cao showing McNamara captured enemy weapons: VA038335, Lee Baker Collection, Vietnam Center and Sam Johnson Vietnam Archive, Texas Tech University

During a TV interview in his Pentagon office: CBS Photo Archive/Getty Images

With General Nguyen Khanh: Larry Burrows/The LIFE Picture Collection/Shutterstock

Greeting South Vietnamese children in the village of Hoa Hao: AP Photo

Veteran mountain climber McNamara: Photo by Werner Pfändler/RDB/ullstein bild via Getty Images

Pointing out to American journalists where two American destroyers were reportedly attacked in the Tonkin Gulf: Bettmann/Getty Images

Getting a firsthand report on frontline action: Bettmann/Getty Images

With President Johnson in the White House Cabinet Room: LBJ Library photo by Yoichi Okamoto

With President Johnson, March 1967: VA052891, Barry & Margaret Zorthian Collection, Vietnam Center and Sam Johnson Vietnam Archive, Texas Tech University

With Jacqueline Kennedy and John F. Kennedy Jr.: WWD/Getty Images. Photo by Guy DeLort/WWD/Penske Media

Watching from a Pentagon window: Bettmann/Getty Images

President Johnson and McNamara, showing their fatigue: LBJ Library photo by Yoichi Okamoto

McNamara and his family with President and Lady Bird Johnson: Courtesy of Craig McNamara

Arriving at the World Bank: President Robert S. McNamara's first day of work at the World Bank, May 1968, Folder 1894060, World Bank Group Archives, Washington, DC, United States

With his son, Craig, at Craig's California farm: Courtesy of Craig McNamara

The front cover of the paperback edition of Craig McNamara's book: Cover design by Julianna Lee. Cover Composite: Black-and-white photo provided by the author, photo insert by Bettmann/Getty Images. Cover ©2023 Hachette. From *Because Our Fathers Lied* by Craig McNamara, copyright ©2022. Reprinted by permission of Little, Brown, an imprint of Hachette Book Group, Inc.

Robert McNamara and his wife, Marg: Photo by Craig McNamara. Courtesy of Craig McNamara

As World Bank president on the outskirts of Lima, Peru: President Robert S. McNamara on a trip to Latin America, March 12, 1976, Folder 1800560, World Bank Group Archives, Washington, DC, United States

With Joan Braden at a book launch party: Photo by Thomas Iannaccone/WWD/Penske Media via Getty Images

With Washington Post *publisher Katharine Graham:* Photo by Guy DeLort/WWD/Penske Media via Getty Images

With General Vo Nguyen Giap at the Critical Oral History Conference in Hanoi, Vietnam: Photo by HOANG DINH NAM/AFP/Stringer via Getty Images

At the Critical Oral History Conference on the Cuban missile crisis in Havana, Cuba: Photo by ADALBERTO ROQUE/AFP via Getty Images

With Craig McNamara at Craig's California home: Courtesy of Craig McNamara

With his second wife, Diana McNamara: Photo by Craig McNamara. Courtesy of Diana McNamara

With the weight of the world: Photo by John McDonnell/*The Washington Post* via Getty Images

TEXT CREDITS

Joan Braden, from *Just Enough Rope: An Intimate Memoir* (Villard Books, 1989). Copyright © 1989 by Joan Braden. Used by permission of Villard Books, an imprint of Random House, a division of Penguin Random House LLC. All rights reserved.

Paul Hendrickson, excerpts from *The Living and the Dead: Robert McNamara and Five Lives of a Lost War* (Vintage Books, 1997). Text copyright © 1996 by Paul Hendrickson. First published in 1997 in the United Kingdom by Macmillan, an imprint of Pan Macmillan. Used by permission of Alfred A. Knopf, an imprint of the Knopf Doubleday Publishing Group, a division of Penguin Random House LLC, and by permission of Macmillan Publishers International Limited. All rights reserved.

H. R. McMaster, from *Dereliction of Duty: Johnson, McNamara, the Joint Chiefs of Staff, and the Lies That Led to Vietnam* (HarperCollins, 1998). Copyright © 1997 by H. R. McMaster. Used by permission of HarperCollins Publishers.

Craig McNamara, from *Because Our Fathers Lied: A Memoir of Truth and Family, from Vietnam to Today* (Little, Brown and Company, 2022). Copyright © 2022 by Craig McNamara. Reprinted by permission of Little, Brown, an imprint of Hachette Book Group, Inc., and SLL/Sterling Lord Literistic, Inc.

Robert McNamara, from *In Retrospect: The Tragedy and Lessons of Vietnam* (Vintage Books, 1993). Copyright © 1995 by Robert S. McNamara. Used by permission of Crown Books, an imprint of the Crown Publishing Group, a division of Penguin Random House LLC. All rights reserved.

John T. McNaughton, *Unclassified Personal Diary of John T. McNaughton, January 1, 1966–April 22, 1967,* transcribed by Asheley Smith, 2003. Courtesy of Alex McNaughton.

INDEX